Ordnance Survey

STREET
East Kent

Contents

III   *Key to map symbols*

IV-V   *Key to map pages*

VI   *Administrative and post code boundaries*

1   *Street maps*

206   *Town plans of Bromley and Dartford*

207   *Town plans of Gravesend and Royal Tunbridge Wells*

208   *Town plans of Sevenoaks and Tonbridge*

209   *Index of hospitals, railway stations, schools, shopping centres, street names and universities*

245   *Town and village index*

PHILIP'S

First edition published 1994
First colour edition published 1997
Reprinted in 1999, 2000 by

George Philip Ltd, a division of
Octopus Publishing Group Ltd
2-4 Heron Quays, London E14 4JP

ISBN 0-540-07287-7 (pocket)

Digital Data

The exceptionally high-quality mapping
found in this book is available as
digital data in TIFF format, which is
easily convertible to other bit-mapped
(raster) image formats.

The index is also available in digital
form as a standard database table.
It contains all the details found in the
printed index together with the
National Grid reference for the map
square in which each entry is named
and feature codes for places of
interest in eight categories such as
education and health.

For further information and to discuss
your requirements, please contact
Philip's on 020 7531 8440 or
george.philip@philips-maps.co.uk

Key to map symbols

Motorway (with junction number)	
Primary routes (dual carriageway and single)	
A roads (dual carriageway and single)	
B roads (dual carriageway and single)	
Minor through road (dual carriageway and single)	
Minor roads	
Roads under construction	
Railways	
Tramway, miniature railway	
Rural track, private road or narrow road in urban area	
Gate or obstruction to traffic (restrictions may not apply at all times or to all vehicles)	
All paths, bridleways, byway open to all traffic, road used as a public path	

The representation in this atlas of a road, track or path is no evidence of the existence of a right of way

45
140   **Adjoining page indicators**

𝔇𝔬𝔳𝔢𝔯 ℭ𝔞𝔰𝔱𝔩𝔢   **Non-Roman antiquity**

ROMAN FORT   **Roman antiquity**

Acad	**Academy**	Mon	**Monument**
Cemy	**Cemetery**	Mus	**Museum**
C Ctr	**Civic Centre**	Obsy	**Observatory**
CH	**Club House**	Pal	**Royal Palace**
Coll	**College**	PH	**Public House**
Ex H	**Exhibition Hall**	Resr	**Reservoir**
Ind Est	**Industrial Estate**	Ret Pk	**Retail Park**
Inst	**Institute**	Sch	**School**
Ct	**Law Court**	Sh Ctr	**Shopping Centre**
L Ctr	**Leisure Centre**	Sta	**Station**
LC	**Level Crossing**	TH	**Town Hall/House**
Liby	**Library**	Trad Est	**Trading Estate**
Mkt	**Market**	Univ	**University**
Meml	**Memorial**	YH	**Youth Hostel**

⇌	**British Rail station**
(🚂)	**Private railway station**
⬛	**Bus, coach station**
♦	**Ambulance station**
♦	**Coastguard station**
♦	**Fire station**
♦	**Police station**
✚	**Casualty entrance to hospital**
✛	**Church, place of worship**
H	**Hospital**
i	**Information centre**
P	**Parking**
PO	**Post Office**
The Canterbury High School	**Important buildings, schools, colleges, universities and hospitals**
·—·—·	**County boundaries**
Great Stour	**Water name**
	Stream
	River or canal (minor and major)
	Water
	Tidal water
	Woods
	Houses

■ The dark grey border on the inside edge of some pages indicates that the mapping does not continue onto the adjacent page

■ The small numbers around the edges of the maps identify the 1 kilometre National Grid lines

The scale of the maps is 3.92 cm to 1 km (2½ inches to 1 mile)

0	¼	½	¾	1 mile
0	250m	500m	750m	1 Kilometre

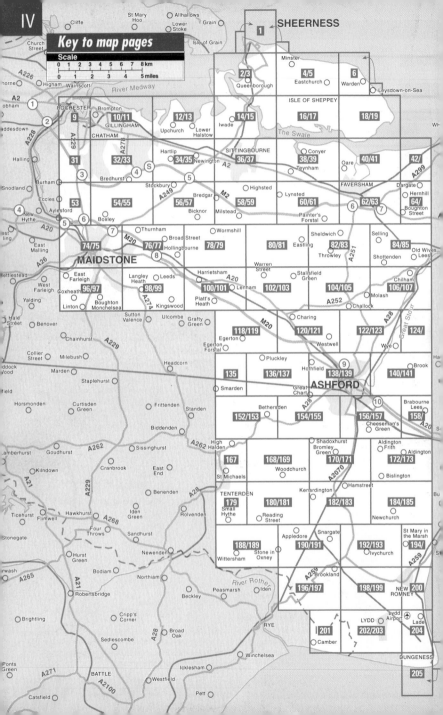

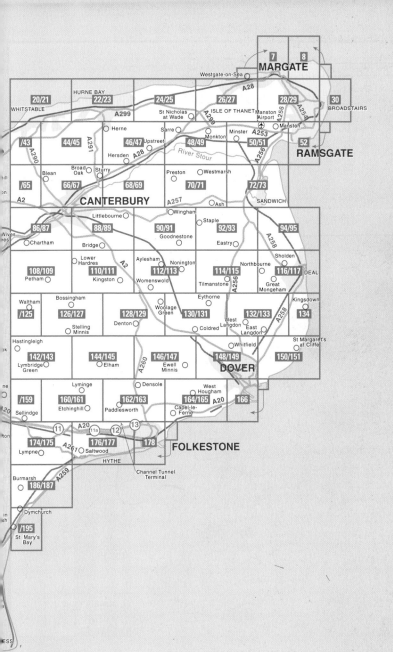

WESTGATE-ON-SEA

MARGATE **7** **8**

WHITSTABLE **20/21** HURNE BAY **22/23** **24/25** **26/27** ISLE OF THANET **28/29** **30** BROADSTAIRS

A299 St Nicholas at Wade A28 Manston Airport A256 A254 Manston

/43 **44/45** A291 **46/47** Upstreet **48/49** Monkton **50/51** Minster A253 **52** RAMSGATE

Herne Sarre River Stour A256

Broad Oak Sturry **66/67** **68/69** Preston Westmarsh **70/71** **72/73**

Blean **/65** CANTERBURY A257 Ash SANDWICH

Littlebourne Wingham

86/87 **88/89** **90/91** Goodnestone Staple **92/93** **94/95** A258

Chartham Bridge Eastry

Lower Hardres Aylesham Nonington Northbourne Sholden

108/109 Petham **110/111** Kingston A2 **112/113** Womenswold **114/115** Tilmanstone A256 **116/117** Great Mongeham DEAL

Waltham Bossingham Eythorne Kingsdown

/125 **126/127** **128/129** Woolage Green **130/131** West Langdon **132/133** **134**

Stelling Minnis Denton Coldred East Langdon

Hastingleigh Whitfield St Margaret's at Cliffe

142/143 Lymbridge Green **144/145** Elham A260 **146/147** Ewell Minnis **148/149** DOVER **150/151**

Lyminge Densole West Hougham

/159 **160/161** Etchinghill **162/163** Paddlesworth **164/165** A20 **166**

Sellindge Capel-le-Ferne

11 A20 **12** **13** 11a

174/175 A261 **176/177** **178** FOLKESTONE

Lympne Saltwood HYTHE Channel Tunnel Terminal

Burmarsh **186/187** A259

Dymchurch

/195 St Mary's Bay

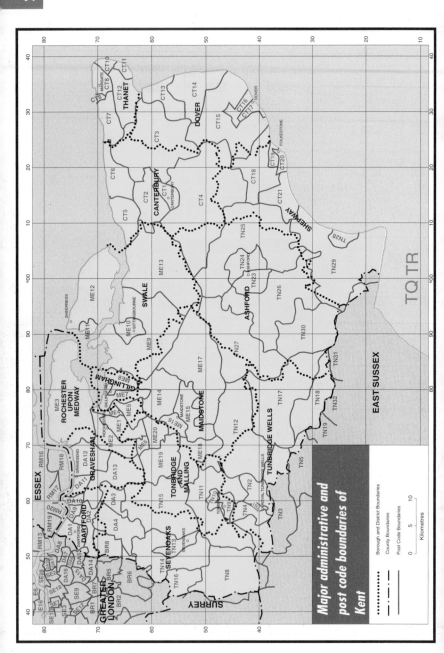

Major administrative and post code boundaries of Kent

Borough and District Boundaries
County Boundaries
Post Code Boundaries

0   5   10
Kilometres

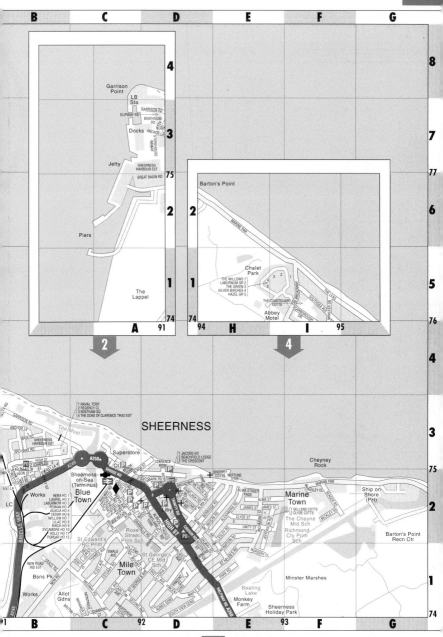

The Lappel

River Medway

NEWLAND RD

BRIELLE WAY

WHITEWAY RD

West Swale

Factory

Deadmans Island

Shepherds Creek

COURT HALL

NORTH RD

HIGH ST

SOUTH ST

CORONATION CRES

JUBILEE CRES

PH

The Hard

Works

Tailness Marshes

KLONDYKE IND EST

Ladies Hole Point

West Point

Works

Loading Hope Reach

The Swale

Piers

Rushenden Hill

FIRST AVE

SECOND AVE

SWALE AVE

WYKEMALD CL

RIVER VIEW

TERRY VIEW

MARSH RD

Long Reach

Rushenden

Chetney Marshes

Saxon Shore Way

Rushenden Marshes

Joan Fleet

Sewage Works

Horse Reach

Chetney Canal

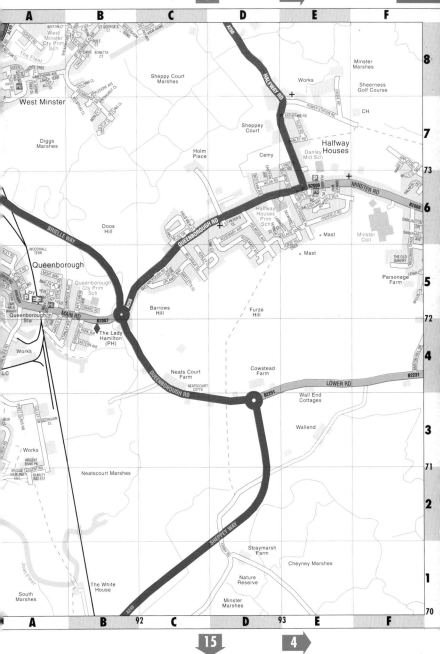

5

| A | B | C | D | E | F |

8

71

2 Leysdown-on-Sea

GROVE AVE

P

EASTERN RD

SAND CT

B2231 LEYSDOWN RD

PO

MANOR WAY

B2231

THAMES CT

PH

PROSPECT

7

73

1 Holiday Villages

SHELLNESS RD

WING RD

6

70

03 **G** **H** 04

19

Fletcher Battery Camp Site

Swanley Farm

Barrows Brook

THIRD AVE

NORMAN RD

SIXTH AVE

Cartts Farm

COASTGUARD COTTS

MANOR WAY

Warden Point

Warden Spring Caravan Pk

Wheatsheaf Inn (PH)

WARDEN RD

WARDEN WAY

5

72

Barnland

Thorn Hill

DEAL AV

PRESTON HALL GDNS

SEA APP

ST JAMES CT

IMPERIAL GDNS

WATERSIDE

SEA VIEW

BASAN PL

KNOLL WAY

EMPRESS GDNS

MELODY

WINDSOR GDNS

SEA APP

Warden

BEACH VIEW

CLARENCE GDNS

LEICESTER GDNS

SEA VIEW GDNS

BEACH APP

SEA VIEW GDNS

4

Rayham

Mustards

Warden Bay Hotel (PH)

Holiday Villages

WARDEN RD

3

71

B2231

B2231

Bay View

CORONATION DR

ST CLEMENTS

MILTON RD

Cemy

DANES DR

BAY VIEW

WARDEN VIEW GDNS

Paradise Farm

CROSS WAY

OLIVET RD

2

Old Rides Farm

HARTY FERRY RD

Rides Farm

LEYSDOWN RD

Bay View (PH)

1

70

00 **A** **B** 01 **C** **D** 02 **E** **F**

5

18

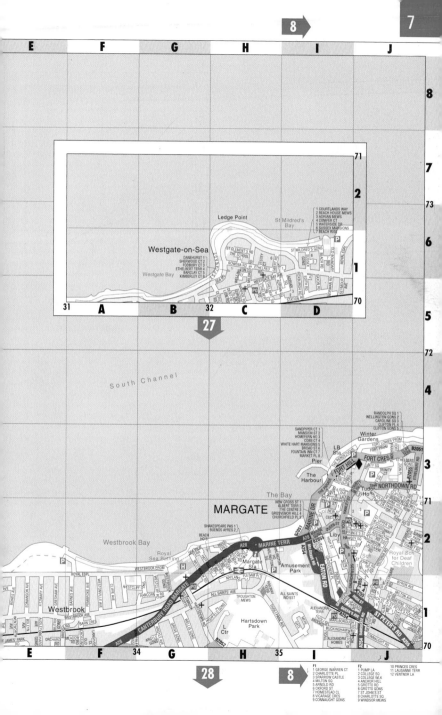

E   F   G   H   I   J

8

7

73

2

6

1

71

70

5

72

4

3

71

2

1

70

Westgate-on-Sea

1 COURTLANDS WAY
2 BEACH HOUSE MEWS
3 ADRIAN MEWS
4 CONIFER CT
5 WATERSIDE DR
6 SUSSEX MANSIONS
7 BEACH RISE

Ledge Point

St Mildred's Bay

ST MILDRED'S GDNS

DANEHURST 1
SHERWOOD CT 2
FODBURY CT 3
ETHELBERT TERR 4
BARCLAY CT 5
KIMBERLEY CT 6

Westgate Bay

ST CLEMENT'S RD
THE SCHOOL

ROWENA RD

31   A   32   B   C   D   70

South Channel

72

RANDOLPH SQ 1
WELLINGTON GDNS 2
CAROLINE SQ 3
CLIFTON PL 4
CLIFTON GDNS 5

Winter
Gardens

FORT LOWER PROM
FORT PROM

B2051

SANDPIPER CT 1
MANSION ST 2
HOMEFERN HO 3
COBB CT 4
WHITE HART MANSIONS 5
BROAD ST 6
FOUNTAIN INN CT 7
MARKET PL 8

LB
Sta

Pier

FORT HILL

FORT CRES

ETHELBERT
GDNS

TRINITY

The
Harbour

NORTHDOWN RD

Tudor
Ho

MARGATE

The Bay

NEW CROSS ST 1
ALBERT TERR 2
THE CENTRE 3
GROSVENOR HILL 4
CHURCHFIELD PL 5

MARINE DR

LOVE

Lib'y

SHAKESPEARE PAS 1
BUENOS AYRES 2

BEACH

Westbrook Bay

Royal
Sea Bathing

A28   MARINE TERR   A254

Margate
Sta

Amusement
Park

EATON RD

Royal Sch
for Deaf
Children

Westbrook

WESTBROOK PROM

H

ALL SAINTS' AVE

TROUGHTON
MEWS

ALL SAINTS
IND EST

BYRON AVE

ROYAL ESP

ROYAL AVE
WESTCLIFF AVE
WESTCLIFF RD
CLIFFE AVE
RANCORN RD

CANTERBURY ROAD MARGATE

A28

B2052

ALEXANDRA
TERR

ST PETER'S RD

CONNAUGHT RD

A254

A256

ORCHARD RD
MEADOW RD
BARN CRES
WESTBROOK AVE

L
Ctr

Hartsdown
Park

BUCKINGHAM
RD

ALEXANDRA
HOMES

70

E   F   34   G   H   35   I   J

A B C D E F

8

3 Botany Bay

71 Neptune's Tower

2 Captain Digby Inn (PH) Kingsgate Bay

Kingsgate Castle
Castle Keep Hotel

6 Kingsgate Hackemdown Point

Port Regis

1 Tower

70

39 G 40 H

30

7

73

5

72

4 Long Nose Spit

ETHELBERT TERR 1
CLIFTONVILLE CT 2
CLIFTONVILLE MEWS 3
QUEENS PAR 4
HATHERLEY CT 5
CARLTON MANSIONS 6
GODWIN COTTS 7
SANDOWN COTTS 8

Walpole Bay Palm Bay

MARGATE

Miniature Golf Course

FLORENCE CT 1
LYNTON COURT MANSIONS 2
Queen's Prom

NEWGATE LOWER PROM
NEWGATE PROM

NORTHUMBERLAND CT

PRINCE'S WLK

ROBINA CT 1
LEICESTER CT 2

B2051

ETHELBERT

LEWIS CRES

EASTERN ESPL

PALM BAY AVE

3

Palm Bay Cty Prim Sch

GODWIN RD/WS

Cliftonville

ST PAUL'S

ALBION RD

71

Princess Mary's Day

Cliftonville Cty Prim Sch

2

BROCKLEY RD
FAIRVIEW CL

PHILIP RD

Dane Park

THE AVENUE

LALEHAM CL

Laleham Sch

INVICTA HO 1
APPLEDORE CL 2

Liby

WALTHAM CT 1
ROSEACRE CT 2

Northdown Park

1

ST ANTHONY'S WAY
WALTHAM WAY 2
ROCKMAIDEN CL
DENTON WAY
ELHAM CL
LYNSTED WAY 5

Northdown

VICTORIA AVE

NORTHDOWN PARK RD

QUEEN ELIZABETH AVE

GEORGE HILL RD

GREYFRIARS CT

COLLEGE RD

Drapers Windmill (dis)

LALEHAM WLK 1
WINDSOR CT 2

MILLMEAD RD

Cty Prim Sch

B2052

Nursery

70

36 A B 37 C D 38 E F

B2
1 ADAM CT
2 JAMES CT
3 RUTLAND HO
4 WESTMOUNT HO
5 HIGHFIELD CT
6 REBECCA CT
7 RICHARD CT
8 LEONA CT

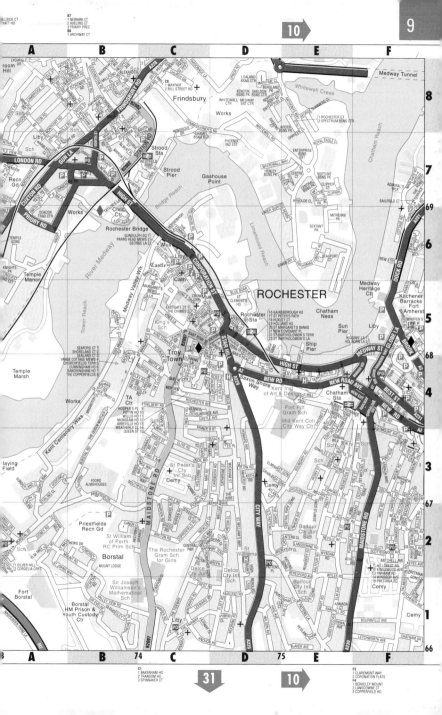

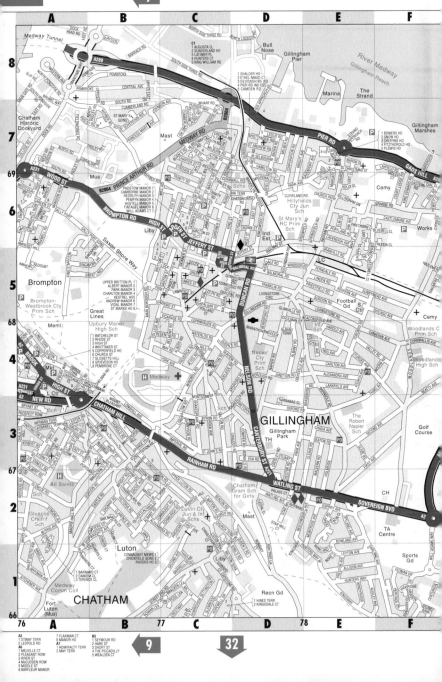

A B C D E F

8

River Medway

7

69

Bartlett Creek

Rainham Creek

Bayford

Ham Green Farm

6

Ham Green

Sewage Works

Motney Hill

Poultry Farm

Wetham Green

5

Saxon Shore Way

Otterham Creek

68

Horsham Marsh

Saxon Shore Way

Street Farm

4

Wharf

Horsham Farm

Horsham Hill

The Crown (PH)

Upchurch

Horsham La

Wharf

Caravan Pk

Horsham La

Holywell Cty Prim Sch

3

B2004

PH

Nature Reserve

Lower Rainham Rd

PH

Mill Farm

Windmill Hill

Wallbridge La

Bishop Cl

Dills Terr

67

Otterham Quay

Angel Cotts

Hubbards Cotts

River Valley Golf Course

Chaffes Terr

2

Station Rd

The Three Sisters (PH)

Kent Terr

Natal Farm

Gore

CH

Gore Cotts

Canterbury La

William St

Henry St

B2004

Wakeley Cty Jun Sch

1 ST EDMUNDS WAY
2 HARWOOD RD

1

P

Meredale Cty Inf Sch

Vineyard Cres

66

82 A B 83 C D 84 E F

A   B   C   D   E   F

8

Chetney
Hill

The Shade

Horse Reach

7

Funton Reach

River Medway

Saxon Shore Way

69

Ferry Marshes

Chetney
Cottages

Willow
Cottages

Marshbank

Rushan Fleet

Saxon Shore Way

Raspberry
Hill

RASPBERRY HILL LA

SHEPPEY WAY

OLD FERRY RD

6

Raspberry Hill
Park

5

Saxon Shore Way

68

Iwade Cty Prim
Sch

Wool Pack
Inn

EVERGREEN

MEADOW CL

TANS LA

LIBRARY

SPRINGVALE

FERRY RD

4

Iwade

SCHOOL LA

MEADOW DR

EASTON

COLESHALL
COTTS

PINK'S
CNR

3

Moat Farm
Cottages

Culnell's
Cottages

Coleshall
Farm

Orchard
Farm

Coleshall

67

2

Culnells

Great
Grovehurst
Farm

LC

FEATHERBED LA

SHEPPEY WAY

BERGIN

GROVEHURST RD

1 FLANDERS CL
2 LIEGE CL
3 MELLOR ROW

The Kemsley
Arms
(PH)

Corbiere

Pheasants

Cambray
Farm

Cambray
Cottages

BINGHAM LA

PARSONAGE LA

WOODSTOCK

BRAMBLEFIELD LA

Kemsley
Halt

B2006

Kemsley

1

66

88   A   B   89   C   D   90   E   F

A B C D E F

8

Joan Fleet

Ferry Reach

Minster Marshes

Stray Marshes

Kingsferry
Bridge

Ferry Marshes

7

The Dray

69

Swale
Halt

Ridham
Marshes

6

Ridham
Dock

Saxon Shore Way

5

Coldharbour
Marshes

Clay Reach

68

Kings Hill
Farm

Coldharbour Fleet

4

The Swale

Elmley
Hills

3

Jetty

67

Conveyor

Elmley Reach

2

Kemsley
Marshes

THE
CRESCENT

Chy

Chy

The
Lilies

1

Mill

COLDHARBOUR

RIDHAM AVE

Sittingbourne &
Kemsley Light Rly

Milton Creek

Saxon Shore Way

66

Kemsley Down

Oyster
Pond
(dis)

A B C D E F

92   93

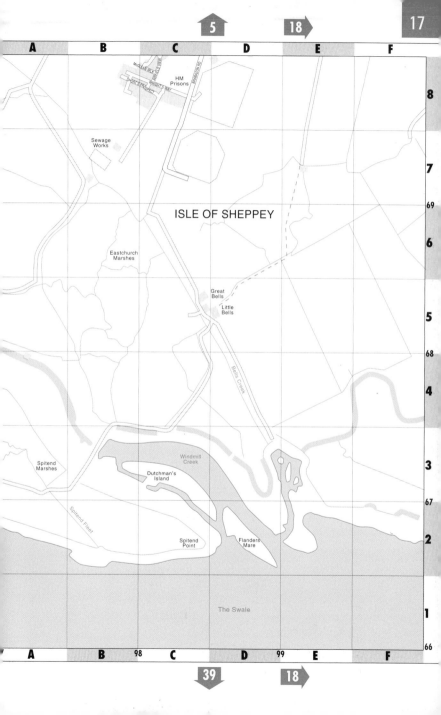

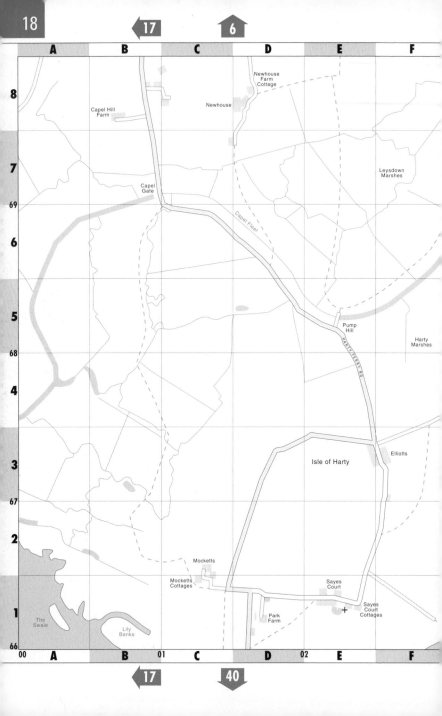

A B C D E F

8

Newhouse
Farm
Cottage

Capel Hill
Farm

Newhouse

7

Leysdown
Marshes

Capel
Gate

69

Capel Fleet

6

5

Pump
Hill

Harty
Marshes

68

HARTY FERRY RD

4

Isle of Harty

3

Elliotts

67

2

Mocketts

Mocketts
Cottages

1

The
Swale

Lily
Banks

Park
Farm

Sayes
Court

Sayes
Court
Cottages

66

00 A B 01 C D 02 E F

A B C D E F

8

North
Sea

Priory
Hill

Coastal
Park

SEAVIEW AVE

WINDS RD

SHELLNESS RD

Muswell Manor
Country Club

Leysdown
Marshes

Capel Fleet

7

69

SHELLBEACH

6

Harty
Marshes

5

TAMARISK
YELLOW
SANDS

Hamlet of Shellness

COASTGUARD
COTTS

68

Nature
Reserve

Shell
Ness

4

Brewers
Hill

3

67

2

The Swale

1

66

03 A B 04 C D 05 E F

WHITSTABLE

Tankerton Bay

Kingsdown
Park

1 WYNN ELLIS HO
2 SOUTH LODGE CL

Harbour

Saxon Shore Way

TOWER PAR

TANKERTON RD

B2205

IRB
Sta

Mus

D2
1 STARVATION CNR
2 NEW ST
3 FOUNTAIN ST
4 LEGGETT'S LA
5 RED LION LA
6 HARTS LA
7 VICTORIA HO
8 SQUEEZE GUT ALLEY
9 BEACH ALLEY
10 THE SALTINGS
11 HAYES ALLEY
12 EVELINGS ALLEY
13 BONNERS ALLEY
14 KNIGHTS ALLEY
15 SALT MARSH LA
16 ALBERT CT

Westmeads
Cty Inf Sch

St Mary's
RC Prim Sch

NORTHWOOD RD
STRANGFORD RD
GLOUCESTER RD
QUEEN'S RD
BRIDGEWAY

PETTMANS
MEWS

Whitstable &
Tankerton Sta

White Marsh
CT

WHEATLEY RD

THE BRIDGE APP

SHIPWRIGHTS
LEE

MARINE TERR 1
COASTGUARD ALLEY 2

MARINE LEA

Thurston
Park

Church
Street

NAVE
CREST

Sch

HIGH ST

OXFORD ST

Lower
Island

CH

Liby &
L Hall

Mus

BELMONT RD

WINDSOR
HO

43

D1
1 REEVES ALLEY
2 KEMP ALLEY
3 SKINNER'S ALLEY

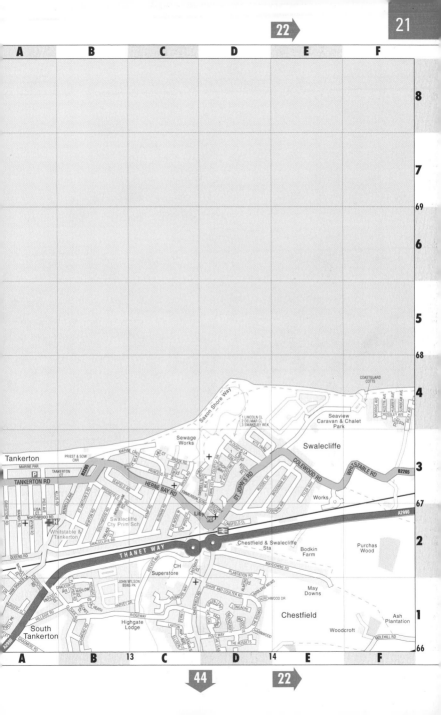

A　　B　　C　　D　　E　　F

8

7

69

6

5

68

4

3

67

2

1

66

Tankerton

MARINE PAR

P

TANKERTON CT

TANKERTON RD

PRIEST & SOW CNR

MARINE CRES

HERNE BAY RD

B2205

Saxon Shore Way

Sewage Works

1 LINCOLN CL
2 DELMAR CL
3 SWAKELEY WLK

KITE FARM

COLEWOOD RD

WHITSTABLE RD

B2205

Seaview Caravan & Chalet Park

Swalecliffe

COASTGUARD COTTS

MORRIS AVE
AUSTIN AVE
WEBBER AVE
SUNBEAM AVE
CRESTA
RILEY AVE
CROSSLEY AVE

ST JOHN'S RD

EMMERSON GDNS

Works

Swalecliffe City Prim Sch

SWALECLIFFE AVE

BRIDGEFIELD RD

Whitstable & Tankerton

GRAYSTONE RD

NORTHWOOD RD
PIER AVE
ELLIS RD

MANOR RD

QUEENS RD

Liby

MANSFIELD CL

THANET WAY

A2990

Chestfield & Swalecliffe Sta

Bodkin Farm

Purchas Wood

CH Superstore

JOHN WILSON BSNS PK

HARVEY DR

PLANTATION RD

MAYDOWNS RD

May Downs

CHURCHWOOD DR

Ash Plantation

CHAUCER AVE
MARLOW
THE HEATH

RIDGEWAY

SHARE AND COULTER RD

SADDLERS MEWS

CONIGAR

Highgate Lodge

LAXTON

POLO WAY

CHARNWOOD

THE JUGSETS

Chestfield

Woodcroft

MOLEHILL RD

South Tankerton

A2990

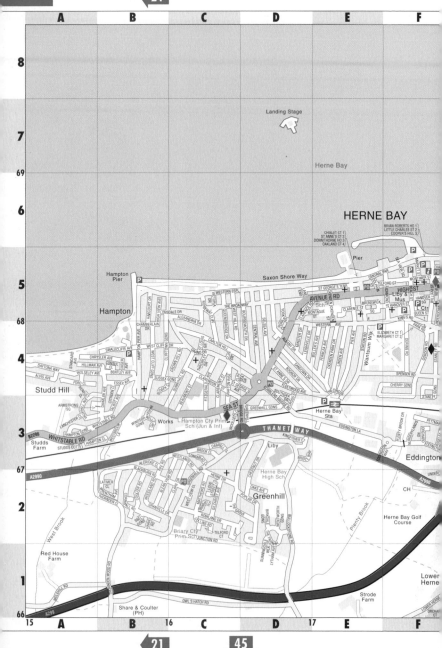

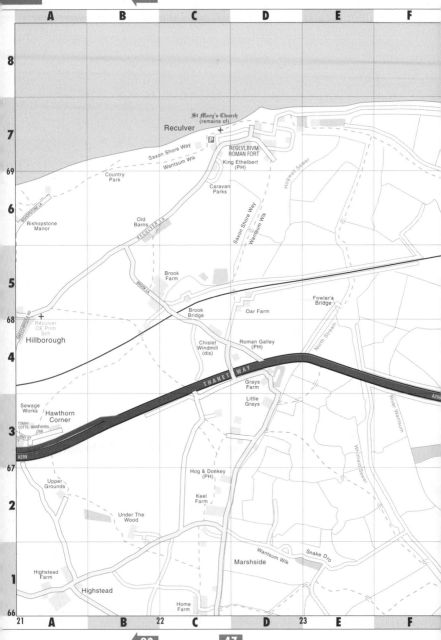

| | A | B | C | D | E | F |

8

St Mary's Church
(remains of)
Reculver

7

P

Saxon Shore Way
Wantsum Wlk
69

REGLVLBIVM
ROMAN FORT
King Ethelbert
(PH)

Hogwell Sewer

Country
Park

Caravan
Parks

6

BISHOPSTONE LA

Bishopstone
Manor

Old
Barns

RECULVER LA

Saxon Shore Way

Wantsum Wlk

Brook
Farm

5

BROOK LA

Fowler's
Bridge

68

SHEPPEY WAY

Reculver
CE Prim
Sch

Hillborough

Brook
Bridge

Oar Farm

North Stream

Chislet
Windmill
(dis)

Roman Galley
(PH)

4

THANET WAY

Grays
Farm

Little
Grays

A299

River Wantsum

Sewage
Works

Hawthorn
Corner

TOM AY
COTTS

HAWTHORN
CNR

MAY LA

Whitehead Sewer

3

A299

67

Upper
Grounds

Hog & Donkey
(PH)

Keel
Farm

2

Under The
Wood

Wantsum Wlk

Snake Dro

Marshside

1

Highstead
Farm

Highstead

Home
Farm

66

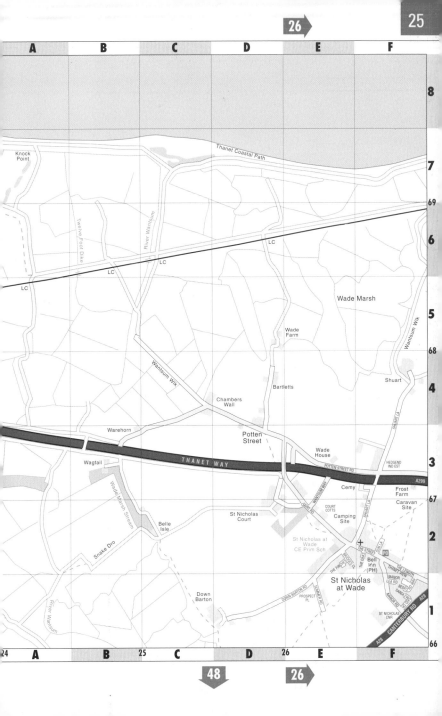

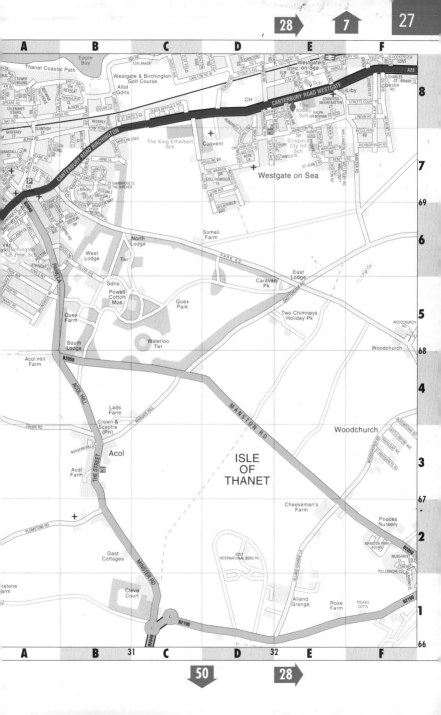

A B C D E F

8

7

69

6

5

68

4

3

67

2

1

66

ST JAMES'
PARK RD
BRIARY CT
A28 CANTERBURY ROAD MARGATE

MICHELLE GDNS
ALICIA AVE
DENT-DE-LION RD
WELLESDENE RD
KINGFISHER CL

MUTRIX RD

B2052 GEORGE V AVE

B2052

HARTSDOWN RD

A254
COLLEGE RD P6 B2052

Que
Elizabe
Queens

RAMSGATE RD

Garlinge

Dent-de-Lion
Farm
1 OLD CROSSING RD
2 CAMELLIA CL
3 ROSELAWN GDNS
4 BALMORAL RD
5 EDINBURGH WLK
6 GLEBE GDNS

Zeila Farm

Hartsdown
Sch

MARGATE

Garlinge Cty
Inf Sch

Allot
Gdns

Shottendane
Farm

St Gregory's
RC Prim Sch

Salmestone
Grange

Crem

Crem

Twenties

California
Farm

HILL VIEW

SHOTTENDANE RD

Hengrove
Farm

HALFMILE RIDE

Chapel Bottom

Wks

Nash
Court

Grove Villas

Chalkhole
Farm

Flete

Piggeries
NORFOLK RD
VICTORIA
RD
WELLINGTON RD

Lydden
Farm

Red House
Farm

Retreat
Farm

WOODCHURCH RD

WESTGATE AVE

MANSTON RD

Vincent
Farm

VINCENT RD

Flete Farm

Lydden

Caravan
Park

The Nook
Hackthorn Farm

QUEENDOWN RD

The
Bungalow

Nursery

Fleete
Court Farm

COLDSWOOD RD

Coldswood
Farm

Haine

Masts

B2060

B2190

MANSTON COURT
COTTS

Mus

Manston
Court

Caravan
Parks

MANSTON RD

Kent
International
Airport

Worlds
Wonder

Wood
Farm

Jolly Farmer
(PH)

THE
LEYS

THE LEYS

Grove
Farm

B2054

SPRATLING ST

Spratling Street
Farm

Manston

Haine
Cottage

HAINE RD

A256

SPRATLING LA

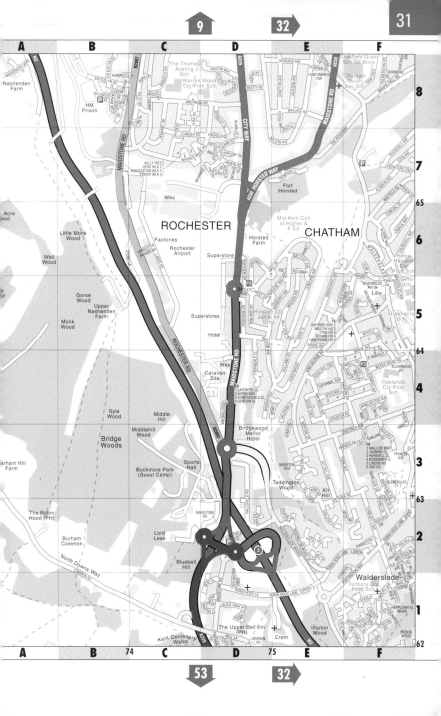

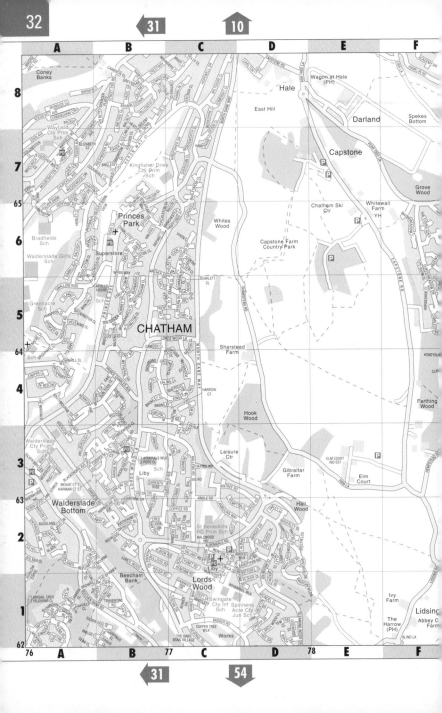

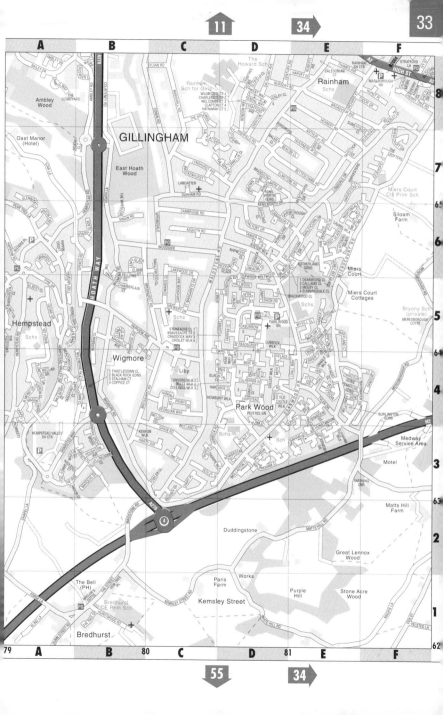

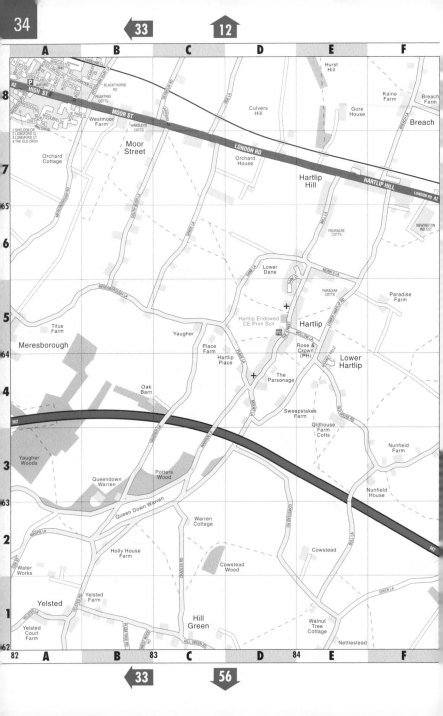

A   B   C   D   E   F

8

A2
HIGH ST
P
WINCHESTER
GLOUCESTER
SUNDERLAND
CHERRY DR
AMFORD
FARNHAM CL
BLACKTHORNE RD
PEARTREE COTTS
MIDDLEFIELDS
PARK RD
MOOR ST
WAKELEYS COTTS
THE MALTINGS
1 SHELDEN DR
2 LONGFORD CL
3 LONGFORD CT
4 THE OLD ORCH

Westmoor Farm

Moor Street

Hurst Hill

Kaine Farm

Breach Farm

Breach

Culvers Hill

Gore House

7

Orchard Cottage

Moor Street

LONDON RD

Orchard House

Hartlip Hill

HARTLIP HILL

LONDON RD A2

65

FOURACRE COTTS

NEWINGTON IND EST

6

MERESBOROUGH LA

SOUTH BUSH LA

BRICE LA

DANE LA

Lower Dane

MUNN'S LA

PARADISE COTTS

Paradise Farm

5

Titus Farm

Yaugher

Hartlip Endowed CE Prim Sch

Hartlip

LOWER HARTLIP RD

Meresborough

Place Farm

Hartlip Place

ROSE ST

HOLLOW LA

Rose & Crown (PH)

Lower Hartlip

64

Oak Barn

+

The Parsonage

Sweepstakes Farm

Oldhouse Farm Cotts

Nunfield Farm

4

M2

Nunfield House

CHERRY LA

LOWER HARTLIP RD

HILL LA

OLD HOUSE RD

SEA LA

3

Yaugher Woods

Queendown Warren

Potters Wood

Queen Down Warren

GREENSTED RD

Warren Cottage

Cowstead

63

MAPLE LA

CHARLES RD

Holly House Farm

2

Cowstead Wood

SEA LA

GREEN LA

M2

Water Works

YELSTED LA

Yelsted

Yelsted Farm

PLUM TREE RD

Hill Green

Walnut Tree Cottage

Nettlestead

1

Yelsted Court Farm

HILL GREEN RD

62

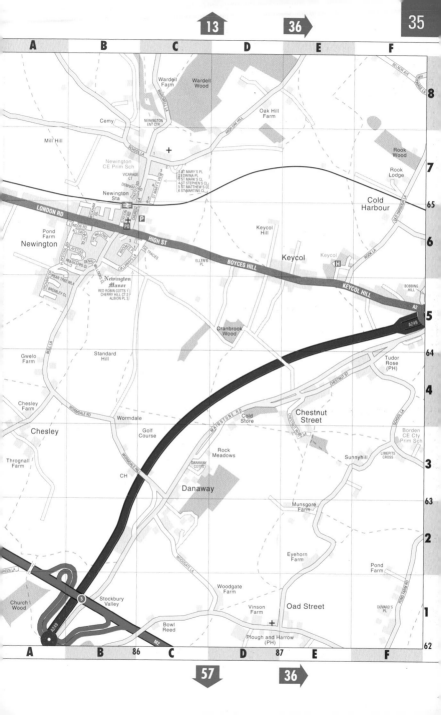

A B C D E F

Parsonage Farm

Stickfast Farm

PH

Upper Toes

Nether Toes

Blue Houses

Cricketers Cl

Beauford

8

Quinton Farm House

Alexandra Cl

LC

Sch

Sch

Saffron Way

7

Church Farm

Bobbing Cty Prim Sch

Regis Manor Cty Prim Sch

The Butts Trad Est

Trinity Trad Est

65

Bobbing

SITTINGBOURNE

Cross La 1
Oyster Cl 2
Albion Terr 3

Recn Gd

Liby

Mill Way

Bobbing Court

B2006

Milton Regis

Hall

Work

6

Bobbing Hill

Grove Park Cty Prim Sch

1 Norwood Wlk F
2 Wentworth Ho

Staplehurst Rd

B2005

Milton Creek

Saxon Shore Way

Denham Ho 1
Roentgen Ho 2
Pinous Ho 3

St Paul's St

St Paul's St
Prentis Quay

E5
1 St Paul's St.
2 Pear Tree Alley
3 Tannery Ct
4 Bishop Ct
5 Perinwick Ct
6 Alexander Ct

Crown Quay

5

Allenby Wlk 1
Nelson Wlk 2
Collingwood Wlk 3
Norwood Wlk 4
Andrews Wlk 5
Gainsborough Cl 6

A2 KEY ST

Key Street

Wilton Terr

Cavell La

London Rd

Chalkwell Rd

B2006

Sittingbourne Sta

Ind Pk

64

Cherry Fields

Grove Park

LONDON RD

Chalkwell

Hollybrook Hill

Westbourne Gro

Eurolink Way

4

The Westlands High Sch

Playing Field

Cryalls Bsns Est

Victoria Terr

London Road Trad Est

West St

Dover St

Station Rd

St Michael's Rd

Cryalls

Homewood Cty Inf Sch

Johnson House

School La

Liby

PO

3

Borden Hall

Maypole Inn (PH)

Borden

L Ctr

Barrow Grove Cty Jun Sch

Borden Gram Sch for Boys

Trotts Hall Gdns 1
The Burrs 2

Glovers Cres

Memorial (General)

H

63

Hall

Home Farm

The Barn

St Peter's RC Prim Sch

Manterne Cty Inf Sch

Hill Brow

Cemys

Spicer Homes

Highste Sch

2

Pond House

Harman's Corner

Fernleigh

The Oaks Cty Inf Sch

Park Ave

Fulston Ma Sch

1

Hearts Delight

Waymarks

Chedworth

62

88 A B 89 C D 90 E F

E4
1 Dover St
2 Fountain St
3 Freeman Ct
4 Mockett Ct
5 Church St
6 Pembury Ct
7 The Cloisters
8 Middleton Ct

F4
1 Crescent St
2 The Forum
3 Lion Yd
4 Does Alley
5 St Michael's Cl
6 Banks Yd

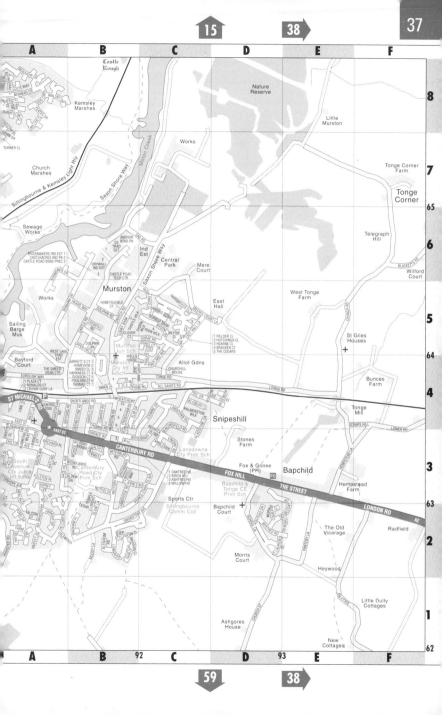

A   B   C   D   E   F

8

Saxon Shore Way

The Swale

Conyer Creek

Wharf

7

Blacketts

BLACKETTS COTTS

Works

Rifle Rang (dis)

65

BLACKETTS RD

Wilford Court Farm

Ship Inn (PH)

QUAY COTTS

THE QUAY

1 COASTGUARD COTTS
2 BRUNSWICK COTTS

6

Cheke's Court

Dock

EASTWOOD COTTS

THE MOORINGS

1 2

Conyer

BRUNDWICK RD

5

Stone Chimney Farm

Banks Farm

Peete House

64

NEW COTTS

Teynham Street

CONYER RD

4

Bax

Teynham Court

LC

Teynham Court Farm

+

LC

Fair View

LOWER RD

LC

Frognal

Sewage Works

Barrow Green

Osiers Farm

3

CHURCHILL HD 1

Teynham Sta

STATION ROW

RAILWAY COTTS

THE CRESCENT

Teynham

BROAD

OSIER RD

63

Little Radfield

CLAXFIELD COTTS

Teynham Parochial CE Prim Sch

BELLE FRIDAY CL

HONEYBALL WK

ROPER'S CL

RENE

1 ROUNDEL CL
2 TRIGG'S ROW
3 BRIDGE COTTS

LOWER RD

2

A2

Radfield

Depot

Comet Motel

FRIARY

Liby

FROGNAL GDNS

DIEBOLD MOOR AVE

ROBEL CL

NUTBERRY CL

Whent's Farm

Claxfield Farm

CLAXFIELD RD

P

NEW GARDENS

LONDON RD

1

+

CELLAR MILL

White Hall

SANDOWN COTTS

A2

Cellarhill

VIGO TERR

Cellar Hill Farm

Orchard House

PHEASANT RD

62

94   A   B   95   C   D   96   E   F

The Swale

Saxon Shore Way

Fowley Island

South Deep

Rifle Range (dis)

Luddenham Gut

Teynham Level

Little Uplees

Howletts

UPLEES COTTS

Luddenham Marshes

Poplar Hall

A 251

Luddenham Court

+

CHERRY TREE DR

BROOK COTTS

Deerton Street

Elverton

The Mounted Rifleman (PH)

Hawks & Beetles Farm

Nash's Farm

Lower Newlands

THE ELMS

The Old Farmhouse

Wildmarsh

LC

The Old Rectory

Luddenham Cty Prim Sch

BYSING WOOD RD

Mockbeggar

LOWER RD

Bysing Wood

BYSING WOOD COTTS

Mockbeggar Farm

LC

Stone Farm

BYSING WOOD RD

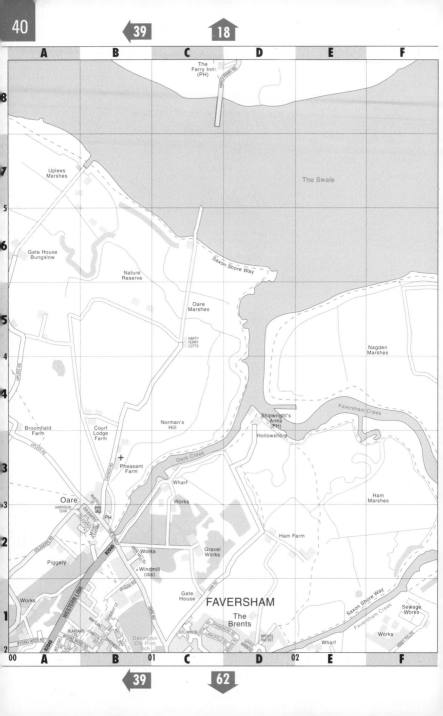

A B C D E F

8

The Ferry Inn (PH)

HARTY FERRY RD

7

Uplees
Marshes

The Swale

5

6

Gate House
Bungalow

Nature
Reserve

Saxon Shore Way

Oare
Marshes

5

HARTY
FERRY
COTTS

Nagden
Marshes

4

Faversham Creek

4

Broomfield
Farm

Court
Lodge
Farm

Norman's
Hill

Shipwright's
Arms
(PH)

Hollowshore

Pheasant
Farm

Oare Creek

3

Ham
Marshes

Wharf

Oare

Works

HARRISON
TERR

PH

Ham Farm

2

Works

Gravel
Works

Piggery

Windmill
(dis)

Ham
Farm

1

Gate
House

FAVERSHAM

The
Brents

Saxon Shore Way

Faversham Creek

Sewage
Works

Works

Davington
C\of\E\Prim
Sch

GOLDFINCH

Wharf

Works

2

00 A B 01 C D 02 E F

Whitstable Bay

Saxon Shore Way

FAVERSHAM RD

Caravan & Chalet Site

Blue Anchor (PH)

PRESTON PARA

ST MARY'S DR

ALMA RD

LUCERNE

LUCERNE DR

KIMBERLEY RD

BEACONSFIELD

ROBERTS RD

LADY GR

Caravan Park

Ye Old Sportsman (Inn)

Caravan Park

Caravan Parks

Graveney Marshes

Seasalter Level

Mount Pleasant

Denly Hill

Brookdene Farm

Hern Hill Nursery

Yorkletts

Brookhill Farm

Monkshill Farm

Ind Est

DARGATE RD

MONKSHILL RD

Waterham

HIGHSTREET RD

THANET WAY

HIGHSTREET RD

Highstreet

Horse Hill Farm

Waterham Farm

WATERHAM RD

Horse Hill

Brook Hall Farm

A299

ALBERSHELMS LA

Lamberhurst Farm

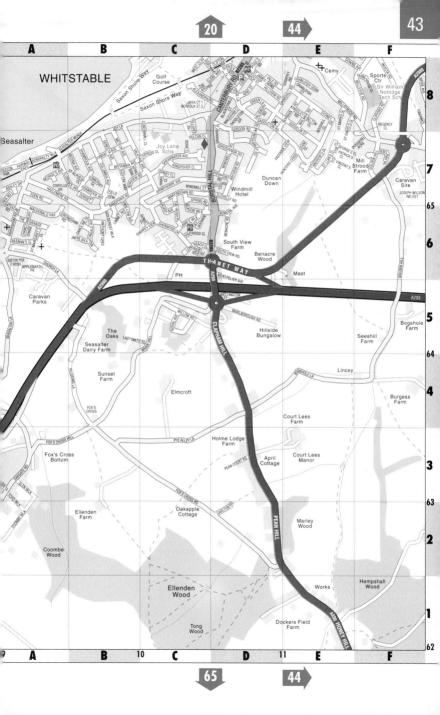

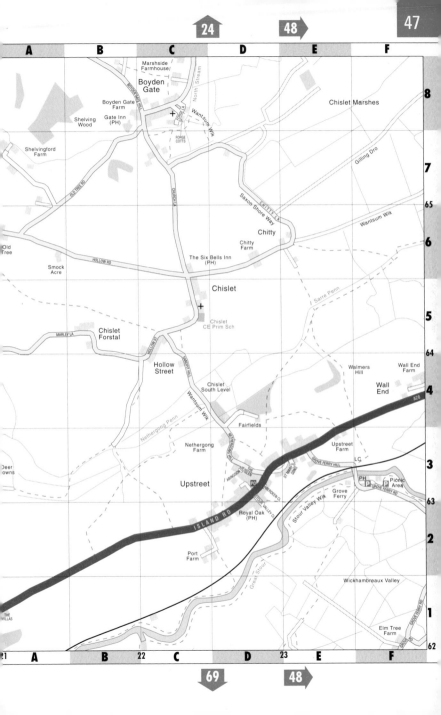

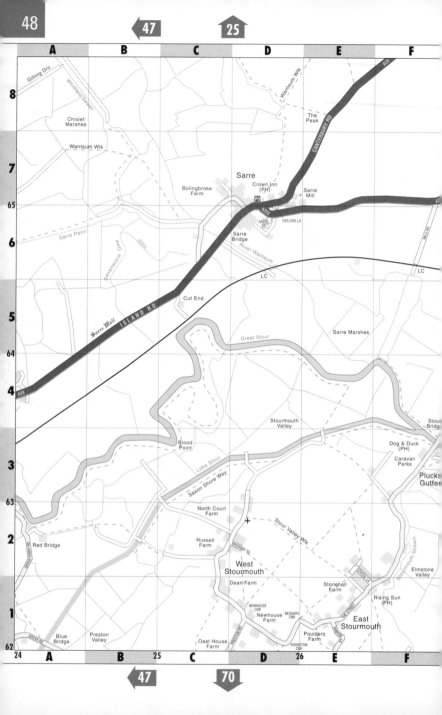

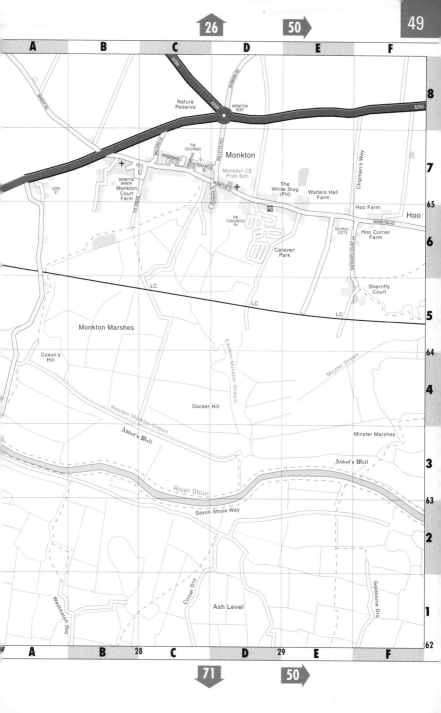

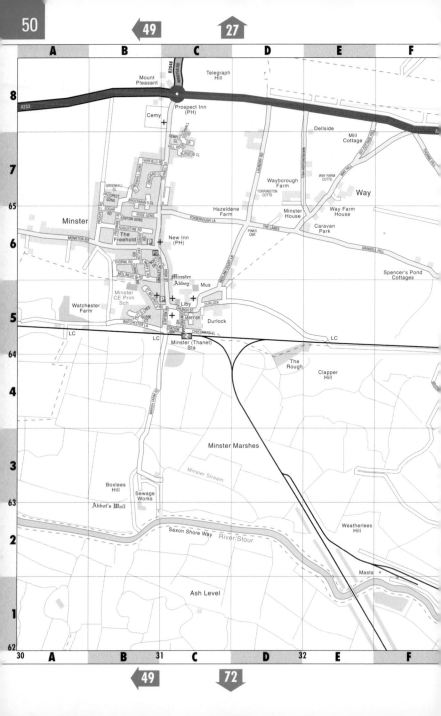

8
7
65
6
5
64
4
3
63
2
1
62

A253
R204B
RAMSGATE RD

Mount Pleasant
Telegraph Hill
Prospect Inn (PH)
Cemy
Dellside
Mill Cottage

SEMPLE COTTS
HILL HOUSE
BURGESS CL
FAIRFIELD RD
GREENHILL CL
PROSPECT GDNS
BROCKMAN'S CL
ROSE GDNS
EDGAR RD
KENTON GDNS
AUGUSTINE RD
MONKTON RD
THORNE RD
MOLINEUX RD
FOXBOROUGH LA

Wayborough Farm
TORRINGTON COTTS
WAY FARM COTTS
Way
WAY HILL
OLD COTTAGE HILL

Hazeldene Farm
Minster House
Way Farm House
Caravan Park

Minster
New Inn (PH)
The Freehold
PINKS CNR
THE LANES
LAURISTON RD
MARSHBOROUGH RD
GRINSELL HILL

Watchester Farm
Minster Abbey
Mus
Minster CE Prim Sch
Liby
Durlock
BETHEL COURT LA
Spencer's Pond Cottages

GLEBE
WATCHESTER LA
STATION APP
CHURCH ST
ABBEY GR
CHEESMAN'S CL
DURLOCK

LC
LC
Minster (Thanet) Sta
LC
The Rough
Clapper Hill

Minster Marshes

MARSH HARRIER RD

Minster Stream

Boxlees Hill
Sewage Works
Abbot's Wall

Weatherlees Hill

Saxon Shore Way
River Stour

Ash Level

Masts

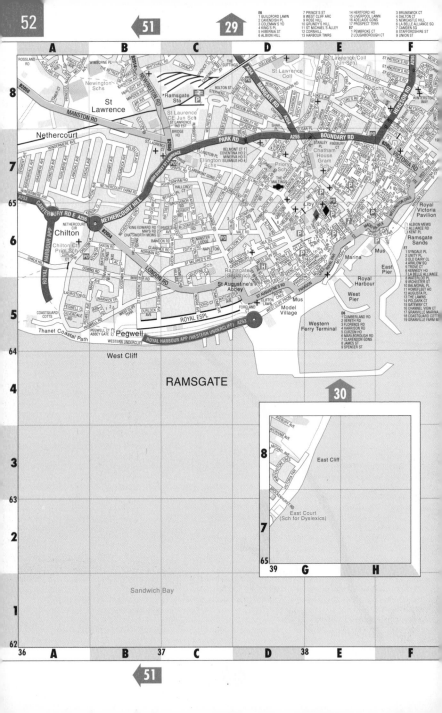

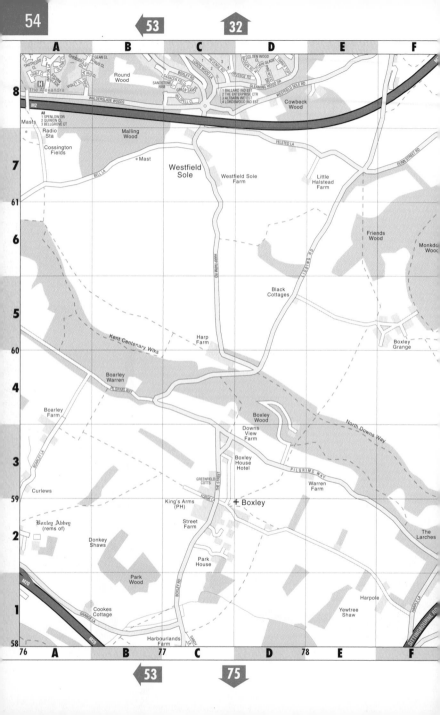

53
32

A **B** **C** **D** **E** **F**

M2

Troywood

Round Wood

The Alexandra

8

M2

A8
1 SPENLOW DR
2 QUINION CL
3 BELLGROVE CT

WALDERSLADE WOODS

SANDSTONE RISE

GINGER LANE

BOXLEY RD

1 BALLARD IND EST
2 THE ENTERPRISE CTR
3 ALTBARN IND EST
4 LORDSWOOD IND EST

GOLDEN WOOD

JOHN GLADE

GLEAMING WOOD DR

WESTFIELD SOLE RD

Cowbeck
Wood

Masts

Radio
Sta

Cossington
Fields

Malling
Wood

Mast

YELSTED LA

DUNN STREET RD

7

BELL LA

Westfield
Sole

Westfield Sole
Farm

Little
Halstead
Farm

61

6

Friends
Wood

Monkdown
Wood

HARP FARM RD

Black
Cottages

YELSTED LA

5

Kent Centenary Wlks

Harp
Farm

Boxley
Grange

60

Boarley
Warren

PILGRIMS WAY

4

Boarley
Farm

Boxley
Wood

BOARLEY LA

Downs
View
Farm

North Downs Way

3

Boxley
House
Hotel

Greenfield
Cotts

THE STREET

FORGE LA

PILGRIMS WAY

Warren
Farm

Curlews

59

King's Arms
(PH)

+ Boxley

2

Boxley Abbey
(rems of)

Donkey
Shaws

Street
Farm

Park
House

The
Larches

BOXLEY RD

Park
Wood

M20

1

Cookes
Cottage

GRANGE LA

M20

Harpole

Yewtree
Shaw

HARPER LA

SITTINGBOURNE RD

58

SANDLING

Harbourlands
Farm

76 **A** **B** 77 **C** **D** 78 **E** **F**

53
75

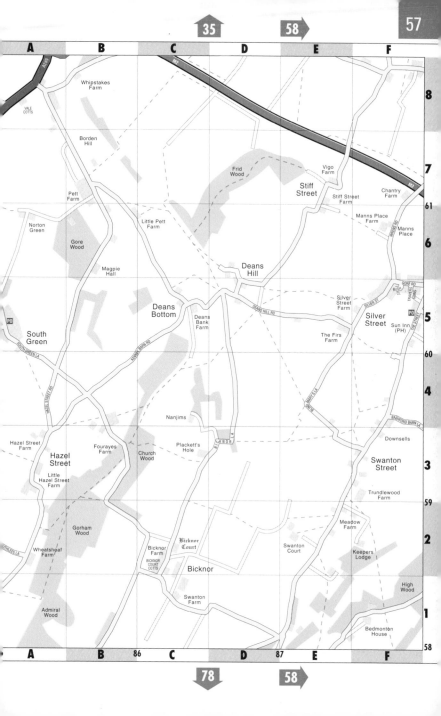

8

7

61

6

5

60

4

3

59

2

1

58

A B C D E F

VALE COTTS

Whipstakes Farm

Borden Hill

Frid Wood

Vigo Farm

Stiff Street

Chantry Farm

Stiff Street Farm

Pett Farm

Manns Place Farm

Manns Place

Norton Green

Little Pett Farm

Gore Wood

Magpie Hall

Deans Hill

South Green

Deans Bottom

Deans Bank Farm

DEANS HILL RD

Silver Street Farm

GORE RD

Silver Street

Sun Inn (PH)

PO

The Firs Farm

PO

BICKNOR BARN RD

HAZEL STREET RD

SOUTH GREEN LA

Nanjims

Hazel Street Farm

Fourayes Farm

Church Wood

Plackett's Hole

LA N D R

Downsells

Swanton Street

Hazel Street

Little Hazel Street Farm

Gorham Wood

Wheatsheaf Farm

Bicknor Farm

BICKNOR COURT COTTS

Bicknor Court

Bicknor

Swanton Court

Meadow Farm

Keepers Lodge

Trundlewood Farm

Admiral Wood

Swanton Farm

High Wood

Bedmonton House

86 87

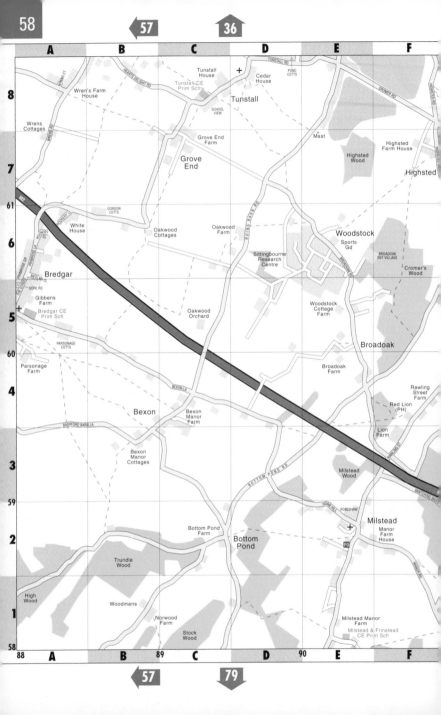

A **B** **C** **D** **E** **F**

8

Wren's Farm House

Tunstall House

Tunstall CE Prim Sch

Cedar House

POND COTTS

SCHOOL VIEW

Tunstall

Wrens Cottages

Grove End Farm

Mast

Highsted Wood

Highsted Farm House

7

Grove End

Highsted

61

GORDON COTTS

White House

Oakwood Cottages

Oakwood Farm

Woodstock

6

Sittingbourne Research Centre

Sports Gd

BROADOAK ENT VILLAGE

Cromer's Wood

Bredgar

Gibbens Farm

Bredgar CE Prim Sch

Oakwood Orchard

Woodstock Cottage Farm

5

PARSONAGE COTTS

Broadoak

60

Parsonage Farm

Broadoak Farm

Rawling Street Farm

4

BEXON LA

Red Lion (PH)

Bexon

Bexon Manor Farm

Lion Farm

BASHFORD BARN LA

Bexon Manor Cottages

3

BOTTOM POND RD

Milstead Wood

59

HOPE HILL

ROBESHAW

Milstead

Bottom Pond Farm

Bottom Pond

Manor Farm House

2

Trundle Wood

PO

High Wood

Woodmans

Norwood Farm

Milstead Manor Farm

1

Stock Wood

Milstead & Frinstead CE Prim Sch

58

88 **A** **B** **89** **C** **D** **90** **E** **F**

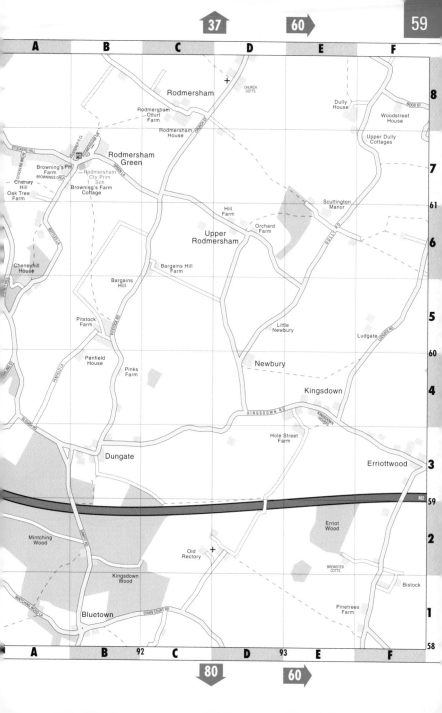

59 38

| | A | B | C | D | E | F |

A2 LONDON RD

8

Sunderland Farm

Sunderland

Cambridge Farm

CELLAR HILL

Cherry Gardens

Nouds House

Upper Newlands

Orchard House

Norton Ash

Bogle

Lewson Street

Batteries Farm

Bogle

The Plough Inn (PH)

7

Swedish Houses

BOWL RD

Nouds Farm

Norton Court

Lynsted & Norton Cty. Prim Sch

Bumpit Farm

61

Black Lion (PH)

ST PETERS PL

THE TREFOIL

6

Lynsted

Tickham

Tickham Farm

Aymers

UPPER TICKHAM COTTS

THE VALLANCE

NORTON RD

PROVENDER RD

Lynsted Court

Green Acres

5

Park Farm

MILL LA

TICKHAM LA

Loyterton

60

Park View

Monks Farm

4

Dadman's

Rushett

Lynsted Park

Wren's Hill

Colyers Farm

CHRISTOPHER'S ROW

Stuppington Cottages

3

Homestall

Stuppington Farm

M2

M2

59

Little Sharsted Farm

Moonfield Farm

2

Sharsted Plantation

Martlesham

College Wood

FAVERSHAM RD

1

Sharsted Court

Whitehall

NORTH EASTLING RD

58

Keepers Cottage

Champion Court

| 94 | A | B | 95 | C | D | 96 | E | F |

61
40

C7
1 CURTIS WAY
2 CASLOCKE ST
3 HATCH ST
4 BECKETT ST
5 MENDFIELD ST
6 WATER LA

C7
7 REEVES PAS
8 WESTBROOK WLK

D7
1 MARKET PL
2 MIDDLE ROW
3 GANGE MEWS
4 GARFIELD PL
5 HUGH PL
6 BACK LA

7 CROSS LA
8 JACOB YD
9 GATEFIELD LA
10 HERBERT DANE CT
11 JOHN ANDERSON CT
12 QUEENS PAR

13 ST MARY CT
14 WILLIAM GIBBS CT
15 LIMES PL

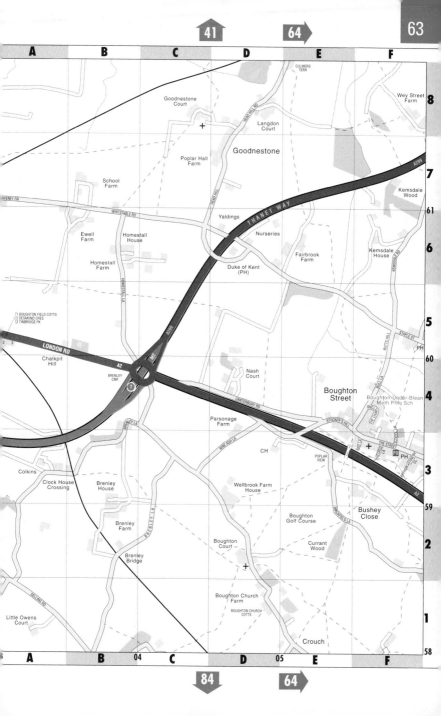

8

A299

Meadow Grange Nursery

Butler's Court Wood

Denstroude

DENSTROUDE LA

HONEY HILL

Brook Lodge

Honey Hill

Blean Bird Park

Clay Hill

Royal Oak (PH)

7

Parsonage Farm

Honey Hill Farm

WOODLANDS

BLEAN COMM A299

Denstroude Farm

Nature Reserve

61

Mincing Wood

Little Den Lees

6

Crawford's Rough

Great Den Lees

North Bishopden Wood

5

Grimshill Wood

60

Crooked Oak

4

Church Wood

Nature Reserve

NEW RD

3

Manson Wood

59

Landing Strip

Homestall Wood

2

Willows Wood

FAWSETT LA

Stumps Farm

Staines Farm

Plough Inn (PH)

Harbledown Lodge

GLEMSFORD COTTS

Upper Harbledown

NEW COTTS

THE

LITTLE LONDON

PROSPECT COTTS

1

Poldhurst Farm

A2050

A2

58

A   B   C   D   E   F

Walnut Tree Farm

Well Court

Frog Hall

8

Amery Court

Timber Wood

Arbele House

Daw's Wood

The Radfall

7

BROADLANDS IND EST

Honey Wood

Great Hall Wood

61

BLEAN COMMON

The Halt

Hothe Court Farm

Tyler Hill

6

Blean

Church Cottage

Little Hall Wood

Hillside Farm

BLEAN HILL

Hare & Hounds (Inn)

5

Luckett's Farm

TILE KILN HILL

Brotherhood Wood

Darwin Coll

Little Hall Farm

60

Blean Cty Prim Sch

LYEAT CT

PURCHAS CT

1 CLOWES CT
2 HOMESTALL CT
3 SUMMERFIELD CT
4 THORNDEN CT

Park Wood

Univ of Kent at Canterbury

Templeman Liby

GREEN DELL

4

Masts

ELLENDEN CT

BISHOPDEN CT

FARTHINGS

MARLEY CT

Rutherford Coll

Eliot Coll

MOORFIELD

DENSTEAD CT

WILLOWS CT

BROTHERWOOD RD

Keynes Coll

The Archbishop's CE Sec Sch

THE TERRACE

MOAT LA

WHITSTABLE RD

OAKS AV

The Grove

3

NEW RD

RAVENSCOURT RD

Kent Coll

St Edmund's Sch

CRANBOURNE WLK

Schs

FIRTREE CL

LOVELL RD

Wtr Twr

Chaucer Coll

Rough Common

The Close (St Edmunds SGH)

ST THOMAS HILL

59

Dog & Bear (PH)

Neal's Place

St Stephen's

STOCKWOOD CHASE

WHITSTABLE RD

NURSERY WLK

VIKING CL

STEPHEN LODG

LC

2

Stock Wood

GARDEN CL

St Dunstan's

HACKINGTON TEBB

Recn Ctr

HALL PLACE

The Grove

CHANCEL CT

JOSEPH CONRAD HOUSE

RUNCIE PL

Cemy

HANSCOMB RD

DEANS MILL

1

Hall Place

ST DUNSTAN'S ST

LC

58

FAULKNERS LA

A2050

Vernon Holme (Kent Coll Inf & Jun Sch)

CHURCH HILL

The Mint

Harbledown

SUMMER CT

SUMMER HILL

A2050   RHEIMS WAY

QUEENS RD

12   A   B   13   C   D   14   E   F

E1
1 ROSIERS CT
2 CROSS ST
3 LIONARD HO

F1
1 RIVERSIDE CT
2 STOURSIDE STUDIOS
3 WESTGATE HALL RD
4 CHANTRY CT
5 BLACKFRIARS ST
6 ST ALPHEGE LA
7 THE CLOISTERS

A B C D E F

8
7
61
6
5
60
4
3
59
2
1
58

Mayton Farm
Brookside
Langton Lodge
Nook Farm
Golden Lion (PH)
Foxhill House
Kemberland Wood
Little Hall Wood
Goose Farm
Broad Oak
Sweech Farm
Barton Wood
Sturry
Alcroft Grange
Shelford Farm
Den Grove Wood
Brickhouse Wood
Broad Oak Lodge Farm
Sturry Sta
Barton Down
Broadoak Crossing
Great Stour
King's Sch (Jun)
George & Dragon Hotel
1 HALSTEAD CL
2 FRENCHAM CL
Sewage Works
Folly Farm
Vauxhall Lakes (Nature Reserve)
(Park & Ride)
Recn Gd
Chequers Wood
Hales Place
Stour Valley Wlk
Parkside Cty Prim Sch
Kingsmead Stadium
TA Ctr
Canterbury Golf Course
Scotland Hills
Northgate
CANTERBURY
DVROVERNVM
Old Park Farm
Christ-Church Coll Post Graduate Ctr
Crown & Cty Cts

CLYDE ST
ALMA PL
NOTLEY TERR
UNION PL
LANFRANC HO
ST JOHN'S HOSPL
KINGS MEWS
HIGH ST
ST GREGORY'S

10 DRAGOON HO
11 ARTILLERY ST
12 ARTILLERY GDNS
13 ARTILLERY HO
14 DEAN CT
15 THE FORRENS
16 THE PRECINCTS
17 PALACE ST
18 COBDEN PL
19 HOMESPIRE HO

20 KNOTT'S LA
21 CHURCH LA
22 ST RADIGUND ST
B1
1 KNOWLTON WLK
2 JESSICA MEWS
3 PYATT MEWS
4 PAYTON MEWS
5 PLUMPTON WLK
6 MANNOCK HO

7 THE RIDINGS
8 CRADDOCK DR
B2
1 METCALFE MEWS
2 GREEN CLOTH MEWS
3 GORE MEWS
4 ARRAN MEWS
5 MARY GREEN WLK
6 CALCROFT MEWS
7 KEYWORTH MEWS

8 ANNE GREEN WLK
9 GILLON MEWS
10 HALLETT WLK
11 PETCHELL MEWS
12 REMSTON MEWS
13 WEMYSS CT
14 WEMYSS HO
15 ANZIO HO
16 CASSINO HO
17 MALTA HO

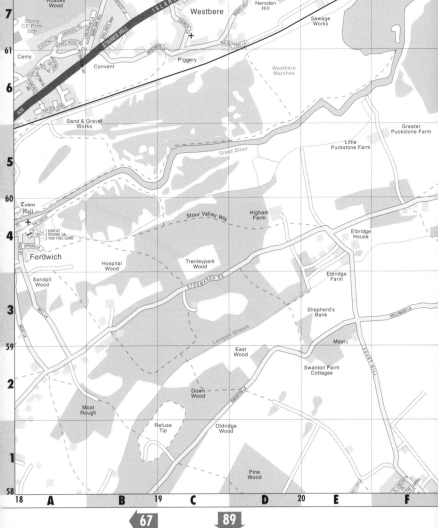

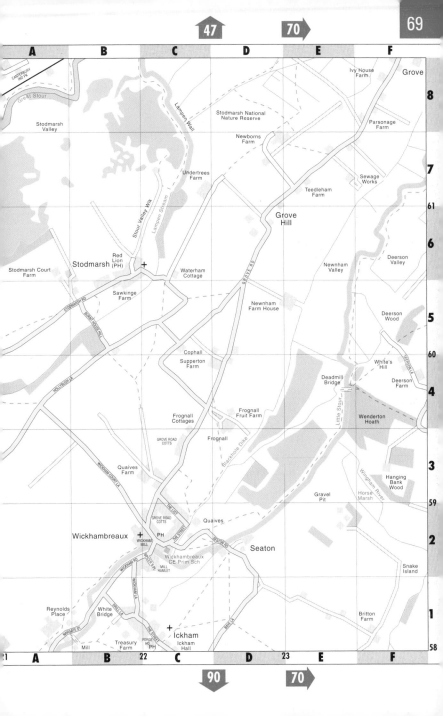

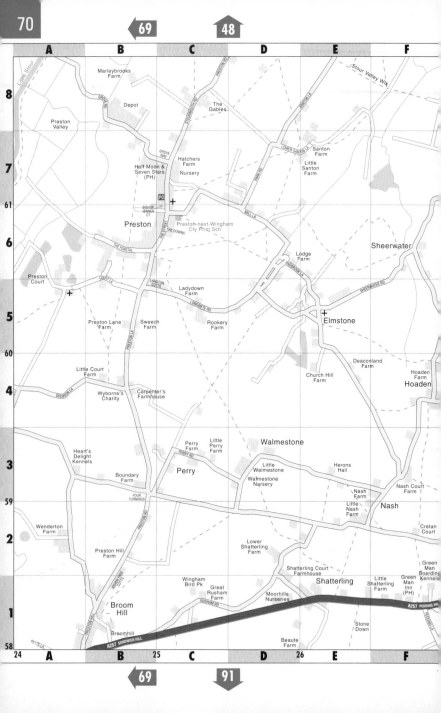

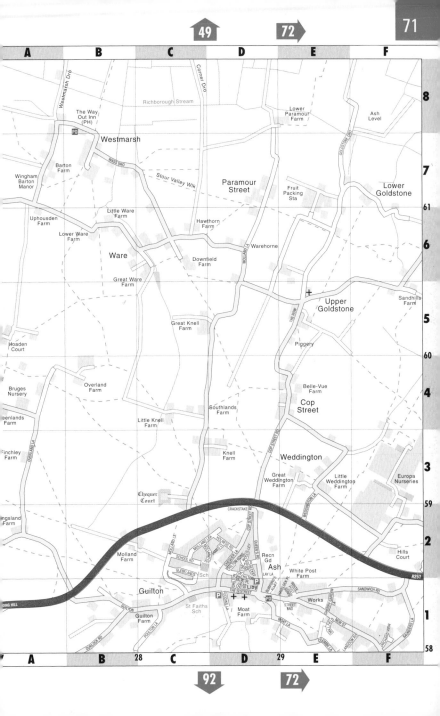

A   B   C   D   E   F

8

Ash Level

Potts Farm Dro

7

White
House

61

Richborough Stream

WHITE HOUSE DRO

RUSHEY DRO

Bride
Farm

Guston
Farm

6

Sparrow
Castle

Richborough
Farm

Fleet
Farm

Richborough Castle
ROMAN FORT
(remains of)

Castle
Farm

5

CASTLE
COTTS

Cooper Street
Farmhouse

Mus

Swallows
Brook Farm

60

Sewage
Works

COOPER STREET DRO

COOPER STREET DRO

Cooper
Street

Goshall Valley

Stour Valley Wlk

4

Goshall Stream

River Stour

3

Brookestreet
Farmyard

LC

The Minks Wall

Little East Street
Farm

Saxon Shore Way

RICHBOROUGH RD

59

East
Street

East Street
Farm

North Poulders Stream

2

Goss
Hall

EACH END LA

GOSS HALL LA

North
Poulders

White Mill
Folk Mus

Ind
Est

Nature
Reserve

WHITE MILL CLEES

MILL CL

A257   SANDWICH RD

A257

SANDWICH RD

A257

THE CAUSEWAY

ASH RD

LC

Sandwich
City Inf Sch

STROND ST

Each End

Each End
House

South Poulders

A256

The
Butts

LOOP COURT MEWS 1
WANTSUM MEWS 2
CHURCH STREET ST MARYS 3
VICARAGE LA 4
GUILDCOUNT LA 5
HARNET ST 6
WATTS YD 7
WHITEFRIARS WAY 8

THOMAS ST

P

1

Each Manor
Farm

Caravan
Park

Mary-le-bone
Hill

THOMAS HOSPL

LC

P

58

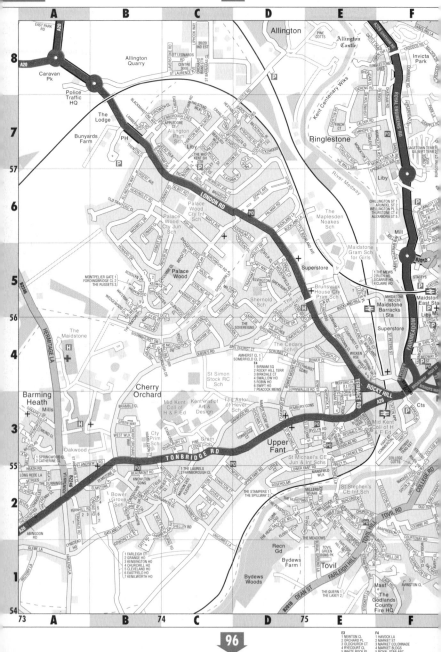

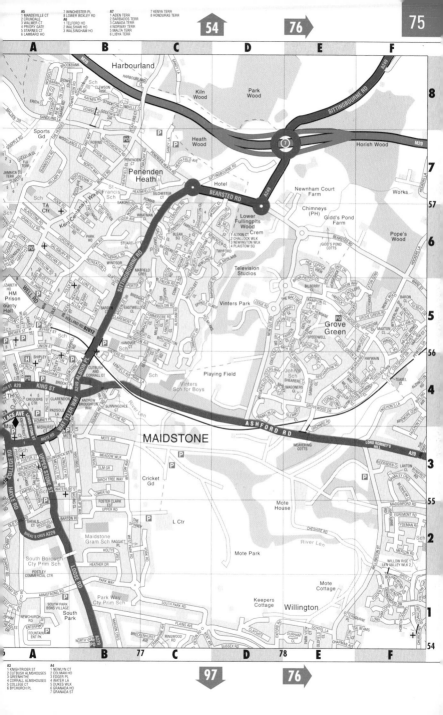

A B C D E F

Coldharbour

Eastfield
Farm

Hucking Hill
House

Admiral
House

SCRAGGED OAK RD
BOUGHBRIDGE LA

North Downs Way

Little
Scragged Oak
Farm

Smokes
Wood

London
Wood

Cat's
Mount

Scragged
Oak

Chitt's
Wood

BROAD STREET HILL

Bolton's
Wood

hitehall

WHITCHALL

Broad Street
Farm

Broad
Street

PILGRIMS WAY

North Downs Way

Ripple

Allington
Farm

Little
Allington

HOLLINGBOURNE HILL

Newlands
Wood

BANK
COTTS

Snarkhurst Wood

Stricketts
Garden

Manor
House PH

PILGRIMS WAY

Hollingbourne
Sta

Little
Snagbrook

Hollingbourne

White
Heath

MUSKET LA

Eyhorne
Farm

Eyhorne
Street

Hollingbourne
Cty Prim
Sch

MUSKET LA

ASHFORD RD

Musketstone

Godfrey
House

HADLEY
GDNS

Oak Meadow
Farm

Eyhorne
Green

PH P

UPPER ST

Target
Cottage

ASHFORD RD

Old Mill
Farm

The
Great Danes
Hotel

PENFOLD HILL

B2163

Oakfield

A20

M20

Coombe
Wood

HARPSWOOD

River Len

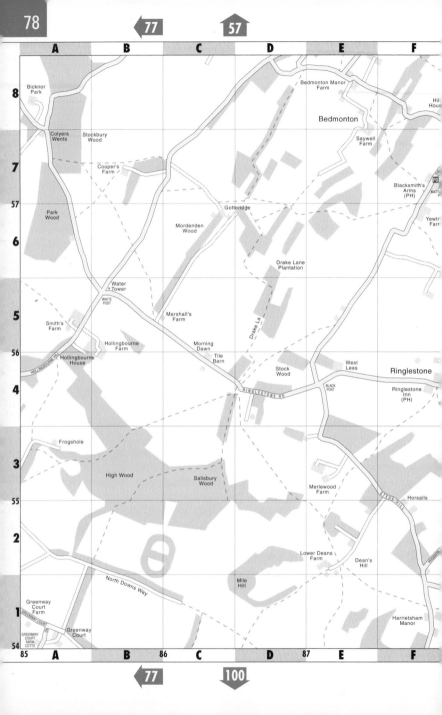

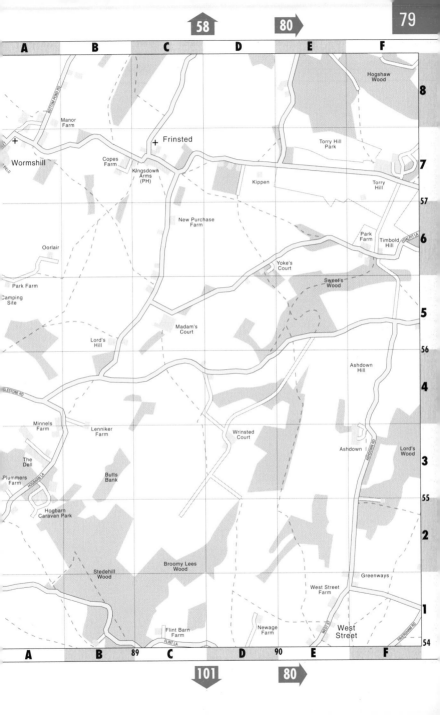

79
59

Hollybushes

Great Higham

Down Court Rd

Down Court

PALACE COTTS

Palace Farm

Doddington

Home Farm

PH

Lodge

Little Higham

THE RETREAT

WEST END COTTS

SUNNYSIDE

THE STREET

PO

BUTTERDOWN

Doddington Cty Prim Sch

Endings Wood

Ppg Sta

West End

Jackson's Wood

Shulla Woo

COAL PIT LA

COAL PIT LA

Sprats Hill

Green Farm

The Yew Tree (PH)

Temple Farm

Frangbury

Wichling

Syndale Bottom

Solomon's Cottages

King's Acre

Filmer Wood

Wichling Wood

TAVERSHAM RD

Takarazuka

Birchwo

Broomhill Farm

Bank Farm

Greet

Wellwood Farm

Lone Barn Farm

Maitlands Farm

Lady Margaret Manor

Rhode Farm

Wyeban

Oakenpole Wood

Sparks Wood

Centre Slade Farm

Slade

Forge Cottage

LONE BARN RD

RHODES ST

SLADE RD

Upper Slade Farm

Payden Street

Payden Street Farm

LONE BARN RD

Otterden Plantation

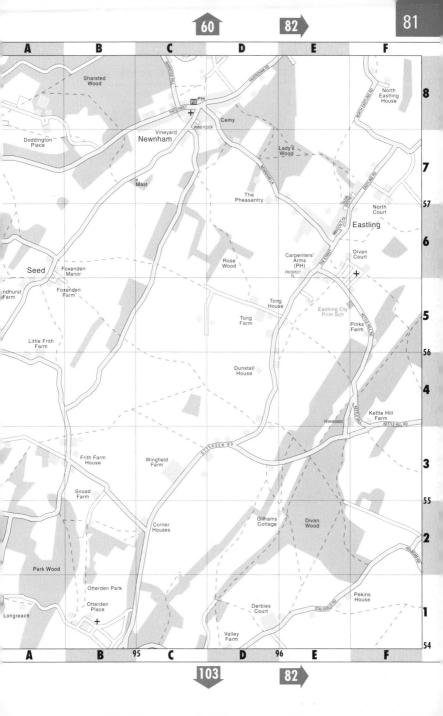

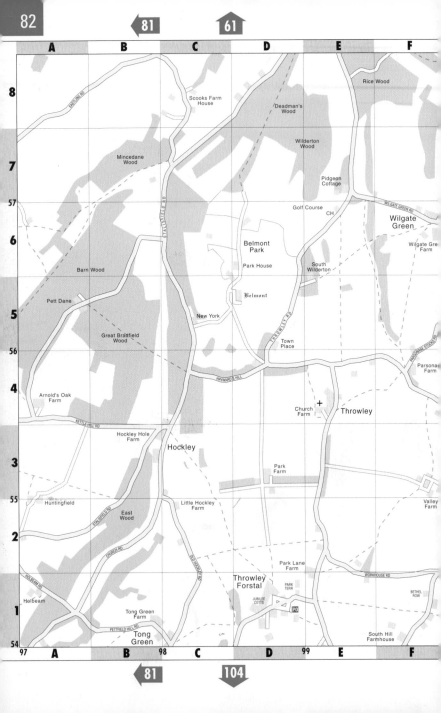

A   **B**   **C**   **D**   **E**   **F**

8

Rice Wood

Scooks Farm
House

Deadman's
Wood

7

Wilderton
Wood

Mincedane
Wood

Pidgeon
Cottage

57

WILGATE GREEN RD

Golf Course

CH.

Wilgate
Green

6

Belmont
Park

Wilgate Gre
Farm

Barn Wood

Park House

South
Wilderton

Pett Dane

Belmont

5

New York

Great Bradfield
Wood

Town
Place

PILGRIMS STOCKS RD

56

Parsonas
Farm

HAYWARD'S HILL

4

Arnold's Oak
Farm

Church
Farm

Throwley

KETTLE HILL RD

Hockley Hole
Farm

Hockley

3

Park
Farm

55

Huntingfield

STALISFIELD RD

East
Wood

Little Hockley
Farm

Valley
Farm

2

CHURCH RD

OLD HOCKLEY RD

Park Lane
Farm

WORKHOUSE RD

HOLBEAM RD

Throwley
Forstal

PARK
TERR

BETHEL
ROW

Helbeam

JUBILEE
COTTS

PO

1

Tong Green
Farm

PETTFIELD HILL RD

South Hill
Farmhouse

54

Tong
Green

97   **A**   **B**   **98**   **C**   **D**   **99**   **E**   **F**

A	B	C	D	E	F

Baggin Wood

North Street

OAST COTTS

OWENS COURT COTTS

Owens Court

Saffery Farm

8

PLUMFORD RD

Gosmere

NEWHOUSE LA

Newhouse Farm

7

57

WINDING HILL

Throwley House

Sheldwich

THE STOCKS

Church Plantation

Winding Hill Wood

6

OLD BADGINS RD

Cobrahamsole Farm

Sheldwich Cty Prim Sch

HUNTER'S WAY

LEE'S COURT RD

AMOS CL

NURSERY LA

BEST HARROW

MAJOR KIRBY'S GDN

THE CARRIAGE HO

5

Sheldwich Lees

Lees Court

56

Lords Farm

Lees Court Park

4

BADGSHILL RD

Little Lords

LORDS COTTS

ASHFORD RD

Stocking Wood

3

Poultry Farm

MILLEN'S ROW

DAYTON RD

Badlesmere Court

55

LEAVELAND COTTS

lack haw

Leaveland Court

Woods Court

2

Leaveland Wood

Badlesmere Park Wood

Holly Grove

FISHER STREET RD

Stringmans Farm

1

Workhouse Wood

Tenant Wood

Badlesmere

A251

Leaveland

54

A	01	C	02	E	F

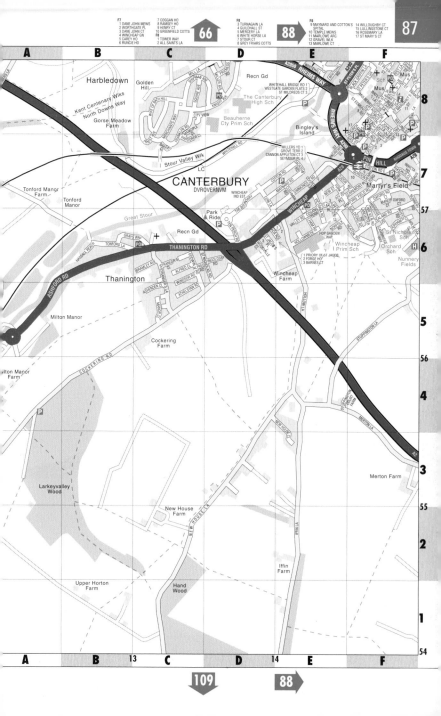

88

All
1 BUTCHERY LA
2 LONGMARKET
3 IRON BAR LA
4 BURGATE LA
5 LADY WOOTTON'S GN
6 CHURCH ST (ST PAULS)
7 ALMSHOUSES

87
67

A   B   C   D   E   F

Cath
THE PRECINCTS
St AUGUSTINE'S
Christ Church
Coll

Ct HM
Prison

CH

LITTLEBOURNE RD

1 DYMCHURCH HO
2 EDENBRIDGE HO

Howe
Barracks

TALAVERA
RD

8

St AUGUSTINE'S
Coll

St MARTIN'S HILL
Coll

WINDMILL
CL

St Martin's

Camping
Site

LONGPORT

St Martin's

HETFORD CT 1
ELISANS WLK 2
CONFERENCE WLK 3
LAMBOURNE WLK 4

Barton Cl

Canterbury
Coll

1 CHAUCER CT
2 ABBOTS BARTON WLK

St AUGUSTINE'S RD

Chaucer
Tech Coll

ORCHARD
FLATS

Little Barton
House

The Hoath
Farm

7

3 FIESTA WLK
5 PEARMAIN WLK
7 EYNDON HO

SUSSEX
WLK

DUROVERNUM

The
Pilgrims Way
Cty Prim Sch

CHAUCER CL

BARTON
BSNS PK

57

YH

SCD

Little Barton
Farm

6

Kent
Cty Cricket
Club

North Downs Way

NEW DOVER RD

Elham Valley Way

Haystack
Wood

John Graham Ct

RIDLANDS

Kent &
Canterbury

1 UNDERWOOD CT
2 NACKINGTON CT
3 BOUNDARY CT

5

Simon Langton
Sch for Girls

Old Gate Inn
(Hotel)

Hode
Farm

56

St Anselm's
Catholic
Comp Sch

CANTERBURY

Chaucer

DVROVERNVM

LANGTON LA

4

Simon Langton
Sch for Boys

Milestone

NACKINGTON RD

NACKINGTON RD

MERTON LA

A2
Winter's
Farm

Renville
Farm

3

A2050

BEKESBOURNE RD

55

THE
CLOSE

2

Meml

Nackington

CHURCH LN

1

MILL LN

BRIDGE RD

54

15   A   B   16   C   D   17   E   F

87
110

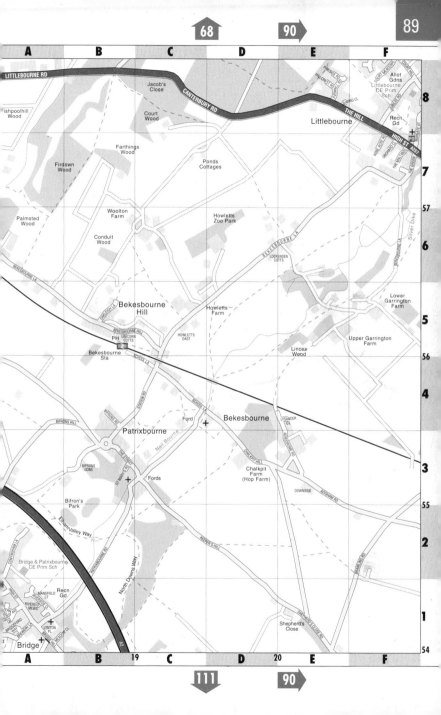

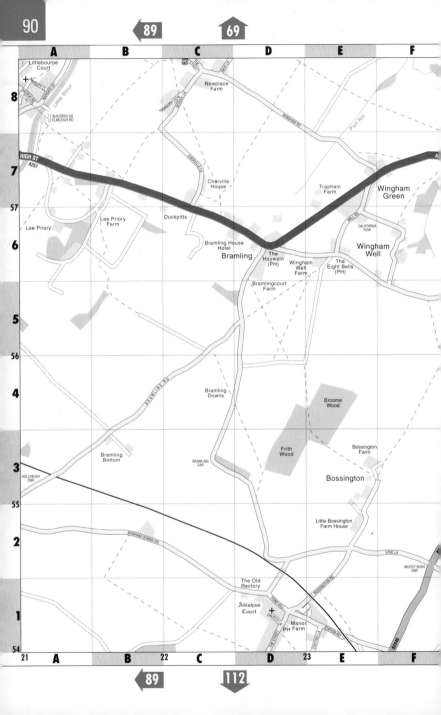

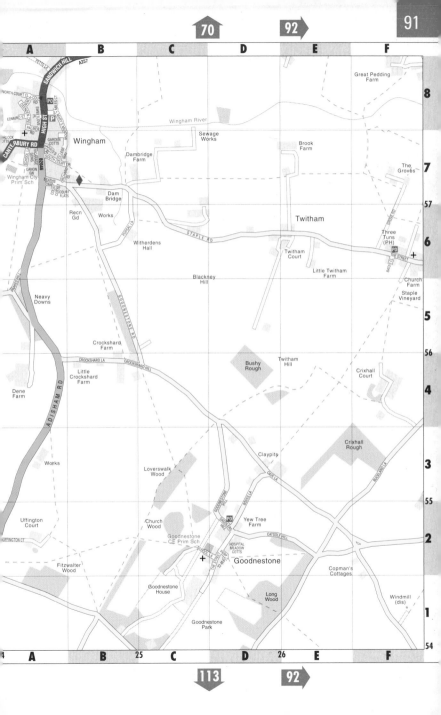

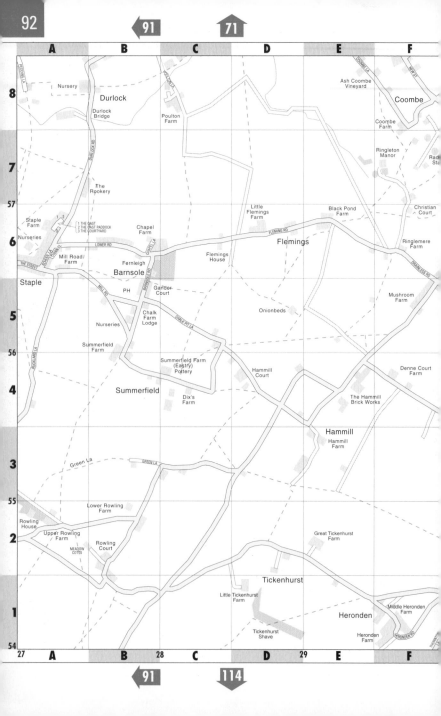

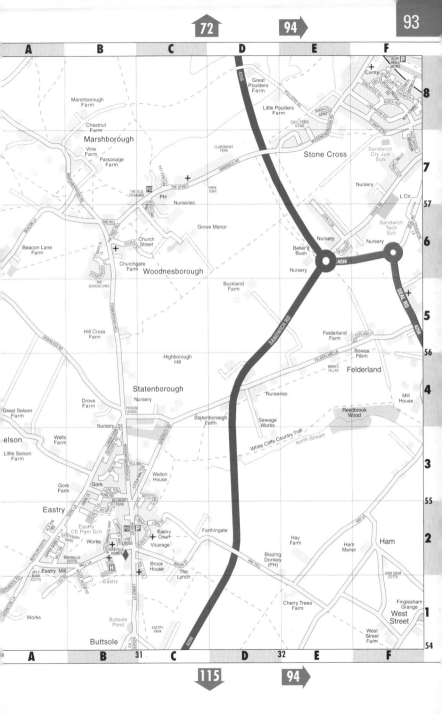

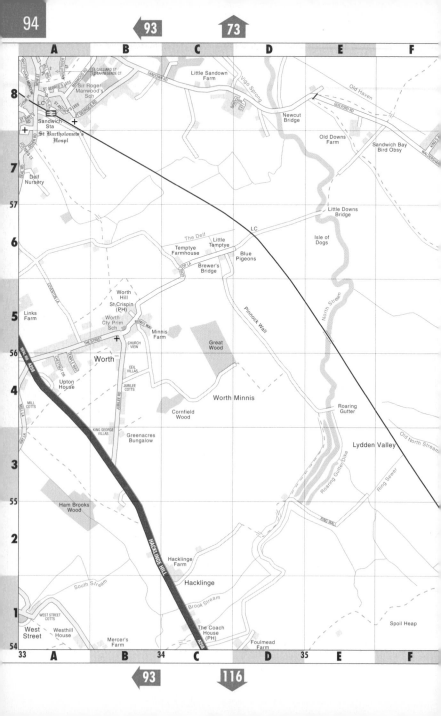

A   B   C   D   E   F

Royal
George's
Golf Links

Sandwich Bay

8

KING'S AVE.

COASTGUARD
COTTS.

Sandwich Bay
Estate

PRINCE'S DR.

FIRTH RD.

WALDERSHARE AVE.

SANDOWN AVE.

7

FRANCIS AVE.

CAMBRIDGE AVE.

57

DICKSON'S
CNR

6

Lyddcourt
Stile

Lydden

Mary Bax's
Stone

5

56

Chequers
(PH)

Caravan
Park

Royal Cinque Ports Golf Links

White Cliffs Country Trail

Saxon Shore Way

4

3

Tennants
Hills

55

Rd. No. 1 Stream

Walnut Tree
Farm

2

Sandhills

CH

REDHOUSE WAY

GOLF RD.

Sandown Castle
(remains of)

1 CASTLE WLK
2 CANUTE WLK

1

Penfold Sewer

Spoil
Heap

CANUTE RD.

SANDOWN RD.

THE MAIYAR

THELBERT RD.

GOLF CT 1
LINKS CT 2

54

A   B   37   C   D   38   E   F

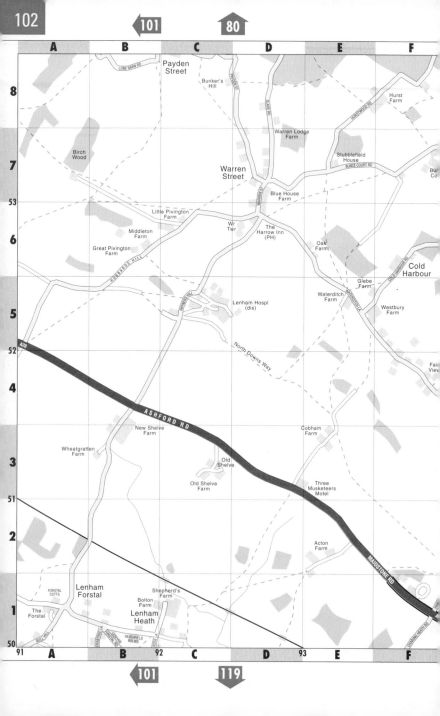

Payden Street

LONE BARN RD

Bunker's Hill

Hurst Farm

Warren Lodge Farm

Birch Wood

Stubblefield House

WINCE COURT RD

Bur Co

Warren Street

Blue House Farm

Little Pivington Farm

Wr Twr

The Harrow Inn (PH)

Middleton Farm

Oak Farm

Cold Harbour

Great Pivington Farm

Glebe Farm

Waterditch Farm

Westbury Farm

Lenham Hospl (dis)

North Downs Way

Fair View

A20

Ashford Rd

New Shelve Farm

Cobham Farm

Wheatgratten Farm

Old Shelve

Old Shelve Farm

Three Musketeers Motel

Acton Farm

Maidstone Rd

Forstal Cotts

Lenham Forstal

Shepherd's Farm

The Forstal

Bolton Farm

Lenham Heath

Heathfield Bglws

Tong Green

Dodds Willows

Hazel Wood

Bell's Forstal

8

Heel Farm

Cadman's Farm

LOOSE DOWN RD

7

53

Almhouse Cottages

HOUSEFIELD RD

OAST LA

6

Hurst Wood

Rushmere Farm

Snoad Street Manor

Codling Wood

5

Snoad Street Cottage

52

Newlands Farm

4

NEWLANDS FARM COTTS

Tir Beg

Landew's Farm

Monkery Farm

FAVERSHAM RD

3

Wagon & Horses (PH)

STALISFIELD RD

51

Longbeech Wood

MONKERY LA

Snoad Lodge

2

GREEN LA

Paddock

Brisley Farm

Cedar House Farm

A252

CANTERBURY RD

1

The Woodlands Inn (PH)

RAG LA

Great Paddock Fram

Beech Court

Burnt Oak Farm

50

97 **A** **B** 98 **C** **D** 99 **E** **F**

Leaveland
Red Lion (PH)
GODFREYS COTTS
Collington Farm
ASHFORD RD
A251
Dennis Nash Wood
Beacon Hill
Bagshot Cottage
SHOTTENDEN RD
Birchetts Wood
Willow Wood
Dryland Farm
Bowerland Shaw
BOUNDSGATE CNR
Jeffreys Bank Wood
Works
Cradle Bottom Wood
Pontus
Broomfield Farm
FAVERSHAM RD
Hegdale Farm
Howlett's Farm
Hillibus Farm
Great Pested Farm
Pested
Molash
Bird Farm
PO
George Inh (PH)
CHURCH RD
A252
Harbour Farm
Knock Wood
PESTED LA
PESTED LA
Butt House Wood
Crispin Farm
Brushdane Wood
Tower Farm
Loamhole Wood
Oathill Farm
Round Wood
Green Lane Farm
Halfway House (PH)
Carpet Wood
GREEN LA
CLEVEDON CT
HIGH HALDEN RD
BUCK ST
ORCHARD LA
CLOCKHOUSE
PO
CANTERBURY RD
FOREST COTTS
Nine Chimneys Farm
FAVERSHAM RD
The Lees
Challock
Challock Cty Prim Sch
KILN LA
Rattle Hall
A251

8

Chequers
Farm

Little Hurst
Wood

Great Hurst
Wood

Harts
Farm

Dolfinch
Wood

Maggrllyden

7

Little
Bower

Wytherling
Court

Denne Manor
Farm

Pigeonhouse
Wood

Danecourt
Shaw

Dane
Court

53

Great Bower

Old Park Shaw

Dane
Street

6

Park Wood

Young Manor
Farm

Flemings

Ridge
Wood

5

Stanners Wood

Cutlers

Cutlers
Wood

52

Coppins Farm

4

Godmersham
Park

North Downs Way

3

51

King's Wood

2

1

Godmersham
Downs

Biltin

50

109
88

A B C D E F

8

Whitehill
Wood

Middle Pett
Farm

Warren
Wood

7

North Court
Farm

Little Pett
Farm

Redhill
Wood

The
Shave

53

+

Lower
Hardres

Lenhall
Farm

BUTTS CT

6

PO

BUTTS
MEADOW

PH

Little
Eaton
Farm

Avenue
Wood

Stockfield
Wood

5

Pett
Bottom

The
Duck
(PH)

52

Cook's
Farm

Gorsley
Wood

4

Peaceful
Retreat
Farm

Pilot's
Wood

Langham
Park
Farm

Broxhall
Farm

3

Broxhall
Wood

St Andrew's
Wood

Bursted
Manor

WOODGATE

51

BOW HILL

2

+

Upper
Hardres
Court

Hardres
Court
Farm

Bursted
Wood

Park
Rough

Reed
Farm

1

The
Manor
House

Westwood
Farm

Marley
Wood

50

15 A B 16 C D 17 E F

BRIDGE RD

WHITE HILL CL

SCHOOL LA

PETT BOTTOM RD

HARDRES COURT RD

PILOT'S LANE

BUTTS HILL

PILOT'S LANE RD

BROXHALL LN

BURSTED LN

PRARAM'S HILL RD

GROVE CAMP RD

REED HILL LA

109
127

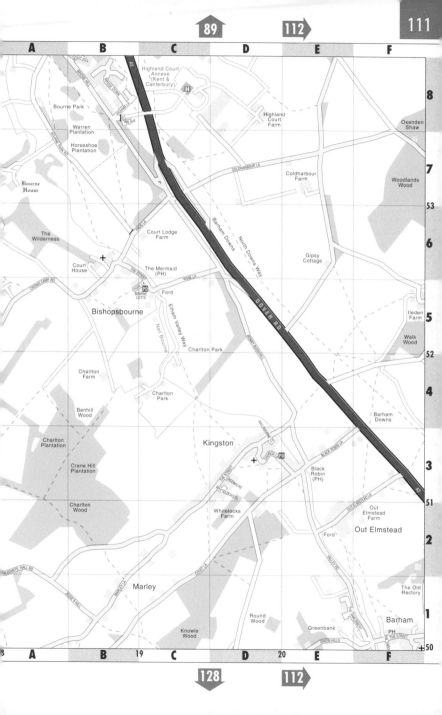

8

7

53

6

5

52

4

3

51

2

1

50

Highland Court Annexe (Kent & Canterbury)

Highland Court Farm

Oxenden Shaw

Bourne Park

Warren Plantation

Horseshoe Plantation

Coldharbour La

Coldharbour Farm

Woodlands Wood

Bourne House

The Wilderness

Court Lodge Farm

Barham Downs

North Downs Way

Gipsy Cottage

Dover Rd

Court House

The Mermaid (PH)

Rose La

Bishopsbourne

Ford

Elham Valley Way

Nail Bourne

Penny Bishop

Ileden Farm

Walk Wood

Charlton Park

Charlton Farm

Charlton Park

Benhill Wood

Charlton Plantation

Crane Hill Plantation

Kingston

Nail Bourne

Barham Downs

Black Robin La

Church Hill PH

Black Robin (PH)

Charlton Wood

The Street

The Greenacre

Whitelocks Sq

Whitelocks Farm

Out Elmstead La

Out Elmstead

Out Elmstead Farm

Pleasants Hall Rd

Marley

Dover La

Ford

Valley Rd

The Old Rectory

Barham

Jesse's Hill

Round Wood

Green Hills

Greenbank

PH

The Street

Knowle Wood

A2

111
90

A B C D E F

8

7

53

6

52

5

4

3

51

2

1

50

21 A B 22 C D 23 E F

Twelve Acre Shaw

Adisham CE Prim Sch

Adisham Sta

Bloodden

Ratling Court

Adisham

Woodlands Manor

WOODLANDS RD

DUCK ST

ICE ST

COTTON LA

Oxenden Wood

Cooting Farm

STATION RD

B2046

Pitt Wood

Woodlands Wood

1 ULLSWATER GDNS
2 ENNERDALE GDNS

TENNYSON RD
COLERIDGE RD
THIRLMERE
WORDSWORTH GDNS
CORNWALLIS AV

DORMAN AV E

Aylesham Cty Prim Sch

Aylesham

Well Wood

Cooting Downs

WOODLAND AVE

Liby
MEADOW
DOWN

QUEENS RD
HYDE PL

CLARENDON RD
SPINNEY LA

EASTRY CT

Ileden Wood

Aylesham Wood

COOTING RD

HAWTHORN CL

Ind Est

COVERT RD

SPINNEY LA

Ackholt Wood

Barham Downs

Upper Digges Farm

A2

AYLESHAM CNR

Willow Wood

Chalk Wood

DOVER RD

ADISHAM RD

North Downs Way

Cemy

POND LA

Well Wood

Nethersole Farm

Snow Down

Aylesham Farm

CHURCH LA

Womenswold

Woodpeckers Country Hotel

Westmore Ho

OLD DOVER RD

A2

GRAND CASTLE LA

B2046

A260

Woolage Village

NETHERSOLE RD

PO

PO

111
129

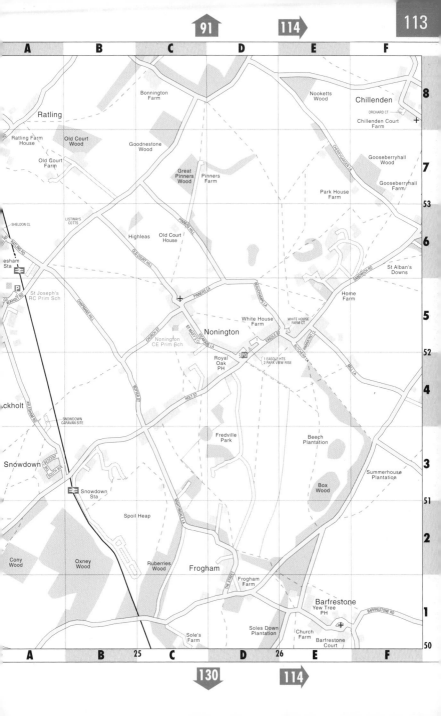

A   B   C   D   E   F

8

Bonnington
Farm

Nooketts
Wood

Chillenden

Ratling

ORCHARD CT

Ratling Farm
House

Old Court
Wood

Chillenden Court
Farm

Old Court
Farm

Goodnestone
Wood

Gooseberryhall
Wood

7

Great
Pinners
Wood

Pinners
Farm

Gooseberryhall
Farm

SHELDON CL

LISTWAYS
COTTS

Park House
Farm

53

esham
Sta

Highleas

Old Court
House

6

P

St Joseph's
RC Prim Sch

St Alban's
Downs

Home
Farm

5

White House
Farm

WHITE HOUSE
FARM CT

Nonington
CE Prim Sch

Nonington

52

Royal
Oak
PH

1 EASOLE HTS
2 PARK VIEW RISE

ckholt

4

HOLT ST

SNOWDOWN
CARAVAN SITE

Fredville
Park

Beech
Plantation

Snowdown

Summerhouse
Plantation

3

Snowdown
Sta

Box
Wood

51

Spoil Heap

2

Cony
Wood

Oxney
Wood

Ruberries
Wood

Frogham

Frogham
Farm

Barfrestone

Yew Tree
PH

BARFRESTONE RD

1

Sole's
Farm

Soles Down
Plantation

Church
Farm

Barfrestone
Court

50

A   B   25   C   D   26   E   F

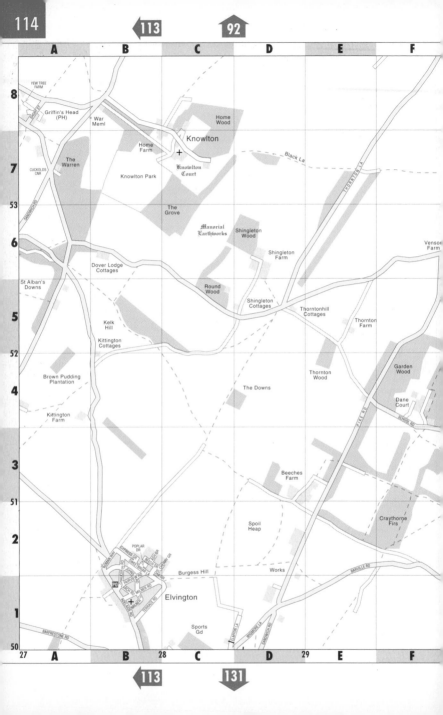

113
92

A B C D E F

8

YEW TREE FARM

Griffin's Head (PH)
War Meml

7

The Warren
CUCKOLDS CNR

Home Farm

Knowlton

Home Wood

Black La

53

Knowlton Park

Knowlton Court

The Grove

6

St Alban's Downs

Dover Lodge Cottages

Manorial Earthworks

Shingleton Wood

Shingleton Farm

Vensor Farm

5

Kelk Hill

Round Wood

Shingleton Cottages

Thorntonhill Cottages

Thornton Farm

52

Kittington Cottages

Thornton Wood

Garden Wood

4

Brown Pudding Plantation

The Downs

Dane Court

SCHOOL RD

Kittington Farm

3

Beeches Farm

Craythorne Firs

51

2

POPLAR DR

Burgess Hill

Spoil Heap

Works

BARVILLE RD

PO

Elvington

1

BARFRESTONE RD

Sports Gd

50

27 A B 28 C D 29 E F

113
131

8

7

53

6

5

52

4

3

51

2

1

50

Updown Farm

Sangrado's Wood

Updown House

Nursery

Lower Venson Farm

Betteshanger

Scawsby

Longlands

Northbourne Park Sch (Annexe)

HOME FARM COTTS

Northbourne Park Sch (Prep)

Home Farm

Little Betteshanger

Northbourne CE Prim Sch

Mill House

New Park

North Court Plantation

North Court

Lower Longlands

Admiral's Hole

Coldharbour

DOVES CNR

ST MARY'S GR

SCHOOL RD

Tilmanstone

ST ANDREW'S WAY

CHAPEL RD

PH

WHITE HILL

The Old Vicarage

Telegraph Farm

Stoneheap Wood

Nine Acre Wood

Stoneheap Farm

Fairlight Bungalow

BARVILLE RD

Boys' Firs Mast

Willow Wood

Pilgrim's Nook

Brighton Bungalow Farm

Barville Farm

DOVER RD

NORTH COURT LA

SANDWICH RD

MILL LA

STONEHEAP RD

NORTHBOURNE RD

A256

A256

A B 31 C D 32 E F

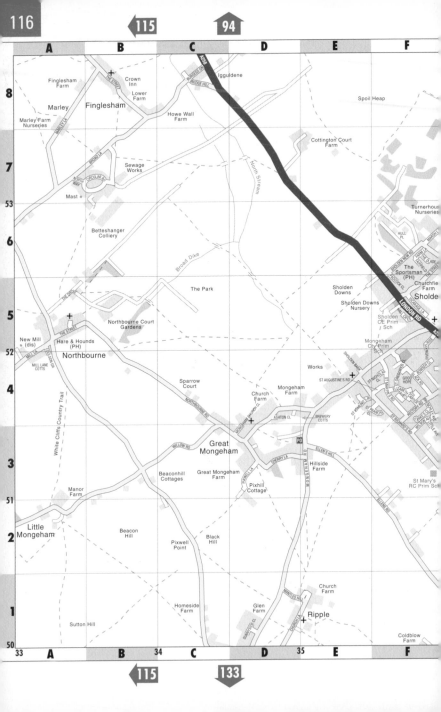

115
94

8

Finglesham Farm
Crown Inn
THE STREET
Lower Farm
Iggulden
Marley
Finglesham
Howe Wall Farm
Marley Farm Nurseries
MARLEY LA
BRIDGE HILL
A256
Spoil Heap

7

Cottington Court Farm
BROAD LA
Sewage Works
NORTH CIRCULAR RD
North Stream

53

Mast
Turnerhour Nurseries

6

Betteshanger Colliery
Broad Dike
MARGT
HULL PL
CLADE
SHOLDEN NEW RD
The Sportsman (PH)
Churchfie Farm
Sholde
LONDON RD
A258

5

THE DRO
THE STREET
Northbourne Court Gardens
The Park
Sholden Downs
Sholden Downs Nursery
Sholden CE Prim Sch
New Mill (dis)
Hare & Hounds (PH)
Northbourne
Mongeham Cty Prim Sch

52

MILL LA
MILL LANE COTTS
Works
SHOLDEN BANK
GOOD HOPE
St Augustine's Rd

4

Sparrow Court
NORTHBOURNE RD
Church Farm
Mongeham Farm
ST AUGUSTINE'S RD
White Cliffs Country Trail
ASHTON CL
BREWERY COTTS
PO

3

WILLOW RD
Great Mongeham
Great Mongeham Farm
CHERRY LA
Hillside Farm
MANOR RD
MONGEHAM RD
ELLEN'S HILL
St Mary's RC Prim Sch
Beaconhill Cottages
Pixhill Cottage
Manor Farm
ELLEN RD

51

2

Little Mongeham
Beacon Hill
Pixwell Point
Black Hill

1

Homeside Farm
Glen Farm
Church Farm
Ripple
MANOR HILL
CHERRY LA
BIRDSFOOT CL
Coldblow Farm
Sutton Hill

50

33   34   35
115   133

DEAL

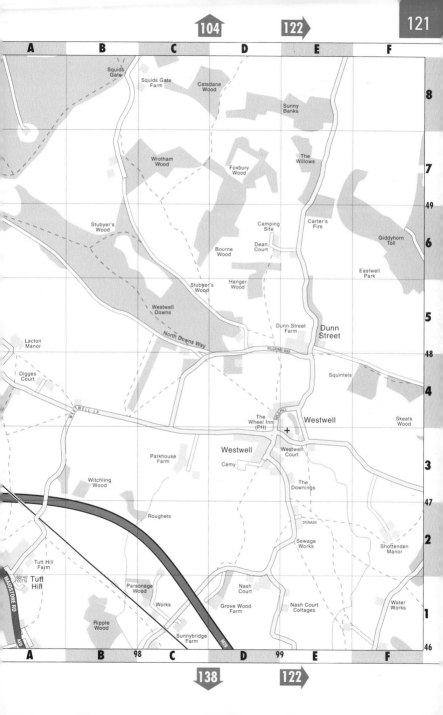

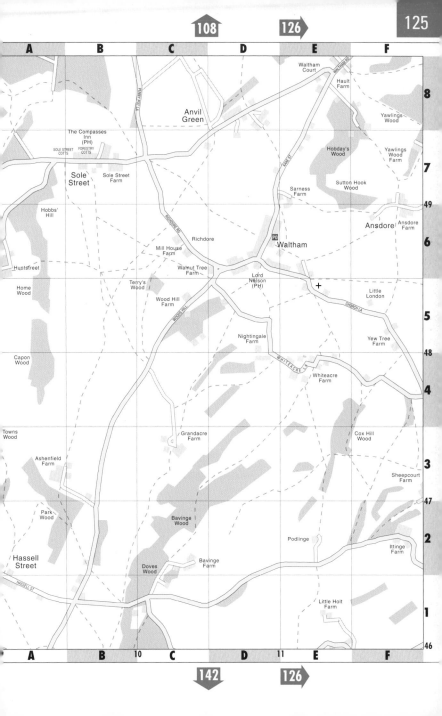

125
109

A   B   C   D   E   F

8

New Barn
Farm

Dane
Chantry

Homestead
Farm

Upper Hardres
Wood

Rou
Woo

Waddenhall
Wood

Nursery

7

Stubb's
Wood

Little Bossingham
Farm

Dunlies
Wood

The
Hollies

49

Stelling Lodge
Farm

HOMESIDE FAR

6

Little Wadden
Hall

Parkmead

Yockletts
Banks

WADDENHALL
FARM

Stelling Minnis
CE Prim Sch

Wadden Hall
Cottages

Doghouse
Farm

5

Syngate
Wood

Syngate
House

Church
Wood

STONE ST

SPIL LA

48

Yockletts
Farm

Cherry Gard
Farm

4

WHITEACRE LA

Nature
Reserve

Common

Butts
Farm

Holly Tree
Farm

Yewtree
Farmhouse

Mead
Farm

3

Westcroft
Farm

North
Leigh

Gaylees
Farmhouse

Prim
Farm
Malt
Farm

The
Laurels

CROWN LA

47

Little Buckett
Farm

Rose & Crown
(PH)

PO

Stelling
Minnis

Chapel
Farm

2

THORN LA

CURTIS LA

Little
North Leigh
Farm

Thorn
Farm

Knowler
Farm

1 MINNIS ON
2 MINNISFIELD

MILL L

Windmill
(dis)

Dean
Farm

Scarp's
Farm

1

Courthope
Farm

46

Great Dowles
Farm

B2068

12   A   B   13   C   D   14   E   F

125
143

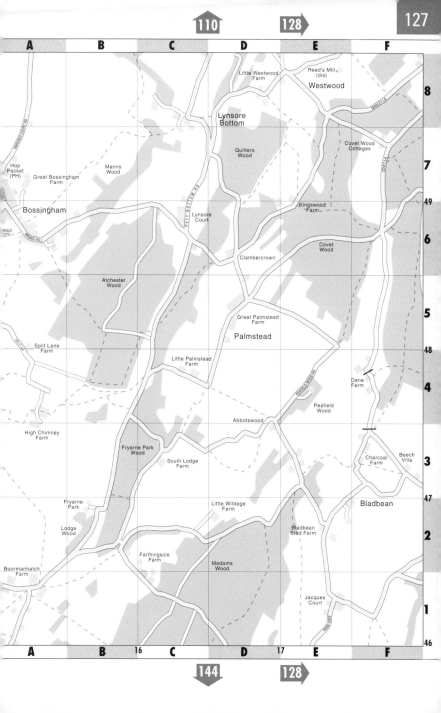

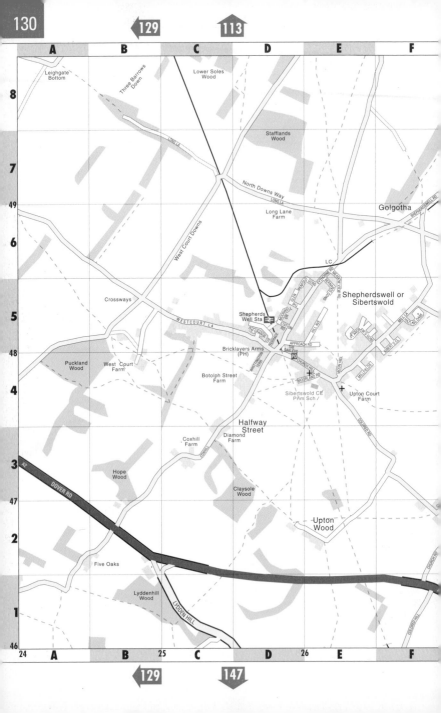

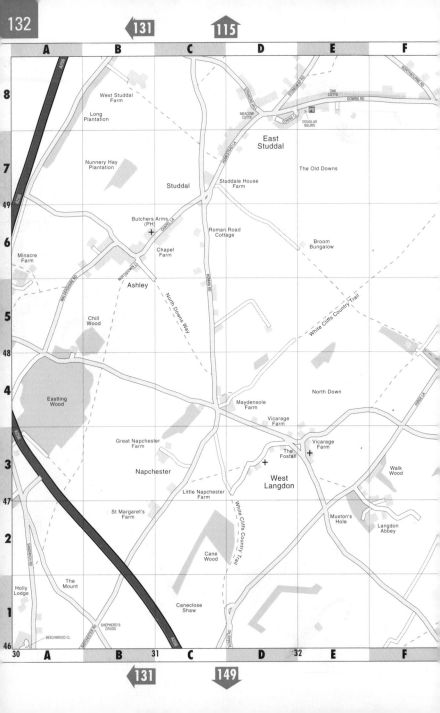

White Cliffs Country Trail

Coldblow Farm

Sutton Vale Country Club

CRANSWICK COTTS

SUTTON LA

Ripple Cty Prim Sch

MAYTREE COTTS

CHAPEL LA

PORTLAND TERR

The Plough Inn (PH)

Homestead Farmhouse

Ripplevale Sch

8

Upper Farm

Parsonage Farm

CHURCH

Ripple Farm

VALE RD

Sutton Court Farm

Sutton

Wingleton Farm

CROOKED S RD

7

PINNER'S LA

CHAPEL LA

49

Ripple Court

Holly Lodge

RIPPLE RD

6

Sutton Downs

PINNER'S LA

Winkland Oaks Farm

The Forest

Ringwould

RIPPLE RD

CHURCH LA

RIPPLE GROVE

SUTTON LA

MARKLAND

HANGMAN'S LA

PD

5

BACK ST

MATT RISE

CHURCH HAVEN

A258

48

HANGMAN'S LA

RINGWOULD RD

Nursery

DOVER RD

4

Appleton Manor

WATERWORKS HILL

Martin

Martin Lodge

THE STREET

THE STREET

Oxneybottom Wood

3

The Old Lantern Inn

The Grange

47

St Nicholas Church (rems of)

2

Hollands Hill

Martin Mill

MARTIN DALE RD

STATION RD

Martin Mill Sta

The Ugly Duckling (PH)

Oxney Court

A258

East Langdon

Langdon Cty Prim Sch

OLD ROMAN RD

MILL LA

PD

Martin Vale

GREEN LA

SCHOOL RD

1

Church Farm

THE STREET

WEST LA

MILL HILL

Jossingbrock

Hawthorn Farm Caravan & Camping Site

STATION RD

A258

VICTORY RD

NELSON PARK RD

THE CHASE

BERESFORD RD

46

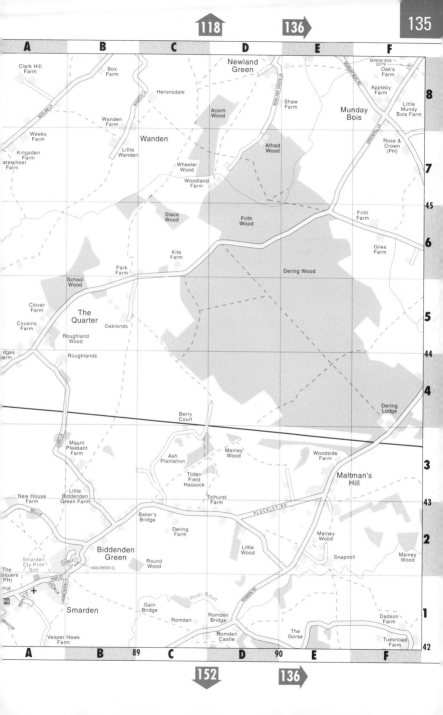

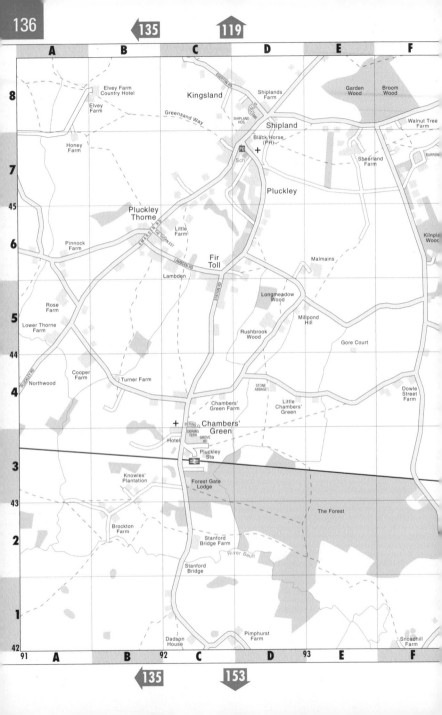

Ford Mill
Swan Inn (PH)
Little Chart Forstal
Greensand Way
Coldham Wood
RAM LA
Oaks Wood
Coldham Acres
Hothfield Common Nature Reserve
Hothfield Bogs
8

Rooting Street Farm
Brown Mill
Brownmill Bridge
Conyer Wood
Turners
WEST ST
Sch
7
Rooting Manor
Rooting Alders
Brownmill Spinney
45

Hall Farm
Mitchell Plantation
Thanet Copse
THE STREET
Egg Hole
6
Knight's Wood
Glebe Shaw
Fred's Spinney
THE BUNGALOW

Stour Valley Wlk
Great Stour
Ash Plantation
Bert's Walk
5
Saracen's Dairy
Benacre Wood
Paddocks Farm
Park Spinney
44

PLUCKLEY RD
Benacre Lodge
High Ridge
Burntoak Wood
Ripper's Cross Farm
Ripper's Cross
Worten Wood
Worten House
4
Hurst Hill
Hurst Hill Farm
BETHERSDEN RD

March Wood
Worten
3
Newlands Wood
RAM ST LA
Bear's Lane Wood
43

Golf Driving Range
Pumpfields
NINN LA
2
Dynes Farm
Hoad's Wood
Bridge Farm
Brickhurst Wood
Goldwell
South Landing
GOLDWELL

Belmont Farm
ETCHDEN RD
Goldwell
1
BELMONT FARM BSNS CTR
Etchden Wood
Etchden

River Beult
Mill Land Wood
42
A B 95 C D 96 E F

8

Castle Farm

Ripple Court

Beechbrook Farm

Foxenhill Toll

Beechbrook

Crouchers Manor

Kingsland

Beechbrook Wood

Sch

COMMON WAY

Tollhill Wood

7

MAIDSTONE RD

CH

PLANTATION
CLIFTON
FLAG

Hothfield

Yonsea Farm

Depot

45

PARK DR
MEADOW VIEW
THE STREET

Home Farm

Mill House

Woodside

PH

POTTERS CNR

Potters Corner

6

BEATHFIELD RD

The Larches

Broomfield Wood

Potters Corner Wood

POTTERS CNR

Hoad's Wood

Marble Wood

Eyesend Plantation

Nursery

Mansion Copse

Pigsbrook Wood

Godinton Plantation

GODINTON LA

Eyesend

Th War

5

Balls Wood

ASHGROVE

44

West Lodge

Balls Wood

Petts Hole

Lodge Wood

ORCHARD
KINGSNORTH RD

4

Godinton

Godinton Park

Chestnut Tell Plantation

LONG WLK

Worten Mill

Swinford Manor Sch

Jubilee Plantation

Greensand Way

MANOR WAY

ORCHARD LA

3

Worten Home Farm

River Spinney

Great Stour

Stour Valley Wlk

Loudon Wood

Chimneys (PH)

Godinton Cty Prim Sch

LOUDON PATH

EAST LODGE RD

LOUDON
LOCKHOLT

CHESTNUT DR

CEDAR

Willow Bed

Chart Ave

MAPLE
SPRINGWOOD DR

ROWAN CL

CHART RD

2

NINN LA

Godinton Park

ST GEORGE'S BSNS CTR

BRUNSWICK RD

COBBS WOOD IND EST

Depot

Ninn Lodge Farm

Bucksford Manor

1

Bucksford Bridge

CHART RD

Buxford Mill

Singleton Lake

BROOKFIELD RD

Riverside Sch

MONTPELIER LA
MONTPELIER BSNS PK

BROOKFIELD IND PK

Great Chart

PH

THE STREET

Playing Field

A28

OAKLANDS

42

97

98

C

99

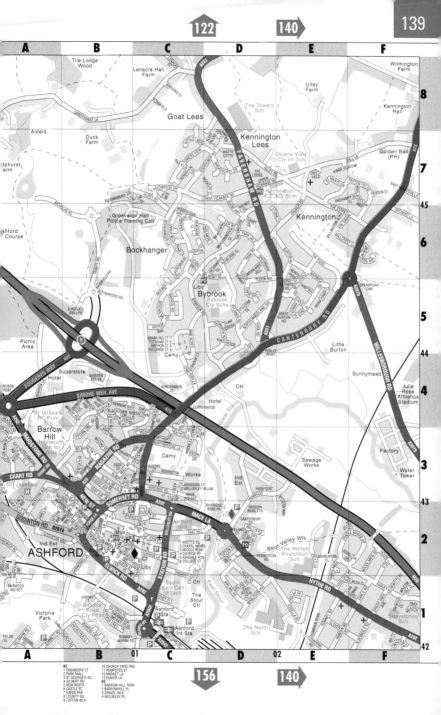

A 122 140 139

B2
1 ENGINEERS CT
2 PARK MALL
3 ST GEORGE'S SQ
4 GILBERT RD
5 NEW RENTS
6 CASTLE ST
7 KINGS PAR
8 COUNTY SQ
9 TUFTON WLK

10 CHURCH YARD PAS
11 HEMPSTED ST
12 MARKET LA
13 ELWICK LA

B3
1 BARROW HILL TERR
2 BARROWHILL PL
3 GRAVEL WLK
4 WOLSELEY PL

156 140

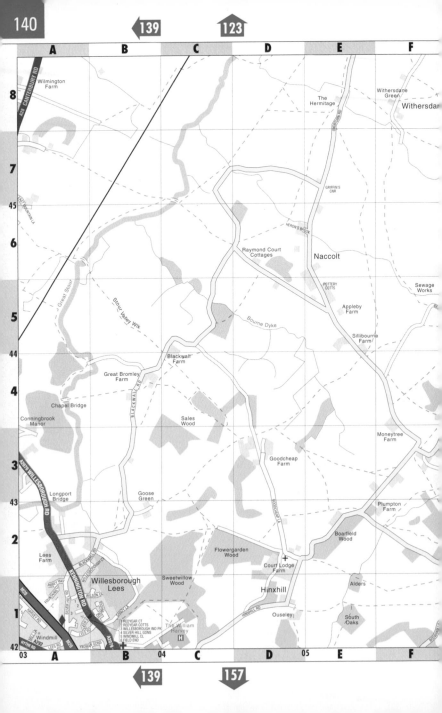

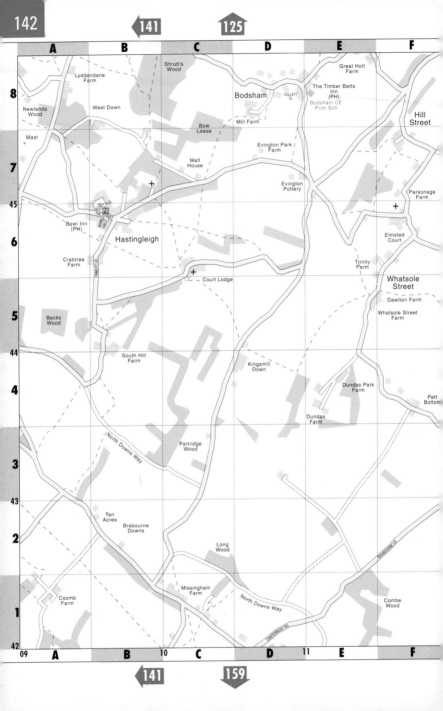

141
125

Shrub's Wood

Lyddendane Farm

Newlands Wood

West Down

Mast

Bow Lease

Malt House

Bodsham

Great Holt Farm

The Timber Batts Inn (PH)

Bodsham CE Prim Sch

COLLETT CL

Mill Farm

Hill Street

Evington Park Farm

Bowl Inn (PH)

THE STREET

Hastingleigh

Crabtree Farm

TAMELY LA

Court Lodge

Evington Pottery

Parsonage Farm

Elmsted Court

Trinity Farm

Whatsole Street

Dawlton Farm

Becks Wood

South Hill Farm

Kingsmill Down

Whatsole Street Farm

Dundas Park Farm

Pett Bottom

North Downs Way

Partridge Wood

Dundas Farm

Ten Acres

Brabourne Downs

Long Wood

Coomb Farm

Missingham Farm

North Downs Way

CANTERBURY RD

BRABOURNE LA

Combe Wood

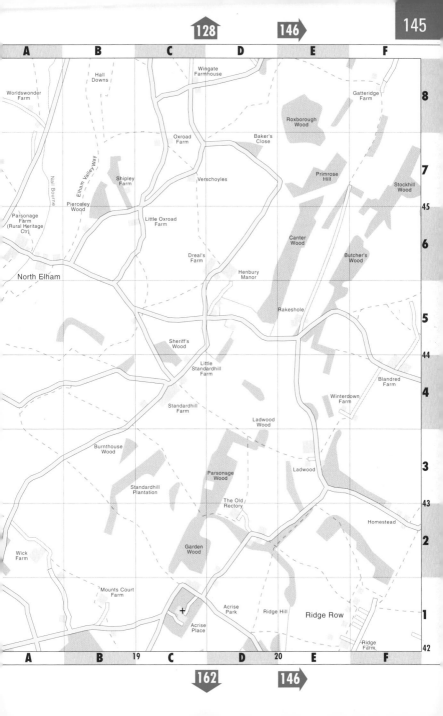

A   B   C   D   E   F

Worldswonder
Farm

Hall
Downs

Wingate
Farmhouse

Gatteridge
Farm

8

Roxborough
Wood

Oxroad
Farm

Baker's
Close

Elham Valley Way

Shipley
Farm

Verschoyles

Primrose
Hill

7

Stockhill
Wood

Nai Bourne

Pierceley
Wood

Little Oxroad
Farm

45

Parsonage
Farm
(Rural Heritage
Ctr)

Canter
Wood

6

Dreal's
Farm

Butcher's
Wood

North Elham

Henbury
Manor

Rakeshole

5

Sheriff's
Wood

44

Little
Standardhill
Farm

Blandred
Farm

4

Standardhill
Farm

Ladwood
Wood

Winterdown
Farm

Burnthouse
Wood

Parsonage
Wood

Ladwood

3

Standardhill
Plantation

The Old
Rectory

43

Homestead

Wick
Farm

Garden
Wood

2

Mounts Court
Farm

Acrise
Park

Ridge Hill

Ridge Row

1

Acrise
Place

Ridge
Farm

42

19

20

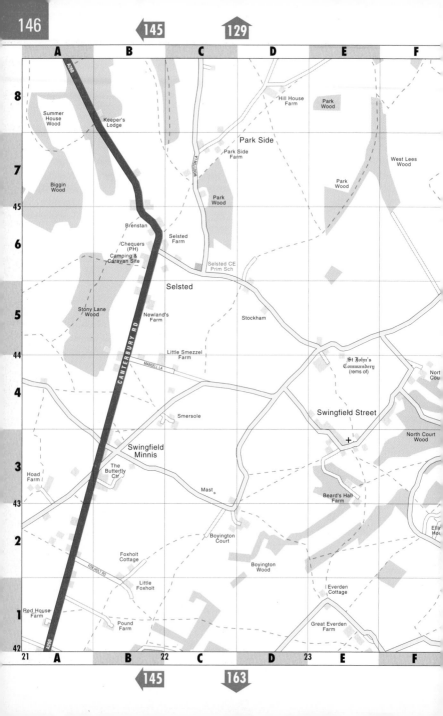

145
129

A   B   C   D   E   F

A2060

Summer House Wood

Keeper's Lodge

Hill House Farm

Park Wood

8

Park Side

Park Side Farm

WOOTTON LA

West Lees Wood

7

Biggin Wood

Park Wood

Park Wood

45

Brenstan

Selsted Farm

6

Chequers (PH)
Camping & Caravan Site

Selsted CE Prim Sch

Selsted

Stony Lane Wood

Newland's Farm

St John's Commandery (rems of)

5

Stockham

Nort Cou

Little Smezzel Farm

44

MANSELL LA

CANTERBURY RD

Smersole

Swingfield Street

4

North Court Wood

Swingfield Minnis

The Butterfly Ctr

+

3

Hoad Farm

Mast

Beard's Hall Farm

43

Boyington Court

Elli Ho

2

Foxholt Cottage

Boyington Wood

FOXHOLT RD

Little Foxholt

Everden Cottage

1

Red House Farm

Pound Farm

Great Everden Farm

42

21   A   B   22   C   D   23   E   F

A2060

145
163

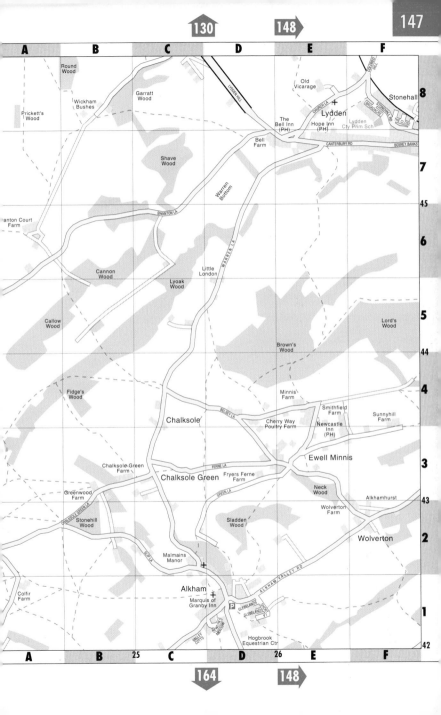

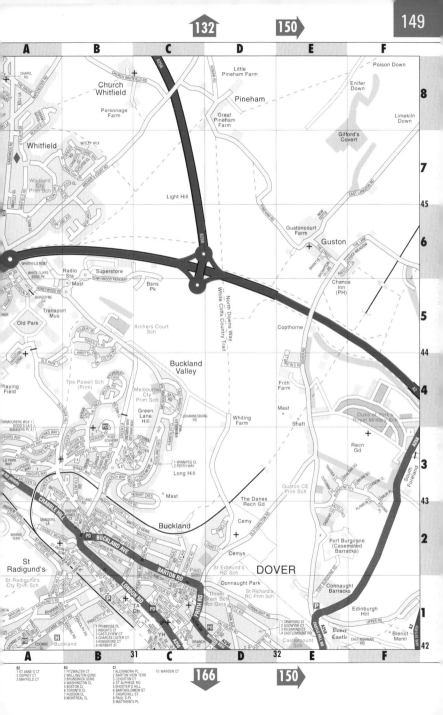

CHAPEL RD
Church Whitfield
Parsonage Farm
Whitfield
Whitfield Cty Prim Sch
Little Pineham Farm
Pineham
Great Pineham Farm
Poison Down
Enifer Down
Limekiln Down
Gifford's Covert
Light Hill
Gustoncourt Farm
Guston
Radio Sta
Mast
Superstore
WHITE CLIFFS BSNS PK
HONEYWOOD PARKWAY
Bsns Pk
WHITFIELD RDBT
BURGOYNE GR
Transport Mus
Old Park
OLD PARK CL
Archers Court Sch
North Downs Way
White Cliffs Country Trail
Chance Inn (PH)
Copthorne
Playing Field
The Powell Sch (Prim)
Buckland Valley
Melbourne Cty Prim Sch
Green Lane Hill
Johannesburg RD
Whiting Farm
Frith Farm
Mast
Shaft
Duke of York's Royal Military Sch
Recn Gd
1 WINNIPEG CL
2 PERTH WAY
Long Hill
Mast
Guston CE Prim Sch
CRABBLE HILL
MANGERS LA
CRABBLE MEADOW
BUCKLAND AVE
Buckland
The Danes Recn Gd
Cemy
OLD DOVER RD
South Foreland
St Radigund's
St Radigund's Cty Prim Sch
BARTON RD
LONDON RD
FRITH RD
St Andrew's
Cemys
St Edmund's RC Sch
Prim Sch
Connaught Park
DOVER
Fort Burgoyne (Casemated Barracks)
Connaught Barracks
H
Buckland
TA Ctr
Dover Gram Sch for Girls
St Richard's RC Prim Sch
Castlemount Sch
Edinburgh Hill
UPPER RD
Dover Castle
Bleriot Meml
EAST NORMAN RD
1 CRAFFORD ST
2 GODWYNE CT
3 RICHMOND CT
4 CASTLEMOUNT RD
YH
BRANCH ST

B2
1 ST ANNE'S CT
2 OSPREY CT
3 MAYFIELD CT

B3
1 FITZWALTER CT
2 WELLINGTON GDNS
3 BRUNSWICK GDNS
4 WASHINGTON CL
5 BOSTON CL
6 TORONTO CL
7 HUDSON CL
8 MONTREAL CL

C1
1 ALEXANDRA PL
2 BARTON VIEW TERR
3 LEIGHTON CT
4 ST ALPHEGE RD
5 SHOOTER'S HILL
6 BARTHOLOMEW ST
7 CHURCHILL ST
8 PAUL'S PL
9 MATTHEW'S PL

10 WARDEN CT

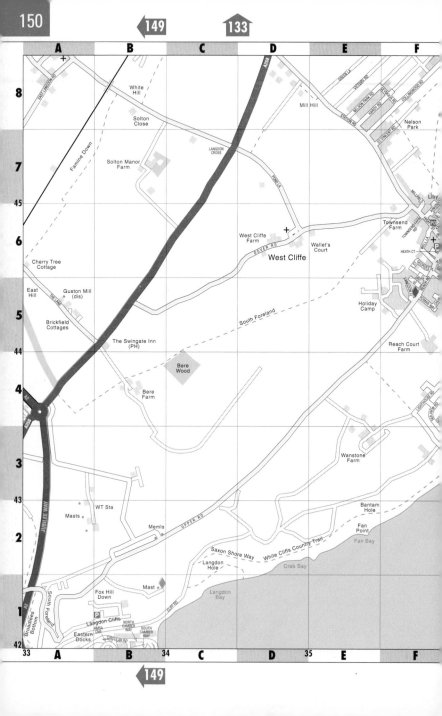

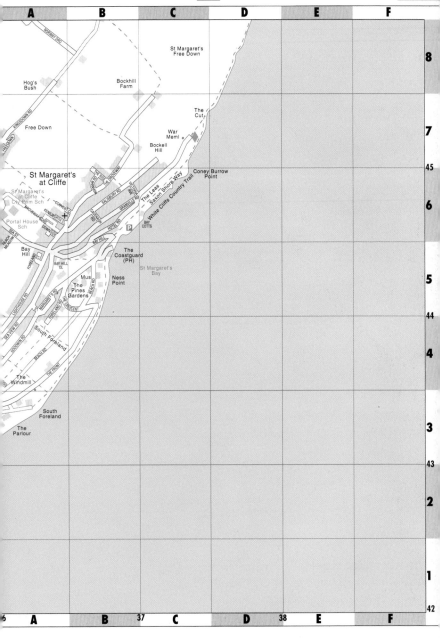

St Margaret's
Free Down

Hog's
Bush

Bockhill
Farm

Free Down

The
Cut

War
Meml

Bockell
Hill

St Margaret's
at Cliffe

St Margaret's
at Cliffe
Cty. Prim Sch

Coney Burrow
Point

The Leas

Saxon Shore Way

White Cliffs Country Trail

Portal House
Sch

BAY
COTTS

Bay
Hill

The
Coastguard
(PH)

St Margaret's
Bay

Mus

Ness
Point

The
Pines
Gardens

South Foreland

The
Windmill

South
Foreland

The
Parlour

135

167

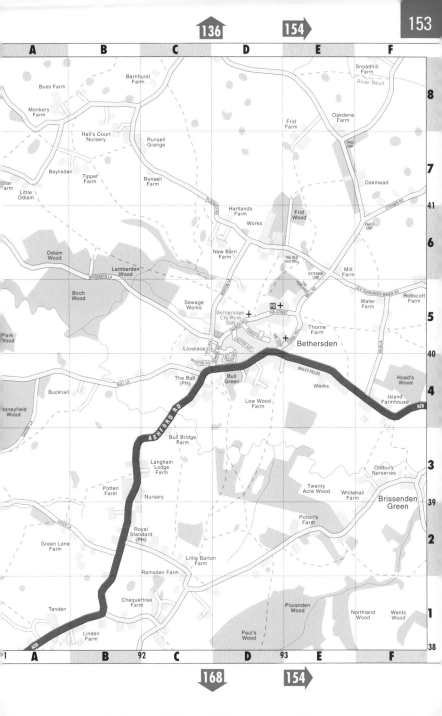

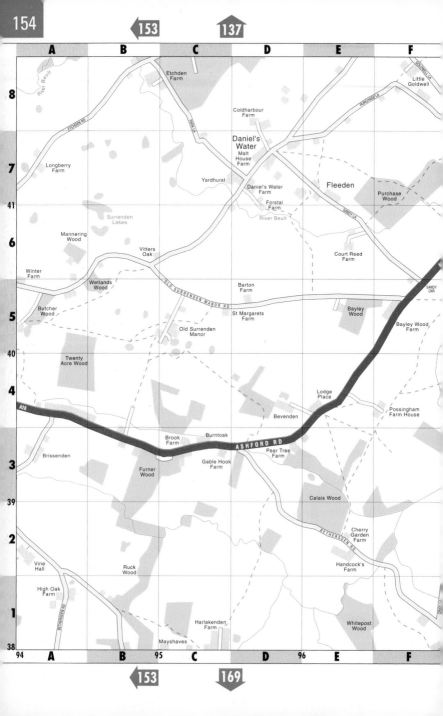

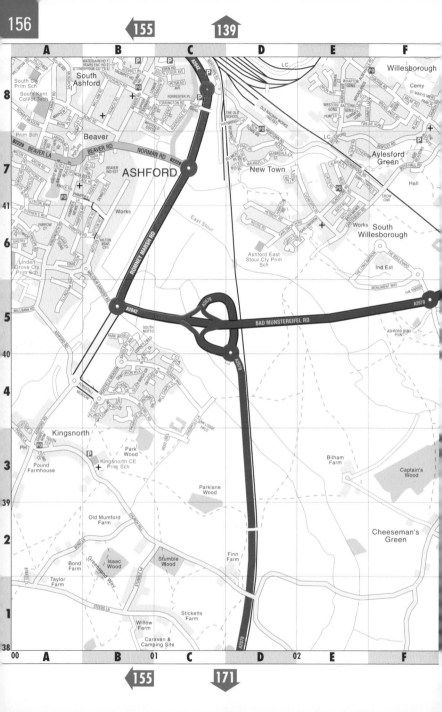

157
141

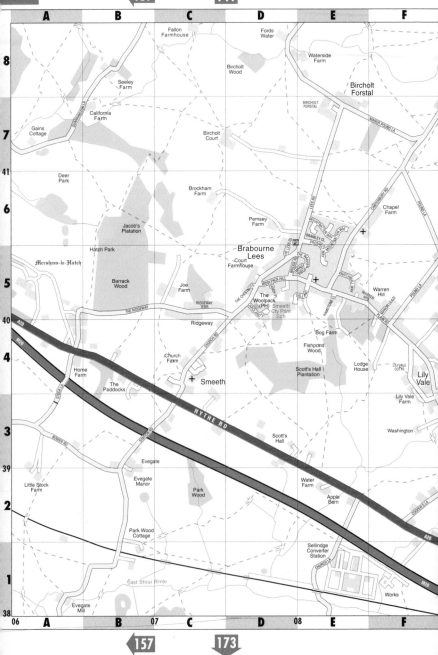

157
173

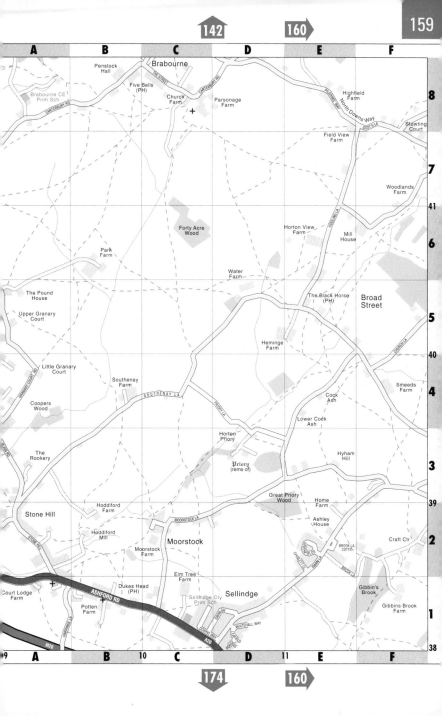

159
143

8

Mill Farm
Stowting CE Prim Sch
Round Down Wood
Ridge Farm
Hemsted
Stowting
Curteis Farm
Hill Top Farm
Woodland

Tiger Inn (PH)
Palmer's Wood
FLORENCE WAY
Golf Course
Cobb's Hill
Wick Wood
Skeete
Dingleden Wood

7

STONE ST
SKEETE RD

Whiteway
Skeete

41

Skeete Wood
Little Hollow Farm

6

CHURCH LA
North Downs Way
Nursery

Horton Wood
Horton Court
Hempton Farm
Nursery

Hempton Lodge Farm
Farthing Common

5

BRADY RD

40

HAMPTON HILL

Brickclamp Wood
Monks Horton Manor

4

Pent Farm

BLINDHOUSE LA
Blindhouse

3

STONE ST

Hayton Wood
Postling Court Farm
Page Farm

39

Postling

ORCHARD FIELDS
Vicarage Farm

Hayton Manor Farm
East Stour River

2

HAYTON RD
CUCKOLD LA

Lees Farm

The Drum Inn (PH)
Douglas Farm

1

Stanford

CHURCH HILL
STONE ST
B2068

KENNETT LA
VIEW TREE CL

38

159
175

A | B | C | D | E | F
12 | 13 | 14

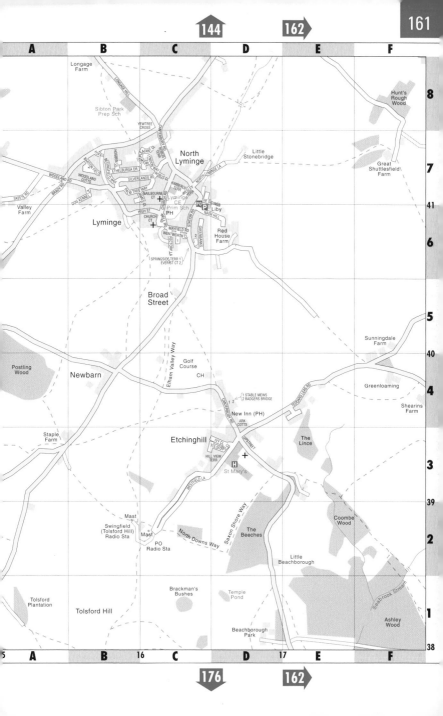

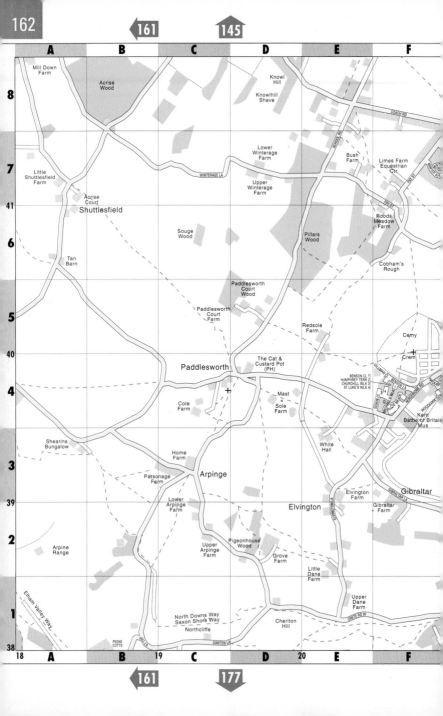

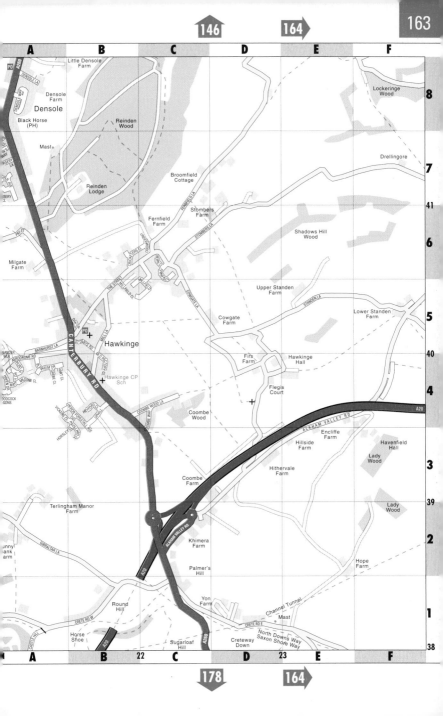

A B C D E F

PO

Little Densole
Farm

DENSOLE LA

PENDLE WAY

8

Lockeringe
Wood

Densole
Farm

Densole

Black Horse
(PH)

Reinden
Wood

Drellingore

7

Mast

Broomfield
Cottage

Reinden
Lodge

41

Stombers
Farm

PINE RD

Fernfield
Farm

Shadows Hill
Wood

6

KENFIELD LA

Milgate
Farm

STOMBERS LA

CHALK PIT RD

FIRS RD

THE STREET

PEAK LA

Upper Standen
Farm

5

Lower Standen
Farm

Cowgate
Farm

STANDEN LA

CANTERBURY RD

BARNHURST LA

Hawkinge

CHURCHILL RD

Firs
Farm

40

Hawkinge
Hall

SANDLE
MEA

AERODROME RD

HART CL

DEENE CL

HEIM DR

Hawkinge CP
Sch

Flegis
Court

4

COOMBE WOOD LA

VIKING CL

HORSLEY RD

COOMBE WAY

Coombe
Wood

A20

Encliffe
Farm

ALKHAM VALLEY RD

Havenfield
Hall

Hillside
Farm

Lady
Wood

3

Terlingham Manor
Farm

Hithervale
Farm

Lady
Wood

39

GIBRALTAR LA

Coombe
Farm

ALKHAM VALLEY RD

Khimera
Farm

A260

2

nny
ank
arm

Palmer's
Hill

Hope
Farm

Round
Hill

CRETE RD W

Channel Tunnel

Mast

1

CASTLE HILL

CRETE RD

Horse
Shoe

A20

Yon
Farm

North Downs Way
Saxon Shore Way

Sugarloaf
Hill

A260

Creteway
Down

38

A B 22 C D 23 E F

◄ 163

147 ▲

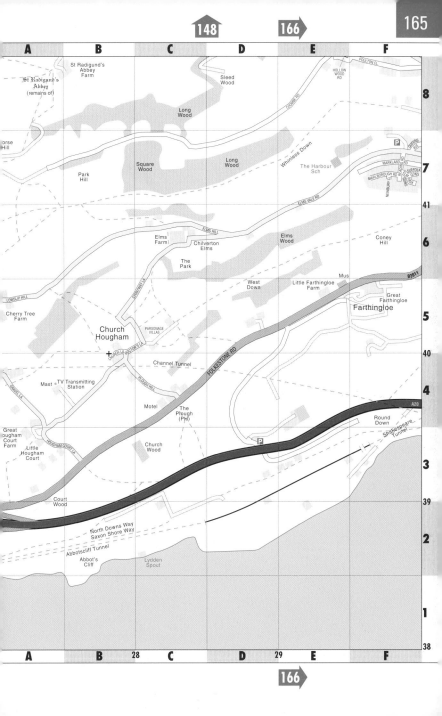

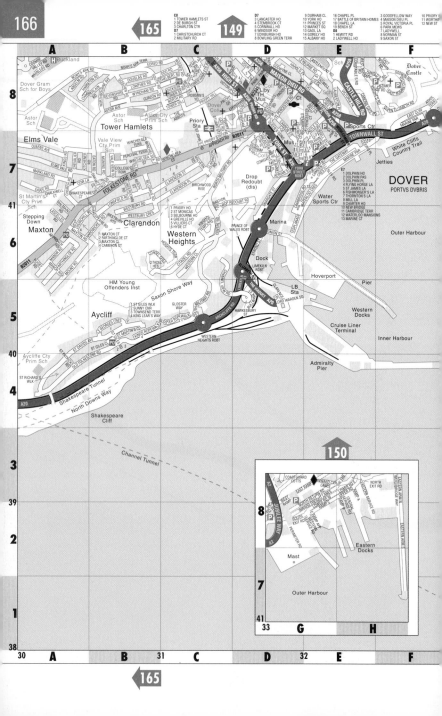

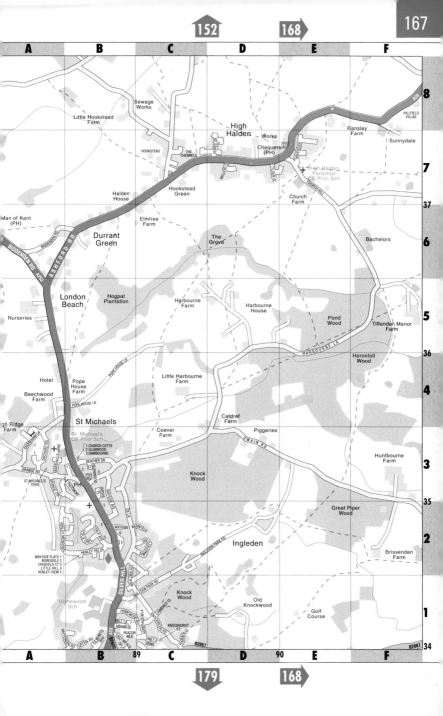

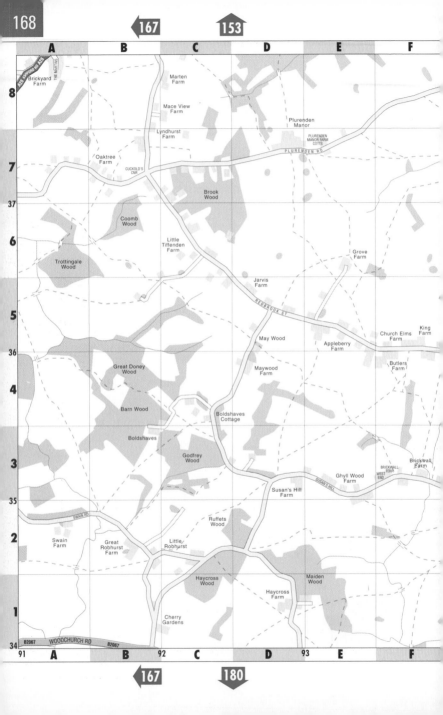

St PETER'S WAY

RIDGE CL

Shadoxhurst

Coxland
Wood

Kenilworth
Farm

8

THE STREET

Nursery

Woodside
Farm

HORNASH LA

Works

BUCK LA

Alex
Farm

7

Hillcrest
Farm

Great Turrels
Wood

Manor
Farm

Forty Acre
Wood

Upper Toke's
Wood

CHURCH LA

Nursery

37

Nursery

Nickley
Wood

Bambridge Wood

Bromley
Green

BROMLEY GREEN RD

6

NICKLEY WOOD RD

Kennels

Poplar
Farm

Little
Hurst

Moat
Farm

Dering
Wood

Bromley Green
Farm

Courthope
Wood East

Jenkey
Farm

Long-Hurst

5

HAMSTREET RD

Capel Wood

36

Bayland
Wood

Birchett
Wood

4

Longrope
Wood

Capel
House

Sir Edward Street's
Wood

Sugarloaf

CAPEL RD

3

ST THOMAS
CROSS

Spot House
Farm

35

Forest Walks

Picnic
P Site

2

Parsonage
Farm

Orlestone

Burnt
Oak

Cour
Lod

Tucker
Farm

SALT HOUSE LA

Fifty Acre Wood

Faggs
Wood

Apsley
Wood

ASHFORD RD

1

Lord's Wood

34

Adams Wood

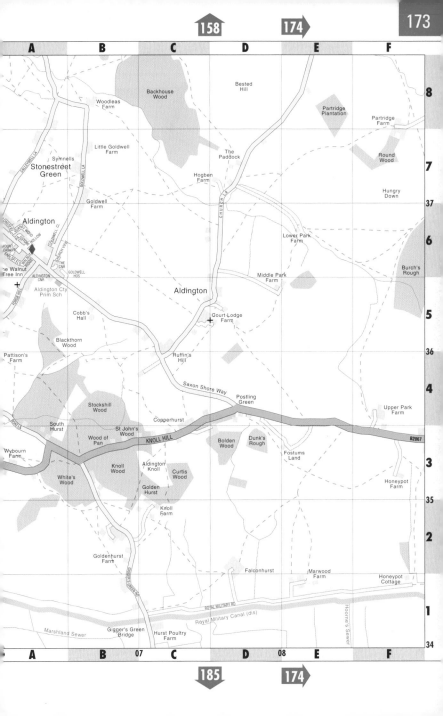

A   B   C   D   E   F

8

Backhouse Wood

Bested Hill

Partridge Plantation

Partridge Farm

Woodleas Farm

Little Goldwell Farm

Symnells

The Paddock

Round Wood

7

Stonestreet Green

Hogben Farm

Hungry Down

37

Goldwell Farm

Aldington

Lower Park Farm

6

The Walnut Tree Inn

GOLDWELL HOS

ALDINGTON CNR

THE CNR

Middle Park Farm

Burch's Rough

Aldington Cty Prim Sch

Aldington

5

Cobb's Hall

Court Lodge Farm

Blackthorn Wood

Ruffin's Hill

36

Pattison's Farm

Saxon Shore Way

Postling Green

4

Stockshill Wood

Copperhurst

Upper Park Farm

South Hurst

St John's Wood

Wood of Pan

KNOLL HILL

Bolden Wood

Dunk's Rough

B2067

3

Wybourn Farm

White's Wood

Knoll Wood

Aldington Knoll

Curtis Wood

Fostums Land

Honeypot Farm

Golden Hurst

35

Knoll Farm

2

Goldenhurst Farm

Falconhurst

Marwood Farm

Honeypot Cottage

1

Marshland Sewer

Gigger's Green Bridge

Hurst Poultry Farm

ROYAL MILITARY RD

Royal Military Canal (dis)

Hoorne's Sewer

34

A   B   07   C   D   08   E   F

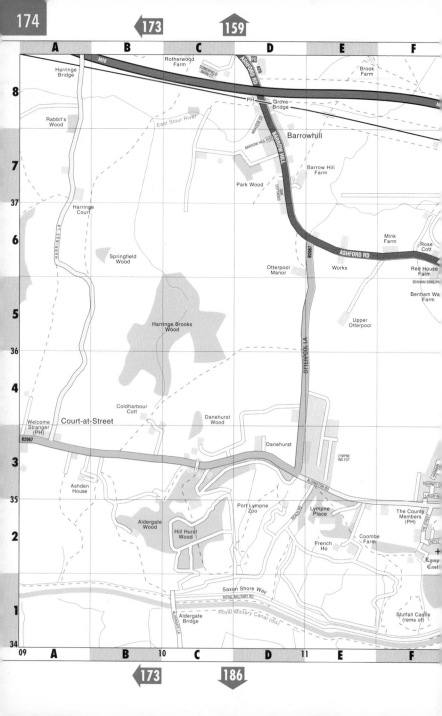

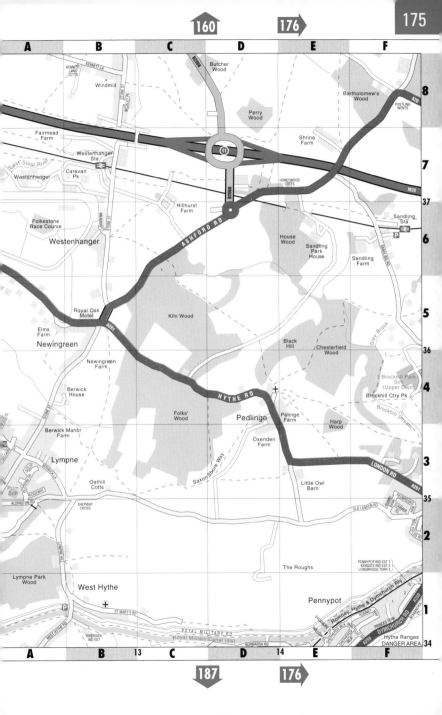

F5
1 WOLMER WAY
2 CHURCHILL HO
3 SPENCER HO
4 WINSTON HO
5 TURNER CT

E3
1 HILLSIDE
2 SOUTHOVER CT
3 HOMEVALE HO
4 TOWER CT
5 SIR JOHN MOORE CT
6 RIVIERA CT
7 NORTH LA
8 WHITE CT

F3
1 MARTELLO TERR
2 LACHLAN WAY
3 JAMES MORRIS CT
4 CASTLE CL
5 VARNE LODGE
6 VARNE CT
7 BEACH MARINE
8 ZARENA CT

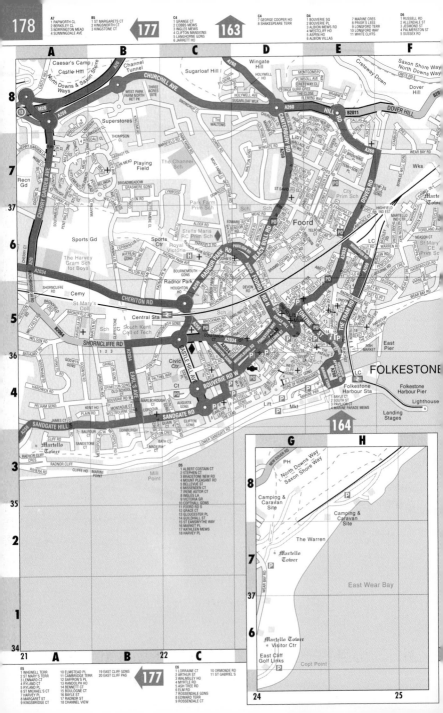

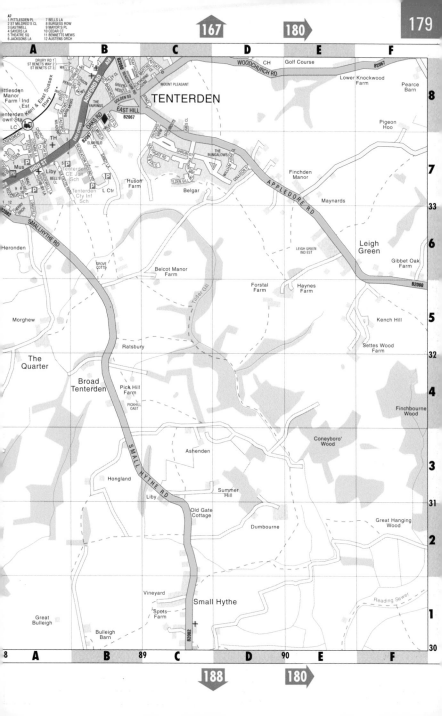

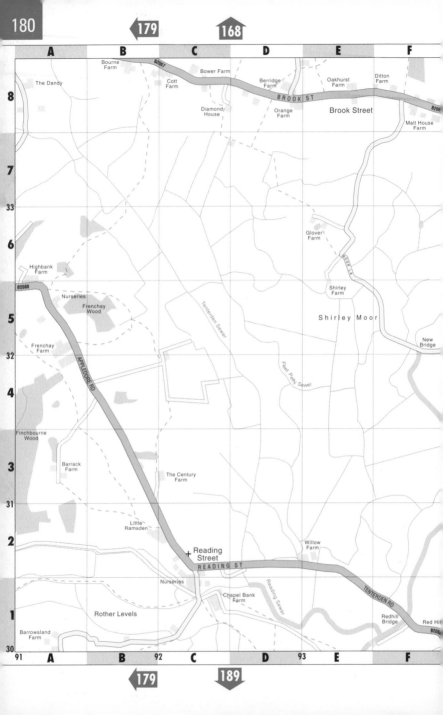

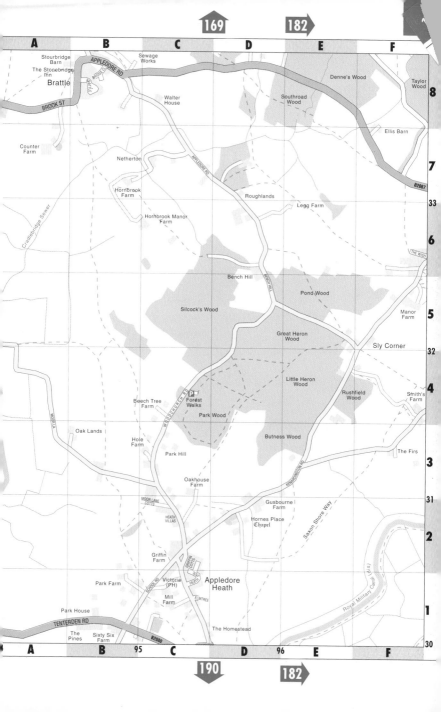

A   B   C   D   E   F

Stourbridge
Barn
The Stonebridge
Inn
Brattle

APPLEDORE RD

Sewage
Works

Denne's Wood

Taylor
Wood

8

BROOK ST

BRATTLE

Walter
House

Southroad
Wood

Ellis Barn

Counter
Farm

Netherton

APPLEDORE RD

7

Cradlebridge Sewer

Hornbrook
Farm

Roughlands

Legg Farm

33

Hornbrook Manor
Farm

THE WISH

6

Bench Hill

BENCH HILL

Pond Wood

Silcock's Wood

Manor
Farm

5

Great Heron
Wood

Sly Corner

32

Little Heron
Wood

Beech Tree
Farm

WOODCHURCH RD

P
Forest
Walks

Park Wood

Rushfield
Wood

Smith's
Farm

4

Oak Lands

Hole
Farm

Butness Wood

The Firs

MOOR LA

Park Hill

The Firs

3

Oakhouse
Farm

Gusbourne
Farm

KENARDINGTON RD

Saxon Shore Way

31

MOOR LANE
COTTS

HEATH
VILLAS

Hornes Place
Chapel

Griffin
Farm

GRIFFIN COTTS
HEATH

Appledore
Heath

2

Park Farm

SCHOOL RD

Victoria
(PH)

ELMTREE

Royal Military Canal (dis)

1

Mill
Farm

Park House

TENTERDEN RD

The Homestead

30

The Pines

Sixty Six
Farm

B2080

A   B   95   C   D   96   E   F

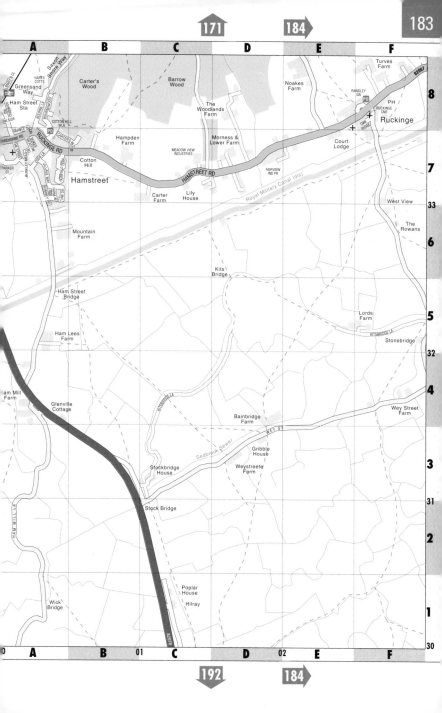

183
172

| A | B | C | D | E | F |

Herne House

B2067

Sewage Works

8

Royal Military Canal (dis)

Marsh Cottage

Bridge Farm

7

Sedbrook Sewer

Sedbrook Sewer

Wallstool Sewer

KITSBRIDGE LA

Marshland Sewer

33

Pear Tree Farm

Honeywood Farm

6

Hans Farm

Rock Cottage

Oak Farm

Toll Farm

Blisington Sewer

5

32

The Chestnuts

4

Wallstool Sewer

Newchurch

Black Bull (PH)

Mill House

Will's Farm

PILCHER'S LA

CHURCH HO

Tower Windmill

3

Langdon

Brooker Cottage

Brooker Farm

CLARKLANDS

Langdon Cottages

Manor House

31

Four Winds

Stone Bridge

Brenzen Sewer

Rosedale

New Barn Farm

2

Shearly Sewer

Millbank

Hill's Farm

Squires Farm

1

Norwood Farm

BURGROVE LA

MEAD LA

NORTH RD

Lodgeland Bungalow

30

| 03 | A | B | 04 | C | D | 05 | E | F |

183
193

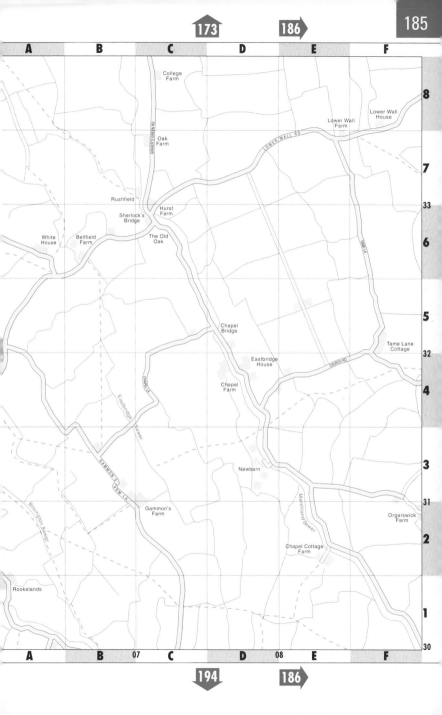

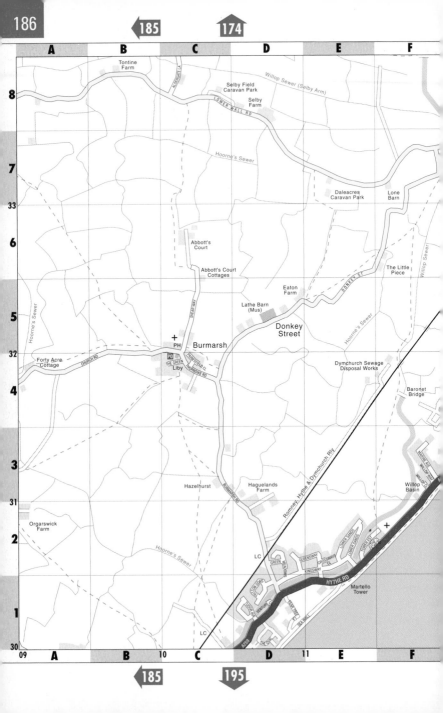

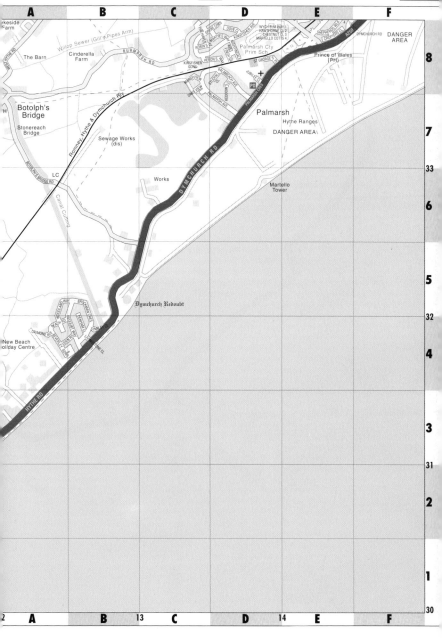

A   B   C   D   E   F

8

7

33

6

5

32

4

3

31

2

1

30

Botolph's
Bridge

The Barn

Cinderella
Farm

Stonereach
Bridge

Sewage Works
(dis)

Works

Romney, Hythe & Dymchurch Rly

Canal Cutting

DYMCHURCH RD

BURMARSH RD

Willop Sewer (Gill's Pipes Arm)

LC

New Beach
Holiday Centre

Dymchurch Redoubt

HYTHE RD

Palmarsh Cty
Prim Sch

Palmarsh

Hythe Ranges
DANGER AREA

Prince of Wales
(PH)

Martello
Tower

DANGER
AREA

DYMCHURCH RD

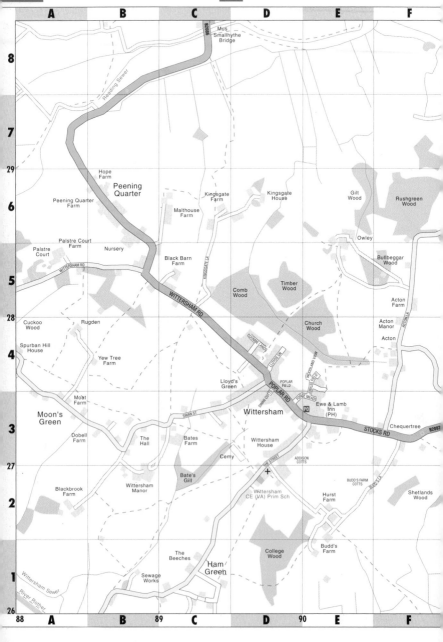

A | B | C | D | E | F

8

7

29

6

5

28

4

3

27

2

1

26

88 A | B | 89 C | D | 90 E | F

Mus
Smallhythe
Bridge

Reading Sewer

Hope
Farm

Peening
Quarter

Peening Quarter
Farm

Kingsgate
Farm

Kingsgate
House

Gilt
Wood

Rushgreen
Wood

Malthouse
Farm

Palstre Court
Farm

Palstre
Court

Nursery

Black Barn
Farm

Owley

Bullbeggar
Wood

WITTERSHAM RD

Comb
Wood

Timber
Wood

Church
Wood

Acton
Farm

Acton
Manor

Acton

Cuckoo
Wood

Rugden

Spurban Hill
House

Yew Tree
Farm

COOMBE LANE

LLOYDS DR

POPLAR
FIELD

PROLD AND VIEW

Lloyd's
Green

POPLAR RD

Moat
Farm

Moon's
Green

SWAN ST

MILLER COTTS

VICTORIA MEAD

Ewe & Lamb
Inn
(PH)

PO

Chequertree

STOCKS RD

B2082

Dobell
Farm

The
Hall

Bates
Farm

Wittersham

Wittersham
House

Cemy

OAK STREET

ADDISON
COTTS

Blackbrook
Farm

Wittersham
Manor

Bate's
Gill

Wittersham
CE (VA) Prim Sch

Hurst
Farm

BUDD'S FARM
COTTS

BUDDS LA

Shetlands
Wood

The
Beeches

Ham
Green

College
Wood

Budd's
Farm

Wittersham Sewer

River Rother

Sewage
Works

8

High House
Farm

Hayes
Farm

Ramsden
Farm

Chapel Bank

Reading Sewer

7

STONE
CNR

Stone Corner
Farm

29

Whole
Farm

6

Saxon Shore Way

Little Odiam
Farm

LOWER RD

Stemp's
Wood

Rosehill
Farmhouse

Odiam
Farm

Stone Farm

Luckhurst

5

28

Isle of Oxney

Curteis
Wood

Luckhurst
Wood

Stone in Oxney

The Crown
(PH)

THE STREET

4

Green Acres

Maynes Farm

Twelve Acre
Wood

STONE DR

Catt Farm

Lord's
Wood

Scrub's
Wood

CATT'S HILL

The Stocks

Wr
Twr

Four Acre
Wood

WATTLE
CNR

Huggit's
Farm

3

STOCKS RD

WITTERSHAM RD

QUARRY
COTTS

WADDLE
CNR

TOP RD

CHURCH HILL

Windmill
(dis)

Stocks Farm

Holman's
Farm

Oxenden

27

Prospect
House

Little Prawls
Farm

Tighe Farm

Rook
Wood

STOCK HILL

2

Tophill
Farm

RYE RD

Great Prawls
Farm

Saxon Shore Way

Cliff Farm

Underhill
Farmhouse

Rother Levels

Stone Cliff

1

A92292

26

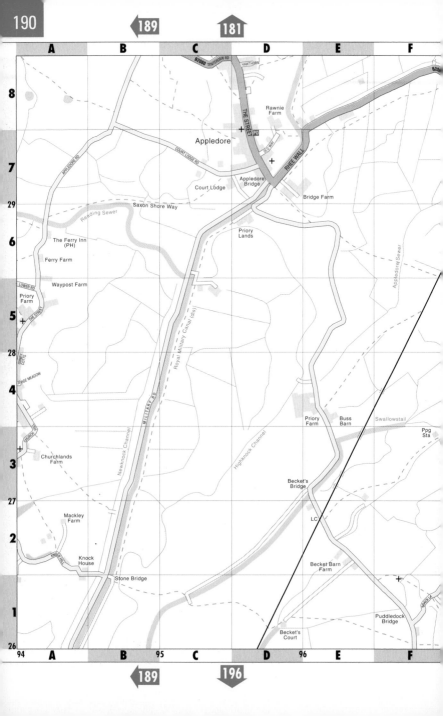

189
181

B2080 TENTERDEN RD
HAWTHORN

THE STREET

Rawnie
Farm

Appledore

APPLEDORE RD

COURT LODGE RD

OLD WAY

RHEE WALL

B2080

Court Lodge

Appledore
Bridge

Bridge Farm

Saxon Shore Way

Reading Sewer

Priory
Lands

Appledore Sewer

The Ferry Inn
(PH)

Ferry Farm

LOWER RD

Waypost Farm

THE STREET

Priory
Farm

Royal Military Canal (dis)

SCOTTS
ROAD

GEORGE MEADOW

Priory
Farm

Buss
Barn

Swallowstail

Ppg
Sta

Churchlands
Farm

Newknock Channel

MILITARY RD

Highknock Channel

Becket's
Bridge

Mackley
Farm

LC

Knock Hill

Knock
House

Stone Bridge

Becket Barn
Farm

Puddledock
Bridge

GRACK LA

Becket's
Court

189
196

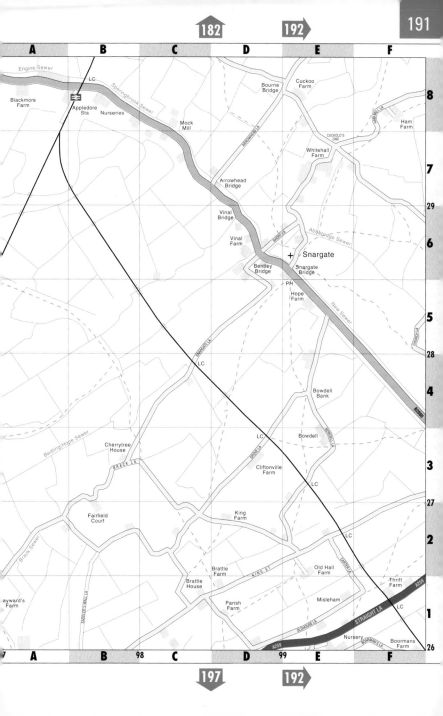

182
192

A **B** **C** **D** **E** **F**

Engine Sewer

LC

Springbrook Sewer

8

Blackmore
Farm

Appledore
Sta

Nurseries

Mock
Mill

Bourne
Bridge

Cuckoo
Farm

HAM MILL LA

Ham
Farm

CUCKOLD'S
CNR

Whitehall
Farm

7

Arrowhead
Bridge

29

Vinal
Bridge

Abakridge Sewer

SHORT LA

6

Vinal
Farm

Vinal
Farm

Bentley
Bridge

+ Snargate

Snargate
Bridge

New Sewer

PH

Hope
Farm

5

CHURCH LA

28

LC

STRAIGHT LA

Bedling Hope Sewer

Bowdell
Bank

B2080

4

Cherrytree
House

LC
BRACK LA

LC
BRIDLE LA

Bowdell

Bowdell

BOWDELL LA

Cliftonville
Farm

LC

3

Fairfield
Court

King
Farm

27

LC

2

Brack Sewer

SADDLER'S WALL LA

Brattle
Farm

KING ST

Old Hall
Farm

CHURCH LA

LC

Thrift
Farm

A259

Brattle
House

ayward's
Farm

Parish
Farm

Misleham

STRAIGHT LA

LC

1

OLDHOUSE LA

Nursery

Boormans
Farm

BOARMANS LA

26

A 98 **B** **C** **D** 99 **E** **F**

A259

A259

197
192

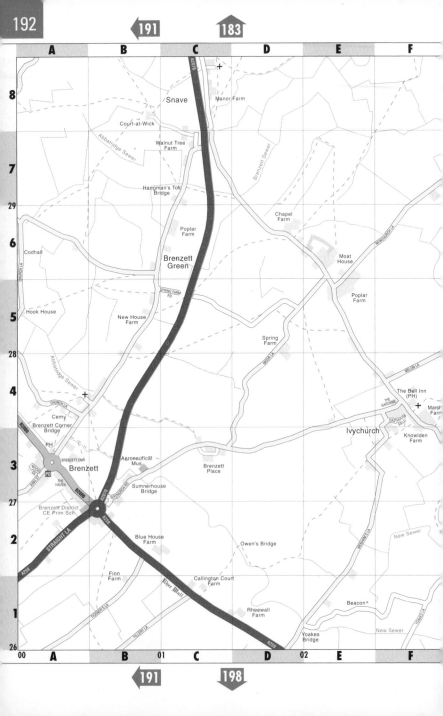

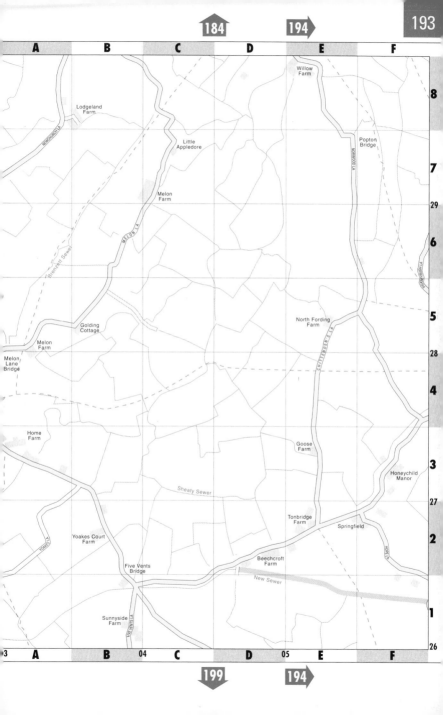

184
194

A B C D E F

8

Willow Farm

Lodgeland Farm

7

Little Appledore

NEWCHURCH LA

29

Melon Farm

6

MELON LA

NORWOOD LA

Popton Bridge

Brenzett Sewer

5

Golding Cottage

North Fording Farm

ASHFORD LA

Melon Farm

Melon Lane Bridge

28

CHITTENDEN LA

4

Home Farm

Goose Farm

3

Honeychild Manor

Sheafy Sewer

27

Yoakes Court Farm

Tonbridge Farm

Springfield

2

Beechcroft Farm

Five Vents Bridge

HOPE LA

New Sewer

FIVE VENTS LA

1

Sunnyside Farm

HORN LA

26

3 A B 04 C D 05 E F

199
194

	A	B	C	D	E	F

Oldhouse Bridge

Blue House Farm

Blackmanstone Bridge

Eastbridge Sewer

Pickneybush Bridge

Tatnam Farm

Pickney Bush Farm

Clobsden Sewer

Tatnam Bridge

Sellinge Farm

Jefferstone La

Steady Sewer

Pickney Bush Farm Cotts

Marten Farm

Swallowtail Bridge

Turngates Bridge

Wild Refuge

Sports Gd

Golden Sands Holiday Centre

Jefferstone Lane Sta

Haffenden Farm

ST MARY'S RD

Shingle Hall Farm

Jefferstone La

Jesson Court Caravan Park

LC

Star Inn

St Mary in the Marsh

Jefferstone Sewer

OLD BAKERY

School Farm

Brodnyx

Romney, Hythe & Dymchurch Rly

New Sewer

Slinches

New Sewer

Winford Bridge

DYMCHURCH RD

The Warren

Littlestone Golf Course

Paternosterford Bridge

Marlie Farm Caravan & Camping Park

Brodynex Farm

Marlie Farm

06	A		B	07	C		D	08	E		F

Marshall's
Bridge

Sutton
Farm

Dymchurch
Cty Prim Sch

NEW HALL

Mus

HYTHE RD

M259

COOPERS QUARTER

SYCAMORE
GDNS

SYCAMORE
CL

Dymchurch

Caravan
Pks

Dunkirk End

Dymchurch
Sta

Mill

LC

PO

Liby

Martello Tower

Martello Tower

Romney, Hythe & Dymchurch Rly

Dymchurch Wall

HIGH ST

Chorlden Beach

St Mary's
Bay

DYMCHURCH RD

ST MARY'S GDNS

BROOKSIDE

COBSDEN RD

SPRING HOLLOW

KINGSLAND
HOLLOW

HIGHLANDS
CRES

St Mary's Bay

1 SHEARWATER HO
2 DUNLIN CT
3 TURNSTONE CT

MARISHLANDS
CL

ST MARY'S RD

8

29

7

6

5

28

4

3

27

2

1

26

190

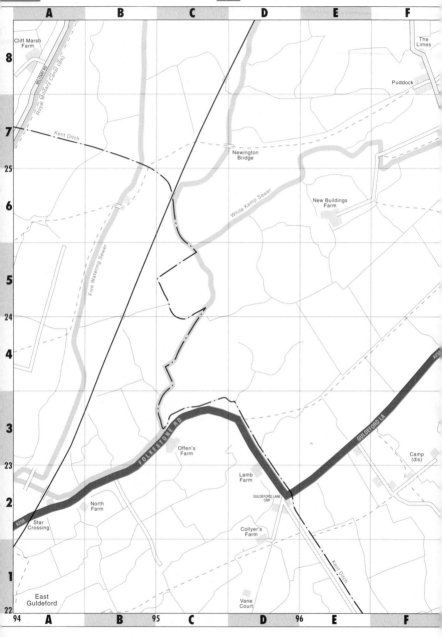

8

Cliff Marsh Farm

The Limes

Puddock

7

Kent Ditch

Newington Bridge

25

White Kemp Sewer

New Buildings Farm

6

Royal Military Canal (dis)

Five Watering Sewer

5

24

4

A259

GULDEFORD LA

3

FOLKESTONE RD

Offen's Farm

Camp (dis)

23

Lamb Farm

2

North Farm

GULDEFORD LANE CNR

A259

Star Crossing

Collyer's Farm

Kent Ditch

1

East Guldeford

Vane Court

22

| A | B | 95 | C | D | 96 | E | F |

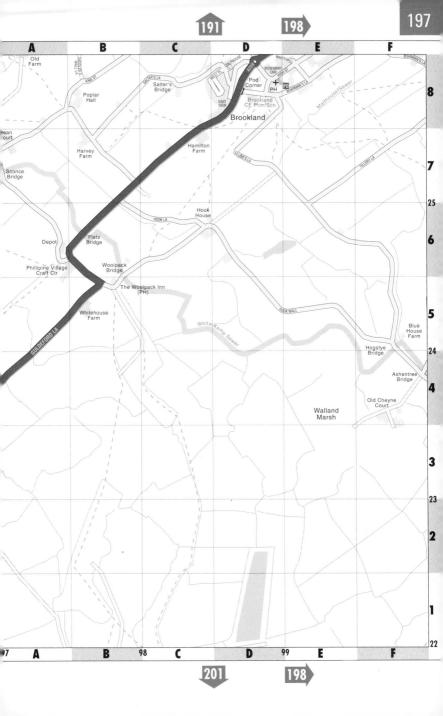

A B C D E F

Old
Farm

SADDLER'S WALL LA

KING ST

Poplar
Hall

SALTER'S LA

Salter's
Bridge

WEST PL

SALTHOUSE RD

WHITEHALL

ROSEMARY CNR
HIGH ST

Pod
Corner

PH

BOARMAN'S LA

BOARMAN'S LA

8

EAST
VIEW

Brookland
CE Prim Sch

Malthouse Sewer

Brookland

Bean
Court

Harvey
Farm

Hamilton
Farm

GLEBE ST LA

TILLERY LA

7

Sconce
Bridge

25

HOOK LA

Hook
House

6

Depot

Flats
Bridge

Phillipine Village
Craft Ctr

Woolpack
Bridge

The Woolpack Inn
(PH)

HOOK WALL

Blue
House
Farm

5

GUILDFORD LA

Whitehouse
Farm

White Kemp Sewer

Hogstye
Bridge

24

Ashentree
Bridge

4

Walland
Marsh

Old Cheyne
Court

3

23

2

1

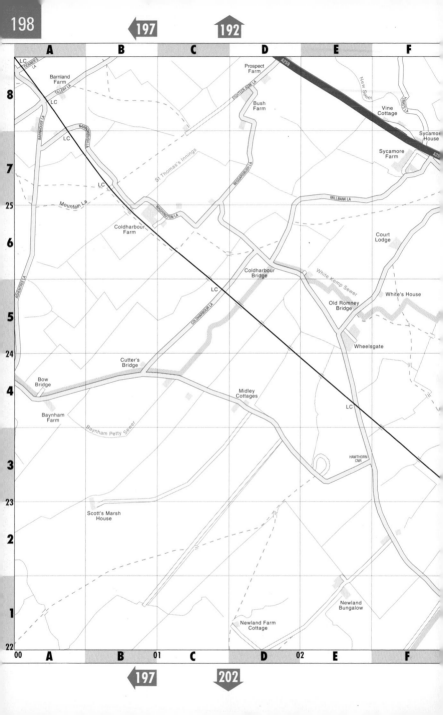

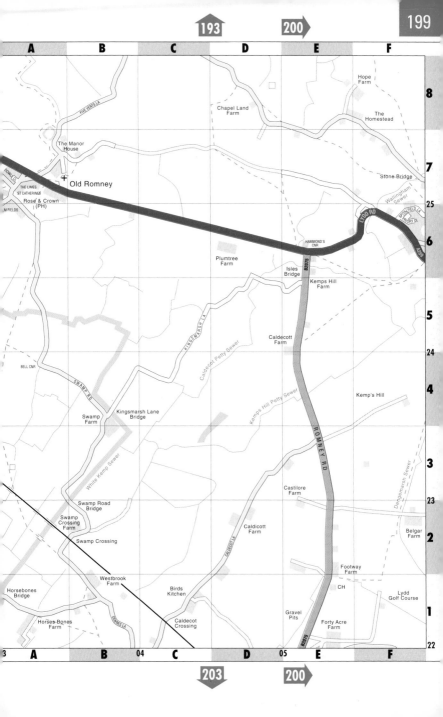

A B C D E F

8

Hope Farm

Chapel Land Farm

The Homestead

7

The Manor House

Stone Bridge

FIVE VENTS LA

ROWLES CL

+ Old Romney

THE LIMES
ST CATHERINES

Rose & Crown
(PH)

M FIELDS

Wallingham
Sewer

LYDD RD

SPITALFIELD ℃
PRIORY CL

25

A259

6

HAMMOND'S
CNR

Plumtree Farm

Isles Bridge

B2075

Kemps Hill Farm

5

KINGSMARSH LA

Caldecot Petty Sewer

Caldecott Farm

24

BELL CNR

SWAMP RD

Kemps Hill Petty Sewer

Kemp's Hill

4

Swamp Farm

Kingsmarsh Lane Bridge

ROMNEY RD

Dengemarsh Sewer

3

White Kemp Sewer

Castilore Farm

23

Swamp Road Bridge

Belgar Farm

Swamp Crossing Farm

Caldicott Farm

2

Swamp Crossing

CALDICOT LA

Footway Farm

Horsebones Bridge

Westbrook Farm

Birds Kitchen

CH

Lydd Golf Course

1

VENTS LA

Horses-Bones Farm

Caldecot Crossing

Gravel Pits

Forty Acre Farm

B2075

22

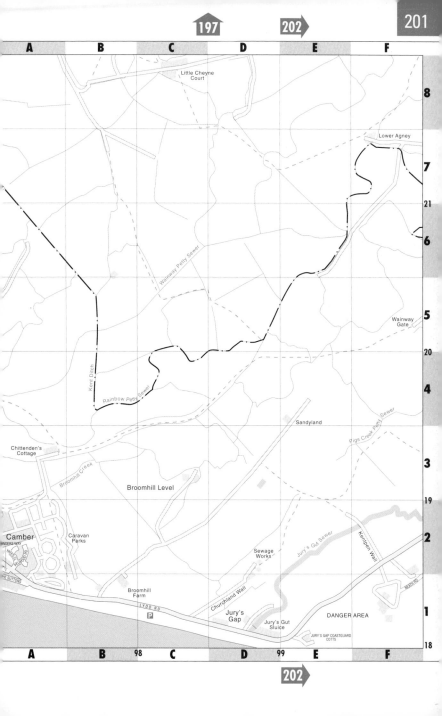

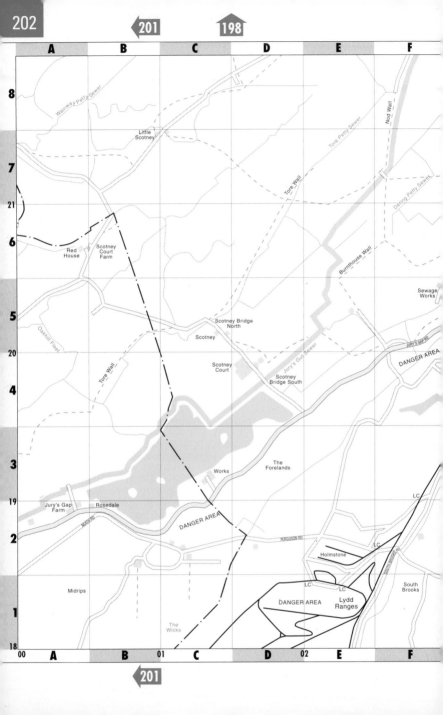

203
200

| | A | B | C | D | E | F |

8

7

21

6

5

20

4

3

19

2

1

18

Romney Sands
Holiday Village

Romney Sands
Sta

LC

Caravan
Park

LA ROCCO
LA TAUSCO
LA GALAMINA

BEACHMONT CL.

PRIOR RD

CHANNON RD

DERVILLE RD

WALLER RD

COLEVILLE CRES

BEATRICE
MEWS

THE PARADE

HULL RD

The Ship
(PH)

LCs

P

TAYLOR RD

FOLEY CT

VIEW POINT RES

LADE FORT
COTTS

LC

WILLIAMSON RD

SEXTON RD

Lade

LPOOL BRI

COAST RD

COAST RD

Lydd
Airport

Mockmill Sewer

Works

Boulderwall
Farm

Conveyor

DUNGENESS RD

Halfway
Bush

Romney, Hythe & Dymchurch Railway

PLEASANCE ROAD CENTRAL

GORDON RD

PLEASANCE RD

PLEASANCE RD N

Lydd-on-Sea

Mast

Denge
Marsh

Walkers Outland
(RSPB Reserve)

Coastguard
Cottages

BATTERY RD

PLEASANCE RD S

| 06 | A | | B | 07 | C | | D | 08 | E | | F |

203
205

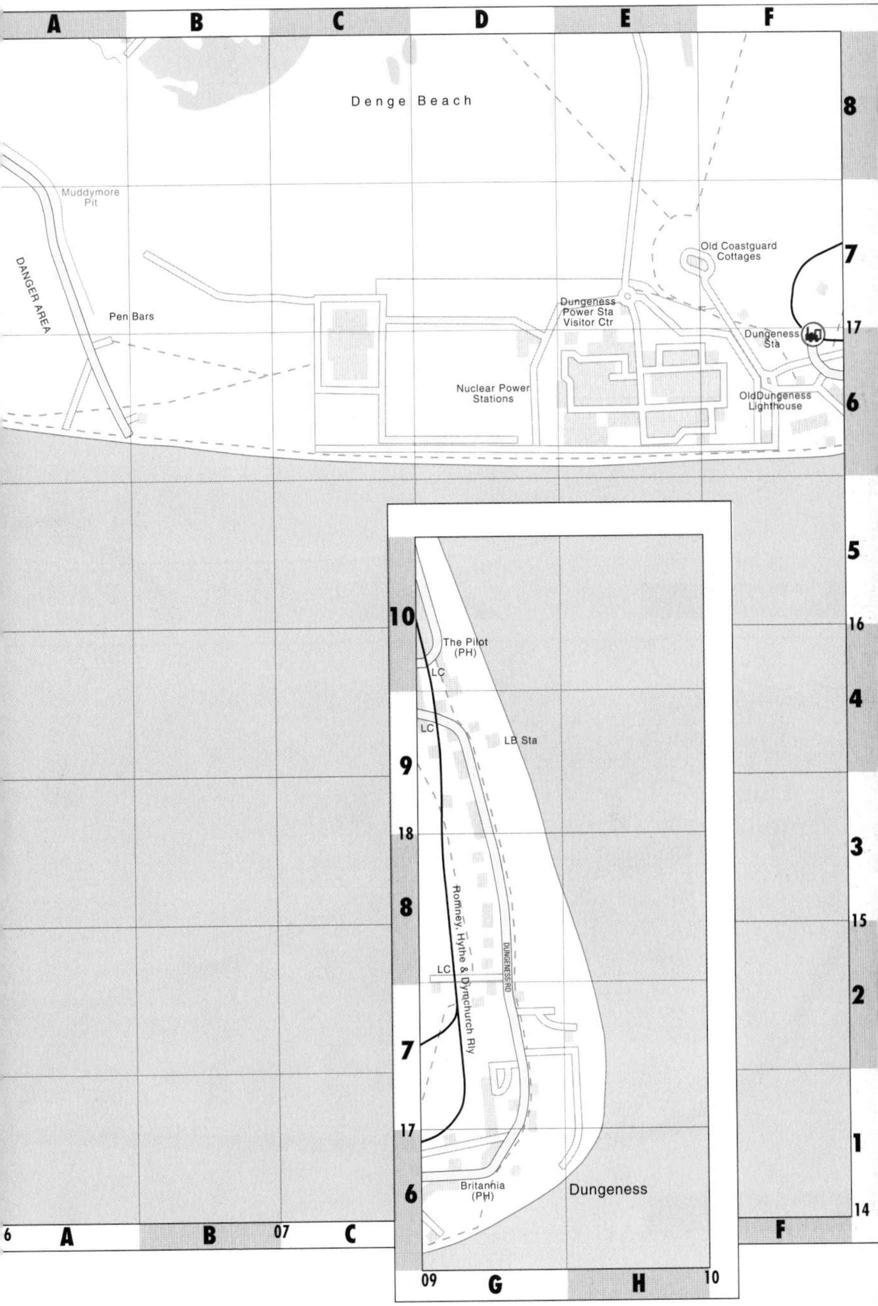

Denge Beach

Muddymore Pit

DANGER AREA

Pen Bars

Old Coastguard Cottages

Dungeness Sta

Dungeness Power Sta Visitor Ctr

Nuclear Power Stations

Old Dungeness Lighthouse

The Pilot (PH)

LC

LC

LB Sta

Romney, Hythe & Dymchurch Rly

DUNGENESS RD

LC

Britannia (PH)

Dungeness

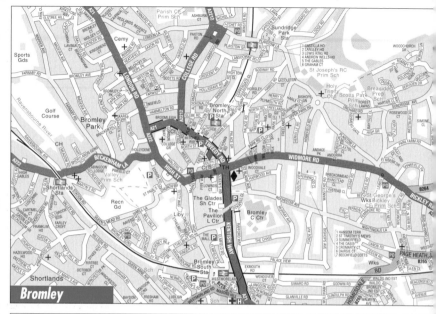

Bromley

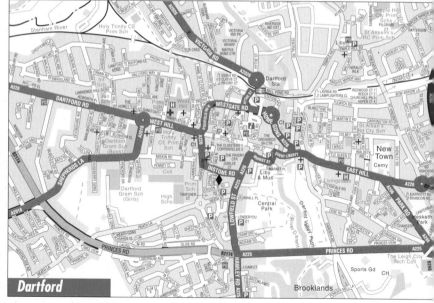

Dartford

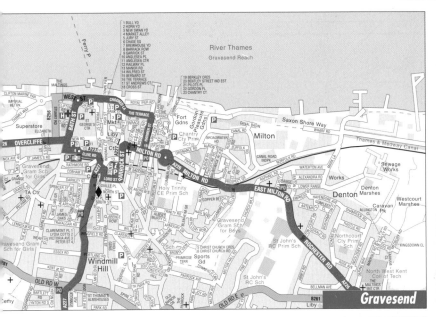

Gravesend

Index (Gravesend):
1 BULL YD
2 HORN YD
3 NEW SWAN YD
4 MARKET ALLEY
5 JURY ST
6 CHASE SQ
7 BREWHOUSE YD
8 BARRACK ROW
9 GARRICK ST
10 ANGLESEA PL
11 ANGLESEA CTR
12 RAILWAY ST
13 MANOR RD
14 WILFRED ST
15 BERNARD ST
16 THE TERRACE
17 ST ANDREWS CT
18 CROSS ST

19 BERKLEY CRES
20 BENTLEY STREET IND EST
21 PILOTS PL
22 GORDON PL
23 CHANTRY CT

River Thames
Gravesend Reach

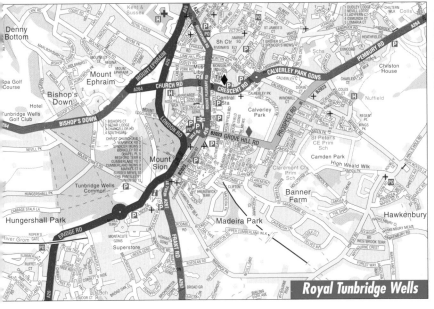

Royal Tunbridge Wells

Index (Royal Tunbridge Wells):
1 DUDLEY LODGE
2 NEVILL LODGE
3 LADYFERN CT
4 OSMUNDA CT
5 LOMARIA CT

1 BISHOPS CT
2 CEDAR LODGE
3 CHANCELLOR RD
4 SOUTHGATE

CHRIST CHURCH AVE
1 WARWICK RD
2 SPENCER MEWS
3 BERKELEY RD
4 CHAPEL RD
5 REDFORD TERR
6 CUMBERLAND MEWS
MARKET ST
7 SUSSEX MEWS
THE PANTILES
CHURCH RD

1 GROVE MEWS
2 SPENCER'S MEWS

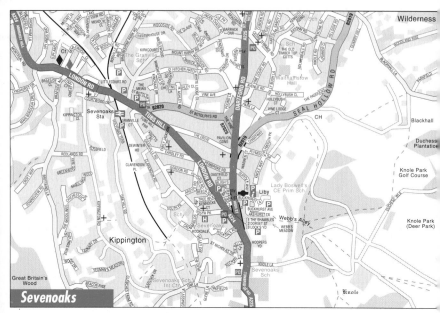

Sevenoaks

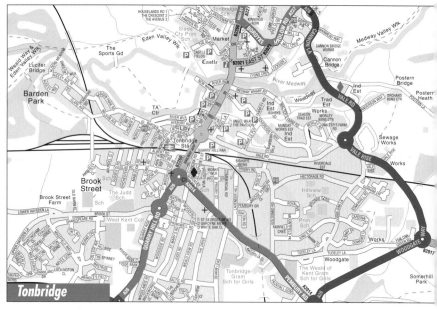

Tonbridge

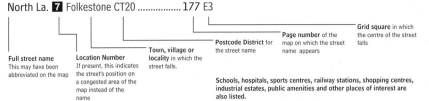

Index

Street names are listed alphabetically and show the locality, the Postcode District, the page number and a reference to the square in which the name falls on the map page

North La. **7** Folkestone CT20 .... 177 E3

Full street name
This may have been abbreviated on the map

Location Number
If present, this indicates the street's position on a congested area of the map instead of the name

Town, village or locality in which the street falls.

Postcode District for the street name

Page number of the map on which the street name appears

Grid square in which the centre of the street falls

Schools, hospitals, sports centres, railway stations, shopping centres, industrial estates, public amenities and other places of interest are also listed.

Abbreviations used in the index

App	Approach	Cl	Close	Espl	Esplanade	N	North	S	South
Arc	Arcade	Comm	Common	Est	Estate	Orch	Orchard	Sq	Square
Ave	Avenue	Cnr	Corner	Gdns	Gardens	Par	Parade	Strs	Stairs
Bvd	Boulevard	Cotts	Cottages	Gn	Green	Pk	Park	Stps	Steps
Bldgs	Buildings	Ct	Court	Gr	Grove	Pas	Passage	St	Street, Saint
Bsns Pk	Business Park	Ctyd	Courtyard	Hts	Heights	Pl	Place	Terr	Terrace
Bsns Ctr	Business Centre	Cres	Crescent	Ho	House	Prec	Precinct	Trad Est	Trading Estate
Bglws	Bungalows	Dr	Drive	Ind Est	Industrial Estate	Prom	Promenade	Wlk	Walk
Cswy	Causeway	Dro	Drove	Intc	Interchange	Ret Pk	Retail Park	W	West
Ctr	Centre	E	East	Junc	Junction	Rd	Road	Yd	Yard
Cir	Circus	Emb	Embankment	La	Lane	Rdbt	Roundabout		

20/20 Ind Est. ME16 .... 74 C8
Abbeville Ho. ME1 .... 9 C4
Abbey Cl. Deal CT14 .... 117 A5
Abbey Cl. Minster ME12 ...... 4 D6
Abbey Fields. ME13 .... 62 E7
Abbey Fields Ct. ME13 .... 62 E7
Abbey Gate. CT11 .... 52 B5
Abbey Gate Cotts. ME20 .... 53 E2
Abbey Gdns. CT2 .... 67 A2
Abbey Gr. Minster, Thanet
  CT12 .... 50 C5
Abbey Gr. Ramsgate CT11 ... 52 B5
Abbey Pl. ME13 .... 62 D8
Abbey Rd.
  Faversham ME13 .... 62 D8
Abbey Rd. Gillingham ME8 .. 11 A2
Abbey Rd. Kearsney CT16 . 148 D4
Abbey Rd.
  River CT15 & CT17 ...... 148 E1
Abbey St. ME13 .... 62 D8
Abbey Way. TN24 .... 140 A1
Abbeyview Dr. ME12 .... 4 B6
Abbot's Hill. CT11 .... 52 E6
Abbots Barton Wlk. CT1 ..... 88 B7
Abbots Field. ME16 .... 74 B2
Abbots Pl. CT1 .... 66 F1
Abbots Rd. ME3 .... 62 F7
Abbots The. CT17 .... 166 C1
Abbots Wlk. TN25 .... 123 E2
Abbotsbury Hts. CT2 .... 67 B4
Abbott Rd. CT20 .... 178 E6
Abbotts Cl. ME1 .... 9 B3
Aberdeen Cl. CT3 .... 47 D3
Aberdeen Ho. **8** ME15 .... 97 E7
Abigail Cres. ME5 .... 32 A1
Abingdon Gr. CT3 .... 47 D3
Abingdon Rd. ME16 .... 74 A2
Abinger Dr. ME5 .... 32 D2
Absalam Ct. ME8 .... 11 C2
Acacia Ho. ME12 .... 1 C2
Acacia Terr. ME10 .... 36 C4
Academy Dr. ME7 .... 10 F1
Achilles Rd. ME5 .... 32 C2
Ackerny Ct. TN23 .... 155 F6
Ackholt Rd. CT3 .... 113 A5
Acol Hill. CT7 .... 27 B4
Acorn Pl. ME15 .... 97 E6
Acorn Rd. ME7 .... 10 F4
Acorn St. ME12 .... 1 D1
Acre Cl. ME4 .... 9 E1
Acre Ct. CT17 .... 166 C8
Acre The. CT16 .... 148 F8

Acton La. TN30 .... 188 F4
Acton Rd. CT5 .... 20 D2
Ada Rd. CT1 .... 87 D6
Adam Cl. ME17 .... 96 D3
Adam Ct. **1** CT9 .... 8 B2
Adams St. ME15 .... 167 B1
Adbert Dr. ME15 .... 96 B4
Addelam Cl. CT14 .... 117 A4
Addelam Rd. CT14 .... 117 A4
Addington Pl. CT11 .... 52 E6
Addington Rd. Margate CT9 .. 7 J2
Addington Rd.
  Sittingbourne ME10 ...... 36 E3
Addington Sq. CT9 .... 7 J2
Addington St. Margate CT9 ... 7 J2
Addington St.
  Ramsgate CT11 .... 52 D6
Addiscombe Gdns. CT9 ...... 7 J1
Addiscombe Rd. CT9 .... 8 A1
Addison Cotts. TN30 .... 188 D3
Adelaide Dr. ME10 .... 36 C4
Adelaide Gdns.
  Halfway Houses ME12 ...... 3 E3
Adelaide Gdns. **16**
  Ramsgate CT11 .... 52 E6
Adelaide Pl. CT1 .... 87 F8
Adelaide Rd.
  Elvington CT15 .... 114 B1
Adelaide Rd.
  Gillingham ME7 .... 10 C4
Aden Terr. **1** ME14 .... 75 A7
Adie Rd. TN28 .... 200 D3
Adie Rd N. TN28 .... 200 D4
Adisham
  CE Prim Sch. CT3 .... 112 D8
Adisham Downs Rd.
  CT3 & CT4 .... 90 B2
Adisham Dr. ME16 .... 74 B7
Adisham Gn. ME10 .... 36 F8
Adisham Rd.
  Bekesbourne CT4 .... 89 E3
Adisham Rd. Wingham CT3 .. 91 A4
Adisham Rd.
  Womenswold CT3 & CT4 .. 112 C2
Adisham Sta. CT3 .... 112 E8
Adisham Way. CT9 .... 8 C1
Admiral's Wlk. ME4 .... 9 F7
Admirals Wlk.
  Chatham ME5 .... 32 B3
Admirals Wlk.
  Halfway Houses ME12 ...... 3 E6
Admirals Wlk.
  Hythe CT21 .... 176 C1

Admirals Wlk.
  Tenterden TN30 .... 167 C1
Admiralty Terr. **1** ME4 ... 10 A7
Admiralty Wlk. CT5 .... 43 A7
Adrian Mews. CT8 .... 7 D1
Adrian Sq. CT8 .... 7 D1
Adrian St. CT16 & CT17 ... 166 D7
Aerodrome Rd.
  Bekesbourne CT3 & CT4 .. 89 E3
Aerodrome Rd.
  Hawkinge CT18 .... 163 A4
Afghan Rd.
  Broadstairs CT10 .... 29 F8
Afghan Rd. Chatham ME4 .... 9 E4
Agester La. CT14 .... 129 A4
Ainsdale Cl. CT19 .... 178 B7
Aintree Ho. **1** ME15 ...... 97 F6
Aintree Rd. ME5 .... 32 C3
Airedale Cl. CT9 .... 8 A1
Airfield View. ME12 .... 17 C8
Aisne Dr. CT1 .... 67 D1
Ajax Rd. ME1 .... 9 D3
Alamein Ave. ME5 .... 31 F7
Alamein Cl. CT16 .... 149 F3
Albany Dr. CT6 .... 22 D4
Albany Ho. **1** CT17 .... 166 D7
Albany Pl. CT17 .... 166 D7
Albany Rd.
  Capel-le-F CT18 .... 164 C1
Albany Rd. Chatham ME4 ... 10 B8
Albany Rd. Gillingham ME7 .. 10 D4
Albany Rd. Rochester ME1 .... 9 C4
Albany Rd.
  Sittingbourne ME10 ...... 36 E3
Albany St. ME14 .... 75 B5
Albany Terr. Chatham ME4 ... 9 E4
Albany Terr.
  Gillingham ME7 .... 10 C4
Albemarle Rd.
  Ashford TN24 .... 139 F1
Albemarle Rd.
  Chatham ME5 .... 32 C2
Albert Costain Ct. **1**
  CT20 .... 178 D5
Albert Ct. **16** CT5 .... 20 D2
Albert La. CT21 .... 176 C1
Albert Manor. ME7 .... 10 B5
Albert Pl. ME2 .... 9 B7
Albert Rd. Ashford TN24 ... 139 B3
Albert Rd. Broadstairs CT10 .. 29 E8
Albert Rd. Canterbury CT1 ... 88 B8
Albert Rd. Capel-le-F CT18 . 164 C2
Albert Rd. Chatham ME4 .... 10 A3

Albert Rd. Deal CT14 .... 117 C6
Albert Rd. Dover CT16 .... 149 D1
Albert Rd.
  Folkestone CT19 .... 178 D6
Albert Rd. Gillingham ME7 .. 10 C4
Albert Rd. Hythe CT21 .... 176 B1
Albert Rd. Margate CT9 ...... 7 H2
Albert Rd. Ramsgate CT11 .. 52 F7
Albert Rd. Rochester ME1 .... 9 C3
Albert St. Maidstone ME14 .. 74 F6
Albert St. Ramsgate CT11 .. 52 E6
Albert St. Whitstable CT5 ... 20 D2
Albert Terr. Margate CT9 .... 7 I2
Albert Terr. Minster ME12 .... 5 A5
Alberta Cl. CT16 .... 149 B3
Albion Cl. CT6 .... 46 A8
Albion Hill. **6** CT11 .... 52 E6
Albion La. CT6 .... 46 A8
Albion Mews. CT11 .... 52 F6
Albion Mews Rd. **3** CT20 178 D4
Albion Pl. Ashford TN24 ... 156 E7
Albion Pl. Canterbury CT1 ... 67 A1
Albion Pl. Faversham ME13 .. 62 E7
Albion Pl. Hythe CT21 ...... 176 D2
Albion Pl. Maidstone ME14 .. 75 B4
Albion Pl. Newington ME9 ... 35 B8
Albion Pl. Ramsgate CT11 .. 52 E6
Albion Pl. Sheerness ME12 ... 1 D2
Albion Rd. Birchington CT7 .. 27 A7
Albion Rd. Broadstairs CT10 29 F6
Albion Rd. Chatham ME5 ... 32 B2
Albion Rd. Deal CT14 ...... 117 D8
Albion Rd. Eastry CT13 ...... 93 A2
Albion Rd.
  Folkestone CT19 .... 178 D6
Albion Rd. Margate CT9 ...... 8 B3
Albion Rd. Ramsgate CT11 .. 52 F7
Albion St. CT10 .... 30 B4
Albion Terr. ME10 .... 36 E6
Albion Villas. **6** CT20 ... 178 D4
Albuhera Sq. CT1 .... 67 D2
Alchorne Cl. ME5 .... 32 D2
Alchins Cotts. ME17 .... 96 E2
Alder Cl. ME12 .... 3 A8
Alder Rd. CT19 .... 178 C6
Aldergate La.
  CT21 & TN29 .... 174 C1
Alderney Gdns. CT10 .... 29 E5
Aldershot Rd. ME5 .... 32 A7
Aldington Cl. ME5 .... 32 B5
Aldington Cnr. TN25 .... 173 A6
Aldington
  Cty Prim Sch. TN25 ..... 173 A5

Aldington La. ME14 .... 76 D8
Aldington Rd.
  Lympne CT21 .... 174 E3
Aldington Rd.
  Maidstone ME14 .... 75 F4
Aldon Cl. ME14 .... 75 C6
Aldon Ct. ME14 .... 75 C6
Aldred Rd. ME13 .... 62 C6
Aldridge Ct. CT6 .... 22 B3
Alexander Cl. ME13 .... 62 B8
Alexander Ct.
  Rochester ME2 .... 9 B8
Alexander Dr. **6**
  Sittingbourne ME10 ...... 36 E5
Alexander Dr. ME13 .... 62 B7
Alexandra Ave. ME7 .... 10 E4
Alexandra Cl. ME10 .... 36 E7
Alexandra Cl. CT21 .... 176 A1
Alexandra Gdns. CT20 .... 178 D4
Alexandra Glen. ME5 .... 32 A1
Alexandra Homes. CT9 .... 7 I1
Alexandra Hospl The. ME5 .. 54 A8
Alexandra Pl. **1** CT16 ... 149 C1
Alexandra Rd.
  Birchington CT7 .... 27 A5
Alexandra Rd.
  Broadstairs CT10 .... 30 B4
Alexandra Rd.
  Capel-le-F CT18 .... 164 C2
Alexandra Rd.
  Chatham ME4 .... 10 B2
Alexandra Rd. Deal CT14 .. 117 D2
Alexandra Rd.
  Kingsdown CT14 .... 134 C5
Alexandra Rd. Margate CT9 . 28 E3
Alexandra Rd.
  Ramsgate CT11 .... 52 D8
Alexandra Rd.
  Sheerness ME12 .... 1 E2
Alexandra Rd.
  Whitstable CT5 .... 43 C8
Alexandra St.
  Maidstone ME14 .... 74 F6
Alexandra Terr. CT9 .... 7 I1
Alexandria Dr. CT6 .... 22 D5
Alfred Cl. Canterbury CT1 ... 87 C6
Alfred Cl. Chatham ME4 ..... 10 B2
Alfred Cotts. CT11 .... 52 E7
Alfred Rd. Ashford TN24 ... 156 E7
Alfred Rd. Birchington CT7 .. 26 D8
Alfred Rd. Canterbury CT1 ... 87 C6

Alfred Rd. Dover CT16 .... 149 B2
Alfred Rd.
Littlestone-on-S TN28 ... 200 D3
Alfred Rd. Margate CT9 .... 8 B1
Alfred Sq. CT14 .... 117 D7
Alicia Ave. CT9 .... 28 A8
Alison Cl. Birchington CT7 .... 27 B8
Alison Cl. Whitfield CT16 ... 149 A6
Alison Cres. CT16 .... 149 A7
Alkham Cl. CT9 .... 8 F2
Alkham Rd.
Maidstone ME14 .... 75 C5
Alkham Rd. Temple
Ewell CT15 & CT16 .... 148 C4
Alkham Valley Rd.
Alkham CT15 .... 147 E1
Alkham Valley Rd.
Hawkinge CT18 & CT15 ... 163 E4
All Saints' Ave. CT9 .... 7 H1
All Saints' CE Prim Sch.
Chatham ME14 .... 10 A3
All Saints CE Prim Sch.
Maidstone ME15 .... 75 A3
All Saints' Cl. CT5 .... 20 F1
All Saints Hospl. ME4 .... 10 A2
All Saints Ind Est. CT9 .... 7 I1
All Saints La. 2 CT1 .... 87 F8
All Saints Rd. ME10 .... 37 C4
All Saints View. ME13 .... 41 E2
All Souls
CE Prim Sch. CT19 .... 177 E6
Allan Rd. CT5 .... 42 E6
Alland Grange La. CT12 .... 27 E2
Allen Ave. CT8 .... 27 D7
Allen Cl. ME5 .... 32 C6
Allen Ct. ME12 .... 4 A5
Allen Field. TN23 .... 155 F8
Allen St. ME14 .... 75 B5
Allenby Ave. CT14 .... 117 B5
Allenby Rd. CT12 .... 29 C2
Allenby Wlk. ME10 .... 36 B5
Allendale St. 2 CT19 .... 178 D6
Alliance Rd. CT11 .... 52 F6
Allington Prim Sch. ME16 ... 74 C7
Allington Rd. ME8 .... 11 A3
Allington Way. ME16 .... 74 B6
Allison Ave. ME7 .... 10 E1
Allnutt Mill Cl. ME15 .... 74 E2
Allsworth Cl. ME8 .... 35 B6
Alma Pl. 2 Canterbury CT1 ... 67 A1
Alma Pl. Ramsgate CT11 ...... 52 F7
Alma Rd. Folkestone CT19 ... 177 D5
Alma Rd. Herne Bay CT6 ...... 23 C5
Alma Rd. Margate CT9 .... 7 J1
Alma Rd. Ramsgate CT11 .... 52 E8
Alma Rd. Sheerness ME12 ..... 1 D2
Alma St. Canterbury CT1 ...... 67 A1
Alma St. Sheerness ME12 ..... 1 E2
Alma Street Pas. ME12 .... 1 E2
Almon Pl. ME1 .... 9 D5
Almond Cl. Ashford TN23 ... 138 F5
Almond Cl.
Broadstairs CT10 .... 29 C4
Almond Cl. Whitstable CT5 ... 21 D1
Almond Gr. ME7 .... 33 A4
Almond Tree Cl. ME2 .... 3 A8
Almonds The. ME14 .... 76 A4
Almshouse Rd. ME13 .... 104 C7
Almshouses. 7 CT1 .... 88 A8
Alpha Rd. Birchington CT7 ... 27 A7
Alpha Rd. Ramsgate CT11 ... 52 D6
Alsager Ave. ME11 .... 2 F3
Alsops Rd. TN24 .... 156 E7
Alston Cl. ME12 .... 4 C7
Altbarn Ind Est. ME5 .... 54 C8
Alvis Ave. CT6 .... 22 A4
Amage Rd. TN25 .... 141 C8
Amage Road Cotts. TN25 . 124 B1
Amanda Cl. ME5 .... 31 F3
Amber Cl. ME9 .... 38 D2
Amber La. ME17 .... 98 A1
Amber Way. ME17 .... 98 B1
Ambleside.
Faversham ME13 .... 62 E6
Ambleside.
Sittingbourne ME10 .... 37 C3
Ambley Gn. ME7 .... 33 A8
Ambley Rd. ME7 .... 33 B8
Ambrose Hill. ME4 & ME5 ... 10 C2
Amels Hill. ME9 .... 56 F8
Ames Ave. ME14 .... 76 A4
Amethyst Ave. ME5 .... 31 E6
Amherst Cl.
Maidstone ME14 .... 74 D4
Amherst Cl. Margate CT9 ...... 8 C1
Amherst Hill. ME4 .... 10 A6

Amherst Rd. ME1 .... 9 D3
Amherst Redoubt. ME4 ...... 10 A5
Amies Ho. ME15 .... 96 F3
Amos Cl. Herne Bay CT6 ..... 23 C3
Amos Cl. Sheldwich ME13 .... 83 C5
Amsa Cnr. CT16 .... 150 B1
Amsbury Rd. ME17 .... 96 B2
Amshurst Villas. ME15 .... 96 A4
Anchor Bsns Pk. ME10 .... 37 B6
Anchor Hill. 4 CT9 .... 7 J2
Anchor La. Deal CT14 .... 117 C6
Anchor La. Sheerness ME12 ... 1 B3
Anchor Rd. ME1 .... 9 C5
Ancress Cl. CT2 .... 67 A4
Andover Wlk. 12 ME15 .... 97 F6
Andrew Broughton Way.
ME14 .... 75 B4
Andrew Manor. ME7 .... 10 C6
Andrews Wlk. ME10 .... 36 B5
Anerley Cl. ME16 .... 74 D7
Angel Cotts. ME8 .... 12 A2
Anglesey Ave. ME15 .... 97 A7
Anglesey Cl. ME5 .... 32 B7
Ann's Rd. CT11 .... 52 E8
Anna Pk. CT7 .... 26 F8
Anne Boleyn Cl. ME2 .... 5 E3
Anne Cl. CT7 .... 27 B7
Anne Green Wlk. 8 CT1 ...... 67 B2
Anne Roper Cl. TN28 .... 200 E6
Anne's Rd. CT10 .... 30 C7
Ansell Ave. ME4 .... 10 A1
Anselm Cl. ME10 .... 36 E4
Anselm Rd. CT17 .... 166 A8
Anson Cl. Broadstairs CT10 . 29 D3
Anson Cl. Chatham ME5 ...... 32 C6
Anstee Rd. CT16 & CT17 ... 149 C1
Anthony Cres. CT5 .... 43 B6
Anthonys Way. ME2 .... 9 E8
Anvil Cl. CT7 .... 27 A6
Anzio Cres. CT16 .... 149 E2
Anzio Ho. 15 CT1 .... 67 B2
Apartments The. TN28 ...... 200 D5
Apollo Ho. ME5 .... 32 A6
Appleby Cl. ME1 .... 31 D7
Appledore Ave. ME12 .... 3 A8
Appledore Cl. CT19 .... 177 D7
Appledore Cres. CT19 .... 177 D7
Appledore Ct. ME16 .... 74 D8
Appledore Rd.
Appledore TN26 & TN30 .. 190 A7
Appledore Rd.
Brattle TN26 .... 181 B8
Appledore Rd.
Brattle TN26 & TN30 ... 181 C7
Appledore Rd.
Gillingham ME8 .... 11 A3
Appledore Rd.
Shepherdswell CT15 ..... 130 D5
April Rise. Birchington CT7 .. 26 D8
April Rise. Whitstable CT5 ... 43 B7
Apsley Cotts. CT4 .... 86 D3
Apsley St. TN23 .... 155 E7
Aragon Cl. TN23 .... 155 E7
Archbishop's
CE Sec Sch The. CT2 .... 66 E3
Archcliffe Rd. CT17 .... 166 C5
Archer Rd. Chatham ME5 .... 32 B6
Archer Rd.
Folkestone CT19 .... 178 D6
Archer's Court Rd.
CT15 & CT16 .... 149 B7
Archers Court Rd. CT16 .... 149 B5
Archery Sq. CT14 .... 117 D3
Archway Ct. 1 ME2 .... 9 B8
Archway Rd.
Ramsgate CT11 .... 52 E6
Archway Rd.
Sheerness ME12 .... 1 B3
Arcon Cl. TN23 .... 156 A7
Arcon Rd. TN23 .... 156 A7
Arden Bsns Pk. ME2 .... 9 E8
Arden Cty Jun Sch. ME7 ..... 10 D6
Arden Dr. TN24 .... 139 C3
Arden Rd.
Faversham ME13 .... 62 E7
Arden Rd. Herne Bay CT6 .... 23 C2
Arden St. ME7 .... 10 C6
Ardenlee Dr. ME14 .... 75 B5
Arethusa Rd. ME1 .... 31 C8
Argent Bsns Pk. ME11 .... 3 A3
Argent Rd. ME11 .... 3 A2
Argyle Ave. CT9 .... 7 G1

Argyle Cl. ME1 .... 31 E8
Argyle Gdns. CT9 .... 7 G1
Argyle Rd. CT5 .... 20 D1
Argyll Dr. CT10 & CT11 ..... 29 F1
Ark Cotts. CT18 .... 161 D4
Ark La. CT14 .... 117 D7
Arkley Rd. CT6 .... 22 F4
Arklow Sq. 4 CT11 .... 52 F7
Arlington. TN23 .... 155 B8
Arlington Gdns. CT9 .... 29 C8
Arlington Ho. CT9 .... 7 H2
Arlington Sq. CT9 .... 7 H2
Arlott Cl. ME14 .... 74 F6
Armada Cl. TN28 .... 200 E5
Armada Ct. ME4 .... 9 E1
Armada Way. ME4 .... 9 F3
Armourers Wlk. CT16 .... 149 A3
Armstrong Rd. ME15 .... 75 A1
Armstrong Sq. CT6 .... 22 A3
Arnhem Dr. ME5 .... 31 F7
Arnold Rd. Chartham CT4 ... 86 C2
Arnold Rd. 5
Margate CT9 .... 7 J1
Arnolde Cl. ME2 .... 9 E7
Arran Mews. 4 CT1 .... 67 B2
Arran Rd. ME15 .... 97 A6
Arrowhead La. TN26 .... 191 D7
Arthur Kennedy Cl. ME13 ... 63 F3
Arthur Rd. Birchington CT7 .. 26 D8
Arthur Rd. Deal CT14 .... 117 A3
Arthur Rd. Gillingham ME8 . 33 E7
Arthur Rd. Hythe CT21 ..... 176 C1
Arthur Rd. Margate CT9 .... 8 A3
Arthur Rd. Rochester ME1 .... 9 D3
Arthur Salmon Cl. ME14 ..... 62 B7
Arthur St. 2
Folkestone CT19 .... 178 E6
Arthur St.
Sittingbourne ME10 .... 36 E4
Artillery Gdns. 12 CT1 .... 67 A1
Artillery Ho. 3 CT1 .... 67 A1
Artillery Rd. CT11 .... 52 F7
Artillery St. 11 CT1 .... 67 A1
Arundel Ave. ME10 .... 36 E1
Arundel Cl. ME5 .... 32 D1
Arundel Rd. Cliffs End CT12 . 51 D7
Arundel Rd. Margate CT9 ..... 8 B2
Arundel St. ME14 .... 74 F6
Ascot Cl. ME5 .... 32 C2
Ascot Gdns. CT8 .... 27 E7
Ascot Ho. 8 ME15 .... 97 F6
Ash Cl. Ashford TN23 .... 138 E3
Ash Cl. Broadstairs CT10 .... 29 C4
Ash Cl. Chatham ME5 .... 10 C1
Ash Cl. Gillingham ME8 ...... 11 A3
Ash Cl. Herne Bay CT6 .... 22 F1
Ash Cl. River CT17 .... 148 E3
Ash Cres. CT3 .... 46 E1
Ash Gr. Elvington CT15 ..... 114 B2
Ash Gr. Lydd TN29 .... 203 D7
Ash Gr. Maidstone ME16 .... 74 C6
Ash Meadows. TN24 .... 156 F7
Ash Rd. Aylesham CT3 .... 112 E5
Ash Rd. Sandwich CT13 ...... 72 E2
Ash Tree Cl. TN29 .... 194 F3
Ash Tree La. ME5 .... 10 D1
Ash Tree Rd. 5 CT19 .... 178 E6
Ashbank Cotts. ME17 .... 99 B7
Ashbee Gdns. CT6 .... 23 C5
Ashborne Cl. TN24 .... 139 D6
Ashburn Gdns. CT6 .... 23 C5
Ashburnham Rd.
Maidstone ME14 .... 75 B8
Ashburnham Rd.
Ramsgate CT11 .... 52 C7
Ashburton Cl. TN24 .... 139 E2
Ashdale Hos. TN23 .... 139 C2
Ashdown Cl.
Herne Bay CT6 .... 23 B2
Ashdown Cl.
Maidstone ME16 .... 74 D3
Ashdown Cres. TN28 .... 200 B6
Ashdown Cl. TN24 .... 139 C3
Ashdown Rd. ME17 & ME9 .. 79 F3
Ashen Tree Cotts. CT3 .... 70 B1
Ashen Tree La. CT16 .... 166 E8
Ashenden Cl. CT1 .... 87 C5
Ashendene Gr. CT2 .... 68 A6
Ashentree La. TN29 .... 198 A5
Ashford Bsns Pk. TN24 ..... 157 A6
Ashford Bsns Point.
TN24 .... 156 F5
Ashford Dr. ME17 .... 99 D3
Ashford East Stour
Cty Prim Sch. TN24 ...... 156 D6
Ashford Golf Course.
TN24 .... 139 A6
Ashford Hospl. TN23 .... 139 A3
Ashford Int Sta. TN23 ...... 139 C1
Ashford Rd. Bethersden
TN26 & TN23 .... 153 C4

Ashford Rd.
Chartham CT4 & CT1 ...... 86 C3
Ashford Rd.
Folkestone CT18 & CT19 .. 177 B7
Ashford Rd.
Godmersham CT4 .... 107 C4
Ashford Rd.
Great Chart TN23 .... 155 B8
Ashford Rd.
Hamstreet TN26 .... 170 F1
Ashford Rd.
Harrietsham ME17 .... 100 C6
Ashford Rd.
Kingsnorth TN23 & TN26 . 156 A4
Ashford Rd. Maidstone,
Grove Green ME14 & ME15 .. 75 D4
Ashford Rd.
Maidstone,Silver Hill ME14 . 76 D3
Ashford Rd.
New Romney TN28 .... 200 A6
Ashford Rd.Sellindge TN25 . 159 B1
Ashford Rd.
Sheldwich ME13 .... 83 C4
Ashford Rd.
Tenterden TN30 .... 179 B8
Ashford Rd.
Westenhanger TN25 ...... 174 E6
Ashford Rd. Westenhanger
CT21 & TN25 & CT18 ... 175 C6
Ashford Sch. TN23 .... 139 C2
Ashford Sta. TN23 .... 139 C1
Ashgrove. TN23 .... 138 F5
Ashington Cl. ME10 .... 36 C5
Ashley Ave. CT19 .... 177 E6
Ashley Cl.
Halfway Houses ME12 ..... 3 C5
Ashley Cl. Ramsgate CT12 ... 29 B2
Ashley Dr. CT5 .... 43 A7
Ashley Ho. CT19 .... 177 E6
Ashley Mill Cotts. CT19 .... 177 E7
Ashley Rd. ME8 .... 11 C2
Ashmead Cl. ME5 .... 32 C3
Ashtead Dr. ME9 .... 37 D2
Ashton Cl. CT14 .... 116 D4
Ashtree Ho. ME10 .... 37 B3
Ashtrees. CT6 .... 23 B3
Ashurst Ave. CT5 .... 43 C6
Ashurst Gdns. CT9 .... 8 E3
Ashurst Rd. ME14 .... 75 C5
Askes Ct. TN23 .... 155 D8
Aspen Cl. TN29 .... 194 F3
Aspen Cl. CT20 .... 178 D4
Aspen Way. 2 ME5 .... 31 F4
Aspian Dr. ME17 .... 96 D3
Asquith Rd. ME8 .... 33 C6
Association Wlk. ME1 .... 31 C7
Astley Ave. CT16 .... 149 C2
Astley St. ME14 .... 75 A4
Aston Cl. ME5 .... 32 A2
Astor Ave. CT17 .... 166 B8
Astor Cty Prim Sch. CT17 . 166 B8
Astor Dr. CT14 .... 117 C5
Astor of Hever Sch The.
ME16 .... 74 C3
Astor Rd. CT10 .... 29 F8
Astor Sch. Dover CT17 ..... 166 A8
Astor Sch. Dover CT17 ..... 166 B8
Astrid Rd. CT14 .... 117 A2
Athelstan Gn. ME17 .... 77 C2
Athelstan Pl. CT14 .... 117 C8
Athelstan Rd.
Canterbury CT1 .... 87 C5
Athelstan Rd. Chatham ME4 .. 9 F2
Athelstan Rd.
Faversham ME13 .... 62 C6
Athelstan Rd.
Folkestone CT19 .... 178 D7
Athelstan Rd. Margate CT9 ... 8 A3
Athol Pl. ME13 .... 62 A8
Athol Rd. Ashford TN23 ... 155 F7
Athol Rd. Whitstable CT5 .... 20 F7
Athol Terr. CT16 .... 166 F8
Atlanta Ct. ME1 .... 9 D3
Attlee Ave. CT3 .... 112 E5
Attlee Way. ME10 .... 36 E8
Atwater Ct. ME17 .... 101 D5
Aubretia Wlk. ME10 .... 37 A3
Auckland Ave. CT12 .... 52 A8
Auckland Cres. CT16 .... 149 C3
Auckland Dr. ME10 .... 36 C5
Audley Ave. Gillingham ME7 . 10 E1
Audley Ave. Margate CT9 ..... 7 E1
Audley Cl. ME16 .... 74 B5
Audley Rd. CT20 .... 177 F5
Augusta Cl. 1 ME7 .... 10 C7
Augusta Gdns. CT20 .... 178 C4
Augusta Pl. 12 CT11 .... 52 F7
Augusta Rd. CT11 .... 52 F7
Augustine Rd. Minster,
Thanet CT12 .... 50 B6

Austell Manor. ME7 .... 10 C6
Austens Orch. 12 TN30 .... 179 A7
Austin Ave. CT6 .... 21 F4
Austin Cl.
Gillingham ME5 & ME7 .... 10 E2
Austin Cl.
Sittingbourne ME10 .... 37 A8
Austin Rd. TN23 .... 156 B6
Austins La. 4 CT13 .... 73 A1
Autumn Glade. ME14 .... 54 D8
Avebury Ave. CT11 .... 52 G8
Aveling Ct. 2 ME2 .... 9 B7
Avenue Gdns. CT9 .... 8 C3
Avenue of Remembrance.
ME10 .... 36 F3
Avenue Rd. Dover CT16 .... 149 C1
Avenue Rd. Herne Bay CT6 . 22 E5
Avenue Rd. Ramsgate CT11 . 52 F7
Avenue The. Deal CT14 ..... 117 C7
Avenue The. Hersden CT3 .. 46 E1
Avenue The. Hythe CT21 .. 176 C2
Avenue The.
Kingsdown CT14 .... 134 D4
Avenue The. Margate CT9 .... 8 A1
Avenue The. St Margaret's
at Cliffe CT15 .... 150 F6
Avenue The.
Temple Ewell CT16 .... 148 E5
Averenches Rd. ME14 .... 75 F5
Avereng Gdns. CT19 .... 178 B6
Avereng Rd. CT19 .... 178 B6
Avery Cl. ME15 .... 74 F1
Avery La. ME15 .... 98 D6
Aviemore Gdns. ME14 .... 75 F4
Avington Cl. ME15 .... 74 F1
Avocet Wlk. ME5 .... 32 D2
Avon Cl. CT1 .... 88 C8
Avondale Cl. CT5 .... 44 A8
Avondale Rd.
Capel-le-F CT18 .... 164 C2
Avondale Rd.
Gillingham ME7 .... 10 D5
Axford Ct. ME8 .... 34 A8
Aycliffe
Cty Prim Sch. CT17 ...... 166 A4
Aylesford Cres. ME8 .... 11 B4
Aylesford Pl. TN24 .... 156 E7
Aylesham Cnr. CT3 .... 112 D3
Aylesham
Cty Prim Sch. CT3 .... 112 E5
Aylesham Rd. CT15 & CT3 . 113 A4
Aylesham Sta. CT3 .... 113 A5
Aylewyn Gn. ME10 .... 36 F8
Aynsley Ct. 1 CT13 .... 73 A1
Ayton Rd. CT11 .... 52 C6

Babs Oak Hill. CT2 & CT3 ... 68 B7
Back La. 6
Faversham ME13 .... 62 D7
Back La. Marlpit ME17 .... 97 E1
Back La. Minster ME12 .... 4 D6
Back Rd W. CT16 .... 166 G8
Back St.
Langley Heath ME17 .... 98 E6
Back St. Ringwould CT14 ... 133 F5
Backfields. ME1 .... 9 B4
Bad Munstereifel Rd.
TN23 & TN24 .... 156 D5
Baddlesmere Rd. CT5 .... 21 A2
Baden Rd. ME7 .... 10 D7
Bader Cres. ME5 .... 32 A7
Badger Rd. ME5 .... 32 C1
Badgers Bridge. CT18 ...... 161 D4
Badgers Cl. CT2 .... 66 A7
Badgers Ct. TN23 .... 156 A7
Badgers Oak. TN23 .... 155 D8
Badgers Rise. Deal CT14 ... 134 C8
Badgers Rise.
River CT17 .... 148 D3
Badlesmere Cl. TN23 .... 155 E6
Baffin Cl. ME4 .... 9 F2
Bagham La. CT4 .... 107 D8
Bagham Rd. CT4 .... 107 C8
Bagshill Rd. ME13 .... 83 A3
Bailey Dr. ME7 .... 11 A1
Bailey Fields. TN26 .... 153 E4
Baileys Field. TN23 .... 138 F1
Baird's Hill. CT10 .... 29 F6
Bairdsley Cl. CT10 .... 29 F6
Bakenham Ho. 1 ME1 .... 9 C1
Baker Cl. ME9 .... 38 C2
Baker Rd. CT19 .... 177 E6
Baker St. ME1 .... 9 C3
Baker's La. CT4 .... 86 D2
Baker's Wlk. ME1 .... 9 C6
Bakers Cl. CT2 .... 87 C7
Balcomb Cres. CT9 .... 29 C8
Baldric Rd. CT20 .... 177 F5
Baldwin Rd.
Greatstone-on-S TN28 ... 200 D1
Baldwin Rd. Minster ME12 ... 4 D7

aldwin Terr. CT19 .... 178 D6
alfour Ct. CT20 .... 178 B3
alfour Cty Inf Sch. ME4 .... 9 E1
alfour Cty Jun Sch. ME4 .... 9 E2
alfour Rd. Chatham ME4 .... 9 F1
alfour Rd. Deal CT14 .... 117 C2
alfour Rd. Dover CT16 .... 149 C1
alliol Rd. CT5 .... 20 E2
all La. TN24 .... 139 F7
allard Ind Est. ME5 .... 54 C8
allard Rd. TN28 .... 200 D1
allens Rd. ME5 .... 32 C3
alliemoor Ct. CT11 .... 29 F1
alliol Rd. CT10 .... 29 F8
almer Cl. ME8 .... 33 D7
almoral Ho. 6 ME15 .... 97 F5
almoral Pl. 10 CT11 .... 52 F7
almoral Rd.
  Gillingham ME7 .... 10 D5
almoral Rd.
  Kingsdown CT14 .... 134 C6
almoral Rd. 4
  Margate CT9 .... 28 B8
amford Way. CT14 .... 117 C4
ank Cotts. ME17 .... 77 E3
ank Rd. TN25 .... 172 E8
ank Side. TN26 .... 183 A8
ank St. Ashford TN23 .... 139 B2
ank St. Chatham ME4 .... 10 B3
ank St. Faversham ME13 .... 62 C7
ank St. Herne Bay CT6 .... 22 F5
ank St. Hythe CT21 .... 176 C2
ank St.
  Maidstone ME14 & ME15 ..... 75 A4
anks Rd. Ashford TN23 .... 156 A7
anks Rd. Rochester ME2 .... 9 C8
anks The. CT10 .... 29 F6
anks Yd. 8 ME10 .... 36 F4
ankside. Canterbury CT1 .... 88 D7
ankside. Chatham ME5 .... 32 B8
anky Fields. ME8 .... 12 B1
anner Way. ME12 .... 3 E6
anning St. ME2 .... 9 B8
anningbrook Ct. CT14 .... 117 D4
annister Hall. ME14 .... 97 F5
annister Hos. TN26 .... 120 A1
annister Rd. ME14 .... 75 A7
apchild & Tonge
  CE Prim Sch. ME10 .... 37 D3
arbados Terr. 2 ME14 .... 75 F4
arberry Ave. ME5 .... 31 E5
archam Ct. ME15 .... 96 F5
arclay Ct. CT7 .... 7 C1
ardell Terr. ME1 .... 9 D5
arden Ct. ME14 .... 75 D5
arfleur Manor. 6 ME4 .... 10 A6
arfrestone Rd. CT15 .... 114 A1
argates. TN23 .... 155 E6
argrove Rd. ME14 .... 75 C5
arham CE Prim Sch. CT4 .... 128 F8
arham Cl. ME15 .... 97 E5
arham's Mill Rd. TN27 .... 118 B3
arker Rd. ME16 .... 74 F2
arkers Ct. ME10 .... 36 B4
arkis Cl. ME1 .... 31 D7
arkir Pl. ME1 .... 3 A5
arley Cl. Herne Bay CT6 .... 23 D2
arley Ct. Martin Mill CT15 .. 133 C2
arley Fields. ME4 .... 9 F2
arleycorn Dr. ME8 .... 33 C2
arleymow Cl. ME5 .... 32 C7
arlow Cl. ME1 .... 31 D1
arlow Cl. ME8 .... 33 E5
arn Cl. Borden ME9 .... 36 A2
arn Cl. Hoath CT3 .... 46 E5
arn Cl. Yorklets CT5 .... 43 A3
arn Cres. CT5 .... 7 F1
arn Platt. TN23 .... 156 A8
arn The. ME9 .... 36 A2
arnaby Terr. ME1 .... 9 D2
arnard Ct. ME4 .... 10 A5
arnberry Cl. TN23 .... 155 E8
arncroft Cl. ME14 .... 75 F4
arncroft Dr. ME7 .... 32 F4
arnes Ave. CT13 .... 62 B8
arnes Ct. CT1 .... 87 D6
arnesende Ct. CT14 .... 94 A8
arnett's La. CT2 .... 67 D8
arnett Cl. CT12 .... 29 B1
arnett Field. TN23 .... 155 F8
arnfield. Chatham ME5 .... 32 A8
arnfield. Herne Bay CT6 .... 22 C2
arnfield.
  St Michaels TN30 .... 167 C2
arnfield Rd.
  Faversham ME13 .... 62 C8
arnfield Rd.
  Folkestone CT19 .... 178 C3
arnhouse La. TN29 .... 198 A8

Barnhurst La. CT18 .... 163 A5
Barnsell Rd. ME14 .... 75 A8
Barnsley Cl. ME12 .... 1 F5
Barnsole Cty Inf Sch. ME7 .... 10 E4
Barnsole
  Cty Jun Sch. ME7 .... 10 E4
Barnsole Rd.
  Gillingham ME7 .... 10 E4
Barnsole Rd. Staple CT3 .... 92 B5
Barntye Cl. CT15 .... 149 E6
Barnwood Cl. ME1 .... 31 B8
Baron Cl. Gillingham ME7 ...... 10 E7
Baron Cl. Maidstone ME14 ... 75 F5
Barrack Hill. CT21 .... 176 A2
Barrack Rd. ME4 .... 10 B8
Barrey Rd. TN24 .... 157 A6
Barrier Rd. ME4 .... 9 F5
Barrington Cl. ME5 .... 31 F5
Barrington Cres. CT7 .... 27 B7
Barrow Gr. ME8 .... 36 D3
Barrow Grove
  Cty Jun Sch. ME10 .... 36 D3
Barrow Hill.
  Ashford TN23 & TN24 ..... 139 B2
Barrow Hill.
  Sellindge TN25 .... 174 D7
Barrow Hill Cotts. TN23 ..... 139 A2
Barrow Hill Rise. TN25 ...... 174 D7
Barrow Hill Terr. 1 TN23 .. 139 B3
Barrowfields. ME5 .... 32 D1
Barrowhill Pl. 2 TN23 .... 139 B3
Barrows Cl. CT7 .... 27 A6
Bartholomew Cl. CT21 .... 176 B3
Bartholomew La. CT21 .... 176 B3
Bartholomew St. 6
  Dover CT16 .... 149 C1
Bartholomew St.
  Hythe CT21 .... 176 B2
Bartlett Cl. ME5 .... 32 C1
Bartlett Dr. CT5 .... 21 A1
Bartletts Cl. ME12 .... 3 C5
Barton Court
  Gram Sch. CT1 .... 88 D8
Barton Cty Jun Sch. CT16 .. 149 C2
Barton Field. CT18 .... 161 B7
Barton Hill Dr. ME12 .... 4 A5
Barton Mill Rd. CT1 .... 88 C6
Barton Rd. Canterbury CT1 ... 88 C6
Barton Rd. Dover CT16 .... 149 C2
Barton Rd. Maidstone ME15 . 75 A2
Barton Rd. Rochester ME2 ...... 9 A7
Barton View Terr. 2
  CT16 .... 149 C1
Barton's Point Recn Ctr.
  ME12 .... 1 F2
Barville Rd. CT15 .... 114 E2
Barwick Rd. CT17 .... 148 F1
Bashford Barn La. ME9 .... 58 A4
Basing Cl. ME15 .... 75 B3
Baskerville. TN24 .... 139 B3
Basmere Cl. ME14 .... 75 C6
Bassett Cl. CT21 .... 176 E4
Bassett Gdns. CT21 .... 176 D4
Bassett Rd. ME10 .... 36 D4
Bastion Rd. CT17 .... 166 C6
Batchelor St. ME4 .... 10 A4
Bateman Cnr. TN26 .... 153 E6
Bates Cl. CT3 .... 91 F6
Bath Ct. CT20 .... 178 B3
Bath Hard. ME1 .... 9 D5
Bath Mews. TN24 .... 156 E6
Bath Pl. CT9 .... 7 J2
Bath Rd. Ashford TN24 ...... 156 E6
Bath Rd. Margate CT9 .... 7 J2
Bathurst Cl. CT12 .... 29 B1
Bathurst Rd. CT20 .... 178 A5
Batteries Cl. ME7 .... 60 B8
Batteries Terr. ME9 .... 60 B8
Battery Point. CT21 .... 177 B2
Battery Rd. TN29 .... 204 F2
Battle of Britain Homes. 17
  CT16 .... 166 D7
Bawden Cl. CT2 .... 67 A4
Baxendale Cl. TN24 .... 156 C7
Bay Banks. ME13 .... 64 E2
Bay Cotts. CT15 .... 151 C6
Bay Hill. CT15 .... 151 B6
Bay Hill Cl. CT15 .... 151 A5
Bay Mus The. CT15 .... 151 B5
Bay View Gdns. ME12 .... 6 B2
Bay View Hts. CT7 .... 26 D8
Bay View Rd. CT10 .... 30 A2
Baye La. CT3 .... 69 D1
Bayfield. ME13 .... 61 E2
Bayford Rd. ME10 .... 37 A4
Bayhill. ME13 .... 61 E2
Bayle Ct. CT20 .... 178 E4
Bayle St. 16 CT20 .... 178 E5
Bayle The. CT20 .... 178 E4
Bayswater Dr. ME8 .... 33 E4

Bayview Rd.
  Kingsdown CT14 .... 134 C4
Bayview Rd.
  Whitstable CT5 .... 43 D7
Beach Alley. 9 CT5 .... 20 D2
Beach App. ME12 .... 6 E3
Beach Ave. CT7 .... 26 F8
Beach Flats. 2 CT21 .... 176 B2
Beach Ho's. CT9 .... 7 G2
Beach House Mews. CT8 ...... 7 D1
Beach Marine. 7 CT20 ...... 177 F3
Beach Rd.
  Dymchurch TN29 .... 187 A4
Beach St Margaret's
  at Cliffe CT15 .... 151 B5
Beach Rd.
  Westgate-on-S CT8 & CT9 .. 7 D1
Beach Rise. CT9 .... 7 D1
Beach St. Deal CT14 .... 117 D8
Beach St. Folkestone CT20 . 178 E14
Beach St. Herne Bay CT6 ..... 22 F5
Beach St. Sheerness ME12 ..... 1 C3
Beach Terr. ME12 .... 1 C2
Beach The. CT14 .... 117 D3
Beach Wlk. CT5 .... 20 E3
Beachborough Rd.
  CT19 & CT20 .... 178 A5
Beachfield Lodge. ME12 .... 1 C2
Beachmont Cl. TN29 .... 204 E8
Beacon Ave. CT6 .... 23 A4
Beacon Cl. ME8 .... 33 D7
Beacon Hill. Chatham ME5 ... 10 D2
Beacon Hill. Herne Bay CT6 .. 23 B5
Beacon La. CT13 .... 93 A6
Beacon Oak Rd. TN30 .... 179 B8
Beacon Rd.
  Broadstairs CT10 .... 29 F7
Beacon Rd. Chatham ME5 .... 10 C2
Beacon Rd. Herne Bay CT6 .. 23 A5
Beacon Rd. Lenham ME17 .. 101 C5
Beacon Way. CT21 .... 174 F3
Beacon Wlk. Herne Bay CT6 . 23 A5
Beacon Wlk.
  Tenterden TN30 .... 167 B1
Beacons The. ME17 .... 96 C2
Beaconsfield Ave.
  Dover CT16 .... 149 C1
Beaconsfield Ave.
  Gillingham ME7 .... 10 E5
Beaconsfield Gdns. CT10 .... 29 F5
Beaconsfield Rd.
  Canterbury CT1 .... 66 F2
Beaconsfield Rd.
  Chatham ME4 .... 9 F3
Beaconsfield Rd.
  Deal CT14 .... 117 D5
Beaconsfield Rd.
  Dover CT16 .... 149 C1
Beaconsfield Rd.
  Maidstone ME15 .... 74 E2
Beaconsfield Rd.
  Sittingbourne ME10 .... 37 C4
Beamont Cl. CT12 .... 27 F2
Beams The. ME15 .... 75 F1
Bean Cl. TN23 .... 138 C1
Beaney Inst (Liby & Mus).
  CT1 .... 87 F8
Beaney's Cl. CT4 & ME13 .... 84 C1
Bear's La. TN26 .... 137 E3
Bears End Ho. TN23 .... 156 B8
Bearsted Cl. ME8 .... 11 B3
Bearsted Green Bsns Ctr.
  ME14 .... 76 C4
Bearsted Rd. ME14 .... 75 E6
Bearsted & Thurnham Sta.
  ME14 .... 76 C6
Beatrice Mews. TN28 .... 204 E7
Beatrice Rd.
  Capel-le-F CT18 .... 164 C2
Beatrice Rd. Margate CT9 ... 28 B8
Beatty Ave. ME7 .... 1 C7
Beatty Cl. CT19 .... 178 E8
Beatty Rd. Chatham ME1 .... 31 D8
Beatty Rd.
  Folkestone CT19 .... 178 B7
Beauchamp Ave. CT14 ...... 117 A3
Beauchamp Cl. TN24 .... 139 E5
Beauchamps La. CT15 .... 113 D5
Beaufort Ave. CT12 .... 52 B8
Beaufort Cl. ME2 .... 9 A1
Beaufort Wlk. ME15 .... 97 F4
Beaufoy Rd. CT17 .... 149 A1
Beaufoy Terr. CT17 .... 148 F1
Beauherne
  Cty Prim Sch. CT2 .... 87 D8
Beaulieu Rise. ME1 .... 9 D1
Beaulieu Wlk. ME16 .... 74 C7
Beaumanor. CT6 .... 23 A3
Beaumont Davy Cl. ME13 .... 62 C5
Beaumont Rd. ME16 .... 74 D7

Beaumont St. CT6 .... 22 C4
Beaumont Terr. ME13 .... 62 D6
Beauvoir Dr. ME10 .... 37 A8
Beauworth Pk. ME15 .... 97 E8
Beauxfield. CT16 .... 149 A7
Beaver Ct. TN23 .... 156 A5
Beaver Green
  Cty Inf Sch. TN23 .... 155 E7
Beaver Ind Est. TN23 .... 156 B7
Beaver La. Ashford TN23 ... 138 E1
Beaver La.
  Ashford, Beaver TN23 ..... 156 A7
Beaver Rd. TN23 .... 156 B8
Beazley Ct. TN24 .... 156 D7
Beckenham Dr. ME16 .... 74 D7
Becket Ave. CT2 .... 66 D1
Becket Cl. Ash CT3 .... 71 D2
Becket Cl. Deal CT14 .... 117 C8
Becket Cl. Whitstable CT5 ... 21 B1
Becket Mews. CT2 .... 66 F1
Becket's Cl. TN25 .... 142 B6
Becket St. 4 ME13 .... 62 C7
Becketts Terr. CT21 .... 176 B4
Beckley Mews. ME5 .... 31 F5
Beckley Pl. TN25 .... 175 B8
Beckley Rd. ME12 .... 1 F2
Becksbourne Cl. ME14 .... 75 A8
Beckwith Gn. CT20 .... 177 E5
Beddow Way. ME20 .... 53 A2
Bede Ho. CT14 .... 117 D8
Bedford Ave. ME8 .... 11 C1
Bedford Pl. ME16 .... 74 E4
Bedford Sq. CT12 .... 29 B2
Bedford Way. CT7 .... 25 F1
Bedgebury Cl.
  Chatham ME1 .... 31 D8
Bedgebury Cl.
  Maidstone ME14 .... 75 C6
Bedingfield Way. CT18 ...... 161 B7
Bedlam Court La. CT12 .... 50 C6
Bedlam La. TN12 .... 135 A8
Bedson Wlk. ME8 .... 12 B1
Bedwin Cl. ME1 .... 31 D7
Beech Cl. Faversham ME13 .. 62 B7
Beech Cl. Folkestone CT19 . 178 C6
Beech Ct. Canterbury CT1 .... 88 A7
Beech Dr. Broadstairs CT10 . 29 D4
Beech Dr. Elvington CT15 ... 114 B2
Beech Dr. Hothfield TN26 ... 138 A7
Beech Dr. Maidstone ME16 .. 74 C5
Beech Gr. CT12 .... 51 C5
Beech Green Cl. CT15 .... 131 C7
Beech Hill. CT4 .... 111 B8
Beechcroft. CT5 .... 21 D1
Beechcroft Gdns. CT11 .... 52 F6
Beechen Bank Rd. ME5 .... 32 A1
Beeches The. ME5 .... 32 B3
Beeching Gn. ME8 .... 11 C3
Beeching Way. ME8 .... 11 C3
Beechmore Dr. ME5 .... 32 A2
Beecholme Dr. TN24 .... 139 C5
Beechwood Ave.
  Chatham ME5 .... 10 D2
Beechwood Ave.
  Deal CT14 .... 117 A4
Beechwood Ave.
  Sittingbourne ME10 .... 36 E6
Beechwood Cl.
  St Mary's Bay TN29 .... 194 F3
Beechwood Cl.
  Whitfield CT16 .... 132 A1
Beechwood Ct. CT16 .... 148 E4
Beecroft Cl. CT2 .... 67 A4
Beer Cart La. CT1 .... 87 F8
Beggars Cnr. CT3 .... 48 D1
Beggarsbush La. TN29 ...... 198 D7
Begonia Ave. ME8 .... 11 C2
Beke Rd. ME8 .... 33 D4
Bekesbourne Hill. CT4 .... 89 E6
Bekesbourne La.
  Bekesbourne CT3 & CT4 ... 89 E6
Bekesbourne La. Canterbury
  CT1 & CT3 & CT4 .... 88 F7
Bekesbourne La.
  Littlebourne CT3 .... 89 F6
Bekesbourne Rd. CT4 .... 88 F2
Bekesbourne Sta. CT4 .... 89 B5
Belcaire Cl. CT21 .... 175 A3
Belgrave Cl. CT11 .... 52 D7
Belgrave Rd. Dover CT17 .. 166 B7
Belgrave Rd.
  Halfway Houses ME12 .... 3 C6
Belgrave Rd. Margate CT9 .... 7 I2
Belinda Ct. CT19 .... 178 B7
Bell Chapel Cl. TN23 .... 156 C4
Bell Cnr. TN29 .... 199 A4
Bell Cres. ME1 .... 53 A8
Bell Farm La. ME12 .... 5 A6
Bell Gr. CT3 .... 113 A5

Bell La. Burham ME1 .... 53 A8
Bell La. Maidstone ME14 ..... 76 A5
Bell La. Sandwich CT13 .... 73 A1
Bell La.
  Westfield Sole ME14 .... 54 B7
Bell Rd. Park Wood ME15 .... 97 E5
Bell Rd. Sittingbourne ME10 . 36 F3
Bell Way. ME17 .... 99 E2
Bell Wood
  Cty Inf Sch. ME15 .... 97 E5
Bell La. Sun ME15 .... 97 E5
Bell-Davies Dr. CT12 .... 28 A1
Belle Friday Cl. ME9 .... 38 C2
Belle Vue Rd. CT6 .... 23 B5
Bellevue Ave. CT11 .... 52 F7
Bellevue Rd. Minster ME12 .... 4 C6
Bellevue Rd.
  Ramsgate CT11 .... 52 F7
Bellevue Rd.
  Whitstable CT5 .... 43 F8
Bellevue St. 5 CT20 .... 178 D5
Bellgrove Ct. ME5 .... 54 A8
Bellmeadow. ME15 .... 97 E6
Bells La. 7 TN30 .... 179 A7
Belmont CT14 .... 117 B1
Belmont Ct. CT11 .... 52 D7
Belmont Farm Bsns Ctr.
  TN26 .... 137 A1
Belmont Pl. TN24 .... 156 D7
Belmont Rd.
  Ashford TN24 .... 139 D6
Belmont Rd.
  Broadstairs CT10 .... 30 A4
Belmont Rd.
  Faversham ME13 .... 62 C6
Belmont Rd.
  Gillingham ME7 .... 10 C4
Belmont Rd.
  Halfway Houses ME12 .... 3 E6
Belmont Rd.
  Ramsgate CT11 .... 52 D7
Belmont Rd.
  Sittingbourne ME10 .... 36 E3
Belmont Rd.
  Westgate-on-S CT8 .... 27 F8
Belmont St. CT11 .... 52 E7
Belmont Terr. CT13 .... 93 B3
Belmore Pk. TN24 .... 139 B3
Belnor Ave. ME9 .... 13 F1
Belsey La. CT15 .... 147 D4
Belting Dr. CT6 .... 23 E5
Beltinge Rd. CT6 .... 23 B5
Belton Cl. CT5 .... 43 E8
Belvedere Rd.
  Broadstairs CT10 .... 30 B4
Belvedere Rd.
  Faversham ME13 .... 62 D8
Benacre Rd. CT5 .... 43 D6
Bench Hill. TN30 .... 181 D5
Bench St. 19 CT16 .... 166 D7
Bendon Way. ME8 .... 33 D8
Benenden Manor. ME8 .... 11 B3
Bengal Rd. CT12 .... 29 A1
Benham Bsns Pk. TN25 ..... 174 F5
Bennells Ave. CT5 .... 21 B3
Bennett Ct. 14 CT20 .... 178 E5
Bennetts Cotts. ME7 .... 55 A8
Bennetts Gdns. ME13 .... 61 D8
Bennetts Mews. 11
  TN30 .... 179 A7
Benson Cl. CT18 .... 162 F4
Benson La. CT18 .... 162 F4
Bensted. TN23 .... 155 F5
Bensted Gr. ME13 .... 62 A7
Benstede Cl. CT16 .... 23 A1
Bentham Sq. ME12 .... 1 B3
Bentley Ave. CT6 .... 23 D3
Bentley Cl. ME5 .... 32 D2
Bentley Rd. TN24 .... 156 F7
Bentlif Cl. ME16 .... 74 D5
Berber Rd. ME2 .... 9 B8
Berengrave La. ME8 .... 11 F2
Berengrave Lane Chalk Pit
  (Nature Reserve). ME8 .... 12 A3
Beresford Ave. ME4 .... 9 E2
Beresford Gap. CT7 .... 26 F8
Beresford Gdns. CT9 .... 8 C3
Beresford Rd.
  Gillingham ME7 .... 10 C4
Kit's Coty ME20 .... 53 D7
Beresford Rd.
  Ramsgate CT11 .... 52 D6
Beresford Rd. River CT17 .. 148 E3

Beresford Rd.St Margaret's
  at Cliffe CT15 .... 133F1
Beresford Rd.
  Whitstable CT5 .... 20 D1
Beresfords Hill. ME17 .... 97 B4
Bergland Pk. ME2 .... 9 D8
Berkeley Cl.
  Boughton Street ME13 .... 64 B3
Berkeley Cl. Chatham ME1 ... 31 D8
Berkeley Cl. **2**
  Folkestone CT19 .... 178 A7
Berkeley Ct. ME10 .... 36 C3
Berkeley Mount. **1** ME4 .... 9 F4
Berkeley Rd. CT7 .... 26 F8
Berkshire Cl. ME5 .... 32 C8
Bernard Sunley Hall.
  TN25 .... 124 A2
Bernards Gdns. CT15 .... 130 E5
Berridge Rd. ME2 .... 1 D2
Berry St. ME10 .... 36 F4
Berwick La. CT21 .... 175 A3
Berwyn Gr. ME15 .... 97 A6
Best La. CT1 .... 87 F8
Best St. ME4 .... 9 F4
Bethel Row. ME13 .... 82 F1
Bethersden Ct. ME15 .... 97 F7
Bethersden
  Cty Prim Sch. TN26 .... 153 D5
Bethersden Rd.
  Bethersden TN27 & TN26 . 152 C5
Bethersden Rd.
  Hothfield TN26 .... 137 D4
Bethersden Rd.
  Shadoxhurst TN26 .... 154 E2
Bethersden Rd.
  Woodchurch TN26 .... 169 A6
Betony Gdns. ME14 .... 75 F5
Betsham Rd. ME15 .... 97 F6
Bettescombe Rd. ME8 .... 33 E7
Betty Shelvey Ct. CT14 ...... 117 D4
Beult Meadow. TN27 .... 135 A1
Bevan Way. CT3 .... 112 E5
Beverley Cl. ME8 .... 33 F8
Beverley Gdns. TN29 .... 187 A4
Beverley Rd.
  Canterbury CT2 .... 66 E2
Beverley Rd.
  Maidstone ME16 .... 74 A1
Beverley Way. CT12 .... 29 C1
Beverly Cl. CT7 .... 27 B8
Bewsbury Cres. CT16 .... 148 F7
Bewsbury Cross La. CT16 ... 148 F7
Bexley St. CT5 .... 20 D2
Bexon La. ME9 .... 58 C4
Bicknor Cl. CT2 .... 67 B4
Bicknor Court Cotts. ME9 ... 57 C2
Bicknor La. ME9 .... 57 D3
Bicknor Rd. ME15 .... 97 F4
Biddenden Cl.
  Maidstone ME15 .... 75 F3
Biddenden Cl. Margate CT9 .. 8 C1
Biddenden Rd. TN26 .... 167 A6
Bierce Ct. CT7 .... 26 F7
Bifrons Gdns. CT4 .... 89 B3
Bifrons Hill. CT4 .... 89 B4
Bifrons Rd. CT4 .... 89 B4
Bigbury Rd. CT2 & CT4 .... 86 E7
Biggin St. CT16 .... 166 D8
Biggins Wood Rd. CT19 ...... 177 E7
Bilberry Cl. ME14 .... 75 E5
Bill Street Rd. ME2 .... 9 C8
Billington Gdns. TN24 .... 139 E6
Bilsington Cl. ME5 .... 32 B5
Bilsington Cross. TN24 .... 172 C1
Binbury La. ME14 .... 56 A5
Bindon Blood Rd. CT16 ..... 149 A5
Bingley Rd. ME1 .... 9 E4
Binland Gr. ME5 .... 31 D5
Binnacle Rd. ME1 .... 31 C8
Binnie Cl. CT10 .... 29 F2
Birch Cl. Ashford TN24 ...... 139 F2
Birch Cl. Broadstairs CT10 . 29 C3
Birch Ct. CT4 .... 128 F8
Birch Dr. ME5 .... 32 D1
Birch Gr. ME7 .... 33 A5
Birch Hill Ct. CT7 .... 27 B7
Birch Ho. Sheerness ME12 .... 1 C2
Birch Ho.
  Sittingbourne ME10 .... 37 B3
Birch Rd. CT5 .... 44 A8
Birch Tree Way. ME15 .... 75 B3
Birches The. CT7 .... 27 B7
Birchett. TN23 .... 138 E1
Birchfield Cl. ME15 .... 97 B6
Birchfields. ME5 .... 32 A3
Birchington
  CE Prim Sch. CT7 .... 27 A6
Birchington Cl. ME14 .... 75 C5

Birchington-On-Sea Sta.
  CT7 .... 26 F7
Bircholt Forstal. TN25 .... 158 E7
Bircholt Rd. ME15 .... 97 F4
Birchwood Rd. ME16 .... 74 C5
Birchwood Rise. CT17 .... 166 C7
Birchwood Wlk. CT2 .... 66 E2
Bird Farm. CT4 .... 105 E4
Birds Ave. CT9 .... 28 B7
Birdwood Ave. CT14 .... 117 A5
Birkdale Cl. **3** ME8 .... 74 E4
Birkdale Dr. CT19 .... 178 A8
Birkdale Gdns. CT6 .... 22 D2
Birling Ave.
  Maidstone ME14 .... 76 A4
Birling Cl. ME14 .... 76 A4
Birling Rd. TN24 .... 139 D1
Birnam Sq. **1** ME16 .... 74 E4
Bishop Cl. **4** ME10 .... 36 E5
Bishop Jenner Ct. CT3 .... 70 C6
Bishop La. ME9 .... 12 E3
Bishop's Ave. CT10 .... 30 B6
Bishopbourne Gn. ME8 .... 11 B4
Bishopden Ct. CT2 .... 66 C4
Bishops Gn. TN23 .... 155 E7
Bishops Way.
  Canterbury CT2 .... 66 D1
Bishops Way.
  Maidstone ME15 .... 74 F4
Bishops Wlk. ME1 .... 9 C5
Bishopstone La. CT6 .... 23 F6
Bishopstone La. CT6 .... 23 F5
Black Bull Rd. CT19 .... 178 D6
Black Griffin La. CT1 .... 87 F8
Black Post. ME17 .... 78 E4
Black Robin La. CT4 .... 111 E3
Blackburn Rd. CT4 .... 22 B2
Blackdown Dr. TN24 .... 139 B4
Blacketts Cotts. ME9 .... 38 B7
Blacketts Rd. ME9 .... 38 A6
Blackfriars St. **5** CT1 .... 66 F1
Blackhouse Hill.
  CT18 & CT21 .... 176 D4
Blackhouse Rise. CT21 .... 176 D3
Blackleys. ME13 .... 84 F7
Blackmanstone Way. ME16 . 74 B7
Blacksmith Dr. ME14 .... 75 D5
Blackstable Ct. CT5 .... 43 D8
Blackthorn Ave. ME5 .... 32 A3
Blackthorne Rd. ME8 .... 34 B8
Blackwall Rd.
  TN24 & TN25 .... 140 B4
Blake Cl. CT14 .... 134 C8
Blake Ct. TN24 .... 156 F8
Blakeney Cl. ME14 .... 76 B4
Blaker Ave. ME1 .... 9 E1
Blandford Gdns. ME10 .... 36 E1
Blatcher Cl. ME12 .... 4 B6
Blaxland Cl. ME13 .... 62 B8
Bleak Ho. CT10 .... 30 B4
Bleak Rd. TN29 .... 203 C6
Bleakwood Rd. ME5 .... 31 F4
Blean Bird Pk. CT2 .... 65 F8
Blean Comm. CT2 .... 66 A6
Blean Cty Prim Sch. CT2 ...... 66 B4
Blean Hill. CT2 .... 66 A5
Blean Rd. ME8 .... 11 C2
Blean Sq. ME14 .... 75 C6
Blean View Rd. CT6 .... 22 B2
Blendon Rd. ME4 .... 75 C5
Blenheim Ave.
  Canterbury CT1 .... 67 D1
Blenheim Ave.
  Chatham ME1 & ME4 .... 9 E2
Blenheim Ave.
  Faversham ME13 .... 62 E5
Blenheim Cl.
  Broadstairs CT10 .... 29 D3
Blenheim Cl.
  Herne Bay CT6 .... 23 A1
Blenheim Cl.
  Maidstone ME15 .... 75 F3
Blenheim Dr. Dover CT16 ... 149 C3
Blenheim Dr.
  Hawkinge CT18 .... 163 A4
Blenheim Pl. CT20 .... 177 F4
Blenheim Rd. Deal CT14 .... 117 D5
Blenheim Rd.
  Littlestone-on-S TN28 ...... 200 D6
Blenheim Rd.
  Sittingbourne ME10 .... 37 B2
Bleriot Meml. CT16 .... 149 F1
Billig Cnr. TN25 .... 171 F8
Blind La. Bredhurst ME7 ...... 33 A1
Blind La. Chalock TN25 ...... 105 C2
Blind La. Lidsing ME7 .... 32 F1
Blind La.
  Mersham TN24 & TN25 ... 157 D5

Blind Mary's La. ME9 .... 57 E4
Blindgrooms La.TN26 .... 155 C1
Blindhouse La. TN25 .... 160 B3
Blockmakers Ct. ME4 .... 10 B1
Bloomsbury Rd. CT11 .... 52 C6
Bloomsbury Way. TN24 .... 139 B7
Bloors La. Gillingham ME8 . 11 D1
Bloors La. Gillingham ME8 . 11 E3
Bloors Wharf Rd. ME7 .... 11 F4
Blowers Grove Wood. ME7 . 33 B3
Blue Boar La. ME1 .... 9 D5
Blue House La. CT21 .... 176 B8
Blue Line La. TN24 .... 139 B3
Bluebell Cl. Gillingham ME7 . 10 F6
Bluebell Cl.
  Kingsnorth TN23 .... 156 A4
Bluebell Rd. TN23 .... 156 B4
Bluett St. ME14 .... 75 A5
Bluett St. ME14 .... 75 A5
Blyth Cl. ME10 .... 37 C5
Blythe Cl. CT21 .... 176 D2
Blythe Rd. ME15 .... 75 B4
Boarley Ct. ME14 .... 53 F1
Boarley La. ME14 .... 53 F2
Boarman's La. TN29 .... 197 E8
Boat La. TN25 .... 173 A4
Boathouse Rd. ME12 .... 1 A3
Bob Amor Cl. ME13 .... 62 E7
Bobbin Lodge Hill. CT4 .... 86 B2
Bobbing
  Cty Prim Sch. ME10 .... 36 B7
Bobbing Hill. ME10 & ME9 .. 36 A6
Bockham Cotts. TN25 .... 157 E8
Bockham La. Hinxhill TN25 141 A1
Bockham La.
  Mersham TN24 & TN25 .. 157 E8
Bockhanger La. ME14 .... 139 C6
Bockingford La. ME15 .... 96 F8
Bodenham Rd. CT20 .... 178 A4
Bodiam Cl. ME8 .... 11 C3
Bodsham
  CE Prim Sch. TN25 .... 142 E8
Bodsham Cres. ME15 .... 76 B3
Bogle Rd. ME9 .... 60 C7
Bognor Dr. CT6 .... 22 D4
Bogshole La.
  Herne Bay CT6 .... 23 D3
Bogshole La.
  Whitstable CT5 .... 43 E4
Boley Hill. ME4 .... 9 C6
Boleyn Ave. CT9 .... 7 E1
Bolner Cl. ME5 .... 31 F2
Bolton Rd. CT19 .... 178 D6
Bolton St. CT11 .... 52 D8
Bolts Hill. CT4 .... 86 C2
Bombay Ho. **1** ME15 .... 97 F3
Bond La. TN23 .... 156 A2
Bond Rd. Ashford TN23 ...... 156 B8
Bond Rd. Gillingham ME8 ... 33 E5
Bonetta Ct. ME12 .... 3 B8
Bonham Dr. ME10 .... 37 B5
Bonners Alley. **13** CT5 .... 20 D2
Bonnington Cross. TN25 .... 172 E3
Bonnington Gn. ME8 .... 11 C3
Bonnington Rd. ME14 .... 75 C6
Bonny Bush Hill. CT4 .... 111 D5
Bonsor Rd. CT19 .... 178 D6
Booth Pl. CT9 .... 7 J3
Booth Rd. ME4 .... 9 F2
Borden
  CE Cty Prim Sch. ME9 ...... 35 F3
Borden Gram Sch for Boys.
  ME10 .... 36 F3
Borden La. ME10 & ME9 ...... 36 C3
Boresisle. TN30 .... 167 B2
Bornefields. TN23 .... 156 A7
Borough. CT1 .... 67 A1
Borough Rd.
  Queenborough ME11 .... 3 B4
Borough Rd.
  Gillingham ME7 .... 10 D4
Borrowdale Ave. CT11 .... 52 A7
Borstal Ave. CT5 .... 43 D6
Borstal Hill. CT5 .... 43 D7
Borstal HM Prison & Youth
  Custody Ctr. ME1 .... 9 B1
Borstal Rd. ME1 .... 9 B3
Borstal St. ME1 .... 9 A2
Boscombe Rd. CT19 .... 178 C6
Bosney Banks. CT15 .... 148 A7
Bossingham Rd. CT4 .... 126 F3
Bossington Rd. CT3 .... 90 E1
Boston Cl. **5** CT16 .... 149 B3
Boston Gdns. ME8 .... 11 C1
Boston Rd. ME5 .... 32 C2
Botany Cl. ME1 .... 1 C1
Botany Rd. CT10 & CT9 .... 8 F2
Boteler Cotts. CT13 .... 93 A2
Botolph's Bridge Rd.
  CT21 .... 187 A6
Bottles La. ME9 .... 59 A6
Bottlescrew Hill. ME17 .... 97 B4

Bottom Pond Rd. ME9 .... 58 D3
Boughton Ave. CT10 .... 30 A2
Boughton Church Cotts.
  ME13 .... 63 D1
Boughton Cl. ME8 .... 11 B3
Boughton Cnr. TN25 .... 123 C5
Boughton Field Cotts.
  ME13 .... 63 A5
Boughton Golf Course.
  ME13 .... 63 E2
Boughton Hill. ME13 .... 64 C3
Boughton La. ME15 .... 97 B6
Boughton Monchelsea
  Cty Prim Sch. ME17 .... 97 B2
Boughton Par. ME15 .... 97 A7
Boughton Pl ace Cotts.
  ME17 .... 118 A8
Boughton Rd. ME17 .... 101 B2
Boulevard Courrieres.
  CT20 .... 112 E5
Boulevard The. CT1 .... 87 D7
Boulonge La. **15** CT20 ...... 178 E5
Boundary Cl. ME12 .... 4 E6
Boundary Ct. CT1 .... 88 B6
Boundary Rd.
  Chatham ME1 & ME4 .... 9 E3
Boundary Rd. Hythe CT21 . 176 A2
Boundary Rd.
  Kingsdown CT14 .... 134 D6
Boundary Rd.
  Ramsgate CT11 .... 52 E7
Boundary The. CT1 .... 87 D7
Bounds La. ME13 .... 64 A3
Boundsgate Cnr. ME13 ...... 105 B7
Bourne. CT2 .... 66 A7
Bourne Cotts. CT4 .... 111 C5
Bourne Gr. ME10 .... 36 C5
Bourne La. TN26 .... 183 A8
Bourne Park Rd. CT4 .... 111 A7
Bourne Rd. TN25 .... 172 D5
Bourne View. CT4 .... 88 F1
Bournemouth Dr. CT6 .... 22 D4
Bournemouth Gdns. CT19 . 178 C6
Bournemouth Rd. CT19 .... 178 C5
Bournes Cl. CT2 .... 67 F7
Bournes Pl. TN26 .... 169 A2
Bourneside Terr. ME17 .... 77 D2
Bournewood. TN26 .... 183 A8
Bournwood Cl. ME15 .... 75 F1
Bournville Ave. ME4 .... 9 F1
Bournewood Cl. ME15 .... 75 F1
Bouverie Pl. **2** CT20 .... 178 D4
Bouverie Rd. CT20 .... 178 D4
Bouverie Rd W. CT20 .... 178 C4
Bouverie Sq. **1** CT20 .... 178 D4
Bow Hill. CT4 .... 109 F2
Bowdell La. TN29 .... 191 E3
Bowden Cres. CT20 .... 177 C6
Bowen Rd. CT19 .... 177 E6
Bowens Field. TN23 .... 139 B1
Bower Cl. ME16 .... 74 E4
Bower Gr. ME5 .... 32 C1
Bower Grove Sch. ME16 .... 74 B2
Bower La. Maidstone ME16 .. 74 E3
Bower La. Maidstone ME16 .. 74 E3
Bower Mount Rd. ME16 .... 74 D4
Bower Pl. ME16 .... 74 E3
Bower Rd. TN25 .... 158 A3
Bower St. ME16 .... 74 E4
Bower Terr. ME16 .... 74 E3
Bowerland La. Chilham CT4 . 85 E1
Bournville Ave.
  Old Wives Lees CT4 .... 85 C2
Bowers Ho. ME7 .... 10 E7
Bowes Ave. CT9 .... 7 E1
Bowes La. CT6 .... 23 A2
Bowes Rd. ME2 .... 9 B8
Bowes Villas. CT14 .... 93 E4
Bowl Field. TN25 .... 142 B6
Bowl Rd. TN27 .... 103 D2
Bowland Cl. CT6 .... 23 C2
Bowles Well Gdns. CT19 ... 178 F7
Bowley La. ME17 .... 118 D8
Bowling Green La. CT14 .... 117 B5
Bowling Green Terr. **8**
  CT17 .... 166 D7
Bowling Sq. CT13 .... 72 F1
Bowman Cl. ME5 .... 32 C5
Bowman Ct. CT17 .... 149 A1
Bower Cl. CT14 .... 116 F4
Bowyer Rd. CT5 .... 42 F7
Boxley. TN23 .... 155 F8
Boxley Cl. Maidstone ME14 . 75 B8
Boxley Cl.
  West Minster ME12 .... 3 B7
Boxley Rd. Chatham ME5 .... 32 B2
Boxley Rd.
  Maidstone ME14 .... 75 B7
Boxmend Ind Est. ME15 ...... 97 F3
Boxted La. ME13 .... 13 A1
Boyces Hill. ME9 .... 35 D6

Boyden Gate Hill. CT3 .... 47 B[?]
Boyes La. CT3 .... 91 D[?]
Boyke La. CT4 .... 144 C[?]
Boyne Rd. CT15 .... 134 A[?]
Boys Hall Rd. TN24 .... 156 F[?]
Boystown Pl. CT13 .... 93 C[?]
Brabazon Rd. ME2 .... 5 C[?]
Brabner Cl. CT19 .... 178 E[?]
Brabourne Ave. ME8 .... 11 C[?]
Brabourne
  CE Prim Sch. TN25 .... 159 A[?]
Brabourne Cl. CT2 .... 67 A[?]
Brabourne Gdns. CT20 ...... 177 E[?]
Brabourne La. TN25 .... 142 F[?]
Brabourne Rd. TN25 .... 141 D[?]
Brack La. TN29 .... 191 B[?]
Bracken Cl. TN24 .... 139 C[?]
Bracken Ct.
  Broadstairs CT10 .... 29 E[?]
Bracken Ct.
  Sittingbourne ME10 .... 37 C[?]
Bracken Hill. ME5 .... 32 A[?]
Bracken Lea. ME5 .... 10 C[?]
Brackley Cl. ME14 .... 75 C[?]
Brackwood Cl. ME8 .... 33 D[?]
Bradbridge Gn. TN23 .... 155 D[?]
Braddick Cl. ME15 .... 97 B[?]
Bradfield Ave. ME9 .... 38 D[?]
Bradfield Rd. TN24 .... 139 B[?]
Bradfields Ave. ME5 .... 31 F[?]
Bradfields Ave W. ME5 .... 31 F[?]
Bradfields Sch. ME5 .... 32 A[?]
Bradley Dr. ME10 .... 36 E[?]
Bradley Rd.
  Folkestone CT19 .... 178 F[?]
Bradley Rd.
  Ramsgate CT12 .... 29 C[?]
Bradshaw Cl. ME9 .... 12 E[?]
Bradstone Ave. CT19 .... 178 D[?]
Bradstone New Rd. **3**
  CT20 .... 178 D[?]
Bradstone Rd. CT20 .... 178 D[?]
Bradstow Way. CT10 .... 30 A[?]
Brady Rd. CT18 .... 161 A[?]
Braeside. CT10 .... 30 B[?]
Braggs La. CT6 .... 45 E[?]
Brake Ave. ME5 .... 31 E[?]
Bramble Cl.
  Maidstone ME16 .... 74 B[?]
Bramble Cl. Wye TN25 .... 123 D[?]
Bramble La. TN25 .... 123 C[?]
Brambledown.
  Chatham ME5 .... 32 B[?]
Brambledown.
  Folkestone CT19 .... 178 D[?]
Bramblefield La. ME10 .... 14 E[?]
Bramblefields Cl. CT6 .... 23 B[?]
Bramblehill Rd. ME13 .... 62 C[?]
Brambles Wildlife Pk.
  CT2 &CT6 .... 45 C[?]
Brambley Cres. CT20 .... 177 E[?]
Bramley Ave.
  Canterbury CT1 .... 87 C[?]
Bramley Ave.
  Faversham ME13 .... 62 E[?]
Bramley Cl.
  Brabourne Lees TN25 ...... 158 E[?]
Bramley Cl.
  Eastchurch ME12 .... 5 D[?]
Bramley Cl.
  Gillingham ME8 .... 34 B[?]
Bramley Cres. ME15 .... 75 F[?]
Bramley Gdns.
  Ashford TN23 .... 156 A[?]
Bramley Gdns.
  Coxheath ME17 .... 96 C[?]
Bramley Way. ME12 .... 5 D[?]
Bramling Gap. CT3 .... 90 C[?]
Bramling Rd. CT3 & CT4 ...... 90 B[?]
Bramshaw Rd. CT2 .... 66 E[?]
Bramshott Cl. ME14 .... 74 C[?]
Bramston Rd. ME12 .... 4 C[?]
Branch Rd. CT4 .... 107 C[?]
Branch St. CT15 .... 149 C[?]
Brandon Rd. CT12 .... 29 A[?]
Brandon Way. CT7 .... 27 B[?]
Bransgore Cl. ME8 .... 33 D[?]
Brasenose Rd. ME7 .... 10 E[?]
Brasier Ct. ME4 .... 45 A[?]
Brassey Ave. CT10 .... 29 F[?]
Brattle. TN26 .... 181 B[?]
Bray Gdns. ME15 .... 96 F[?]
Breach La. ME9 .... 13 A[?]
Breadlands Cl*.TN24 .... 156 F[?]
Breadlands Rd.TN24 .... 156 F[?]
Brecon Chase. ME12 .... 4 C[?]
Brecon Rise. TN24 .... 139 B[?]
Brecon Sq. CT12 .... 29 A[?]
Bredgar
  CE Prim Sch. ME9 .... 58 A[?]
Bredgar Cl. Ashford TN23 ... 155 F[?]

Bredgar Cl.
  Maidstone ME14 .... 75 C5
Bredgar Rd. ME8 .... 11 B4
Bredhurst CE Prim Sch.
  ME7 .... 33 B1
Bredhurst Cl. ME12 .... 3 B7
Bredhurst Rd.
  Gillingham ME8 .... 33 B4
Bredhurst Rd.
  Gillingham ME8 .... 33 C5
Bredlands La. CT3 & CT2 .... 46 C1
Brenchley Ave. CT14 .... 116 F4
Brenchley Cl.
  Ashford TN23 .... 155 E6
Brenchley Cl. Chatham ME1 .... 9 D2
Brenchley Rd.
  Gillingham ME8 .... 11 B2
Brenchley Rd.
  Maidstone ME15 .... 74 F2
Brenchley Rd.
  Sittingbourne ME10 .... 36 F2
Brendon Ave. ME5 .... 32 A3
Brendon Dr. TN24 .... 139 B3
Brenley Cnr. ME13 .... 63 B4
Brenley La. ME13 .... 63 C2
Brent Cl. ME5 .... 31 E5
Brent Hill. ME13 .... 62 C8
Brent Rd. ME13 .... 62 C8
Brents Ind Est. ME13 .... 40 D1
Brentwood. TN23 .... 155 F5
Brenzett Cl. ME5 .... 32 B5
Brenzett Cnr. TN29 .... 192 A3
Brenzett District
  CE Prim Sch. TN29 .... 192 A2
Breton Rd. ME1 .... 9 C2
Brett Wlk. ME8 .... 33 D4
Brewer St. Deal CT14 .... 117 D6
Brewer St.
  Maidstone ME14 .... 75 A5
Brewer's Hill CT20 .... 177 D3
Brewery Cotts. CT14 .... 116 E4
Brewery La. CT4 .... 89 A1
Brewery Rd. ME10 .... 36 E6
Brewery Sq. CT3 .... 48 D2
Brewster Cotts. ME9 .... 59 E2
Brian Roberts Ho. CT6 .... 22 F5
Briar Cl. Ashford TN24 .... 139 C6
Briar Cl. River CT17 .... 148 F2
Briar Fields. ME14 .... 75 E5
Briars Rd. TN29 .... 194 F3
Briars Wlk. CT10 .... 29 F3
Briary Cl. CT7 .... 28 A8
Brice Ave. CT4 .... 86 C1
Brices Alley. CT5 .... 20 D2
Brickfield Cotts. TN25 .... 123 B2
Brickfield La. ME13 .... 63 E2
Brickfield Rd. CT4 .... 128 F7
Brickmakers Ind Est. ME10 .... 37 B6
Brickwall Terr. TN26 .... 168 F3
Bridewell La. TN30 .... 179 A7
Bridewell Pk. CT5 .... 21 A1
Bridge App The. CT5 .... 20 F1
Bridge Cl. Hythe CT21 .... 176 A2
Bridge Cl.
  Woodchurch TN26 .... 181 B8
Bridge Cotts. Selling ME13 .... 84 E7
Bridge Cotts.
  Teynham ME9 .... 38 D2
Bridge Down. CT4 .... 111 B8
Bridge Hill. Bridge CT4 .... 111 B8
Bridge Hill.
  Finglesham CT14 .... 116 C8
Bridge Ho. CT11 .... 52 C7
Bridge Mill Way. ME15 .... 74 D2
Bridge & Patrixbourne
  CE Prim Sch. CT4 .... 89 A2
Bridge Rd. Ashford TN23 .... 138 F2
Bridge Rd.
  Brabourne Lees TN25 .... 158 D5
Bridge Rd. Bridge CT4 .... 88 D1
Bridge Rd. Deal CT14 .... 117 D7
Bridge Rd.
  Faversham ME13 .... 62 D8
Bridge Rd. Gillingham ME7 .... 10 C7
Bridge Rd. Margate CT9 .... 7 E1
Bridge Rd. Rochester ME1 .... 9 C2
Bridge Rd. Sheerness ME12 .... 1 C3
Bridge St. Dover CT16 .... 149 C1
Bridge St.
  Folkestone CT19 .... 178 E6
Bridge St. Loose ME15 .... 96 F5
Bridge St. Wye TN25 .... 123 E2
Bridge View Ind Est. ME11 .... 3 A2
Bridgefield Rd. CT5 .... 21 B3
Bridgeford Way. CT4 .... 89 A1
Bridges Cl. CT7 .... 25 E2
Bridgeside. CT14 .... 117 C6
Bridgewater Rd. ME12 .... 3 B8
Bridgeway. CT5 .... 20 F2
Bridle Way. CT21 .... 177 A3
Bridleway Gdns. CT10 .... 29 E3

Bridleway La. TN23 .... 156 B4
Brielle Way. Queenborough
  ME11 & ME12 .... 3 A6
Brielle Way.
  Sheerness ME12 .... 1 B2
Brier Cl. ME5 .... 32 C8
Brier Rd. ME10 & ME9 .... 36 B4
Bright Rd. ME4 .... 10 B2
Bright's Pl. CT11 .... 52 F7
Brightlingsea Rd. CT13 .... 93 F8
Brindle Way. ME5 .... 32 C1
Brinklow Terr. TN26 .... 155 A1
Brisbane Ave. ME10 .... 36 C4
Brisbane Dr. CT12 .... 29 A1
Brisbane Rd. ME4 .... 10 A3
Brishing Cl. ME15 .... 97 E5
Brishing La. ME17 .... 97 F4
Brishing Rd. ME15 & ME17 .... 97 F3
Brissenden Cl. TN28 .... 200 B8
Bristles Cnr. CT3 .... 46 E6
Bristol Pl. CT11 .... 52 D7
Bristol Rd. CT1 .... 87 F6
Britannia Ave. CT5 .... 43 B7
Britannia Cl. ME10 .... 36 E7
Britannia Rd. CT14 .... 117 D8
Briton Cl. ME12 .... 3 B8
Briton Rd. ME13 .... 62 C7
Britten Cl. CT21 .... 176 A3
Britton St. ME7 .... 10 B5
Broad La. CT14 .... 116 B7
Broad Oak Rd. CT2 .... 67 B3
Broad St. Canterbury CT1 .... 67 A1
Broad St. Canterbury CT1 .... 88 A8
Broad St. Deal CT14 .... 117 D6
Broad St. Margate CT9 .... 7 I3
Broad St. Ramsgate CT11 .... 52 E7
Broad St. Sheerness ME12 .... 1 C2
Broad Street Hill.
  ME14 & ME15 .... 77 D7
Broadacre. Lydden CT15 .... 147 F8
Broadacre. Teynham ME9 .... 38 D2
Broader La. ME14 .... 55 B2
Broadfield Cres. CT20 .... 178 A5
Broadfield Rd.
  Folkestone CT20 .... 178 A5
Broadfield Rd.
  Maidstone ME15 .... 97 A8
Broadhurst Dr. TN24 .... 139 D7
Broadlands Ave. TN28 .... 200 B8
Broadlands Cres. TN28 .... 200 B8
Broadlands Dr. ME5 .... 32 B4
Broadlands Ind Est. CT2 .... 66 A7
Broadley Ave. CT7 .... 26 F5
Broadley Rd. CT9 .... 29 D7
Broadmead. ME13 .... 155 E6
Broadmead Rd. CT19 .... 178 C5
Broadmeadow. CT19 .... 178 B7
Broadoak Ave. ME15 .... 97 A8
Broadoak Rd. ME9 .... 58 E6
Broadsole La. CT15 .... 164 E5
Broadstairs Rd. CT10 .... 29 E5
Broadstairs Sta. CT10 .... 30 A4
Broadview. CT20 .... 177 C6
Broadview Ave. ME8 .... 33 E8
Broadviews. CT21 .... 176 D1
Broadway. Gillingham ME8 .... 11 A3
Broadway.
  Maidstone ME16 .... 74 F4
Broadway. Petham CT4 .... 109 A2
Broadway. Sheerness ME12 .... 1 D2
Broadway The.
  Broadstairs CT10 .... 30 A4
Broadway The.
  Herne Bay CT6 .... 22 C5
Broadway The.
  Minster ME12 .... 4 B7
Brockenhurst Ave. ME15 .... 75 C1
Brockenhurst Cl.
  Canterbury CT2 .... 66 E2
Brockenhurst Cl.
  Gillingham ME8 .... 33 C7
Brockenhurst Rd. CT11 .... 52 G8
Brockhill City Pk. CT21 .... 175 F4
Brockhill Park Sch
  (Lower Dept). CT21 .... 176 A3
Brockhill Park Sch
  (Upper Dept). CT21 .... 175 F4
Brockhill Rd. CT21 .... 176 B3
Brockley Rd. CT9 .... 8 A2
Brockman Cres. TN29 .... 187 B4
Brockman Rd. CT20 .... 178 C5
Brockman's Cl. CT12 .... 50 B7
Brogdale Farm Cotts.
  ME13 .... 62 A3
Brogdale Rd. ME13 .... 62 B5
Brogden Cres. ME17 .... 98 F7
Bromley Cl. Chatham ME5 .... 32 B4
Bromley Cl. Newington ME9 .... 35 A5
Bromley Green Rd. TN26 .... 171 A5
Brompton Hill. ME4 .... 9 F6

Brompton La. ME2 .... 9 A8
Brompton Rd. ME7 .... 10 B6
Brompton Villas. CT15 .... 149 E6
Brompton-Westbrook
  Cty Prim Sch. ME7 .... 10 A5
Bromstone
  Cty Prim Sch. CT10 .... 29 D3
Bromstone Mews. CT10 .... 29 E3
Bromstone Rd. CT10 .... 29 E3
Bronington Cl. ME5 .... 32 A5
Brook. ME4 .... 10 A4
Brook Cl. Herne Bay CT6 .... 22 C3
Brook Cl. Hythe CT21 .... 177 B3
Brook Cotts.
  Dean Street ME15 .... 96 C7
Brook Cotts.
  Teynham ME9 .... 39 A2
Brook Cty Prim Sch. TN25 .... 141 A4
Brook La. Cliffs End CT12 .... 50 F4
Brook La. Reculver CT6 .... 24 B5
Brook La. Sellindge TN25 .... 159 E2
Brook La Cotts. TN25 .... 159 E2
Brook Rd.
  Faversham ME13 .... 40 D1
Brook Rd. Whitstable CT5 .... 21 C3
Brook St. Eastry CT13 .... 93 C2
Brook St.
  Woodchurch TN26 .... 180 D8
Brookbank. Brook TN25 .... 141 A5
Brookbank.
  Maidstone ME14 .... 75 A8
Brooke Ave. CT9 .... 28 B7
Brooke Rd. TN24 .... 139 B3
Brookes Pl. ME9 .... 35 B6
Brookfield Ave. CT16 .... 149 B2
Brookfield Cl. TN23 .... 155 F8
Brookfield Ind Pk. TN23 .... 138 F1
Brookfield Pl. CT16 .... 149 B2
Brookfield Rd.
  Ashford TN23 .... 155 F8
Brookfield Rd.
  Dover CT16 .... 149 A3
Brookland
  CE Prim Sch. TN29 .... 197 D8
Brooklands Cl. CT2 .... 67 F4
Brooklyn Paddock. ME7 .... 10 D6
Brooks Pl. ME14 .... 75 A4
Brooks Way. TN29 .... 203 C5
Brookside.
  St Mary's Bay TN29 .... 195 A5
Brookside.
  Temple Ewell CT16 .... 148 D5
Broom Rd. ME10 .... 37 C5
Broomcroft Rd. ME8 .... 11 F2
Broome Park
  Golf Course. CT4 .... 129 B6
Broomfield Cres. CT9 .... 8 F2
Broomfield Gate. CT5 .... 44 D5
Broomfield Rd.
  Broomfield ME17 .... 99 D4
Broomfield Rd.
  Faversham ME13 .... 62 C8
Broomfield Rd.
  Folkestone CT19 .... 177 E6
Broomfield Rd.
  Herne Bay CT6 .... 23 C2
Brotherhood Cl. CT2 .... 66 D4
Broughton Cl. TN23 .... 138 E1
Brown St. ME8 .... 11 F1
Brownelow Copse. ME5 .... 32 B1
Brownhill Cl. ME5 .... 32 A4
Browning Pl. CT19 .... 178 E7
Brownings Orch. ME9 .... 59 A7
Brucei Rd. CT14 .... 94 C7
Bruce Cl. CT14 .... 117 B4
Bruges Ct. ME10 .... 14 F1
Brundell Terr. CT4 .... 86 B2
Brunel Way. ME4 .... 10 A7
Brunswick Cotts. ME9 .... 38 E6
Brunswick Cl. CT11 .... 52 E7
Brunswick Field. ME9 .... 38 E6
Brunswick Gdns. CT16 .... 149 B3
Brunswick House
  Cty Prim Sch. ME16 .... 74 E5
Brunswick Ind Ctr. TN23 .... 138 F2
Brunswick Rd.
  Ashford TN23 .... 138 F2
Brunswick Rd.
  Birchington CT7 .... 27 A5
Brunswick Sq. CT6 .... 22 E5
Brunswick St.
  Maidstone ME15 .... 75 A3
Brunswick St.
  Maidstone ME15 .... 75 A3
Brunswick St E. ME15 .... 75 A3
Bryant Rd. ME2 .... 9 A7
Bryant St. ME4 .... 10 A3
Brymore Cl. CT1 .... 67 B2
Brymore Rd. CT1 .... 67 B2
Bryony Sch (private). ME8 .... 33 F5
Buck St. TN25 .... 105 C2

Buckhurst Dr. CT9 .... 8 F2
Buckingham Rd. 14
  Broadstairs CT10 .... 30 B4
Buckingham Rd.
  Gillingham ME7 .... 10 D5
Buckingham Rd.
  Margate CT9 .... 7 I1-
Buckingham Row. ME15 .... 97 E7
Buckland Ave. CT16 .... 149 B2
Buckland Cl. ME5 .... 32 A2
Buckland Cotts. ME13 .... 61 B8
Buckland Hill. ME16 .... 74 E5
Buckland Hospl. CT17 .... 149 A1
Buckland La.
  Maidstone ME16 .... 74 D6
Buckland La. Staple CT3 .... 92 A4
Buckland Pl. ME16 .... 74 E4
Buckland Rd. ME16 .... 74 E4
Buckland Cl. ME12 .... 6 E4
Buckmore Park
  (Scout Camp). ME5 .... 31 C3
Bucksford La. TN23 .... 155 C7
Buckstone Cl. CT14 .... 117 C7
Budd's Farm Cotts. TN30 .... 188 F2
Budd's La. TN30 .... 188 F2
Buenos Ayres. CT9 .... 7 H2
Buffs Ave. CT20 .... 177 B6
Builders Sq. CT3 .... 90 A8
Bull Hill. ME17 .... 102 A1
Bull La. Bethersden TN26 .... 153 B4
Bull La.
  Boughton Street ME13 .... 63 F4
Bull La. Eccles ME20 .... 53 A6
Bull La. Stockbury ME9 .... 34 C2
Bulldog Rd. ME5 .... 32 B2
Bulleid Pl. TN24 .... 156 D7
Buller Rd. ME4 .... 9 F2
Buller's Ave. CT6 .... 22 E4
Bullockstone Rd. CT6 .... 45 E7
Bulls Cotts. 4 CT21 .... 176 B2
Bulltown Cnr. TN25 .... 141 F3
Bullwark St. CT17 .... 166 D5
Bulrush Cl. ME5 .... 31 F3
Bulrushes The. TN23 .... 155 D8
Bulwark Rd. CT14 .... 117 D7
Bumbles Cl. ME1 .... 31 D7
Bunce Court Rd.
  ME13 & ME17 .... 102 E7
Bungalow The. TN26 .... 137 F5
Bungalows The.
  Faversham ME13 .... 62 A4
Bungalows The.
  Tenterden TN30 .... 179 D7
Bungalows The.
  Woodnesborough CT13 .... 93 B5
Bunker's Hill. CT17 .... 149 B2
Bunkers Hill Ave. CT17 .... 149 B1
Bunkers Hill Rd. CT17 .... 149 A1
Bunkley Meadow. TN26 .... 183 A7
Burberry La. ME17 .... 99 B5
Burch Ave. CT13 .... 93 F8
Burford's Alley. CT3 .... 71 D1
Burgate. CT1 .... 88 A8
Burgate La. 4 CT1 .... 88 A8
Burgess Terr. TN25 .... 157 E4
Burgess Cl. Minster,
  Thanet CT12 .... 50 C7
Burgess Gn. CT14 .... 116 C8
Burgess Hall Dr. ME17 .... 98 F6
Burgess Rd. Aylesham CT3 .... 112 F6
Burgess Rd. Rochester ME2 .... 9 B7
Burgess Row. 8 TN30 .... 179 A7
Burghclere Dr. ME16 .... 74 B2
Burgoyne Cl. ME14 .... 74 F7
Burgoyne Gr. CT16 .... 149 A5
Burgoyne Hts. CT16 .... 149 E3
Burial Ground La. ME15 .... 74 E1
Burkestone Cl. ME10 .... 37 A8
Burleigh Dr. ME14 .... 53 F1
Burleigh Rd. TN27 .... 120 C7
Burley Rd. ME10 .... 36 E4
Burlington Dr. CT6 .... 23 D5
Burlington Gdns.
  Gillingham ME8 .... 33 E4
Burlington Gdns.
  Margate CT9 .... 28 C8
Burma Cres. CT1 .... 67 D1
Burma Way. ME5 .... 31 F6
Burmarsh Cl. ME5 .... 32 B5
Burmarsh Rd.
  Burmarsh TN29 .... 186 C3
Burmarsh Rd. Hythe CT21 .... 187 C8
Burn's Rd. ME7 .... 10 C7
Burnan Rd. CT5 .... 21 C2
Burnham Cl. ME10 .... 36 E8
Burnham Wlk. ME8 .... 33 E3
Burns Rd. ME14 .... 74 C2
Burnt House Hill. CT3 .... 69 B5

Burnt Oak Terr. ME7 .... 10 D6
Burnt Oast Rd. ME13 .... 64 A3
Burntwick Dr. ME9 .... 13 B3
Burnup Bank. ME10 .... 37 C5
Burrow Rd. CT19 .... 178 F6
Burrs The. ME10 .... 36 F3
Burrstock Way. ME4 .... 12 B2
Bursill Cres. CT12 .... 29 B1
Bursted Hill. CT4 .... 110 B2
Bursted Hill. ME7 .... 96 B2
Burton Cl. CT19 .... 178 A7
Burton Fields. CT6 .... 23 B4
Burton Rd. TN24 .... 139 C6
Busbridge Rd. ME15 .... 96 C6
Bush Ave. CT12 .... 29 B1
Bush Cl. ME9 .... 57 F5
Bush Row. ME20 .... 53 A3
Busheyfields Rd. CT6 .... 45 F6
Bushmeadow Rd. ME8 .... 11 F2
Bushy Gr. ME17 .... 99 D2
Bushy Hill Rd. CT2 .... 68 D7
Bushy Royds. TN24 .... 156 D6
Bushy Ruff Cotts. CT16 .... 148 D4
Butchers La. CT15 .... 113 E5
Butchery La. 1 CT1 .... 88 A8
Butchery The. 2 CT13 .... 73 A1
Butler's Hill. ME13 .... 64 D7
Butt Field Rd. TN23 .... 155 F7
Butter St. CT15 .... 113 C4
Butterfly Ctr The. CT15 .... 146 B3
Buttermere. ME13 .... 62 E6
Buttermere Cl.
  Folkestone CT19 .... 178 B6
Buttermere Cl.
  Gillingham ME7 .... 11 A5
Buttermere Gdns. CT3 .... 112 F6
Button La. ME15 .... 76 B2
Butts Cl. CT14 .... 110 A6
Butts Cty Prim
  Inf Sch The. ME10 .... 36 E6
Butts Hill. ME13 .... 63 F5
Butts Meadow. CT4 .... 110 A6
Butts The. Sandwich CT13 .... 72 F1
Butts The.
  Maidstone ME10 .... 36 F4
Buxton Cl. Chatham ME5 .... 32 D1
Buxton Cl. Maidstone ME15 .... 97 A8
Buxton Rd. CT12 .... 139 C4
Bybrook Ct. TN24 .... 139 C4
Bybrook
  Cty Inf Sch. TN24 .... 139 D5
Bybrook
  Cty Jun Sch. TN24 .... 139 D5
Bybrook Field. CT20 .... 177 E3
Bybrook Rd. TN24 .... 139 C5
Bybrook Way. CT20 .... 177 E4
Bychurch Pl. 6 ME15 .... 75 A3
Byllan Rd. CT17 .... 148 E3
Byron Ave. CT9 .... 7 J1
Byron Cl. CT1 .... 88 C7
Byron Cres. CT16 .... 149 B4
Byron Cty Prim Sch. ME7 .... 10 C3
Byron Rd. Gillingham ME7 .... 10 C3
Byron Rd. Maidstone ME14 .... 75 B7
Bysing Wood Cotts. ME13 .... 39 F1
Bysing Wood
  Cty Prim Sch. ME13 .... 62 A8
Bysing Wood Rd. ME13 .... 39 F1
Bythorne Ct. ME8 .... 12 B1

C Ramp App. CT16 .... 166 G8
Cade Rd. TN23 .... 156 B7
Cades Orch. ME13 .... 61 E3
Cadnam Cl. CT2 .... 66 E3
Caernarvon Dr. ME15 .... 74 F1
Caesar's Way. CT19 .... 177 E7
Cage La. TN27 .... 135 A1
Calais Hill. CT2 .... 66 E6
Calcroft Mews. 6 CT1 .... 67 B2
Calcutta Ho. 3 ME15 .... 97 E5
Caldecot La. TN29 .... 199 D2
Caldecote Cl. ME8 .... 12 B1
Calder Rd. ME14 .... 74 E7
Caldew Ave. ME8 .... 11 C1
Caldew Gr. ME10 .... 37 A7
Caledon Terr. CT1 .... 88 A8
Caledon La. CT1 .... 33 E8
Calehill Cl. ME14 .... 75 C6
Calgary Cres. CT19 .... 178 E8
California Row. CT13 .... 90 E6
Callams Cl. ME8 .... 33 D6
Calland. TN25 .... 158 E5
Callaways La. ME9 .... 35 B6
Calleywell La. TN25 .... 173 A7
Callis Court Rd. CT10 .... 29 F6
Callis Grange
  Cty Inf Sch. CT10 .... 29 F7

Calverden Rd. CT12 29 A1
Camborne Manor. ME7 10 C6
Cambourne Ave. CT8 27 D8
Cambrai Ct. CT1 67 D1
Cambridge Ave. CT13 95 B7
Cambridge Cl. CT7 27 B7
Cambridge Cres. ME15 97 D7
Cambridge Gdns. CT20 178 D5
Cambridge Ho. 3 ME15 97 D7
Cambridge Rd. Canterbury CT1 87 F6
Cambridge Rd. Deal CT14 117 D3
Cambridge Rd. Dover CT16 & CT17 166 D7
Cambridge Rd. Faversham ME13 62 B6
Cambridge Rd. Gillingham ME8 33 C6
Cambridge Rd. Rochester ME2 9 A8
Cambridge Rd. Sittingbourne ME10 37 B3
Cambridge Terr. Chatham ME4 9 F4
Cambridge Terr. 11 Dover CT16 166 E7
Cambridge Terr. 11 Folkestone CT20 178 E5
Cambridge Terr. Margate CT9 8 B1
Cambridge Way. CT1 87 F6
Camden Cl. ME5 32 B5
Camden Cres. CT16 166 E7
Camden Rd. Broadstairs CT10 29 E7
Camden Rd. Gillingham ME7 10 D7
Camden Rd. Ramsgate CT11 52 E6
Camden Sq. 7 CT11 52 E7
Camden St. ME14 75 A5
Camden Terr. TN24 139 E1
Camellia Cl. Gillingham ME8 33 D7
Camellia Cl. 2 Margate CT9 28 B8
Cameron Cl. ME5 32 B8
Cameron Ct. CT17 166 A6
Camomile Dr. ME14 75 F5
Camp Way. ME15 97 C6
Campbell Cl. CT6 23 C3
Campbell Rd. Deal CT14 117 D4
Campbell Rd. Maidstone ME15 75 A3
Campion Cl. ME5 31 E3
Campleshon Rd. ME8 33 D5
Campus Way. ME7 33 A8
Canada Cl. CT18 & CT19 177 C6
Canada Rd. CT14 117 D3
Canada Terr. 3 ME14 75 A7
Canadian Ave. ME7 10 F4
Canal Rd. ME2 9 C7
Canberra Gdns. ME10 36 C4
Canning St. ME14 75 A6
Cannon Appleton Ct. CT1 87 E7
Cannon Rd. CT11 52 D7
Cannon St. Deal CT14 117 C7
Cannon St. Dover CT16 166 D8
Cannon St. Lydd TN29 203 C6
Cannon St. New Romney TN28 200 B7
Cannonbury Rd. CT11 52 D6
Cannongate Ave. CT21 176 D3
Cannongate Cl. CT21 176 E2
Cannongate Gdns. CT21 176 E3
Cannongate Rd. CT21 176 D3
Canon Cl. ME1 9 B2
Canon Gn. CT3 91 A7
Canon Woods Way. TN24 139 F6
Canons Gate Rd. CT16 166 E8
Canterbury Cl. CT10 29 D5
Canterbury Coll. CT1 88 A7
Canterbury Ct. TN24 139 D2
Canterbury East Sta. CT1 87 F7
Canterbury Equestrian Ctr. CT6 22 D3
Canterbury Golf Course. CT2 67 E2
Canterbury High Sch The. CT2 87 D8
Canterbury Hill. CT2 66 E5
Canterbury Ho. 2 ME15 97 D7
Canterbury Ind Pk. CT3 69 A8
Canterbury La. Canterbury CT1 88 A8
Canterbury La. Gillingham ME8 & ME9 12 C1
Canterbury Rd. Ashford, Bybrook TN24 139 E5
Canterbury Rd. Ashford, South Willesborogh TN24 156 E6
Canterbury Rd. Barham CT4 129 C5
Canterbury Rd. Boughton Aluph CT4 & TN25 & TN24 123 C5
Canterbury Rd. Boughton Street ME13 63 D4
Canterbury Rd. Brabourne TN25 159 C8
Canterbury Rd. Brabourne Lees TN25 158 F6
Canterbury Rd. Challock TN25 & TN27 104 C1
Canterbury Rd. Chilham CT4 85 E1
Canterbury Rd. Denton CT4 129 A1
Canterbury Rd. Dunkirk ME13 64 E2
Canterbury Rd. Elham CT4 144 E3
Canterbury Rd. Etchinghill CT18 161 D4
Canterbury Rd. Faversham ME13 62 E5
Canterbury Rd. Folkestone CT19 178 D7
Canterbury Rd. Folkestone, Foord CT19 178 E6
Canterbury Rd. Hawkinge CT18 & CT19 & CT15 & CT4 163 B4
Canterbury Rd. Herne CT3 & CT6 45 E5
Canterbury Rd. Herne Bay CT6 23 A3
Canterbury Rd. Littlebourne CT3 89 C8
Canterbury Rd. Lydden CT15 147 E7
Canterbury Rd. Lyminge CT18 161 C7
Canterbury Rd. Sarre CT7 48 E7
Canterbury Rd. Sittingbourne ME10 37 B3
Canterbury Rd. Whitstable CT5 43 D8
Canterbury Rd. Wingham CT3 91 A7
Canterbury Rd E. CT11 & CT12 52 A6
Canterbury Rd W. CT12 51 D7
Canterbury Road Birchington. CT7 27 B7
Canterbury Road Cty Prim Sch. ME10 37 B3
Canterbury Road Margate. CT9 7 G1
Canterbury Road Westgate. CT8 & CT9 27 E8
Canterbury St. ME7 10 C4
Canterbury West Sta. CT2 66 F1
Canute Rd. Birchington CT7 26 D7
Canute Rd. Deal CT14 95 C1
Canute Rd. Faversham ME13 62 C6
Capel Cl. Broadstairs CT10 8 F1
Capel Cl. Gillingham ME8 33 D4
Capel Rd. Faversham ME13 62 B7
Capel Rd. Petham CT4 108 F3
Capel Rd. Ruckinge TN25 & TN26 171 B4
Capel Rd. Sittingbourne ME10 36 E2
Capel St. CT18 164 B3
Capel-le-Ferne Cty Prim Sch. CT18 164 C3
Capell Cl. ME17 96 C3
Capetown Ho. 1 ME15 97 F5
Capstan Row. CT14 117 D7
Capstone Farm Country Pk. ME7 32 D5
Capstone Rd. Chatham ME5 10 D1
Capstone Rd. Gillingham ME7 32 F6
Cardine Cl. ME10 36 E7
Carey Cl. TN28 200 B6
Carey Ho. 5 CT1 87 F7
Caring La. ME15 76 E1
Caring Rd. ME15 76 C1
Carisbrooke Dr. ME16 74 D4
Carlsden Cl. CT16 149 A3
Carlton Ave. Broadstairs CT10 30 A5
Carlton Ave. Gillingham ME7 10 E4
Carlton Ave. Ramsgate CT11 52 D6
Carlton Ave. Sheerness ME12 1 C1
Carlton Cres. ME5 32 D8
Carlton Gdns. ME15 97 B8
Carlton Hill. CT6 22 C4
Carlton Leas. CT20 178 C4
Carlton Mansions. CT10 8 A3
Carlton Rd. Ashford TN23 139 A2
Carlton Rd. Kingsdown CT14 134 C6
Carlton Rd. Whitstable CT5 43 D2
Carlton Rd E. CT8 27 D8
Carlton Rd W. CT8 27 D8
Carlton Rise. CT8 27 C8
Carman's Cl. ME15 & ME17 96 F3
Carmel Ct. 2 CT7 26 F8
Caroland Cl. TN25 158 D5
Caroline Cl. CT5 43 B6
Caroline Cres. Broadstairs CT10 29 E6
Caroline Cres. Maidstone ME16 74 D7
Caroline Sq. CT9 7 J3
Carpeaux Cl. ME4 10 A4
Carpenters Cl. ME4 9 E2
Carpinus Cl. ME5 32 B1
Carriage Ho The. ME13 83 D5
Carriage Mus. ME15 75 A3
Carrie Ho. ME16 74 E5
Carroway's Pl. CT9 7 J2
Carter La. TN29 191 E2
Carter's Rd. CT20 177 F5
Carter's Wood. TN26 183 B7
Carton Cl. ME1 9 D2
Cartwright & Kelsey CE Prim Sch The. CT3 71 C2
Carvoran Way. ME8 33 C5
Caslocke St. 2 ME13 62 C7
Cassino Ho. 16 CT1 67 B2
Cassino Sq. CT16 149 E2
Castalla Cotts. CT14 117 D3
Castle Ave. Broadstairs CT10 30 B6
Castle Ave. Dover CT16 149 D1
Castle Ave. Hythe CT21 176 B3
Castle Ave. Rochester ME1 9 C4
Castle Bay. CT20 177 D3
Castle Cl. 4 Folkestone CT20 177 F3
Castle Cl. Lympne CT21 174 F2
Castle Comm Sch. CT14 117 C4
Castle Cotts. CT13 72 E5
Castle Cres. CT21 176 C4
Castle Dene. ME14 74 F8
Castle Dr. CT16 148 F7
Castle Hill. Folkestone CT19 & CT18 178 A8
Castle Hill. Rochester ME1 9 C6
Castle Hill. Thurnham ME14 55 D1
Castle Hill Ave. CT20 178 C4
Castle Hill Rd. CT16 166 E8
Castle Mayne Ave. CT7 27 F3
Castle Mews. CT14 117 A4
Castle Rd. Chatham ME4 10 B2
Castle Rd. Folkestone CT20 177 F3
Castle Rd. Hythe CT21 176 B4
Castle Rd. Maidstone ME16 74 D7
Castle Rd. Sittingbourne ME10 37 B5
Castle Rd. Whitstable CT5 20 F2
Castle Road Bsns Prec. ME10 37 B6
Castle Road Tech Ctr. ME10 37 B6
Castle Rough La. ME10 14 F1
Castle Row. CT1 87 F7
Castle St. 6 Ashford TN23 139 B2
Castle St. Canterbury CT1 87 F8
Castle St. Dover CT16 166 E8
Castle St. Queenborough ME11 3 A5
Castle View Rd. ME2 9 A7
Castle Wlk. CT14 95 D1
Castleacres Ind Pk. ME10 37 B6
Castlemaine Ave. ME7 10 F6
Castlemere Ave. ME11 3 B5
Castlemount Rd. CT16 149 D1
Castlemount Sch. CT16 149 E1
Castleview Ct. CT17 149 B1
Cathedral View. CT2 67 A2
Catherine Cl. ME16 74 A3
Catherine St. ME1 9 D3
Catherine Way. CT10 30 A6
Catkin Cl. ME5 31 F1
Catsole Hill. CT3 91 D2
Catt's Hill. TN30 189 E3
Catt's Wood Rd. CT4 109 F4
Catterick Rd. ME5 32 D2
Cattle Market. CT13 72 F1
Cauldham Cl. CT18 164 B1
Cauldham La. CT18 164 B3
Causeway The. Canterbury CT2 66 F1
Causeway The. Sandwich CT13 72 D2
Cavalry Ct. CT20 177 D5
Cave Hill. ME15 74 F1
Cave La. CT3 91 D3
Cavell Sq. CT14 117 A3
Cavell Way. ME10 36 D5
Cavenagh Rd. CT15 151 B6
Cavendish Ave. ME7 10 E6
Cavendish Ct. CT6 23 A5
Cavendish Pl. 2 CT11 52 E6
Cavendish Rd. Herne Bay CT6 23 A5
Cavendish Rd. Rochester ME1 9 D3
Cavendish St. CT11 52 E6
Cavendish Way. ME15 76 B3
Caversham Cl. ME8 11 F1
Cavour Rd. Faversham ME13 62 C7
Cavour Rd. Sheerness ME12 1 D2
Caxton Rd. CT9 28 C8
Cayser Dr. ME17 99 E2
Cazeneuve St. ME1 9 C5
Cecil Ave. Gillingham ME8 11 A2
Cecil Ave. Rochester ME2 9 B8
Cecil Ave. Sheerness ME12 1 C1
Cecil Ct. Ashford TN24 139 B3
Cecil Ct. Herne Bay CT6 23 A4
Cecil Pk. CT6 23 A4
Cecil Rd. Kingsdown CT14 134 D7
Cecil Rd. Rochester ME1 9 C3
Cecil Sq. CT9 7 I2
Cecil St. CT9 7 I2
Cecilia Gr. CT10 29 F6
Cecilia Rd. CT11 52 E8
Cedar Cl. Ashford TN23 138 E3
Cedar Cl. Broadstairs CT10 29 F7
Cedar Cl. Margate CT9 8 B1
Cedar Cl. Sittingbourne ME10 37 B2
Cedar Cres. TN29 194 F3
Cedar Ct. Folkestone CT20 177 E5
Cedar Ct. 10 Tenterden TN30 179 A7
Cedar Gdns. ME9 56 E8
Cedar Gr. ME7 33 A5
Cedar Ho. ME12 1 C2
Cedar Rd. CT2 68 A6
Cedar Terr. ME13 62 A4
Cedars Sch The. Maidstone ME16 74 D4
Cedars Sch The. Rochester ME1 9 C4
Cedars The. ME10 37 C5
Cedarview. CT2 66 C1
Cedarwood Ho. ME15 96 B6
Cedric Rd. CT8 7 C1
Ceil Villas. CT14 94 B4
Celestine Cl. ME5 32 A1
Cellar Hill. ME9 60 C8
Celtic Rd. CT14 117 A2
Cemetery La. TN24 139 C4
Centenary Cl. TN27 120 C8
Centenary Gdns. CT13 93 A2
Central Ave. Gillingham ME4 10 B8
Central Ave. Herne Bay CT6 22 D4
Central Ave. Sittingbourne ME10 36 F4
Central Bsns Pk. ME2 9 E7
Central Par. Herne Bay CT6 22 E5
Central Par. Rochester ME1 9 D2
Central Park Gdns. ME1 9 E2
Central Rd. Ramsgate CT11 52 D8
Central Rd. Rochester ME2 9 A7
Central Service Rd. CT16 166 H8
Central Sta. CT19 178 C5
Centre 2000. Maidstone ME16 74 C8
Centre 2000. Sittingbourne ME10 37 A4
Centre Ct. ME2 9 E7
Centre Rd. CT17 166 C6
Centre The. Margate CT9 7 I2
Centre The. Ramsgate CT12 29 A1
Centurion Cl. ME7 10 F1
Centurion Wlk. TN23 156 B4
Century Rd. Faversham ME13 62 E7
Century Rd. Gillingham ME8 33 D8
Century Wlk. CT14 117 C6
Ceres Ct. ME10 37 C5
Chada Ave. ME7 10 E3
Chaffe's La. ME9 12 E3
Chaffes Terr. ME9 12 E2
Chaffinch Cl. ME5 32 A7
Chafy Cres. CT2 67 F5
Chain Gate. TN27 118 A8
Chain The. 6 CT13 73 A1
Chalcroft Rd. CT20 177 E4
Chalfont Dr. Gillingham ME8 33 D6
Chalfont Dr. Herne Bay CT6 23 D2
Chalk Ave. TN30 167 B2
Chalk Cl. CT19 178 A7
Chalk Hill. CT11 & CT12 51 F6
Chalk Hill Rd. CT14 134 C5
Chalk Pit Hill. ME4 10 A3
Chalk Pit La. CT13 & CT3 92 C5
Chalk Rd. ME11 3 A5
Chalkenden Ave. ME8 11 A2
Chalkpit Hill. CT4 89 D3
Chalksole Green La. CT15 147 B2
Chalkwell Ct. CT17 166 A7
Chalkwell Rd. ME10 36 D5
Chalky Bank Rd. ME8 11 F2
Chalky Rd. ME9 56 C6
Challenger Cl. ME10 36 E7
Challock Ct. CT9 8 F2
Challock Cty Prim Sch. TN25 105 B1
Challock Wlk. ME14 75 C6
Chamberlain Ave. ME16 74 C2
Chamberlain Ct. ME8 33 B5
Chamberlain Dr. CT6 22 B4
Chamberlain Rd. Chatham ME4 10 B2
Chamberlain Rd. Dover CT17 166 B8
Chance Meadow. CT15 149 E6
Chancel Ct. CT2 66 D1
Chancery La. ME15 75 B3
Chanctonbury Chase. CT5 43 A6
Chandos Rd. 16 CT10 30 B4
Chandos Sq. 15 CT10 30 B4
Channel Cl. CT19 178 F7
Channel Lea. CT14 117 C1
Channel Rd. CT9 29 A6
Channel Sch The. CT19 178 C7
Channel Tunnel Terminal. CT18 177 B8
Channel View. 18 CT19 178 E5
Channel View Ct. 16 CT11 52 F7
Channel View Rd. CT17 166 C5
Channel Watch. TN28 200 E4
Channon Rd. TN29 204 E7
Chantry Ct. 4 CT1 66 F1
Chapel Cotts. ME17 98 F5
Chapel Hill. Eythorne CT15 131 C7
Chapel Hill. Margate CT9 29 A6
Chapel Hill Cl. CT9 28 F7
Chapel La. Blean CT2 66 A7
Chapel La. Broad Oak CT2 67 D7
Chapel La. 18 Dover CT16 166 D7
Chapel La. East Studdal CT15 132 C6
Chapel La. Gillingham,Hempstead ME7 33 A4
Chapel La. Gillingham,Lidsing ME7 33 A2
Chapel La. Maidstone ME14 76 A5
Chapel La. Newchurch TN29 185 C4
Chapel La. Potter's Forstal TN27 118 B2
Chapel La. Rhodes Minnis CT4 144 B4
Chapel La. Ripple CT14 133 D8
Chapel La. St Margaret's at Cliffe CT15 150 F6
Chapel La. Staple CT3 92 B6
Chapel La. Sturry CT2 67 F5
Chapel Mews. TN23 139 C2
Chapel Pl. 16 Dover CT16 & CT17 166 D7
Chapel Pl. Ramsgate CT11 52 D7
Chapel Place La. CT11 52 D7
Chapel Rd. Dymchurch TN29 195 C7
Chapel Rd. Ram Lane TN26 120 F1
Chapel Rd. Ramsgate CT11 52 C7
Chapel Rd. Tilmanstone CT14 115 A3
Chapel Rd. Whitfield CT16 149 A8
Chapel Row. Herne CT6 46 A8
Chapel Row. Kingsnorth TN23 156 A3
Chapel Row. Ram Lane TN26 120 F2
Chapel St. Deal CT14 117 D6
Chapel St. Faversham ME13 62 D6
Chapel St. Herne Bay CT6 23 A5
Chapel St. Hythe CT21 176 B2
Chapel St. Minster ME12 4 D6
Chapel St. Sheerness ME12 1 B2
Chapman Ave. ME15 97 F8
Chapman Ho. CT14 117 B3
Chapmans Cl. TN25 105 C2

Chapmans Hill.
CT15 & CT3 .... 113 B5
Chappell Way. ME10 ...... 36 E6
Charing CE Prim Sch.
TN27 .... 120 C8
Charing Cl. CT12 .... 52 C8
Charing Cres. CT8 ...... 27 D7
Charing Heath Rd.
Charing TN27 .... 119 F8
Charing Heath Rd.
Coppins Corner TN27 ... 120 A6
Charing Hill. TN27 .... 103 E1
Charing Rd. ME8 .... 11 B3
Charing Sta. TN27 .... 120 B7
Charlbury Cl. ME16 ...... 74 C3
Charlecote Ct. ME8 ...... 33 D8
Charles Cobb Cl. TN29 .. 195 D8
Charles Cres. CT19 ...... 177 E7
Charles Ct. CT8 .... 27 F8
Charles Dickens
High Sch The. CT10 ..... 29 E4
Charles Drayson Ct. ME13 .. 62 E7
Charles Ho. CT14 .... 117 B3
Charles Lister Ct. CT17 .. 149 B1
Charles Rd. Ramsgate CT11 . 52 E8
Charles St. Chatham ME4 ... 9 E3
Charles St. Herne Bay CT6 ... 23 A5
Charles St. Maidstone ME16 ... 74 E3
Charles St. Rochester ME2 ... 9 A7
Charles St. Sheerness ME12 .. 1 B3
Charlesford Ave. ME17 ... 99 D3
Charleston Ct. CT10 ...... 30 B3
Charlesworth Dr. CT7 ... 27 B7
Charlotte Ct. ME5 .... 32 B6
Charlotte Cl. CT11 .... 52 E6
Charlotte Dr. ME8 .... 11 C1
Charlotte Pl. 2 CT9 ...... 7 J1
Charlotte Sq. 3 CT9 ..... 7 J2
Charlotte St. 13
Broadstairs CT10 .... 30 B4
Charlotte St.
Folkestone CT20 .... 178 E5
Charlotte St.
Sittingbourne ME10 ...... 36 E5
Charlton Ave Ct. CT14 .... 149 C1
Charlton CE Prim Sch.
CT16 .... 149 C1
Charlton Cl. Ashford TN24 . 157 A8
Charlton Cl.
Ramsgate CT12 .... 29 B2
Charlton Gn. 3 CT17 ..... 166 C8
Charlton Gn. CT16 .... 149 C1
Charlton La. ME17 .... 99 C1
Charlton Manor. ME7 ..... 10 B5
Charlton St. ME16 .... 74 C2
Charltons The. ME13 ..... 63 F4
Charminster. TN23 .... 155 E6
Charnwood. CT5 .... 21 D1
Charnwood Rd. CT6 ...... 23 B1
Chart Cl. ME13 .... 62 B7
Chart Cnr. ME17 .... 98 B1
Chart Hill Rd. ME17 ...... 98 B1
Chart Pl. ME8 .... 33 C3
Chart Rd. Ashford TN23 .. 138 D1
Chart Rd. Ashford TN23 .. 155 D6
Chart Rd. Ashford,
Godinton Park TN23 ...... 138 F2
Chart Rd. Folkestone CT19 . 177 F6
Chart Road Ind Est. TN23 . 139 A3
Charter Ho. 9 CT10 ...... 166 E7
Charter St. Chatham ME4 . 9 F2
Charter St. Gillingham ME7 .. 10 C7
Chartham
Cty Prim Sch. CT4 ...... 86 C1
Chartham Downs Rd. CT4 . 109 C7
Chartham Sta. CT4 .... 86 D3
Chartway St. ME17 .... 99 C1
Chartwell Ave. CT6 ...... 23 D4
Chartwell Gr. ME10 ...... 36 E5
Chase The. Chatham ME1 .. 9 D2
Chase The. Gillingham ME8 . 11 A2
Chase The. St Margaret's
at Cliffe CT15 .... 133 F1
Claffe Ct. CT14 .... 117 C4
Chatham Cl. CT11 .... 52 D8
Chatham Gr. ME4 .... 9 F1
Chatham
Gram Sch for Boys. ME4 . 31 F8
Chatham
Gram Sch for Girls. ME5 . 10 C2
Chatham Hill. ME4 .... 10 B3
Chatham Historic Dockyard.
ME4 .... 10 A7
Chatham House
Gram Sch for Boys. CT11 . 52 E7
Chatham Pl. CT11 .... 52 E7
Chatham Rd.
Kit's Coty ME20 .... 53 D6

Chatham Rd.
Kit's Coty ME20 .... 53 D7
Chatham Rd.
Maidstone ME14 .... 53 E1
Chatham Rd.
Sandling ME14 .... 53 E4
Chatham Ski Ctr. ME7 .... 32 E6
Chatham South Sec Sch.
ME4 .... 31 F8
Chatham St. CT11 .... 52 E7
Chatham Sta. ME4 .... 9 E4
Chatsworth Dr. ME10 .... 36 B5
Chatsworth Mews. CT11 . 52 C6
Chatsworth Rd. ME7 ..... 10 C6
Chattenden Ct. ME14 ..... 75 B6
Chaucer Ave. CT5 .... 21 B1
Chaucer Cl. Canterbury CT1 . 88 C7
Chaucer Cl. Rochester ME2 ... 9 E8
Chaucer Coll. CT2 .... 66 D3
Chaucer Cres. CT16 ...... 149 B3
Chaucer Ct. CT1 .... 88 B7
Chaucer Hospl. CT1 ...... 88 A4
Chaucer Rd.
Broadstairs CT10 .... 30 A3
Chaucer Rd. Canterbury CT1 . 67 C1
Chaucer Rd.
Elvington CT15 .... 114 B2
Chaucer Rd. Gillingham ME7 . 10 D3
Chaucer Rd.
Sittingbourne ME10 ...... 36 D3
Chaucer Tech Coll. CT1 .. 88 B7
Cheddar Cl. TN24 .... 139 B4
Cheesmans Cl. CT12 ..... 50 C5
Cheffins Ho. ME7 .... 10 E7
Chegwell Dr. ME5 .... 32 B4
Chegworth Gdns. ME10 . 36 E1
Chegworth La. ME17 ..... 100 A6
Chegworth Rd. ME17 ..... 99 F5
Chelmar Rd. ME7 .... 10 B4
Chelsea Cl. CT21 .... 176 C1
Chelsea Rd. CT1 .... 67 C4
Cheltenham Cl. ME15 .... 97 F6
Cheney Cl. ME8 .... 33 D5
Cheney Hill. ME9 .... 59 A5
Cheney Rd. ME13 .... 62 F7
Chennels The. TN26 ...... 167 C7
Chepstow Ro. 3 ME15 ... 97 F6
Chequer La. CT3 .... 71 D2
Chequer's Terr. ME12 .... 5 A5
Chequers Cl. ME5 .... 54 A8
Chequers Ctr. ME15 ...... 75 A4
Chequers Hill. CT4 .... 109 C2
Chequers Orch. CT4 ..... 109 D2
Chequers Pk. TN25 ...... 123 E1
Chequers Rd. ME12 ...... 4 E6
Chequertree. ME25 ...... 172 A7
Cherbourg Cres. ME5 ... 31 F7
Cheriton Ave. CT12 ...... 52 B8
Cheriton Court Rd. CT20 . 177 C6
Cheriton
Cty Prim Sch. CT19 ...... 177 C6
Cheriton Gdns. CT20 ..... 178 C4
Cheriton High St.
CT18 & CT19 & CT20 .. 177 D6
Cheriton Interchange.
CT19 .... 177 C6
Cheriton Pl. Deal CT14 ... 117 D4
Cheriton Rd.
Folkestone CT20 .... 178 D4
Cheriton Rd. Deal CT14 .. 117 C4
Cheriton Rd.
Folkestone CT19 & CT20 .. 178 B5
Cheriton Rd. Folkestone,
Morehall CT19 .... 177 F6
Cheriton Rd.
Gillingham ME8 .... 33 D8
Cheriton Way. ME16 ..... 74 C7
Cheriton Wood Ho. CT19 . 177 D7
Cherries The. ME16 ...... 74 A2
Cherry Amber Cl. ME8 ... 33 F8
Cherry Ave. CT2 .... 66 D2
Cherry Cl. ME10 .... 36 D6
Cherry Cl. Ashford TN23 .. 139 B1
Cherry Ct.
Cherry Cl. CT19 .... 178 A6
Cherry Dr. CT2 .... 66 D2
Cherry Fields. ME10 ..... 36 A5
Cherry Garden Ave. CT19 . 178 A7
Cherry Garden Cres.
TN25 .... 123 F2
Cherry Garden La. Ash CT3 . 71 E1
Cherry Garden La.
Folkestone CT19 .... 177 F7
Cherry Garden La.
Wye TN25 .... 123 F2
Cherry Garden Rd. CT2 .. 66 D2
Cherry Gdns.
Broadstairs CT10 .... 29 C3
Cherry Gdns.
Elham CT4 .... 144 F5
Cherry Gdns.
Herne Bay CT6 .... 22 F4

Cherry Gdns.
Littlebourne-on-S TN28 .. 200 D6
Cherry Gdns.
Teynham ME9 .... 38 C2
Cherry Glebe. TN25 ...... 157 E3
Cherry Gr. CT15 .... 114 B2
Cherry Hill Ct. ME9 ...... 35 B6
Cherry La. CT14 .... 116 D3
Cherry Orch.
Tenterden TN30 .... 179 A6
Cherry Orch.
Whitstable CT5 .... 44 C8
Cherry Orch.
Woodchurch TN26 .... 169 A3
Cherry Orchard La. TN25 . 172 E4
Cherry Orchard Way.
ME16 .... 74 B3
Cherry Tree Ave. CT16 ... 149 C1
Cherry Tree Cl.
Teynham ME9 .... 38 D2
Cherry Tree Cl.
West Minster ME12 ...... 3 A8
Cherry Tree Dr. ME13 .... 39 F3
Cherry Tree Gdns. CT12 .. 29 B3
Cherry Tree Rd.
Charing Heath TN27 ..... 119 C7
Cherry Tree Rd.
Gillingham ME8 .... 33 F8
Cherry View. ME17 .... 97 B2
Cherry Waye. CT15 ...... 131 D7
Cherrybrook Rd. CT20 ... 177 D6
Cherrygarden La.
CT15 & CT3 .... 113 E7
Cherville La. CT3 .... 90 C7
Chervilles. ME16 .... 74 A2
Chesham Dr. ME8 .... 33 E6
Cheshire Rd.
Maidstone,Shepway ME15 . 97 E7
Cheshire Rd.
Maidstone,Willington ME15 . 75 E2
Chessenden La. TN27 .... 135 A1
Chester Ave. TN26 .... 153 D5
Chester Rd. Gillingham ME7 . 10 D2
Chester Rd.
Westgate-on-S CT8 ..... 27 F8
Chestfield Cl. ME8 .... 11 E2
Chestfield Rd. CT5 ...... 44 C7
Chestfield &
Swalecliffe Sta. CT5 .... 21 D2
Chestnut Ave.
Chatham ME5 .... 31 F3
Chestnut Cl. Ashford TN23 .. 138 E3
Chestnut Cl. Hythe CT21 .. 187 E8
Chestnut Cl.
Tenterden TN30 .... 167 C1
Chestnut Cl.
Whitfield CT16 .... 149 A8
Chestnut Cl. ME13 ...... 64 A3
Chestnut Dr.
Broadstairs CT10 .... 29 D4
Chestnut Dr.
Coxheath ME17 .... 96 B3
Chestnut Dr. Herne Bay CT6 . 22 D3
Chestnut Dr.
Kingswood ME17 .... 99 D2
Chestnut Dr. Sturry CT2 . 68 A7
Chestnut Dr. Worth CT14 . 94 A4
Chestnut La. TN23 .... 156 C4
Chestnut Rd. CT17 .... 166 B7
Chestnut St. ME9 .... 35 E4
Chestnut Terr. CT21 ..... 176 A1
Chestnut Wood La. ME9 . 35 E3
Chestnuts The. TN25 .... 158 D5
Chevalier Rd. CT17 ...... 166 A7
Chevening Cl. ME5 .... 32 A5
Cheviot Cl. CT10 .... 30 B5
Cheviot Gdns. ME15 ..... 76 A1
Cheviot Way. TN24 ...... 139 C4
Cheyne Cl. ME10 .... 36 F8
Cheyne Mid Sch The. ME12 . 1 E2
Cheyne Rd. ME12 .... 5 D3
Chicago Ave. ME7 .... 10 F5
Chichester Cl.
Ashford TN23 .... 139 B1
Chichester Cl.
Gillingham ME8 .... 34 A8
Chichester Rd.
Folkestone CT20 .... 177 C6
Chichester Rd.
Ramsgate CT12 .... 29 B1
Chickfield Gdns. ME5 .... 10 C2
Chiddingfold Cl. ME12 ... 4 D6
Chiddingstone Cl. ME15 . 97 F6
Chieftain Cl. ME7 .... 11 B1
Childscroft Rd. ME8 ..... 11 F2
Chilham Ave. CT6 .... 27 D7
Chilham Castle. CT4 ..... 107 B7
Chilham Cl.
West Minster ME12 ...... 3 B8

Chilham Rd.
Folkestone CT19 .... 177 E6
Chilham Rd. Gillingham ME8 . 11 A3
Chilham Rd.
Maidstone ME16 .... 74 C7
Chilham Sta. CT4 .... 107 D8
Chillington St. ME14 ..... 74 F6
Chilston Rd. ME17 .... 101 D5
Chiltern Cl. ME15 .... 75 F1
Chiltern End. TN24 ...... 139 B3
Chilton Ave.
Kearsney CT16 .... 148 C4
Chilton Ave.
Sittingbourne ME10 ..... 37 A3
Chilton Ct. ME8 .... 11 E1
Chilton
Cty Prim Sch. CT11 ..... 52 A6
Chilton Field. CT3 .... 71 D2
Chilton Gdns. CT3 .... 71 D2
Chilton La. CT11 .... 52 A6
Chilton Pl. CT3 .... 71 D2
Chilton Sq. CT3 .... 71 D2
Chilton Way. CT17 .... 148 D3
Chimes The.
Ashford TN24 .... 139 C3
Chimes The. Rochester ME1 . 9 C5
Chippendale Cl. ME5 ..... 31 F1
Chippendale Dr. ME17 ... 100 D6
Chipstead Cl. ME16 ...... 74 D6
Chipstead Rd. ME8 ...... 33 D4
Chislehurst Cl. ME15 .... 97 F6
Chislet CE Prim Sch. CT3 . 47 C5
Chislet Ct. CT6 .... 22 E5
Chislet Park Cotts. CT3 .. 46 F1
Chislet Wlk. ME8 .... 33 D5
Chislett Cl. TN25 .... 159 E2
Chisnall Rd. CT17 .... 148 E4
Chittenden's La. TN29 ... 193 E5
Chitty La. CT3 .... 47 D6
Christ Church Cath. CT1 .. 88 A8
Christ Church
CE High Sch. TN23 ...... 155 F5
Christ Church CE Jun Sch.
Ramsgate CT11 .... 52 C6
Christ Church
CE Prim Sch. CT20 ...... 178 C5
Christ Church Coll. CT1 .. 88 B8
Christ Church Coll
Post Graduate Ctr. CT2 .. 67 F1
Christ Church Rd. CT20 .. 178 C4
Christchurch Ct.
Chatham ME5 .... 10 C2
Christchurch Ct. 1
Dover CT17 .... 166 D7
Christchurch Ho. 9 ME15 . 97 E5
Christchurch Rd. TN25 .. 156 B8
Christchurch Way. CT16 . 149 B3
Christen Way.
ME15 & ME17 .... 97 F3
Christie Cl. ME5 .... 32 B6
Christmas St. ME7 .... 10 E7
Christopher's Row. ME9 . 60 A3
Chrysler Ave. CT6 .... 22 B4
Chunnel Ind Est. TN23 ... 139 B1
Church App. TN28 .... 200 A6
Church Cl. Mersham TN25 . 157 E3
Church Cl.
New Romney TN28 ...... 200 B6
Church Cliff. CT14 .... 134 D6
Church Cotts.
Rodmersham ME9 .... 59 D8
Church Cotts.
St Michaels TN30 .... 167 B3
Church Court Gr. CT10 ... 29 E6
Church Cres. ME17 ...... 100 F6
Church Ct. CT18 .... 161 C6
Church Farm Rd. ME9 ... 12 E3
Church Field. TN25 ...... 160 B1
Church Gn. ME2 .... 9 C8
Church Haven. CT14 ..... 133 F5
Church Hill.
Bethersden TN26 .... 153 D5
Church Hill.
Boughton Street ME13 .. 64 A5
Church Hill.
Canterbury CT2 .... 66 C1
Church Hill. Charing
Heath ME17 & TN27 ..... 119 C7
Church Hill. Chatham ME5 . 10 C2
Church Hill. Chilham CT4 . 107 B8
Church Hill.
Doddington ME9 .... 80 F8
Church Hill.
Eythorne CT15 .... 131 C8
Church Hill.
High Halden TN26 .... 167 E7
Church Hill. Hythe CT21 .. 176 C2
Church Hill.
Kingsnorth TN23 & TN25 . 156 B2

Church Hill. Ramsgate CT11 . 52 E7
Church Hill.
Shepherdswell CT15 ..... 130 D4
Church Hill. Stockbury ME9 . 56 F7
Church Hill.
Stone in Oxney TN30 .... 189 F3
Church Hill. Sutton CT15 .. 133 A7
Church Hill.
Temple Ewell CT16 ...... 148 D5
Church Ho. CT14 .... 117 C7
Church La. Adisham CT3 . 90 C1
Church La. Aldington TN25 . 173 D7
Church La.
Boughton Aluph TN25 ... 123 B4
Church La.
Boyden Gate CT3 .... 47 C7
Church La. Brenzett TN29 . 192 A4
Church La. Brenzett TN29 . 192 A5
Church La. 21
Canterbury CT1 .... 67 A1
Church La. Canterbury CT1 . 87 F8
Church La. Challock TN25 . 122 B8
Church La. Chatham ME4 . 9 F6
Church La.
Church Hougham CT15 .. 165 B5
Church La. Deal CT14 .... 117 B6
Church La.
Harrietsham ME17 .... 100 E6
Church La. Kingston CT4 .. 111 D3
Church La.
Lower Hardres CT4 ...... 88 B2
Church La. Lydden CT15 .. 147 E8
Church La. Maidstone ME14 . 76 B4
Church La.
New Romney TN28 ...... 200 B5
Church La. Newington ME9 . 35 B6
Church La. Petham CT4 ... 109 C3
Church La. Ringwould CT14 . 133 F5
Church La. Ripple CT14 .. 116 D1
Church La. Selling ME13 . 84 B6
Church La.
Shadoxhurst TN26 ...... 170 A7
Church La. Stockbury ME9 . 56 E8
Church La. Stowting TN25 . 160 A6
Church La. Sturry CT2 ... 67 F5
Church La. Waltham CT4 . 125 F5
Church La. Westbere CT2 . 68 C7
Church La. Whitstable CT5 . 43 A6
Church La.
Womenswold CT4 .... 112 D2
Church Meadows. CT14 .. 117 A6
Church Mews. ME8 ...... 33 F8
Church Path. Deal CT14 .. 117 B5
Church Path.
Gillingham ME7 .... 10 E6
Church Rd. Ashford TN23 . 139 C2
Church Rd. Ashford TN24 . 157 A8
Church Rd.
Ashford,Kennington TN24 . 139 E6
Church Rd. Boughton
Malherbe ME17 .... 118 A8
Church Rd. 1
Broadstairs CT10 .... 30 B4
Church Rd.
Burmarsh TN29 .... 185 E4
Church Rd. Charing TN27 . 103 D2
Church Rd.
Chart Sutton ME17 ...... 98 C1
Church Rd. Coldred CT15 . 131 A3
Church Rd.
Coldred Street CT15 ..... 130 F2
Church Rd. Dover CT17 .. 166 A7
Church Rd. Eastchurch ME12 . 5 D7
Church Rd. Eastling ME13 . 82 B2
Church Rd.
Faversham ME13 .... 62 D7
Church Rd.
Faversham ME13 .... 62 D8
Church Rd.
Folkestone CT20 .... 177 C6
Church Rd.
Harrietsham ME17 .... 100 E6
Church Rd. Hoath CT3 ... 46 E5
Church Rd. Hucking ME17 . 56 E1
Church Rd. Hythe CT21 .. 176 C2
Church Rd.
Kenardington TN26 ...... 182 A5
Church Rd.
Littlebourne CT3 .... 90 A8
Church Rd. Lydd TN29 ... 203 C6
Church Rd. Lyminge CT18 . 161 C7
Church Rd.
Maidstone,Shepway ME15 . 97 F7
Church Rd.
Maidstone,Tovil ME15 ... 74 E2
Church Rd. Margate CT9 .. 7 J1
Church Rd. Mersham TN25 . 157 E3
Church Rd. Molash CT4 .. 105 F5

Church Rd.
New Romney TN28 .... 200 A6
Church Rd. Oare ME13 .... 40 B3
Church Rd. Ramsgate CT11 . 52 E7
Church Rd.
Sevington TN24 .... 157 A7
Church Rd.
Sevington TN24 .... 157 B6
Church Rd.
Sittingbourne ME9 .... 37 E5
Church Rd. Sittingbourne,
Murston ME10 .... 37 B5
Church Rd. Smeeth TN25 .. 158 C4
Church Rd.
Stalisfield Green ME13 .... 103 F5
Church Rd.
Tenterden TN30 .... 179 A7
Church Sq. **2**
Broadstairs CT10 .... 30 B4
Church Sq. Lanham ME17 . 101 D5
Church St. Boughton
Monchelsea ME17 .... 97 B2
Church St. Broadstairs CT10 29 E6
Church St. Canterbury CT1 .. 66 E1
Church St. Chatham ME4 .... 10 A4
Church St. Deal CT14 .... 117 B1
Church St. Dover CT16 ...... 166 D7
Church St. Eastry CT13 ...... 93 C2
Church St. Faversham ME13 62 D8
Church St.
Folkestone CT20 .... 178 D4
Church St. Gillingham ME7 .. 10 E6
Church St. Loose ME15 ...... 96 F5
Church St. Maidstone ME14 .. 74 A4
Church St.
Maidstone,Tovil ME15 ...... 74 E2
Church St. Margate CT9 .... 7 J1
Church St. Minster,
Thanet CT12 .... 50 C5
Church St. Nonington CT15 113 C5
Church St. Rochester ME1 .... 9 D4
Church St.
Rodmersham ME9 .... 59 C8
Church St. **7**
Sandwich CT13 .... 73 A1
Church St. **5**
Sittingbourne ME10 .... 36 E6
Church St.
Sittingbourne ME10 .... 36 E5
Church St. Whitstable CT5 .. 20 F1
Church St.
Woodnesborough CT13 .... 93 B6
Church St. Wye TN25 ...... 123 E2
Church Street St Mary's.
CT13 .... 72 F1
Church Street (St Pauls). **6**
CT1 .... 88 A8
Church Terr. ME5 .... 10 C2
Church View.
Aldington TN25 .... 173 A6
Church View.
Herne Bay CT6 .... 23 C4
Church View.
Newchurch TN29 .... 184 E3
Church View. Worth CT14 .. 94 B5
Church Way. CT5 .... 21 D3
Church Whitfield Rd.
CT15 .... 149 B8
Church Wlk. CT4 .... 144 F4
Church Wood Cl. CT2 .... 66 B2
Church Yard Pas. **10**
TN23 .... 139 B2
Church Yd. TN23 .... 139 C2
Churchfield Pl. CT9 .... 7 I2
Churchfield Way. TN25 .... 123 E2
Churchfields.
Broadstairs CT10 .... 29 F7
Churchfields. Margate CT9 .... 7 J1
Churchfields Terr. ME1 .... 9 B4
Churchill Ave.
Chatham ME5 .... 32 A7
Churchill Ave. Deal CT14 .. 117 C2
Churchill Ave.
Folkestone CT19 .... 178 C8
Churchill Ave.
Herne Bay CT6 .... 23 D4
Churchill Cl. Bridge CT4 .... 88 F1
Churchill Cl.
Folkestone CT19 .... 178 D8
Churchill Cl.
St Margaret's at Cliffe CT15 .. 150
F5
Churchill Cotts. ME17 .... 98 F6
Churchill Ct. CT21 .... 176 B1
Churchill Ho. **2**
Folkestone CT20 .... 177 F5
Churchill Ho.
Maidstone ME16 .... 74 B2

Churchill Ho.
Sittingbourne ME10 .... 37 C4
Churchill Ho. Teynham ME9 . 38 C3
Churchill Rd.
Canterbury CT1 .... 88 C6
Churchill Rd. Dover CT17 .. 166 A6
Churchill Rd. Minster ME12 .. 4 D6
Churchill Way. ME1 .... 40 B1
Churchill Wlk. CT18 .... 162 F4
Churchlands Ho. TN28 ...... 200 B6
Churchlands The. TN28 .... 200 B6
Churchwood Dr. CT5 .... 21 D1
Chute Cl. ME8 .... 33 D8
Cinder Path. CT10 .... 30 A4
Cinnabar Cl. ME5 .... 32 A1
Cinque Ports Ave. CT21 .... 176 B1
Circular Rd. Dover CT16 .... 150 B1
Circular Rd.
Finglesham CT14 .... 116 B7
Circus The. CT6 .... 22 E4
Citadel Cres. CT17 .... 166 B6
Citadel Hts. CT17 .... 166 B6
Citadel Rd. CT17 .... 166 C6
Citroen Cl. CT6 .... 22 B4
City Bsns Pk. CT1 .... 67 C3
City View. CT2 .... 87 C8
City Way. ME1 .... 9 D2
Claire Ct. Birchington CT7 .. 26 F7
Claire Ct. Broadstairs CT10 .. 30 B5
Claire Ho. ME16 .... 74 E5
Clandon Rd. ME5 .... 32 D2
Clanwilliam Rd. CT14 ...... 117 D5
Clapham Hill. CT5 .... 43 D5
Clapton Ct. ME8 .... 33 D8
Clare Dr. CT6 .... 22 C2
Clare Rd. CT5 .... 20 E2
Claremont Cl. CT14 .... 134 C6
Claremont Gdns. CT11 ...... 52 C7
Claremont Pl. CT1 .... 87 F7
Claremont Rd. Deal CT14 . 117 B5
Claremont Rd.
Folkestone CT20 .... 178 C5
Claremont Rd.
Kingsdown CT14 .... 134 C6
Claremont Rd.
Maidstone ME14 .... 75 B5
Claremont St. CT6 .... 22 C4
Claremont Terr. CT13 .... 93 D7
Claremont Way. **1** ME4 ...... 9 F3
Clarence Ave. Wye CT9 ...... 8 D2
Clarence Ave.
Rochester ME1 .... 9 C4
Clarence Ct. ME14 .... 75 E4
Clarence Gdns. ME12 .... 6 E3
Clarence Pl. Deal CT14 .... 117 D7
Clarence Pl. Dover CT17 .. 166 D5
Clarence Rd.
Capel-le-F CT18 .... 164 B2
Clarence Rd. Chatham ME4 . 10 B2
Clarence Rd. Deal CT14 .... 117 D3
Clarence Rd.
Herne Bay CT6 .... 22 D5
Clarence Rd.
Ramsgate CT11 .... 52 C7
Clarence Row. ME12 .... 1 C2
Clarence St.
Folkestone CT20 .... 178 D5
Clarence St. Herne Bay CT6 . 22 E5
Clarendon Cl.
Maidstone ME14 .... 76 A4
Clarendon Cl.
Sittingbourne ME10 .... 36 F1
Clarendon Gdns. **7** CT11 .. 52 D6
Clarendon House
Gram Sch. CT11 .... 52 E6
Clarendon Mews.
Broadstairs CT10 .... 30 A4
Clarendon Mews.
New Romney TN28 .... 200 C8
Clarendon Pl. Dover CT17 . 166 C7
Clarendon Pl.
Maidstone ME14 .... 75 A4
Clarendon Rd.
Aylesham CT3 .... 112 F5
Clarendon Rd.
Broadstairs CT10 .... 30 A4
Clarendon Rd. Dover CT17 166 C7
Clarendon Rd. Margate CT9 . 8 A2
Clarendon St. Dover CT17 . 166 C7
Clarendon St.
Herne Bay CT6 .... 22 C4
Claridge Cl. ME7 .... 32 F4
Claridge Mews. CT21 ...... 176 C2
Clarke Rd. TN28 .... 200 E4
Clarke's Cl. CT14 .... 116 F4
Clarklands. TN29 .... 184 E3
Clavell Cl. ME8 .... 33 E4
Claxfield Cotts. ME9 .... 38 A2
Claxfield Rd. ME9 .... 60 A8
Claygate. Ashford TN23 .. 155 F5

Claygate. Maidstone ME15 .. 75 D1
Clearmount Dr. TN27 ...... 120 C8
Cleave Rd. ME7 .... 10 E3
Clease La. CT11 .... 52 E7
Clematis Ave. ME8 .... 33 B5
Clement Cl. CT1 .... 67 B1
Clement Ct. ME16 .... 74 D5
Clement's Rd. CT12 .... 29 C2
Clementine Cl. CT6 .... 23 D4
Clerke Dr. ME10 .... 37 A8
Clermont Ct. ME7 .... 33 A4
Clevedon Ct. TN25 .... 105 B2
Cleveland Cl. CT16 .... 149 B3
Cleveland Ho. ME16 .... 74 B2
Cleveland Rd. ME7 .... 10 D6
Cleveley Lodge. CT11 .... 29 E2
Cleves Way. TN23 .... 155 E8
Clewson Rise. ME14 .... 75 B8
Cliff Ave. CT6 .... 23 C5
Cliff Cl. CT21 .... 176 D3
Cliff Dr. Herne Bay CT6 .... 22 C4
Cliff Dr. Warden ME12 .... 6 E4
Cliff Field. CT8 .... 27 C8
Cliff Gdns. ME12 .... 4 E7
Cliff Hill. ME17 .... 97 D4
Cliff Hill Rd. ME17 .... 97 C4
Cliff Prom. CT10 .... 30 C7
Cliff Rd. Birchington CT7 .. 26 F8
Cliff Rd. Broadstairs CT10 .. 30 B7
Cliff Rd.
Dover CT15 & CT16 .... 150 C1
Cliff Rd. Folkestone CT20 .. 178 A3
Cliff Rd. Hythe CT21 .... 176 E3
Cliff Rd. Whitstable CT5 .... 20 F3
Cliff Sea Gr. CT6 .... 22 C4
Cliff St. CT11 .... 52 E6
Cliff Terr. CT9 .... 7 J3
Cliff View Gdns.
Leysdown-on-S ME12 .... 6 D1
Cliff View Gdns.
Warden ME12 .... 6 E4
Cliff View Rd. CT12 .... 51 D6
Cliffe Ave. CT9 .... 7 F1
Cliffe Ho. CT20 .... 178 A3
Cliffe Rd. Kingsdown CT14 134 D6
Cliffe Rd. Rochester ME2 .... 9 B8
Cliffestone Ct. CT20 .... 178 B5
Clifford Gdns. CT14 .... 117 B2
Clifford Rd. CT5 .... 43 F8
Cliffs End Gr. CT12 .... 51 D5
Cliffs End Rd. CT12 .... 51 E5
Cliffside Dr. CT10 .... 30 A1
Clifftown Gdns. CT6 .... 22 B4
Clifton Cl. ME14 .... 75 B5
Clifton Cres. CT20 .... 178 B3
Clifton Gdns.
Canterbury CT2 .... 66 D2
Clifton Gdns.
Folkestone CT20 .... 178 C4
Clifton Gdns. Margate CT9 .... 7 J3
Clifton Lawn. CT11 .... 52 D5
Clifton Mansions. **4**
CT20 .... 178 C4
Clifton Pl. CT9 .... 8 A3
Clifton Rd.
Folkestone CT20 .... 178 C4
Clifton Rd. Gillingham ME7 . 10 C7
Clifton Rd. Margate CT9 ...... 8 A2
Clifton Rd. Ramsgate CT11 . 52 B8
Clifton Rd. Whitstable CT5 .. 20 D1
Clifton St. CT9 .... 7 J3
Cliftonville Ave. Margate CT9 8 A2
Cliftonville Ave.
Ramsgate CT12 .... 29 B1
Cliftonville Ct. CT9 .... 8 A3
Cliftonville Cty Prim Sch.
CT9 .... 8 C2
Cliftonville Mews. CT9 .... 8 A3
Clim Down. CT14 .... 134 D6
Clinton Cl. ME17 .... 96 B3
Clints La. CT14 .... 129 D4
Clipper Cl. ME2 .... 9 E7
Clipper Ct. ME2 .... 9 E7
Clive Dennis Ct. TN24 .... 139 E1
Clive Rd. Cliffs End CT12 .. 51 D6
Clive Rd. Margate CT9 ...... 29 A5
Clive Rd. Rochester ME1 .... 9 C3
Clive Rd.
Sittingbourne ME10 .... 36 B5
Clockhouse. TN23 .... 138 F1
Clockhouse Pk. TN25 ...... 105 C2
Cloisterham Rd. ME1 .... 31 D7
Cloisters The. **7**
Canterbury CT1 .... 66 F1
Cloisters The.
Lenham ME17 .... 101 C5
Cloisters The.
Ramsgate CT11 .... 52 D5
Cloisters The. **7**
Sittingbourne ME10 .... 36 E4
Close The. Ashford TN23 .. 155 F7

Close The. Bridge CT4 .... 88 F1
Close The. Canterbury CT2 .. 66 F4
Close The. Faversham ME13 62 C6
Close The.
Folkestone CT19 .... 178 E8
Close The. Hythe CT21 .... 176 B4
Close The. Lydden CT15 .... 147 F8
Close The. Rochester ME1 .... 9 C4
Close The. Wye TN25 ...... 123 E2
Close The
(St Edmunds Sch). CT2 .. 66 C3
Cloudesley Cl. ME1 .... 9 B1
Clovelly. TN28 .... 200 E6
Clovelly. Dr. ME12 .... 4 B8
Clovelly Rd. CT5 .... 43 D7
Clover Bank View. ME5 .... 32 B6
Clover Ct. ME10 .... 37 B5
Clover Rise. CT5 .... 21 B1
Clover St. ME4 .... 9 F4
Clowes Ct. CT2 .... 66 C4
Clubb's La. TN29 .... 197 D7
Cluny Rd. ME13 .... 62 F7
Clyde Cotts. ME12 .... 1 E2
Clyde St. **1**
Canterbury CT1 .... 67 A1
Clyde St. Sheerness ME12 .... 1 E2
Clynton Way. TN23 .... 156 A7
Coach Dr. TN26 .... 138 A7
Coach Rd. Densole CT18 .. 162 F8
Coach Rd. Egerton TN27 .. 118 E6
Coalpit La. ME9 .... 80 A6
Coast Dr.
Littlestone-on-S TN28 .... 200 E3
Coast Dr. Lydd-on-S TN29 . 204 F4
Coast Dr.
St Mary's Bay TN29 ...... 194 F2
Coast Rd. TN28 & TN29 .. 200 F7
Coastguard Alley. CT5 .... 20 C1
Coastguard Cotts.
Conyer ME9 .... 38 E6
Coastguard Cotts.
Dover CT16 .... 166 G8
Coastguard Cotts.
Herne Bay CT6 .... 21 F4
Coastguard Cotts.
Hythe CT21 .... 176 B1
Coastguard Cotts.
Kingsdown CT14 .... 134 D4
Coastguard Cotts.
Leysdown-on-S ME12 .... 19 E4
Coastguard Cotts.
Minster ME12 .... 5 C5
Coastguard Cotts.
Ramsgate CT11 .... 52 A5
Coastguard Cotts. **10**
Ramsgate CT11 .... 52 F7
Coastguard Cotts.
Sandwich CT13 .... 95 B7
Coastguard Cotts The. ME12 . 1 I1
Coastguard Ho. ME12 .... 6 C5
Coats Ave. ME12 .... 3 A8
Cobay Cl. CT21 .... 176 D2
Cobb Ct. CT9 .... 7 I3
Cobb Wlk. ME13 .... 62 B8
Cobblers Bridge Rd. CT6 .... 22 D3
Cobblestones. ME7 .... 32 F5
Cobbs Hill. CT4 .... 85 C2
Cobbs Mews. **2** CT20 .... 178 C4
Cobbs Pl. CT9 .... 7 I3
Cobbs Wood Ind Est.
TN23 .... 138 F2
Cobden Pl. **16** CT1 .... 67 A2
Cobden Rd. CT21 .... 176 B1
Cobdown Gr. ME8 .... 12 A2
Cobfield. ME17 .... 98 A1
Cobham Ave. ME10 .... 36 E1
Cobham Chase. ME13 ...... 62 A8
Cobham Cl.
Canterbury CT1 .... 88 C6
Cobham Cl.
Maidstone ME16 .... 74 E4
Cobsden Cl. TN29 .... 195 A4
Cobsden Rd. TN29 .... 195 A4
Cobtree Cl. ME5 .... 32 C8
Cobtree Rd. ME17 .... 96 C3
Cobtree Wharf. ME20 ...... 53 C2
Cock La. Elham CT4 .... 144 F4
Cock La. Hamstreet TN26 .. 183 A7
Cockering Rd. CT1 & CT4 .. 87 B4
Cockreed La. TN28 .... 200 B7
Codrington Rd. CT11 .... 52 D7
Cogans Terr. CT1 .... 87 E6
Coggan Ho. **7** CT1 .... 87 F7
Coinston Ave. CT10 .... 52 A7
Colburn Rd. CT10 .... 52 A8
Colchester Cl. ME5 .... 32 A7
Cold Harbour. CT1 .... 67 A2
Cold Harbour La. ME9 ...... 35 F6
Cold Harbour Rd.
ME13 & ME17 .... 103 A7
Coldblow. CT14 .... 117 A1

Coldharbour La.
Thurnham ME14 .... 56 A2
Coldblow La.
Woodchurch TN26 .... 169 D4
Coldbridge La. TN27 ...... 118 B5
Coldharbour La.
Aylesford ME20 .... 53 A1
Coldharbour La.
Bekesbourne CT4 .... 111 D7
Coldharbour La.
Hucking ME14 .... 56 B1
Coldharbour La.
Old Romney TN29 .... 198 C5
Coldharbour La.
Sittingbourne ME10 .... 14 F1
Coldharbour La.
Wye TN25 .... 124 A2
Coldred Hill. CT15 .... 130 F1
Coldred Rd. Coldred CT15 . 131 B5
Coldred Rd.
Park Wood ME15 .... 97 F4
Coldred Rd.
Shepherdswell CT15 ...... 130 E3
Coldswood Rd. CT12 .... 28 F2
Cole Rd. ME13 .... 62 E7
Cole Terr. ME17 .... 101 C4
Colegate Dr. ME14 .... 76 C4
Colegates Cl. ME13 .... 40 B2
Colegates Ct. ME13 .... 40 B2
Colegates Rd. ME13 .... 40 A2
Coleman Cres. CT12 .... 29 C1
Coleman's Stairs Rd. CT7 .. 27 A8
Coleman's Yd. **3** CT11 ...... 52 E6
Colemans Cl. TN29 .... 203 D7
Coleridge Gdns. CT3 ...... 112 F6
Coleshall Cl. ME15 .... 97 F6
Coleshall Cotts. ME9 ...... 14 D3
Colette Cl. CT10 .... 8 G2
Coleville Cres. TN29 ...... 204 E7
Colewood Rd. CT5 .... 21 E3
Colfe Way. ME10 .... 37 A8
Colin's Way. CT21 .... 177 A3
Collard Cl. CT6 .... 23 A4
Collard Rd. TN24 .... 157 A8
Collards La. CT12 .... 49 D7
Collards La. CT4 .... 144 E3
College Ave.
Gillingham ME7 .... 10 C2
College Ave.
Maidstone ME15 .... 74 F3
College Cotts. ME16 .... 74 F3
College Ct. Ashford TN23 .. 139 C2
College Ct. **5**
Maidstone ME15 .... 75 A3
College Rd. Canterbury CT1 . 67 B1
College Rd. Chatham ME4 .. 10 A7
College Rd. Deal CT14 .... 117 D8
College Rd.
Maidstone ME15 .... 74 F2
College Rd. Margate CT9 .... 8 A1
College Rd. Margate CT9 .. 28 F8
College Rd. Ramsgate CT11 . 29 E1
College Rd.
Sittingbourne ME10 .... 36 D3
College Row. CT17 .... 166 B7
College Sq. **2** CT9 .... 7 J2
College Way. CT3 .... 91 A7
College Wlk. **3** CT9 .... 7 J2
College Yd. ME1 .... 9 C6
Collet Wlk. ME8 .... 33 D4
Collett Cl. TN25 .... 142 D8
Collingbourne. TN23 ...... 155 E6
Collings Wlk. ME8 .... 33 D4
College Wlk. Tent. ME15 .. 97 E4
Collingwood Cl.
Broadstairs CT10 .... 29 E4
Collingwood Cl.
Westgate-on-S CT20 ...... 27 D7
Collingwood Ct. CT20 .... 177 E5
Collingwood Ind Ctr. ME17 . 98 E2
Collingwood Rd.
Kit's Coty ME20 .... 53 C7
Collingwood Rd St Margaret's
at Cliffe CT15 .... 150 F8
Collingwood Rd.
Whitstable CT5 .... 20 C1
Collingwood Rd E.
CT14 & CT15 .... 134 A1
Collingwood Rise. CT20 .. 177 E5
Collingwood Wlk. ME10 .. 36 B5
Collins Rd. CT6 .... 22 C2
Collis St. ME2 .... 9 A8
Collison Pl. TN30 .... 179 D7
Colman Ho. **18** ME14 .... 75 A4
Colombo Sq. CT12 .... 29 A1
Colonel's La. ME13 .... 64 A3
Colorado Cl. CT16 .... 149 B3
Colton Cres. CT14 .... 149 B4
Coltsfoot Dr. ME14 .... 75 F4
Columbia Ave. CT5 .... 43 B7
Command Rd. ME14 .... 74 F8

Commercial Rd. ME2 .... 9 A7
Commissioner's Rd. ME2 .... 9 C8
Commodore Rd. ME14 .... 75 C5
Common La. CT17 .... 148 E3
Common Rd. ME1 .... 31 B1
Common The. ME1 .... 9 C6
Common Way. TN26 .... 138 A7
Commonwealth Cl. ME10 .... 37 B3
Compass Cl. ME1 .... 9 C1
Compass Ctr. ME4 .... 10 B8
Compton Cl. ME5 .... 32 C2
Concord Ave. ME5 .... 31 E5
Conduit St. ME13 .... 62 D8
Conference Wlk. CT1 .... 88 C8
Conifer Ct. CT8 .... 7 D1
Conifer Dr. ME5 .... 32 D1
Coniston Ave. ME7 .... 11 A6
Coniston Dr. CT3 .... 112 F6
Coniston Rd. CT19 .... 178 B7
Connaught Barracks.
  CT16 .... 149 E1
Connaught Cl. ME15 .... 97 F4
Connaught Gdns. 9 CT9 ...... 7 J1
Connaught Rd. ME14 .... 10 C2
Connaught Rd.
  Chatham ME4 .... 10 C2
Connaught Rd.
  Dover CT16 .... 149 D1
Connaught Rd.
  Folkestone CT20 .... 178 C5
Connaught Rd.
  Gillingham ME7 .... 10 D5
Connaught Rd. Margate CT9 . 7 J1
Connaught Rd.
  Sittingbourne ME10 .... 36 E3
Conquest Ind Est. ME2 .... 9 A6
Conrad Ave. CT1 .... 67 C3
Conrad Cl. ME8 .... 33 D4
Consort Cl. ME14 .... 75 B5
Constable Rd. CT7 .... 27 A8
Constable's Rd. CT16 .... 166 E8
Constancia Ct. CT20 .... 178 C5
Constitution Hill. ME4 .... 10 B3
Constitution Rd. ME4 .... 10 C2
Consul Cl. CT6 .... 22 B4
Continental App. CT19 .... 28 F6
Convent Cl. CT15 .... 151 B6
Convent Rd. CT10 .... 8 G1
Convent Wlk. CT11 .... 52 B5
Conway Cl. CT7 .... 26 E7
Conway Mews. ME7 .... 10 A6
Conway Rd. ME16 .... 74 C6
Conyer Rd. ME9 .... 38 F4
Conyers Wlk. ME8 .... 33 D4
Conyngham Cl. CT12 .... 29 B2
Conyngham La. CT4 .... 89 A2
Conyngham Rd.
  Herne Bay CT6 .... 23 D5
Conyngham Rd.
  Minster, Thanet CT12 ...... 50 C5
Cooden Cl. ME8 .... 12 A2
Cook Cl. ME5 .... 32 C6
Cook's Lea. CT13 .... 93 B2
Cookham Hill. ME1 .... 9 A2
Cookham Wood Rd. ME1 .... 31 B8
Cooks La. ME10 .... 36 F6
Cooling Cl. ME14 .... 75 C6
Coolinge La. CT20 .... 177 F4
Coolinge Rd. CT20 .... 178 D5
Coombe Cl. Chatham ME5 .. 32 B3
Coombe Cl. Dover CT17 ... 149 A1
Coombe Ct. CT17 .... 149 A1
Coombe Dr. ME10 .... 37 C4
Coombe La. Ash CT3 .... 92 E8
Coombe La.
  Tenterden TN30 .... 179 A7
Coombe Lands. TN30 .... 188 D4
Coombe Rd. Dover CT17 ... 148 F1
Coombe Rd.
  Dover CT15 & CT17 ...... 165 E8
Coombe Rd.
  Folkestone CT19 .... 177 F6
Coombe Rd.
  Maidstone ME15 .... 74 F2
Coombe Valley Rd. CT17 ... 149 A1
Coombe Way. CT18 .... 163 C4
Coombe Wlk. CT5 .... 43 A2
Coombe Wood La. CT18 ... 163 C4
Cooper Rd. ME5 .... 32 B3
Cooper Street Dro. CT3 .... 72 B4
Cooper's Hill. CT6 .... 22 F5
Cooper's La. TN25 .... 158 F2
Coopers La. CT1 .... 87 E7
Cooting La. CT3 .... 112 D8
Cooting Rd. CT3 .... 112 E4
Cop Street Rd. CT3 .... 72 A4
Copenhagen Rd. ME7 .... 10 C4
Copinger Cl. CT2 .... 67 A4
Copland Ave. ME12 .... 4 C6
Copper Tree Ct. ME15 .... 97 A5
Copper Tree Wlk. ME5 .... 32 C1

Copperfield. ME12 .... 5 F6
Copperfield Cl. TN24 .... 139 C6
Copperfield Ct. CT10 .... 30 B5
Copperfield Dr. ME17 .... 98 E4
Copperfield Ho. ME4 .... 10 A4
Copperfield Rd. ME1 .... 9 C2
Copperfields. TN29 .... 203 B6
Copperfields The. ME1 .... 9 B4
Coppergate. Canterbury CT2 66 F2
Coppergate.
  Gillingham ME7 .... 32 F5
Copperhouse La. ME7 .... 11 B6
Copperhurst Wlk. CT9 .... 8 F2
Copperwood. TN24 .... 139 C4
Coppice Ct. ME7 .... 33 B4
Coppice Rd. ME5 .... 32 C2
Coppice The. CT2 .... 67 A2
Coppice View. ME14 .... 75 E6
Coppin St. CT14 .... 117 D6
Coppins La. ME9 .... 36 B2
Copse The. TN23 .... 138 D3
Copsewood Way. ME15 ...... 76 A3
Copt Cl. CT2 .... 67 F7
Copthall Gdns. 10 CT20 .... 178 D5
Cordingham Rd. CT5 .... 43 A6
Cordova Ct. CT20 .... 178 B4
Corkwell St. ME4 .... 9 E3
Corner Cotts. TN26 .... 182 A6
Corner Field. TN23 .... 156 B5
Corner The. TN25 .... 173 A6
Cornerways. CT21 .... 176 B4
Cornflower Cl. ME14 .... 75 E4
Cornford Rd. CT7 .... 27 A7
Cornhill. 12 CT11 .... 52 E6
Corniche The. CT20 .... 177 C3
Cornwall Ave. CT11 .... 52 F8
Cornwall Cl. ME15 .... 97 E7
Cornwall Gdns.
  Canterbury CT1 .... 88 D7
Cornwall Gdns. Margate CT9 . 8 B3
Cornwall Ho. Deal CT14 ... 117 A5
Cornwall Ho. 5
  Dover CT17 .... 166 D7
Cornwall Rd. Deal CT14 ... 117 C3
Cornwall Rd.
  Gillingham ME7 .... 10 D5
Cornwall Rd. Herne Bay CT6 22 B2
Cornwall Rd. Rochester ME1 . 9 C3
Cornwallis Ave.
  Aylesham CT3 .... 112 F6
Cornwallis Ave.
  Chatham ME4 .... 9 E1
Cornwallis Ave.
  Folkestone CT19 .... 178 B6
Cornwallis Ave.
  Gillingham ME8 .... 11 A4
Cornwallis Ave.
  Herne Bay CT6 .... 23 C3
Cornwallis Circ. CT5 .... 20 D1
Cornwallis Cl.
  Ashford TN24 .... 157 B7
Cornwallis Cl.
  Folkestone CT19 .... 178 B6
Cornwallis Cotts. ME17 ...... 96 E2
Cornwallis Gdns. CT10 ...... 30 A6
Cornwallis Rd. ME16 .... 74 D4
Cornwallis Sch The. ME15 .. 96 F2
Coronation Rd. CT10 .... 29 E7
Coronation Rd. CT19 .... 177 D6
Coronation Cres.
  Margate CT9 .... 28 B8
Coronation Cres.
  Queenborough ME11 .... 2 F5
Coronation Dr.
  Bay View ME12 .... 6 D2
Coronation Dr.
  Great Chart TN23 .... 138 C1
Coronation Flats. 2 ME4 ... 9 F3
Coronation Rd.
  Chatham ME5 .... 10 C2
Coronation Rd.
  Sheerness ME12 .... 1 E1
Coronation Sq. TN29 .... 203 C6
Corone Cl. CT19 .... 178 A7
Corporation Rd. ME7 .... 10 D7
Corporation St. ME1 .... 9 C6
Corral Cl. ME5 .... 10 D2
Corrall Almshouses. 4
  ME15 .... 75 A3
Corrance St. ME15 .... 97 A8
Corsican Wlk. CT5 .... 23 C3
Cortland Cl. ME10 .... 36 E6
Cortland Mews. ME10 .... 36 E6
Corunna Cl. CT21 .... 176 A2
Corunna Pl. CT16 .... 149 E3
Corylus Dr. CT5 .... 43 A7
Cossack St. ME1 .... 9 D3
Cossington Rd.
  Canterbury CT1 .... 88 A7

Cossington Rd.
  Chatham ME5 .... 32 B1
Cosway Cotts. TN25 .... 172 C1
Cotswold Cl. TN24 .... 139 B4
Cotswold Gdns. ME15 .... 76 A2
Cottage Rd. Chatham ME4 .... 9 F6
Cottage Rd. Ramsgate CT11 52 E6
Cottage Row. CT13 .... 72 F1
Cottall Ave. ME4 .... 9 F2
Cottington Rd. CT12 .... 51 B5
Cotton Hill Wlk. TN26 ...... 183 A7
Cotton Rd. CT1 .... 87 E7
Coulman St. ME7 .... 10 D5
Coulson Gr. CT14 .... 116 A5
Coulter Rd. CT6 .... 22 A2
Coulters Cl. ME14 .... 75 D5
Council Cotts. ME15 .... 96 A4
Countess Mountbatten Ct.
  CT8 .... 27 E8
Country's Field. TN29 ...... 195 C8
County Rd. ME14 .... 75 A5
County Sq. 3 TN23 .... 139 B2
Court Cotts. CT7 .... 25 E2
Court Dr. ME16 .... 74 D4
Court Flats. CT3 .... 91 A7
Court Hall. ME11 .... 2 F5
Court Hill. CT3 .... 68 E2
Court Hill Ho. CT16 .... 148 E4
Court House Farm. CT15 .. 113 E5
Court La. Detling ME14 ...... 55 C5
Court La. Preston CT3 .... 70 B6
Court Lodge Cotts. ME15 ... 96 A7
Court Lodge Rd.
  Appledore TN26 .... 190 C7
Court Lodge Rd.
  Gillingham ME7 .... 10 F6
Court Meadow. ME8 .... 11 B2
Court Meadows. CT3 .... 89 F8
Court Pl. CT20 .... 178 C4
Court Rd. Deal CT14 .... 117 B1
Court Rd. Eccles ME20 .... 53 A6
Court Rd.
  Sittingbourne ME10 .... 36 F7
Court Rd.
  St Nicholas at Wade CT7 .. 25 E2
Court St. ME13 .... 62 D7
Court Wurtin. TN23 .... 156 A7
Courtenay Rd. Boughton
  Street CT2 & ME13 .... 64 E5
Courtenay Rd. Deal CT14 . 117 C8
Courtenay Rd.
  Maidstone ME15 .... 74 F2
Courteney Rd. ME8 .... 33 B8
Courtfield Ave. ME5 .... 32 B3
Courtland Ave. CT16 .... 149 A6
Courtland Dr. CT16 .... 148 E4
Courtlands. Herne Bay CT6 . 23 B3
Courtlands.
  Kingsdown CT14 .... 134 D6
Courtlands Way. CT8 .... 7 D1
Courts The. CT9 .... 7 E1
Courtyard The.
  Gillingham ME7 .... 33 A8
Courtyard The. Staple CT3 .. 92 A6
Coventina Ho. CT11 .... 52 D7
Coventon La. CT13 & CT14 .. 94 A5
Coventry Gdns. CT6 .... 23 E5
Coverdale Ave. ME15 .... 97 D6
Coverdale Cl. ME5 .... 32 B7
Covert. TN23 .... 138 E1
Covert Rd. CT3 .... 112 E4
Covert The. ME5 .... 32 B1
Covet La. CT4 .... 111 C2
Cow La. Canterbury CT1 .... 87 D7
Cow La. Dover CT17 .... 166 A7
Cowbeck Cl. ME8 .... 33 C6
Cowden Rd. ME14 .... 75 C5
Cowdray Rd. CT14 .... 117 A3
Cowdray Sq. CT14 .... 117 A3
Cowdrey Cl. Ashford TN24 157 A7
Cowdrey Cl.
  Maidstone ME16 .... 74 B2
Cowdrey Cl. Rochester ME1 .. 9 B2
Cowdrey Pl. CT11 .... 88 B6
Cowgate Hill.CT16 & CT17 166 D7
Cowgate La. CT18 .... 163 C5
Cowley Rise. CT9 .... 29 C8
Cowper Cl. CT5 .... 21 D3
Cowper Rd. Deal CT14 ..... 117 C5
Cowper Rd. Gillingham ME7 10 C3
Cowper Rd. Margate CT9 ..... 7 J1
Cowper Rd. River CT17 .... 148 E3
Cowper Rd.
  Sittingbourne ME10 .... 37 B4
Cowstead Rd. ME9 .... 34 D2
Cox St. ME14 .... 55 E6
Coxes Ave. CT12 .... 29 B3
Coxes La. CT12 .... 29 B3
Coxett Hill. ME13 .... 61 D5
Coxheath
  Cty Prim Sch. ME17 .... 96 C3

Coxhill. CT15 .... 130 C3
Coxhill Cres. CT17 .... 148 D3
Coxhill Gdns. CT17 .... 148 D3
Cozenton Cl. ME8 .... 11 E1
Crabble Ave. CT17 .... 149 A2
Crabble Cl. CT17 .... 148 F2
Crabble Hill CT16 & CT17 . 149 A2
Crabble La. CT15 & CT17 .. 148 E2
Crabble Meadows. CT17 ... 149 A2
Crabble Rd. CT17 .... 149 A3
Crabble Water Mill. CT17 . 148 F3
Crabtree La. ME17 .... 119 B8
Crabtree Rd. ME8 .... 33 D8
Crackstake. CT3 .... 71 D2
Craddock Dr. 8 CT1 .... 67 B1
Craddock Rd. CT1 .... 67 B1
Craddock Way. ME8 .... 33 D5
Cradle Bridge Dr. TN24 ... 139 F2
Cradles Rd. ME9 .... 34 C2
Crafford St. CT16 .... 149 D1
Cragie Wlk. ME8 .... 33 E4
Crampton Cl. CT10 .... 30 A4
Cranborne Ave. ME15 .... 75 C1
Cranbourne Ave. ME15 ...... 97 B8
Cranbourne Cl. CT11 .... 52 F8
Cranbourne Wlk. CT2 .... 66 E3
Cranbrook Cl.
  Gillingham ME8 .... 11 C3
Cranbrook Cl.
  Maidstone ME15 .... 97 F7
Cranbrook Cl. Margate CT9 . 8 E1
Cranbrook Dr. ME16 .... 36 D1
Cranbrooks. TN25 .... 157 D4
Cranford Cl. ME8 .... 11 D1
Cranleigh Dr. CT16 .... 149 B7
Cranleigh Gdns.
  Chatham ME1 .... 9 D3
Cranleigh Gdns.
  Maidstone ME16 .... 74 C7
Cranleigh Gdns.
  Whitstable CT5 .... 43 E8
Cranmer Ct. ME15 .... 97 B8
Cranswick Cotts. CT14 .... 133 C8
Craufurd Gn. CT20 .... 177 D5
Craven Cl. CT9 .... 28 C8
Crawford Gdns. CT9 .... 8 B2
Crawford Rd. CT10 .... 29 F5
Crayford Cl. ME14 .... 75 C6
Craythorne. TN30 .... 179 B8
Craythorne Cl. Hythe CT21 177 F4
Craythorne Cl.
  New Romney TN28 .... 200 B8
Craythorne La. TN28 .... 200 B7
Cremer Cl. CT14 .... 86 C1
Cremer Pl. ME13 .... 62 A8
Cremers Rd. ME10 .... 37 B5
Crescent Rd.
  Birchington CT7 .... 27 A7
Crescent Rd.
  Broadstairs CT10 .... 30 C8
Crescent Rd.
  Faversham ME13 .... 62 D7
Crescent Rd. Margate CT9 . 7 H2
Crescent Rd.
  Ramsgate CT11 .... 52 D7
Crescent St. 1 ME10 .... 36 F4
Crescent The.
  Aylesham CT15 .... 113 A3
Crescent The.
  Boughton Street ME13 ..... 64 A3
Crescent The.
  Canterbury CT2 .... 66 F4
Crescent The.
  Chartham CT4 .... 86 D1
Crescent The.
  Folkestone CT20 .... 177 E3
Crescent The.
  Halfway Houses ME12 .... 3 E6
Crescent The.
  Lower Halstow ME9 .... 13 C3
Crescent The.
  Maidstone ME14 .... 74 F8
Crescent The.
  Sandwich CT13 .... 93 E6
Crescent The.
  Sheerness ME12 .... 1 D2
Crescent The.
  Sittingbourne ME10 .... 15 A1
Crescent The. St Margaret's
  at Cliffe CT15 .... 151 A5
Crescent Way. ME5 .... 31 D5
Cress Way. ME13 .... 62 A7
Cressey Ct. ME4 .... 9 E4
Cressfield. TN23 .... 138 F1
Crest Rd. ME1 .... 31 A5
Cresta Cl. CT6 .... 21 F4
Crestway. ME5 .... 32 A6
Crete Rd E. CT18 & CT19 . 163 D1
Crete Rd W. CT18 .... 163 B1

Creteway Cl. CT19 .... 178 E8
Creve Coeur Cl. ME14 .... 76 A5
Cricketers Cl.
  Harrietsham ME17 .... 100 D6
Cricketers Cl.
  Hawkinge CT18 .... 163 B6
Cricketers Cl.
  Sittingbourne ME10 .... 36 F8
Crimond Ave. TN29 .... 187 A4
Criol La. TN26 .... 155 A2
Cripple Hill. TN26 .... 132 D7
Cripple St. ME15 .... 97 A7
Cripps Cl. CT3 .... 112 E5
Cripps' La. CT15 .... 150 F6
Crisfield Cl. TN30 .... 167 B2
Crismill La. ME14 .... 76 F4
Crismill Rd. ME14 .... 76 F3
Crispe Cl. ME8 .... 33 D4
Crispe Rd. CT7 .... 27 A3
Crispin Cl. ME13 .... 62 D8
Crispin Ct. ME17 .... 96 C3
Crittenden Bglws. ME15 .... 96 A4
Crittenden Cotts. ME15 ..... 96 A4
Crocken Hill Rd. TN27 ..... 118 C2
Crockham La. ME14 .... 64 B6
Crockham Rd. ME14 .... 64 C6
Crockshard Hill. CT3 .... 91 B4
Crockshard La. CT3 .... 91 B4
Croft Cl. ME5 .... 32 C1
Croft Gdns. ME17 .... 101 D4
Croft La. CT20 .... 177 F5
Croft Rd. TN24 .... 139 D2
Croft's Pl. 3 CT10 .... 30 B4
Crofters Cl. CT21 .... 187 E8
Crofters The. ME8 .... 33 F7
Crofton Cl. TN24 .... 139 C6
Crofton Rd. CT8 .... 27 E7
Croftwood. TN23 .... 155 D6
Croidene Ct. ME12 .... 4 A6
Cromer Rd. Rochester ME2 .. 9 B8
Cromer Rd.
  Sittingbourne ME10 .... 58 F8
Cromwell Park Pl. CT20 ... 177 D4
Cromwell Rd.
  Canterbury CT1 .... 88 A6
Cromwell Rd.
  Maidstone ME14 .... 75 B5
Cromwell Rd. West
  Minster ME11 & ME12 .... 2 F7
Cromwell Rd.
  Whitstable CT5 .... 20 E1
Cromwell Terr. ME4 .... 10 A3
Crook's Court La. CT15 .... 164 F4
Crooked S Rd. CT14 .... 133 E7
Crookenden Pl. CT4 .... 128 F8
Crosier Ct. ME9 .... 12 E3
Crosley Rd. ME7 .... 10 D3
Cross Dr. ME7 .... 99 B1
Cross Keys. ME14 .... 76 C4
Cross La. Faversham ME13 . 62 C7
Cross La.
  Sittingbourne ME10 .... 36 E6
Cross La.
  Throwley Forstal ME13 .... 104 C7
Cross Rd. Birchington CT7 . 27 B8
Cross Rd. Deal CT14 .... 117 A2
Cross Rd. St Margaret's
  at Cliffe CT15 .... 151 A4
Cross St. 2
  Canterbury CT2 .... 66 E1
Cross St. Chatham ME4 ..... 10 A4
Cross St. Gillingham ME7 .. 10 C6
Cross St. Herne Bay CT6 ... 22 B3
Cross St. Maidstone ME14 .. 75 A6
Cross St. Rochester ME2 ..... 9 B8
Cross Stile. TN23 .... 155 F8
Cross The. CT13 .... 93 B2
Cross Way. ME1 .... 9 C3
Crossley Ave. CT6 .... 21 F4
Crossway. ME5 .... 31 E6
Crossways. Canterbury CT2 . 66 C7
Crossways.
  Chart Sutton ME17 .... 98 B1
Crossways.
  Sittingbourne ME10 .... 36 F1
Crossways Ave. CT9 .... 29 A5
Crossways Cl. TN29 .... 186 E2
Crouch Cotts. ME13 .... 84 E8
Crouch Hill Ct. ME9 .... 13 C3
Crouch La. ME13 .... 84 E8
Crow Cnr. Ashford TN24 ... 156 F7
Crow Cnr. Rochester ME1 ... 9 C5
Crow Hill. CT10 .... 30 B5
Crow Hill Rd. CT9 .... 28 B8

Crow La. ME1 .... 9 C5
Crowbridge Rd. TN24 .... 156 E7
Crown Ct. CT14 .... 117 D6
Crown Gdns. CT2 .... 66 E1
Crown Hill Rd. CT6 .... 22 C4
Crown La. CT4 .... 126 E3
Crown Quay. ME10 .... 36 F5
Crown Quay La. ME10 ...... 37 A4
Crown Rd. ME10 .... 36 E6
Crown St. ME7 .... 10 D6
Crownfield Rd. TN23 ...... 155 F8
Crownfields. ME14 .... 75 F4
Crows Camp Rd. CT4 ...... 111 A5
Croydon Cl. ME5 .... 32 C4
Cruise Liner Terminal.
CT17 .... 166 E4
Crundale. **2** ME14 .... 75 A5
Crundale Cl. TN23 .... 155 F6
Crundale Rd. ME8 .... 11 C3
Crundale Way. CT10 & CT9 ... 8 E1
Crusader Cl. ME7 .... 33 B8
Cryalls Bsns Est. ME10 .... 36 C4
Cryalls La. ME10 & ME9 .... 36 C3
Cryol Rd. TN23 .... 156 A7
Crystal Bsns Ctr. CT13 ... 73 B2
Ctr for European
Agricultural Studies.
TN25 .... 124 A1
Cubitt Ho. CT19 .... 178 D6
Cuckmere Ho. **3** ME15 ... 97 E8
Cuckold's Cnr.
High Halden TN26 .... 168 B7
Cuckold's Cnr.
Snargate TN29 .... 191 E7
Cuckolds Cnr. CT3 .... 114 A7
Cuckoo La. Ashford TN23 ... 155 D6
Cuckoo La. Ashford TN23 ... 155 E7
Cuckoo La. Postling CT21 ... 160 F2
Cuckoowood Ave. ME14 ... 53 F1
Cudham Cl. ME14 .... 75 C6
Cudham Gdns. CT9 .... 8 E2
Cudworth Rd. TN24 .... 156 E7
Cullens Hill. CT4 .... 144 F4
Cullet Dr. ME11 .... 3 A3
Culling's Hill. CT4 .... 144 F4
Culmers Terr. ME13 .... 41 E1
Culpeper Cl.
Hollingbourne ME17 ...... 77 E2
Culpeper Cl. Rochester ME2 ... 9 B4
Culpeper Cl. CT2 .... 67 A4
Culpepper Rd.
Coxheath ME17 .... 96 B3
Culpepper Rd.
Gillingham ME8 .... 33 D4
Culter Field. TN23 .... 155 E8
Culver's La. TN29 .... 203 D5
Cumberland Ave.
Broadstairs CT10 .... 30 A5
Cumberland Ave.
Canterbury CT1 .... 88 D7
Cumberland Ave.
Maidstone ME15 .... 97 D8
Cumberland Dr. ME9 ...... 13 C3
Cumberland Rd.
Gillingham ME4 & ME7 ... 10 B7
Cumberland Rd.
Gillingham ME7 .... 10 C7
Cumberland Rd.
Margate CT9 .... 8 B3
Cumberland Rd. **1**
Ramsgate CT11 .... 52 D6
Cundishall Cl. CT5 .... 43 C8
Cunningham Cres.
Birchington CT7 .... 26 E7
Cunningham Cres.
Chatham ME5 .... 32 A8
Cunningham Ho. ME1 .... 9 B4
Curlew Ave. ME9 .... 13 B3
Curlew Cl. CT6 .... 23 C2
Curlinge Cl. CT11 .... 52 A6
Curteis Rd. TN30 .... 167 B1
Curtis La. CT4 .... 126 C2
Curtis Rd. TN24 .... 156 E7
Curtis Way. **1** ME13 ...... 62 C7
Curtis Wood Park Rd. CT6 ... 46 A7
Curtis Wood Rd. CT6 ...... 45 F7
Curzon Cl. CT14 .... 117 C3
Curzon Rd. **5** CT11 ...... 52 C6
Curzon Rd. Chatham ME4 ... 9 F3
Curzon Rd. Dover CT17 ... 166 B8
Curzon Rd. Maidstone ME14 ... 75 A6
Cushman Rd. CT1 .... 87 E7
Cutbush Almshouses. **2**
ME15 .... 75 A3
Cutbush and Corrall Cl.
ME14 .... 75 B4
Cuthbert Rd. CT8 .... 27 E8
Cuttings The. CT12 .... 52 C8

Cuxton Rd.
Park Wood ME15 .... 97 F5
Cuxton Rd. Rochester ME2 ... 9 A7
Cygnet Rd. ME5 .... 32 C2
Cygnet Way. TN23 .... 138 F1
Cylinder Rd. CT21 .... 176 B4
Cypress Ave. TN23 .... 138 E2
Cypress Cl. CT5 .... 43 C7
Cypress Ct. ME7 .... 10 F6
Cypress Gr. CT15 .... 114 B2
Cyprus Rd. ME13 .... 62 E7

D'este Rd. CT11 .... 52 F7
D2 Trad Est. ME10 .... 37 B6
Daglish Cl. TN28 .... 200 B6
Dagmar Rd. ME4 .... 10 B2
Dalby Rd. CT9 .... 8 A3
Dalby Sq. CT9 .... 8 A3
Dale Rd. ME1 .... 9 C3
Dale St. ME4 .... 9 E2
Dale Wlk. TN24 .... 139 C7
Dalewood. ME10 .... 37 A2
Dallas-Brett Cres. CT19 ... 178 E8
Dallinger Rd. **1** CT7 ...... 26 F8
Dalmatia Ct. CT17 .... 149 A1
Dalmeny Ave. CT9 .... 8 D1
Dalton Cl. **4** CT11 .... 52 E7
Dalton St. ME7 .... 10 C6
Dame Janet
Cty Inf Sch. CT12 .... 29 B2
Dame Janet
Cty Jun Sch. CT12 .... 29 B2
Damerham Cl. CT12 .... 66 E3
Damien Cl. ME4 .... 10 A2
Dan Dr. ME13 .... 62 A8
Danaway Cotts. ME9 ..... 35 C3
Dane Cl. Chatham ME5 ... 32 A7
Dane Cl. Hartlip ME9 ..... 34 D6
Dane Court Gdns. CT10 ... 29 D5
Dane Court Gram Sch.
CT10 .... 29 E4
Dane Court Rd. CT10 & CT9 ... 29 E6
Dane Cres. CT11 .... 52 E8
Dane Ct. ME7 .... 96 C2
Dane End Rd. CT8 .... 27 D8
Dane Gdns. CT9 .... 29 B8
Dane Hill. CT9 .... 7 J3
Dane Hill Gr. CT9 .... 7 J2
Dane Hill Row. CT9 .... 7 J2
Dane John Ct. **3** CT1 ... 87 F7
Dane John Mews. **1** CT1 ... 87 F7
Dane La. ME9 .... 34 D6
Dane Mount. CT9 .... 29 C8
Dane Park Rd. Margate CT9 ... 7 J2
Dane Park Rd.
Ramsgate CT11 .... 52 E8
Dane Rd. Birchington CT7 ... 26 D7
Dane Rd. Margate CT9 .... 8 A2
Dane Rd. Ramsgate CT9 ... 52 E8
Dane Valley Rd.
CT10 & CT9 .... 29 C8
Danecourt Sch The. ME8 ... 11 A2
Danedale Ave. ME12 .... 4 F6
Danefield Ct. ME14 .... 76 B4
Danehurst. CT7 .... 7 C1
Danemore. TN30 .... 179 B8
Danes Ct. CT16 .... 149 D2
Danes Dr. ME12 .... 6 D2
Danes Hill. ME7 .... 11 A6
Danes Mead. ME10 .... 14 F1
Danesmead Terr. CT9 .... 7 J2
Daniels Ct. CT5 .... 20 C1
Danley Mid Sch. ME12 ...... 5 F7
Danley Rd. ME12 .... 3 F7
Danson Way. ME8 .... 11 C1
Danton La. CT18 & CT19 ... 162 C1
Darby Pl. CT20 .... 178 D5
Darby Rd. CT20 .... 178 D5
Darenth Cl. CT6 .... 23 B3
Darenth Ho. **2** ME15 ... 97 D8
Darenth Rise. ME5 .... 32 B3
Dargate Cl. ME16 .... 74 D7
Dargate Rd.
Dargate CT2 & ME13 ..... 64 F7
Dargate Rd. Yorklets CT5 ... 43 A3
Dargets Rd. ME5 .... 32 A3
Dark Hill. ME13 .... 62 C8
Darland Ave. ME7 .... 10 E1
Darlinghurst Rd. CT19 ... 177 E7
Darlington Dr. ME12 .... 4 A6
Darlington St. CT20 ...... 178 D5
Darnley Cl.
Broadstairs CT10 .... 29 F3
Darnley Cl.
Folkestone CT20 .... 177 F4
Darnley Rd. ME2 .... 9 A1
Darracott Cl. CT14 .... 117 B5
Darrell Cl. CT6 .... 22 C3
Darren Gdns. CT12 .... 29 F2
Darwin Coll. CT2 .... 66 E5
Darwin Rd. CT7 .... 26 F8
Daryngton Ave. CT7 .... 26 C7
Davenport Ave. ME7 ...... 10 E7
David Ave. CT9 .... 8 D2
Davids Cl. CT10 .... 30 B3
Davidson Rd. CT2 .... 66 D1
Dave Cl. ME12 .... 3 B8
Davis Cl. ME12 .... 3 B8
Davington
Cty Prim Sch. ME13 ...... 62 C8
Davington Hill. ME13 ...... 62 C8
Davis Ave. CT14 .... 117 A4
Dawbourns. TN30 .... 167 B3
Dawes St. ME13 & ME13 ... 64 F7
Dawes St. ME7 .... 10 C5
Dawn Rise. ME12 .... 5 F6
Dawn Rd. CT19 .... 178 D6
Dawson's Rd. ME13 ...... 62 A6
Dayton Rd. ME13 .... 83 C3
Daytona Way. CT6 .... 22 A4
De Burgh Hill. CT17 ..... 149 C1
De Burgh St. **2** CT17 ... 166 C8
De Haviland Cl. CT18 ... 163 B4
De L'angle Row. CT4 .... 86 D3
De Mere Cl. ME8 .... 33 D6
Deacon Est The. ME20 ... 53 A2
Deacon Trad Ctr. ME2 ...... 9 A6
Deacons Cl. CT14 .... 117 D6
Deal Castle. CT14 .... 117 D5
Deal Castle Rd. CT14 ... 117 D5
Deal Parochial
CE Prim Sch. CT14 .... 117 C5
Deal Rd. CT13 & CT14 ... 93 F5
Deal Sta. CT14 .... 117 C6
Dean Croft. CT6 .... 23 B2
Dean Ct. **16** CT1 .... 67 A1
Dean Hill CT4 & TN25 ... 126 B2
Dean Mead. CT19 .... 178 B7
Dean Rd. ME10 .... 36 F6
Dean St. ME15 .... 96 C6
Dean Wood
Cty Prim Inf Sch. ME8 ... 33 D3
Dean Wood
Cty Prim Jun Sch. ME8 ... 33 D4
Dean's Wlk. TN23 .... 155 F7
Deane Cl. CT5 .... 43 E7
Deans Hill Rd. ME9 .... 57 D5
Deans Mill Ct. CT2 .... 66 F1
Deansway Ave. CT2 .... 67 F7
Deanwood Cl. ME8 .... 33 D6
Deanwood Dr. ME8 .... 33 E4
Deanwood Rd. CT17 .... 148 E2
Deborah Cl. CT5 .... 43 F7
Deedes Cl. CT21 .... 176 C3
Deerhurst Gdns. ME16 ... 74 D4
Deerson La. CT3 .... 70 A4
Defiant Cl. ME5 .... 32 B6
Defoe Cl. ME5 .... 32 B6
Delacourt Cl. CT12 .... 51 D5
Delamark Rd. ME12 .... 1 C2
Delane Rd. CT14 .... 117 A5
Delaware Cl. CT2 .... 67 F6
Delce Cty Inf Sch. ME1 .... 9 D2
Delce Cty Jun Sch. ME1 ... 9 C2
Delce Rd. ME1 .... 9 D4
Delft St. CT13 .... 72 F1
Delfside. CT13 .... 94 A8
Delmaney Cl. CT10 .... 30 B5
Delmar Cl. CT5 .... 21 D3
Denbigh Ave. ME8 .... 11 D1
Denbigh Cl. ME10 .... 36 E7
Denbigh Rd. CT12 .... 29 A1
Dence Cl. CT6 .... 23 B5
Dence Pk. CT6 .... 23 B4
Dencora Way. TN23 .... 139 A1
Dene. The.
Bethersden TN26 .... 153 D5
Dene The. Canterbury CT1 ... 88 B5
Dene The. Hythe CT21 ... 176 C2
Dene Wlk. CT9 .... 28 F7
Dengemarsh Rd. TN29 ... 203 C3
Denham Cl. TN29 .... 187 B4
Denham Ho. ME10 .... 36 D5
Denham Rd. ME9 .... 35 B7
Denmark Rd. CT11 .... 52 E8
Denmark St. CT11 .... 178 E6
Dence Cl. CT7 .... 67 F7
Denne Manor La. CT4 ... 106 C8
Dennes La. TN29 .... 203 C8
Dennes Mill La. TN25 ... 123 D2
Denness Rd. TN23 .... 156 B7
Dennis Way. CT19 .... 177 E7
Dennis Willocks Cl. ME9 ... 35 C5
Densole La. CT18 .... 163 A8
Densole Way. CT18 ..... 163 A8
Denstead Cotts. CT4 .... 86 B8
Denstead Ct. CT2 .... 66 C4
Denstead La. CT4 & ME13 ... 86 C7
Denstead Oast. CT4 ...... 86 B8
Denstead Wlk. **11** ME15 ... 97 F8
Denstroude La. CT2 ...... 65 D8
Dent-De Lion Rd. CT9 .... 28 A8

Dent-De-Lion Rd.
Margate CT9 .... 28 A8
Dent-De-Lion Rd.
Westgate-on-S CT8 .... 7 C1
Dental St. CT21 .... 176 C2
Denton Cl. ME15 .... 97 E8
Denton Way. CT9 .... 8 C1
Derby Cl. ME10 .... 36 A6
Derby Rd. Chatham ME5 ... 10 E2
Derby Rd. Gillingham ME15 ... 10 E5
Derby Rd. Maidstone ME15 ... 97 C8
Dering Cl. Bridge CT4 ..... 88 F1
Dering Cl.
Chamber's Green TN27 ... 136 C4
Dering Rd. Ashford TN24 ... 139 D2
Dering Rd. Bridge CT4 .... 89 A1
Dering Rd. Herne Bay CT6 ... 22 F4
Dering Terr. TN27 .... 136 C3
Derings The. TN29 .... 203 B6
Deringwood Dr. ME15 .... 75 F1
Derringstone Downs. CT4 ... 128 F6
Derringstone Hill. CT4 ... 128 F6
Derringstone St. CT4 ... 128 F7
Derville Ho. TN28 .... 200 B6
Derville Rd. TN29 .... 204 E7
Derwent Ave. CT11 .... 52 A7
Derwent Ho. **5** ME15 ... 97 E7
Derwent Way.
Aylesham CT3 .... 112 F6
Derwent Way.
Gillingham ME8 .... 33 D8
Desmond Cres. ME13 .... 63 A5
Detling Ave. CT10 .... 30 A1
Detling Cl.
CE Prim Sch. ME14 .... 55 A1
Detling Ct. Gillingham ME8 ... 11 C2
Detling Cl.
West Minster ME12 .... 3 B7
Detling Hill. ME14 .... 55 B2
Devon Ave. CT14 .... 117 C3
Devon Cl. Chatham ME5 ... 32 C7
Devon Cl. Gillingham ME8 ... 11 F1
Devon Ct. CT12 .... 29 B2
Devon Gdns. CT7 .... 26 F8
Devon Rd. Canterbury CT1 ... 88 D8
Devon Rd.
Folkestone CT19 .... 178 D5
Devon Rd. Maidstone ME15 ... 97 C8
Devonshire Gdns. CT9 ..... 6 J2
Devonshire Rd.
Dover CT17 .... 166 B8
Devonshire Rd.
Gillingham ME7 .... 10 D7
Devonshire Terr. CT10 .... 30 B5
Dhekelia Cl. ME14 .... 75 A7
Dial Cl. ME7 .... 10 F6
Dial Rd. ME7 .... 10 F6
Diamond Ct. ME12 .... 1 C1
Diamond Rd. CT5 .... 20 E2
Diana Gdns. CT14 .... 117 A5
Dibdin Rd. CT14 .... 117 D7
Dickens Ave. CT1 .... 67 D2
Dickens Cl. ME7 .... 98 E4
Dickens Ct. ME2 .... 9 D8
Dickens Rd.
Broadstairs CT10 .... 30 B5
Dickens Rd.
Maidstone ME14 .... 74 E8
Dickens Rd. Rochester ME1 ... 9 C2
Dickens Wlk. CT10 .... 30 B4
Dickley La. ME17 .... 101 A6
Dickson Cl. ME10 .... 37 B4
Dickson Rd. CT17 .... 166 C8
Dickson's Cnr. CT13 ...... 95 A6
Dicksons Bourne. TN25 ... 172 F6
Dieu Stone La. CT16 .... 166 D8
Digby Rd. CT20 .... 177 E5
Dignals Cl. ME8 .... 11 F2
Dignash. TN25 .... 121 E2
Diligent Dr. ME10 .... 36 F7
Diocesan & Payne Smith
CE Prim Sch. CT1 .... 67 A1
Discovery Wlk. CT1 .... 88 C7
Disraeli Cl. ME15 .... 97 E5
Dixon Cl. ME15 .... 74 F2
Dixwell Cl. ME8 .... 33 D5
Dixwell Rd. CT20 .... 178 A4
Dobbie Cl. ME10 .... 36 E6
Dock Exit Rd. CT16 ..... 166 F8
Dock Head Rd. ME4 ...... 10 A8
Dock Rd. Chatham ME4 .... 9 F6
Dock Rd. Gillingham ME4 ... 10 A7
Doctor's La. CT15 .... 165 B5
Dodd's La. CT15 .... 149 A3
Doddington Cl. ME16 .... 74 E5
Doddington Rd.
Cty Prim Sch. ME9 .... 80 F7
Doddington Rd. ME8 ...... 11 D3
Does Alley. ME4 .... 36 F4
Dog Kennel La. CT18 .... 161 B7
Doggerel Acre. CT5 .... 43 F7

Doggett's Sq. ME2 .... 9 C7
Dogwood Cl. ME5 .... 32 D1
Dola Ave. CT14 .... 117 B6
Dolphin Cl. CT10 .... 8 G3
Dolphin Dr. ME8 .... 33 E5
Dolphin Ho. **1** CT16 ... 166 E7
Dolphin La. CT16 .... 166 E7
Dolphin Pas. **2** CT16 ... 166 E7
Dolphin Pk. ME10 .... 37 B5
Dolphin Pl. **3** CT16 ..... 166 E7
Dolphin Rd. Lydd TN29 ... 203 C6
Dolphin Rd.
Sittingbourne ME10 ...... 37 B5
Dolphin St. Deal CT14 ... 117 D7
Dolphin St. Herne Bay CT6 ... 22 E5
Dolphins Rd. CT19 ...... 178 D7
Dombey Cl. ME1 .... 9 C3
Domneva Rd. Minster,
Thanet CT12 .... 50 B6
Domneva Rd.
Westgate-on-S CT8 .... 27 D8
Donald Moor Ave. ME9 ... 38 C2
Doncaster Cl. **7** ME15 ... 97 F6
Donegal Rd. CT1 .... 88 C8
Donemowe Dr. ME10 .... 36 F8
Donet Cl. ME8 .... 33 C5
Dongola Rd. ME7 .... 9 A8
Donkey La. CT3 .... 112 C8
Donkey St. CT21 & TN29 ... 186 E5
Donnahay Rd. CT12 .... 29 C3
Donnithorne Ho. CT6 ..... 22 E5
Dorcas Gdns. CT10 .... 30 A6
Doric Ct. CT11 .... 52 C5
Dorman Ave N. CT3 ...... 112 E6
Dorman Ave S. CT3 ...... 112 F5
Dornden Gdns. ME5 ...... 32 B2
Dorne Cotts. TN27 ...... 118 E6
Dorothy Dr. CT12 .... 29 C2
Dorrit Way. ME1 .... 9 D2
Dorset Cl. CT5 .... 43 B7
Dorset Ct. Deal CT14 ... 117 D2
Dorset Ct. Ramsgate CT12 ... 29 B2
Dorset Gdns.
Birchington CT7 .... 26 F7
Dorset Gdns. Deal CT14 ... 117 C2
Dorset Pl. ME13 .... 62 C7
Dorset Rd. Canterbury CT1 ... 88 D7
Dorset Rd.
West Minster ME12 .... 3 A8
Dorset Sq. ME8 .... 11 D1
Dorset Way. ME15 .... 97 C8
Dossett Ct. CT14 .... 117 A2
Dotterel Cl. ME5 .... 32 D2
Doubleday Dr. ME9 .... 37 E2
Douglas Almshouses.
ME17 .... 101 D5
Douglas Ave. Hythe CT21 ... 176 C2
Douglas Ave.
Whitstable CT5 .... 20 E1
Douglas Bglws. CT15 ... 132 E8
Douglas Cl. CT10 .... 29 E5
Douglas Rd. Deal CT14 ... 117 A3
Douglas Rd. Dover CT17 ... 166 B8
Douglas Rd. Herne Bay CT6 ... 23 A4
Douglas Rd.
Lenham ME17 .... 101 D5
Douglas Rd.
Maidstone ME16 .... 74 C3
Douglas Terr. CT14 ...... 117 D5
Dour Side. CT17 .... 148 F3
Dour St. CT16 .... 166 D8
Douro Cl. CT1 .... 67 D1
Douro Pl. CT16 .... 166 E7
Dove Cl. Chatham ME5 ... 32 B6
Dove Cl. Hythe CT21 .... 187 D8
Dove Cl. Whitstable CT5 ... 43 C7
Dove Lea Gdns. CT17 ... 148 E3
Dovedale. CT7 .... 27 B7
Dovedale Ct. CT17 .... 148 E3
Dover Castle. CT16 ..... 166 F8
Dover Coll. Dover CT17 ... 166 C8
Dover Coll. Dover CT16 ... 166 D7
Dover Gram Sch
for Boys. CT17 .... 166 A8
Dover Gram Sch
for Girls. CT16 .... 149 C1
Dover Hill. CT19 .... 178 F8
Dover Pl. TN23 .... 139 C1
Dover Rd. Barham CT4 ... 112 A1
Dover Rd.
Bishopsbourne CT4 ..... 111 D5
Dover Rd.
Folkestone CT19 & CT20 ... 178 E2
Dover Rd. Guston CT15 ... 149 E4
Dover Rd.
Ringwould CT14 & CT15 ... 134 A6
Dover Rd. Sandwich CT13 ... 93 F6
Dover Rd. St Margaret's
at Cliffe CT15 .... 150 D6
Dover Rd.
Tilmanstone CT13 & CT14 ... 115 B5

Dover Rd. Woolage
Green CT4 & CT15 .... 129 D6
Dover St. Canterbury CT1 ..... 88 A7
Dover St. Maidstone ME16 ... 74 C2
Dover St. **1**
Sittingbourne ME10 .... 36 E4
Doves Cnr. CT14 .... 115 A4
Dowle Cl. TN29 .... 199 A7
Down Barton Rd. CT7 .... 25 E1
Down Court Rd. ME9 .... 59 C1
Down Ct. TN23 .... 155 E5
Downer Ct. ME4 .... 31 E8
Downhill Cl. CT16 .... 148 D6
Downings The. CT6 .... 23 A2
Downland Ct. TN24 .... 139 B3
Downlands. Deal CT14 .... 134 B8
Downlands.
Harrietsham ME17 .... 100 F6
Downs Ave. CT5 .... 20 E1
Downs
CE Prim Sch The. CT14 . 117 B2
Downs Cl. Charing TN27 ...... 120 C8
Downs Cl.
East Studdal CT15 .... 132 D8
Downs Cl. Maidstone ME14 .. 75 B8
Downs Cl.
Sittingbourne ME10 .... 36 D2
Downs Pk. CT6 .... 23 A5
Downs Rd. Canterbury CT2 .. 66 F4
Downs Rd. Deal CT14 .... 117 C3
Downs Rd.
East Studdal CT15 .... 132 E8
Downs Rd.Folkestone CT19 178 C7
Downs Rd. Maidstone ME14 75 B8
Downs Rd. Ramsgate CT11 .. 52 B6
Downs The. Chatham CT4 ..... 86 E1
Downs The. Chatham CT4 ... 31 D1
Downs The. Preston CT3 .... 70 C6
Downs View
Cty Inf Sch. TN24 .... 139 E7
Downs View Rd. ME14 .... 75 B8
Downs Way. Charing TN27 .. 120 C8
Downs Way.
Sellindge TN25 .... 159 C1
Downside.
Bekesbourne CT4 .... 89 E3
Downside.
Folkestone CT19 .... 178 C7
Downside. Rochester ME2 ...... 9 A7
Downside. St Margaret's
at Cliffe CT15 .... 151 A6
Downside Rd. CT16 .... 149 B7
Downsview. ME5 .... 32 C8
Dragonfly Cl. TN23 .... 155 D8
Dragoon Ho. **10** CT1 .... 67 A1
Drainless Rd. CT13 .... 93 A5
Drake Ave. ME12 .... 4 D5
Drake Rd. TN24 .... 157 B7
Drakes Cl. ME9 .... 12 E2
Drapers Almshouses. CT9 ... 29 A8
Drapers Ave. CT9 .... 28 F8
Drapers Cl. CT9 .... 29 A8
Drapers Mills
Cty Prim Sch. CT9 .... 29 A8
Drapers Windmill (dis). CT9 . 8 A1
Dray's Field. ME9 .... 79 A7
Dreadnought Ave. ME12 .... 4 B6
Drew La. CT14 .... 117 C4
Drewery Dr. ME8 .... 33 C5
Drill La. CT3 .... 69 B1
Drive The. Canterbury CT1 ... 88 B6
Drive The. Whitstable CT5 .... 44 D8
Drivers Rdbt. TN24 .... 139 A4
Drop Redoubt Rd. CT17 .... 166 D7
Drove Rd. ME12 .... 3 E7
Drove The. Fordwich CT2 .... 68 A4
Drove The. Monkton CT12 ... 49 B6
Drove The.
Northbourne CT14 .... 116 A5
Drove The. Whitfield CT16 . 149 A8
Drove The. Whitstable CT5 .. 44 D8
Droveway Gdns. CT15 .... 151 A6
Droveway The. CT15 .... 151 B6
Drum La. TN23 .... 139 B2
Drury Rd. TN30 .... 179 B8
Drybeck Ave. CT11 .... 51 F7
Dryden Cl. CT1 .... 88 C7
Dryden Rd. CT10 .... 149 B3
Drywall Ind Est. ME10 .... 37 B6
Duchess Of Kent Dr. ME5 .... 32 B3
Duck La. Canterbury CT1 ..... 67 A1
Duck La. Shadoxhurst TN26 169 F7
Duck St. CT4 .... 144 F4
Duckpit Rd. CT4 .... 126 A6
Duckworth Cl. TN24 .... 157 B7
Dudley Ave. CT8 .... 27 C8
Dudley Rd. Ashford TN24 ... 139 E5
Dudley Rd.
Folkestone CT19 .... 178 E5
Duke of Clarence
Trad Est The. ME12 .... 1 B3

Duke of York's Royal
Military Sch. CT15 .... 149 F4
Duke St. Deal CT14 .... 117 D7
Duke St. Margate CT9 .... 7 J1
Dukes Meadow. TN26 .... 183 A7
Dukes Meadow Dr. ME7 ...... 32 F6
Dukes Wlk. **5** ME15 .... 75 A4
Dukeswood. CT5 .... 44 D6
Dully Rd. ME9 .... 59 E6
Dumergue Ave. ME11 .... 3 B5
Dumpton Gap Rd. CT10 ...... 30 A2
Dumpton La. CT11 .... 29 E1
Dumpton Park Dr.
CT10 & CT11 .... 30 A2
Dumpton Park Rd. CT11 ...... 52 E8
Dumpton Park Sta. CT11 ..... 29 F1
Duncan Dr. CT7 .... 26 E8
Duncan Rd. Gillingham ME7 . 10 D5
Duncan Rd. Ramsgate CT11 . 52 D7
Duncan Rd. Whitstable CT5 . 43 D7
Dundein Dr. CT16 .... 149 B3
Dundonald Rd. **11**
Broadstairs CT10 .... 30 B4
Dundonald Rd.
Ramsgate CT11 .... 52 C7
Dunedin Cl. ME10 .... 36 C3
Dunedin Rd. CT12 .... 29 A1
Dunera Dr. ME14 .... 75 A7
Dunes Rd. TN28 .... 200 D3
Dungeness Power Sta
Visitor Ctr. TN29 .... 205 E6
Dungeness Rd. TN29 .... 204 C3
Dungeness Sta. TN29 .... 205 F6
Dunkery Rise. TN24 .... 139 B4
Dunkirk Cl. TN29 .... 195 B7
Dunkirk
Cty Prim Sch. ME13 .... 64 D2
Dunkirk Dr. ME5 .... 31 F6
Dunkirk Rd.
Boughton Street ME13 .... 64 B1
Dunkirk Rd.
Boughton Street ME13 ...... 64 B2
Dunkin Sq. CT16 .... 149 F3
Dunlin Ct. TN29 .... 195 A3
Dunn Street Rd. ME7 .... 55 A8
Dunnett Rd. CT19 .... 177 E6
Dunning's La. ME1 .... 9 C4
Dunnings The. ME16 .... 74 A2
Dunoon Ct. CT11 .... 29 F1
Dunstall Cl. TN29 .... 195 A5
Dunstall Gdns. TN29 .... 195 A5
Dunstall La. TN29 .... 195 A5
Dunstan Ave. CT8 .... 27 D7
Dunston Cl. CT2 .... 66 E1
Dunston Ho. CT14 .... 117 D8
Durban Cl. CT12 .... 29 A2
Durban Cres. CT16 .... 149 C4
Durban Ho. **7** ME15 .... 97 E5
Durban Rd. CT9 .... 8 A1
Durham Cl. Canterbury CT1 . 87 F6
Durham Cl. **9** Dover
CT17 .... 166 D7
Durham Cl.
Maidstone ME15 .... 75 E1
Durham Hill. CT16 & CT17 166 D7
Durham Rd. ME8 .... 33 C7
Durling Ct. ME8 .... 12 A1
Durlock Ct12 .... 50 C5
Durlock Ave. CT11 .... 52 B5
Durlock Rd. CT3 .... 92 B7
Durlocks The. CT19 .... 178 E5
Durnford Cl. CT2 .... 66 E2
Durovernum Ct. CT1 .... 88 A7
Durrell Gdns. ME5 .... 10 C1
Duval Dr. ME1 .... 31 E8
Duvard's Pl. ME9 .... 35 F1
Dyke Rd. CT19 .... 178 E5
Dymchurch
Cty Prim Sch. TN29 .... 195 C8
Dymchurch Ho. CT1 .... 88 B8
Dymchurch Rd.
Hythe CT21 .... 176 A2
Dymchurch Rd.
Hythe CT21 .... 187 C6
Dymchurch Rd St Mary's
Bay TN29 & TN29 .... 195 A5
Dymchurch Sta. TN29 .... 195 B7
Dyngley Cl. ME10 .... 36 E6

Eagle Hill. CT11 .... 52 D7
Eagles Cl. ME10 .... 37 C4
Ealham Cl. Ashford TN24 .. 157 A8
Ealham Cl. Canterbury CT1 .. 88 B5
Ealing Cl. ME5 .... 32 C4
Earl Cl. ME5 .... 32 B4
Earl La. ME14 .... 74 F4
Earl's Ave. CT20 .... 178 B4
Earls Ave. TN24 .... 139 F1
Earlsfield. TN25 .... 173 A6
Earlsfield Rd. CT21 .... 176 D2
Earlsmead Cres. CT12 .... 51 C5

Earlsworth Ct. TN24 .... 156 E6
Earlsworth Rd. TN24 .... 156 D6
Easole Hts. CT15 .... 113 D5
Easole St. CT15 .... 113 D5
East Borough
Cty Prim Sch. ME14 .... 75 B5
East Cliff. Dover CT16 .... 166 F8
East Cliff. Folkestone CT19 178 F6
East Cliff Gdns. **19** CT19 .. 178 E5
East Cliff Golf Links.
CT19 .... 178 G6
East Cliff Par. CT6 .... 23 A5
East Cliff Pas. **20** CT19 ... 178 E5
East Court
(Sch for Dyslexics). CT11 . 52 G7
East Cross. TN30 .... 179 B7
East Farleigh
Cty Prim Sch. ME15 .... 96 B6
East Farleigh Sta. ME16 ..... 96 B8
East Gn. ME10 .... 15 A1
East Hall La. ME10 .... 37 C5
East Hill.
Ashford TN23 & TN24 ...... 139 C2
East Hill. Tenterden TN30 ... 179 B8
East Kent Light Railway.
CT15 .... 131 C8
East La. ME12 .... 1 B2
East Langdon Rd. CT15 ..... 149 F7
East Lodge Rd. TN23 .... 138 F3
East Mountain La. TN24 .... 139 F7
East Norman Rd. CT16 ...... 149 E1
East Northdown Cl. CT9 .... 8 E1
East Park Rd. ME20 .... 74 A8
East Ramp. CT16 .... 166 G8
East Rd. Chatham ME4 .... 10 A7
East Rd. Folkestone CT20 ... 177 D4
East Rd. Gillingham ME4 .... 10 A8
East Rd.
Sandwich CT12 & CT13 ..... 73 A8
East Rise. CT12 .... 29 B1
East Roman Ditch. CT16 .... 166 F8
East Row. ME1 .... 9 C5
East St. Ashford TN23 .... 139 B2
East St. Canterbury CT1 ..... 67 C3
East St. Chatham ME4 .... 10 A3
East St. Dover CT17 .... 166 C8
East St. Faversham ME13 ... 62 D7
East St. Folkestone CT19 ... 178 E5
East St. Gillingham ME7 ..... 10 D6
East St. Harrietsham ME17 100 E5
East St. Herne Bay CT6 .... 23 A5
East St. Hythe CT21 .... 176 D2
East St. Sittingbourne ME10 . 37 A4
East Stour St. TN24 .... 139 D1
East View.
Brookland TN29 .... 197 D8
East View. Hersden CT3 ...... 46 F1
East Weald Dr. TN30 .... 167 B1
East Wootton Cotts. CT4 ... 109 A4
Eastbridge Rd. TN29 .... 195 B8
Eastbrook Pl. CT16 .... 166 E8
Eastchurch
CE Prim Sch. ME12 .... 5 D3
Eastchurch Rd. Margate CT9 . 8 E3
Eastchurch Rd.
Minster ME12 .... 5 B5
Eastcourt Gn. ME8 .... 11 B4
Eastcourt La.
Gillingham ME8 .... 11 B3
Eastcourt La. Gillingham,
Lower Twydall ME7 & ME8 . 11 B4
Eastern Arm N. CT16 .... 166 H8
Eastern Arm S. CT16 .... 166 H8
Eastern Ave. Ashford TN23 139 A2
Eastern Ave.
Halfway Houses ME12 .... 3 D6
Eastern Espl.
Queenborough ME11 .... 3 B4
Eastern Espl.
Broadstairs CT10 .... 30 B5
Eastern Espl. Margate CT9 ... 8 B3
Eastern Gdns. TN24 .... 156 E8
Eastern Rd. Gillingham ME7 . 10 F6
Eastern Rd.
Leysdown-on-S ME12 .... 6 G2
Eastern Rd. Lydd TN29 ...... 203 D7
Eastern Service Rd. CT16 . 166 H8
Eastfield Ho. ME16 .... 74 B2
Eastfield Rd. CT7 .... 27 A7
Eastfields. CT19 .... 178 D6
Eastgate. ME1 .... 9 D5
Eastgate Cl. CT6 .... 23 B3
Eastgate Ct. ME1 .... 9 C5
Eastgate Rd. TN30 .... 179 C8
Eastgate Terr. ME1 .... 9 C5
Eastling Cl. ME8 .... 11 D3
Eastling
Cty Prim Sch. ME13 .... 81 F5
Eastling Rd. Bayfield ME13 .. 61 D2
Eastling Rd. Eastling ME13 .. 81 F7
Eastmead Ave. TN23 .... 156 C8

Easton's Cnr. TN25 .... 172 F4
Eastry CE Prim Sch. CT13 ... 93 B2
Eastry Cl. Ashford TN23 .... 156 A6
Eastry Cl. Maidstone ME16 .. 74 C7
Eastry Ct. CT13 .... 112 F5
Eastry Hospl. CT13 .... 93 B2
Eastry Park. CT13 .... 93 C1
Eastwell. **3** TN30 .... 179 B7
Eastwell Barn Mews.TN30 . 179 A8
Eastwell Cl.
Maidstone ME14 .... 75 C5
Eastwell Cl.
Shadoxhurst TN26 .... 155 B1
Eastwell Meadows. TN30 .. 179 A8
Eastwell Terr. TN25 .... 122 E3
Eastwood Cotts. ME9 .... 38 E6
Eastwood Rd. ME10 .... 36 D5
Eaton Hill. CT9 .... 7 J2
Eaton Rd. Dover CT17 .... 166 B7
Eaton Rd. Margate CT9 .... 7 J1
Eaves Rd. CT17 .... 166 A7
Ebbsfleet La. CT12 .... 51 A3
Ebony Cotts. TN30 .... 189 A6
Eccleston Rd. ME15 .... 74 F2
Echo Cl. ME15 .... 97 F6
Echo Ho. ME10 .... 37 B3
Echo Wlk. ME12 .... 4 D6
Eddington Cl. ME15 .... 97 B6
Eddington La. CT6 .... 22 F3
Eddington Way. CT6 .... 22 E3
Eden Ave. ME5 .... 32 A7
Eden Ho. TN23 .... 156 C8
Eden Rd. CT5 .... 43 A7
Edenbridge Dr. ME12 .... 3 B8
Edenbridge Ho. CT1 .... 88 B6
Edenfield. CT7 .... 27 B7
Edgar Cl. CT5 .... 21 D3
Edgar Ho. CT14 .... 117 B3
Edgar Rd. Canterbury CT1 .. 67 B1
Edgar Rd. Dover CT17 .... 149 B1
Edgar Rd. Margate CT9 .... 8 A3
Edgar Rd. Minster.
Thanet CT12 .... 50 B6
Edge End Rd. CT10 .... 29 F4
Edgehill Cl. CT20 .... 177 D4
Edger Pl. **3** ME15 .... 75 A4
Edinburgh Ho. Deal CT14 . 117 A5
Edinburgh Ho. **7**
Dover CT17 .... 166 D7
Edinburgh Pl. CT20 .... 178 B3
Edinburgh Rd.
Ashford TN23 & TN24 ...... 139 B2
Edinburgh Rd.
Chatham ME4 .... 10 C2
Edinburgh Rd.
Gillingham ME7 .... 10 D5
Edinburgh Rd.Margate CT9 28 B8
Edinburgh Sq.
Maidstone ME15 .... 97 C7
Edinburgh Wlk. **5** CT9 ... 28 B8
Edith Rd. Faversham ME13 .. 62 C6
Edith Rd. Ramsgate CT11 ... 52 C6
Edith Rd.
Westgate-on-S CT8 .... 7 D1
Edmanson Ave. CT9 .... 7 E1
Edmund Cl. ME16 .... 74 A3
Edmund St. CT13 .... 91 A8
Edna Rd. ME14 .... 74 F8
Edred Rd. CT17 .... 166 B8
Edward Cl. ME5 .... 10 C1
Edward Dr. CT7 .... 27 B7
Edward Rd. Canterbury CT1 . 88 A8
Edward Rd.
Folkestone CT19 .... 178 D6
Edward Rd.
Kingsdown CT14 .... 134 C6
Edward Rd.
Queenborough ME11 .... 3 B5
Edward St.
Whitstable CT5 .... 43 C5
Edward St. Chatham ME4 ... 10 A3
Edward Terr. **8** CT20 .... 178 E6
Edwards Cl. ME8 .... 33 C5
Edwards Rd. CT16 .... 166 D8
Edwin Rd. ME8 .... 33 C8
Edwina Ave. ME12 .... 4 A7
Edwina Pl. ME9 .... 35 C7
Edyngham Cl. ME10 .... 37 A8
Effingham Cres.
CT16 & CT17 .... 166 D8
Effingham St. Dover CT17 . 166 D8
Effingham St.
Ramsgate CT11 .... 52 E6
Egbert Rd. Birchington CT7 . 26 D8
Egbert Rd.
Faversham ME13 .... 62 C6
Egbert Rd. Minster.
Thanet CT12 .... 50 B6

Egbert Rd.
Westgate-on-S CT8 .... 7 C1
Egerton
CE Prim Sch.TN27 .... 118 F3
Egerton Dr. CT9 .... 8 E2
Egerton House Rd. TN27 .. 118 E4
Egerton Rd.
Maidstone ME14 .... 74 E7
Egerton Rd. Pluckley TN27 119 B1
Egerton Rd.
Temple Ewell CT16 .... 148 E5
Eggarton La. CT4 .... 107 C2
Eggringe. TN23 .... 138 E1
Egremont Rd. ME15 .... 75 F2
Eighteen Acre La. TN29 .... 198 D8
Elder Cl. ME17 .... 99 D2
Elder Cl. ME8 .... 33 B6
Elders The. CT3 .... 68 F1
Eldon Pl. **4** CT10 .... 30 B4
Eldon St. ME4 .... 10 A4
Elfrida Cl. CT9 .... 29 C8
Elgar Pl. CT11 .... 52 D7
Elham CE Prim Sch. CT4 .. 144 F4
Elham Cl. Gillingham ME8 ... 11 B3
Elham Cl. Margate CT9 .... 8 C1
Elham Rd. CT1 .... 87 E6
Elham Way. CT10 .... 30 A2
Eling Cl. ME15 .... 97 A8
Eliot Coll. CT2 .... 66 E4
Elisans Wlk. CT1 .... 88 C8
Elizabeth Carter Ave.
CT14 .... 116 F4
Elizabeth Ct.
Broadstairs CT10 .... 30 B6
Elizabeth Ct.
Gillingham ME8 .... 11 C1
Elizabeth Ct.
Herne Bay CT6 .... 22 F5
Elizabeth Dr. CT18 .... 164 B2
Elizabeth Gdns. CT21 .... 176 B1
Elizabeth Ho. ME16 .... 75 A6
Elizabeth Kemp Ct. CT12 ... 29 C1
Elizabeth Rd. Dover CT17 . 166 D6
Elizabeth Rd.
Ramsgate CT11 .... 52 F6
Elizabeth Way. CT6 .... 23 B3
Elizabethen Ct. TN27 .... 120 C7
Ellen Ave. CT11 .... 29 E2
Ellen's Hill. CT14 .... 116 E3
Ellen's Pl. ME9 .... 35 C6
Ellenden Ct. CT2 .... 66 C4
Ellens Rd. CT14 .... 116 F2
Ellenswood Cl. ME15 .... 76 A1
Ellesmere Mews. TN28 ..... 200 C8
Ellingham Leas. ME15 .... 97 C7
Ellingham Way. TN23 .... 156 A5
Ellington Ave. CT9 .... 28 B8
Ellington
Cty Inf Sch. CT11 .... 52 C7
Ellington High Sch. CT11 ... 52 C7
Ellington Pl. CT11 .... 52 C7
Ellington Rd. CT11 .... 52 D7
Elliots Pl. ME13 .... 62 D7
Elliott Park Sch. ME12 .... 4 A7
Ellis Dr. TN28 .... 200 C8
Ellis Rd. CT5 .... 21 A3
Ellis Way. CT6 .... 23 C2
Ellison Cl. CT5 .... 21 C1
Ellison Ct. ME13 .... 62 E6
Ellison Way. ME8 .... 12 A2
Elm Ave. ME4 .... 9 F1
Elm Cl. TN27 .... 118 F3
Elm Cotts. TN25 .... 122 E3
Elm Court Ind Est. ME7 ...... 32 E3
Elm Ct. CT8 .... 27 E8
Elm Fields. TN29 .... 199 A6
Elm Gdns. CT21 .... 176 E2
Elm Gr. Maidstone ME15 .... 75 B3
Elm Gr.
Sittingbourne ME10 .... 37 B4
Elm Gr. Westgate-on-S CT8 .. 27 E8
Elm Ho. **11** CT21 .... 176 B2
Elm La. ME12 .... 4 E5
Elm Park Gdns. CT17 .... 165 F7
Elm Pl. TN23 .... 155 F7
Elm Rd. Aylesham CT3 ...... 112 E5
Elm Rd. **6**
Folkestone CT19 .... 178 E6
Elm Rd. Gillingham ME7 ..... 10 E6
Elm Rd.
St Mary's Bay TN29 .... 194 F3
Elm Tree Dr. ME1 .... 9 A2
Elm Wood Cl. CT5 .... 21 C2
Elm Wood W. CT5 .... 21 C2
Elmfield. Sittingbourne ME8 . 11 A3
Elmfield. Tenterden TN30 .. 179 B8
Elmfield Ct. Coxheath ME17 96 C3

Elmfield Ct.
Tenterden TN30 .... 179 B8
Elmhurst Gdns. ME1 .... 9 E3
Elmleigh Rd. CT3 .... 90 A8
Elmley Ind Est. ME11 .... 3 A2
Elmley Rd. ME12 .... 4 D3
Elmley Way. CT9 .... 28 F6
Elms Ave. CT11 .... 52 D6
Elms Hill. CT15 .... 165 D6
Elms The. Hersden CT3 .... 46 E1
Elms The. Teynham ME9 ...... 39 A2
Elms Vale Rd.
CT15 & CT17 .... 165 E7
Elmstead Pl. **10** CT20 .... 178 E5
Elmstone Cl. ME16 .... 74 B2
Elmstone Gdns. CT9 .... 8 E2
Elmstone Hole Rd. ME17 .... 100 D1
Elmstone La. ME16 .... 74 B2
Elmstone Rd.
Gillingham ME8 .... 33 D7
Elmstone Rd.
Ramsgate CT11 .... 52 D7
Elmton La. CT15 .... 114 C1
Elmtree. TN26 .... 181 C1
Elmway. ME12 .... 5 F6
Elmwood Ave. CT10 .... 30 A8
Elmwood Cl. CT10 .... 30 A7
Elventon Cl. CT19 .... 177 E7
Elverland La. ME13 & ME9 ... 61 B2
Elvington Cl. ME16 .... 74 D5
Elvington La. CT18 .... 162 E2
Elwick La. **18** TN23 .... 139 B2
Elwick Rd. TN23 .... 139 B2
Ely Cl. ME8 .... 11 E2
Embassy Cl. ME7 .... 10 F1
Emerald Cl. ME1 .... 31 D7
Emerald View. ME12 .... 6 E4
Emily Rd. ME5 .... 32 B6
Emmerson Gdns. CT5 .... 21 D3
Empire Terr. CT9 .... 28 E8
Empress Gdns. ME12 .... 6 D4
Emsworth Gr. ME14 .... 75 D6
Enbrook Rd. CT20 .... 177 E4
Enbrook Valley. CT20 .... 177 E5
Encombe. CT20 .... 177 D3
Enfield Rd. CT14 .... 117 D7
Engineers Ct. **1** TN23 .... 139 B2
English Martyrs'
RC Prim Sch. ME2 .... 9 B8
Ennerdale. ME13 .... 62 E6
Ennerdale Gdns. CT13 ...... 112 F6
Enterprise Bsns Est. ME2 ..... 9 E7
Enterprise Cl. ME2 .... 9 D8
Enterprise Ctr The. ME5 .... 54 C8
Enterprise Rd.
Maidstone ME15 .... 75 A1
Enterprise Rd. Margate CT9 .. 29 A6
Enticott Cl. CT5 .... 21 A1
Epaul La. ME1 .... 9 C6
Epping Cl. CT6 .... 23 B2
Epple Bay Ave. CT7 .... 27 B8
Epple Bay Rd. CT7 .... 27 A8
Epple Rd. CT7 .... 27 B8
Epps Rd. ME10 .... 36 E3
Epsom Cl. ME15 .... 97 F6
Eric Rd. CT17 .... 149 B2
Erith Cl. ME14 .... 75 A8
Erith St. CT17 .... 149 B1
Ernest Dr. ME16 .... 74 B5
Ernest Rd. ME4 .... 10 A3
Ernwell Rd. CT19 .... 178 D6
Ersham Rd. CT1 .... 88 A7
Eskdale Ave. CT11 .... 52 A7
Esmonde Dr. CT12 .... 27 F2
Esplanade. Dover CT17 .... 166 D6
Esplanade. Rochester ME1 ... 9 C5
Esplanade.
Westgate-on-S CT8 & CT9 .... 7 C1
Essella Pk. TN24 .... 139 E1
Essella Rd. TN24 .... 139 E1
Essetford Rd. TN23 .... 156 A7
Essex Ave. CT6 .... 22 B4
Essex Gdns. CT7 .... 26 F6
Essex Rd. Canterbury CT1 .... 88 D7
Essex Rd. Maidstone ME15 ... 97 E6
Essex Rd.
Westgate-on-S CT8 .... 7 C1
Essex St. CT5 .... 43 D8
Estelle Cl. ME1 .... 31 D7
Esther Cl. ME10 .... 36 E8
Estuary Rd. ME12 .... 1 C1
Etchden Rd. TN26 .... 154 A8
Ethel Rd. CT10 .... 29 F5
Ethel-Maud Ct. ME7 .... 10 D7
Ethelbert Cres. CT9 .... 8 A3
Ethelbert Gdns. CT9 .... 7 J3
Ethelbert Rd.
Birchington CT7 .... 26 D8

Ethelbert Rd.
Canterbury CT1 .... 88 B6
Ethelbert Rd. Deal CT14 ..... 95 C1
Ethelbert Rd. Dover CT17 .. 166 C8
Ethelbert Rd.
Faversham ME13 .... 62 C6
Ethelbert Rd.
Folkestone CT19 .... 178 D7
Ethelbert Rd. Margate CT9 ... 7 J3
Ethelbert Rd.
Ramsgate CT11 .... 52 D6
Ethelbert Rd. Rochester ME1 . 9 C4
Ethelbert Road
Cty Inf Sch. ME13 .... 62 C6
Ethelbert Sq. CT8 .... 7 C1
Ethelbert Terr. Margate CT9 .. 8 A3
Ethelbert Terr.
Westgate-on-S CT8 .... 7 C1
Ethelburga Dr. CT18 .... 161 B7
Ethelred Ct. ME13 .... 62 C6
Ethelred Rd. CT8 .... 7 C1
Eton Cl. ME5 .... 31 F4
Eurogate Bsns Pk. TN24 ... 139 B5
Eurolink Way. ME10 .... 36 F4
Eva Rd. ME7 .... 10 D3
Evans Rd. TN24 .... 157 A7
Evelings Alley. **12** CT5 .... 20 D2
Evelyn Ct. CT21 .... 177 A2
Evelyn Rd. ME16 .... 74 E3
Evenhill Rd. CT3 .... 89 E8
Everard Way. ME13 .... 62 B8
Everglades The. ME7 .... 32 F6
Evergreen Cl.
Gillingham ME7 .... 33 A5
Evergreen Cl. Iwade ME9 ... 14 D4
Everist Ct. CT18 .... 161 C6
Eversley Cl. ME16 .... 74 C6
Eversley Codr. CT20 .... 177 F4
Eversley Rd. CT21 .... 177 B3
Eversley Way. CT20 .... 177 F5
Evison Cl. CT16 .... 149 B2
Ewart Rd. ME4 .... 9 E1
Exchange St. CT14 .... 117 D7
Exeter Cl. CT19 .... 177 D6
Exeter Wlk. ME1 .... 31 C7
Exmoor Rise. TN24 .... 139 B4
Exmouth Rd. ME7 .... 10 C7
Exton Cl. ME5 .... 32 C2
Exton Gdns. ME14 .... 75 B5
Eyhorne St. ME17 .... 77 D2
Eylesden Court Sch. ME14 . 76 B4
Eynsford Cl. CT9 .... 8 F2
Eynsford Rd. ME16 .... 74 D7
Eythorne Elvington
Cty Prim Sch. CT15 .... 131 C8
Eythorne Rd. CT15 .... 130 E6
Eythorne Sta. CT15 .... 131 C8
Fagus Cl. ME5 .... 32 B1
Fair St. CT10 .... 29 E4
Fair View
Jun & Inf Schs. ME8 .... 33 C5
Fairacre. CT10 .... 29 E4
Fairacres Cl. CT6 .... 23 C4
Fairbourne Heath Cotts.
ME17 .... 100 B1
Fairbourne La. ME17 .... 100 C4
Fairfax Bsns Ctr. ME15 ...... 97 F4
Fairfax Cl.
Folkestone CT20 .... 177 D5
Fairfax Cl. Gillingham ME8 ... 33 D5
Fairfax Dr. CT6 .... 23 C5
Fairfield. Deal CT14 .... 116 F6
Fairfield. Elham CT4 .... 144 F5
Fairfield Cl. TN28 .... 200 B7
Fairfield Pk. CT10 .... 29 F4
Fairfield Rd.
Broadstairs CT10 .... 29 E4
Fairfield Rd. Minster,
ThanetCT12 .... 50 B7
Fairfield Rd.
New Romney TN28 .... 200 B7
Fairfield Rd.
Ramsgate CT11 .... 29 E2
Fairfield Terr. TN26 .... 183 A7
Fairhurst Dr. ME15 .... 96 B4
Fairings The. TN30 .... 179 B8
Fairlawn. CT5 .... 21 D1
Fairlawn Rd. CT10 & CT12 ... 29 B3
Fairlead Rd. ME1 .... 9 D1
Fairleas. ME10 .... 37 B2
Fairlight Ave. CT12 .... 52 B8
Fairlight Rd. CT21 .... 176 A3
Fairmeadow. ME14 .... 74 F4
Fairoaks. CT6 .... 23 B3
Fairservice Cl. ME10 .... 37 C5
Fairview Ave. ME8 .... 33 B5
Fairview Cl. CT9 .... 8 A2
Fairview Cotts. ME15 .... 96 F5

Fairview Gdns. Deal CT14 . 117 A2
Fairview Gdns. Sturry CT2 .. 68 A6
Fairview Ind Pk. TN26 ...... 183 D7
Fairview Rd.
Elvington CT15 .... 114 B1
Fairview Rd.
Sittingbourne ME10 .... 37 A3
Fairway Cl. CT19 .... 178 A7
Fairway Cl. Rochester ME1 ... 9 C1
Fairway Cl.
St Mary's Bay TN29 .... 194 F3
Fairway Cres. CT5 .... 44 A1
Fairway The. Deal CT14 .... 117 C8
Fairway The.
Herne Bay CT6 .... 22 D2
Fairway The. Hythe CT21 .. 176 C1
Fairway The.
Littlestone-on-S TN28 ..... 200 D6
Fairway The. Rochester ME1 . 9 C1
Fairway The.
Sittingbourne ME10 .... 36 E1
Fairway The.
St Mary's Bay TN29 .... 195 A5
Fairways The. ME13 .... 61 A8
Fairwood Ind Est. TN23 ... 139 A1
Falcon Cl. ME10 .... 37 A2
Falcon Gdns. ME12 .... 4 D7
Falcon Way. TN23 .... 155 E7
Falkland Pl. ME5 .... 31 E1
Fallowfield. Chatham ME5 ... 32 B8
Fallowfield.
Sittingbourne ME10 .... 37 A2
Fallowfield Cl. ME14 .... 75 E4
Fan The. CT16 .... 166 H8
Fanconi Rd. ME5 .... 32 B3
Fancy Row. ME14 .... 76 C5
Fane Way. ME8 .... 33 D4
Fans La. ME9 .... 14 D4
Fant La. ME16 .... 74 B2
Faraday Rd. ME14 .... 75 C7
Fareham Wlk. **10** ME15 .... 97 F6
Farleigh Cl. ME16 .... 74 A2
Farleigh Hill. ME15 .... 74 A1
Farleigh Hill Ret Pk. ME15 .. 74 E1
Farleigh Hill Sch. ME15 ..... 74 A1
Farleigh Rd. CT2 .... 67 A3
Farleigh Trad Est. ME15 ... 74 E1
Farley Cl. Chatham ME5 .... 32 D2
Farley Cl.
Shadoxhurst TN26 .... 155 D1
Farley Rd. CT9 .... 28 F7
Farm Cl. TN23 .... 155 E7
Farm Cres. ME10 .... 37 A2
Farm House Cl. CT5 .... 43 F8
Farm La. CT14 .... 116 F6
Farm Rd. Chatham ME5 ..... 31 E3
Farm Rd. Hamstreet TN26 . 183 A7
Farmer Cl. Hythe CT21 .... 176 D3
Farmer Cl. Leeds ME17 ..... 99 A6
Farmhouse Cl. CT4 .... 128 F7
Farnborough Cl. ME16 ...... 74 C2
Farncombe Way. CT16 ...... 149 B7
Farne Cl. ME15 .... 97 A6
Farnham Cl. ME8 .... 12 E2
Farningham Cl. ME14 .... 75 C6
Farraday Cl. ME1 .... 31 D8
Farrar Rd. CT7 .... 27 A7
Farrers Wlk. TN23 .... 156 B4
Farrier Cl. Ashford TN23 .. 138 F5
Farrier Cl. Maidstone ME14 . 75 E5
Farrier St. CT14 .... 117 C8
Farriers Cl. ME8 .... 34 C8
Farrow Ct. TN23 .... 156 A6
Farthing Cnr. ME9 .... 35 B3
Farthingloe Ct. CT17 ...... 166 A6
Farthingloe Rd. CT17 ...... 166 A6
Farthings Cotts. ME14 ...... 53 F1
Farthings Ct. CT2 .... 66 C4
Fauchon's Cl. ME14 .... 75 F3
Fauchon's La. ME14 .... 75 F4
Faulkners La. CT2 .... 66 A1
Faussett Hill. CT4 .... 109 F8
Faversham Cottage Hospl.
ME13 .... 62 C7
Faversham Rd. Boughton
Lees TN24 & TN25 .... 122 E5
Faversham Rd.
Charing TN27 .... 103 E1
Faversham Rd.
Faversham ME13 & ME9 ... 61 B5
Faversham Rd.
Lenham ME17 .... 101 E7
Faversham Rd. Paddock
ME13 & TN25 & TN27 .... 104 C3
Faversham Rd. Pested
CT4 & ME13 & TN25 ..... 105 B4
Faversham Rd.
Whitstable CT5 .... 42 C6
Faversham Rd.
Wichling ME17 & ME9 ..... 80 B4
Faversham Reach. ME13 .... 62 D8

Faversham Sta. ME13 .... 62 D6
Fawley Cl. ME14 .... 74 E7
Featherbed La.
Selling ME13 .... 84 A7
Featherbed La.
Sittingbourne ME9 .... 14 E2
Featherby Cty Prim Inf Sch.
ME8 .... 11 A3
Featherby Jun Sch. ME8 .... 11 A3
Featherby Rd. Gillingham,
Lower Twydall ME7 .... 11 A5
Featherby Rd.
Gillingham,Twydall ME8 ... 11 A3
Felborough Cl. CT4 .... 107 C8
Felderland Cl.
Park Wood ME17 .... 97 E5
Felderland Cl.
Sandwich CT14 .... 93 F5
Felderland Dr. ME17 .... 97 E5
Felderland La. CT13 & CT14 . 93 E4
Felderland Rd. ME17 .... 97 E5
Feldspar Cl. ME5 .... 32 A1
Fellows Cl. ME8 .... 33 B6
Fenner Cl. CT20 .... 177 E4
Fenoulhet Way. CT6 .... 23 A5
Ferdi Lethert Ho. TN24 .... 139 E5
Ferguson Cl. CT21 .... 176 F2
Ferguson Rd. TN29 .... 202 D2
Fern Bank Cres. CT19 ...... 178 D6
Fern Cl. Hawkinge CT18 .. 163 C6
Fern Cl. Whitstable CT5 ..... 21 C1
Fern Ct. CT10 .... 30 B5
Fern Wlk. ME10 .... 37 A2
Fernbank Cl. ME5 .... 31 F2
Ferndale Cl. ME12 .... 3 D6
Ferndale Ct. CT7 .... 27 A6
Ferndale Rd. CT4 .... 109 F8
Ferndown. CT7 .... 26 D8
Ferndown Cl. ME7 .... 33 A5
Ferne Way. CT20 .... 177 E6
Fernfield. CT18 .... 163 C6
Fernfield La. CT18 .... 163 C7
Fernhill Rd. ME14 .... 74 E4
Fernlea Ave. CT6 .... 22 E4
Fernleigh Cl. ME13 .... 64 B3
Fernlee Cl. ME8 .... 33 E4
Ferry Rd. Iwade ME9 .... 14 E4
Ferry Rd. Queenborough
ME11 & ME12 .... 3 D1
Ferry View. ME11 .... 2 F3
Fiddling La. TN25 .... 159 E6
Field Ave. CT1 .... 67 C8
Field Cl. ME5 .... 31 E6
Field End. TN24 .... 140 A1
Field End Pl. ME13 .... 64 A3
Field Mill Rd. TN27 .... 119 B5
Field View.
Kingsnorth TN23 .... 156 B4
Field View. Whitstable CT5 .. 43 B7
Field View. Cl. ME12 .... 3 C6
Field Way. CT2 .... 67 F5
Fielder Cl. ME10 .... 37 C5
Fielding St. ME13 .... 62 C7
Fieldings The. ME10 .... 36 E2
Fieldworks Rd. ME4 & ME7 . 10 A7
Fiesta Wlk. CT1 .... 88 C7
Fife Rd. CT6 .... 22 B3
Fifth Ave. CT9 .... 8 B3
Fig Tree Rd. CT10 .... 29 F7
Fiji Terr. ME14 .... 75 A7
Filer Rd. ME12 .... 3 E4
Filmer Rd. CT4 .... 88 F1
Finch Cl. ME14 .... 75 A2
Finch Gr. CT21 .... 187 D8
Finch Mews. CT14 .... 117 C4
Finches The.
Sittingbourne ME10 .... 36 F3
Finches The.
St Nicholas at Wade CT7 ... 25 E2
Findlay Cl. ME8 .... 33 D6
Findley Cl. **9** CT21 .... 176 B2
Finglesham Ct. ME15 .... 97 C8
Finlay Cl. ME13 .... 62 B7
Finsbury Ct. CT11 .... 52 E8
Finsbury Rd. CT11 .... 52 E8
Fintonagh Dr. ME14 .... 75 B6
Finwell Rd. ME8 .... 12 A2
Fir Ct. TN24 .... 139 F1
Fir Tree Cl. CT11 .... 52 C6
Fir Tree Gr. Bredhurst ME7 . 33 B1
Fir Tree Gr. Chatham ME5 ... 32 D1
Fir Tree Hill. CT13 .... 93 B6
Firbank Gdns. CT9 .... 28 D7
Firbanks. CT5 .... 43 B7
Firethorn Cl. ME7 .... 10 E6
Firs Cl. CT19 .... 177 D7
Firs La. CT19 .... 177 D7
Firs Rd. CT4 .... 112 F1
Firs The. Deal CT14 .... 117 C8
Firs The. Hersden CT3 ...... 46 E1

First Ave. Broadstairs CT10 ... 8 F2
First Ave. Chatham ME4 .... 10 C2
First Ave. Eastchurch ME12 .. 5 E5
First Ave. Gillingham ME7 ... 10 E3
First Ave. Margate CT9 .... 8 B3
First Ave. Rushenden ME11 ... 2 F3
First Ave. Sheerness ME12 .... 1 D1
First La. ME15 .... 76 E2
Firtree Cl. CT14 .... 66 B3
Fish Market. CT19 .... 178 E5
Fisher Cl. CT21 .... 176 D1
Fisher Rd. Canterbury CT2 .. 66 D1
Fisher Rd. Chatham ME5 .... 32 B7
Fisher St. Maidstone ME14 .. 75 A6
Fisher St. Sandwich CT13 .. 73 A1
Fisher Street Rd. ME13 ..... 83 C2
Fishermans Ctyd. CT14 .... 117 D3
Fishmonger's La. **6** CT16 . 166 E7
Fitzgerald Ave. CT6 .... 22 C4
Fitzmary Ave. CT9 .... 7 E1
Fitzroy Ave.
Broadstairs CT10 .... 8 G2
Fitzroy Ave. Margate CT9 ... 8 B1
Fitzroy Ave.
Ramsgate CT12 .... 29 B2
Fitzroy Rd. CT5 .... 20 E7
Fitzthorold Ho. ME7 .... 10 E7
Fitzwalter Cl. **1** CT16 .... 149 B3
Fitzwilliam Rd. ME14 .... 75 F5
Five Acre Wood Sch. ME15 . 97 B7
Five Bells La. ME1 .... 9 D4
Five Vents La. TN29 .... 199 B8
Fiveways L. Ctr. ME4 .... 10 A4
Fiveways Rise. CT14 .... 116 F5
Flamingo Cl. ME5 .... 32 A7
Flanders Cl. ME10 .... 14 F1
Flanders Field. TN25 ...... 157 E4
Flax Court La. CT15 .... 131 C7
Flaxman Ct. **7** ME7 .... 10 A6
Flaxman Dr. ME16 .... 74 C6
Flaxpond Rd. TN23 .... 155 F7
Fleet Ave. ME12 .... 1 C1
Fleet Rd. Rochester ME1 .... 9 D1
Fleet Rd. St Margarets'
at Cliffe CT15 .... 134 A1
Fleet Villas. TN24 .... 139 D7
Fleets La. CT2 .... 66 D7
Fleetwood Ave. CT6 .... 22 D4
Fleetwood Cl. ME12 .... 4 A4
Fleming Rd. CT13 & CT3 .... 92 D6
Fleming Way. CT19 .... 178 E8
Fletcher Rd. CT5 .... 21 B1
Flete Rd. CT9 .... 28 D5
Flimwell. TN23 .... 155 D6
Flint Gn. ME5 .... 32 C3
Flint La. ME17 .... 79 C1
Flood Hatch. ME15 .... 74 D2
Flood La. ME13 .... 62 C8
Flood St. TN25 .... 157 D2
Flora Rd. CT11 .... 52 E8
Florence Ave. CT5 .... 43 B7
Florence Cres. CT9 .... 8 B3
Florence Rd.
Maidstone ME16 .... 74 E3
Florence Rd. **3**
Ramsgate CT11 .... 52 D6
Florence St. ME2 .... 9 C3
Florida Cl. CT16 .... 149 B3
Flower Rise. ME14 .... 74 F7
Flume End. ME16 .... 74 D4
Flying Horse La. **4** CT16 . 166 E7
Foads Hill. CT12 .... 51 D6
Foads La. CT12 .... 51 D5
Fodbury Ct. CT8 .... 7 C1
Foley Cl. TN24 .... 157 A7
Foley St. ME14 .... 75 A5
Folkestone Harbour Sta.
CT20 .... 178 E4
Folkestone Race Course.
TN25 .... 175 A6
Folkestone Rd.
Church Hougham CT15 .... 165 D4
Folkestone Rd.
Dover CT17 & CT15 .... 166 B7
Folkestone Rd.
East Guildford TN31 .... 196 C3
Folkestone
Sch for Girls. CT20 .... 177 F4
Folkestone West Sta.
CT18 .... 177 F5
Folkstone Ho. **4** ME15 .... 97 F6
Folly Rd. CT20 .... 178 E6
Fonblanque Rd. ME12 .... 1 D2
Fontwell Cl. **6** ME15 ..... 97 F6
Foord Almshouses. ME1 .... 9 B8
Foord Rd. ME17 .... 101 D5
Foord Rd N. CT19 & CT20 . 178 D5
Foord Rd S. CT19 & CT20 . 178 C5
Foord St. **11** CT20 .... 178 C5
Foord St. ME1 .... 9 D4
Forbes Rd. ME13 .... 64 D3
Ford Cl. Bridge CT4 .... 88 F1

Ford Cl. Herne Bay CT6 .... 22 A4
Ford Hill. CT13 .... 46 E8
Ford Wlk. CT5 .... 43 A3
Fordcombe Cl. ME15 .... 97 F7
Fordingbridge Cl. ME16 ...... 74 B5
Fordoun Rd. CT10 .... 29 F5
Fordwich Cl. ME6 .... 74 B7
Fordwich Gn. ME8 .... 11 C3
Fordwich Gr. CT10 .... 29 E7
Fordwich Pl. CT13 .... 93 F8
Fordwich Rd. CT2 .... 67 F4
Foreland Ave.
 Folkestone CT19 .... 178 F6
Foreland Ave. Margate CT9 .... 8 D1
Foreland Ct.
 Ramsgate CT11 .... 52 D5
Foreland St. St Margaret's
 at Cliffe CT15 .... 151 A5
Foreland Park Ho. CT10 ...... 30 B7
Foreland Rd. CT15 .... 151 A4
Foreland Sch The. CT10 ...... 30 A6
Forelands The. CT1 .... 88 B5
Forelands Sq. CT14 .... 117 B3
Forelands Cl. CT10 & CT9 .... 8 G3
Forest Cotts. TN25 .... 105 C2
Forest Dr. ME5 .... 31 F2
Forestall Meadow. TN23 ... 156 B4
Forestdale Rd. ME5 .... 54 A8
Foresters Cl. ME5 .... 31 F2
Foresters Way. CT20 .... 178 D5
Forestry Cotts. CT4 .... 125 B7
Forge Cl. Eythorne CT15 ... 131 C7
Forge Cl. Sellindge TN25 ... 159 D1
Forge Cl. Sturry CT2 .... 67 F5
Forge Cotts. CT3 .... 47 C8
Forge Field. CT15 .... 164 E5
Forge Hill. Aldington TN25 . 173 A5
Forge Hill.
 Bethersden TN26 .... 153 E5
Forge Ho. Canterbury CT1 ... 87 E6
Forge La. Ashford TN23 .... 139 B2
Forge La. Boxley ME14 ...... 54 C2
Forge La. Boyden Gate CT3 . 47 C8
Forge La. Bredhurst ME7 .... 33 A1
Forge La. Dean Street ME15 . 96 C7
Forge La.
 Egerton Forstal TN27 ...... 118 C1
Forge La. Gillingham ME7 .... 10 E7
Forge La. Leeds ME17 .... 98 F7
Forge La. Ramsgate CT12 ... 52 C7
Forge La. Sutton CT15 ..... 133 A6
Forge La. Upchurch ME9 .... 12 F3
Forge La. Whitfield CT16 ... 149 A8
Forge La. Whitstable CT5 ... 43 D8
Forge Lane
 Cty Inf Sch. ME7 .... 10 E6
Forge Meadow.
 Harrietsham ME17 .... 100 D6
Forge Meadow.
 Stone in Oxney TN30 ..... 190 A4
Forge Meads. TN30 .... 188 E3
Forge Path. CT16 .... 149 A8
Forge Rd. ME10 .... 36 E6
Forgefield. TN26 .... 153 D5
Forgefields. CT6 .... 46 B8
Forrens The. **13** CT1 .... 67 A1
Forrester Cl. CT7 .... 67 C2
Forson Cl. TN30 .... 179 B8
Forstal Cotts.
 Lenham Heath ME17 ..... 102 A1
Forstal Cotts.
 Pratling Street ME20 ...... 53 B2
Forstal La. ME17 .... 96 D4
Forstal Rd.
 Egerton Forstal TN27 ...... 118 C1
Forstal Rd. Forstal ME20 ... 53 C2
Forstal Rd.
 Woolage Village CT4 ...... 112 E1
Forstal The. Preston CT3 .... 70 B6
Forstal The. Wye TN25 .... 123 E2
Forsters. ME17 .... 98 E4
Fort Burgoyne (Casemated
 Barracks). CT16 .... 149 E2
Fort Burgoyne Rd. CT16 ... 149 E1
Fort Cres. CT9 .... 204 E6
Fort Hill. CT9 .... 7 J3
Fort Lower Prom. CT9 ...... 7 J3
Fort Luton (Mus). ME4 ..... 10 A1
Fort Paragon. CT9 .... 7 J3
Fort Pitt Gram Sch. ME1 .... 9 E4
Fort Pitt Hill. ME1 & ME4 ... 9 E4
Fort Pitt St. ME4 .... 9 E3
Fort Prom. CT9 .... 7 J3
Fort Rd. Broadstairs CT10 ... 30 B4
Fort Rd. Hythe CT21 ...... 176 A2
Fort Rd. Margate CT9 ...... 7 J3
Fort St. ME1 .... 9 D4

Fortuna Ct. CT11 .... 52 D7
Forty Acres Hill. ME12 ...... 1 B3
Forty Acres Rd. CT2 .... 66 E2
Forum The. **2** ME10 .... 36 F4
Fostall Rd. ME13 .... 155 F7
Fostall Rd. ME13 .... 40 C1
Foster Cl. CT19 .... 177 E7
Foster Clark Est. ME15 ..... 75 B2
Foster Rd. TN24 .... 157 A6
Foster St. ME15 .... 75 A3
Foster Way. CT14 .... 117 B5
Foster's Ave. CT13 .... 29 E7
Foster's Cl. CT13 .... 94 A7
Fostington Way. ME5 .... 31 F1
Foulds Cl. ME8 .... 33 B5
Fountain Ent Pk. ME15 ..... 75 A1
Fountain La. CT19 .... 7 I3
Fountain La. ME16 .... 74 A2
Fountain St. **2**
 Sittingbourne ME10 .... 36 E4
Fountain St. **3**
 Whitstable CT5 .... 20 D2
Fountains Cl. TN24 .... 140 A1
Four Oaks. ME13 .... 61 E8
Four Turnings. CT3 .... 70 B3
Four Wents.
 Langley Heath ME17 ...... 98 E3
Four Wents. Marlpit ME17 .. 97 F2
Fouracre Cotts. ME9 .... 34 F6
Fourth Ave.
 Eastchurch ME12 .... 5 F5
Fourth Ave. Gillingham ME7 . 10 E4
Fowey Cl. ME5 .... 32 C5
Fowler Cl. ME8 .... 33 C2
Fox Cl. CT18 .... 161 B7
Fox Hill. ME10 & ME9 ...... 37 D3
Fox Holt Rd. CT15 .... 146 B2
Fox St. ME7 .... 10 C6
Fox Way. CT14 .... 128 F8
Fox's Cross Cl. CT5 .... 43 B4
Fox's Cross Hill. CT5 .... 43 A3
Fox's Cross Rd. CT5 .... 43 C3
Foxborough Cl. CT13 .... 93 B6
Foxborough Hill. CT13 ...... 93 B5
Foxborough La. CT12 .... 50 C6
Foxburrow Cl. ME8 .... 33 D5
Foxden. Dr. ME15 .... 75 F1
Foxdown Cl. CT2 .... 66 E2
Foxglove Cres. ME5 .... 31 E4
Foxglove Gn. TN24 .... 139 F2
Foxglove Rd. TN24 .... 139 E1
Foxglove Rise. ME14 .... 74 E7
Foxgrove. ME10 .... 36 E7
Foxgrove Rd. CT5 .... 43 A5
Foxhunter Pk The. CT12 ... 49 D6
Foxley Rd. ME11 .... 3 A5
Frampton Rd. CT21 .... 176 A2
France Rd. CT16 .... 149 A5
Francis Gdns. CT11 .... 52 F8
Francis Ave. CT13 .... 95 B7
Francis Dr. ME5 .... 32 A2
Francis La. ME15 .... 97 F5
Francis Rd. Ashford TN23 .. 156 B8
Francis Rd.
 Broadstairs CT10 .... 30 B7
Frank Walters
 Bsns Pk The. CT10 .... 29 D3
Frankapps Cl. ME9 .... 35 B6
Franklin Dr. ME14 .... 75 D4
Franklin Rd. ME7 .... 10 D5
Franklins Cotts. ME15 ...... 96 C5
Franklyn Rd. CT2 .... 87 C8
Fraser Ave. ME8 .... 11 B2
Freda Cl. CT10 .... 29 F1
Frederick Rd. Deal CT14 ... 117 A3
Frederick Rd.
 Gillingham ME7 .... 10 A4
Fredom St. ME10 .... 36 E4
Freedown The. CT15 ...... 151 A7
Freeman Ct. **3** ME10 ..... 36 E4
Freeman Gdns. ME4 .... 9 F2
Freeman Way. ME15 ...... 97 E7
Freeman's Cl. CT5 .... 43 A6
Freeman's Rd. CT12 ...... 50 B6
Freemen's Way. CT14 ..... 117 B3
Freesia Cl. ME7 .... 10 E5
Fremantle Rd. CT20 ...... 177 E5
Fremlins Rd. ME14 .... 76 C4
French's Row. ME1 .... 38 D2
Frencham Cl. CT20 .... 67 A4
Frensham Cl. ME10 .... 37 B4
Frensham Wlk. ME5 .... 31 F1
Freshfield La. CT21 ...... 176 B4
Freshland Rd. ME16 .... 74 B4
Freshlands. CT6 .... 23 E5
Freshwater Rd. ME5 .... 32 B7
Friars Ave. ME5 .... 31 F2
Friars Cl. CT5 .... 21 A1
Friars Sch. TN3 .... 155 B8
Friars The. CT1 .... 66 F1
Friars Way. CT16 .... 149 A3

Friary Pl. **3** ME2 .... 9 B7
Friary Prec. ME2 .... 9 B7
Friary Way. CT2 .... 66 D2
Frid Cnr. TN27 .... 153 E7
Friendly Cl. CT9 .... 8 D1
Friends Ave. CT9 .... 29 D8
Frindsbury Rd. ME2 .... 9 B8
Frinstead Wlk. ME16 .... 74 B7
Frinsted Cl. ME9 .... 11 C3
Friston Way. ME1 .... 31 D8
Frith Rd. Aldington TN25 .. 172 C6
Frith Rd. Dover CT16 ..... 149 C1
Frithwood Cl. ME15 .... 75 F1
Frittenden Cl. TN23 ...... 155 F6
Frobisher Cl. ME10 .... 36 E7
Frobisher Gdns. ME1 .... 9 C2
Frog Farm Cotts. ME9 .... 13 A4
Frog La. CT4 .... 111 C6
Frogmore Wlk. ME17 ..... 101 C5
Frognal Cl. ME9 .... 38 B2
Frognal Gdns. ME9 .... 38 C2
Frognal La. ME9 .... 38 B2
Front Brents. ME13 .... 62 D8
Front Rd. TN26 .... 169 A1
Front St. CT15 .... 133 C5
Front The. CT15 .... 151 A4
Front Cres. ME5 .... 32 A7
Froyle Rd. ME16 .... 74 C6
Fruiterer's Cl. ME9 .... 59 B7
Fulbert Dr. ME14 .... 75 F5
Fulbert Rd. CT16 .... 149 B5
Fulham Ave. CT9 .... 28 B7
Fullers Cl. ME14 .... 76 A4
Fulmar Ct. TN29 .... 194 F3
Fulston Cl. CT9 .... 7 H1
Fulston Manor Sch. ME10 . 36 F2
Fulston Pl. ME10 .... 37 A3
Furfield Cl. ME17 .... 97 E5
Furrell's Rd. ME1 .... 9 D5
Furze Hill Cres. ME12 ...... 3 E6
Fusilier Ave. CT20 .... 177 B5
Fyndon Ho. CT1 .... 88 C7

Gabriel's Hill.
 ME14 & ME15 .... 75 A4
Gadby Rd. ME10 .... 36 C5
Gads Hill. ME7 .... 10 F6
Gadsby La. TN26 .... 153 A3
Gagetown Terr. ME14 ..... 74 F7
Gainsboro Rd. **4** CT7 ..... 26 F8
Gainsborough Cl.
 Folkestone CT19 .... 178 A7
Gainsborough Cl.
 Gillingham ME8 .... 33 D6
Gainsborough Cl.
 Sittingbourne ME10 .... 36 B5
Gainsborough Dr.
 Herne Bay CT6 .... 23 E5
Gainsborough Dr.
 Maidstone ME16 .... 74 B4
Gainsborough Ho. ME1 .... 9 D5
Galahad Ave. ME4 .... 9 F2
Galena Cl. ME5 .... 32 A1
Gallants La. ME15 .... 96 A4
Galleon Cl. ME1 .... 21 C8
Galliard St. CT13 .... 94 A8
Gallow's Cnr. CT21 ...... 176 A2
Galloways Rd. TN29 ..... 203 C5
Gallwey Ave. CT7 .... 26 E7
Galway Rd. ME12 .... 1 D1
Gammon's Farm La.
 TN29 .... 185 B3
Gandy's La. ME17 .... 97 C2
Gange Mews. **3** ME13 ... 62 D7
Gann Rd. CT5 .... 20 F2
Gaol La. **13** CT16 .... 166 D7
Gap House Sch. CT10 ..... 30 B2
Gap The. Bean CT2 .... 66 A7
Gap The. Canterbury CT1 .. 88 B5
Garden Cl. Maidstone ME15 . 97 F7
Garden Cl.
 Rough Common CT2 ..... 66 A2
Garden Cotts. CT3 .... 91 A7
Garden Hall The. TN25 .... 124 A1
Garden of Pkland
 (Mobile Home Pk)ME17 100 B7
Garden Rd. CT19 .... 178 D6
Garden St. ME7 .... 10 A6
Gardens The.
 Coxheath ME17 .... 96 C3
Gardens The.
 Ivychurch TN29 .... 192 F4
Gardiner St. ME7 .... 10 C6
Garfield Pl. **4** ME13 ..... 62 D7
Garfield Rd.
 Gillingham ME7 .... 10 D6
Garfield Rd. Margate CT9 .. 7 H2
Garlinge Cty Inf Sch. CT9 . 28 C8
Garlinge Cty Jun Sch. CT9 . 28 B8
Garlinge Green Rd. CT4 .. 108 E6
Garrard Ave. CT9 .... 28 B8
Garrington Cl. ME14 ...... 75 C6

Garrison Rd. ME12 .... 1 B3
Gas House Rd. ME1 .... 9 C6
Gas La. ME13 .... 63 F3
Gas Rd. Sittingbourne ME10 . 36 F5
Gas Rd. Sittingbourne ME10 . 37 C6
Gas St. CT1 .... 87 F7
Gasworks La. TN23 .... 139 B2
Gatcombe Cl.
 Chatham ME5 .... 32 A5
Gatcombe Cl.
 Maidstone ME16 .... 74 B5
Gateacre Rd. CT5 .... 43 A6
Gatefield La. **9** ME13 .... 62 D7
Gateway The. **5** CT11 .... 52 F7
Gateway The. CT14 ...... 166 E7
Gatland La. ME16 .... 74 B2
Gault Cl. ME15 .... 76 A2
Gaunt's Cl. CT14 .... 117 A4
Gayhurst Cl. ME8 .... 33 D6
Gayhurst Dr. ME10 .... 36 C5
Gaze Hill Ave. ME10 ...... 37 A3
Gazedown. TN29 .... 194 F3
Gean Cl. ME5 .... 54 A8
Genesta Ave. CT5 .... 43 B7
Genesta Cl. ME10 .... 36 C7
Geneva Ave. ME8 .... 11 A2
Gentian Cl. **4**
 Chatham ME5 .... 31 E4
Gentian Cl.
 Maidstone ME14 .... 75 E5
Geoffrey Ct. CT7 .... 27 D7
George Alley. CT14 ..... 117 D6
George Cooper Ho. **7**
 CT20 .... 178 C4
George Gurr Cres. CT19 .. 178 D8
George Hill Rd. CT10 ..... 29 F8
George La.
 Boughton Street ME13 ... 63 F3
George La.
 Folkestone CT19 .... 178 D4
George La. Leeds ME17 ... 99 B7
George St. Ashford TN23 . 139 B1
George St. Deal CT14 .... 117 D7
George St. Dover CT17 ... 149 C1
George St.
 Maidstone ME15 .... 75 A3
George St.
 Ramsgate CT11 .... 52 E7
George St.
 Sittingbourne ME10 ...... 37 B4
George Summers Cl. ME2 . 9 E8
George Warren Ct. **1** CT9 7 J1
George Wood Cl. TN29 .. 203 C6
George's Ave. CT5 .... 43 A7
George's Cl. CT5 .... 43 A7
Georgian Cl. ME11 .... 3 A3
Georgian Dr. ME17 .... 96 D3
Georgian Way. ME8 .... 33 C4
Gerald Palmby Ct. CT14 . 117 C7
Geraldine Rd. CT19 ..... 177 F6
Gerrard Ave. ME1 .... 31 E8
Gerrards Dr. ME10 .... 36 C5
Gibbons Rd. ME10 .... 36 B5
Gibraltar Ave. ME7 ...... 10 B7
Gibraltar Hill. ME4 .... 9 F4
Gibraltar La.
 Hawkinge CT18 .... 163 A2
Gibraltar La.
 Maidstone ME14 .... 74 F8
Gibraltar Sq. CT16 ..... 149 E3
Gibson St. ME10 .... 36 E4
Gidd's Pond Cotts. ME14 .. 75 E6
Giddyhorn La. ME16 ...... 74 C5
Gifford Cl. ME8 .... 11 C3
Gigger's Green Rd. TN25 . 185 C2
Gilbert Cl. ME7 .... 33 A5
Gilbert Rd. **4**
 Ashford TN23 .... 139 B2
Gilbert Rd. Ramsgate CT11 52 D8
Gilbert Terr. ME14 .... 74 F7
Gilchrist Ave. CT6 .... 22 C2
Giles Gdns. CT9 .... 28 F8
Giles La. CT2 .... 66 D4
Gilford Rd. CT14 .... 117 D5
Gilham Gr. CT14 .... 117 B7
Gill La. Mersham TN25 ... 172 A8
Gill La. Ruckinge TN26 .. 171 C2
Gillett Rd. TN29 .... 203 D7
Gillham Wood Ave. CT10 . 29 F3
Gillingham Gn. ME7 ...... 10 E6
Gillingham Rd. ME7 ...... 10 D5
Gillingham Sta. ME7 ..... 10 D5

Gillman Cl. CT18 .... 162 F4
Gillon Mews. **9** CT1 ..... 67 B2
Gills Terr. ME8 .... 12 C3
Ginsbury Cl. ME2 .... 9 E6
Giraud Dr. ME13 .... 62 B8
Glack Rd. CT14 .... 116 F4
Glade The. Chatham ME5 . 32 A2
Glade The. Deal CT14 ... 116 F6
Gladstone Dr. ME10 ...... 37 C4
Gladstone Rd.
 Ashford TN24 .... 156 E7
Gladstone Rd.
 Broadstairs CT10 .... 29 F4
Gladstone Rd. Chatham ME4 . 9 F2
Gladstone Rd. Deal CT14 . 117 C4
Gladstone Rd.
 Folkestone CT19 .... 178 E6
Gladstone Rd.
 Margate CT9 .... 7 I1
Gladstone Rd.
 Whitstable CT5 .... 20 D2
Gladwyn Cl. ME8 .... 33 D4
Glamis Cl. ME5 .... 32 A5
Glanville Rd.
 Gillingham ME7 .... 10 D5
Glanville Rd.
 Rochester ME2 .... 9 A8
Glasgow Ho. **7** ME15 ... 97 E7
Gleaming Wood Dr. ME5 .. 54 D8
Gleaners Cl. ME14 .... 75 E4
Glebe Cl.
 Biddenden Green TN27 .. 135 B2
Glebe Cl. St Margaret's
 at Cliffe CT15 .... 150 F6
Glebe Cotts. ME13 .... 81 E7
Glebe Ct. CT12 .... 50 B5
Glebe Gdns. Lenham ME17 101 E5
Glebe Gdns. **6**
 Margate CT9 .... 28 B8
Glebe La. Maidstone ME16 . 74 A1
Glebe La.
 Sittingbourne ME10 ...... 37 B2
Glebe Rd. Gillingham ME7 . 10 E3
Glebe Rd. Margate CT9 ... 28 B8
Glebe The. TN27 .... 120 D7
Glebe Way. Ashford TN24 . 139 D6
Glebe Way. Whitstable CT5 . 43 D8
Glebeland. TN27 .... 120 D7
Glebelands. Alkham CT15 . 147 D1
Glebelands. Ash CT3 ...... 71 C2
Glebelands.
 Mersham TN25 .... 157 A4
Glemsford Cotts. CT2 ..... 65 E1
Glen Ave. CT6 .... 23 C5
Glen Gr. CT17 .... 166 B7
Glen Iris Ave. CT2 .... 66 C2
Glen Iris Cl. CT2 .... 66 C2
Glen Rd. CT14 .... 134 C6
Glen The. Minster ME12 ... 4 B7
Glen The. Minster ME12 ... 4 C7
Glen The.
 Shepherdswell CT15 ..... 130 D5
Glen The. Upstreet CT3 ... 47 D3
Glen Wlk. CT5 .... 43 A3
Glenavon Ho. CT10 ...... 30 B7
Glenbervie Dr. CT6 .... 23 E5
Glenbrook Cl. CT16 ...... 23 D5
Glenbrook Gr. ME10 ..... 36 E7
Glencoe Cty Inf Sch. ME4 . 10 A2
Glencoe
 Cty Prim Sch. ME4 ...... 10 A2
Glencoe Rd. Chatham ME4 . 10 A2
Glencoe Rd. Margate CT9 .. 8 A1
Glendale Rd. ME12 .... 4 B7
Gleneagles Cl. ME5 .... 31 F2
Gleneagles Dr. ME15 ..... 75 A1
Glenfield Rd. CT16 ...... 149 B3
Glenside. CT5 .... 44 A8
Glenside Ave. CT1 .... 67 B2
Glenwood Cl. Chatham ME5 10 C1
Glenwood Cl.
 Gillingham ME7 .... 33 A7
Glenwood Cl.
 Maidstone ME16 .... 74 C5
Glenwood Cl.
 St Michaels TN30 .... 167 B3
Glenwood Dr. ME12 .... 3 E6
Glistening Glade. ME8 ... 33 E6
Globe La. ME4 .... 9 F5
Gloster Ropewalk. CT17 .. 166 C5
Gloster Way. CT17 ...... 166 C5
Gloucester Ave.
 Broadstairs CT10 .... 29 F3
Gloucester Ave.Margate CT9 8 D2
Gloucester Cl. ME8 ...... 34 A8
Gloucester Mews. TN28 .. 200 C8

Gloucester Pl. **13** CT20 .... 178 D5
Gloucester Rd.
Maidstone ME15 .... 97 D8
Gloucester Rd.
Whitstable CT5 .... 20 E2
Glover Rd. TN24 .... 139 E1
Glovers Cres. ME10 .... 36 F3
Goad Ave. ME5 .... 32 B3
Godden Rd. CT2 .... 67 A4
Goddings Dr. ME1 .... 9 A3
Goddington La. ME17 .... 100 B6
Goddington Rd. ME2 .... 9 B8
Godfrey Ho. CT5 .... 43 E8
Godfrey Wlk. TN23 .... 156 B8
Godfrey's Grave. ME13 .... 64 B7
Godfreys Cotts. ME13 .... 105 C8
Godinton
Cty Prim Sch. TN23 ...... 138 D3
Godinton La. TN23 & TN26 . 138 D5
Godinton Park. TN23 .... 138 C4
Godinton Rd. TN23 .... 139 A2
Godinton Way. TN23 .... 139 A2
Godwin Bglws. CT9 .... 8 B3
Godwin Cl. ME10 .... 14 F1
Godwin Cotts. CT9 .... 8 A3
Godwin Rd. Canterbury CT1 . 87 C6
Godwin Rd. Dover CT16 ..... 166 F8
Godwin Rd. Margate CT9 ...... 8 A3
Godwyn Gdns. CT20 .... 178 A4
Godwyn Rd. Deal CT14 ..... 117 C8
Godwyn Rd.
Folkestone CT20 .... 178 A4
Godwyne Cl. CT16 .... 166 D8
Godwyne Ct. CT16 .... 149 D1
Godwyne Rd. CT16 .... 149 D1
Gogway. CT4 .... 126 B4
Gold Hill. TN25 .... 121 D4
Goldcrest Wlk. CT5 .... 43 B6
Golden Acre La. CT8 .... 27 D7
Golden Cl. CT8 .... 27 D7
Golden Hill. CT5 .... 43 F6
Golden Sq.
New Romney TN28 .... 200 A6
Golden Sq.
Tenterden TN30 .... 179 B8
Golden St. CT14 .... 117 D7
Golden Wood Cl. ME5 .... 54 D8
Goldfinch Cl.
Faversham ME13 .... 40 C1
Goldfinch Cl. Herne Bay CT6 23 C2
Goldings The.
Gillingham ME8 .... 33 C8
Goldings The.
Monkton CT12 .... 49 C7
Goldsmith Rd. ME8 .... 33 E5
Goldstone Dro. CT3 .... 71 E7
Goldstone Wlk. ME5 .... 32 A1
Goldthorne Cl. ME14 .... 75 C5
Goldups La. CT4 & ME13 .... 84 C1
Goldups Lane Cotts. CT4 ..... 84 C1
Goldwell Cl. TN25 .... 173 A6
Goldwell Hos. TN25 .... 173 A6
Goldwell La.
Aldington TN25 .... 173 B7
Goldwell La.
Great Chart TN23 & TN26 . 154 F8
Golf Cl. CT14 .... 95 C1
Golf Rd. CT14 .... 117 C8
Golf Road Pl. CT14 .... 117 C8
Good Hope. CT14 .... 116 F4
Good Intent Cotts. TN27 ... 119 A5
Goodall Cl. ME8 .... 33 E5
Goodban Sq. CT3 .... 71 D1
Goodcheap La.
TN24 & TN25 .... 140 D2
Goodfellow Way. **3**
CT16 .... 166 D8
Goodneston
CE Prim Sch. CT3 .... 91 C2
Goodnestone Hill. CT3 .... 91 D2
Goodnestone Ho. CT3 .... 91 C1
Goodnestone Rd.
Sittingbourne ME10 .... 37 B4
Goodnestone Rd.
Wingham CT3 .... 91 B5
Goodwin Ave. CT5 .... 21 E2
Goodwin Dr. ME14 .... 75 B8
Goodwin Rd.
Ramsgate CT11 .... 52 B5
Goodwin Rd. St Margaret's
at Cliffe CT15 .... 151 A4
Goodwood Cl. ME15 .... 97 F6
Goose Cl. ME5 .... 32 A7
Gordon Ave. ME11 .... 3 A4
Gordon Cl. ME10 .... 37 C4
Gordon Cotts. ME9 .... 58 B6
Gordon Ct. ME17 .... 96 E3
Gordon Cty Jun Sch. ME2 ..... 9 A8

Gordon Gr. CT8 .... 7 C1
Gordon Rd. Canterbury CT1 . 87 F7
Gordon Rd. Chatham ME4 .... 10 B2
Gordon Rd.
Faversham ME13 .... 62 E8
Gordon Rd.
Folkestone CT20 .... 177 D6
Gordon Rd. Gillingham ME7 . 10 E5
Gordon Rd.
Gillingham,Brompton ME4 .. 10 A7
Gordon Rd. Herne Bay CT6 .. 22 F4
Gordon Rd. Margate CT9 ...... 8 A3
Gordon Rd.
Margate, Westwood CT9 .... 29 A5
Gordon Rd. Ramsgate CT11 . 52 D8
Gordon Rd. Rochester ME2 .... 9 A8
Gordon Rd. Whitfield CT16 . 149 A5
Gordon Rd. Whitstable CT5 .. 43 D8
Gordon Sq. Birchington CT7 . 26 F7
Gordon Sq.
Faversham ME13 .... 62 E7
Gordon Terr. ME1 .... 9 C4
Gore Cl. CT13 .... 93 B3
Gore Cotts. ME9 .... 12 E1
Gore Court Rd.
Park Wood ME15 .... 97 F5
Gore Court Rd.
Sittingbourne ME10 .... 36 E2
Gore End Cl. CT7 .... 26 F7
Gore La. CT13 .... 93 B2
Gore Mews. **3** CT1 .... 67 B2
Gore Rd. Eastry CT13 .... 93 B3
Gore Rd. Silver Street ME9 .. 57 F5
Gore St. CT12 .... 49 A7
Gore Terr. CT13 .... 93 B3
Goreham Rd. CT14 .... 94 C6
Gorham Dr. ME15 .... 76 A1
Gorrell Rd. CT5 .... 20 E1
Gorse Ave. ME5 .... 31 F5
Gorse La. CT6 .... 23 C2
Gorse Mead. TN23 .... 155 F8
Gorse Rd. ME10 .... 37 C5
Goschen Rd. CT17 .... 166 B8
Gosfield Rd. CT6 .... 23 A4
Goss Hall La. CT3 .... 72 A2
Gosselin St. CT5 .... 43 E8
Gothic Mere. TN24 .... 139 C7
Gothic Cl. CT14 .... 117 B1
Gothic Cotts. TN25 .... 121 A1
Goudhurst Cl.
Canterbury CT2 .... 67 A4
Goudhurst Cl.
Maidstone ME16 .... 74 E4
Goudhurst Rd. ME8 .... 11 B3
Gough Rd. CT20 .... 177 E3
Gould Rd. ME5 .... 32 B3
Grace Ave. ME16 .... 74 D6
Grace Ct. **12** CT20 .... 178 D5
Grace Hill. CT20 .... 178 D5
Grace Meadow. CT16 ...... 149 A7
Grace Rd. ME12 .... 1 B1
Grace Wlk. CT14 .... 117 A5
Grafton Ave. ME1 .... 31 E8
Grafton Rd.
Broadstairs CT10 .... 29 F8
Grafton Rd.
Sittingbourne ME10 .... 36 F4
Grafton Rise. CT6 .... 22 C4
Grain Rd. ME8 .... 33 C3
Grainey Field. ME9 .... 34 E4
Gram's Rd. CT14 .... 134 C8
Grampian Way. ME15 .... 76 A1
Grampion Cl. TN24 .... 139 C4
Granada Ho. **6** ME15 .... 75 A4
Granada St. **8** ME15 .... 75 A4
Granary Cl. Gillingham ME8 . 11 F1
Granary Cl.
Maidstone ME14 .... 75 E5
Granary Court Rd. TN25 ... 159 A4
Granary Pl. CT5 .... 43 D8
Grand Ct. TN28 .... 200 E5
Grand Dr. CT6 .... 22 C4
Grand Par. TN28 .... 200 E5
Grange Cres. TN30 .... 167 A3
Grange Cl. **1** CT20 .... 178 C4
Grange Hill. ME10 .... 10 B3
Grange Ho. ME16 .... 74 A2
Grange La. ME5 .... 54 A1
Grange Rd.
Broadstairs CT10 .... 29 F6
Grange Rd. Deal CT14 ..... 117 B5
Grange Rd.
Folkestone CT19 .... 177 E6
Grange Rd. Gillingham ME7 . 11 B5
Grange Rd. Herne Bay CT6 .. 23 C4
Grange Rd. Hythe CT21 .... 176 B4
Grange Rd. Ramsgate CT11 . 52 C6
Grange Rd. Rochester ME2 .... 9 B7
Grange Rd.
St Michaels TN30 .... 167 A3

Grange The.
Shepherdswell CT15 ...... 130 D5
Grange The. Whitstable CT5 . 43 A6
Grange Way.
Broadstairs CT10 .... 29 F2
Grange Way. Rochester ME1 . 9 C3
Grant Cl. Broadstairs CT10 .. 29 E6
Grant Cl. Gillingham ME7 .... 11 B1
Grant's Cotts. ME17 .... 101 B5
Grantham Ave. CT14 .... 117 A5
Grantley Cl. TN23 .... 156 A8
Granville Ave.
Broadstairs CT10 .... 30 B3
Granville Ave.
Ramsgate CT12 .... 29 B1
Granville Cl. ME13 .... 62 C7
Granville Dr. CT6 .... 22 B2
Granville Farm Mews. **19**
CT11 .... 52 F7
Granville Marina. **17**
CT11 .... 52 F7
Granville Par. CT20 .... 177 E3
Granville Pl. ME12 .... 1 D2
Granville Rd.
Broadstairs CT10 .... 30 B3
Granville Rd.
Gillingham ME7 .... 10 E5
Granville Rd.
Kingsdown CT14 .... 134 D3
Granville Rd.
Maidstone ME14 .... 75 A6
Granville Rd.
Sheerness ME12 .... 1 D2
Granville Rd. St Margaret's
at Cliffe CT15 .... 151 B6
Granville Rd E. CT20 .... 177 F3
Granville Rd S. CT20 .... 177 D5
Granville St. Dover CT16 ... 149 C1
Grapple Rd. ME14 .... 75 A7
Grasmere Ave. CT11 .... 52 A7
Grasmere Gdns. CT19 ...... 178 B7
Grasmere Rd.
Whitstable CT5 .... 44 B8
Grasmere Way. CT3 .... 112 F6
Grasslands. Ashford TN23 . 155 D7
Grasslands.
Langley Heath ME17 .... 98 E4
Grassmere. TN29 .... 194 E3
Grassy Glade. ME7 .... 33 B6
Gravel Castle Rd. CT4 ..... 129 A8
Gravel Hill. ME13 .... 103 C8
Gravel La. CT15 .... 165 A4
Gravel Wlk. **3**
Ashford TN23 .... 139 B3
Gravel Wlk. **12**
Canterbury CT1 .... 87 F8
Gravel Wlk. Rochester ME1 .. 9 D5
Gravelly Bottom Rd. ME17 .. 99 B2
Graveney
Cty Prim Sch. ME13 .... 41 E1
Graveney Rd.
Faversham ME13 .... 62 F7
Graveney Rd.
Maidstone ME15 .... 97 F7
Graylings Ct. ME10 .... 36 C2
Grays Way. CT1 .... 87 B6
Grayshott Cl. ME10 .... 36 F3
Graystone Rd. CT5 .... 21 A2
Great Basin Rd. ME12 .... 1 A2
Great Burton Ho. TN24 .... 139 E5
Great Chart
Cty Prim Sch. TN23 ...... 155 D8
Great Conduit St. CT21 .... 176 C2
Great Ivy Mill Cotts. ME15 . 96 F7
Great Lines. ME7 .... 10 B5
Great South Ave. ME4 ...... 10 A1
Greatstone Halt. TN28 .... 200 D3
Greatstone
Prim Sch. TN28 .... 200 D2
Grebe Apartments. **13**
ME15 .... 97 E5
Grebe Cl. CT18 .... 163 A4
Grebe Cres. CT21 .... 187 C8
Grecian St. ME14 .... 75 A6
Green Acres. CT15 .... 131 D7
Green Acres Cl. CT6 .... 23 B3
Green Bank Cl. ME7 .... 33 A5
Green Cl. ME1 .... 9 D2
Green Cloth Mews. **2** CT1 . 67 B2
Green Ct. Bridge CT4 .... 89 A1
Green Ct. Folkestone CT19 . 178 E7
Green Dell. CT2 .... 66 F4
Green Gates. CT16 .... 149 A8
Green Hedges. TN30 ...... 179 B8
Green Hill. ME15 .... 76 B1
Green Hill La. ME17 ...... 100 D1
Green Hills. CT4 .... 128 D8
Green La. Ashford TN23 ... 155 E5

Greenhouse La. CT2 .... 66 E2
Greenly Way. TN28 .... 200 C6
Greensand Rd. ME15 .... 76 A2
Greenside.
High Halden TN26 .... 167 E7
Greenside.
Maidstone ME15 .... 75 B3
Greenvale Gdns. ME8 ...... 11 B2
Greenview Wlk. ME8 .... 11 A4
Greenway. Chatham ME5 ... 31 D6
Greenways.
Faversham ME13 .... 62 B8
Greenway Court
Farm Cotts. ME17 .... 78 A1
Greenway Court Rd. ME17 .. 78 A1
Greenway La. ME17 .... 100 A7
Greenways.
Lower Halstow ME9 .... 13 B3
Greenways.
Maidstone ME14 .... 75 F5
Greenways.
Sittingbourne ME10 .... 37 B3
Greenwich Cl.
Chatham ME5 .... 32 B4
Greenwich Cl.
Maidstone ME16 .... 74 D4
Gregory Cl. Gillingham ME8 . 33 E4
Gregory Cl.
Sittingbourne ME10 .... 37 A8
Gregory Ct. TN25 .... 123 E2
Grenham Bay Ave. CT7 ..... 26 E8
Grenham Rd. CT7 .... 26 F8
Grenville Gdns. CT7 .... 26 E8
Grenville Way. CT10 .... 29 E4
Gresham Ave. CT9 .... 7 E1
Gresham Rd. ME17 .... 96 D3
Greville Homes. CT13 ...... 93 B2
Grey Friars Gdns. **6** CT1 .. 87 F8
Grey Wethers. ME14 .... 53 E4
Grey Willow Gdns. TN23 .. 155 D8
Greyfriars Cl. ME16 .... 74 D5
Greyfriars Ct. CT10 .... 8 F1
Greystones Rd. ME15 ...... 76 A2
Greystones Sch. TN24 .... 139 F1
Grieveson Ho. ME4 .... 10 A4
Griffin Cotts. TN26 .... 181 C2
Griffin St. CT14 .... 117 D7
Griffin's Cnr. TN25 .... 140 E7
Grimshill Ct. CT2 .... 66 C4
Grimshill Rd. CT5 .... 43 E8
Grimston Ave. CT20 .... 178 B4
Grimston Gdns. CT20 ...... 178 B4
Grimthorpe Ave. CT5 .... 43 C7
Grinsell Hill. CT12 .... 50 E6
Grisbrook Farm Cl. TN29 . 203 D6
Grisbrook Rd. TN29 .... 203 D6
Grizedale Cl. ME1 .... 31 D8
Groombridge Sq. **13**
ME15 .... 97 F6
Grosvenor Ave. ME1 & ME4 . 9 E3
Grosvenor Gdns. CT9 .... 7 I1
Grosvenor Hill. CT9 .... 7 I2
Grosvenor Pl. CT9 .... 7 I2
Grosvenor Rd.
Ashford TN24 .... 139 D7
Grosvenor Rd.
Broadstairs CT10 .... 30 A4
Grosvenor Rd.
Gillingham ME7 .... 11 A1
Grosvenor Rd.
Ramsgate CT11 .... 52 C7
Grosvenor Rd.
Whitstable CT5 .... 43 D7
Grotto Gdns. CT9 .... 7 J2
Grotto Hill. CT9 .... 7 J2
Grotto Rd. **5** CT9 .... 7 J2
Grove Ave. ME12 .... 6 G2
Grove Cl. ME13 .... 62 A6
Grove Cotts. TN30 .... 179 B6
Grove Court Farm. ME13 ... 64 A3
Grove Ferry Hill. CT3 .... 47 E3
Grove Ferry Rd. CT3 .... 48 A2
Grove Gdns. **6** CT9 .... 7 G1
Grove Green La. ME14 ...... 75 E5
Grove Green Rd. ME14 ..... 75 F5
Grove Ho. TN27 .... 136 C3
Grove La. TN29 .... 191 D3
Grove Park Ave. ME10 ...... 36 B5
Grove Park
Cty Prim Sch. ME10 .... 36 B6
Grove Rd. Chatham ME4 .... 10 B2
Grove Rd. Deal CT14 ...... 117 D3
Grove Rd. Folkestone CT20 178 E6
Grove Rd. Gillingham ME7 .. 11 A6
Grove Rd. Maidstone ME15 . 97 C7
Grove Rd. Preston CT3 ...... 70 B8
Grove Rd. Ramsgate CT11 .. 52 B8
Grove Rd. Rochester ME2 .... 9 B8
Grove Rd. Selling ME13 .... 84 B1
Grove Rd. Staple CT3 .... 91 F6

Green La.
Bethersden TN26 .... 153 A2
Green La. Boughton
Monchelsea ME17 .... 97 C3
Green La. Broadstairs CT10 . 29 E5
Green La. Capel-le-F CT18 . 164 B3
Green La. Challock TN25 ... 105 A2
Green La. Chilham CT4 ...... 85 D7
Green La. Deal CT14 .... 117 B1
Green La. Dover CT16 ...... 149 B3
Green La.
Ewell Minnis CT15 .... 147 D3
Green La. Eythorne CT15 .. 131 D7
Green La. Folkestone CT19 . 178 E7
Green La.
Goodnestone CT3 .... 92 B3
Green La. Hythe CT21 ...... 176 A2
Green La.
Langley Heath ME17 .... 98 E3
Green La. Margate CT9 ...... 29 E8
Green La.
Platt's Heath ME17 .... 100 F2
Green La.
Rhodes Minnis CT4 .... 143 E2
Green La.
Rodmersham ME9 .... 59 B7
Green La. Smarden TN27 ... 135 A1
Green La. St Margaret's
at Cliffe CT15 .... 133 F1
Green La. Stockbury ME9 ... 34 F1
Green La.
Temple Ewell CT16 .... 148 E8
Green La. Whitfield CT16 .. 148 E7
Green La. Whitstable CT5 .. 44 B8
Green Lane Ave. CT21 ..... 176 A2
Green Lane Cotts. ME17 .... 98 E3
Green Leas. CT5 .... 21 D1
Green Lees. ME13 .... 61 E2
Green Meadows. TN29 .... 186 D2
Green Porch Cl. ME10 ...... 36 F7
Green Rd. Birchington CT7 . 26 F8
Green Rd.
Stalisfield Green ME13 ... 103 C6
Green Sands. ME14 .... 54 C8
Green St. ME7 .... 10 C5
Green The. Blean CT2 ...... 66 A6
Green The.
Burmarsh TN29 .... 189 A4
Green The. Chartham CT4 .. 86 D3
Green The.
East Farleigh ME15 .... 96 B7
Green The.
Harbledown CT2 .... 65 E1
Green The. Hythe CT21 .... 176 B4
Green The. Littlebourne CT3 89 F7
Green The.
Lower Halstow ME9 .... 13 B3
Green The. Lydd TN29 ..... 203 B5
Green The. Manston CT12 .. 28 D1
Green The. Sheerness ME12 .. 1 I1
Green The.
Woodchurch TN26 .... 169 A2
Green The. Wye TN25 ..... 123 C2
Green Way. Lydd TN29 .... 203 C5
Green Way.
Maidstone ME16 .... 74 B3
Green's Cotts. ME15 .... 96 A4
Greenacre. CT4 .... 111 D3
Greenacre Cl. ME5 .... 32 A5
Greenacre Dr. CT14 .... 117 C1
Greenacre Sch. ME5 .... 31 F5
Greenbank. Ashford TN24 . 139 D6
Greenbank. Chatham ME5 .. 32 B8
Greenbanks. CT18 .... 161 C6
Greenborough Cl. ME15 .... 97 E6
Greenfinches. ME7 .... 32 F6
Greenhill Bridge Rd. CT6 ... 22 D3
Greenhill Cl. CT12 .... 50 B7
Greenhill Gdns.
Herne Bay CT6 .... 22 D3
Greenhill Gdns.
Minster, Thanet CT12 ...... 50 B7
Greenhill La. TN27 .... 135 F8
Greenhill Rd. CT6 .... 22 C2
Greenhithe. **3** ME15 .... 75 A3

Grove Rd.
Wickhambreaux CT3 .... 69 D6
Grove Road Cotts.
Wickhambreaux CT3 .... 69 C2
Grove Road Cotts.
Wickhambreaux CT3 .... 69 C3
Grove Terr. CT1 .... 87 E7
Grove The. Ashford TN24 .... 139 E6
Grove The. Barham CT4 .... 128 F8
Grove The. Deal CT14 .... 117 C6
Grove The. Dover CT16 .... 149 C1
Grove The. Herne Bay CT6 .... 22 C2
Grove The.
Maidstone ME14 .... 76 A3
Grove The.
Westgate-on-S CT8 .... 27 F8
Grove Way. CT3 .... 70 C7
Grovehurst Ave. ME10 .... 14 F1
Grovehurst Rd.
ME10 & ME9 .... 14 E2
Grovelands. ME17 .... 101 E5
Groveway. ME2 .... 6 F2
Growewood Dr. ME14 .... 75 E4
Grummock Ave. CT11 .... 52 B7
Grundy's Hill. CT11 .... 52 E6
Guardian Ct. CT4 .... 88 C1
Guildcourt La. CT13 .... 72 F1
Guildford Ave. CT6 .... 27 E8
Guildford Lawn. **1** CT11 .... 52 E6
Guildford Rd. CT11 .... 87 F6
Guildhall St. **4**
Canterbury CT1 .... 87 F8
Guildhall St. **14**
Folkestone CT20 .... 178 D5
Guildhall St N.
CT19 & CT20 .... 178 D5
Guilford Ave. CT16 .... 149 A8
Guilford Ct. CT14 .... 117 D2
Guilford Rd. CT13 .... 94 E8
Guilton. CT3 .... 71 B1
Guldeford La.
TN29 & TN31 .... 196 F3
Guldeford Lane Cnr.
TN31 .... 196 D2
Gullands. ME17 .... 98 E4
Gun La. ME2 .... 9 B7
Gundulph Rd. ME1 & ME4 ...... 9 E4
Gundulph Sq. ME1 .... 9 E4
Gunnis Cl. ME8 .... 33 D4
Gurling Rd. CT15 .... 133 F1
Guston
CE Prim Sch. CT16 .... 149 E3
Guston Rd. ME14 .... 75 C6
Guy Cl. CT10 .... 30 A7
Gwyn Rd. CT12 .... 29 C2
Gypsy Cnr. CT2 .... 44 D3

Hackfield. TN23 .... 138 F1
Hackington Cl. CT2 .... 66 E4
Hackington Pl. CT2 .... 66 F2
Hackington Rd. CT2 .... 66 E7
Hackington Terr. CT2 .... 66 F2
Hacklinge Hill. CT14 .... 94 B2
Hackney Rd. ME16 .... 74 C2
Haddon Dene Sch. CT10 ...... 29 F4
Hadleigh Ct. ME7 .... 33 B3
Hadleigh Gdns. CT6 .... 23 B5
Hadley Gdns. ME17 .... 77 E2
Hadlow Coll of Agriculture &
Horticulture (Horticultural
Unit). CT1 .... 88 B8
Hadlow Dr. CT9 .... 8 E2
Hadlow Rd. ME14 .... 75 C5
Haffenden Meadow.
TN27 .... 120 C8
Haffenden Rd. TN30 .... 167 B1
Haig Ave. Chatham ME1 ...... 9 D1
Haig Ave.
Chatham,Luton ME4 .... 10 A2
Haig Ave. Gillingham ME7 ...... 10 E4
Haine Hospl. CT12 .... 29 A4
Haine Ind Est. CT12 .... 28 F1
Haine Rd. CT12 & CT10 ...... 28 F2
Halden Cl. ME15 .... 97 F6
Hales Cl. TN30 .... 179 B8
Hales Ct. TN30 .... 179 B8
Hales Dr. CT2 .... 66 F3
Hales Rd. ME10 .... 36 D1
Haleys Pl. ME1 .... 53 A8
Halfmile Ride. CT9 .... 28 E6
Halford Cl. CT6 .... 23 B2
Halfpenny Cl. ME16 .... 74 A2
Halfway Houses
Prim Sch. ME12 .... 3 D6
Halfway Rd. ME12 .... 3 D8
Halifax. ME5 .... 32 B6
Hall Cl. ME10 .... 36 E6
Hall Cres. CT14 .... 116 F5
Hall Rd. ME5 .... 32 C3
Hallcroft Ct. CT11 .... 52 C7
Hallett Wlk. **10** CT1 .... 67 B2

Halliday Ct. CT21 .... 176 A2
Hallsfield Rd. ME5 .... 31 D2
Hallwood Cl. ME8 .... 33 D5
Hallwood Ho. ME5 .... 32 C2
Halstatt Rd. CT14 .... 117 A3
Halstead Cl. CT2 .... 67 B4
Halstead Gdns. CT9 .... 8 F3
Halstead Wlk. ME16 .... 74 C7
Halstow Cl. ME15 .... 97 B6
Halstow Way. ME3 .... 155 F8
Halt The. Elham CT4 .... 144 F4
Halt The. Whitstable CT5 ...... 44 A7
Ham Farm Cotts. CT14 ...... 93 F2
Ham La. Gillingham ME5 ...... 32 E3
Ham La. Lenham ME17 ...... 101 C5
Ham Mill La.
Snargate TN29 .... 191 F8
Ham Mill La.
Warehorne TN26 & TN29 ...183 A2
Ham Rd. ME12 .... 40 C1
Ham Shades La. CT5 .... 21 A1
Ham Street Sta. TN26 ...... 183 A8
Hambledon Cl. ME16 .... 74 B3
Hambrook Cl. CT4 .... 107 B8
Hambrook La. CT14 .... 107 C8
Hambrook Wlk. ME10 ...... 36 F8
Hamele The. CT2 .... 67 F5
Hamelin Rd. ME7 .... 32 F8
Hamilton Cl. CT12 .... 29 B1
Hamilton Cres. ME16 .... 36 C3
Hamilton Ho. ME17 .... 96 C3
Hamilton Rd.
Ashford TN24 .... 156 D6
Hamilton Rd. Deal CT14 ...... 117 C4
Hamilton Rd. Dover CT17 .... 166 B8
Hamilton Rd.
Gillingham ME7 .... 10 D7
Hamilton Rd. Lydd TN29 .... 203 C6
Hamilton Rd.
Whitstable CT5 .... 20 D1
Hammond Cl. CT15 .... 113 E5
Hammond's Cnr. TN29 ...... 199 E6
Hammond's Rd. CT20 ...... 177 E5
Hamond Hill. ME4 .... 9 E4
Hampden La. TN23 .... 156 A7
Hampden Mews. TN23 .... 156 A7
Hampden Rd. TN23 .... 156 A6
Hampshire Cl. ME5 .... 32 C7
Hampshire Dr. ME15 .... 97 C8
Hampshire Rd. CT1 .... 88 D7
Hampson Way. ME14 ...... 76 A4
Hampton Cl. Chatham ME5 .. 32 A5
Hampton Cl. Herne Bay CT6 . 22 A3
Hampton Cty Prim Sch
(Jun & Inf). CT6 .... 22 C4
Hampton Gdns. CT6 .... 22 A3
Hampton La. TN25 .... 141 C3
Hampton Pier Ave. CT6 ...... 22 B4
Hampton Rd. ME14 .... 75 C6
Hampton Vale. CT21 .... 177 B4
Hamstreet Rd.
Bromley Green TN26 ...... 170 E5
Hamstreet Rd.
Hamstreet TN25 & TN26 ... 183 C7
Hamwick Gn. ME5 .... 32 C1
Hancocks Field. CT14 .... 117 A5
Hangman's La.
Ringwould CT14 .... 133 F5
Hangman's La.Ripple CT14 .. 133 D5
Hanover Cl. Ashford TN23 ... 138 F2
Hanover Cl. Deal CT14 ...... 117 D2
Hanover Cl. Margate CT9 ...... 8 E2
Hanover Cl.
Sittingbourne ME10 .... 36 E2
Hanover Ct.
Faversham ME13 .... 62 B8
Hanover Ct. Hythe CT21 .... 176 C1
Hanover Ct.
Maidstone ME14 .... 75 B5
Hanover Dr. ME8 .... 33 C4
Hanover Pl. CT2 .... 66 F2
Hanover Rd. ME17 .... 96 C3
Hanover Sq. CT6 .... 22 F5
Hanover St. CT6 .... 22 F5
Hanscomb Ho. CT2 .... 66 E2
Hanslett's La. ME13 .... 61 D3
Hanway. ME8 .... 11 A2
Harbledown Gdns. CT9 ...... 8 E3
Harbledown Manor. ME8 ...... 11 B3
Harbledown Pk. CT2 .... 66 C1
Harbour Approach Rd.
CT20 .... 178 E4
Harbour Par. CT11 .... 52 E6
Harbour Point. CT19 .... 178 F5
Harbour Sch The. CT15 .... 165 E7
Harbour St.
Broadstairs CT10 .... 30 B4
Harbour St.
Folkestone CT20 .... 178 E5
Harbour St.
Ramsgate CT11 .... 52 E6

Harbour St.
Whitstable CT5 .... 20 D2
Harbour Twrs. **13** CT11 ...... 52 E6
Harbour Way. CT20 .... 178 E5
Harbourland Cl. ME14 ...... 75 B8
Harbourne La.
TN26 & TN30 .... 167 E5
Harbour Dr.
Canterbury CT2 .... 66 D2
Harcourt Dr.
Herne Bay CT6 .... 22 B5
Harcourt Gdns. ME8 .... 33 E4
Harcourt Prim Sch. CT19 .... 177 E7
Harcourt Rd. CT19 .... 177 F7
Harden Rd. TN29 .... 203 D7
Hardinge Cl. ME8 .... 33 D4
Hardinge Rd. TN24 .... 139 C3
Hardres Court Rd.
Lower Hardres CT4 .... 110 A3
Hardres Court Rd.
Stelling Minnis CT4 .... 126 F6
Hardres Rd. CT11 .... 52 E8
Hardres St. CT11 .... 52 E7
Hards Town. ME4 .... 10 A4
Hardwick Ho. **1** ME4 ...... 9 F8
Hardwick Rd. CT20 .... 178 A4
Hardwicke Rd. CT17 .... 166 B6
Hardy Cl. Ashford TN24 .... 157 A7
Hardy Cl. Canterbury CT2 .... 66 C1
Hardy Cl. Chatham ME5 ...... 32 B6
Hardy Rd.
Littlestone-on-S TN28 ...... 200 D3
Hardy Rd. St Margaret's
at Cliffe CT15 .... 150 E8
Hardy St. ME14 .... 75 A6
Hare St. **2** ME4 .... 10 B3
Harebell Cl. **3**
Chatham ME5 .... 31 F4
Harebell Cl.
Maidstone ME14 .... 75 E5
Haredale Cl. ME1 .... 31 D7
Harkness Cl. ME10 .... 37 B4
Harkness Dr. CT2 .... 66 E2
Harman Ave. CT21 .... 174 F3
Harman Ct. ME5 .... 32 B3
Harmers Way. TN27 .... 118 F3
Harmsworth Gdns. CT10 ...... 30 A5
Harnet St. CT13 .... 72 F1
Harold Ave. Gillingham ME7 . 10 E4
Harold Ave.
Westgate-on-S CT8 .... 27 E8
Harold Cl. ME13 .... 62 C6
Harold Rd. Birchington CT7 ... 26 E8
Harold Rd. Deal CT14 ...... 117 D8
Harold Rd. Margate CT9 ...... 8 B3
Harold Rd.
Sittingbourne ME10 .... 37 B4
Harold St. Dover CT16 ...... 166 D8
Harold St.
Queenborough ME11 .... 3 A4
Harold's Rd. CT16 .... 166 E8
Harp Farm Rd. ME14 ...... 54 C6
Harper Rd. TN23 .... 155 F8
Harple La. ME14 .... 54 F1
Harps Ave. ME12 .... 4 C6
Harpswood. ME17 .... 77 F1
Harpswood La. CT21 .... 176 A4
Harptree Dr. ME5 .... 31 F5
Harrier Dr. ME10 .... 37 A2
Harrietsham Sta. ME17 .... 100 D6
Harringe La. TN25 .... 174 A6
Harriot Cl. CT19 .... 178 B7
Harris Gdns. ME10 .... 37 C5
Harris Rd. ME12 .... 1 D2
Harris's Alley. CT15 .... 91 A7
Harrison Rd. **4** CT11 ...... 52 D6
Harrison Terr. ME13 .... 40 A2
Harrow Ct. Chatham ME5 .... 32 C4
Harrow Ct. Stockbury ME9 .. 56 D8
Harrow Dene. CT10 .... 29 E6
Harrow Rd. ME7 .... 32 F6
Harrow Way. ME14 .... 75 E5
Harry Wells Rd. CT6 .... 22 B3
Harrys Rd. ME9 .... 38 D3
Hart Cl. CT18 .... 163 A4
Hart Hill. TN27 .... 103 A2
Hart St. ME16 .... 74 F3
Hart St Commercial Ctr.
ME16 .... 74 F3
Hartington St. ME4 .... 10 A3
Hartley Cl. ME15 .... 97 F6
Hartlip Cl. ME12 .... 4 A6
Hartlip Endowed
CE Prim Sch. ME9 .... 34 D5
Hartlip Hill. ME9 .... 34 F7
Hartnup St. ME16 .... 74 C2
Hartpiece Cl. ME8 .... 11 F2
Harts Cotts. TN26 .... 183 A8
Harts La. **6** CT5 .... 20 D2
Hartsdown Sch. CT9 .... 28 D8

Harty Ave. ME8 .... 33 C3
Harty Ferry Cotts. ME13 ...... 40 C5
Harty Ferry Rd. ME12 .... 18 E4
Harty Terr. ME12 .... 5 A5
Harvest Way. TN23 .... 155 D7
Harvesters Cl. ME8 .... 33 E7
Harvesters Way. ME14 ...... 75 D4
Harvey Dr.
Sittingbourne ME10 .... 37 A2
Harvey Dr. Whitstable CT5 ... 21 B1
Harvey Gram Sch
for Boys The. CT19 .... 178 B6
Harvey Rd. **8**
Folkestone CT20 .... 178 D5
Harvey Rd. **7**
Folkestone CT20 .... 178 E5
Harvey Rd. Ashford TN24 ... 139 F1
Harvey Rd. Gillingham ME8 .. 33 E8
Harvey St. CT20 .... 178 E5
Harville Rd. TN25 .... 123 C2
Harwich St. CT5 .... 43 D8
Harwick Dr. TN28 .... 200 C8
Harwood Ho. TN25 .... 123 E1
Harwood Rd. ME8 .... 12 B1
Hasborough Rd. CT19 .... 178 F6
Haskard Cl. CT18 .... 162 F4
Haslemere Est. ME15 .... 97 F5
Haslewood Cl. TN27 .... 135 B2
Hassall Reach. CT1 .... 87 B6
Hassell St. CT4 & TN25 ...... 124 F2
Haste Hill Cl. ME17 .... 97 B3
Haste Hill Rd. ME17 .... 97 B3
Hasted Dr. ME9 .... 35 B7
Hasteds. ME17 .... 77 D2
Hastings Ave. CT9 .... 8 A1
Hastings Pl. CT13 .... 93 F8
Hastings Rd. ME15 .... 75 B3
Hatch La. CT4 .... 86 C5
Hatch Rd. ME17 .... 101 C5
Hatch St. **3** ME13 .... 62 C7
Hatfield Rd. Margate CT9 ...... 7 G2
Hatfield Rd.
Ramsgate CT11 .... 52 D7
Hatfield Rd. Rochester ME2 ... 9 A8
Hathaway Cl.
Gillingham ME8 .... 33 D8
Hathaway Ct.
Rochester ME1 .... 9 B5
Hatherall Rd. ME14 .... 75 B6
Hatherley Ct. CT9 .... 8 A3
Hatton Rd. ME5 .... 32 C3
Havant Wlk. **8** ME15 ...... 97 F6
Havelock Pl. CT3 .... 117 C3
Havelock Rd. CT14 .... 117 C3
Havelock St. CT1 .... 67 A1
Haven Cl. ME1 .... 9 C2
Haven Dr. Hawkinge CT18 ... 163 A4
Haven Dr. Herne Bay CT6 ...... 23 F6
Haven The. Ashford TN23 .. 155 F5
Haven The. Brenzett TN29 .. 192 A3
Haven The. Hythe CT21 .... 187 C8
Haventhorpe. TN24 .... 139 C3
Havisham Cl. ME1 .... 9 D2
Havock La. **1** ME14 ...... 74 F4
Hawbeck Rd. ME8 .... 33 C3
Hawe Cl. CT2 .... 67 A4
Hawe Farm Way. CT6 .... 23 B2
Hawe La. CT2 & CT3 .... 68 A7
Hawes Ave. CT11 .... 52 B7
Hawk Cl. CT5 .... 43 C7
Hawk's La. CT1 .... 87 F8
Hawkesbury St. CT17 ...... 166 D5
Hawkhurst Cl. CT7 .... 27 B8
Hawkhurst Rd. ME8 .... 11 B3
Hawkhurst Way. CT10 ...... 30 A2
Hawkinge CP Sch. CT18 .... 163 B4
Hawkins Cl. Chatham ME4 .. 10 A6
Hawkins Cl.
Sittingbourne ME10 .... 36 E7
Hawkins Rd. CT19 .... 177 D6
Hawkins Rd. CT6 .... 22 B2
Hawks Way. TN23 .... 155 E7
Hawksdown. CT14 .... 134 B8
Hawksdown Rd. CT14 .... 134 C8
Hawkshill Activity Ctr.
CT14 .... 134 C7
Hawkshill Rd. CT14 .... 134 D8
Hawkwood. ME16 .... 74 B5
Hawkwood Cl. ME15 .... 9 D5
Hawley Cl. ME16 .... 74 E4
Hawley Sq. CT9 .... 7 I2
Hawley St. CT9 .... 7 I2
Hawser Rd. ME1 .... 9 C1
Hawthorn. TN26 .... 190 D8
Hawthorn Ave.
Canterbury CT2 .... 67 A2
Hawthorn Ave.
West Minster ME12 .... 3 A8
Hawthorn Cl. Hythe CT21 ... 187 E8
Hawthorn Cl.
Ramsgate CT11 .... 29 E1

Hawthorn Cl. River CT17 ...... 148 E2
Hawthorn Cl.
St Mary's Bay TN29 .... 194 F3
Hawthorn Cl.
Womenswold CT3 .... 112 E4
Hawthorn Cnr.
Herne Bay CT6 .... 24 A3
Hawthorn Cnr.
Old Romney TN29 .... 198 E3
Hawthorn Ho. **5** ME5 ...... 31 F5
Hawthorn Rd.
Kingsnorth TN23 .... 156 B4
Hawthorn Rd.
Sittingbourne ME10 .... 36 E4
Hawthorne Ave. ME8 .... 11 C2
Hawthorne Cl. CT15 .... 131 D7
Hawthorns. ME5 .... 31 F1
Hawthorns The. CT10 ...... 29 C4
Hay Hill. CT13 & CT14 ...... 93 D2
Hay La. CT14 .... 93 F2
Hayes Alley. **11** CT5 ...... 20 D2
Hayes La. ME9 .... 56 F6
Hayfields. ME5 .... 32 D2
Hayle Mill Cotts. ME15 ...... 96 F8
Hayle Mill Rd. ME15 .... 96 F8
Hayle Rd. ME15 .... 75 A3
Haymakers La. TN23 ...... 155 D8
Haymen St. ME4 .... 9 E3
Hayrick Cl. ME14 .... 75 E5
Haysel. ME10 .... 37 A2
Hayton Rd. TN25 .... 160 A2
Haywain Cl. ME14 .... 75 F4
Hayward Ave. ME2 .... 9 B8
Hayward Cl. Ashford TN24 .. 157 A8
Hayward Cl. Deal CT14 .... 117 A4
Hayward's Hill. CT13 .... 82 C4
Hayward's Hill. ME13 .... 82 C4
Hazebrouck Rd. ME13 ...... 62 A7
Hazel Ave. ME16 .... 74 C5
Hazel Cl. CT15 .... 131 C7
Hazel Gr. Chatham ME5 ...... 32 B8
Hazel Gr. Sheerness ME12 ...... 1 H1
Hazel Street Rd. ME9 .... 57 A4
Hazel Wlk. CT10 .... 29 C4
Hazeldene. ME12 .... 5 F6
Hazeldown Cl. CT17 .... 148 E2
Hazelmere Dr. CT6 .... 23 D5
Hazels The. ME8 .... 33 B5
Hazelwood Dr. ME16 ...... 74 B4
Hazelwood Meadow. CT13 ... 93 F7
Hazelmere Dr. ME7 .... 11 A5
Hazelmere Rd. CT15 .... 43 A7
Hazling Dane. CT15 .... 130 F5
Hazlitt Dr. ME16 .... 74 D5
Head Hill. ME13 .... 63 D7
Head Hill Rd. ME13 .... 63 D8
Head Race The. ME15 ...... 74 D2
Headcorn Dr. CT2 .... 67 B4
Headcorn Gdns. CT9 .... 8 E2
Headcorn Rd.
Gillingham ME8 .... 11 B4
Headcorn Rd.
Sandway ME17 .... 101 A2
Headingley Rd. ME16 ...... 74 B6
Head Way. ME10 .... 37 B5
Heart In Hand Cot. CT6 ...... 23 F2
Heart In Hand Rd. CT6 ...... 23 F2
Hearts Delight Rd. ME9 ...... 36 B1
Heath Cl. CT2 .... 67 F7
Heath Cl. CT15 .... 150 F6
Heath Dr. ME16 .... 74 A2
Heath Ho. CT3 .... 46 E5
Heath Rd. Coxheath ME17 ... 96 C3
Heath Rd.
Langley Heath ME17 ...... 98 E4
Heath Rd.
Maidstone ME16 .... 74 A2
Heath The. CT5 .... 21 B1
Heath Villas. TN26 .... 181 C2
Heather Cl. Chatham ME5 .... 31 F4
Heather Cl. Margate CT9 ...... 28 C8
Heather Cl.
Sittingbourne ME10 .... 37 A3
Heather Dr.
Maidstone ME15 .... 75 B2
Heather Dr.
St Michaels TN30 .... 167 B3
Heatherwood Cl. ME17 .... 99 E2
Heatherwood Dr. ME17 .... 98 E4
Heathfield Ave.
Dover CT15 .... 149 B2
Heathfield Ave.
Maidstone ME14 .... 75 C7
Heathfield Bglws. ME17 .... 102 B1
Heathfield Cl.
Chatham ME5 .... 32 B7
Heathfield Cl.
Maidstone ME14 .... 75 B7

Heathfield Rd.
Ashford TN24 .... 139 C3
Heathfield Rd.
Maidstone ME14 .... 75 C7
Heathfield Way. CT4 .... 128 F8
Heathorn St. ME14 .... 75 B5
Heathside. TN26 .... 181 C1
Heathside Ave. ME17 .... 96 C4
Heathwood Dr. CT11 .... 29 E1
Heaton Rd. CT1 .... 87 F6
Hedgend Ind Est. CT7 .... 25 F3
Hedgerow The. ME14 .... 75 E5
Hedgerows. TN23 .... 155 D7
Hedges The. ME14 .... 75 A7
Hedley St. ME14 .... 75 A5
Heel La. CT2 .... 67 C8
Heel Rd. ME13 .... 104 B7
Heights Terr. CT17 .... 166 C6
Heights The. CT5 .... 43 C6
Helding Cl. CT6 .... 23 B2
Helena Ave. CT9 .... 28 E8
Helena Corniche. CT20 ..... 177 C3
Helena Rd. CT18 .... 164 C2
Helmdon Cl. CT12 .... 29 C2
Helvellyn Ave. CT11 .... 52 B7
Hempstead
  Cty Jun Sch. ME7 .... 33 A5
Hempstead
  Cty Prim Sch. ME7 .... 33 A5
Hempstead La. ME9 .... 37 E3
Hempstead Rd.
  Gillingham ME7 .... 33 A5
*Hempstead Rd.
  Gillingham ME8 .... 33 B6
Hempstead Valley Dr. ME7 . 33 A4
Hempstead Valley Sh Ctr.
  ME7 .... 33 A4
Hempsted St. **11** TN23 ..... 139 B2
Henbane Cl. ME4 .... 31 C3
Hendon Bsns Ctr. TN24 ... 139 D2
Hengest Rd. CT14 .... 117 D7
Hengist Ave. CT9 .... 8 B1
Hengist Rd. Birchington CT7 26 C7
Hengist Rd.
  Westgate-on-S CT8 .... 27 E8
Henley Bsns Pk. ME2 .... 9 D7
Henley Cl. Chatham ME5 ..... 32 A6
Henley Cl. Gillingham ME8 ... 33 D8
Henley Fields.
  Maidstone ME14 .... 75 E6
Henley Fields.
  St Michaels TN30 .... 167 B2
Henley Meadows. TN30 ... 167 A2
Henley View. TN30 .... 167 B2
Henniker Cl. CT16 .... 149 A5
Henry Ct. **9** CT1 .... 87 F7
Henry Rd. CT1 .... 87 F7
Henry St. Chatham ME4 .... 10 B3
Henry St. Gillingham ME8 ... 12 A1
Henwood. TN24 .... 139 D3
Hera Ho. ME12 .... 1 C2
Herbert Dane Ct. **10**
  ME13 .... 62 D7
Herbert Rd. Ashford TN24 . 156 D6
Herbert Rd. Chatham ME4 ... 10 A3
Herbert Rd.
  Gillingham ME8 .... 33 E8
Herbert Rd.
  Ramsgate CT11 .... 52 C6
Herbert St. CT17 .... 149 B1
Herdson Rd. CT20 .... 178 A5
Hereford Cl. ME8 .... 11 D2
Hereford Gdns. CT7 .... 26 F6
Hereford Rd. ME15 .... 97 D7
Hereson Rd. CT11 .... 52 F8
Hereson Sch The. CT11 ..... 52 F8
Hereward Ave. CT7 .... 26 E8
Heritage Dr. ME7 .... 10 F1
Heritage Rd. Chatham ME5 . 32 A6
Heritage Rd.
  Folkestone CT20 .... 177 D6
Herman Terr. ME4 .... 10 A3
Hermitage Cl. CT21 .... 176 B2
Hermitage La.
  Detling ME14 .... 55 B4
Hermitage La.
  Maidstone ME16 .... 74 A4
Herne Ave. CT6 .... 23 A4
Herne Bay
  Cty Prim & Inf Sch. CT6 .. 22 F4
Herne Bay Golf Course.
  CT6 .... 22 F2
Herne Bay High Sch. CT6 .. 22 D3
Herne Bay Jun Sch. CT6 ... 22 F4
Herne Bay Rd.
  Whitstable CT5 .... 21 C3

Herne Bay Sta. CT6 .... 22 E3
Herne CE Inf Sch. CT6 .... 46 B8
Herne CE Jun Sch. CT6 ...... 46 A8
Herne Ct. CT19 .... 177 C6
Herne Dr. CT6 .... 22 C2
Herne Rd. ME8 .... 11 C2
Herne St. CT6 .... 46 A8
Herneville Gdns. CT6 .... 23 B4
Hernhill
  CE Prim Sch. ME13 .... 64 B6
Hero Wlk. ME1 .... 31 C7
Heron Apartments. **8**
  ME15 .... 97 F5
Heron Cl. ME9 .... 13 B3
Heron Forestall Ave.
  CT18 .... 163 B4
Heron Way. ME5 .... 32 B7
Heron Wlk. TN23 .... 155 E8
Heron's Brook. TN25 .... 140 E6
Heron's Way. CT21 .... 187 D8
Heronden Rd. Eastry CT13 .. 92 F1
Heronden Rd.
  Park Wood ME15 .... 97 F4
Herons Cl. CT4 .... 107 C8
Herschell Rd. CT7 .... 26 F8
Herschell Rd E. CT14 ...... 117 C3
Herschell Rd W. CT14 ..... 117 C3
Herschell Sq. CT14 .... 117 C3
Hersden Cty Prim Sch. CT3 46 E1
Hertford Ho.
  Herne Bay CT6 .... 23 A5
Hertford Ho. **14**
  Ramsgate CT11 .... 52 E6
Hertford Pl. CT11 .... 52 E6
Hertford Rd. CT9 .... 29 C8
Hertford St. CT11 .... 52 E6
Herts Cres. ME15 .... 96 F3
Hetford Ct. CT1 .... 88 C3
Hever Cl. ME15 .... 97 F6
Hever Gdns. ME16 .... 74 E3
Hever Pl. CT2 .... 67 A3
Hewitt Cl. ME7 .... 10 F6
Hewitt Rd. **1** CT16 .... 166 D8
Hewitts Pl. TN24 .... 139 F1
Hextable Cl.
  Ashford TN23 .... 155 F6
Hextable Cl.
  Maidstone ME16 .... 74 D7
Heyford Cl. CT18 .... 163 B4
Hibernia St. **8** CT11 .... 52 E6
Hickory Dell. ME7 .... 33 A5
Hicks Forstal Rd.CT3 & CT6 . 46 B5
Higgins' La. ME4 .... 9 F5
High Banks. Loose ME15 .... 96 F5
High Banks. Rochester ME1 .. 9 F5
High Dewar Rd. ME8 .... 34 A8
High Elms. ME8 .... 11 E1
High Halden Parochial
  CE Prim Sch. TN26 .... 167 E7
High Knocke. TN29 .... 195 B6
High Meadow. CT17 .... 149 C1
High Minnis. CT4 .... 143 F8
High Oak Hall. ME9 .... 13 E1
High Snoad Wood. TN25 .. 105 A1
High St. Ashford TN23 ..... 139 C2
High St. Aylesford ME20 ... 53 A2
High St. Bridge CT4 .... 89 A1
High St. Broadstairs CT10 .. 29 E5
High St. Broadstairs,
  St Peter's CT10 .... 30 A4
High St. Brookland TN29 ... 197 E8
High St. **3** Canterbury CT1 . 67 A1
High St. Canterbury CT1 .... 87 F8
High St. Chatham ME4 .... 9 E4
High St. Chatham ME4 ...... 10 C6
High St. Deal CT14 .... 117 D6
High St.
  Dover CT16 & CT17 ...... 166 C7
High St. Dymchurch TN29 .. 195 C8
High St. Eastchurch ME12 ... 5 D3
High St. Eastry CT13 .... 93 B2
High St. Elham CT4 .... 144 F5
High St. Fordwich CT2 ...... 68 A4
High St. Gillingham ME7 .... 10 B6
High St. Gillingham ME7 ... 10 C5
High St.
  Gillingham,Brompton ME4 . 10 A6
High St.
  Gillingham,Rainham ME8 .. 33 F8
High St. Herne Bay CT6 .... 22 F5
High St. Hythe CT21 .... 176 C2
High St. Lenham ME17 ..... 101 D5
High St. Littlebourne CT3 ... 89 F7
High St. Lydd TN29 .... 203 B6
High St. Lyminge CT18 .... 161 C6
High St. Maidstone ME14 .. 74 F4
High St. Manston CT12 ..... 51 D8
High St. Margate CT9 .... 7 I2
High St. Margate CT9 .... 7 J1
High St.
  Margate, Garlinge CT9 ..... 28 B7

High St. Minster ME12 .... 4 D6
High St. Minster,
  Thanet CT12 .... 50 C6
High St. New Romney
  TN28 .... 200 B6
High St. Newington ME9 .... 35 C6
High St. Queenborough
  ME11 .... 2 F5
High St. Ramsgate CT11 .... 52 D7
High St. Rochester ME2 ...... 9 B7
High St. Rochester ME1 ...... 9 C6
High St. Rochester ME4 ...... 9 E4
High St. Sandwich CT13 .... 73 A1
High St. Sheerness ME12 .... 1 B3
High St. Sheerness ME12 ... 1 D2
High St. Sittingbourne ME10 . 36 E6
High St. Sittingbourne ME10 . 36 F4
High St. Smarden TN27 .... 135 A1
High St. St Margaret's
  at Cliffe CT15 .... 150 F6
High St. Sturry CT2 .... 67 F5
High St.
  Temple Ewell CT16 .... 148 D5
High St. Tenterden TN30 ... 179 A7
High St. Whitstable CT5 ..... 20 D2
High St. Wingham CT3 .... 91 A8
High St. Wye TN25 .... 123 E2
High St. The TN27 .... 120 C7
High Street St Lawrence.
  CT11 .... 52 B7
High Trees Cl. TN24 .... 157 A8
High View Ave. CT9 .... 22 B5
Higham Cl. ME15 .... 74 E2
Higham La. CT4 .... 111 B8
Higham View. ME14 .... 53 E4
Highbury Gdns. CT12 ...... 29 B3
Highbury La. TN30 .... 179 A7
Highbury Wlk. CT12 .... 29 B2
Highcroft Gn. ME15 .... 97 F4
Highfield Cl.
  Gillingham ME8 .... 33 D7
Highfield Cl. Hythe CT21 ... 176 A4
Highfield Cl.
  Ramsgate CT12 .... 29 B3
Highfield Ct.
  Rough Common CT2 ...... 66 B3
Highfield Ct. **5**
  Margate CT9 .... 8 B2
Highfield Ct.
  Ramsgate CT12 .... 29 B2
Highfield Gdns. CT9 .... 7 H1
Highfield Ind Est. CT19 .... 178 F6
Highfield La. TN24 .... 157 C6
Highfield Rd.
  Ashford TN24 .... 157 A8
Highfield Rd.
  Gillingham ME8 .... 33 D7
Highfield Rd.
  Halfway Houses ME12 ...... 3 E6
Highfield Rd.
  Ramsgate CT12 .... 29 B3
Highfields Ave. CT6 .... 23 D4
Highfields View. CT6 .... 23 C3
Highgate Rd. CT5 .... 21 B1
Highgrove Rd. ME5 .... 32 A5
Highland Cl. CT20 .... 177 F4
Highland Court Annexe
  (Kent & Canterbury
  Hospl). CT4 .... 111 C8
Highland Rd.
  Chartham CT4 .... 86 D1
Highland Rd.
  Maidstone ME15 .... 97 E6
Highlands Cres. TN29 ...... 195 A4
Highlands Farm
  Rare Breeds Ctr. TN26 ... 169 D1
Highpoint. TN24 .... 139 D3
Highridge. Gillingham ME7 .. 11 A4
Highridge. Hythe CT21 ..... 177 A3
Highridge Cl. ME14 .... 75 F5
Highsted Rd. ME9 &10 ...... 36 F1
Highsted Sch. ME10 .... 36 F2
Highsted Valley. ME9 .... 58 F7
Highstreet Rd.
  Waterham ME13 .... 42 D2
Highstreet Rd.
  Yorklets CT5 & ME13 ...... 42 E2
Highview Cl.
  Boughton Street ME13 ..... 64 B3
Highview Cl.
  Maidstone ME15 .... 97 A8
Highview Dr. ME5 .... 31 D5
Highview Rd. ME12 .... 4 C7
Highview Sch. CT19 .... 178 D6
Highworth Gram Sch
  for Girls. TN24 .... 139 A3
Hilary Cl. CT16 .... 149 C4
Hilda Rd. Chatham ME4 .... 10 A3
Hilda Rd.
  Halfway Houses ME12 ...... 3 D6
Hildenborough Cres. ME16 . 74 C7

Hildersham Cl. CT10 .... 29 E5
Hill Ave. CT15 .... 130 E5
Hill Brow. Maidstone ME14 . 76 A5
Hill Brow.
  Sittingbourne ME10 .... 36 D2
Hill Chase. ME5 .... 31 E3
Hill Cres. Aylesham CT3 ... 112 E5
Hill Cres. Lenham ME17 ... 101 D5
Hill Crest. TN23 .... 155 B8
Hill Ct. TN27 .... 103 E1
Hill Dr. CT13 .... 93 B3
Hill Green Rd. ME9 .... 56 D8
Hill House Dr. CT12 .... 50 C7
Hill La. CT18 .... 162 B1
Hill Rd. Chatham ME1 .... 31 A3
Hill Rd. Folkestone CT19 ... 178 E7
Hill Rd. Folkestone CT19 ... 178 E8
Hill Rd. Rochester ME1 ...... 9 A2
Hill The. Charing TN27 .... 120 D8
Hill The. Littlebourne CT3 .. 89 F8
Hill Top Cotts. ME17 .... 96 E2
Hill Top Rd. CT6 .... 23 B5
Hill View. Ashford TN24 ... 139 C3
Hill View. Margate CT9 ...... 28 D2
Hill View Terr. CT18 .... 161 D3
Hill View Way. ME5 .... 31 E5
Hill's Terr. ME4 .... 9 F3
Hillary Rd. ME14 .... 75 A7
Hillborough Dr. CT6 .... 23 F5
Hillborough Gr. ME5 .... 32 A3
Hillborough Rd. CT6 .... 23 B5
Hillbrow Ave.
  Herne Bay CT6 .... 23 B2
Hillbrow Ave. Sturry CT2 ... 67 F7
Hillbrow La. TN23 .... 138 F1
Hillbrow Rd.
  Ashford TN23 .... 139 A1
Hillbrow Rd.
  Ramsgate CT11 .... 52 D8
Hillcrest Cl. TN24 .... 139 A1
Hillcrest Gdns. Deal CT14 . 117 A2
Hillcrest Gdns.
  Ramsgate CT11 .... 52 B6
Hillcrest Rd. Chatham ME4 .. 9 F2
Hillcrest Rd. Hythe CT21 .. 176 B3
Hillcrest Rd.
  Kingsdown CT14 .... 134 D4
Hillcrest Rd.
  Littlebourne CT3 .... 89 E8
Hillcroft Rd. CT6 .... 23 B3
Hillden Shaw. ME15 .... 97 A8
Hiller Cl. CT10 .... 30 A6
Hillfield Villas. TN26 .... 167 F8
Hillman Ave. CT6 .... 22 A4
Hillside. **1** CT20 .... 177 E3
Hillside Ave.
  Canterbury CT2 .... 66 C2
Hillside Ave. Rochester ME2 .. 9 B8
Hillside Ave.
  Rushenden ME11 .... 2 F3
Hillside Ct. Hythe CT21 ... 176 C2
Hillside Ct. **1**
  Rochester ME2 .... 9 A7
Hillside Ind Est. CT20 .... 177 E4
Hillside Rd. Chatham ME4 .. 10 A4
Hillside Rd. Dover CT17 ... 149 A2
Hillside Rd. Minster ME12 ... 4 B7
Hillside Rd.
  Stalisfield Green ME13 .... 103 E6
Hillside Rd. Whitstable CT5 .. 21 A1
Hillside St. CT21 .... 176 C2
Hilltop Rd. ME12 .... 4 A7
Hillview Rd. Canterbury CT2 . 66 C2
Hillview Rd. Whitstable CT5 . 43 D8
Hillyfield Rd. TN23 .... 156 A8
Hillyfields
  Cty Jun Sch. ME7 .... 10 E6
Hillyfields Rise. TN23 ...... 139 A1
Hilton Bsns Ctr. TN23 ..... 156 B6
Hilton Dr. ME10 .... 36 B6
Hilton Rd. TN23 .... 138 F2
Hinchliffe Way. CT9 .... 29 D8
Hind Cl. TN29 .... 195 C8
Hinde Cl. ME10 .... 36 F7
Hines Terr. ME15 .... 10 C1
Hinton Cres. ME7 .... 33 A6
Hinxhill Rd. TN24 & TN25 . 140 D1
Hirst Cl. CT16 .... 149 B4
Hither Field. TN27 .... 120 C7
Hoades Wood Rd. CT2 ...... 68 A7
Hoath Cl. ME7 .... 33 B7
Hoath Cty Prim Sch. CT3 ... 46 E5
Hoath La. ME8 .... 33 B8
Hoath Rd. CT3 .... 46 C3
Hoath Way. ME7 & ME8 .... 33 B5
Hobart Cres. CT16 .... 149 C3
Hobart Gdns. ME10 .... 36 C4
Hobart Rd. CT12 .... 29 A1
Hockeredge Gdns.
  CT8 & CT9 .... 27 F8
Hockers Cl. ME14 .... 76 A8

Hockers La. ME14 .... 76 A7
Hodge's Gap. CT9 .... 8 C3
Hodgson Rd. CT5 .... 42 F7
Hog Gn. CT4 .... 144 F4
Hog Hill. ME14 .... 76 B5
Hogarth Cl. CT6 .... 23 E5
Hogbarn La. ME17 .... 79 A3
Hogben Cl. CT18 .... 161 B7
Hogg La. CT4 .... 109 E2
Holbeam Rd. ME13 .... 82 A1
Holborn La. ME4 .... 9 F5
Holbourn Cl. CT6 .... 46 B8
Holbrook Dr. CT12 .... 29 B1
Holcombe Rd. Chatham ME4 . 9 F2
Holcombe Rd.
  Rochester ME1 .... 9 C3
Holdenhurst. TN23 .... 155 E6
Holder Cl. ME5 .... 32 C6
Holding St. ME8 .... 11 D2
Holland Cl. Broadstairs CT10 . 8 G2
Holland Cl. Sheerness ME12 .. 1 C1
Holland Ho. ME1 .... 9 D5
Holland Rd. Chatham ME5 .. 31 E4
Holland Rd.
  Maidstone ME14 .... 75 B5
Hollands Ave. CT19 .... 178 F7
Hollicondane Rd. CT11 ..... 52 E8
Hollingbourne
  Cty Prim Sch. ME17 .... 77 E2
Hollingbourne Hill. ME17 .. 77 F4
Hollingbourne Rd. ME8 .... 11 C2
Hollingbourne Sta. ME17 .. 77 C3
Hollington Pl. TN24 .... 139 B3
Hollington Sch. TN24 ..... 139 B3
Hollingworth Rd. ME15 .... 97 F5
Hollow La. Canterbury CT1 .. 87 E5
Hollow La. Hartlip ME9 ...... 34 E5
Hollow Rd. CT3 .... 47 B6
Hollow St. CT3 .... 47 C5
Hollow Wood Rd. CT17 .... 165 E8
Hollowmede. CT1 .... 87 E6
Holly Cl. Broadstairs CT10 .. 29 C4
Holly Cl. Chatham ME5 ..... 32 C8
Holly Cl. Eastry CT13 .... 93 B2
Holly Cl. Folkestone CT19 . 178 E7
Holly Cl. Gillingham ME7 ... 10 E6
Holly Farm Rd. ME15 .... 98 C6
Holly Gdns. CT9 .... 8 C2
Holly Hill Rd. ME13 .... 64 D5
Holly Ho. ME12 .... 1 C2
Holly La. CT9 .... 8 C2
Holly Rd. Ramsgate CT11 .. 52 E8
Holly Rd.
  St Mary's Bay TN29 .... 194 F4
Holly Tree Cl. ME17 .... 99 E2
Hollybrook Hill. ME10 .... 36 D4
Hollybush Cnr. CT4 .... 90 A3
Hollybush La. CT13 .... 69 A4
Holm Mill La. ME17 .... 100 B6
Holm Oak Cl. CT1 .... 87 F6
Holm Oak Gdns. CT10 ...... 29 F4
Holmesdale Cl. ME15 .... 96 F3
Holmestone Rd.
  CT15 & CT17 .... 148 E1
Holmlea Cl. TN24 .... 139 E1
Holmoaks. Gillingham ME8 .. 11 E2
Holmoaks.
  Maidstone ME14 .... 75 C5
Holmscroft Rd. CT6 .... 23 D5
Holmside. ME7 .... 10 E3
Holmside Ave. ME12 .... 3 D6
Holmwood Rd. TN23 ...... 155 E7
Holness Rd. CT3 .... 71 D2
Holt St. CT15 .... 113 C4
Holton Cl. CT7 .... 27 A6
Holtwood Cl. ME8 .... 33 D6
Holtye Cres. ME15 .... 75 B2
Holy Cross
  RC High Sch The. CT10 ... 30 A3
Holy Family RC
  Prim Sch The. ME15 .... 97 F4
Holy Trinity CE Prim Sch.
  CT10 .... 30 A1
Holy Trinity & St John's
  CE Prim Sch. CT17 .... 7 J2
Holyrood Dr. ME12 .... 4 A5
Holywell Ave. CT19 .... 178 D8
Holywell Cty Prim Sch.
  ME9 .... 12 F3
Holywell Ho. CT19 .... 178 D8
Holywell La. ME9 .... 12 E2
Home Farm Cotts. CT14 ... 115 E6
Homebirch Ho. **6** CT7 .... 26 F8
Homefern Ho. CT9 .... 7 I3
Homefield Ave. CT14 ...... 117 B6
Homefield Row. CT14 ...... 117 B6
Homefleet Ho. **11** CT11 .. 52 F7
Homeleigh Rd. CT12 .... 29 A4
Homepeak. **12** CT21 ..... 176 B2
Homeside Farm. CT4 ...... 126 F6
Homespire Ho. **19** CT1 ... 67 A1

Homestall Ct. CT2 .... 66 C4
Homestall La. ME13 .... 63 B5
Homestead. TN23 .... 155 D8
Homestead Ct. ⑦ CT19 ...... 7 J1
Homestead La. CT15 .... 132 C7
Homestead View. ME9 .... 36 B2
Homestead Village. CT11 .... 52 C5
Homestreet
  Cty Prim Sch. TN26 ...... 182 F8
Homevale Ho. ❸ CT20 ...... 177 E3
Homeview. ME10 .... 37 B4
Homewood Ave. ME10 .... 36 D3
Homewood Cty Inf Sch.
  ME10 .... 36 D4
Homewood Rd. Sturry CT2 .. 68 A6
Homewood Rd.
  Tenterden TN30 .... 167 B1
Homewood Sch. TN30 .... 167 B1
Homewood Terr. ❻ ME14 .... 75 A7
Hone St. ME2 .... 9 B8
Honey Bee Glade. ME8 .... 33 E6
Honey La. ME11 .... 33 A5
Honey Hill. CT2 & CT5 .... 65 F8
Honey La. ME15 .... 98 B6
Honeyball Wlk. ME9 .... 38 C2
Honeycrock Hill. ME9 .... 56 F8
Honeyfield. TN23 .... 138 E1
Honeypot Cl. ME2 .... 9 B8
Honeysuckle Cl. ❸
  Chatham ME5 .... 31 E4
Honeysuckle Cl.
  Gillingham ME7 .... 32 F4
Honeysuckle Ct.
  Margate CT9 .... 28 C8
Honeysuckle La. ME10 .... 37 B5
Honeysuckle Rd. CT11 .... 52 F8
Honeysuckle Way. CT6 ...... 23 D2
Honeywood Cl.
  Canterbury CT1 .... 67 B2
Honeywood Cl.
  Lympne CT21 .... 175 A4
Honeywood Parkway.
  CT15 .... 149 B5
Honeywood Rd.
  CT15 & CT16 .... 149 A5
Honflaur Rd. CT13 .... 93 F8
Honiton House Sch. CT9 ...... 8 B2
Honywood Rd. ME17 .... 101 C4
Hook Cl. Folkestone CT20 .. 177 F5
Hook Cl. Maidstone ME15 .... 31 E5
Hook La. Brookland TN29 .. 197 C6
Hook La. Charing TN27 ..... 120 A7
Hook La.
  Harrietsham ME17 .... 100 C4
Hook St. ME17 .... 118 F8
Hook Wall. TN29 .... 197 E5
Hookstead. TN26 .... 167 C7
Hooper's Pl. ME1 .... 9 C4
Hooper's Rd. ME1 .... 9 C4
Hoopers La. CT6 .... 23 D3
Hop Garden Way. CT1 .... 87 E6
Hope La.
  New Romney TN28 .... 200 A8
Hope La. St Mary in
  the Marsh TN28 & TN29 .. 193 F2
Hope Rd. CT14 .... 117 D5
Hope St. Chatham ME4 .... 10 A3
Hope St. Maidstone ME14 ... 74 F6
Hope St. Sheerness ME12 .... 1 C2
Hope's La. CT12 .... 29 C3
Hope's Gr. TN26 .... 167 C7
Hopeville Ave. CT10 .... 29 E6
Hopewell Dr. ME5 .... 32 C8
Hopewell Sch. TN23 .... 155 D7
Hoppers Way. TN23 .... 155 D8
Hopsons Pl. ME12 .... 4 C5
Horn Hill. ME9 .... 58 E2
Horn St.
  CT19 & CT20 & CT21 .... 177 B4
Hornash La. TN26 .... 170 D8
Hornbeam Ave. ME5 .... 32 B2
Hornbeam Cl. TN23 .... 138 F3
Hornes Place Chapel.
  TN26 .... 181 D2
Hornet Cl. CT10 .... 29 D3
Horsa Rd. Birchington CT7 .. 26 D7
Horsa Rd. Deal CT14 .... 117 D8
Horsebridge Rd. CT5 .... 20 D2
Horselees Rd. ME13 .... 64 A2
Horseshoe Cl.
  Gillingham ME7 .... 32 F5
Horseshoe Cl.
  Maidstone ME14 .... 75 E5
Horseshoes La. ME17 .... 98 E4
Horsewash La. ME1 .... 9 C6
Horsford Wlk. ME13 .... 62 A8
Horsham Hill. ME8 & ME9 .. 12 E4
Horsham La. ME8 .... 12 D3
Horshams The. CT6 .... 23 D5
Horsley Cl. CT18 .... 163 B4
Horsley Rd. ME1 .... 9 B4

Horsted Ave. ME4 .... 9 E1
Horsted Cty Inf Sch. ME4 .. 31 D5
Horsted Cty Jun Sch. ME5 .. 31 D5
Horsted Way. ME1 .... 31 D7
Horton Cotts. CT4 .... 86 E4
Horton Downs. ME15 .... 75 F1
Horton Gdns. CT4 .... 86 E4
Horwood Cl. ME1 .... 31 B8
Hoser Gdns. CT7 .... 27 A7
Hospital Rd. CT20 & CT21 . 177 C3
Hospital La.
  Canterbury CT1 .... 87 F8
Hospital La. Chatham ME1 ... 9 E4
Hospital Meadow Cotts.
  CT3 .... 91 D2
Hospital Rd. ME17 .... 99 E8
Hotel Rd. Gillingham ME8 .. 11 A2
Hotel Rd. St Margaret's
  at Cliffe CT15 .... 151 B6
Hothfield Common
  Nature Reserve. TN26 ... 137 F8
Hothfield
  Cty Prim Sch. TN26 ..... 138 A7
Hothfield Rd. ME8 .... 11 F1
Hougham Court La. CT15 .. 165 A3
Houghton Ave. ME7 .... 33 B3
Houghton Ho. CT19 .... 178 C5
House Field. TN24 .... 139 F2
Housefield Rd. ME13 .... 104 C6
Hovenden Cl. CT2 .... 67 A4
Howard Ave.
  Rochester ME1 .... 9 D3
Howard Ave.
  Sittingbourne ME10 ...... 36 D6
Howard Cl. ME12 .... 4 C7
Howard Dr. ME16 .... 74 B5
Howard Rd. CT10 .... 30 A3
Howard Sch The. ME8 .... 33 D8
Howbury Wlk. ME8 .... 33 D4
Howfield La. CT4 .... 86 E5
Howletts Oast. CT4 .... 89 C5
Howletts Zoo Pk. CT4 .... 89 D6
Hoxton Cl. TN23 .... 139 C3
Hoystings Cl The. CT1 .... 88 A7
Hubbard's La. ME15 .... 97 A3
Hubbards Cotts. ME8 .... 12 C2
Hubbards Hill. ME17 .... 102 B6
Hubble Dr. ME15 .... 97 E7
Hubert Way. CT10 .... 29 E6
Huckleberry Cl. ME5 .... 32 B3
Hudson Cl. ❼
  Dover CT16 .... 149 B3
Hudson Cl.
  Gillingham ME8 .... 11 C1
Hudson Rd. Sturry CT2 ...... 67 F6
Hudson Rd. CT1 .... 67 B2
Hugh Pl. ❺ ME13 .... 62 D7
Hugh Price Cl. ME10 .... 37 C5
Hugin Ave. CT10 .... 29 E7
Hull Cl. CT18 .... 163 A4
Hull Pl. CT14 .... 116 F6
Hull Rd. TN29 .... 204 E6
Humber Ave. CT6 .... 21 F4
Humber Ho. ❺ ME15 .... 97 E8
Hume Ct. CT21 .... 176 D1
Humphrey Terr. CT18 ...... 162 F4
Hundreds Cl. CT8 .... 27 D7
Hunger Hatch La. TN27 ... 119 F4
Hunstanton Cl. ME8 .... 33 E3
Hunt Cl. CT18 .... 163 A4
Hunter Ave. TN24 .... 156 E8
Hunter Cl. TN24 .... 156 E8
Hunter Rd. TN24 .... 139 E1
Hunters Chase.
  Herne Bay CT6 .... 23 C2
Hunters Chase.
  Whitstable CT5 .... 43 C6
Hunters Ct. ❹ ME7 .... 10 C7
Hunters Forstal Rd. CT6 .... 23 C2
Hunters Way.
  Gillingham ME8 .... 10 E1
Hunters Way.
  Sheldwich ME13 .... 83 C5
Hunters Way W.
  ME5 & ME7 .... 10 E1
Hunters Wlk. CT14 .... 117 B6
Huntersfield Cl. ME5 .... 32 C1
Hunting Gate. CT7 .... 26 F8
Hunting Rd. CT7 .... 26 F8
Huntingdon Wlk. ❹ ME15 .. 97 E7
Huntingdon Rd. ME17 .... 96 B3
Hunton Gdns. CT2 .... 67 A4
Hunton Hill. ME15 .... 96 A2
Huntsfield Ind Est. CT7 .... 177 D4
Huntsman La. ME14 .... 75 B4
Huntsman's Cnr. ME4 .... 31 E8
Huntsmans Cl. ME14 .... 31 F8
Huntswood. TN23 .... 138 E1
Hurst Cl. ME5 .... 31 E4
Hurst Gr. CT12 .... 29 C1
Hurst Hill. ME5 .... 31 E4
Hurst La. Capel-le-F CT18 . 164 B4

Hurst La.
  Charing Heath TN27 .... 119 E6
Hurst La.
  Sittingbourne ME10 ...... 14 F1
Hurst Pl. ME8 .... 33 F8
Hurst Rd. TN24 .... 139 C7
Hurstford La.
  TN26 & TN27 .... 120 C2
Hurstings The. ME16 .... 74 D2
Hurstwood. ME5 .... 31 E4
Hurstwood Rd.
  Bredhurst ME7 .... 33 B1
Hurstwood Rd.
  Detling ME14 .... 55 B7
Hurstwood Rd. Warren
  Street ME13 & ME17 ... 102 E8
Hutchings Cl. ME10 .... 37 C5
Hutsford Cl. ME8 .... 33 D5
Huxley Cl. ME1 .... 9 D4
Hybrid Cl. ME1 .... 9 D1
Hyde Cl. CT17 .... 166 C7
Hyde Pl. CT3 .... 112 F5
Hyde Rd. ME16 .... 74 D6
Hyde The. CT4 .... 86 B2
Hythe Cl. CT20 .... 177 F5
Hythe Cty Inf Sch. CT21 .. 176 B1
Hythe Light Railway Sta.
  CT21 .... 176 A2
Hythe Pl. CT13 .... 94 A8
Hythe Rd. Ashford TN24 .. 139 E1
Hythe Rd.
  Dymchurch TN29 .... 186 E1
Hythe Rd. Pedlinge CT21 .. 175 D4
Hythe Rd.
  Sittingbourne ME10 ...... 36 D5
Hythe Rd.
  Smeeth TN25 & TN24 ... 158 C3

Ian's Wlk. CT21 .... 177 A3
Iden La. TN27 .... 119 B4
Idenwood Cl. ME8 .... 33 D6
Iffin La. CT1 & CT4 .... 87 E2
Ifield Cl. ME15 .... 97 F7
Ilex Rd. CT19 .... 177 F6
Illustrious Cl. ME5 .... 32 A6
Imbert Cl. TN28 .... 200 C6
Imperial Ave. ME12 .... 4 D7
Imperial Dr. ME12 .... 6 E4
Imperial Rd. ME7 .... 10 C3
Impton La. ME5 .... 32 A1
Ince Rd. CT7 .... 67 F7
Ingle Cl. CT7 .... 27 B7
Ingle Rd. ME4 .... 9 F2
Ingleden Cl. ME10 .... 36 F8
Ingleden Park Rd. TN30 ... 167 C1
Ingles La. ❹ CT20 .... 178 D5
Ingles Mews. ❷ CT20 ..... 178 C4
Ingles Rd. CT20 .... 178 C4
Ingoldsby Rd.
  Birchington CT7 .... 26 E7
Ingoldsby Rd.
  Canterbury CT1 .... 87 D6
Ingoldsby Rd.
  Folkestone CT19 .... 178 E7
Ingram Rd. ME7 .... 10 D6
Institute Rd. Chatham ME4 . 10 A4
Institute Rd.
  Faversham ME13 .... 62 D7
Inverary Ct. CT11 .... 29 C3
Inverness Ho. ❻ ME15 ..... 97 E7
Inverness Terr. CT10 .... 30 A3
Invicta Ct. ME10 .... 36 F7
Invicta Gram Sch
  for Girls. ME14 .... 75 C4
Invicta Ho. Canterbury CT1 . 87 F7
Invicta Ho. Margate CT9 .... 8 C1
Invicta Rd.
  Folkestone CT19 .... 178 D7
Invicta Rd. Lydd TN29 .... 203 A2
Invicta Rd. Margate CT9 .... 29 B8
Invicta Rd. Sheerness ME12 . 1 D2
Invicta Rd. Whitstable CT5 .. 43 F8
Invicta Villas. ME14 .... 76 C4
Inward Car Lanes. CT16 ... 166 G8
Inward Freight Lanes.
  CT16 .... 166 G8
Iona Cl. ME5 .... 32 C8
Iona Rd. ME15 .... 97 A7
Irchester St. ❾ CT11 .... 52 F7
Ireland Ct. TN24 .... 139 D2
Irene Astor Ct. ❼ CT20 ... 178 D5
Iris Cl. ME5 .... 54 A8
Iron Bar La. ❸ CT1 .... 88 A8
Ironside Cl. ME5 .... 32 A8
Irvine Dr. CT9 .... 29 C8
Isis Cl. CT21 .... 175 A3
Island Rd.
  Upstreet CT3 & CT7 ...... 47 D2
Island Rd.
  Westbere CT2 & CT3 ..... 68 C7
Island Wall. CT5 .... 20 C1

Ivanhoe Rd.
  Herne Bay CT6 .... 23 A4
Ivanhoe Rd.
  Westgate-on-S CT8 .... 7 C1
Ivens Way. ME17 .... 100 D6
Iversgate Ct. ME8 .... 11 F2
Ivory Cl. ME13 .... 40 A1
Ivy Cl. Etchinghill CT18 .... 161 D3
Ivy Cl. Kingswood ME17 .... 99 D2
Ivy Cottage Hill. CT12 ...... 50 E7
Ivy Cotts. TN23 .... 155 C8
Ivy Ct. CT2 .... 66 E6
Ivy House Rd. CT5 .... 20 F1
Ivy La. Canterbury CT1 ..... 88 A8
Ivy La. Ramsgate CT11 ..... 52 D6
Ivy Pl. Canterbury CT1 ...... 87 E7
Ivy Pl. Deal CT14 .... 117 D7
Ivy St. ME8 .... 33 F8
Ivy Way. CT19 .... 178 E7
Ivychurch Gdns. CT9 .... 8 E2
Ivychurch Rd. TN29 .... 192 B3
Iwade Cty Prim Sch. ME9 .. 14 E2

Jaarlen Rd. TN29 .... 203 B6
Jackdaw La. ME5 .... 31 F2
Jackson Ave. ME13 .... 40 B8
Jackson Cl. ME8 .... 11 C1
Jackson Ct. ME1 .... 87 E7
Jacksons La. ❻ TN30 ...... 179 A7
Jacob Cl. CT9 .... 28 E7
Jacob Yd. ❽ ME13 .... 62 D7
Jacobs Ho. ME12 .... 1 D2
Jaffa Ct. CT5 .... 43 D8
Jamaica Terr. ME14 .... 75 A7
James Cl. Ash CT3 .... 71 D2
James Cl. Lyminge CT18 .. 161 C7
James Ct.
  Folkestone CT20 .... 178 A4
James Ct. ❷ Margate CT9 .. 8 B2
James Hall Gdns. CT14 .... 117 C3
James Morris Ct. ❸ CT20 . 177 F3
James St. Ashford TN23 ... 139 A2
James St. Chatham ME4 ..... 9 F4
James St.
  Folkestone CT19 .... 178 D6
James St. Gillingham ME7 .. 10 D6
James St. Maidstone ME14 . 75 A5
James St.
  Ramsgate CT11 .... 52 D6
James St. Rochester ME1 .... 9 C4
James St. Sheerness ME12 .. 1 E2
James Whatman Way.
  ME14 .... 74 F5
Japonica Cl. ME5 .... 32 C2
Jarman's Field. TN25 ...... 123 F2
Jarrett Ho. ❻ CT20 .... 178 C4
Jarrett's Ct. ME10 .... 37 B4
Jarvis Dr. TN24 .... 157 A7
Jarvis Pl. TN30 .... 167 B3
Jarvist Pl. CT14 .... 134 D6
Jasmine Cl. ❷ ME5 .... 31 F4
Jasper Ave. ME7 .... 9 D2
Jayne Wlk. CT5 .... 43 D8
Jefferson Cl. TN23 .... 138 F1
Jefferson Dr. ME8 .... 11 C1
Jefferson Rd. ME7 .... 10 A7
Jefferson Gdns. TN29 ..... 194 E4
Jefferson La. TN29 .... 194 E4
Jefferson Lane Sta.
  TN29 .... 194 E4
Jeffery St. ME7 .... 10 C6
Jeffrey St. ME14 .... 75 A5
Jellicoe Cl. TN24 .... 157 A7
Jemmett La. TN25 .... 157 D3
Jemmett Rd. TN23 .... 156 A8
Jenkins' Dale. ME4 .... 9 F3
Jenkins Dr. ME15 .... 97 F5
Jenner Rd. ME1 .... 9 C4
Jenner's Way. TN23 .... 194 F3
Jennifer Gdns. CT9 .... 29 C8
Jersey La. CT4 .... 109 C6
Jersey Rd. ME2 .... 9 A8
Jesmond St. ❸ CT19 ...... 178 D6
Jesse's Hill. CT4 .... 111 B1
Jessica Mews. ❷
Jessica Mews.
  Sittingbourne ME10 ...... 36 E7
Jesuit Cl. CT2 .... 67 A4
Jesus Hospl. CT1 .... 67 A1
Jetty Rd. Sheerness ME12 .. 1 B3
Jetty Rd. Warden ME12 ...... 6 F4
Jewry La. CT1 .... 87 F8
Jeyes Rd. ME7 .... 10 C4
Jezreels Rd. ME7 .... 10 D3
Jillian Way. TN23 .... 155 E7
Jiniwin Rd. ME1 .... 31 D7
Joey's La. TN24 .... 139 E2
Johannesburg Ho. ❷
  ME15 .... 97 F5
Johannesburg Rd. CT16 .. 149 C4

John Anderson Ct. ❶
  ME13 .... 62 D7
John Bowley Ho. CT19 .... 177 F6
John Graham Ct. CT1 .... 88 A8
John Hall Cl. ME13 .... 40 B2
John St. Broadstairs CT10 .. 30 B4
John St. Maidstone ME14 .. 75 A6
John St. Rochester ME1 ..... 9 C4
John Tapping Cl. CT14 .... 117 B1
John Wilson Bsns Pk. CT5 .. 21 B1
John's Gn. CT13 .... 93 E6
Johnson Ave. ME7 .... 10 C7
Johnson Cl. TN24 .... 157 A7
Johnson Ct. ME13 .... 40 B1
Johnson Rd. ME10 .... 36 D4
Johnson Way. ME12 .... 4 A7
Joiners Ct. ME4 .... 10 B2
Jointon Rd. CT20 .... 178 B4
Jordan Cl. ME15 .... 97 E5
Joseph Conrad Ho. CT2 .... 66 D1
Joseph Wilson Ind Est.
  CT5 .... 44 A7
Joss Gap Rd. CT10 .... 8 H1
Joy La. CT5 .... 43 B8
Joy Lane
  Cty Prim Inf Sch. CT5 .... 43 C7
Joy Lane
  Cty Prim Jun Sch. CT5 ... 43 C7
Joyes Cl. Folkestone CT19 . 178 E7
Joyes Cl. Whitfield CT16 .. 149 B7
Joyes Rd. Folkestone CT19 178 E7
Joyes Rd. Whitfield CT16 .. 149 B7
Jubilee Cl. CT21 .... 187 D8
Jubilee Cotts.
  Throwley ME13 .... 82 D1
Jubilee Cotts. Worth CT14 . 94 B4
Jubilee Cres. ME11 .... 2 F5
Jubilee Ct. CT18 .... 30 B4
Jubilee Field. TN30 .... 188 E4
Jubilee Rd.
  Littlebourne CT3 .... 89 F8
Jubilee Rd. Sandwich CT13 . 93 F8
Jubilee Rd. Worth CT14 .... 94 B4
Jubilee Terr. ME12 .... 1 C6
Jubilee Way. Dover CT16 . 166 G8
Jubilee Way.
  Guston CT15 & CT16 .... 150 A2
Judd Rd. ME13 .... 62 A7
Judkins Cl. ME5 .... 32 C6
Julian Rd. CT19 .... 178 B6
Julie Cl. CT10 .... 30 A7
Julien Pl. TN24 .... 157 A8
Junction Rd.
  Gillingham ME7 .... 10 D4
Junction Rd.
  Herne Bay CT6 .... 22 C2
Juniper Cl. Ashford TN23 .. 138 E2
Juniper Cl. Canterbury CT1 . 88 A6
Juniper Cl. Chatham ME5 ... 32 A4
Juniper Cl. Whitstable CT5 . 20 F1
Jury's Gap
  Coastguard Cotts. TN31 . 201 E1
Jury's Gap Rd. TN29 ...... 203 A5

Kake St. CT4 .... 125 E7
Katherine Ct. ME5 .... 32 B2
Kathleen Mews. ❶❼
  CT20 .... 178 D5
Kearsley Abbey. CT16 .... 148 D4
Kearsney Ave. CT16 .... 148 E4
Kearsney Ct. CT16 .... 148 D4
Kearsney Sta. CT16 .... 148 E4
Keat Farm Cl. CT6 .... 23 F5
Keddow's Cl. CT21 .... 187 D8
Keefe Cl. ME5 .... 31 D1
Keeper's Hill. CT4 .... 89 C2
Keith Ave. CT12 .... 52 A8
Kellaway Rd. ME5 .... 32 A2
Kelly Dr. ME7 .... 10 C7
Kelly Ho. ME1 .... 31 C7
Kelvedon Rd. CT14 .... 117 C2
Kemp Alley. ❷ CT5 .... 20 D1
Kemp Cl. ME5 .... 32 C1
Kemp Rd. CT5 .... 21 C2
Kempes Pl. TN25 .... 123 E2
Kempton Cl. ME8 .... 32 C2
Kemsdale Rd. ME13 .... 63 F6
Kemsing Gdns. CT2 .... 67 B4
Kemsley Halt. ME10 .... 14 E1
Kemsley Street Rd. ME14 .. 33 C1
Kenardington Rd. TN26 .. 181 E3
Kenbrook. TN24 .... 139 C7
Kendal Cl. CT11 .... 52 A6
Kendal Rise. CT10 .... 30 A5
Kendal Way. ME8 .... 33 D8
Kendon Bsns Pk. ME2 .... 9 D8
Kenfield Rd. CT4 .... 109 A6

Kengate Ind Est. CT21 ... 175 F1
Kenilworth Cl. CT15 ... 151 A6
Kenilworth Ct. ME10 ... 36 C5
Kenilworth Dr. ME8 ... 33 B7
Kenilworth Gdns. ME8 ... 33 D7
Kenilworth Ho. ME16 ... 74 B2
Kennedy Cl. ME13 ... 62 D8
Kennedy Dr. CT14 ... 117 B2
Kennedy Ho. 6 CT11 ... 52 F7
Kennel Barn Rd. ME9 ... 57 C5
Kennel Hill. CT15 ... 131 E6
Kennelling Rd.
 ME13 & TN27 ... 103 D5
Kennett Dr. CT14 ... 117 A2
Kennett La. TN25 ... 175 B8
Kennett Lane Cotts. TN25 175 B8
Kennington
 CE Jun Sch. TN24 ... 139 E7
Kennington Cl.
 Gillingham ME8 ... 11 B4
Kennington Cl.
 Maidstone ME15 ... 97 F7
Kensington Ho. ME16 ... 74 A2
Kensington Rd. CT1 ... 67 C4
Kent Ave. Ashford TN24 ... 139 B3
Kent Ave. Canterbury CT1 ... 88 D8
Kent Ave. Maidstone ME15 .. 75 C1
Kent Ave. Minster ME12 ... 4 B6
Kent Ave.
 Sittingbourne ME10 ... 36 D3
Kent Battle of Britain Mus.
 CT18 ... 162 F4
Kent & Canterbury Hospl.
 CT1 ... 88 A5
Kent Cl. ME1 ... 31 C8
Kent Coll. CT2 ... 66 C3
Kent County Opthalmic
 & Aural Hospl. ME14 ... 75 A4
Kent County Show Gd.
 ME14 ... 75 A4
Kent Gdns. CT7 ... 26 F7
Kent Ho. CT20 ... 178 B4
Kent Inst of Art & Design.
 Chatham ME1 ... 9 E4
Kent Inst of Art & Design.
 Maidstone ME16 ... 74 C3
Kent Int Bsns Pk. CT12 ... 27 D2
Kent International Airport.
 CT12 ... 28 B1
Kent Music Sch. CT2 ... 66 F1
Kent Pl. CT11 ... 52 F6
Kent Rd. Folkestone CT19 ... 177 E7
Kent Rd. Margate CT9 ... 28 B8
Kent Rd. Sheerness ME12 ... 1 C1
Kent St. CT5 ... 43 D8
Kent Terr. Gillingham ME8 ... 12 C2
Kent Terr. Ramsgate CT11 ... 52 F6
Kent View Dr. ME12 ... 5 D1
Kentmere Ave.
 CT11 & CT12 ... 51 F7
Kenton Gdns. CT12 ... 50 B6
Kenward Rd. ME16 ... 74 C5
Kenwood Ave. ME5 ... 32 A4
Kenya Terr. 7 ME14 ... 75 A7
Kenyon Wlk. ME8 ... 33 B3
Kerton Rd. TN29 ... 204 F3
Kestrel Cl. ME10 ... 37 A2
Kestrel Ho. 7 ME7 ... 10 B6
Kestrel Rd. ME5 ... 32 C2
Keswick Dr. ME16 ... 74 B5
Keswick Rd. ME10 ... 37 C3
Kettle Hill. ME13 ... 81 F4
Kettle Hill Rd.
 Eastling ME13 ... 81 F5
Kettle Hill Rd.
 Hockley ME13 ... 82 A4
Kevin Dr. CT11 ... 52 B6
Kewlands. ME14 ... 75 C6
Key St. ME10 ... 36 A5
Keycol Hill.
 Key Street ME10 & ME9 ... 36 A5
Keycol Hill.
 Sittingbourne ME9 ... 35 F5
Keycol Hospl. ME9 ... 35 E6
Keyes Ave. ME4 ... 9 F2
Keyes Rd. CT19 ... 178 E7
Keyes Coll. CT2 ... 66 D4
Keyworth Mews. 7 CT11 ... 67 B2
Khartoum Rd. Chatham ME4 . 9 F5
Khartoum Rd.
 Gillingham ME4 ... 10 A6
Khartoum Sq. CT16 ... 149 A6
Khyber Rd. ME4 & ME7 ... 10 B7
Kilbride Ct. CT11 ... 29 F1
Kiln Cl. Challock TN25 ... 105 B1
Kiln Cl. Sittingbourne ME10 .. 37 A3
Kiln Cnr. CT21 ... 176 B4

Kiln Field. TN30 ... 179 C7
Kiln La. TN26 ... 153 F5
Kiln Rd. TN25 ... 172 F4
Kilndown Cl. Ashford TN23 155 E6
Kilndown Cl.
 Maidstone ME16 ... 74 C7
Kilndown Gdns.
 Canterbury CT2 ... 67 A4
Kilndown Gdns.
 Margate CT9 ... 8 E2
Kimberley Cl. CT16 ... 149 C3
Kimberley Cnr. CT10 ... 29 E5
Kimberley Ct. CT7 ... 7 C1
Kimberley Gr. CT5 ... 42 F6
Kimberley Rd.
 Gillingham ME7 ... 10 D3
Kimberley Rd.
 Ramsgate CT12 ... 29 A1
Kimberly Terr. CT18 ... 161 C7
King Arthur Rd. CT12 ... 51 D7
King Charles Ct. CT14 ... 117 D2
King Edward Ave.
 Broadstairs CT10 ... 30 A4
King Edward Ave.
 Herne Bay CT6 ... 23 B4
King Edward Ct. CT6 ... 23 B4
King Edward Rd.
 Birchington CT7 ... 27 A5
King Edward Rd.
 Chatham ME4 ... 9 F2
King Edward Rd.
 Deal CT14 ... 117 D8
King Edward Rd.
 Gillingham ME7 ... 10 F6
King Edward Rd.
 Maidstone ME15 ... 74 F2
King Edward Rd.
 Ramsgate CT11 ... 52 C6
King Edward Rd.
 Rochester ME1 ... 9 C5
King Edward St. CT5 ... 20 D1
King Ethelbert
 Sch The. CT8 ... 27 C7
King George Rd. ME5 ... 31 E4
King George V Meml Hos.
 ME8 ... 11 C2
King George Villas. CT14 ... 94 B3
King Lear's Way. CT17 ... 166 B5
King St. Brookland TN29 ... 191 D2
King St. Canterbury CT1 ... 66 F1
King St. Chatham ME4 ... 10 A4
King St. Deal CT14 ... 117 D6
King St.
 Maidstone ME14 & ME15 .. 75 A4
King St. Margate CT9 ... 7 J3
King St. Ramsgate CT11 ... 52 E7
King St. Rochester ME1 ... 9 C5
King St. Sandwich CT13 ... 73 A1
King St. Sheerness ME12 ... 1 B2
King St. Sittingbourne ME10 .. 36 E5
King William Rd. 8 ME7 ... 10 C7
King's Ave. Ashford TN23 .. 139 A2
King's Ave. Birchington CT7 . 26 D7
King's Ave.
 Broadstairs CT10 ... 30 B6
King's Ave. Ramsgate CT12 . 29 B1
King's Ave. Rochester ME1 ... 9 C3
King's Ave. Sandwich CT13 .. 95 A8
King's Ave. Whitstable CT5 .. 20 E1
King's Bastion. ME7 ... 10 A5
King's Cl. CT14 ... 134 C6
King's Head Alley. ME12 ... 1 B3
King's Orch. ME1 ... 9 C5
King's Pk. CT1 ... 67 B1
King's Pl. 4 CT11 ... 52 E6
King's Rd. Birchington CT7 .. 27 A6
King's Rd. Chatham ME5 .... 10 D1
King's Rd. Faversham ME13 . 62 C7
King's Rd. Herne Bay CT6 ... 22 F5
King's Rd. Ramsgate CT11 .. 52 D8
King's Sch. Canterbury CT1 .. 67 A1
King's Sch. Rochester ME1 ... 9 C5
King's Sch (Jun). CT2 ... 67 A2
Kingfisher Apartments. 11
 ME15 ... 97 E5
Kingfisher Ave. CT21 ... 187 D8
Kingfisher Cl.
 Sevington TN24 ... 157 A7
Kingfisher Cl.
 Whitstable CT5 ... 43 C7
Kingfisher Ct. CT5 ... 22 D3
Kingfisher Dr. ME5 ... 32 C7
Kingfisher Drive
 Prim Sch. ME5 ... 32 B7
Kingfisher Gdns. CT21 ... 187 C8
Kingfisher Ct. Margate CT9 .. 28 B8

Kingfisher Wlk. CT10 ... 29 F5
Kings Acre. ME15 ... 76 A1
Kings Cotts. ME17 ... 98 F6
Kings Ct. CT14 ... 117 D3
Kings Mews. ME7 ... 67 A1
Kings Mill Cl. ME10 ... 36 E5
Kings Par. 7 TN23 ... 139 B2
Kings Rd. Aylesham CT3 .... 112 F6
Kings Rd. Dover CT17 ... 166 A7
Kings Rd.
 Folkestone CT20 ... 177 D6
Kings Rd. Minster ME12 ... 4 D4
Kings Ropewalk. CT17 ... 166 B5
Kingsbridge Ct. 9 CT20 ... 178 E5
Kingsdale Ct. ME5 ... 31 E5
Kingsdown Cl.
 Gillingham ME7 ... 33 B4
Kingsdown Cl.
 Maidstone ME16 ... 74 E4
Kingsdown Hill. CT14 ... 134 D7
Kingsdown Hos. ME9 ... 59 E4
Kingsdown Pk. CT5 ... 20 F2
Kingsdown Rd.
 Erriottwood ME9 ... 59 D4
Kingsdown Rd.
 Kingsdown CT14 ... 134 D7
Kingsdown Rd. St Margaret's
 at Cliffe CT15 ... 151 A7
Kingsfield Rd. CT6 ... 23 B2
Kingsford Cl. TN25 ... 157 E4
Kingsford Ct. CT17 ... 149 B1
Kingsford St.
 TN24 & TN25 ... 157 D5
Kingsgate Ave. CT10 ... 8 F1
Kingsgate Bay Rd. CT10 ... 8 F2
Kingsgate Cl. ME16 ... 74 C4
Kingsgate Coll. CT10 ... 30 A8
Kingsgate La. TN30 ... 188 C5
Kingsland Gdns. CT14 ... 134 B8
Kingsland Hollow. TN29 ... 195 A4
Kingsland La. TN27 ... 118 E1
Kingsley Rd.
 Maidstone ME15 ... 75 A3
Kingsley Rd.
 Whitstable CT5 ... 43 E8
Kingsmarsh La. TN29 ... 199 C5
Kingsmead. CT19 ... 178 B8
Kingsmead
 Cty Prim Sch. CT1 ... 67 A1
Kingsmead Rd. CT1 & CT2 .. 67 A2
KIngsmead Stadium. CT1 ... 67 A2
Kingsnorth
 CE Prim Sch. TN23 ... 156 B3
Kingsnorth Cl. 2 CT20 ... 178 B5
Kingsnorth Gdns. CT20 ... 178 C5
Kingsnorth Rd.
 Ashford TN23 ... 156 A6
Kingsnorth Rd.
 Faversham ME13 ... 62 C6
Kingsnorth Rd.
 Gillingham ME8 ... 11 C4
Kingston Ave. CT9 ... 28 C7
Kingston Cl.
 Herne Bay CT6 ... 23 F5
Kingston Cl.
 Ramsgate CT12 ... 29 B2
Kingston Cl. River CT17 ... 148 F3
Kingston Cres. ME5 ... 32 C4
Kingston Dr. ME15 ... 97 A8
Kingston Ct. 3 CT20 ... 178 B5
Kingsway. Chatham ME5 ... 10 D1
Kingsway.
 Dymchurch TN29 ... 186 E2
Kingsway. Gillingham ME7 ... 10 E1
Kingswood. TN24 ... 139 D5
Kingswood Ave. ME4 ... 9 F2
Kingswood
 Cty Prim Sch. ME17 ... 99 C2
Kingswood Rd.
 Gillingham ME7 ... 10 D6
Kit's Coty ME1 & ME20 ... 53 D8
Kinross Cl. ME5 ... 32 B7
Kipling Rd. TN23 ... 139 B2
Kirby's La. CT2 ... 66 F1
Kirk Gdns. CT14 ... 117 B2
Kirkdale. ME15 ... 96 F5
Kirkdale Cl. ME15 ... 32 D1
Kirkdale Cotts. ME15 ... 96 F5
Kirkdale Rd. ME15 ... 96 F6
Kirkstone Ave. CT11 ... 51 F7
Kirkwood Ave. TN26 ... 169 A1
Kit Hill. ME13 ... 84 D8
Kit Hill Ave. ME5 ... 31 E3
Kit's Coty Ho. ME20 ... 53 C6
Kitchener Ave. ME4 ... 10 A1
Kitchener Cl. CT14 ... 128 F8
Kitchener Rd. Dover CT17 . 166 A7
Kitchener Rd.
 Rochester ME2 ... 9 A8

Kitchener Sq. CT19 ... 178 E8
Kite Farm. CT5 ... 21 D3
Kitewell La. TN29 ... 203 D8
Kither Rd. TN23 ... 156 A7
Kitsbridge La.
 Hamstreet TN26 ... 183 C4
Kitsbridge La.
 Ruckinge TN26 ... 183 F5
Kitsbridge La.
 Ruckinge TN25 & TN26 ... 184 B6
Klondyke Ind Est. ME11 ... 2 F4
Knatchbull Way. TN25 ... 158 E5
Knavesacre Ct. ME8 ... 33 D5
Knight Ave.
 Canterbury CT2 ... 87 D8
Knight Ave.
 Gillingham ME7 ... 33 B4
Knight's Ave. CT10 ... 30 B6
Knight's Rd. CT16 ... 166 E8
Knightrider Ct. ME15 ... 75 A3
Knightrider St. 1
 Maidstone ME15 ... 75 A3
Knightrider St.
 Sandwich CT13 ... 73 A1
Knights Alley. 14 CT5 ... 20 D2
Knights Cl. CT17 ... 149 B1
Knights Pk. ME2 ... 9 A6
Knights Templars. CT17 ... 166 C6
Knights Way. CT16 ... 149 A3
Knightsfield Rd. ME10 ... 36 D7
Knock Hill. TN30 ... 190 A2
Knock Rd. TN23 ... 156 A7
Knockholt Rd. CT9 ... 8 F1
Knockhurst Ct. TN30 ... 167 C1
Knockhurst Rd. TN30 ... 167 C1
Knold Pk. CT9 ... 28 E8
Knole Rd. ME5 ... 32 C3
Knole The. TN23 ... 62 B7
Knoll Hill. TN25 ... 173 C3
Knoll La. TN23 ... 155 E7
Knoll Pl. CT14 ... 117 C2
Knoll Way. ME12 ... 6 H4
Knott Cres. TN24 ... 157 A7
Knott Ct. ME14 ... 74 F6
Knott's La. 20 CT1 ... 67 B2
Knotts La. CT15 ... 150 F6
Knotts Sq. TN23 ... 139 C2
Knowle Rd. ME14 ... 75 B6
Knowler Way. CT6 ... 23 C5
Knowlton Gdns. ME16 ... 74 B2
Knowlton Wlk. 1 CT1 ... 67 B1
Kohima Pl. CT16 ... 149 F2
Kyetop Wlk. ME8 ... 33 D6
Kymbelne Ct. CT14 ... 117 B4

La Belle Alliance Sq. 6
 Ramsgate CT11 ... 52 E7
La Belle Alliance Sq. 7
 Ramsgate CT11 ... 52 F7
La Galamina. TN28 ... 204 E8
La Rocco. TN28 ... 204 E8
La Tausco. TN28 ... 204 D8
La-Tene. CT14 ... 117 B2
Laburnum Ave. CT13 ... 93 F8
Laburnum Cl. ME16 ... 148 E4
Laburnum Gr. ME12 ... 1 I1
Laburnum Ho. ME12 ... 1 C2
Laburnum La. CT2 ... 68 B7
Laburnum Pl. ME10 ... 36 E4
Labworth Cl. ME12 ... 3 E6
Lacey Cl. ME17 ... 98 E4
Lachlan Way. 2 CT20 ... 177 F3
Lacton Oast. TN24 ... 157 B8
Lacton Way. TN24 ... 157 A8
Ladds Cnr. ME7 ... 11 B5
Lade Fort Cotts. TN28 ... 204 E6
Lade Fort Cres. TN29 ... 204 E6
Lady Garne Rd. CT15 ... 164 F5
Lady J Thornhill's Endowed
 Prim Sch. TN29 ... 123 E2
Lady Wootton's Gn. 5
 CT1 ... 88 A8
Ladyfields. Chatham ME5 ... 32 D2
Ladyfields. Herne Bay CT6 .. 23 D2
Ladysmith Gr. CT5 ... 42 F6
Ladysmith Rd. CT5 ... 43 C5
Ladywell. 7 CT16 ... 166 D8
Ladywell Ho. 2 CT16 ... 166 D8
Ladywood Rd. CT2 ... 67 F7
Lagos Ave. CT12 ... 29 A1
Lakelands.
 Harrietsham ME17 ... 100 E6
Lakelands.
 Maidstone ME15 ... 97 A7
Lakemead. TN23 ... 155 E8
Laker Rd. ME1 ... 31 C6
Lakeside. TN23 ... 155 E8
Lakeside Cabins TN26 ... 120 F1
Lakeside Pk. ME2 ... 9 E7
Lakewood Dr. ME8 ... 33 C6

Laking Ave. CT10 ... 30 B7
Laleham Gdns. CT9 ... 8 B2
Laleham Rd. CT9 ... 8 B1
Laleham Sch. CT9 ... 8 B1
Laleham St. CT9 ... 8 B1
Laleham Wlk. CT9 ... 8 B1
Lamb's Wlk. CT5 ... 43 C6
Lambard Ho. 6 ME14 ... 75 A5
Lambden Rd. TN27 ... 136 C6
Lamberhurst Gn. ME8 ... 11 B3
Lamberhurst Rd. ME16 ... 74 B7
Lamberhurst Way. CT9 ... 8 F3
Lambert Ho. CT14 ... 117 B3
Lambeth Cl. ME5 ... 32 B4
Lambeth Rd. CT1 ... 67 C4
Lambourn Way. ME5 ... 32 C2
Lambourne Pl. ME8 ... 12 A2
Lambourne Rd. ME15 ... 75 F2
Lambourne Wlk. CT1 ... 88 C8
Lambsfrith Gr. ME7 ... 33 B3
Lambton Rd. CT17 ... 149 A1
Laming Rd. CT7 ... 26 A2
Lammas Dr. ME10 ... 36 E6
Lamplighters Cl. ME7 ... 32 F5
Lancashire Rd. ME15 ... 97 E7
Lancaster Ave. CT18 ... 164 C2
Lancaster Cl. CT12 ... 29 B1
Lancaster Ct. ME8 ... 33 C7
Lancaster Gdns.
 Birchington CT7 ... 26 F6
Lancaster Gdns.
 Herne Bay CT6 ... 23 D5
Lancaster Ho. Deal CT14 ... 117 A5
Lancaster Ho. 3
 Dover CT17 ... 166 D7
Lancaster Rd.
 Canterbury CT1 ... 87 F6
Lancaster Rd. Dover CT17 . 166 D7
Lancet La. ME15 ... 97 A6
Lanchester Cl. ME5 ... 22 A3
Landbury Wlk. TN23 ... 138 F4
Landon Rd. CT6 ... 23 C4
Landor Ct. ME7 ... 33 A3
Landrail Rd. ME9 ... 13 B3
Landway The. ME14 ... 76 A4
Lane End. CT6 ... 22 D5
Lane The. CT15 ... 149 F6
Lane's Wlk. CT5 ... 20 E2
Lanes The. CT12 ... 50 C6
Lanfranc Gdns. CT17 ... 66 C1
Lanfranc Ho. 5 CT1 ... 67 A2
Lang Ct. CT5 ... 21 C3
Langdale. TN23 ... 155 E8
Langdale Cl. CT11 ... 52 A7
Langdale Cl. ME8 ... 11 D1
Langdale Rise. ME16 ... 74 C5
Langdon Ave. CT3 ... 71 F1
Langdon Cl. CT15 ... 150 F5
Langdon Cross. CT15 ... 150 C7
Langdon
 Cty Prim Sch. CT15 ... 133 A1
Langdon Rd.
 Folkestone CT19 ... 177 D7
Langdon Rd. Rochester ME1 .. 9 C4
Langham Cr. ME15 ... 7 F1
Langham Gr. ME16 ... 74 C4
Langholm Rd. TN23 ... 156 A7
Langhorne Gdns. 5 CT20 . 178 C4
Langley Gdns. CT9 ... 8 E3
Langley Rd. ME10 ... 36 F7
Langney Dr. TN23 ... 155 E6
Langport Rd. TN28 ... 200 C6
Langton Cl. ME14 ... 75 C5
Langton Cotts. CT3 ... 70 B5
Langton La. CT1 ... 88 A4
Lankester Parker Rd. ME1 .. 31 C6
Lansdown Rd.
 Canterbury CT1 ... 88 A7
Lansdown Rd.
 Sittingbourne ME10 ... 37 C4
Lansdowne Ave. ME15 ... 97 C6
Lansdowne Cl. 2 ME4 ... 9 F4
Lansdowne
 Cty Prim Sch. ME10 ... 37 C3
Lansdowne Rd. ME4 ... 9 E2
Lanthorne Rd. CT10 ... 30 A6
Lapwing Dr. ME9 ... 13 B3
Larch Cl. CT10 ... 29 D4
Larch Rd. CT15 ... 114 B3
Larch Terr. ME12 ... 3 A8
Larch Wlk. TN24 ... 139 C6
Larch Wood Cl. ME5 ... 32 C4
Larchcroft. ME5 ... 32 A1
Larches The.
 Faversham ME13 ... 62 A8
Larches The.
 Whitstable CT5 ... 43 C8
Larkey View. CT4 ... 86 E1
Larkfield Ave.
 Gillingham ME7 ... 10 E4
Larkfield Ave.
 Sittingbourne ME10 ... 36 E6

Larksfield Rd. ME13 .... 40 C1
Larkspur Rd. ME5 .... 31 E4
Lascelles Rd. CT17 .... 166 A6
Laser Quay. ME2 .... 9 D6
Latchgate. CT20 .... 177 C3
Lathe Barn (Mus). TN29 .... 186 B5
Latimer Cl. CT14 .... 22 B2
Latimer Pl. ③ ME7 .... 10 C7
Launder Way. ME15 .... 74 E2
Laundry Rd. CT12 .... 50 D7
Laureate Cl. CT9 .... 8 B2
Laurel Ave. TN29 .... 194 F4
Laurel Cl. CT20 .... 177 E6
Laurel Gr. ME17 .... 99 D2
Laurel Ho. ME12 .... 1 C2
Laurel Rd. ME15 .... 10 C7
Laurel Wlk. ME8 .... 33 E6
Laurels The. ME16 .... 74 C2
Laureston Pl. CT16 .... 166 E8
Laurie Gray Ave. ME5 .... 31 D1
Lauriston Cl. CT11 .... 52 A5
Lauriston Mount. CT10 .... 30 A5
Lausanne Rd. CT9 .... 7 J2
Lausanne Terr. ① CT9 .... 7 J2
Lavenda Cl. ME4 .... 33 A4
Lavender Cl. ①
  Chatham ME5 .... 31 E4
Lavender Cl. Margate CT9 .. 28 C8
Lavender Cl.
  Whitstable CT5 .... 21 C2
Lavender Cl. ME10 .... 37 A3
Laverstoke Rd. ME16 .... 74 C8
Lawley Cl. CT2 .... 29 C1
Lawn Cl. ME4 .... 10 B2
Lawn Rd. Broadstairs CT10 .. 30 A4
Lawn Rd. Deal CT14 .... 117 C1
Lawns The. ⑮ CT11 .... 52 F7
Lawrence Cl.
  Folkestone CT19 .... 177 F6
Lawrence Cl.
  Maidstone ME15 .... 97 A7
Lawrence Cl. CT19 .... 178 E6
Lawrence Gdns. CT6 .... 23 C4
Lawrence St. ME7 .... 10 C5
Laws La. TN25 .... 172 D7
Lawson Cl. CT4 .... 86 D2
Laxey The. ME15 .... 74 E1
Laxton Cl. ME15 .... 75 F3
Laxton Dr. ME17 .... 98 A1
Laxton Way.
  Canterbury CT1 .... 88 C7
Laxton Way.
  Faversham ME13 .... 62 E5
Laxton Way.
  Sittingbourne ME10 .... 36 D6
Laxton Way.
  Whitstable CT5 .... 21 C1
Layfield Rd. ME7 .... 10 F7
Laylam Cl. CT10 .... 29 D5
Lea Cl. CT21 .... 176 B4
Lea Ct. ME4 .... 9 E1
Leacon Cotts. TN27 .... 120 E4
Leacon Cotts The. TN27 .... 120 E4
Leacon Rd. TN23 .... 138 F2
Leafield. TN25 .... 159 D1
Leafy Glade. ME8 .... 33 B6
Leahurst Ct. CT16 .... 148 E4
Leander Rd. ME1 .... 31 C7
Learoyd Rd. TN28 .... 200 C6
Leas Gn. CT10 .... 29 D4
Leas Rd. CT14 .... 117 B4
Leas The.
  Faversham ME13 .... 62 B8
Leas The. Folkestone CT20 . 178 C4
Leas The. Kingsdown CT14 . 134 D3
Leas The. Minster ME12 ...... 4 C8
Leas The. Sheerness ME12 .. 1 I1
Leas The. Whitstable CT5 ... 21 D1
Leaside Cotts. CT21 .... 176 B3
Leatt Cl. CT10 .... 29 F4
Leaveland Cl.
  * Ashford TN23 .... 155 E6
Leaveland Cl.
  Ashford TN23 .... 155 F6
Leaveland Cotts. ME13 ...... 83 B2
Leda Cotts. TN25 .... 120 F3
Leeds & Broomfield
  CE Prim Sch. ME17 .... 99 A7
Leeds Castle. ME17 .... 99 D7
Leeds Rd. ME17 .... 98 E3
Leeds Sq. ME8 .... 11 B3
Leelands Ho. CT14 .... 117 B1
Lees Cl The. TN25 .... 158 D5
Lees Court Rd. ME13 .... 83 C5
Lees Rd. Ashford TN24 ..... 140 A1
Lees Rd.
  Brabourne Lees TN25 ..... 158 E6
Lees Terr. CT4 .... 85 C2
Lees The. Herne Bay CT6 ... 23 C5
Lees The. Herne Bay CT6 ... 23 D5

Leet Cl. ME7 .... 10 E6
Leeward Rd. ME1 .... 9 C1
Leggett's La. ④ CT5 .... 20 D2
Leicester Ave. CT9 .... 8 C2
Leicester Gdns. ME12 .... 6 E2
Leicester Rd. ME15 .... 97 D7
Leigh Ave. ME15 .... 97 B6
Leigh Ct. ME12 .... 3 F5
Leigh Green Ind Est.
  TN30 .... 179 E6
Leigh Rd. CT12 .... 28 F1
Leighton Cl. ③ CT16 .... 149 C1
Leighton Rd. CT16 .... 149 C1
Leighville Dr. CT6 .... 22 D4
Leivers Rd. CT14 .... 117 A3
Len Valley Wlk. ME15 .... 75 F1
Lenacre Ave. CT16 .... 148 F7
Lenacre La. CT16 .... 148 F8
Lenacre St. TN25 .... 122 B2
Lenfield Ave. ME14 .... 75 B4
Length The. CT7 .... 25 F2
Lenham Cl. CT10 .... 30 A2
Lenham
  Cty Prim Sch. ME17 ...... 101 C5
Lenham Forstal Rd. ME17 . 119 B8
Lenham Gdns. CT9 .... 28 B8
Lenham Heath Rd. ME17 ... 101 C2
Lenham Ho. ME17 .... 101 E5
Lenham Rd. ME17 .... 100 C1
Lenham Sta. ME17 .... 101 C4
Lenham Way. ME8 .... 11 A3
Lennard Ct. ③ CT20 .... 178 E5
Lennard Rd. CT20 .... 178 E5
Lenside Dr. ME15 .... 76 A2
Leona Ct. ⑧ CT9 .... 8 B2
Leonard Cl. ME14 .... 74 B6
Leonard Rd. Chatham ME4 . 10 B3
Leonard Rd.
  Greatstone-on-S TN29 .. 204 E7
Leonard's Ave. CT11 .... 29 E1
Leopold Rd. ②
  Chatham ME4 .... 10 A3
Leopold Rd. Ramsgate CT11 52 E8
Leopold St. CT11 .... 52 E6
Lerryn Gdns. CT10 .... 29 F8
Les Spickett Cl. ME13 .... 62 E6
Lesley Ave. CT1 .... 88 A6
Leslie Ave. CT9 .... 28 B8
Leslie Dr. TN30 .... 167 B2
Leslie Pl. ME16 .... 74 E5
Leslie Rd. Birchington CT7 . 27 A8
Leslie Rd. Gillingham ME7 .. 10 D7
Leslie Smith Dr. ME13 .... 62 C7
Lested La. ME17 .... 98 B2
Lester Rd. ME4 .... 10 A3
Letchworth Ave. ME4 .... 9 F1
Lewd La. TN27 .... 135 A3
Lewis Ave. ME8 .... 11 B2
Lewis Cl. ME13 .... 62 A7
Lewis Court Dr. ME17 .... 97 C3
Lewis Cres. CT9 .... 8 B3
Lewis Ct. TN23 .... 155 F7
Lewisham Rd. CT17 .... 148 E3
Lewson Street Rd. ME9 ...... 60 E8
Leybourn Rd. CT10 .... 30 B2
Leybourne Cl. ME5 .... 32 A2
Leybourne Dr. CT9 .... 28 B8
Leyburne Rd. CT16 .... 166 D8
Leycroft Cl. CT2 .... 66 E3
Leys The. CT12 .... 28 D1
Leysdown Rd.
  Eastchurch ME12 .... 6 C1
Leysdown Rd.
  Leysdown-on-S ME12 .... 6 C1
Leyton Ave. ME7 .... 10 E1
Libya Terr. ⑥ ME14 .... 75 A7
Lichfield Ave. CT1 .... 88 B6
Lichfield Cl. ME8 .... 11 D2
Lidsing Rd. ME14 .... 54 F6
Liege Cl. ME10 .... 14 F1
Lighthouse Rd. CT15 .... 151 A5
Lilac Ho. ME12 .... 1 C2
Lilk Hill. ME14 .... 76 C3
Lillian Rd. CT11 .... 52 F8
Lilyvale Cotts. TN25 .... 158 F4
Lime Cl. TN23 .... 138 F3
Lime Ct. ME8 .... 33 C3
Lime Gr.
  Halfway Houses ME12 .... 3 D5
Lime Gr.
  Sittingbourne ME10 .... 37 A4
Lime Kiln Rd. CT1 .... 87 F6
Lime Kiln Wharf. ME11 .... 3 A5
Lime Villas. CT4 .... 144 F5
Limekiln Rdbt. CT17 .... 166 D6
Limekiln St. CT17 .... 166 D5
Limepits Cross. ME9 .... 35 F3
Limes Cl. TN30 .... 179 C8
Limes Pl. ⑱ ME13 .... 62 D7
Limes Rd. Dover CT16 ...... 149 C1
Limes Rd. Folkestone CT19 177 F6

Limes The. Lenham ME17 . 101 D5
Limes The.
  Old Romney TN29 .... 199 A7
Limetree Cl. ME5 .... 32 B8
Limetree Terr. ME17 .... 101 E6
Linces The. CT16 .... 149 B4
Lincoln Ave. CT1 .... 88 B7
Lincoln Cl. CT5 .... 21 D3
Lincoln Gdns. CT 26 F7
Lincoln Rd. ME15 .... 97 D8
Lincon Rd. ME7 .... 10 D7
Linden Ave.
  Broadstairs CT10 .... 30 B5
Linden Ave. Herne Bay CT6 . 22 E4
Linden Ave. Whitstable CT5 . 20 F1
Linden Chase. CT2 .... 66 E1
Linden Cl.
  Sittingbourne ME10 .... 36 D3
Linden Cl.
  Westgate-on-S CT8 .... 27 E7
Linden Cres. CT19 .... 178 D6
Linden Dr. ME12 .... 3 A7
Linden Gr. CT2 .... 66 E1
Linden Grove
  Cty Prim Sch. TN23 ...... 155 F6
Linden Ho. ⑤ ME5 .... 31 F4
Linden Rd. Ashford TN24 .. 139 D1
Linden Rd. Coxheath ME17 . 96 C4
Linden Rd. Gillingham ME7 . 10 E5
Linden Rd.
  Westgate-on-S CT8 .... 27 F8
Lindens. CT21 .... 176 D2
Lindenthorpe Rd. CT10 ...... 30 A6
Lindfield Cotts. ME13 .... 62 A6
Lindridge Cl. CT6 .... 46 A8
Lineacre Cl. ME8 .... 33 D6
Lines Terr. ME4 .... 10 A4
Linington Rd. CT7 .... 27 A6
Linton Hill La. TN27 .... 118 D3
Link La. CT1 .... 88 A8
Link Rd. Broadstairs CT10 .. 29 F7
Link Rd. Tyler Hill CT2 ...... 66 E6
Link The. TN20 .... 155 E7
Links Cl. CT8 .... 23 A3
Links Cl. CT16 .... 23 A3
Links Cres. TN29 .... 195 A4
Links Ct. CT14 .... 95 C1
Links Rd. CT14 .... 117 C8
Links The. ME5 .... 32 B8
Links Way. TN28 .... 200 D6
Linksfield Rd. CT8 .... 27 D7
Linksway. CT19 .... 178 B8
Linksway Cl. CT19 .... 178 B8
Linkway. ME9 .... 14 D4
Linley Ho. CT10 .... 29 E7
Linley Rd. CT10 .... 29 E7
Linnet Ave. CT5 .... 43 B6
Linton Gore. ME17 .... 96 D3
Linton Hill. ME17 .... 96 E1
Linton Hospl. ME17 .... 96 C2
Linton Rd. ME15 .... 96 F4
Lion Field. ME13 .... 62 B7
Lion Yd. Faversham ME13 .. 62 A6
Lion Yd. ③
  Sittingbourne ME10 .... 36 F4
Lion's Rd. TN28 .... 200 A6
Lionard Ho. ③ CT2 .... 66 E1
Liphook Way. ME16 .... 74 C8
Lisa Ct. CT5 .... 21 A2
Lismore Cl. ME15 .... 97 A7
Lismore Rd. Herne Bay CT6 . 23 D5
Lismore Rd.
  Whitstable CT5 .... 44 B8
Liss Rd. CT13 .... 93 A1
List The. CT3 .... 69 C2
Lister Cl. Deal CT14 .... 117 C5
Lister Cl. Dover CT17 .... 149 B1
Lister Ho. CT9 .... 29 A8
Lister Rd. CT9 .... 29 A8
Lister Way. CT20 .... 177 F3
Listmas Rd. ME4 .... 10 B3
Listways Cotts. CT13 .... 113 B6
Little Ave. CT14 .... 116 F3
Little Brook Rd. TN23 ...... 139 A3
Little Buckland Ave. ME16 . 74 D6
Little Charles St. CT6 .... 22 F5
Little Chequers. TN25 ..... 123 E2
Little Cl. ME16 .... 74 D2
Little Glovers. ME10 .... 36 F3
Little Hempen. TN23 .... 155 D8
Little Hill. TN30 .... 167 B2
Little John Ave. ME5 .... 31 F2
Little Kit's Coty Ho. ME20 . 53 C5
Little Knoll. TN23 .... 155 F8
Little Meadow. CT2 .... 65 E1
Little Orch. ME17 .... 96 D3
Little Paddocks. CT5 .... 44 D7
Little Stone Stile Cotts.
  ME13 .... 84 F4
Little Walton. CT13 .... 93 C3
Littlebourne Ave. ME8 ...... 11 B4

Littlebourne
  CE Prim Sch. CT3 .... 89 F8
Littlebourne Rd.
  Canterbury CT1 & CT3 .... 88 E8
Littlebourne Rd.
  Maidstone ME14 .... 75 C6
Littlebrook Cl. TN23 .... 139 A3
Littlemead. CT19 .... 178 A7
Littlestone Golf Course.
  TN28 .... 200 E8
Littlestone Rd. TN28 .... 200 D6
Liverpool Lawn. ⑮ CT11 ... 52 E6
Liverpool Rd. CT14 .... 117 D2
Livingstone Circ. ME10 ..... 10 D5
Livingstone Cl. TN29 ...... 187 B4
Livingstone Rd.
  Broadstairs CT10 .... 29 E6
Livingstone Rd.
  Gillingham ME8 .... 10 E5
Livingstone Wlk. ④ ME15 . 97 F5
Llamas Gate. ME13 .... 62 D8
Lloyd Rd. CT10 .... 30 A4
Lloyds Gn. TN30 .... 188 D4
Loach Ho. ME13 .... 64 A3
Loading Bay App.
  CT12 & CT13 .... 73 A8
Loaland Bsns Ctr. ME2 .... 9 D8
Lobelia Cl. ME7 .... 10 E6
Locarno Ave. ME8 .... 11 A2
Lock La. ME14 & ME16 .... 53 D1
Lock St. ME7 .... 10 C5
Lockenden Cotts. CT3 .... 89 D6
Lockholt Cl. TN23 .... 138 E3
Lockington Gr. ME1 .... 9 C5
Locksley Cl. ME5 .... 31 E2
Lockswood. ME16 .... 74 D7
Loddington La. ME17 .... 97 A1
Loder Cl. ME17 .... 101 B5
Lodge Cl. CT2 .... 66 A5
Lodge Rd. ME14 .... 75 D5
Lodge The. ME4 .... 10 A2
Lodge The. TN24 .... 139 D7
Lomas Rd. ME10 & ME9 .... 37 D4
Lombard St. CT9 .... 7 I3
Lombardy Cl. ME7 .... 33 A6
Lombardy Dr. ME14 .... 75 C5
London Rd. Canterbury CT2 . 66 D1
London Rd. Deal CT14 ...... 117 B5
London Rd.
  Dover CT16 & CT17 .... 149 B1
London Rd.
  Faversham ME13 & ME9 .. 61 C7
London Rd.
  Faversham ME13 .... 63 A5
London Rd. Faversham,
  Ospringe ME13 .... 62 B6
London Rd. Gillingham ME8 . 11 C1
London Rd.
  Hartlip Hill ME8 & ME9 .... 34 D7
London Rd. Hythe CT21 .... 175 F3
London Rd.
  Maidstone ME16 .... 74 C6
London Rd. Newington ME9 . 35 A6
London Rd. Ramsgate CT11 . 52 B6
London Rd. Rochester ME2 .. 9 A7
London Rd.
  Sittingbourne ME10 .... 36 C4
London Rd. Temple Ewell
  CT15 & CT16 .... 148 B8
London Rd. Teynham ME9 .. 38 C1
London Road (River).
  CT16 & CT17 .... 148 F4
London Road Temple Ewell.
  CT16 .... 148 D5
London Road Trad Est.
  ME10 .... 36 D4
London St. CT20 .... 178 E5
Lone Barn Rd. ME17 .... 102 B8
Lonefield. TN26 .... 155 B1
Long Acre Cl. CT2 .... 66 F2
Long Barrow The. CT4 ..... 156 E6
Long Beech. TN23 .... 138 E1
Long Catlis Rd. ME8 .... 33 D4
Long Dr. CT13 .... 93 C2
Long Hill. CT4 .... 85 C1
Long La. CT15 .... 130 D7
Long Length. TN23 .... 155 D4
Long Market. ② CT1 .... 88 A8
Long Meadow Way. CT2 ..... 67 A4
Long Reach Cl. CT5 .... 43 C6
Long Rede La. ME16 .... 74 A3
Long Rock. CT5 .... 21 C3
Long Row. TN25 .... 157 D2
Long Wlk. TN23 .... 138 E4
Long's Acre. TN25 .... 123 E1
Longacre. CT5 .... 21 D1
Longacre Rd. TN23 .... 155 D7
Longage Hill. CT18 & CT4 . 144 A1
Longbridge. TN24 .... 140 B1
Longbridge Terr. CT21 .... 175 F1
Longfellow Rd. ME7 .... 10 C3
Longfield. TN30 .... 179 A6

Longfield Cl. CT5 .... 21 D2
Longfield Pl. ME15 .... 97 C8
Longfield Rd. CT17 .... 166 B3
Longfields Dr. ME14 .... 76 A5
Longford Cl. ME8 .... 34 A8
Longford Ct. ME8 .... 34 A8
Longford Terr. ⑨ CT20 .... 178 D4
Longford Way. ⑩ CT20 .... 178 D4
Longham Copse. ME15 ...... 75 F1
Longhill Ave. ME7 .... 10 B3
Longhurst Dr. ME5 .... 31 F2
Longley Rd.
  Gillingham ME8 .... 11 F1
Longley Rd. Rochester ME1 .. 9 C4
Longmead Cl. CT6 .... 22 C3
Longparish Cl. ME15 .... 97 F6
Longmore Dr. ME12 .... 5 C1
Longparish Cl. ME15 .... 97 F6
Longport. CT1 .... 88 B8
Longridge. ME10 .... 37 B2
Longsfield. TN25 .... 173 A6
Longshaw Rd. ME15 .... 97 F5
Longtye Dr. CT5 .... 44 C7
Longwood. ME5 .... 32 B1
Lonsdale Ave. CT9 .... 8 C3
Lonsdale Dr.
  Gillingham ME8 .... 33 E7
Lonsdale Dr.
  Herne Bay CT6 .... 22 B5
Lonsdale Dr.
  Sittingbourne ME10 .... 36 C5
Lookers La. CT21 .... 176 B3
Loop Court Mews. CT13 .... 72 F1
Loop St. CT13 .... 72 F1
Loose Cty Prim Sch. ME15 . 97 A6
Loose Down Rd. ME13 ..... 104 F7
Lord Nelson Ho. ME15 .... 97 A7
Lord Romney's Hill. ME14 . 75 F3
Lord Warden Ave. CT14 ... 117 D2
Lord Warden Sq. CT17 .... 166 D5
Lords Cl. ME9 .... 37 E2
Lords Cotts. ME13 .... 83 C4
Lords Wood Cl. ME5 .... 32 B2
Lords Wood La. ME5 .... 32 B3
Lordswood
  Cty Prim Sch. ME5 .... 32 B3
Lordswood Ind Est. ME5 ... 54 C8
Lorina Rd. CT12 .... 52 C8
Lorne Cotts. CT14 .... 117 C7
Lorne Rd. Dover CT16 ..... 149 B2
Lorne Rd. Ramsgate CT11 . 52 C6
Lorraine Ct. ① CT19 .... 178 E6
Loudon Ct. TN23 .... 138 E3
Loudon Path. TN23 .... 138 E3
Loudon Way. TN23 .... 138 E3
Loughborough Ct. ② CT11 . 52 E7
Louisville Ave. ME7 .... 10 D4
Love La. Adisham CT3 .... 90 F2
Love La. Canterbury CT1 .... 88 A8
Love La. Faversham ME13 .. 62 F6
Love La. Margate CT9 .... 7 J3
Love La. Minster ME12 .... 4 D7
Love La. Rochester ME1 ...... 9 C5
Love Street Cl. CT6 .... 22 C2
Lovelace Cl. ME8 .... 33 D4
Lovelace Ct. TN26 .... 153 C5
Lovell Rd. Minster ME12 ...... 4 A5
Lovell Rd.
  Rough Common CT2 .... 66 B3
Lovell Rd.
  CT21 .... 176 D3
Lower Boxley Rd. ⑥ ME14 . 75 A5
Lower Bridge St. CT1 .... 88 A8
Lower Chantry La. CT1 ...... 88 A8
Lower Denmark Rd. TN23 . 156 C8
Lower East Rd. ME4 .... 10 B8
Lower Ensden Rd. CT4 ...... 85 D4
Lower Fant Rd. ME16 .... 74 D2
Lower Gore La. CT13 .... 93 B3
Lower Halstow
  Cty Prim Sch. ME9 .... 13 B2
Lower Hartlip Rd. ME9 ...... 34 E5
Lower Herne Rd. CT6 .... 45 E8
Lower Lees Rd. CT4 .... 85 D2
Lower Mill La. CT14 .... 117 C5
Lower Northdown Ave. CT9 . 8 B2
Lower Rainham Rd.
  Gillingham ME8 .... 12 A3
Lower Rainham Rd. Gillingham,
  Lower Twydall ME7 .... 11 D5
Lower Rd.
  East Farleigh ME15 .... 96 B7
Lower Rd.
  Faversham ME13 .... 61 C8
Lower Rd.
  Maidstone ME15 .... 75 B3
Lower Rd. Minster ME12 ..... 3 E4
Lower Rd. Minster ME12 ..... 4 E4

Lyminge Cl. ME8 .... 11 C2
Lyminge Way. CT9 .... 8 C1
Lymington Ct. ME15 .... 97 F4
Lymington Rd. CT8 .... 27 E7
Lympne Castle. CT21 .... 174 F2
Lympne CE Prim Sch.
CT21 .... 175 A3
Lympne Hill. CT21 .... 175 A2
Lympne Ind Est. CT21 .... 174 E3
Lyndhurst Ave.
Gillingham ME8 .... 33 C7
Lyndhurst Ave.
Margate CT9 .... 8 B2
Lyndhurst Cl. CT2 .... 66 E3
Lyndhurst Gr. ME10 .... 36 E2
Lyndhurst Rd.
Broadstairs CT10 .... 30 A6
Lyndhurst Rd.
Dymchurch TN29 .... 195 C8
Lyndhurst Rd.
Maidstone ME15 .... 97 C8
Lyndhurst Rd.
Ramsgate CT11 .... 52 F7
Lyndhurst Rd. River CT17 ... 148 E2
Lyndon Way. CT18 .... 161 C7
Lyngate Cl. CT7 .... 26 E8
Lynmouth Dr. ME12 .... 4 C7
Lynstead Ho. ME16 .... 74 A1
Lynsted La. TN23 .... 155 F6
Lynsted La. ME9 .... 60 B7
Lynsted & Norton
Cty Prim Sch. ME9 .... 60 B7
Lynsted Rd. Gillingham ME8 .. 11 B3
Lynsted Rd.
Halfway Houses ME12 .... 3 E7
Lynton Court Mansions. CT9 .. 8 B3
Lynton Dr. ME5 .... 32 B3
Lynton Pl. CT4 .... 89 A1
Lynton Rd. CT21 .... 176 C1
Lynwood. CT19 .... 178 C7
Lysander Cl.
Broadstairs CT10 .... 29 C3
Lysander Cl.
Littlebourne CT4 .... 89 E4
Lysander Wlk. CT18 .... 163 A4
Lytham Ave. CT6 .... 22 D1

Mableden Ave. TN24 .... 139 D1
Mableden Cl. TN28 .... 200 B6
Macdonald Par. CT5 .... 43 A6
Macdonald Rd.
Dover CT17 .... 149 A1
Macdonald Rd.
Gillingham ME7 .... 10 D6
Mace Ind Est. TN24 .... 139 C3
Mace La. TN23 & TN24 .... 139 C2
Mace Terr. TN26 .... 155 A1
Mackenzie Dr. CT20 .... 177 E5
Mackeson Ct. 6 CT21 .... 176 B2
Macklands Way. ME8 .... 12 A2
Madden Ave. ME5 .... 31 E5
Madeira Ct. CT20 .... 178 B3
Madeira Rd.
Littlebourne-on-S TN28 ...... 200 E6
Madeira Rd. Margate CT9 ...... 8 A2
Madeira Wlk. CT11 .... 52 E6
Madginford Cl. ME15 .... 76 A2
Madginford Park
Cty Inf Sch. ME15 .... 76 A2
Madginford Park
Cty Jun Sch. ME15 .... 76 A2
Madginford Rd. ME15 .... 75 F2
Madras Ho. 2 ME5 .... 97 E5
Mafeking Rd. ME5 .... 31 F3
Magazine Rd. TN24 .... 139 B3
Magdala Rd.
Broadstairs CT10 .... 29 E6
Magdala Rd. Dover CT17 .... 149 B1
Magdalen Cl. ME7 .... 33 A4
Magdalen Ct.
Broadstairs CT10 .... 30 A6
Magdalen Ct.
Canterbury CT1 .... 88 B7
Magness Rd. CT14 .... 117 A2
Magnolia Ave.
Gillingham ME8 .... 33 B8
Magnolia Ave. Margate CT9 .. 8 D2
Magnolia Rise. CT6 .... 23 D2
Magpie Ct. ME12 .... 4 A5
Magpie Hall Rd.
Chatham ME4 .... 10 A2
Magpie Hall Rd.
Stubb's Cross TN26 .... 155 E2
Magpie La.
Rhodes Minnis CT4 .... 144 B3
Magpie La.
Yelstead ME9 & ME14 .... 33 F1
Magwitch Cl. ME1 .... 9 B4

Maida Rd. ME4 .... 10 B2
Maidstone Barracks Sta.
ME16 .... 74 E5
Maidstone East Sta. ME14 ... 74 F5
Maidstone Gram Sch.
ME15 .... 75 B2
Maidstone Gram Sch
for Girls. ME16 .... 74 E5
Maidstone Hospl The.
ME16 .... 74 A4
Maidstone Ind Ctr. ME14 ..... 74 F5
Maidstone Mus &
Art Gallery. ME14 .... 74 F5
Maidstone Rd. Ashford TN23
& TN24 & TN25 & TN26 ... 138 D7
Maidstone Rd. Charing
TN25 & TN26 & TN27 ...... 120 D6
Maidstone Rd.
Chatham ME4 .... 9 F2
Maidstone Rd.
Chatham,Walderslade ME5 . 31 D4
Maidstone Rd.
Chestnut Street ME9 .... 35 D4
Maidstone Rd.
Five Wents ME17 .... 98 E2
Maidstone Rd.
Gillingham ME8 .... 33 C6
Maidstone Rd.
Gillingham,Bredhurst ME7 .. 33 B2
Maidstone Rd.
Lenham ME17 .... 101 D5
Maidstone Rd.
Rochester ME1 .... 9 C3
Maidstone St Francis Sch.
ME14 .... 75 A5
Maidstone West Sta. ME16 .. 74 F3
Mailyns The. ME8 .... 33 D7
Main Gate Rd. ME4 .... 9 F7
Main Rd. Queenborough
ME11 & ME12 .... 3 B5
Main Rd. Sheerness ME12 ..... 1 B3
Maison Des Fleurs. ME16 ..... 74 C2
Maison Dieu Pl. 4 CT16 .... 166 D8
Maison Dieu Rd. CT16 .... 166 D8
Maitland Ct. ME13 .... 40 B1
Makenade Ave. ME13 .... 62 E6
Malcolm Sargent Rd.
TN23 .... 156 B5
Malden Dr. ME14 .... 75 A8
Mall The. ME13 .... 62 C6
Mallard Apartments. 12
ME15 .... 97 E5
Mallard Ct. ME12 .... 4 A6
Mallards. TN24 .... 156 D7
Mallards Way. ME15 .... 76 A1
Malling Terr. ME16 .... 74 C4
Mallings Dr. ME14 .... 76 C4
Mallings La. ME14 .... 76 C4
Mallory Cl. CT12 .... 29 C2
Mallow Way. 1 ME5 .... 31 F4
Mallows The. ME14 .... 74 C2
Malmains Rd. CT17 .... 166 A6
Malt House La. TN30 .... 179 A7
Malta Ave. ME5 .... 32 A7
Malta Ho. 17 CT1 .... 67 B2
Malta Terr. 5 ME14 .... 75 A7
Malthouse Cl. ME17 .... 101 D5
Malthouse Cotts. TN28 ...... 200 A6
Malthouse Hill. 10
Hythe CT21 .... 176 B2
Malthouse Hill.
Loose ME15 .... 96 F4
Malthouse La.
Boughton Aluph TN25 .... 123 A4
Malthouse La.
Hamstreet TN26 .... 170 D1
Malthouse Rd. CT2 .... 66 F2
Maltings The.
Faversham ME13 .... 62 D7
Maltings The.
Gillingham ME8 .... 34 A8
Maltings The.
Littlebourne CT3 .... 89 F7
Maltings The.
Maidstone ME14 .... 75 E5
Maltings The.
Ramsgate CT11 .... 52 D7
Maltings The.
The Quarries ME17 .... 97 B4
Malus Cl. ME5 .... 32 B7
Malvern Meadow. CT6 .... 146 E5
Malvern Pk. CT6 .... 23 D4
Malvern Rd. Ashford TN24 . 139 B4
Malvern Rd. Dover CT17 .... 166 C7
Malvern Rd.
Gillingham ME7 .... 10 E3
Malvern Rd.
Temple Ewell CT16 .... 148 E5
Mamignot Cl. ME14 .... 76 A5
Manchester Cl. ME5 .... 32 C6

Manciple Cl. CT2 .... 87 C8
Mandeville Ct. 1 ME14 .... 75 A5
Mandeville Rd. CT2 .... 66 E2
Mangers La. CT16 .... 149 A2
Mangers Pl. CT16 .... 149 A3
Mangravet Ave. ME15 .... 97 C7
Manktelow Ct. CT10 .... 29 F2
Manley Cl. CT16 .... 149 A7
Mannering Cl. CT17 .... 148 F3
Mannock Ho. 6 CT1 .... 67 B1
Manns Hill. CT4 .... 127 A6
Manor Ave. CT14 .... 117 B4
Manor Cl. Canterbury CT1 ... 87 F5
Manor Cl. Deal CT14 .... 117 A4
Manor Cl. Herne Bay CT6 .... 23 F6
Manor Cl. Maidstone ME14 .. 76 B3
Manor Cl. Rushenden ME11 ... 3 A3
Manor Cotts.
Hernhill ME13 .... 64 B6
Manor Cotts.
Langley ME17 .... 98 C5
Manor Ct. Canterbury CT1 ... 87 F7
Manor Ct. Gillingham ME7 ... 11 C4
Manor Ct. Maidstone ME14 .. 76 B3
Manor Dr. CT7 .... 26 F6
Manor Gdns. ME5 .... 31 F4
Manor Gr. ME10 .... 36 E3
Manor Ho. 8 ME7 .... 10 A6
Manor House Dr. ME16 .... 74 D3
Manor La. ME1 .... 9 A2
Manor Lea Rd. CT7 .... 25 F1
Manor Leaze. TN25 .... 158 F5
Manor Mews. CT14 .... 133 F5
Manor Pound La. TN25 ...... 158 F7
Manor Rd.
Broadstairs CT10 .... 30 A4
Manor Rd. Chatham ME4 .... 9 F4
Manor Rd. Deal CT14 .... 117 A4
Manor Rd. Dover CT17 ...... 166 A6
Manor Rd.
Folkestone CT20 .... 178 E4
Manor Rd. Herne Bay CT6 ... 23 F6
Manor Rd. Lydd TN29 .... 203 C6
Manor Rd. Milstead ME9 ..... 58 F2
Manor Rd.
Mpnkton CT12 & CT7 .... 49 A8
Manor Rd.
Rushenden ME11 .... 3 A3
Manor Rd. Whitstable CT5 .. 21 A2
Manor Rise. Dover CT17 .... 166 A6
Manor Rise.
Maidstone ME14 .... 76 B3
Manor St. ME7 .... 10 A6
Manor Way. Ashford TN23 . 138 F4
Manor Way.
Leysdown-on-S ME12 .... 6 H2
Manor Way. Warden ME12 ..... 6 D6
Manorfield. Ashford TN23 .. 155 E8
Manorfield. Elham CT4 .... 144 F4
Manse Field. TN25 .... 158 E5
Mansel Dr. ME1 .... 9 A2
Mansell La. CT15 .... 146 B4
Mansfield Ct. CT14 .... 89 A1
Mansfield Wlk. ME16 .... 74 E2
Mansion Gdns. CT16 .... 149 A4
Mansion Row. ME7 .... 10 A6
Mansion St. CT9 .... 7 I3
Manston Court Cotts.
CT12 .... 28 C2
Manston Court Rd.
CT12 & CT9 .... 28 D3
Manston Park Bglws. CT12 . 27 F2
Manston Rd.
Acol CT12 & CT7 .... 27 D4
Manston Rd.
Lydden CT12 & CT9 .... 28 C4
Manston Rd.
Ramsgate CT11 & CT12 ...... 52 A8
Mantles Hill. CT14 .... 116 D1
Manwood Ave. CT2 .... 66 F3
Manwood Cl. ME10 .... 36 F2
Manwood Rd. CT13 .... 94 A6
Maple Ave. Gillingham ME7 .. 10 E6
Maple Ave.
Maidstone ME14 .... 74 A6
Maple Cl. Ashford TN23 .... 138 E3
Maple Cl.
Rough Common CT2 .... 66 B3
Maple Cl. CT3 .... 68 E8
Maple Dr. TN29 .... 194 F4
Maple Gdns. CT3 .... 68 E8
Maple St. ME12 .... 1 D1
Maples The.
Broadstairs CT10 .... 29 D4
Maples The. Minster ME12 .... 4 B6
Maplesden Noakes
Sch The. ME16 .... 74 C6
Maplins Cl. ME8 .... 11 F1
Marathon Paddock. ME7 ..... 10 D4
Mardale Cl. ME14 .... 12 A1
Marden Ave. CT12 .... 52 B8

Mardol Rd. TN24 .... 139 C5
Maresfield Cl. CT16 .... 149 B2
Margaret Ct. CT6 .... 22 F4
Margaret St. 8 CT20 .... 178 E5
Margarets Rd. CT15 .... 134 A1
Margate Cl. ME7 .... 10 E6
Margate Hill. CT7 .... 27 C4
Margate Rd. Herne Bay CT6 . 23 C3
Margate Rd. Herne Bay,
Broomfield CT6 .... 23 D2
Margate Rd. Ramsgate
CT10 & CT12 & CT11 .... 29 B3
Margate Sta. CT9 .... 7 H2
Marian Ave. ME12 .... 4 A7
Marilyn Cres. CT7 .... 27 B7
Marina Ct. CT14 .... 117 D8
Marina Dr. ME12 .... 4 A7
Marina Espl. CT11 .... 52 F7
Marina Rd. CT11 .... 52 F7
Marina The. CT14 .... 117 D8
Marina Way. TN29 .... 186 F3
Marine Cres. 7
Folkestone CT20 .... 178 D4
Marine Cres.
Whitstable CT5 .... 21 B3
Marine Ct. 13 CT16 .... 166 E7
Marine Dr. Broadstairs CT10 .. 8 G3
Marine Dr. Margate CT9 ...... 7 I2
Marine Gap. CT5 .... 20 C1
Marine Gdns. CT9 .... 7 I2
Marine Par. Dover CT16 .... 166 E7
Marine Par. Dover CT16 .... 166 F8
Marine Par.
Folkestone CT20 .... 178 E4
Marine Par. Hythe CT21 .... 176 C1
Marine Par.
Littlebourne-on-S TN28 .... 200 E5
Marine Par.
Sheerness ME12 .... 1 F2
Marine Parade Mews.
CT20 .... 178 E4
Marine Point. CT20 .... 178 A3
Marine Rd. CT14 .... 117 D4
Marine Terr. 7 H2
Marine Terr. Margate CT9 ..... 7 H2
Marine Terr.
Whitstable CT5 .... 20 C1
Marine Wlk St. CT21 .... 176 C2
Marion Cl. ME5 .... 32 A2
Marion Cres. ME15 .... 97 B8
Maritime Cl. ME2 .... 9 D8
Maritime Way. ME4 .... 10 A8
Marjan Cl. CT17 .... 149 A1
Mark Ave. CT11 .... 52 B5
Market Bldgs. 4 ME14 .... 74 F4
Market Colonnade. 3
ME14 .... 74 F4
Market Hill. CT21 .... 176 C2
Market La. 12 TN23 .... 139 B2
Market Pl. Aylesham CT3 ... 112 F5
Market Pl. Charing TN27 ... 120 C7
Market Pl. 1
Faversham ME13 .... 62 D7
Market Pl. 16
Folkestone CT20 .... 178 D5
Market Pl. Margate CT9 .... 7 I3
Market Sq. 12 CT16 .... 166 D7
Market St. Deal CT14 .... 117 D6
Market St.
Faversham ME13 .... 62 D7
Market St. Herne Bay CT6 ... 22 F5
Market St. 2
Maidstone ME14 .... 74 F4
Market St. Margate CT9 .... 7 I3
Market St. Sandwich CT13 .. 73 A1
Market View. CT13 .... 112 F5
Market Way. CT2 .... 67 A2
Markland Rd.
CT15 & CT17 .... 165 F7
Marlborough Cl.
Broadstairs CT10 .... 29 E3
Marlborough Cl.
Littlebourne-on-S TN28 .... 200 D6
Marlborough Rd.
Deal CT14 .... 117 A2
Marlborough Rd.
Dover CT15 & CT17 .... 165 F7
Marlborough Rd.
Gillingham ME7 .... 10 B5
Marlborough Rd.
Margate CT9 .... 7 I1
Marlborough Rd. 6
Ramsgate CT11 .... 52 D6

Marlborough Rd.
Whitstable CT5 .... 43 D5
Marlborough Way. TN24 ... 139 F7
Marler Rd. CT19 .... 177 E6
Marley Ct. CT2 .... 66 C4
Marley La. Chislet CT3 ..... 47 A5
Marley La.
Finglesham CT14 .... 116 A8
Marley La. Kingston CT4 ... 111 B1
Marley La. Westwood CT4 .. 127 F8
Marley Rd. ME17 .... 100 F6
Marley Way. ME1 .... 9 C2
Marlow Cl. CT5 .... 21 B1
Marlow Copse. ME5 .... 31 F1
Marlowe Ave. CT1 .... 87 F8
Marlowe Ave. CT1 .... 87 F8
Marlowe Ct. [13] CT1 ..... 87 F8
Marlowe Rd.
Ashford TN23 .... 139 B2
Marlowe Rd. Dover CT16 .. 149 B3
Marlowe Rd. Margate CT9 .. 29 C8
Marpit Cotts. ME17 .... 97 E2
Marquis Dr. ME7 .... 33 B3
Marr Cl. ME12 .... 3 F7
Marrose Ave. CT12 .... 29 B3
Marrowbone Hill. ME12 .... 5 B5
Marsh Cres. TN28 .... 200 B6
Marsh Farm Rd. CT12 ..... 50 B4
Marsh La. CT14 .... 117 A7
Marsh St. ME2 .... 9 B7
Marsh View. CT21 .... 187 C8
Marshall Cres.
Broadstairs CT10 .... 29 E4
Marshall Cres.
Rushenden ME11 .... 2 F3
Marshall Rd. ME8 .... 33 C8
Marshall St. CT19 .... 178 E7
Marshalls Land. TN30 ..... 167 A3
Marsham Cres. ME17 ...... 98 B1
Marsham St. ME14 .... 75 A4
Marshborough Rd. CT13 ... 93 B7
Marshlands. TN29 .... 195 B7
Marshlands Cl. TN29 ...... 195 B7
Marshwood Cl. CT1 .... 67 C3
Marstan Cl. ME9 .... 12 E2
Marston Cl. ME5 .... 31 E3
Marston Dr. ME14 .... 75 C5
Marston Wlk. ME5 .... 31 E3
Martello Cotts. CT21 ...... 187 E8
Martello Dr. CT21 .... 175 F1
Martello Ind Ctr. CT19 .... 178 F6
Martello Rd.
Folkestone CT20 .... 178 E7
Martello Rd. Folkestone,
Sandgate CT20 .... 177 E3
Martello Terr. [1] CT20 ... 177 F3
Marten Rd. CT20 .... 178 B5
Martha Cl. CT19 .... 178 B7
Martin Cl. ME7 .... 33 A3
Martin Dale Cres. CT15 ... 133 C2
Martin Ho. TN25 .... 123 E2
Martin Mill Sta. CT15 ..... 133 C2
Martin Rd. ME2 .... 9 B8
Martin's Cl. CT12 .... 29 C2
Martin's Way. CT21 ...... 187 D8
Martindale Cl. CT1 .... 88 A7
Martindown Rd. CT5 ...... 43 C7
Martins Cl. TN30 .... 179 C8
Martins The. TN26 .... 168 A8
Martyrs' Field Rd. CT1 .... 87 F7
Mary Green Wlk. [5] CT1 .. 67 B2
Mary Haugham
Almshouses. CT14 ..... 117 D7
Mary Rd. CT14 .... 117 A3
Maryland Ct. ME8 .... 33 E5
Mason's Rise. CT10 ...... 30 A5
Masons Rd. CT17 .... 149 B1
Mate Hall Villas. ME14 .... 76 C4
Matfield Cres. ME14 ...... 75 C5
Matilda Cl. ME7 .... 33 A2
Matthew's Pl. [9] CT16 .... 149 C1
Matthews Cl. CT14 .... 117 C6
Matthews Rd. CT6 .... 22 C2
Mattinson Pl. ME9 .... 78 F7
Matts Hill Rd. ME9 .... 33 E2
Maugham Ct. CT5 .... 43 D8
Maundene
Cty Prim Sch. ME5 ..... 32 B5
Maunders Cl. ME5 .... 32 C8
Maunsell Pl. TN24 .... 156 D7
Maxine Gdns. CT10 ...... 29 F5
Maxted Ct. CT6 .... 23 C4
Maxton Cl. Dover CT17 .... 166 A6
Maxton Cl.
Maidstone ME14 .... 75 F5
Maxton Cl. CT17 .... 166 A6
Maxton Rd. CT17 .... 166 A6
Maxwell Dr. ME16 .... 74 B6
Maxwell Pl. CT14 .... 117 C4
Maxwell Rd. ME7 .... 10 A6
May Lodge. CT14 .... 117 D5

May Rd. Gillingham ME7 ... 10 C4
May Rd. Rochester ME1 .... 9 C3
May St. CT6 .... 23 F4
May Terr. [2] ME4 .... 10 A7
Maybrook Ind Est. CT1 .... 67 C3
Maydowns Rd. CT5 .... 21 D2
Mayers Rd. CT14 .... 117 A1
Mayfair. ME2 .... 9 C8
Mayfair Ave. ME5 .... 97 A8
Mayfield Ave. CT16 ...... 149 C2
Mayfield Cl. Chatham ME5 .. 32 A1
Mayfield Cl.
Gillingham ME8 .... 11 E2
Mayfield Cl. [3] CT16 .... 149 B2
Mayfield Gdns. CT16 ..... 149 C2
Mayfield Rd.
Herne Bay CT6 .... 23 A3
Mayfield Rd.
Lyminge CT18 .... 161 C6
Mayfield Rd.
Whitfield CT16 .... 149 A7
Mayfly Dr. CT18 .... 163 A4
Mayford Rd. ME5 .... 32 D2
Mayforth Gdns. CT11 ..... 52 B6
Mayhew Cl. TN23 .... 156 A8
Maymills Cotts. CT13 ..... 93 B2
Maynard and Cotton's
Spital. [9] CT1 .... 87 F8
Maynard Ave. CT9 .... 28 B8
Maynard Pl. ME5 .... 10 D2
Maynard Rd. CT1 .... 87 E7
Mayor's Pl. [7] TN30 ...... 179 A7
Maypits. TN23 .... 155 F8
Maypole La. CT3 .... 46 E6
Maypole Rd. CT3 .... 46 E6
Mays Rd. CT11 .... 52 C6
Maystreet Cross. CT6 ..... 23 F3
Mayton La. CT2 .... 45 C1
Maytree Cotts. CT14 ..... 133 D8
Mayville Rd. CT10 .... 29 E6
Mayweed Ave. ME5 ...... 31 E4
Mc Kenzie Rd. ME5 ...... 32 A3
McAlpine Cres. ME15 .... 96 F3
McCarthy Ave. CT2 ...... 67 F7
McClean Wlk. ME12 ...... 17 C8
McCudden Row. [4] ME4 .. 10 A6
McKinlay Ct. CT7 .... 26 D8
Mead Rd. Ashford TN24 ... 156 E7
Mead Rd. Folkestone CT19 . 178 D6
Mead Way. CT2 .... 66 E1
Mead Wlk. TN23 .... 155 E8
Meade The. CT18 .... 162 F4
Meadow Bank. ME13 ..... 61 F7
Meadow Brook Ct. CT20 .. 177 E4
Meadow Cl. Bagham CT4 .. 107 E8
Meadow Cl. Bridge CT4 .... 89 A1
Meadow Cl. Chatham ME5 . 31 F5
Meadow Cl. Herne Bay CT6 . 23 C4
Meadow Cl. Iwade ME9 .... 14 D4
Meadow Cotts.
East Studdal CT15 ..... 132 D8
Meadow Cotts.
Goodnestone CT3 ...... 92 A2
Meadow Ct. TN25 .... 175 B6
Meadow Dr. CT5 .... 44 D8
Meadow Gr. TN25 .... 174 D8
Meadow Rd. Ashford TN23 139 A4
Meadow Rd.
Canterbury CT2 .... 66 C2
Meadow Rd. Margate CT9 .. 7 F1
Meadow Rd. Sturry CT2 ... 67 F6
Meadow View. TN26 ...... 138 A6
Meadow View Industries.
TN26 .... 183 C7
Meadow View Rd. Boughton
Monchelsea ME17 ...... 97 B3
Meadow View Rd.
Shepherdswell CT15 .... 130 E5
Meadow Wlk.
Maidstone ME15 .... 75 B3
Meadow Wlk.
Whitstable CT5 .... 43 C6
Meadowbank Rd. ME4 .... 10 A4
Meadowbrook. CT20 ...... 177 E4
Meadowbrook Cl. TN24 ... 139 D6
Meadowbrook Rd. TN24 .. 139 D6
Meadowdown. ME14 ..... 75 E4
Meadowdown Cl. ME7 .... 33 A4
Meadows The.
Herne Bay CT6 .... 23 D2
Meadows The.
Maidstone ME15 .... 74 E2
Meadows The.
Sittingbourne ME10 .... 36 D7
Meads Ave The. ME10 .... 36 D7
Meads Way. TN29 .... 194 E3
Meadside Wlk. ME5 ...... 31 F6
Meadway. CT17 .... 148 E3
Medina Ave. CT5 .... 43 B7
Medlar Cl. ME8 .... 58 A6

Medlar Gr. ME7 .... 33 A4
Medlars The. ME14 .... 75 D6
Medway Cl. ME10 .... 10 A1
Medway Com Coll. ME14 .. 10 A1
Medway Ent Ctr. ME2 ..... 9 D8
Medway Gdns. ME4 .... 9 F7
M:.dway Heritage Ctr. ME4 .. 9 F5
Medway Ho. [1] ME15 .... 97 D8
Medway Hospl. ME7 ...... 10 B4
Medway Rd.
Gillingham ME7 .... 10 C7
Medway Rd. Gillingham,
Rainham ME8 .... 11 F1
Medway Rd.
Sheerness ME12 .... 1 C1
Medway Service Area. ME8 . 33 F3
Medway St. Chatham ME4 . 9 F5
Medway St.
Maidstone ME15 .... 74 F4
Medway Trad Est. ME16 ... 74 F3
Medway Villas. ME15 ...... 96 B7
Meehan Rd. TN28 .... 200 E4
Meehan Rd S. TN28 ...... 200 E3
Meeres Court La. ME10 ... 37 C5
Meeson's Cl. ME13 .... 62 A6
Meeting House La. ME4 ... 9 F4
Meeting St. CT11 .... 52 E7
Megby Cl. ME8 .... 33 D6
Megone Cl. CT18 .... 163 A4
Meirs Court Rd. ME8 ..... 33 E6
Melbourne Ave.
Dover CT16 .... 149 C4
Melbourne Ave.
Ramsgate CT12 .... 29 B1
Melbourne
Cty Prim Sch. CT16 .... 149 C4
Melbourne Rd. ME4 ...... 10 A3
Melbury Mews. ME5 ...... 38 C2
Melford Dr. ME16 .... 74 C4
Mellanby Cl. CT7 .... 27 A6
Mellor Row. ME10 .... 14 F1
Melody Cl. Gillingham ME8 . 33 C4
Melody Cl. Warden ME12 .. 6 E4
Melon La. TN26 & TN29 ... 193 B6
Melrose Cl. ME15 .... 97 A7
Melsetter Cl. CT17 .... 27 B7
Melville Ct. ME4 .... 9 E1
Melville Lea. CT13 .... 93 C7
Melville Rd. ME15 .... 75 A3
Memorial (General) Hospl.
ME10 .... 36 F3
Mendfield St. [5] ME13 ... 62 C7
Mendip Rise. TN24 ...... 139 B4
Menin Rd. ME10 .... 14 F1
Mentmore Ho. CT12 ...... 29 C3
Mentmore Rd.CT10 & CT12 . 29 C3
Menzies Ave. CT14 ...... 117 B1
Menzies Cl. ME12 .... 4 A5
Mercer Dr. ME17 .... 100 F6
Mercer Way. ME17 .... 98 B1
Mercery La. [5] CT1 ...... 87 F8
Merchants Way. CT2 ...... 87 C8
Mercury Cl. ME1 .... 9 A3
Mere Gate. CT9 .... 7 I1
Meredale Cty Inf Sch. ME8 . 12 A1
Meresborough Cots. ME8 .. 33 F5
Meresborough La.
ME8 & ME9 .... 34 B5
Meresborough Rd. ME8 ... 34 A7
Merewerth Cl. ME8 ...... 11 A3
Meridian Ct. TN23 .... 155 E7
Meridian Pk. ME2 .... 9 E6
Merivale Gr. ME5 .... 32 B4
Merleburgh Dr. ME10 .... 36 F8
Merlin Cl. ME7 .... 10 A3
Mermaid Cl. ME5 .... 32 A6
Merritt Rd. TN28 .... 200 E2
Mersham
Cty Prim Sch. TN25 .... 157 E3
Merton Cl. ME5 .... 32 C5
Merton La. CT1 & CT4 .... 87 F4
Merton Rd. ME15 .... 75 F2
Meryl Gdns. CT14 .... 117 C1
Metcalfe Mews. [1] CT1 ... 67 B2
Meteor Ave. CT5 .... 43 B7
Metropole Rd E. CT20 .... 178 B3
Metropole Rd W. CT20 .... 178 B3
Meverall Ave. CT12 ...... 51 E5
Mews The. Maidstone ME16 74 E5
Mews The.
Sittingbourne ME10 .... 36 F2
Meyrick Rd. ME12 .... 1 D2
Micawber Cl. ME5 .... 32 A1
Michael Ave. CT11 .... 52 G8
Michelle Gdns. CT9 ...... 28 A8
Mickleburgh Ave. CT6 .... 23 B4
Mickleburgh Hill. CT6 .... 23 B4
Mid Kent Coll
(City Way Ctr). ME1 ..... 9 E4
Mid Kent Coll of H & F Ed.
Maidstone ME16 .... 74 E3

Mid Kent Coll of H & F Ed.
Maidstone,Cherry Orchard
ME16 .... 74 C3
Mid Kent Coll of H & F Ed.
ME1 & ME4 .... 31 E6
Mid Kent Sch for Girls.
ME14 .... 75 B5
Mid Kent Sh Ctr The. ME16 . 74 C7
Middelburg Ho. CT19 ..... 177 D6
Middelburg Sq. CT20 ..... 178 D4
Middle Cl. TN23 .... 138 C1
Middle Deal Rd. CT14 .... 117 B5
Middle Mead. CT19 ...... 178 A7
Middle Row. Ashford TN23 139 C2
Middle Row. [2]
Faversham ME13 .... 62 D7
Middle Row. [6]
Maidstone ME15 .... 74 F4
Middle St. Ashford TN23 ... 139 B2
Middle St. Deal CT14 ..... 117 D6
Middle St. [5]
Gillingham ME4 .... 10 A6
Middle Wall. CT5 .... 20 D2
Middle Way. ME10 .... 37 B3
Middlefields. ME8 .... 34 A8
Middlesex Rd. ME15 ...... 97 D7
Middleton Cl. ME8 .... 33 E4
Middleton Cotts. TN25 ... 122 E3
Middleton Cl. [8] ME10 ... 36 E4
Middletune Ave. ME10 .... 36 E7
Midhurst Cr. ME15 .... 75 A3
Midley Cl. ME16 .... 74 C7
Midsummer Hill. TN24 ... 139 D6
Miers Court
Cty Prim Sch. ME8 ..... 33 F7
Mierscourt Cl. ME8 ...... 34 A8
Mierscourt Rd. ME8 ...... 33 E6
Mikyle Ct. CT1 .... 88 A6
Milbourne Gr. ME10 ...... 36 E7
Milburn Rd. ME7 .... 10 C7
Mildred Cotts. CT19 ...... 177 F7
Mile Rd. CT12 & CT3 ...... 48 F6
Miles Ct. CT3 .... 91 A8
Miles Rd. ME15 .... 75 A3
Milesend CT19 .... 178 A7
Milestone Cl. CT19 ...... 178 A7
Milestone Rd. CT14 ...... 117 B5
Milford Cl. ME16 .... 74 D5
Military Rd. Canterbury CT1 . 67 B1
Military Rd. Canterbury CT1 . 67 B1
Military Rd. Chatham ME4 .. 9 F5
Military Rd. [2]
Dover CT17 .... 166 D7
Military Rd.
Folkestone CT20 .... 177 E4
Military Rd. Hythe CT21 ... 176 B2
Military Rd. Ramsgate CT11 . 52 E6
Military Rd. Stone in Oxney
TN26 & TN30 .... 190 B4
Mill Bank. TN29 .... 203 B6
Mill Bank Cotts. CT13 .... 93 A2
Mill Bay. CT20 .... 178 E5
Mill Cl. Hareblwen CT2 .. 101 C4
Mill Cl. River CT17 .... 148 F2
Mill Cl. Sandwich CT13 .... 72 E2
Mill Cotts. Ramsgate CT11 . 52 D6
Mill Cotts. Worth CT14 .... 94 A4
Mill Ct. ME10 .... 37 A3
Mill Field. Ash CT3 .... 71 E1
Mill Field. Broadstairs CT10 . 29 F5
Mill Fields Rd. CT21 ...... 175 F2
Mill Gn. CT13 .... 93 A2
Mill Hamlet. CT3 .... 69 C2
Mill Hill. CT14 .... 117 A3
Mill Hill. La. Aldington TN25 172 E5
Mill La. Ashford TN24 ..... 140 A1
Mill La. Bagham CT4 ..... 107 D7
Mill La.
Biddenden Green TN27 .. 135 A2
Mill La. Birchington CT7 .. 26 F6
Mill La. Bridge CT4 ...... 88 F1
Mill La. Canterbury CT1 ... 66 F1
Mill La. Canterbury,
Harbledown CT2 .... 87 C8
Mill La.
Chatham,Bluebell Hill ME5 . 31 D1
Mill La. Chatham,Luton ME5 . 10 C1
Mill La. Coxheath ME17 .... 96 D4
Mill La. [8] Dover CT16 ... 166 E7
Mill La. Eastry CT13 ...... 93 B2
Mill La. Hartlip Hill ME9 ... 34 E6
Mill La. Hawkinge CT18 ... 163 B5
Mill La. Herne Bay CT6 .... 23 B2
Mill La. Lynsted ME9 ...... 60 C5
Mill La. Maidstone ME14 .. 74 F6
Mill La. Margate CT9 ...... 7 I2
Mill La. Nonington CT15 .. 113 A5
Mill La. Northbourne CT14 . 115 F4
Mill La. Preston CT3 ...... 70 D6
Mill La.
Shepherdswell CT15 .... 130 F5

Mill La. Stelling Minnis CT4 . 126 C2
Mill La. Tenterden TN30 ... 167 B1
Mill La. Whitfield CT16 .... 149 A8
Mill La. Worth CT14 .... 94 A4
Mill Lane Cotts. CT14 ..... 116 A4
Mill Mews. CT14 .... 117 B4
Mill Pl. ME13 .... 62 D8
Mill Rd. Bethersden TN26 . 153 E5
Mill Rd. Bramling CT3 .... 90 E6
Mill Rd. Deal CT14 .... 117 C4
Mill Rd. Dymchurch TN29 . 195 B7
Mill Rd. Gillingham ME7 ... 10 C6
Mill Rd. Hoath CT3 .... 46 F5
Mill Rd. Hythe CT21 ...... 176 D2
Mill Rd. Lydd TN29 ...... 203 D7
Mill Rd. Rochester ME2 .... 9 B8
Mill Rd. Staple CT3 .... 92 B5
Mill Rd. Sturry CT2 .... 67 F5
Mill Row. CT7 .... 26 F6
Mill St. Loose ME15 ...... 96 F5
Mill St. Maidstone ME15 .. 74 F4
Mill St. Sittingbourne ME10 . 36 E5
Mill St.
Temple Ewell CT16 ..... 148 D5
Mill Terr. Bridge CT4 ..... 88 F1
Mill Terr. Chartham CT4 ... 86 D3
Mill View. Ashford TN24 .. 156 F8
Mill View.
Woodchurch TN26 ...... 169 A3
Mill View Rd. CT6 .... 23 A1
Mill Wall Pl. CT13 .... 94 A8
Mill Way. ME10 .... 36 F6
Milk. ME16 .... 74 A3
Millais Rd. CT16 .... 149 C1
Millbank La. TN29 .... 198 E7
Millbank Rd. TN23 .... 155 F5
Millbrook. CT21 .... 176 D2
Millbrook Cl. ME15 ...... 74 F1
Millbrook Meadow. TN23 . 138 C1
Milldale Cl. CT14 .... 117 B4
Millen Rd. ME10 .... 36 E5
Millen's Row. ME13 ...... 83 B3
Miller Ave. CT2 .... 87 D8
Miller Cl. ME10 .... 37 A8
Miller Ct. ME12 .... 4 A5
Millers Cl. CT5 .... 43 D7
Millers La. CT12 .... 49 C7
Millers Wharf. ME16 ..... 74 E2
Millfield. Ashford TN23 ... 155 D8
Millfield. Folkestone CT20 . 178 D5
Millfield. Hawkinge CT18 .. 163 C6
Millfield.
High Halden TN26 ...... 167 D3
Millfield.
Sittingbourne ME10 ..... 37 A3
Millfield. St Margaret's
at Cliffe CT15 .... 150 F7
Millfield Cl. CT18 .... 163 B5
Millfield Manor. CT5 ...... 20 E1
Millfield Rd.
Faversham ME13 .... 62 E7
Millfield Rd.
Ramsgate CT12 .... 29 B3
Millfields. Chatham ME5 ... 32 D2
Millfields.
Shepherdswell CT15 .... 130 E5
Millmead Ave. CT9 .... 8 D1
Millmead Gdns. CT9 ...... 8 D1
Millmead Rd. CT9 .... 8 C1
Millpond Cl. ME2 .... 9 B8
Mills Cl. ME12 .... 3 F6
Mills Terr. ME4 .... 10 A3
Millstock Terr. ME15 ...... 74 E2
Millstream Cl.
Faversham ME13 .... 62 C7
Millstream Cl.
Whitstable CT5 .... 20 E1
Millstrood Rd. CT5 .... 43 E8
Milne Rd. TN24 .... 156 F8
Milner Cl. CT15 .... 114 B1
Milner Cres. CT3 .... 112 E5
Milner La. CT2 .... 67 F5
Milner Rd. Elvington CT15 . 114 B1
Milner Rd. Gillingham ME7 . 10 D7
Milner Rd. Whitstable CT5 . 43 A6
Milstead Cl.
Maidstone ME14 .... 75 C5
Milstead Cl.
West Minster ME12 .... 3 B7
Milstead & Frinstead
CE Prim Sch. ME9 ...... 58 E1
Milsted Rd. ME8 .... 11 C3
Milton Ave. CT9 .... 7 J1
Milton Cl. Canterbury CT1 . 88 C6
Milton Cl. Dover CT16 ..... 149 B4
Milton Rd. Ashford TN23 .. 139 B2
Milton Rd. Canterbury CT1 . 88 A6
Milton Rd. Dover CT16 ..... 149 B4

Milton Rd. Gillingham ME7 .... 10 C3
Milton Rd.
  Sittingbourne ME10 .... 36 E4
Milton Rd. **4** CT9 .... 7 J1
Milton St. ME16 .... 74 C2
Mincers Cl. ME5 .... 32 C2
Minerva Ave. CT16 .... 149 C2
Minerva Ho. CT11 .... 52 D7
Minerva Rd. ME2 .... 9 A8
Minnis Field. CT4 .... 126 E2
Minnis Gn. CT4 .... 126 E2
Minnis La. CT15 & CT17 ...... 148 C2
Minnis Rd. CT7 .... 26 E7
Minnis Terr. CT17 .... 149 A2
Minnis Way. CT14 .... 94 B5
Minster Abbey.
  Minster ME12 .... 4 D6
Minster Abbey.
  Minster, Thanet CT12 .... 50 C5
Minster CE Prim Sch. CT12 . 50 B5
Minster Cl. CT10 .... 30 A2
Minster Coll. ME12 .... 3 F6
Minster Dr. Herne Bay CT6 .. 22 D4
Minster Dr. Minster ME12 .... 4 A8
Minster Lodge. CT11 .... 52 C6
Minster Rd.
  Acol CT12 & CT7 .... 27 C2
Minster Rd.
  Faversham ME13 .... 62 E7
Minster Rd. Gillingham ME8 . 11 C3
Minster Rd. Minster ME12 ... 4 B6
Minster Rd. Ramsgate CT11 . 52 B5
Minster Rd.
  Westgate-on-S CT8 .... 27 F7
Minster (Thanet) Sta.
  CT12 .... 50 C5
Minster-in-Sheppey
  Cty Prim Sch. ME12 .... 4 C7
Mint The. CT2 .... 66 C1
Mintching Wood La. ME9 .... 58 F2
Minster Ave. CT18 .... 162 F7
Minter Cl. CT18 .... 162 F7
Minterne Ave. ME10 .... 36 D2
Minterne
  Cty Jun Sch.ME10 .... 36 D2
Miranda Ct. ME2 .... 1 C1
Misling La. CT4 & TN25 ...... 143 C7
Missenden Ct. **6** CT20 ...... 178 D5
Mitcham Rd. TN29 .... 195 C8
Mitchell Ave. ME4 .... 9 F7
Mitchell Cl. ME17 .... 101 C5
Mitchell St. CT19 .... 177 D6
Mitre Rd. ME1 .... 9 B4
Mittell Ct. TN29 .... 203 B6
Moat Farm Rd. CT19 .... 178 C7
Moat Farm Rd. CT19 .... 178 C7
Moat Ho. Canterbury CT1 ... 87 F7
Moat Ho. Charing TN27 ..... 120 E7
Moat La. Ash CT3 .... 71 E1
Moat La.
  Fordwich CT2 & CT3 .... 68 A3
Moat La.
  Rough Common CT2 .... 66 B4
Moat Pk. TN27 .... 120 C6
Moat Sole. CT13 .... 72 F1
Moat The. TN27 .... 120 C7
Moat Way. ME11 .... 3 A5
Moatfield Meadow. TN23 .. 156 B4
Mock La. TN23 .... 155 B6
Mockett Cl. **4** ME10 .... 36 E4
Mockett Dr. CT10 .... 29 F7
Molehill Cnr. CT5 .... 44 D8
Molehill Copse
  Cty Prim Sch. ME15 .... 97 D7
Molehill Rd.
  Herne Bay CT6 & CT5 ...... 22 A1
Molehill Rd.
  Whitstable CT5 & CT6 ...... 44 E8
Molineux Rd. CT12 .... 50 B6
Molland Cl. CT3 .... 71 C2
Molland La. Ash CT3 .... 71 C2
Molland La.
  Westmarsh CT3 .... 71 D6
Molland Lea. CT3 .... 71 C2
Molloy Rd. TN26 .... 155 B1
Monarch Cl. ME5 .... 32 A6
Monastery St. CT1 .... 88 A8
Monckton's Ave. ME14 .... 74 F7
Monckton's Dr. ME14 .... 74 F7
Moncktons La. ME14 .... 74 F7
Moncrif Cl. ME14 .... 74 B4
Mongeham Church Cl.
  CT14 .... 116 D3
Mongeham
  Cty Prim Sch. CT14 .... 116 F4
Mongeham Rd. CT14 .... 116 E3
Monins Rd. CT17 .... 166 B7
Monkdown. ME15 .... 76 A1

Monkery La. ME13 & TN25 .. 104 D2
Monks Cl. Canterbury CT2 ... 67 A2
Monks Cl.
  Faversham ME13 .... 62 B8
Monks Way. CT16 .... 149 A3
Monks Wlk. TN27 .... 120 C7
Monkshill Rd. ME13 .... 42 B2
Monkton CE Prim Sch.
  CT12 .... 28 D2
Monkton Court La. CT15 .. 131 D7
Monkton Gdns. CT9 .... 8 E3
Monkton Manor. CT12 .... 49 B7
Monkton Pl. CT11 .... 52 D7
Monkton Rd. CT12 .... 50 A6
Monkton Rdbt. CT12 .... 49 D8
Monkton St. CT12 .... 49 D7
Monkwood Cl. ME1 .... 31 B8
Monmouth Cl. ME8 .... 11 D2
Mons Ct. ME10 .... 14 F1
Montacute Ct. CT20 .... 178 B4
Montague Ct. ME12 .... 1 C1
Montague Rd. CT11 .... 52 E8
Montague St. CT6 .... 22 D5
Montefiore Ave. CT11 .... 29 F1
Montefiore Cotts. CT11 ..... 52 F8
Montfort Cl. Ashford TN23 . 155 F7
Montfort Cl.
  Canterbury CT2 .... 67 A4
Montfort Rd. Chatham ME5 . 31 F2
Montfort Rd.
  Rochester ME2 .... 9 A8
Montgomery Ave. ME5 .... 32 A7
Montgomery GM Sch. CT3 .. 68 C8
Montgomery Rd. ME7 .... 10 C3
Montgomery Way. CT19 ... 178 E8
Montpelier Ave. CT5 .... 43 D6
Montpelier Bsns Pk. TN23 . 138 F1
Montpelier Gate. ME16 ..... 74 B5
Montreal Cl. **8** CT16 ...... 149 B3
Montrose Ave. ME5 .... 10 E2
Monument Way. TN24 ...... 156 F5
Moon Hill. CT15 .... 130 E4
Moonstone Dr. ME5 .... 32 B2
Moor La. Ivychurch TN29 .. 192 D4
Moor La. Woodchurch
  TN26 & TN30 .... 180 E6
Moor Lane Cotts. TN26 ..... 181 C2
Moor Park Cl. ME8 .... 34 A8
Moot St. ME8 .... 34 B8
Moore Cl. TN29 .... 192 A3
Moore St. ME2 .... 9 A8
Moorfield. CT2 .... 66 F4
Mooring Rd. ME1 .... 9 D1
Moorings The. ME9 .... 38 E6
Moorland Rd. CT15 .... 130 E4
Moorstock La. TN25 .... 159 C2
Moorwell Dr. CT15 .... 130 D5
Moray Ave. CT7 .... 26 F8
Mordaunt Ave. CT8 .... 27 E8
Morden St. ME1 .... 9 C4
Morehall Ave. CT19 .... 177 F6
Morehall
  Cty Prim Sch. CT19 .... 177 F6
Morella Wlk. ME17 .... 101 C5
Morello Cl. ME9 .... 38 C2
Moreton Terr. TN26 .... 155 A1
Morgan Kirby's Gdn. ME13 . 83 D5
Morris Ave. CT6 .... 21 F4
Morris Court Cl. ME9 .... 37 D2
Morrison Rd. CT20 .... 178 E6
Morry La. ME17 .... 99 D1
Mortimer Cl. TN23 .... 156 B7
Mortimer Rd. CT16 .... 166 F8
Mortimer St. CT6 .... 22 F5
Mossbank. ME5 .... 32 A3
Mossend Mews. CT11 .... 29 E2
Mossy Glade. ME8 .... 33 E6
Mostyn Rd. ME14 .... 75 C4
Mote Ave. ME15 .... 75 B3
Mote Pk. ME15 .... 75 D2
Mote Rd. ME15 .... 75 A3
Motney Hill Rd. ME8 .... 12 A4
Mouat Ct. ME5 .... 32 A2
Mount Charles Wlk. CT4 .... 88 F1
Mount Dr. ME14 .... 76 B4
Mount Ephraim. ME13 .... 64 A4
Mount Field.
  Faversham ME13 .... 62 B6
Mount Field.
  Queenborough ME11 .... 3 A5
Mount Green Ave. CT12 .... 51 D5
Mount La. Hartlip ME9 .... 34 D4
Mount La. Maidstone ME14 . 76 B4
Mount Lodge. ME1 .... 9 B2
Mount Pleasant.
  Aldington TN25 .... 173 A6
Mount Pleasant.
  Aylesford ME20 .... 53 A3
Mount Pleasant. Blean CT2 . 66 A6
Mount Pleasant.
  Gillingham ME4 .... 10 B3

Mount Pleasant.
  Kingsdown CT14 .... 134 D5
Mount Pleasant.
  Oare ME13 .... 40 B2
Mount Pleasant.
  Tenterden TN30 .... 179 C8
Mount Pleasant Dr. ME4 .... 76 A5
Mount Pleasant Rd. **4**
  CT20 .... 178 D5
Mount Pleasant Terr.
  ME17 .... 100 E2
Mount Rd. Canterbury CT1 .. 88 C6
Mount Rd. Chatham ME4 ..... 9 F3
Mount Rd. Dover CT17 ...... 166 A6
Mount Rd. Rochester ME1 .... 9 B2
Mount St. CT21 .... 176 C2
Mount View. ME13 .... 62 A5
Mount View Rd. CT6 .... 23 A2
Mountain St. CT4 .... 107 B6
Mountbatten Ave. ME5 ...... 32 A7
Mountbatten Way. TN25 .. 158 E6
Mountfield Rd. TN28 .... 200 C6
Mountfield Row. TN30 ...... 200 C6
Mountfield Way. CT8 .... 27 D6
Mountpleasant. CT18 .... 161 C7
Mounts Cl. CT14 .... 117 A5
Mountsfield Cl. ME16 .... 74 D5
Mountview. ME9 .... 36 B2
Moyle Cl. ME8 .... 33 D4
Mozart Ct. ME4 .... 9 E3
Muddy Bush Cnr. CT3 .... 90 F2
Muir Cl. Maidstone ME15 ... 75 A2
Muir Rd. Ramsgate CT11 ..... 52 F8
Mulberry Cl.
  Gillingham ME7 .... 33 A4
Mulberry Cl.
  Ramsgate CT11 .... 52 F8
Mulberry Ct.
  Canterbury CT1 .... 87 F8
Mulberry Ct.
  Littlestone-on-S TN28 .... 200 E5
Mulberry Field. CT13 .... 72 F1
Mulberry Hill. CT4 .... 85 D1
Munday Bois Cotts. TN27 . 135 F8
Munday Bois Rd. TN27 ..... 118 E1
Mundella Cty Prim Sch.
  CT19 .... 178 D6
Mungeam Ho. ME1 .... 9 C4
Munn's La. ME9 .... 34 E6
Murrain Dr. ME15 .... 76 A1
Murray Rd. ME2 .... 9 A8
Murston Cty Inf Sch. ME10 . 37 B4
Murston Jun Sch. ME10 ...... 37 B5
Murston Rd. ME10 .... 37 B4
Murthwaite Ct. ME12 .... 4 A5
Murton Pl. ME13 .... 41 E1
Museum of Kent Rural Life.
  ME14 .... 53 D1
Museum St. ME14 .... 74 F4
Musgrave Cl. CT12 .... 27 F2
Musgrave Rd. ME10 .... 36 F6
Musgrove. TN23 .... 156 A8
Mushroom La.
  Eyhorne Street ME17 .... 77 B2
Musket La. Silver Hill ME17 . 77 A2
Mustards Rd. ME2 .... 6 D2
Mutrix Gdns. CT9 .... 7 E1
Mutrix Rd. CT9 .... 28 B8
Mutton La. ME13 .... 62 A6
Mymms Cl. CT5 .... 44 C8
Mynn Cres. ME14 .... 76 A4
Myrtle Cres. ME5 .... 31 F5
Myrtle Rd. **4** CT19 .... 178 E6
Mystole Cl. CT4 .... 108 C8
Mystole Rd. CT4 .... 108 A8

Nacholt Cl. CT5 .... 21 A2
Nackington Cl. CT1 .... 88 B6
Nackington Pk. CT1 .... 88 A4
Nackington Rd. CT1 & CT4 . 88 A3
Nag's Head La. ME1 .... 9 D4
Nagpur Ho. **4** ME15 .... 97 E5
Nags Head La. ME1 .... 9 D4
Nailbourne Cl. CT4 .... 111 D3
Nailbourne Ct. CT18 .... 161 C7
Naildown Cl. CT21 .... 177 A3
Naildown Rd. CT21 .... 177 A3
Nairne Cl. TN26 .... 170 A8
Namur Pl. CT16 .... 149 F3
Napchester Rd.
  CT15 & CT16 .... 149 A8
Napier Cl. ME10 .... 36 C4
Napier Ct. ME14 .... 75 A2
Napier Cty Prim Sch. ME7 . 10 D4
Napier Gdns. CT21 .... 176 C2
Napier Ho. Dover CT16 ..... 149 F2
Napier Rd. Broadstairs CT10 .29 E6
Napier Rd. Dover CT16 ..... 149 F2
Napier Rd. Gillingham ME7 . 10 D4
Napleton Cl. CT11 .... 52 C6
Napleton Rd.
  Faversham ME13 .... 62 C7

Napleton Rd.
  Ramsgate CT11 .... 52 C6
Napoleon Wlk. ME7 .... 101 C5
Napwood Cl. ME8 .... 33 D6
Nares Rd. ME8 .... 33 D4
Nargate Cl. CT3 .... 90 A8
Nargate St. CT3 .... 90 A8
Narrabeen Rd. CT19 .... 177 E6
Narrowbush La. TN29 .... 198 B7
Naseby Ave. CT20 .... 177 D5
Nash Cl. ME5 .... 32 C2
Nash Court Gdns. CT9 .... 28 F8
Nash Court Rd. CT9 .... 28 F8
Nash Gdns. CT10 .... 30 B4
Nash Hill. CT18 .... 161 D6
Nash La. CT9 .... 28 F7
Nash Rd. CT9 & CT10 .... 28 F7
Nashenden Farm La. ME1 .. 31 A8
Nasmyth Rd. CT7 .... 27 A8
Nat's La. TN25 .... 141 A5
Natal Rd. Chatham ME4 ...... 10 A3
Natal Rd. Dover CT16 .... 149 C4
Nativity Cl. ME10 .... 36 E4
Nautilus Cl. ME12 .... 4 A6
Nautilus Dr. ME12 .... 4 A6
Naval Terr. ME12 .... 1 B3
Naylands. CT9 .... 7 H1
Naylor's Cotts. ME7 .... 33 B1
Neal's Place Rd. CT2 .... 66 C3
Neale St. ME4 .... 9 F2
Neame Rd. CT7 .... 27 A7
Neames Forstal. ME13 .... 84 E7
Neason Ct. CT19 .... 178 F6
Neason Way. CT19 .... 178 F6
Neath Ct. **2** ME15 .... 97 E8
Neath Rd. TN29 .... 202 A2
Neatscourt Cotts. ME12 ...... 3 A4
Nelson Ave. ME12 .... 4 D5
Nelson Cl. Ashford TN24 ... 157 B8
Nelson Cl.
  West Minster ME12 .... 3 A8
Nelson Cres. CT11 .... 52 E6
Nelson Ct. CT7 .... 26 E8
Nelson Ho. **5** ME15 .... 97 F5
Nelson Park Rd. CT15 .... 150 E8
Nelson Pl. CT10 .... 30 B5
Nelson Rd. Gillingham ME7 . 10 D4
Nelson Rd. Whitstable CT5 . 20 D1
Nelson St. Deal CT14 .... 117 D7
Nelson St.
  Faversham ME13 .... 62 C6
Nelson Terr. ME5 .... 10 C1
Nelson Wlk. ME10 .... 36 B5
Neptune Bsns Pk. ME2 .... 9 E7
Neptune Cl. ME2 .... 9 E7
Neptune Terr. ME12 .... 1 E2
Nesbit Rd. TN29 .... 194 F4
Ness Rd. TN29 .... 203 C6
Ness The. CT1 .... 88 B5
Nether Ave. TN28 .... 200 D6
Nethercourt Cir. CT12 .... 52 A6
Nethercourt Farm Rd.
  CT11 .... 52 B7
Nethercourt Gdns. CT11 ... 52 B6
Nethercourt Hill. CT11 ...... 52 B6
Nethergong Hill. CT3 .... 47 D3
Netherhale Farm Rd. CT7 .. 26 B3
Nethersole Cl. CT2 .... 67 A4
Nethersole Rd. CT4 .... 112 F1
Netley Cl. ME14 .... 75 D6
Nettlefield. TN24 .... 139 E5
Nettlepole La. TN27 .... 119 D1
Nevill Gdns. ME10 .... 36 B5
Nevill Rd. ME14 .... 75 B8
Neville Cl. ME4 .... 9 E2
Neville Rd. ME4 .... 9 E2
New Barns Rd. ME4 .... 75 A8
New Beverley Ho. CT2 .... 66 F2
New Bridge. **10** CT16 ... 166 E7
New Cotts. Guston CT15 ... 149 E6
New Cotts.
  Harbledown CT2 .... 65 E1
New Cotts. Teynham ME9 .. 38 A4
New Covenant Pl. ME1 .... 9 D4
New Cross St. CT9 .... 7 I2
New Cut. Chatham ME4 .... 9 F4
New Cut. Dean Street ME15 . 96 D7
New Cut Rd.
  Chilham CT4 & ME13 .... 85 A3
New Cut Rd.
  Maidstone ME14 .... 75 D5
New Delhi Ho. **5** ME15 .. 97 E5
New Dover Rd.
  Canterbury CT1 & CT4 .... 88 D6
New Dover Rd.
  Capel-le-F CT18 .... 164 C2
New Forest La.
  CT4 & ME13 .... 85 B3
New Gardens Rd. ME9 .... 38 C2
New Hall Cl. TN29 .... 195 C8
New Hall Mus. TN29 .... 195 C8
New House Cl. CT1 .... 87 E4

New House La. CT1 & CT4 ... 87 C2
New Inn Cotts. ME15 .... 96 C7
New La. TN29 .... 203 C6
New Rd. Calcott CT2 & CT6 . 45 C4
New Rd. Chatham ME1 .... 9 F4
New Rd. Chatham ME4 .... 9 F4
New Rd. Egerton TN27 ...... 119 A2
New Rd. Elham CT4 .... 144 F4
New Rd. Eythorne CT15 .... 131 C7
New Rd.
  Harbledown CT2 & ME13 . 65 D3
New Rd. Hythe CT21 .... 176 B1
New Rd.
  Hythe, Saltwood CT21 .... 176 B4
New Rd. Langley ME17 .... 98 C5
New Rd. Minster ME12 .... 4 C7
New Rd.
  Rough Common CT2 .... 66 B3
New Rd. Sheerness ME12 .... 1 B1
New Rectory La. TN23 ...... 156 B4
New Rents. **5** TN23 .... 139 B2
New Road Ave. ME4 .... 9 E4
New Road Cotts. CT6 .... 45 E5
New Road
  Cty Prim Sch. ME4 .... 10 A3
New Road Hill. TN25 .... 172 F4
New Road Ind Est. ME12 ...... 1 B1
New Romney
  CE Jun Sch. TN28 .... 200 B7
New Romney
  Cty Inf Sch. TN28 .... 200 B7
New Romney Pl. CT13 .... 93 F8
New Romney Sta. TN28 .... 200 C6
New Ruttington La. CT1 ..... 67 A1
New St. Ash CT3 .... 71 E1
New St.
  Ashford TN23 & TN24 ..... 139 B2
New St. Canterbury CT2 .... 66 E1
New St. Canterbury CT1 .... 87 E7
New St. Chatham ME4 .... 9 E3
New St. Deal CT14 .... 117 D7
New St. **12** Dover CT16 . 166 D8
New St. Folkestone CT20 . 178 D5
New St. Herne Bay CT6 .... 22 F5
New St. Lydd TN29 .... 203 C6
New St. Margate CT9 .... 7 I2
New St. Sandwich CT13 ..... 94 A8
New St. Sheerness ME12 ...... 1 E1
New St. **2** Whitstable CT5 . 20 D2
New Strs. ME4 .... 9 F6
New Town Gn. TN24 .... 156 D8
New Town St.
  Canterbury CT1 .... 67 B2
New Town St.
  Chartham CT4 .... 86 C5
New Villas. ME15 .... 96 C7
Newark Ct. **1** ME2 .... 9 B7
Newark Yd. ME2 .... 9 B7
Newbridge Ave. ME10 .... 36 E7
Newbury Ave. ME16 .... 74 C6
Newbury Cl.
  Birchington CT7 .... 27 B6
Newbury Cl. Dover CT17 ... 165 F7
Newbury Cl.
  Folkestone CT20 .... 177 D5
Newcastle Hill. **5** CT11 .. 52 E7
Newchurch La.
  TN29 & TN26 .... 193 A7
Newchurch Rd. ME15 .... 75 A1
Newcomen Rd. ME12 .... 1 D2
Newenden Cl.
  Ashford TN23 .... 155 F6
Newenden Cl.
  Maidstone ME14 .... 75 D6
Newgate Gap. CT9 .... 8 A3
Newgate Lower Prom. CT9 . 8 A3
Newgate Prom. CT9 .... 8 A3
Newham St. ME4 .... 10 B3
Newhouse Cnr. CT3 .... 48 D1
Newhouse La. ME13 .... 83 D7
Newing Cl. CT3 .... 89 E8
Newington
  CE Prim Sch. ME9 .... 35 B7
Newington
  Cty Inf Sch. CT12 .... 52 B8
Newington Ent Ctr. ME9 .... 35 C8
Newington Ind Est. ME9 .... 34 F6
Newington Jun Sch. CT12 .. 52 A8
Newington Rd.
  Newington CT18 .... 177 A8
Newington Rd.
  Ramsgate CT12 & CT11 .... 29 B1
Newington Sta. ME9 .... 35 B6
Newington Wlk. ME14 .... 75 C6
Newland Green La. TN27 . 135 D8
Newland Rd. ME12 .... 2 F7
Newlands. Ashford TN23 ... 155 F6
Newlands.
  St Mary's Bay TN29 .... 194 F3
Newlands. Whitfield CT16 . 149 B6
Newlands Ave. ME10 .... 36 B5

Newlands Cty Prim Sch. CT11 ... 29 E1
Newlands Dr. CT14 ... 134 B8
Newlands Farm Cotts. ME13 ... 104 C4
Newlands Ho. CT11 ... 29 E2
Newlands La. CT12 ... 29 D2
Newlands Rd. Charing TN27 ... 119 F5
Newlands Rd. Ramsgate CT11 & CT12 ... 29 D1
Newlyn Ct. 1 ME14 ... 75 A4
Newlyn's Meadow. CT15 ... 147 D1
Newman Dr. ME10 ... 37 A8
Newman Rd. CT3 ... 112 E5
Newnham Cl. ME8 ... 11 C2
Newnham La. ME13 & ME9 ... 81 D7
Newport Ct. CT1 ... 88 B6
Newton Cl. Chatham ME5 ... 32 C2
Newton Cl. 1 Maidstone ME16 ... 74 E3
Newton Rd. Faversham ME13 ... 62 D7
Newton Rd. Whitstable CT5 ... 21 B2
Newtown Rd. Ashford TN23 ... 156 C8
Newtown Rd. Ashford TN23 & TN24 ... 156 D7
Nicholas Cl. ME16 ... 74 A3
Nicholas Dr. CT12 ... 51 D5
Nicholas Rd. TN24 ... 139 B6
Nicholls Ave. CT10 ... 29 F2
Nicklaus Dr. ME5 ... 31 F3
Nickle Cotts. CT4 ... 86 A3
Nickleby Cl. ME1 ... 9 C2
Nickley Wood Rd. TN26 ... 170 C6
Nightingale Ave. Hythe CT21 ... 187 D8
Nightingale Ave. Whitstable CT5 ... 43 B6
Nightingale Cl. Chartham CT4 ... 86 C6
Nightingale Cl. Gillingham ME8 ... 33 E6
Nightingale Cl. Sevington TN24 ... 157 B7
Nightingale La. CT15 ... 113 C2
Nightingale Rd. Dover CT16 ... 149 C2
Nightingale Rd. Faversham ME13 ... 62 C7
Nile Rd. ME7 ... 10 C4
Nine Acres. TN24 ... 139 C5
Nine Ash La. ME13 ... 63 D3
Ninn La. TN23 & TN26 ... 138 B2
Nixon Ave. CT12 ... 29 C1
No Name St. 3 CT13 ... 73 A1
Noah's Ark Rd. CT17 ... 166 A8
Noah's Ark Terr. CT17 ... 166 B8
Noakes Meadow. TN23 ... 156 A8
Nobel Cl. ME9 ... 38 C2
Nobel Ct. ME13 ... 62 C7
Noble Ct. CT9 ... 28 A8
Noble Gdns. CT9 ... 28 A8
Nonington CE Prim Sch. CT15 ... 113 C5
Nonsuch Cl. CT1 ... 88 C8
Nore Cl. ME7 ... 10 E1
Noreen Ave. ME12 ... 4 A6
Norfolk Cl. Chatham ME5 ... 32 C3
Norfolk Cl. Gillingham ME8 ... 11 D2
Norfolk Dr. TN23 ... 139 A2
Norfolk Rd. Canterbury CT1 ... 87 E6
Norfolk Rd. Lydden CT9 ... 28 D5
Norfolk Rd. Maidstone ME15 ... 97 C8
Norfolk Rd. Margate CT9 ... 8 B3
Norfolk Sq. CT12 ... 29 B2
Norfolk St. CT5 ... 43 D8
Norman Cl. Gillingham ME8 ... 33 B5
Norman Cl. Maidstone ME14 ... 75 B6
Norman Rd. Ashford TN23 ... 156 B7
Norman Rd. Broadstairs CT10 ... 29 F6
Norman Rd. Canterbury CT1 ... 88 A7
Norman Rd. Faversham ME13 ... 62 C7
Norman Rd. Ramsgate CT11 ... 52 B6
Norman Rd. St Margaret's at Cliffe CT15 ... 151 B6
Norman Rd. Warden ME12 ... 6 A6
Norman Rd. Westgate-on-S CT8 & CT9 ... 7 D1
Norman Rd. Whitstable CT5 ... 43 E8
Norman St. 8 CT16 & CT17 ... 166 D8
Norman Tailyour Ho. CT14 ... 117 D5
Norreys Rd. ME8 ... 33 E7
Norrie Rd. CT7 ... 27 A6
Norrington Mead. 3 CT19 ... 178 A7
Norrington Rd. ME15 ... 97 B6
North Ave. CT11 ... 52 D6
North Barrack Rd. CT14 ... 117 D4
North Borough Cty Jun Sch. ME14 ... 75 A6
North Camber Way. CT16 ... 150 B1
North Cl. CT20 ... 177 D4
North Close Bsns Ctr. CT20 ... 177 D4
North Court Cl. CT3 ... 91 A8
North Court La. CT14 ... 115 A4
North Court Rd. CT3 ... 91 A8
North Cres. ME17 ... 96 D4
North Ct. Deal CT14 ... 117 C7
North Ct. Ramsgate CT12 ... 29 B2
North Dane Way. ME5 ... 32 C4
North Downs Cl. CT4 ... 85 C2
North Eastling Rd. ME13 & ME9 ... 81 F8
North Exit Rd. CT16 ... 166 H8
North Foreland Ave. CT10 ... 30 B7
North Foreland Golf Course. CT10 ... 30 A8
North Foreland Hill. CT10 ... 30 B8
North Foreland Rd. CT10 ... 30 B7
North Holmes Rd. CT1 ... 88 B8
North La. Boughton Street ME13 ... 84 F8
North La. Canterbury CT2 ... 66 F1
North La. Faversham ME13 ... 62 C8
North La. 7 Folkestone CT20 ... 177 E3
North Lea. CT14 ... 117 C7
North Lockside Rd. ME4 ... 10 D8
North Lyminge La. CT18 ... 161 C7
North Military Rd. CT17 ... 166 C7
North Pasley Rd. ME4 ... 10 B7
North Pends. TN24 ... 139 E5
North Pondside Rd. ME4 ... 10 A8
North Rd. Dover CT17 ... 166 C8
North Rd. Folkestone CT20 ... 177 D4
North Rd. Gillingham ME4 & ME7 ... 10 A7
North Rd. Hythe CT21 ... 176 B2
North Rd. Kingsdown CT14 ... 134 D6
North Rd. Queenborough ME11 ... 2 F5
North Rd. Richborough CT12 ... 51 A1
North Rd. Sandwich CT13 ... 95 A7
North Rd W. CT21 ... 176 A3
North Return Rd. CT16 ... 166 G8
North Sch The. TN24 ... 139 D1
North Side Three Rd. ME4 ... 10 C8
North St. Ashford TN23 ... 139 C2
North St. Ashford TN24 ... 139 C3
North St. Deal CT14 ... 117 D7
North St. Dover CT17 ... 166 B7
North St. Folkestone CT19 ... 178 E5
North St. Herne Bay CT6 ... 23 A5
North St. New Romney TN28 ... 200 A6
North St. Rochester ME2 ... 9 B7
North St. Sittingbourne ME10 ... 36 F7
North St. Sutton Valence ME17 ... 98 E1
North View. Hersden CT3 ... 46 F1
North View. Maidstone ME15 ... 75 B1
North View Cotts. ME15 ... 96 C7
North Way. Finglesham CT14 ... 116 A7
North Way. Maidstone ME14 ... 75 B7
Northbourne Ave. CT17 ... 166 B8
Northbourne CE Prim Sch. CT14 ... 115 F5
Northbourne Court Gdns. CT14 ... 116 B5
Northbourne Park Sch (Annexe). CT14 ... 115 D6
Northbourne Park Sch (Prep). CT14 ... 115 C6
Northbourne Rd. East Studdel CT14 & CT15 ... 115 E1
Northbourne Rd. Gillingham ME8 ... 11 B4
Northbourne Rd. Great Mongeham CT14 ... 116 C4
Northbourne Way. CT9 ... 8 E2
Northbrooke. TN24 ... 139 C3
Northbrooke La. TN24 ... 139 C3
Northcliffe Gdns. CT10 ... 30 A7
Northcote Rd. Deal CT14 ... 117 D5
Northcote Rd. Kingsdown CT14 ... 134 D4
Northcote Rd. Rochester ME2 ... 9 A7
Northdown. Ashford TN24 ... 139 C4
Northdown. Doddington ME9 ... 80 F7
Northdown. Stockbury ME9 ... 56 D8
Northdown Ave. CT9 ... 8 B2
Northdown Cl. East Studdal CT15 ... 132 B6
Northdown Cl. Maidstone ME14 ... 75 B7
Northdown Cty Prim Sch. CT9 ... 8 C1
Northdown Hill. CT10 & CT9 ... 29 D7
Northdown Park Rd. CT9 ... 8 C1
Northdown Rd. Broadstairs CT10 ... 29 E6
Northdown Rd. Margate CT9 ... 8 B2
Northdown View. ME17 ... 100 F6
Northdown Way. CT9 ... 8 C1
Northern By-Pass. TN27 ... 120 C8
Northfleet Cl. ME14 ... 75 C5
Northgate. Canterbury CT1 ... 67 A1
Northgate. Rochester ME1 ... 9 C6
Northleigh Cl. ME15 ... 97 A6
Northpoint Bsns Est. ME2 ... 9 D8
Northumberland Ave. Ashford TN24 ... 139 D5
Northumberland Ave. Gillingham ME8 ... 11 E1
Northumberland Ave. Margate CT9 ... 8 C2
Northumberland Ct. Maidstone ME15 ... 97 D7
Northumberland Ct. Margate CT9 ... 8 C3
Northumberland Rd. ME15 ... 97 D8
Northwall Ct. CT14 ... 117 C7
Northwall Mews. CT14 ... 117 C7
Northwall Rd. CT14 ... 117 B8
Northwood Dr. ME10 ... 36 F1
Northwood Rd. Broadstairs, Ramsgate CT10 & CT12 ... 29 C3
Northwood Rd. Whitstable CT5 ... 20 F2
Norton Ave. CT6 ... 46 A8
Norton Dr. CT12 ... 50 B6
Norton Gr. ME5 ... 31 E3
Norton Knatchbull Sch The. TN24 ... 139 E2
Norton La. TN26 ... 153 D5
Norton Rd. Five Wents ME17 ... 98 D1
Norton Rd. Lynsted ME13 & ME9 ... 60 E5
Norview Rd. CT5 ... 43 B7
Norway Dro. CT15 ... 151 A8
Norway Terr. 4 ME14 ... 75 A7
Norwood Gdns. TN23 ... 139 B2
Norwood La. TN29 ... 193 E7
Norwood Rise. ME12 ... 4 C7
Norwood St. TN23 ... 139 B2
Norwood Wlk E. ME10 ... 36 C5
Norwood Wlk W. ME10 ... 36 B5
Notley St. CT1 ... 67 A1
Notley Terr. 3 CT1 ... 67 A1
Nottingham Ave. ME15 ... 97 D7
Nottingham Rd. CT7 ... 26 F5
Nouds Rd. ME9 ... 60 D7
Nunnery Fields. CT1 ... 88 A7
Nunnery Fields Hospl. CT1 ... 88 A6
Nunnery Rd. CT1 ... 87 F7
Nursery Ave. Maidstone ME16 ... 74 B6
Nursery Ave. Maidstone,Bearsted ME14 ... 76 B3
Nursery Cl. Densole CT18 ... 163 A7
Nursery Cl. Ramsgate CT11 ... 52 C7
Nursery Cl. Sheerness ME12 ... 1 E1
Nursery Cl. Whitstable CT5 ... 21 A1
Nursery Fields. Acol CT7 ... 27 B3
Nursery Fields. Hythe CT21 ... 176 A2
Nursery La. Densole CT18 ... 163 A7
Nursery La. Sheldwich ME13 ... 83 D5
Nursery La. Whitfield CT16 ... 148 F7
Nursery Rd. ME8 ... 33 D8
Nursery Wlk. CT2 ... 66 E2
Nurserylands. CT6 ... 22 F3
Nutberry Cl. ME9 ... 38 D2
Nutfield Cl. ME5 ... 32 B8
Nutfields. ME10 ... 37 B3
Nutley Cl. TN24 ... 139 C3
Nutts Ave. ME12 ... 6 G2
Nutwood Cl. ME14 ... 75 E4
Oak Ave. Eythorne CT15 ... 131 D5
Oak Ave. Gillingham ME7 ... 10 E6
Oak Ave. Minster ME12 ... 4 F6
Oak Bglws. TN29 ... 203 C6
Oak Caer. TN25 ... 172 F4
Oak Cotts. East Studdal CT15 ... 132 E8
Oak Cotts. Sellindge TN25 ... 174 D7
Oak Cotts. Selling ME13 ... 84 D4
Oak Dr. Boughton Street ME13 ... 64 A3
Oak Dr. Hawkinge CT18 ... 163 B5
Oak Dr. St Mary's Bay TN29 ... 194 F3
Oak Gr. CT15 ... 114 B2
Oak Hall Pas. CT21 ... 176 C2
Oak Hill. CT13 ... 93 B6
Oak Ho. 6 ME5 ... 31 F4
Oak La. Lydd TN29 ... 203 B6
Oak La. Minster ME12 ... 4 F7
Oak La. Upchurch ME9 ... 12 D2
Oak Lodge Rd. TN28 ... 200 B7
Oak Rd. ME10 ... 37 C5
Oak Ridge. TN25 ... 183 F8
Oak St. CT14 ... 117 D6
Oak Tree Ave. ME15 ... 97 C7
Oak Tree Cty Prim Sch. TN23 ... 155 F8
Oak Tree Gr. CT9 ... 28 A8
Oak Tree Rd. TN23 ... 155 F8
Oak Trees Cty Prim Sch. ME15 ... 97 C7
Oak Wlk. CT21 ... 176 C2
Oakapple La. ME16 ... 74 A3
Oakdale Rd. CT6 ... 23 A4
Oakdene Rd. CT12 ... 29 C1
Oakenpole. TN23 ... 138 E1
Oakfield Ct. CT12 ... 52 B8
Oakfield Rd. TN24 ... 139 D5
Oakfields. ME10 ... 36 C3
Oakhurst Cl. ME5 ... 31 F3
Oakland Cl. ME5 ... 31 F3
Oakland Ct. CT6 ... 22 E5
Oaklands. Ashford TN23 ... 138 F1
Oaklands. Mersham TN25 ... 157 E4
Oaklands Ave. CT10 ... 29 E5
Oaklands Cty Prim Sch.ME5 ... 31 F4
Oaklands Way. CT2 ... 68 B7
Oakleigh Cl. ME5 ... 31 E2
Oakleigh Ho. TN23 ... 155 E8
Oakleigh La. CT4 ... 89 B5
Oakleys The. CT15 ... 130 D5
Oakridge. CT10 ... 8 G1
Oaks Ave. CT6 ... 22 D2
Oaks Bsns Village The. ME5 ... 32 C1
Oaks Cty Inf Sch The.ME10 ... 36 D2
Oaks Dene. ME5 ... 31 F1
Oaks Pk. CT2 ... 66 B3
Oaks Rd. Folkestone CT20 ... 177 D6
Oaks Rd. Tenterden TN30 ... 179 B8
Oaks The. Broadstairs CT10 ... 29 F7
Oaks The. Hersden CT3 ... 46 F1
Oaks The. St Nicholas at Wade CT7 ... 25 F2
Oaks View. CT21 ... 187 C8
Oakside Rd. CT3 ... 112 E5
Oaktree Ho. ME10 ... 37 B3
Oakum Ct. ME4 ... 10 B2
Oakvale Cl. CT17 ... 166 B7
Oakwood Ct. ME16 ... 74 D3
Oakwood Dr. CT5 ... 21 A1
Oakwood Hospl. ME16 ... 74 B3
Oakwood Park Gram Sch. ME16 ... 74 C3
Oakwood Rd. Maidstone ME16 ... 74 D3
Oakwood Rd. Sturry CT2 ... 68 A7
Oare Rd. ME13 ... 40 C1
Oast Cotts. Dargate ME13 ... 64 D8
Oast Cotts. Sheldwich ME13 ... 83 C8
Oast Ct. Margate CT9 ... 28 F8
Oast Ct. Sittingbourne ME10 ... 36 E2
Oast Ho. CT4 ... 85 C2
Oast La. ME13 ... 104 E6
Oast Meadow. TN24 ... 139 F1
Oast Paddock The. CT3 ... 92 A6
Oast The. Canterbury CT1 ... 88 B6
Oast The. Staple CT3 ... 92 A6
Oasthouse Field. TN29 ... 192 F4
Oasts The. ME14 ... 76 C4
Oastview. ME8 ... 34 A8
Oaten Hill. CT1 ... 88 A7
Oaten Hill Pl. CT1 ... 88 A7
Occupation Rd. TN25 ... 123 F2
Ocean Cl. CT7 ... 27 B8
Ocean View. Broadstairs CT10 ... 30 A1
Ocean View. Herne Bay CT6 ... 23 F6
Octavia Ct. ME5 ... 32 B3
Octavian Dr. CT21 ... 175 A3
Odiham Dr. ME16 ... 74 C7
Odo Rd. CT17 ... 166 C8
Officers' Rd. ME4 ... 10 B8
Offley Cl. CT9 ... 8 C1
Ogilvy Ct. CT10 ... 29 E7
Okehampton Cl. TN24 ... 139 F7
Olantigh Ct. CT7 ... 27 A7
Olantigh Rd. TN25 ... 123 F3
Olave Rd. CT9 ... 8 B1
Old Ash Cl. TN24 ... 139 C5
Old Ashford Rd. Charing TN27 ... 120 C7
Old Ashford Rd. Lenham ME17 ... 101 E5
Old Badgins Rd. ME13 ... 83 B6
Old Bakery Cl. TN29 ... 194 F4
Old Bakery The. ME12 ... 3 F5
Old Barn Cl. ME7 ... 32 F6
Old Billet La. ME12 ... 5 C6
Old Boundary Rd. CT9 ... 7 D1
Old Bridge Rd. CT5 ... 20 E1
Old Carriageway The. ME7 ... 32 F4
Old Castle Wlk. ME8 ... 33 D4
Old Charlton Rd. CT16 ... 149 D2
Old Chatham Rd. Kit's Coty ME20 ... 53 D6
Old Chatham Rd. Maidstone ME14 ... 53 F1
Old Court Hill. CT15 ... 113 C6
Old Crossing Rd. 1 CT9 ... 28 B8
Old Dairy Cl. 3 CT11 ... 52 F7
Old Dover Rd. Barham CT4 ... 112 B1
Old Dover Rd. Canterbury CT1 ... 88 B6
Old Dover Rd. Capel-le-F CT18 ... 164 C1
Old Dr. ME15 ... 96 F6
Old Dungeness Lighthouse. TN29 ... 205 F6
Old Farm Cl. CT5 ... 43 C6
Old Farm Rd. CT7 ... 26 D7
Old Ferry Rd. ME9 ... 14 E7
Old Fold. CT5 ... 44 C8
Old Folkestone Rd. CT17 ... 166 A4
Old Forge La. ME9 ... 56 F3
Old Gate Rd. ME13 ... 62 B8
Old Green Rd. Broadstairs CT10 ... 29 F7
Old Green Rd. Margate CT9 ... 8 C1
Old Hall Dr. CT12 ... 51 C5
Old Ham La. ME17 ... 101 A4
Old High St The. CT20 ... 178 E5
Old Hockley Rd. ME13 ... 82 C2
Old Hook Rd. ME12 ... 4 F2
Old House Rd. ME9 ... 34 E4
Old Kingsdown Cl. CT10 ... 29 E3
Old Lain. ME17 ... 100 F6
Old London Rd. CT21 ... 175 F2
Old Loose Hill. ME15 ... 96 F4
Old Mead. CT19 ... 178 A7
Old Mill La. ME20 ... 53 C3
Old Mill Rd. ME17 ... 76 F1
Old Oast Bsns Ctr The. ME20 ... 53 A1
Old Orch. TN23 ... 155 D8
Old Orch The. ME8 ... 34 A8
Old Park Ave. CT1 ... 67 C2
Old Park Cl. CT16 ... 149 A4
Old Park Ct. CT1 ... 67 C2
Old Park Hill. CT16 ... 149 B4
Old Park Rd. CT16 ... 149 B2
Old Park Way. CT16 ... 149 A3
Old Pattens La. ME1 ... 9 D2
Old Pond Rd. TN23 ... 155 F8
Old Railway Works (Ind Est). TN24 ... 156 D8
Old Rd. Chatham ME4 ... 9 F4
Old Rd. Elham CT4 ... 144 F4
Old Rectory Cl. CT18 ... 163 B4
Old Rectory The. TN25 ... 122 E2
Old Roman Rd. CT15 ... 133 C1
Old Ruttington La. CT1 ... 67 A1
Old Saltwood La. CT21 ... 176 B4
Old Saw Mill The. TN26 ... 153 E6
Old School Cl. ME17 ... 101 D4
Old School Ct. Egerton TN27 ... 118 F3
Old School Ct. Folkestone CT20 ... 178 B4
Old School Gdns. CT9 ... 8 A1
Old School Mews. CT4 ... 86 C2
Old School The. TN24 ... 156 D8
Old Surrenden Manor Rd. TN26 ... 154 C5

Old Tovil Rd. ME15 .... 75 A2
Old Trafford Cl. ME16 .... 74 B6
Old Tree La. ME17 .... 97 D3
Old Tree Rd. CT3 .... 47 B7
Old Valley Rd. CT14 .... 128 F7
Old Vicarage The. CT13 ...... 93 C7
Old Way. TN26 .... 190 D7
Oldborough Manor
  Com Coll. ME15 .... 97 B6
Oldchurch Ct. **3** ME16 .... 74 E3
Oldfield Cl. Gillingham ME8 .. 33 D8
Oldfield Cl.
  Maidstone ME15 .... 75 E1
Oldhawe Hill. CT3 & CT6 .... 46 D7
Oldhouse La. TN29 .... 191 E1
Oldstairs Rd. CT14 .... 134 D4
Oliver Cl. ME4 .... 10 B2
Oliver Twist Cl. ME1 .... 9 B4
Olivers Cotts. ME14 .... 76 C4
Olivine Cl. ME5 .... 54 A8
Olliffe Cl. ME5 .... 31 F2
Omer Ave. CT9 .... 8 C2
Onslow Rd. ME1 .... 9 D3
Ontario Way. CT16 .... 149 B3
Opal Gn. ME5 .... 32 B2
Orache Dr. ME14 .... 75 E5
Orange St. CT1 .... 87 F8
Orange Terr. ME1 .... 9 D5
Orbit Cl. ME5 .... 54 A8
Orchard Ave. CT14 .... 117 B5
Orchard Bank. ME17 .... 98 B1
Orchard Bsns Ctr. ME16 .... 74 C8
Orchard Cl.
  Canterbury CT2 .... 66 F4
Orchard Cl.
  Coxheath ME17 .... 96 C3
Orchard Cl..
  Langley Heath ME17 .... 98 E4
Orchard Cl..
  Littlebourne CT3 .... 89 F7
Orchard Cl.
  Mersham TN25 .... 157 C3
Orchard Cl. Minster,
  Thanet CT12 .... 50 B7
Orchard Cl.
  Ramsgate CT12 .... 29 B3
Orchard Cl. Whitfield CT16 . 148 F8
Orchard Cl.
  Whitstable CT5 .... 20 F3
Orchard Cl. Wingham CT3 ... 91 A7
Orchard Cotts. ME16 .... 96 A8
Orchard Ct.
  Chillenden CT3 .... 113 F8
Orchard Ct. Herne Bay CT6 .. 22 F1
Orchard Dr. Ashford TN23 . 138 F4
Orchard Dr.
  Littlestone-on-S TN28 ..... 200 E6
Orchard Dr.
  Newington ME9 .... 35 A5
Orchard Dr. River CT17 .... 148 E3
Orchard Dr. Wye TN25 ...... 123 F1
Orchard Field. TN26 .... 153 D4
Orchard Fields. CT21 .... 160 E2
Orchard Flats. CT1 .... 88 D7
Orchard Gdns. CT9 .... 28 A8
Orchard Gr. ME12 .... 4 C6
Orchard Hts. TN23 .... 138 F5
Orchard Ind Est. ME15 .... 97 F3
Orchard La. Ashford TN24 . 139 F6
Orchard La. Challock TN25 . 105 B2
Orchard Mews. CT14 .... 117 D5
Orchard Pk. CT6 .... 23 D4
Orchard Pl.
  Faversham ME13 .... 62 D7
Orchard Pl. **2**
  Maidstone ME16 .... 74 E3
Orchard Pl.
  Sittingbourne ME10 .... 37 A3
Orchard Rd. Eastry CT13 .... 93 B3
Orchard Rd. Herne Bay CT6 . 22 F3
Orchard Rd.
  Maidstone ME14 .... 75 E4
Orchard Rd. Margate CT9 ... 28 A8
Orchard Rd.
  St Mary's Bay TN29 .... 195 A5
Orchard Rd.
  St Nichaels TN30 .... 167 A3
Orchard Residences The.
  CT1 .... 88 A5
Orchard Row. CT6 .... 23 A1
Orchard Sch. CT1 .... 87 F6
Orchard St. Canterbury CT2 . 66 E1
Orchard St. Gillingham ME8 . 33 E8
Orchard St.
  Maidstone ME15 .... 75 A3
Orchard The. ME14 .... 76 B4
Orchard Valley. CT21 .... 176 A2
Orchard View. Ash CT3 ...... 71 F1

Orchard View.
  Tenterden TN30 .... 179 C8
Orchard View.
  Teynham ME9 .... 38 C3
Orchard Villas. CT16 .... 148 E4
Orchard Way. ME12 .... 5 D1
Orchards The. CT4 .... 144 F4
Ordnance St. ME4 .... 9 E3
Ordnance Terr. ME4 .... 9 E4
Orgarswick Way. TN29 ..... 195 C7
Orgarswick Way. TN29 ..... 195 C7
Oriel Rd. TN23 .... 138 F4
Orient Pl. CT2 .... 66 F1
Orion Rd. ME1 .... 31 C7
Orion Way. TN24 .... 156 E8
Ormonde Ct. CT21 .... 176 C1
Ormonde Rd. **10**
  Folkestone CT20 .... 178 C6
Ormonde Rd. Hythe CT21 . 176 C1
Ormsby Gn. ME8 .... 33 E3
Orwell Ho. **6** ME15 .... 97 E8
Osborne Gdns. CT6 .... 23 D4
Osborne Rd. Ashford TN24 156 F8
Osborne Rd.
  Gillingham ME7 .... 10 C5
Osborne Rd.
  Kingsdown CT14 .... 134 C6
Osborne Terr. CT9 .... 7 J1
Osbourn Ave. CT8 .... 27 E8
Osbourne Rd. CT10 .... 29 F4
Oscar Rd. CT10 .... 30 B4
Osier Field. TN24 .... 139 F7
Osier Rd. ME9 .... 38 E3
Osprey Ave. ME5 & ME7 ..... 10 E2
Osprey Cl. **2** Dover CT16 149 B2
Osprey Ct.
  Sittingbourne ME10 .... 37 A3
Ospringe
  CE Prim Sch. ME13 .... 62 A6
Ospringe Pl. ME13 .... 62 B6
Ospringe Rd. ME13 .... 62 B7
Ospringe St. ME13 .... 62 A6
Ostend Ct. ME10 .... 14 F1
Ostlers La. CT7 .... 48 D6
Oswald Rd. CT17 .... 149 B2
Oswald Rd. CT17 .... 149 B2
Otham Cl. CT2 .... 67 A4
Otham La. ME15 .... 76 C2
Otham St. Maidstone ME15 . 76 C2
Otham St. Otham ME15 ...... 98 B7
Ottawa Cres. CT14 .... 149 C3
Ottawa Way. CT16 .... 149 B3
Otterbourne Pl. ME15 .... 75 E1
Otterden Cl. CT13 .... 155 F6
Otterden Rd. ME13 .... 81 D3
Otterham Quay La. ME8 ..... 12 B2
Otteridge Rd. ME14 .... 76 A3
Otterpool La.
  CT21 & TN25 .... 174 D4
Otway St. ME4 .... 10 A3
Otway Terr. **1** ME4 .... 10 A3
Out Elmstead La. CT4 .... 111 F2
Oval The. TN29 .... 186 D1
Overland La. CT3 .... 71 A3
Owen Sq. CT14 .... 117 B2
Owen's Cl. CT21 .... 177 B3
Owens Court Cotts. ME13 ... 83 F8
Owens Way. ME7 .... 11 A6
Owl's Hatch Rd. CT6 .... 22 C1
Ox La. TN30 .... 167 B2
Oxen Lease. TN23 .... 155 E8
Oxenden Cnr. CT3 .... 23 F1
Oxenden Cres. CT3 .... 91 A8
Oxenden Park Dr. CT6 .... 22 E4
Oxenden Rd. CT20 .... 177 E4
Oxenden St. CT6 .... 22 E5
Oxenden Way. CT14 .... 128 F8
Oxenturn Rd. TN25 .... 140 E8

Paddock Rd.
  Birchington CT7 .... 27 A7
Paddock The.
  Canterbury CT1 .... 88 B8
Paddock The.
  Chatham ME4 .... 9 F4
Paddock The. Chilham CT4 .. 85 C2
Paddock The. Dover CT16 . 166 D8
Paddock View. CT15 .... 43 E7
Paddocks The.
  Broadstairs CT10 .... 29 F7
Paddocks The.
  Gillingham ME7 .... 33 A5
Paddocks The.
  Great Chart TN23 .... 138 C1
Paddocks The.
  Herne Bay CT6 .... 23 F5
Padsole La. ME15 .... 75 A4
Padstow Manor. ME7 .... 10 C6
Padwell La. TN23 .... 155 C8
Paffard Cl. CT2 .... 67 F6
Paffard Ct. CT2 .... 67 F6
Page Pl. CT19 .... 178 D8
Paget Row. ME7 .... 10 C5
Paget St. ME7 .... 10 C5
Pagitt St. ME4 .... 9 E3
Paine Ave. TN29 .... 203 C6
Painesfield Cl. TN29 .... 186 C4
Painter's Forstal Rd. ME13 . 61 E3
Palace Ave. ME15 .... 75 A4
Palace Cl. CT5 .... 21 B2
Palace Cotts. ME9 .... 80 F8
Palace Ct. Chatham ME5 ..... 10 D2
Palace Ct. Hythe CT21 ...... 176 C2
Palace Ind Est. ME15 .... 97 F4
Palace St. **17** CT1 .... 67 A1
Palace Wood
  Cty Inf Sch. ME16 .... 74 C6
Palace Wood
  Cty Jun Sch. ME16 .... 74 C6
Palm Bay Ave. CT9 .... 8 D3
Palm Bay
  Cty Prim Sch. CT9 .... 8 D3
Palm Bay Gdns. CT9 .... 8 D3
Palm Tree Cl. CT15 .... 131 D7
Palm Tree Way. CT18 .... 161 B7
Palmar Rd. ME16 .... 74 D6
Palmarsh Ave. CT21 .... 187 D7
Palmarsh Cres. CT21 .... 187 D7
Palmarsh
  Cty Prim Sch. CT21 .... 187 D8
Palmbeach Ave. CT21 ...... 187 D8
Palmer Cl. CT6 .... 46 B8
Palmer Cres. CT9 .... 29 C8
Palmer Rd. CT3 .... 91 A8
Palmers Cross Hill. CT2 ..... 66 A1
Palmerston Ave.
  Broadstairs CT10 .... 30 B3
Palmerston Ave.
  Deal CT14 .... 117 C2
Palmerston Ct. CT14 .... 117 D2
Palmerston Rd. ME4 .... 9 F1
Palmerston St. **4** CT9 ..... 178 D6
Palmerston Wlk. ME10 ...... 37 C4
Palting Way. CT20 .... 178 B4
Panton Cl. ME5 .... 32 C4
Papion Gr. ME5 .... 31 E2
Papworth Cl. **1** CT19 ..... 178 A7
Parade. CT1 .... 87 F8
Parade Rd. CT20 .... 177 F3
Parade The.
  Birchington CT7 .... 26 D8
Parade The.
  Folkestone CT20 .... 178 E5
Parade The. Greatstone-on-S
  TN28 & TN29 .... 204 E7
Parade The. Margate CT9 ...... 7 I3
Paradise. CT1 .... 156 F5
Paradise Cotts. ME9 .... 52 D7
Paradise Row. CT13 .... 72 F1
Paragon. CT11 .... 52 E5
Paragon St. CT11 .... 52 D5
Paraker Way. CT21 .... 177 B4
Pardoner Cl. CT2 .... 67 C7
Pardoners Way. CT16 .... 149 A3
Parfitt Way. CT16 .... 149 B2
Parham Cl. CT1 .... 67 B2
Parham Rd.
  Canterbury CT1 .... 67 B2
Parham Rd. Chatham ME4 ... 9 F2
Paris Cnr. TN26 .... 153 F6
Parish Rd. Chartham CT4 .... 86 C3
Parish Rd. Minster ME12 ..... 4 A5
Park Ave. Birchington CT7 ... 27 A6
Park Ave. Deal CT14 .... 117 C5
Park Ave. Dover CT16 ...... 149 D1
Park Ave. Gillingham ME7 ... 10 D3

Park Ave.
  Leysdown-on-S ME12 .... 6 G1
Park Ave. Loose ME17 .... 96 E2
Park Ave. Maidstone ME14 .. 75 B6
Park Ave.
  Queenborough ME11 .... 3 B4
Park Ave.
  Sittingbourne ME10 .... 36 E1
Park Ave. Whitstable CT5 ... 20 F3
Park Barn Rd. ME17 .... 99 C5
Park Chase. CT10 .... 29 E2
Park Cl. CT9 .... 8 D1
Park Cotts. CT11 .... 29 E2
Park Cres. ME4 .... 31 F8
Park Crescent Rd. CT9 .... 8 A1
Park Ct. ME13 .... 62 E7
Park Dr.
  Sittingbourne ME10 .... 36 D1
Park Farm Cl.
  Shadoxhurst TN26 .... 155 A1
Park Farm Cl.
  Tyler Hill CT2 .... 66 E6
Park Farm Prim Sch.
  CT19 .... 178 C6
Park Farm Rd. CT19 .... 178 C7
Park Gate. CT10 .... 29 F2
Park Ho. ME14 .... 75 B6
Park La. Bethersden TN26 . 154 C8
Park La. Birchington CT7 ..... 27 A6
Park La.
  Bishopsbourne CT4 .... 111 C5
Park La. Cock Street ME17 .. 97 D2
Park La. Elham CT4 .... 144 F5
Park La. Maidstone ME14 ... 74 F7
Park La. Margate CT9 .... 8 A2
Park Lea. CT14 .... 117 C5
Park Mall. **2** TN23 .... 139 B2
Park Manor. ME7 .... 10 B5
Park Mews. **6** CT16 .... 166 D8
Park Pl. Ashford TN24 ...... 156 F8
Park Pl. Dover CT16 .... 166 D8
Park Pl. Herne CT6 .... 46 A8
Park Pl. Margate CT9 .... 7 I1
Park Rd. Ashford TN24 ..... 139 C6
Park Rd. Broadstairs CT10 .. 30 B6
Park Rd. Dover CT16 .... 149 B2
Park Rd. Faversham ME13 .. 62 D7
Park Rd.
  Folkestone CT19 & CT20 . 177 E6
Park Rd. Herne Bay CT6 ..... 22 F4
Park Rd. Hythe CT21 .... 176 B1
Park Rd.
  Littlestone-on-S TN28 ..... 200 E5
Park Rd. Margate CT9 .... 8 A2
Park Rd. Preston CT3 .... 70 D7
Park Rd.
  Queenborough ME11 .... 2 F5
Park Rd. Ramsgate CT11 .... 52 C7
Park Rd. Sheerness ME12 .... 1 E1
Park Rd.
  Sittingbourne ME10 .... 36 D1
Park Rd.
  Temple Ewell CT16 .... 148 D5
Park Rd. Westgate-on-S
  CT7 & CT8 & CT9 .... 27 D6
Park Rd N. TN24 .... 139 B3
Park St.
  Ashford TN23 & TN24 ...... 139 C2
Park St. Deal CT14 .... 117 D6
Park St. Dover CT16 .... 166 D8
Park St. Lydd TN29 .... 203 C6
Park Terr. Throwley ME13 .. 82 D1
Park Terr.
  Woodnesborough CT13 ...... 93 D7
Park Vale. TN24 .... 139 D6
Park View.
  Folkestone CT19 .... 178 E7
Park View. Sturry CT2 .... 67 F6
Park View Cl. CT3 .... 91 D2
Park View Ct. ME15 .... 75 E1
Park View Rise. CT15 ...... 113 D4
Park Way. Coxheath ME17 .. 96 D3
Park Way. Maidstone ME15 . 75 B1
Park Way
  Cty Prim Sch. ME15 .... 75 B1
Park Wood Cl. TN23 .... 156 B5
Park Wood
  Cty Prim Schs. ME8 .... 33 E5
Park Wood Gn. ME8 .... 33 D5
Park Wood Par. ME15 .... 97 F5
Park Wood Trad Est. ME15 . 97 F4
Parker Cl. Gillingham ME8 .. 33 E5
Parker Cl.
  Hamstreet TN26 .... 183 A7
Parkfield Rd.
  Folkestone CT19 .... 178 C6
Parkfield Rd.
  Gillingham ME8 .... 11 F1

Parkland Ct. CT10 .... 29 F6
Parkside
  Cty Prim Sch. CT1 .... 67 D2
Parkway The. CT7 .... 27 B7
Parkwood Cl. CT10 .... 29 F2
Parr Ave. ME7 .... 10 D6
Parrs Head Mews. ME1 .... 9 C6
Parsonage Chase. ME12 ...... 3 F5
Parsonage Cotts. ME9 .... 58 A5
Parsonage Farm (Rural
  Heritage Ctr). CT4 .... 145 A6
Parsonage Fields. CT12 ..... 49 C3
Parsonage La.
  Bobbing ME9 .... 14 A3
Parsonage La.
  Rochester ME2 .... 9 C8
Parsonage Rd. CT6 .... 23 A3
Parsonage Stocks Rd.
  ME13 .... 82 F5
Parsonage Villas. CT15 .... 165 C5
Partridge La. ME13 .... 62 D7
Pasley Rd. ME7 .... 10 A7
Pasley Rd E. ME7 .... 10 B2
Pasley Rd W. ME4 .... 10 A2
Pasture The. TN24 .... 139 D6
Patchways. TN29 .... 184 E3
Path Field Cotts. CT15 ...... 164 E5
Patricia Way. CT10 .... 29 D3
Patrixbourne Ave. ME8 ...... 11 C2
Patrixbourne Rd. CT4 .... 89 B2
Pattens Gdns. ME4 .... 9 E2
Pattens La. ME4 .... 9 E3
Pattens Pl. ME1 .... 9 D6
Paul's Pl. **8** CT16 .... 149 C8
Pavement The. TN30 .... 167 B3
Pavilion Ct. CT20 .... 178 E4
Pavilion Dr. ME10 .... 14 F1
Pavilion Meadow. CT17 .... 148 E6
Pavilion Rd. CT19 .... 178 D6
Pay St. CT18 .... 162 F2
Payden St. ME17 & ME9 ... 102 D8
Payers Pk. CT20 .... 178 D5
Payne's La. ME15 .... 97 B2
Pays La. TN25 .... 104 D2
Payton Cl. CT9 .... 29 A7
Payton Mews. **4** CT11 ..... 67 B3
Peacock Mews. **7** ME16 .. 74 E6
Peacock Pl. ME13 .... 84 A6
Peafield Wood Rd. CT4 ..... 127 E4
Peak Dr. CT13 .... 93 B7
Pean Court Rd. CT5 .... 43 D3
Pean Hill. CT5 .... 43 D2
Pear Tree Alley. **2** ME10 ... 36 E5
Pear Tree Cl. CT10 .... 29 C4
Pear Tree La.
  Dymchurch TN29 .... 186 D3
Pear Tree La.
  Gillingham ME7 .... 32 C1
Pear Tree La.
  Maidstone ME15 .... 97 B6
Pear Tree Row. ME17 .... 98 B5
Pear Tree Wlk. ME9 .... 35 A5
Pearmain Wlk. CT1 .... 88 C7
Pearman Cl. ME8 .... 12 A3
Pearson's Way. CT10 .... 29 E2
Peartree Cotts. ME8 .... 34 B6
Peartree Rd. CT6 .... 23 C5
Peckham Cl. ME2 .... 9 F8
Pedding Hill. CT3 .... 71 A2
Pedding La. CT3 .... 92 A8
Peel Dr. ME10 .... 37 C4
Peel St. ME14 .... 75 A6
Peene Cotts. CT18 .... 162 B5
Pegwell Ave. CT11 .... 52 A5
Pegwell Cl. CT11 .... 52 A5
Pegwell Ct. CT11 .... 52 B5
Pegwell Rd. CT11 .... 52 B5
Pelham Gdns. CT20 .... 178 A4
Pelwood Rd. TN31 .... 201 A2
Pemberton Ct. CT21 .... 177 B3
Pemberton Rd. TN24 .... 139 D2
Pemberton Sq. ME2 .... 9 C8
Pembroke. ME4 .... 10 B8
Pembroke Ave. CT9 .... 7 F1
Pembroke Ct.
  Chatham ME4 .... 10 A4
Pembroke Ct.
  Ramsgate CT11 .... 52 E7
Pembroke Gdns. ME8 .... 33 E4
Pembroke Mews. TN28 .... 200 C8
Pembroke Rd. ME17 .... 96 C3
Pembury Ct. **6** ME10 .... 36 E4
Pembury Gdns. ME16 .... 74 D3
Pembury St. ME10 .... 36 E4
Pembury Way. ME8 .... 11 E2
Pencester Ct. CT16 .... 166 E8
Pencester Rd. CT16 .... 166 E8
Penderel Mews. TN30 ...... 179 B8
Penenden Cl. ME14 .... 75 B7
Penenden Heath Rd. ME14 . 75 C7
Penenden St. ME14 .... 75 A6

Penfield La. ME9 .... 59 A4
Penfold Cl. Chatham ME5 .... 32 B7
Penfold Cl.
 Park Wood ME15 .... 97 E5
Penfold Gdns. CT15 .... 130 E5
Penfold Hill. ME17 .... 99 B8
Penfold Rd. CT19 .... 178 F6
Penfold Way. ME15 .... 96 F6
Penhurst Cl. ME14 .... 75 F5
Penlee Point. TN24 .... 139 D5
Penn Cl. ME10 .... 37 B2
Penn Hill. TN23 .... 155 E6
Pennant Rd. ME1 .... 31 C7
Pennine Way.
 Ashford TN24 .... 139 B4
Pennine Way.
 Maidstone ME15 .... 76 A1
Pennington Cl. CT2 .... 68 C7
Penny Pot La. CT4 .... 108 B4
Pennypot Ind Est. CT21 ... 175 F1
Penrose Ct. CT21 .... 176 C1
Pensand Ho. CT21 .... 176 D1
Penshurst Cl.
 Canterbury CT2 .... 67 A3
Penshurst Cl.
 Gillingham ME8 .... 11 E2
Penshurst Gdns. CT9 .... 8 F2
Penshurst Rd. CT11 .... 52 F7
Penshurst Rise. ME13 ...... 62 B8
Penstocks The. ME16 ...... 74 D2
Pent Vale Cl. CT19 .... 178 A6
Pent Valley High Sch.
 CT19 .... 177 F7
Pent Valley Sch (annexe).
 CT19 .... 177 F6
Pepys Ave. ME12 .... 1 C2
Percival Terr. CT17 ...... 166 B7
Percy Ave. CT10 .... 8 F2
Percy Rd. Broadstairs CT10 . 29 F5
Percy Rd. Margate CT9 .... 8 A3
Percy Rd. Ramsgate CT11 ... 52 D8
Peregrine Dr. ME10 .... 37 A2
Peri Ct. CT1 .... 87 E6
Perimeter Rd. CT16 .... 166 G8
Periwinkle Cl. ME10 ...... 36 E5
Periwinkle **5** ME10 .... 36 E5
Perkins Ave. CT9 .... 28 F8
Perries Mead. CT19 .... 178 B7
Perry Court
 Rudolf Steiner Sch. CT4 . 108 E7
Perry Rd. CT3 .... 70 C3
Perry St. Chatham ME4 .... 9 E3
Perry St. Maidstone ME14 . 74 F6
Perryfield St. ME14 ...... 74 F6
Perth Gdns. ME10 .... 36 C4
Perth Way. CT16 .... 149 C3
Pested Bars Rd. ME17 ..... 97 D5
Pested La. CT4 & TN25 .... 105 C4
Petchell Mews. **11** CT1 .... 67 B2
Peter St. Deal CT14 ...... 117 D7
Peter St.
 Dover CT16 & CT17 .... 166 C8
Peter St. Folkestone CT20 . 178 E5
Petfield Cl. ME12 .... 4 C6
Petham
 Cty Prim Sch. CT4 .... 109 C3
Petham Gn. ME8 .... 11 C2
Pett Bottom Rd. CT4 ...... 110 C5
Pett Hill. CT4 .... 88 F1
Pett La. TN27 .... 120 D7
Pett's Cres. CT12 .... 50 B5
Pettfield Hill Rd. ME13 .. 82 B1
Pettitts Row. ME13 .... 62 B7
Pettman Cl. CT6 .... 22 F3
Pettmans Mews. CT5 .... 20 C2
Petts La. CT3 .... 91 A8
Peverel Dr. ME14 .... 76 A5
Peverel Gn. ME8 .... 33 D4
Peverell Rd. CT16 .... 149 B4
Pheasant La. ME15 .... 97 B8
Pheasant Rd. ME4 .... 10 C2
Pheasants' Hall Rd. CT4 .. 110 F2
Philip Corby Cl. CT9 ..... 8 B2
Philippa Ho. CT19 .... 178 F6
Phillip Rd. CT19 .... 177 E6
Phillipine Village
 Craft Ctr. TN29 .... 197 A6
Phillippa Ct. ME10 .... 36 E8
Phillips Ct. ME8 .... 11 B2
Phillips Rd. CT7 .... 27 A6
Phoenix Ind Est. ME2 .... 9 D7
Phoenix Pk. ME15 .... 97 F4
Phoenix Rd. ME5 .... 32 B2
Piccadilly The. **4** ME4 ... 10 B3
Pickelden La. CT4 .... 107 F8
Pickering St. ME15 .... 97 B6
Pickhill Oast. TN30 ...... 179 B4
Pickneybush La. TN29 ..... 194 A7
Pickwick Cres. ME1 .... 9 C3
Picton Rd. CT11 .... 52 C7

Pier Approach Rd. ME7 .... 10 D7
Pier Ave. Herne Bay CT6 .. 22 E4
Pier Ave. Whitstable CT5 . 21 A2
Pier Rd. ME7 .... 10 E7
Pier Rd Ind Est. ME7 ..... 10 D7
Pier The. CT16 .... 148 F8
Pierpoint Rd. CT5 .... 43 D7
Pierremont Ave. CT10 ..... 30 A4
Pigeon La. CT6 .... 23 A2
Pigtail Cnr. ME12 .... 4 E6
Pike Cl. CT19 .... 178 A7
Pike Rd. CT14 & CT15 ..... 114 E4
Pikefields. ME8 .... 11 C2
Pilckem Cl. CT1 .... 67 D1
Pilgrim Spring. CT19 ..... 178 D8
Pilgrims Ct. TN27 .... 120 C7
Pilgrims La.
 Whitstable CT5 .... 43 B4
Pilgrims Lakes. ME17 ..... 100 E6
Pilgrims Rd. CT1 .... 88 C7
Pilgrims View. ME14 ...... 53 E3
Pilgrims Way. Boxley ME14 . 54 F3
Pilgrims' Way.
 Brabourne TN25 .... 159 E8
Pilgrims Way.
 Broad Street ME14 & ME17 77 C6
Pilgrims Way.
 Canterbury CT1 .... 88 C7
Pilgrims Way.
 Charing TN27 .... 120 E8
Pilgrims Way.
 Detling ME14 .... 55 B1
Pilgrims Way. Dover CT16 . 149 A3
Pilgrims Way. Eccles ME20 . 53 B6
Pilgrims Way.
 Hollingbourne ME17 ...... 77 F3
Pilgrims Way.
 Lenham ME17 .... 101 B7
Pilgrims Way.
 Westwell TN25 .... 121 D5
Pilgrims Way.
 Cty Prim Sch The. CT1 ... 88 C7
Pilot Rd. ME1 .... 31 C8
Pilot's Farm Rd. CT4 ..... 110 A4
Pilots Ave. CT14 .... 117 A4
Pimp's Court Cotts. ME15 . 96 E6
Pimp's Court Farm Ctr.
 ME15 .... 96 E6
Pimpernel Cl. ME14 .... 76 B4
Pimpernel Way. ME5 .... 31 E4
Pin Hill. CT1 .... 87 F7
Pine Cotts. ME14 .... 74 E8
Pine Gr. Gillingham ME7 .. 33 A5
Pine Gr. Maidstone ME14 .. 75 B6
Pine Ho. **3** ME5 .... 31 F5
Pine Lodge. ME16 .... 74 C3
Pine Tree Ave. CT2 .... 66 E2
Pine Way. CT19 .... 177 D7
Pine Wlk. CT6 .... 23 E5
Pineham Rd. CT15 .... 149 D6
Pines Gardens The. **1** 151 B5
Pines The. CT10 .... 29 D4
Pineside Rd. CT3 .... 89 E8
Pinetree Cl. CT5 .... 20 F3
Pinewood Cl. CT12 .... 29 C1
Pinewood Dr. ME14 .... 54 D8
Pink's Cnr. ME9 .... 14 E3
Pinks Cnr. CT12 .... 50 D6
Pinners Hill. CT15 .... 113 C6
Pinners La. CT15 .... 113 C5
Pinous Ho. ME10 .... 36 E5
Pintail Way. CT6 .... 23 C2
Pioneer Rd. CT16 .... 149 A3
Pippa Ave. CT4 .... 111 B8
Pippin Cl. Coxheath ME17 . 96 B2
Pippin Cl.
 Sittingbourne ME10 ...... 36 D6
Pippin Croft. ME7 .... 33 A6
Pirbright Cl. ME5 .... 32 D2
Pitstock Rd. ME9 .... 59 B5
Pitt Rd.
 Langley Heath ME17 ...... 99 A2
Pitt Rd. Maidstone ME16 .. 74 B1
Pittlesden. TN30 .... 179 A7
Pittlesden Pl. **1** TN30 .... 179 A7
Pittock Ho. CT14 .... 117 B3
Pivington La. TN27 .... 119 C2
Pivington Mill Ind Est.
 TN27 .... 119 C2
Pixwell La. CT13 .... 116 D3
Place La. Hartlip ME9 .... 34 D4
Place La.
 Woodchurch TN26 .... 169 B3
Place The. CT4 .... 112 F1
Plain Rd.
 Brabourne Lees TN25 ..... 158 F5
Plain Rd. Folkestone CT20 . 178 B4
Plains Ave. ME15 .... 75 C1
Plains Of Waterloo. CT11 . 52 F7
Plaistow Sq. ME14 .... 75 C6

Plantation Cl. TN26 ...... 138 A7
Plantation La. ME14 ...... 76 A3
Plantation Rd.
 Faversham ME13 .... 62 C7
Plantation Rd.
 Gillingham ME7 .... 11 A6
Plantation Rd.
 Whitstable CT5 .... 21 A2
Platt's Heath
 Cty Prim Sch. ME17 ...... 100 F2
Platters The. ME8 .... 33 C7
Playstool Cl. ME9 .... 35 B6
Playstool Rd. ME9 .... 35 A6
Plaza Ct. ME10 .... 37 A4
Pleasance Rd N. TN29 ..... 204 E5
Pleasance Rd S. TN29 ..... 204 F2
Pleasance Road Central.
 TN29 .... 204 F3
Pleasant Row. **2** ME4 ...... 10 A6
Pleasant Pl. ME13 .... 3 E6
Plenty Brook Dr. CT6 ..... 22 F3
Plewis Ho. ME7 .... 10 E7
Pleydell Cres. CT7 .... 67 F7
Pleydell Gdns. CT20 ...... 178 D4
Plimsoll Ave. CT19 .... 178 E8
Plomley Cl. ME8 .... 33 D4
Plough Cotts. ME17 .... 98 E2
Plough Ct. CT6 .... 23 D2
Plough Hill. CT15 .... 165 C4
Plough La. CT15 .... 21 D3
Plough Rd. ME12 .... 5 C5
Plough Wents Rd. ME17 .... 98 B2
Ploughmans Way.
 Chatham ME5 .... 32 A1
Ploughmans Way.
 Gillingham ME8 .... 33 E6
Plover Cl. ME5 .... 32 D1
Pluckley CE Prim Sch.
 TN27 .... 136 D7
Pluckley Sta. TN27 .... 136 C3
Pluckley Cl. ME8 .... 11 C3
Pluckley Gdns. CT9 .... 8 E2
Pluckley Rd. Bethersden
 TN26 & TN27 .... 153 C5
Pluckley Rd. Charing TN27 . 120 B5
Pluckley Rd.
 Hothfield TN26 .... 137 B4
Pluckley Rd.
 Maltman's Hill TN27 ..... 135 D2
Pluckley Sta. TN27 .... 136 C3
Plum Tree Gdns. TN26 ..... 169 B1
Plum Tree Rd. ME9 .... 56 B8
Plumford Rd. ME13 .... 62 A2
Plumpton Wlk. **5**
 Canterbury CT1 .... 67 B1
Plumpton Wlk. **9**
 Maidstone ME15 .... 97 F6
Plumpudding La. ME13 ..... 42 E1
Plumstone Rd. CT7 .... 26 F1
Plumtree Gr. ME7 .... 33 A4
Plumtrees. ME16 .... 74 A2
Plurenden Manor
 Farm Cotts. TN26 .... 168 F7
Plurenden Rd. TN26 .... 168 F7
Poachers Cl. ME5 .... 32 C5
Podkin Wood. ME5 .... 53 F8
Poets Cnr. CT9 .... 7 J1
Poets Wlk. CT14 .... 117 C1
Poison Cross. CT13 .... 93 B4
Poldark Ct. **14** CT11 ...... 52 F7
Poles The. ME9 .... 12 E4
Polhill Dr. ME5 .... 31 F2
Pollard Cl. TN23 .... 155 F8
Pollard Cl. ME7 .... 10 C5
Polo Way. CT5 .... 21 D1
Pomfret Ho. CT4 .... 86 D1
Pomfret Rd. CT4 .... 86 D1
Pommeus La. CT14 .... 133 D7
Poncia Rd. TN23 .... 156 A7
Pond Cotts. Herne Bay CT6 . 23 D2
Pond Cotts.
 Sittingbourne ME10 ...... 58 D8
Pond Dr. ME10 .... 37 A2
Pond Farm Rd.
 Hucking ME17 .... 56 D1
Pond Farm Rd.
 Oad Street ME9 .... 35 F1
Pond Hill. CT3 .... 90 D1
Pond Hill Rd. CT20 .... 177 C5
Pond La. St Margaret's at
 Cliffe CT15 .... 150 D7
Pond La.
 Womenswold CT3 & CT4 .... 112 D3
Pondfield. TN25 .... 139 C8
Poorhole La. CT10 .... 29 B5
Poot La. ME9 .... 12 E5
Pope House La. TN30 ...... 167 B4
Pope St. Godmersham CT4 .. 107 E4
Pope St. Maidstone ME16 .. 74 C2
Popes La. CT7 .... 26 F7
Poplar Cl. TN23 .... 138 F3
Poplar Dr. Elvington CT15 . 114 B2

Poplar Dr. Herne Bay CT6 . 22 D2
Poplar Field. TN30 .... 188 D4
Poplar Gr. ME16 .... 74 C5
Poplar Ho. ME12 .... 1 C2
Poplar La. TN29 .... 203 D7
Poplar Rd. Broadstairs CT10 29 G6
Poplar Rd. Ramsgate CT11 . 52 D7
Poplar Rd.
 Wittersham TN30 .... 188 D4
Poplar View. ME13 .... 63 E3
Poplars. TN26 .... 182 A7
Poplars The. Ashford TN23 156 A7
Poplars The.
 Bethersden TN26 .... 153 E5
Poplars The. Hersden CT3 . 46 F1
Poppy Cl. ME7 .... 10 E5
Popsal La. CT3 .... 91 B6
Porchester Cl. ME15 ..... 97 A6
Port Cl. Chatham ME5 .... 32 B3
Port Cl. Maidstone ME14 . 76 A5
Port Lympne Zoo. CT21 ... 174 C2
Port Rise. ME4 .... 9 F3
Portal House Sch. CT15 .. 151 A6
Portbello Ct. CT14 ...... 117 D7
Porter Cl. ME14 .... 4 A6
Porter's La. ME13 .... 62 B2
Porters Wlk. ME17 .... 98 E4
Portland Ave. ME10 ...... 37 C4
Portland Cl. Ashford TN24 . 139 C7
Portland Cl. Hythe CT21 . 176 B2
Portland Ct. **3**
 Hythe CT21 .... 176 B2
Portland Ct.
 Ramsgate CT11 .... 52 E7
Portland Rd.
 Gillingham ME7 .... 10 E6
Portland Rd. Hythe CT21 . 176 B2
Portland St. ME4 .... 10 B2
Portland Terr.
 Ripple CT14 .... 133 D8
Portland Terr.
 Sheerness ME12 .... 1 D2
Portsdown CT16 .... 74 B2
Portway. CT5 .... 43 C8
Post Barn Rd. ME4 .... 9 F2
Postley Commercial Ctr.
 ME15 .... 75 A2
Postley Rd. ME15 .... 75 A1
Posting. TN23 .... 138 E1
Postling Rd. CT19 .... 177 E7
Postling Wents. CT21 .... 175 F8
Postmill Dr. ME15 .... 74 F1
Potten Street Rd. CT7 ... 25 E3
Potter St. CT13 .... 73 A1
Potters Cl. TN24 .... 138 E6
Potters Cnr. TN24 .... 138 E6
Pottery Cotts. TN25 ..... 140 E5
Potyn Ho. ME1 .... 9 C4
Pouces Cotts. CT12 ...... 27 F1
Poulders Gdns. CT13 ..... 93 E8
Poulders Rd. CT13 .... 93 E8
Poulsen Ct. ME10 .... 37 B4
Poulton Cl. CT17 .... 165 F8
Poulton Close Bsns Pk.
 CT17 .... 148 E1
Poulton La. CT3 .... 92 C8
Pound Ct. TN23 .... 156 A3
Pound Farm Cotts. CT18 .. 177 A7
Pound Ho. TN23 .... 156 B8
Pound La. Ashford TN23 .. 155 F4
Pound La.
 Brabourne Lees TN25 .... 158 F5
Pound La.
 Canterbury CT1 & CT2 ... 66 F1
Pound La. Elham CT4 ..... 144 F4
Pound La. Molash CT4 .... 105 F4
Pounshurst Rd. TN26 ..... 171 C3
Powell Cl. ME20 .... 53 A3
Powell Cotton Dr. CT7 ... 27 B6
Powell Cotton Mus. CT7 .. 27 B5
Powell Sch (Prim) The.
 CT16 .... 149 B4
Power Station Rd. ME12 .. 3 E7
Pratling St. ME20 .... 53 C4
Precincts The. **16**
 Canterbury CT1 .... 67 A1
Precincts The.
 Canterbury CT1 .... 88 A8
Prentis Cl. ME10 .... 36 C5
Prentis Quay. ME10 ...... 36 E5
Prescott Cl. CT15 .... 149 E6
Prescott Ho. TN28 .... 200 A7
Prestedge Ave.
 CT10 & CT11 .... 29 E2
Preston Ave.
 Faversham ME13 .... 62 E6
Preston Ave.
 Gillingham ME7 .... 10 E1
Preston Gr. ME13 .... 62 D6
Preston Hill. CT3 .... 70 B1

Preston La.
 Faversham ME13 .... 62 D6
Preston La. Preston CT3 .. 70 B5
Preston Malt Ho. ME13 ... 62 D6
Preston Par. CT5 .... 42 F7
Preston Pk. ME13 .... 62 D6
Preston Rd. Manston CT12 . 28 E2
Preston Rd.
 Stourmouth CT3 .... 48 D1
Preston Rd. Wingham CT3 . 70 B2
Preston St. ME13 .... 62 D7
Preston-next-Wingham
 Cty Prim Sch. CT3 ...... 70 C6
Pretoria Ho. **8** ME15 ..... 97 E5
Pretoria Ho.
 Canterbury CT1 .... 88 B8
Pretoria Rd. Chatham ME4 . 9 F2
Pretoria Rd.
 Gillingham ME7 .... 10 D3
Price's Ave.
 Margate CT9 .... 8 B2
Price's Ave.
 Ramsgate CT11 .... 52 C6
Priest Fields. CT6 ...... 23 F5
Priest & Sow Cnr. CT5 ... 21 B3
Priest Wlk. CT5 .... 21 C3
Priestfield Rd. ME7 ..... 10 E5
Priestfield Stad
 (Gillingham FC). ME7 ... 10 E5
Priestfields. 9 B3
Primrose Ave. ME8 .... 33 B5
Primrose Cl. ME1 .... 31 E7
Primrose Dr. TN23 .... 156 B4
Primrose Gr. ME9 .... 58 A6
Primrose Hill. CT4 ...... 86 B7
Primrose La. ME9 .... 58 A6
Primrose Pl. CT17 .... 149 B1
Primrose Rd. CT17 .... 149 A1
Primrose Way.
 Cliffs End CT12 .... 51 C5
Primrose Way.
 Whitstable CT5 .... 21 C1
Prince Andrew Rd. CT10 .. 29 E7
Prince Arthur Rd. ME7 ... 10 B6
Prince Charles Ave.
 Chatham ME5 .... 32 B4
Prince Charles Ave.
 Minster ME12 .... 4 C6
Prince Charles Ave.
 Sittingbourne ME10 ..... 37 C3
Prince Charles Rd. CT10 . 29 E7
Prince of Wales Rdbt.
 CT17 .... 166 D6
Prince of Wales Terr.
 CT14 .... 117 D5
Prince's Ave. CT12 ...... 29 B1
Prince's Gdns. CT9 ...... 8 C2
Prince's Golf Links. CT13 73 E5
Prince's Rd. CT11 .... 52 D8
Prince's St. Margate CT9 . 7 J2
Prince's St. **7**
 Ramsgate CT11 .... 52 E6
Prince's St. Rochester ME1 9 C4
Prince's Wlk. CT9 .... 8 D3
Princes Ave. Chatham ME5 . 32 B5
Princes Ave. Minster ME12 4 D7
Princes Cl. CT7 .... 26 D7
Princes Cres. **10** CT9 .... 7 J2
Princes Dr. Sandwich CT13 73 F2
Princes Dr. Sandwich CT13 . 95 A8
Princes Par. CT21 .... 176 E2
Princes St. Deal CT14 ... 117 D7
Princes St. **11**
 Dover CT16 & CT17 ...... 166 D7
Princes St.
 Maidstone ME14 .... 75 A5
Princes Terr. CT21 ...... 175 F1
Princes Way.
 Canterbury CT2 .... 66 E1
Princes Way. Detling ME14 55 A1
Princess Anne Rd. CT10 .. 29 E7
Princess Cl. CT5 .... 21 C3
Princess Margaret Ave.
 Margate CT9 .... 8 E2
Princess Margaret Ave.
 Ramsgate CT9 .... 29 A1
Princess Mary Ave. ME7 .. 10 B7
Princess Mary's
 Day Hospl. CT9 .... 8 A2
Princess Rd. CT5 .... 21 C3
Princess St. CT19 .... 178 E6
Prinys Dr. ME8 .... 33 C4
Prior Rd. TN29 .... 204 E8
Prior's Lees. **8** CT20 .... 178 D4
Prioress Rd. CT2 .... 87 D8
Priory Cl. Broadstairs CT10 29 F3
Priory Cl.
 East Farleigh ME15 ..... 96 B8

Priory Cl.
New Romney TN28 ...... 199 F6
Priory Ct. Gillingham ME8 .... 11 A2
Priory Ct.
Leysdown-on-S ME12 .... 6 G1
Priory Cty Inf Sch.
Ramsgate CT11 .... 52 D6
Priory Cty Inf Sch.
Ramsgate CT11 .... 52 D7
Priory Gate. **4** ME14 ...... 75 A5
Priory Gate Rd. CT17 ...... 166 C8
Priory Gdns. CT20 .... 178 D4
Priory Gr. CT17 .... 166 C8
Priory Hill. CT16 & CT17 .... 166 D8
Priory Ho. CT17 .... 166 C7
Priory La. Herne Bay CT6 ...... 23 A3
Priory La. Sellindge TN25 .. 159 D4
Priory of St Jacob. CT11 ...... 87 E6
Priory Rd. Bilsington TN25 .. 172 C4
Priory Rd.
Dover CT16 & CT17 ...... 166 D8
Priory Rd. Faversham ME13 .. 62 C8
Priory Rd. Gillingham ME8 .... 11 A2
Priory Rd. Maidstone ME15 .. 75 A3
Priory Rd. Ramsgate CT11 .. 52 D6
Priory Rd. Rochester ME2 ...... 9 A6
Priory Row. ME13 .... 62 C8
Priory St. **10**
CT16 & CT17 .... 166 D8
Priory Sta. CT17 .... 166 C8
Priory Station Approach Rd.
CT17 .... 166 C7
Priory Way. TN30 .... 179 C7
Progress Est The. ME15 ...... 98 A4
Promenade.
Birchington CT7 .... 26 F8
Promenade. Deal CT14 ...... 117 D3
Promenade The. ME12 .... 6 G2
Prospect Ave. ME2 .... 9 B8
Prospect Cl. CT8 .... 27 E7
Prospect Cotts.
Boughton Lees TN25 ...... 122 E3
Prospect Cotts.
Harbledown CT2 .... 65 E1
Prospect Gdns. CT12 .... 50 B7
Prospect Hill. CT6 .... 23 A5
Prospect Mews. CT21 .... 176 C2
Prospect Pl. **7**
Broadstairs CT10 .... 30 B4
Prospect Pl.
Canterbury CT1 .... 88 A7
Prospect Pl. Dover CT17 .. 149 B1
Prospect Pl. Eastling ME13 .. 81 E6
Prospect Pl.
Maidstone ME16 .... 74 E3
Prospect Pl.
St Nicholas at Wade CT7 .. 25 E1
Prospect Rd.
Birchington CT7 .... 26 F7
Prospect Rd.
Broadstairs CT10 .... 30 B4
Prospect Rd.
Folkestone CT20 .... 177 D3
Prospect Rd. Hythe CT21 .. 176 C2
Prospect Rd. Minster,
Thanet CT12 .... 50 B6
Prospect Row.
Chatham ME4 .... 10 A3
Prospect Row.
Gillingham ME4 .... 10 A6
Prospect Terr. Elham CT4 .. 144 F4
Prospect Terr. **17**
Ramsgate CT11 .... 52 E6
Prospect Way. TN25 ...... 158 E5
Provender Rd. ME13 & ME9 .. 61 A6
Provender Way. ME14 ...... 75 E5
Providence La. ME1 .... 9 C5
Providence St. TN23 ...... 156 C8
Puckle La. CT1 .... 88 A6
Pudding La. Ash CT3 .... 71 D1
Pudding La.
Maidstone ME14 .... 74 F4
Pudding Rd. ME8 .... 33 F8
Pullman Cl. CT12 .... 52 C8
Pump La. Gillingham ME4 .... 11 D2
Pump La.
Gillingham ME7 & ME8 .... 11 D3
Pump La. **1** Margate CT9 ...... 7 J2
Purbeck Rd. ME4 .... 9 E2
Purchas Ct. CT2 .... 66 C4
Purchase La. TN26 .... 154 E8
Purr Wood. CT4 .... 107 B2
Purser Way. ME7 .... 10 C7
Puttney Dr. ME10 .... 37 A8
Pyatt Mews. **3** CT1 ...... 67 B1
Pye Alley La. CT5 .... 43 C3
Pym Ho. TN27 .... 120 D7
Pyrus Cl. ME5 .... 54 A8

Pyson's Rd. CT10 & CT12 ...... 29 D3
Pyson's Road Ind Est.CT10 .. 29 D3

Quain Ct. CT20 .... 178 C4
Quantock Dr.
TN23 & TN24 .... 139 B4
Quantock Gdns. CT12 .... 29 B3
Quarries The. ME17 .... 97 C4
Quarrington La. TN25 ...... 158 A7
Quarry Cotts. TN30 .... 189 C3
Quarry Rd. Hythe CT21 .. 176 B3
Quarry Rd.
Maidstone ME15 .... 75 A2
Quarry Sq. ME14 .... 75 A5
Quarry View. TN23 .... 155 D7
Quarry Wlk. CT21 .... 177 A3
Quarry Wood. TN25 ...... 173 A6
Quay Cotts. ME9 .... 38 E6
Quay La. Faversham ME13 .. 62 D8
Quay La. Sandwich CT13 .... 73 A1
Quay The. ME9 .... 38 E6
Quayside. ME4 .... 10 B8
Queen Anne Rd. ME14 ...... 75 B4
Queen Bertha Rd. CT11 ...... 52 C6
Queen Bertha's Ave.
CT7 & CT8 .... 27 C8
Queen Elizabeth Ave. CT9 ...... 8 D1
Queen Elizabeth Rd. CT16 166 F8
Queen Elizabeth Sq. ME15 .. 97 D6
Queen Elizabeth the Queen
Mother Hospl. CT9 .... 28 F8
Queen Elizabeth's Sch.
ME13 .... 62 D8
Queen Mother Ct The. ME1 .. 9 B4
Queen St. Ashford TN23 .... 139 B2
Queen St. Chatham ME4 ...... 10 A4
Queen St. Deal CT14 ...... 117 D6
Queen St. Dover CT16 .... 166 D7
Queen St.
Folkestone CT20 .... 178 E5
Queen St. Herne Bay CT6 .... 22 F5
Queen St. Margate CT9 ...... 7 I8
Queen St. Ramsgate CT11 .. 52 E6
Queen St. Rochester ME1 ...... 9 C4
Queen Victoria
Meml Hospl. CT6 .... 23 B4
Queen's Ave.
Birchington CT7 .... 26 D7
Queen's Ave.
Broadstairs CT10 .... 30 B6
Queen's Ave.
Maidstone ME16 .... 74 D5
Queen's Ave. Margate CT9 .... 7 I1
Queen's Ave.
Ramsgate CT12 .... 29 B1
Queen's Gate Rd. CT11 .... 52 C8
Queen's Gdns. CT16 ...... 166 D8
Queen's Lea. CT15 .... 164 E5
Queen's Prom. CT9 .... 8 B3
Queen's Rd. Ash CT3 ...... 71 D2
Queen's Rd.
Ashford TN24 .... 140 A1
Queen's Rd.
Broadstairs CT10 .... 30 B4
Queen's Rd. Chatham ME5 .. 10 D1
Queen's Rd.
Faversham ME13 .... 62 B7
Queen's Rd.
Gillingham ME7 .... 10 C4
Queen's Rd.
Littlestone-on-S TN28 .... 200 D6
Queen's Rd. Lydd TN29 .... 203 C6
Queen's Rd.
Maidstone ME16 .... 74 C4
Queen's Rd.
Ramsgate CT11 .... 52 F7
Queen's Rd.
Westgate-on-S CT8 .... 27 F8
Queen's Rise. CT14 .... 133 F5
Queen's Way. ME12 .... 3 A8
Queenborough
Cty Prim Sch. ME11 .... 3 B5
Queenborough Dr. ME12 ...... 4 B7
Queenborough Rd.
Halfway Houses ME12 ...... 3 C6
Queenborough Rd.
Queenborough ME1, ME12 .. 3 C4
Queenborough Sta. ME11 .... 3 A5
Queendown Ave. ME8 ...... 33 D5
Queendown Rd. CT7 .... 28 A8
Queens Ave.
Canterbury CT2 .... 66 E1
Queens Ave. Dover CT17 .. 166 A7
Queens Ave.
Herne Bay CT6 .... 23 D5
Queens Ave. Hythe CT20 .. 177 B6
Queens Ct. Ashford TN24 .. 139 C3
Queens Ct. Hythe CT21 .. 176 B1
Queens Ct. Margate CT9 ...... 8 A3
Queens Gdns.
Broadstairs CT10 .... 30 B3

Queens Gdns.
Herne Bay CT6 .... 22 F5
Queens Mews. CT14 ...... 117 D6
Queens Par. **12**
Faversham ME13 .... 62 D7
Queens Par. Margate CT9 ...... 8 A3
Queens Par.
West Minster ME12 .... 3 A8
Queens Rd. Ashford TN24 .. 139 C3
Queens Rd. Aylesham CT3 .. 112 F5
Queens Rd. Minster ME12 ...... 4 D7
Queens Rd. Whitstable CT5 .. 21 A2
Queens Way. ME14 .... 55 A1
Queensbridge Dr. CT6 ...... 22 C4
Queensdown Rd. CT14 .... 134 D4
Queensway.
Dymchurch TN29 .... 186 E2
Queensway. Lydd TN29 .. 203 C6
Queenswood Rd. ME20 ...... 53 D7
Quern Rd. CT14 .... 117 A2
Quern The. ME15 .... 74 E1
Querns Pl. CT1 .... 88 B8
Querns Rd. CT1 .... 88 C8
Quested Rd. CT19 .... 177 E6
Quested Way. ME17 ...... 100 C6
Quetta Rd. CT12 .... 28 F1
Quex Rd. CT8 .... 27 F8
Quickwater Cres. ME5 ...... 31 E5
Quince Orch. TN26 .... 183 A7
Quinion Cl. ME5 .... 54 A8
Quinnell St. ME8 .... 11 E1
Quinton Rd. ME10 .... 36 C7

Rabbit Hole. CT4 .... 129 A7
Radfall Cnr. CT5 .... 44 C6
Radfall Gate. CT5 .... 44 C6
Radfall Hill. CT5 .... 44 D5
Radfall Rd.
CT2 & CT5 & CT6 .... 44 B6
Radfall Ride. CT5 .... 44 C5
Radleigh Gdns. ME4 .... 9 E1
Radley Cl. CT10 .... 30 A6
Radnor Bridge Rd.
CT19 & CT20 .... 178 E5
Radnor Cl. CT6 .... 23 B1
Radnor Cliff. CT20 .... 178 A3
Radnor Cliff Cres. CT20 .. 178 A3
Radnor Park Ave. CT19 .. 178 C6
Radnor Park Cres. CT19 .. 178 C5
Radnor Park Gdns. CT19 .. 178 C6
Radnor Park Rd. CT19 .... 178 C6
Radnor Pk W. CT19 ...... 178 B6
Radnor St. **17** CT19 .... 178 E5
Raggatt Pl. ME15 .... 75 B2
Raglan Pl. **10** CT10 ...... 30 B4
Ragstone Hollow. TN25 .. 173 A6
Ragstone Rd. ME15 .... 76 A2
Railway Ave. CT5 .... 20 E1
Railway Cotts. ME4 .... 38 D3
Railway Hill. CT4 .... 128 E8
Railway Rd. ME12 .... 1 C2
Railway St. Chatham ME4 ...... 9 F4
Railway St. Gillingham ME7 .. 10 D6
Railway Terr. Margate CT9 ...... 7 H1
Railway Terr.
Queenborough ME11 .... 3 A5
Rainham Cl. ME15 .... 75 A1
Rainham Mark
Gram Sch. ME8 .... 11 D2
Rainham Rd. ME5 & ME7 .... 10 C3
Rainham Sch for Girls.
ME8 .... 33 C8
Rainham Sh Ctr. ME8 ...... 33 F8
Rainham Sta. ME8 .... 11 F1
Raleigh Cl. Ashford TN24 .. 157 A8
Raleigh Cl. Chatham ME5 .. 32 A6
Raleigh Way. ME12 .... 3 E6
Ralph Grimshaw Ct. CT8 .. 27 E8
Ram La. TN26 .... 137 C8
Ramillies Cl. ME5 .... 32 A6
Ramp A. CT16 .... 166 H8
Ramp B. CT16 .... 166 H8
Ramp C. CT16 .... 166 G8
Rampart Rd. CT21 .... 176 B2
Rampion Cl. ME14 .... 75 E5
Ramsey Cl. CT12 .... 66 E1
Ramsey Ho. **8** CT21 ...... 87 F7
Ramsgate Hospl
(Geriatric). CT12 .... 52 D6
Ramsgate Rd.
Broadstairs CT10 & CT11 .... 29 F2
Ramsgate Rd.
Broadstairs CT10 .... 30 B4
Ramsgate Rd.
Margate CT10 & CT9 ...... 29 A6
Ramsgate Rd.
Sandwich CT12 & CT13 .... 73 A7
Ramsgate Sch The. CT12 .. 29 A2
Ramsgate Sta. CT12 .... 52 C8
Ramstone Cl. TN25 .... 158 E5

Rancorn Rd. CT9 .... 7 G1
Randall Rd. ME4 .... 9 E1
Randall St. ME14 .... 74 F6
Randalls Row. ME15 .... 96 F5
Randolph Cl. CT1 .... 88 A7
Randolph Gdns. TN24 .... 139 E5
Randolph Ho. **15** CT20 .. 178 E5
Randolph Rd. Dover CT17 .. 149 B1
Randolph Rd.
Gillingham ME7 .... 10 C5
Randolph Sq. CT9 .... 7 J3
Ranelagh Gdns. CT10 ...... 29 E5
Ranelagh Gr. CT10 .... 29 E5
Ranelagh Rd. Deal CT14 .. 117 D5
Ranelagh Rd.
Sheerness ME12 .... 1 D2
Range Rd. Eastchurch ME12 .. 5 D1
Range Rd. Hythe CT21 .. 176 B1
Range Road Ind Est.
CT21 .... 176 B1
Ransley Gn. TN26 .... 183 F8
Raspberry Hill La. ME9 .... 14 D6
Ratling Rd. CT3 .... 112 F7
Rattington St. CT4 .... 86 E2
Ravenlea Rd. CT20 .... 178 A5
Ravens Dane Cl. ME15 .... 76 A1
Ravensbourne Ave. CT6 .... 23 B3
Ravenscourt Rd.
Deal CT14 .... 117 C5
Ravenscourt Rd.
Rough Common CT2 .... 66 B3
Ravenswood Ave. ME2 ...... 9 B8
Rawdon Dr.
Maidstone ME15 .... 75 A3
Rawdon Rd.
Ramsgate CT11 .... 52 C6
Rawling St. ME9 .... 58 F3
Rayham Rd. CT5 .... 44 A8
Raymer Rd. ME14 .... 75 B8
Raymond Ave. CT1 .... 88 A6
Raymoor Ave. TN29 ...... 195 A4
Rayners Hill. ME17 .... 102 C5
Reach Cl. CT15 .... 150 F5
Reach Meadow. CT15 .... 151 A6
Reach Rd. Lympne CT21 .. 174 D2
Reach Rd. St Margaret's
at Cliffe CT15 .... 150 F5
Reachfields. CT21 .... 176 A1
Reading Cl. CT14 .... 117 B1
Reading Rd. CT17 .... 165 F7
Reading St.
Broadstairs CT10 .... 29 F8
Reading St.
Tenterden TN30 .... 180 C2
Reading Street Rd.
CT10 & CT9 .... 29 E8
Readscroft Rd. ME8 .... 33 D5
Rebecca Ct. **6** CT9 .... 8 B2
Recreation Cl. ME4 .... 75 B6
Recreation Ground Rd.
TN30 .... 179 B7
Rectory Bglws. TN26 .... 169 F8
Rectory Cl. TN26 .... 169 A2
Rectory Gdns. CT5 .... 21 D2
Rectory Grange. ME1 .... 9 C2
Rectory La. Barham CT4 .. 112 A1
Rectory La.
Harrietsham ME17 ...... 100 E5
Rectory La. Hythe CT21 .. 176 B5
Rectory La. Lyminge CT18 .. 161 C6
Rectory La.
Maidstone ME16 .... 74 A1
Rectory Rd.
Broadstairs CT10 .... 30 B5
Rectory Rd. Deal CT14 .. 116 F4
Rectory Rd.
Sittingbourne ME10 ...... 37 B3
Rectory Rd. St Mary
in the Marsh TN29 ...... 194 B4
Rectory Way. TN24 ...... 139 C5
Reculver Ave. CT7 .... 26 E8
Reculver CE Prim Sch. CT6 .. 24 A4
Reculver Cl. CT6 .... 23 E5
Reculver Dr. CT6 .... 23 D5
Reculver La. CT6 .... 24 B6
Reculver Rd. CT6 .... 23 D5
Reculver Wlk.
Maidstone ME15 .... 97 F6
Reculvers Rd. CT8 .... 27 F7
Red Lion Cl. **6** CT21 .... 176 B2
Red Lion La. **5** CT5 ...... 20 D2
Red Lion Sq. **7** CT21 .... 176 B2
Red Rd. CT3 & ME13 ...... 64 D5
Red Robin Cotts. ME9 .... 35 B6
Red Tree Orch. TN23 .... 155 F7
Redbridge Cl. ME5 .... 32 C4
Redbrook St. TN26 .... 169 E3
Redbrooks Way. CT21 .... 175 F2
Redcliffe La. ME14 .... 75 B7

Redcot La. CT2 & CT3 ...... 68 B7
Redfern Ave. ME7 .... 10 E5
Redgates. CT6 .... 23 A5
Redhill Rd. CT8 .... 27 E8
Redhouse La. CT4 .... 109 D6
Redhouse Wall. CT14 ...... 95 B1
Redington. TN24 .... 139 C3
Redland Shaw. ME4 .... 9 E1
Redlands Ct. CT17 .... 148 E4
Redmill Cl. CT20 .... 177 E5
Redoubt Way. TN29 ...... 187 B4
Redruth Manor. ME7 ...... 10 E6
Redsells Cl. ME15 .... 76 A1
Redsull Ave. CT14 .... 117 A3
Redvers Cotts. CT16 ...... 148 E5
Redvers Rd. ME4 .... 10 A2
Redwing Rd. ME5 .... 32 B7
Redwood Cl.
Canterbury CT2 .... 66 E2
Redwood Cl. Chatham ME5 .. 32 B8
Redyear Cotts. TN24 .... 140 A1
Redyear Ct. TN24 .... 140 A1
Reed Ave. CT1 .... 67 D3
Reed Cres. TN23 .... 156 C3
Reedland Cres. ME13 ...... 62 C8
Reedmace Cl. TN23 ...... 155 D8
Reeds Cl. CT6 .... 23 C4
Reeves Alley. **1** CT5 .... 20 D1
Reeves Pas. **7** ME13 .... 62 C7
Reeves Way. CT5 .... 21 C2
Reform Rd. ME4 .... 10 B3
Regency Cl.
Gillingham ME8 .... 33 C3
Regency Cl.
Sheerness ME12 .... 1 B3
Regency Cl. Whitstable CT5 .. 43 F7
Regency Ct. ME10 .... 36 D4
Regency Pl. CT1 .... 67 B2
Regency Villas. CT14 .... 129 C5
Regent Dr. ME15 .... 97 A8
Regent Rd. ME7 .... 10 C4
Regent St. CT5 .... 20 D2
Regents Pl. TN23 .... 139 B2
Regents Wlk. CT6 .... 23 D5
Reginald Rd. ME16 .... 74 E3
Regis Cres. ME10 .... 36 F7
Regis Manor
Cty Prim Sch. ME10 ...... 36 E7
Reglvbivm Roman Fort.
CT6 .... 24 D7
Reinden Gr. ME15 .... 75 F1
Remston Mews. **12** CT1 .. 67 B2
Renault Cl. CT6 .... 22 A4
Rendezvous Cl. CT20 .... 178 D5
Rendezvous The. CT9 .... 7 I3
Renown Rd. ME5 .... 32 C2
Rentain Rd. CT4 .... 86 D2
Repton Cl. CT10 .... 29 F6
Repton Manor Rd. TN23 .. 139 A3
Repton Way. ME5 .... 31 F4
Resolution Cl. ME5 .... 32 A6
Resrvoir Rd. CT5 .... 20 E2
Rest Harrow. ME13 .... 83 D6
Restharrow Rd. ME14 .... 75 E4
Retreat The.
Birchington CT7 .... 27 B8
Retreat The.
Doddington ME9 .... 80 D7
Retreat The.
Ramsgate CT12 .... 52 B8
Revenge Rd. ME5 .... 54 B4
Reynolds Cl. CT6 .... 23 B4
Rhee Wall. TN26 .... 190 D7
Rheims Ct. CT2 .... 66 D1
Rheims Way. CT1 & CT2 .. 87 E8
Rhodaus Cl. CT1 .... 87 F7
Rhodaus Town. CT1 .... 87 F7
Rhode St. ME4 .... 10 A4
Rhodes Gdns. CT10 ...... 30 A6
Rhodes Ho. ME5 .... 10 C2
Rhodewood Cl. ME15 ...... 76 A1
Richard Ct. **7** CT9 .... 8 B2
Richard St. Chatham ME4 ...... 9 F4
Richard St. Rochester ME1 ...... 9 C3
Richborough Bsns Pk.
CT13 .... 73 A3
Richborough Castle. CT13 .. 72 E5
Richborough Rd. CT8 ...... 27 F7
Richbourgh Rd. CT13 .... 72 F3
Richdore Rd. CT4 .... 125 C6
Richmond Ave. CT19 .... 178 C5
Richmond Cl. CT16 ...... 149 D1
Richmond Cty Inf Sch. ME7 10 C6
Richmond
Cty Prim Sch. ME12 .... 1 E2
Richmond Dr.
Herne Bay CT6 .... 23 E5
Richmond Dr.
New Romney TN28 ...... 200 C8

Richmond Dr.
Sittingbourne ME10 ...... 36 E7
Richmond Gdns. CT2 ...... 66 C2
Richmond Rd.
Gillingham ME7 ...... 10 C7
Richmond Rd.
Ramsgate CT11 ...... 52 D6
Richmond Rd.
Whitstable CT5 ...... 21 B1
Richmond St.
Folkestone CT19 ...... 177 D6
Richmond St.
Herne Bay CT6 ...... 22 F5
Richmond St.
Sheerness ME12 ...... 1 E2
Richmond Way. ME15 ...... 97 A8
Riddles ME10 & ME9 ...... 36 C3
Ridge Meadow
Cty Prim Sch. ME5 ...... 31 E6
Ridge The. TN24 ...... 139 E6
Ridgeway. Lympne CT21 ... 175 A3
Ridgeway Cliff. CT6 ...... 22 C5
Ridgeway Rd. CT6 ...... 46 A7
Ridgeway Terr. TN25 ...... 158 C5
Ridgeway The.
Boughton Street ME13 ...... 64 A3
Ridgeway The.
Broadstairs CT10 ...... 29 F3
Ridgeway The.
Chatham ME4 ...... 31 E7
Ridgeway The.
Gillingham ME7 ...... 10 C7
Ridgeway The.
Margate CT9 ...... 8 B1
Ridgeway The. River CT17 148 E2
Ridgeway The.
Smeeth TN25 ...... 158 B5
Ridgeway Wlk. CT6 ...... 46 A7
Ridgway. ME16 ...... 74 B2
Ridham Ave. ME10 ...... 15 A1
Riding Hill. TN24 ...... 139 C6
Ridings The. **7**
Canterbury CT1 ...... 67 B1
Ridings The. Margate CT9 .... 8 F3
Ridings The.
Whitstable CT5 ...... 21 D1
Ridlands. CT1 ...... 88 A5
Ridley Cl. CT6 ...... 46 A8
Ridley Rd. ME1 ...... 9 C4
Rigden Rd. TN23 ...... 156 B7
Rigshill Rd. ME13 ...... 103 B6
Riley Ave. CT6 ...... 21 F4
Ring Wall. CT14 ...... 94 E2
Ringlestone Cres. ME14 ...... 74 E8
Ringlestone Rd. ME14 ...... 78 D4
Ringold Ave. CT12 ...... 52 A8
Ringsloe Ct. CT7 ...... 26 D8
Ringwood Cl.
Canterbury CT2 ...... 66 E3
Ringwood Cl.
Gillingham ME8 ...... 33 D8
Ringwood Rd. ME15 ...... 97 C8
Ringwould Rd.
Ringwould CT4 & CT15 ... 133 D4
Ripley Rd. TN24 ...... 157 A8
Ripon Cl. ME8 ...... 11 D3
Ripper's Cross. TN26 ...... 137 D4
Ripple Cross. CT14 ...... 133 F6
Ripple
Cty Prim Sch. CT14 ...... 133 D8
Ripple Rd. CT14 ...... 133 F7
Ripplevale Sch. CT14 ...... 133 E8
Risborough La.
CT19 & CT20 ...... 177 D5
Risborough Way. CT20 ...... 177 C6
Risdon Cl. CT2 ...... 67 F6
Rise The. Minster ME12 ...... 3 A2
Rise The. Borden ME9 ...... 36 B2
Rise The. Gillingham ME7 .... 33 A3
Rise The.
Halfway Houses ME12 ...... 3 C5
Rise The. Kingsdown CT14 . 134 D5
Rise The. Rochester ME1 ...... 9 D3
Rise The. St Margaret's
at Cliffe CT15 ...... 151 B6
Rising Rd. TN23 ...... 139 A1
River Cl. ME15 ...... 96 A7
River Ct. Chartham CT4 ...... 86 D3
River Ct. River CT17 ...... 148 F2
River Cty Prim Sch. CT17 . 148 E3
River Dale. CT17 ...... 148 F3
River Dr. CT17 ...... 148 F2
River Meadow. CT17 ...... 148 F2
Rise St. **3** Gillingham ME4. 10 A6
River St. River CT17 ...... 148 E3
River Valley Golf Course.
ME8 & ME9 ...... 12 D2
River View. Gillingham ME8 . 11 D3

River View.
Maidstone ME15 ...... 74 F2
River View.
Rushenden ME11 ...... 2 F3
River View. Sturry CT2 ...... 67 F7
Riverdale Rd. CT1 ...... 67 B2
Riverhead Cl.
Maidstone ME16 ...... 74 D6
Riverhead Cl. Margate CT9 .... 8 B1
Riverhead Rd.
Sittingbourne ME10 ...... 36 C3
Rivers Rd. ME9 ...... 38 D2
Rivers Wlk. ME17 ...... 101 C5
Riversdale Rd.
Ashford TN23 ...... 156 C8
Riverside Rd.
Ramsgate CT12 ...... 29 B1
Riverside. CT4 ...... 86 C3
Riverside Bsns Pk. CT14 ... 139 D2
Riverside Cl. Bridge CT4 ...... 89 A1
Riverside Cl.
Kingsnorth TN23 ...... 156 A4
Riverside Cl. **1** CT2 ...... 66 F1
Riverside Ctry Pk. ME7 ...... 11 D5
Riverside Ind Est. CT21 ... 175 B5
Riverside Mews. CT4 ...... 89 A1
Riverside Rd. CT12 ...... 51 A1
Riverside Sch. TN23 ...... 138 F1
Riverview. TN23 ...... 138 E1
Riviera Cl. **6** CT20 ...... 177 E3
Riviera Rd. CT20 ...... 178 A3
Riviera The. CT20 ...... 177 F3
Roach St. ME2 ...... 9 A7
Road View. CT17 ...... 177 C3
Road of Remembrance.
CT20 ...... 178 D4
Robert Napier Sch The.
ME7 ...... 10 E3
Robert St. CT14 ...... 117 D7
Roberts Cl. ME10 ...... 36 D7
Roberts Rd. Gillingham ME8 33 E8
Roberts Rd.
Greatstone-on-S TN28 ... 200 E1
Roberts Rd. Whitstable CT5 . 42 F6
Robeshaw. ME9 ...... 58 E2
Robin Ho. **5** ME6 ...... 74 E4
Robin Hood La.
Chatham ME5 ...... 31 D1
Robin Hood La.
Lydd TN29 ...... 203 C5
Robin Hood Lane
(Lower). ME4 ...... 31 F2
Robin Hood Lane
(Upper). ME4 ...... 31 E1
Robin La. TN29 ...... 203 C6
Robin's Cl. CT21 ...... 187 C8
Robins Ave. ME17 ...... 101 C5
Robins Cl. ME17 ...... 101 C4
Robins Cl. ME14 ...... 75 C8
Robson's Yd. CT17 ...... 166 C8
Robus Cl. CT18 ...... 161 C7
Robus Terr. CT18 ...... 161 C7
Rochester Airport.
ME1 & ME5 ...... 31 C6
Rochester Ave.
Canterbury CT1 ...... 88 B7
Rochester Ave.
Rochester ME1 ...... 9 C4
Rochester Cath. ME1 ...... 9 C6
Rochester Cl. ME2 ...... 9 E8
Rochester Gram Sch
for Girls The. ME1 ...... 9 C2
Rochester Ho. **1** ME15 ... 97 D7
Rochester Rd.
Chatham ME5 ...... 31 C4
Rochester Rd.
Pratling Street ME20 ...... 53 B4
Rochester St. ME4 ...... 9 E3
Rochester Sta. ME1 ...... 9 D5
Rock Ave. ME7 ...... 10 C3
Rock Hill. TN27 ...... 118 E2
Rock Rd. Maidstone ME14 ... 75 A6
Rock Rd.
Sittingbourne ME10 ...... 36 E4
Rockingham Pl. CT6 ...... 23 B2
Rockstone Way. CT12 ...... 29 A1
Rocky Bourne Rd. TN25 ... 172 D5
Rocky Hill. ME16 ...... 74 E4
Rocky Hill Terr. **2** ME16 ... 74 E4
Rodmer Cl. ME12 ...... 4 C8
Rodmersham
Cty Prim Sch. ME9 ...... 59 B7
Rodmersham Gn. ME9 ...... 59 B7
Rodney St. CT11 ...... 52 D6
Roebuck Rd.
Faversham ME13 ...... 62 A7
Roebuck Rd. Rochester ME1 .. 9 C5
Roentgen Ho. ME10 ...... 36 D5
Roethorne Gdns. TN30 ... 179 B8
Roffen Rd. ME1 ...... 9 A2
Rogersmead. TN30 ...... 179 A7

Rokesley Rd. CT16 ...... 149 B5
Rolfe La. TN28 ...... 200 B7
Roll's Ave. ME12 ...... 5 C1
Rolvenden Ave. ME8 ...... 11 C3
Rolvenden Dr. ME10 ...... 36 B5
Roly Eckhoff Ho. CT16 ...... 149 B3
Roman Cl. Chatham ME5 ..... 31 D1
Roman Cl. Deal CT14 ...... 117 B6
Roman Hts. ME14 ...... 75 C6
Roman Rd.
East Studdal CT15 ...... 132 C5
Roman Rd.
Faversham ME13 ...... 62 C7
Roman Rd. Ramsgate CT12 . 29 C2
Roman Rd. Whitfield CT15 . 149 D8
Roman Sq. ME10 ...... 36 F3
Roman Way.
Elvington CT15 ...... 114 B2
Roman Way.
Folkestone CT19 ...... 177 C6
Roman Way.
Kingsnorth TN23 ...... 156 C4
Roman Way. St Margaret's
at Cliffe CT15 ...... 150 F5
Romany Ct. ME5 ...... 10 D1
Romany Rd. ME8 ...... 11 C2
Romden Rd. TN27 ...... 135 D1
Rome House Cnr. TN28 ... 200 A6
Rome Rd. TN28 ...... 200 A6
Romilly Gdns. CT9 ...... 29 C2
Romney Ave. CT20 ...... 177 F5
Romney Cl.
Birchington CT7 ...... 27 A7
Romney Cl.
Maidstone ME14 ...... 76 A3
Romney Cl. ME10 ...... 36 E5
Romney Marsh Rd. TN23 . 156 B6
Romney Pl. ME15 ...... 75 A4
Romney Rd. Ashford TN24 . 139 E1
Romney Rd. Chatham ME5 .. 32 B5
Romney Rd.
Hamstreet TN26 ...... 183 A7
Romney Rd.
New Romney TN29 ...... 199 E3
Romney Sands
Holiday Village. TN28 ... 204 E8
Romney Sands Sta. TN28 . 204 E8
Romney Warren
Golf Course. TN28 ...... 200 E7
Romney Way. CT21 ...... 175 F1
Ronalds Ct. ME10 ...... 37 A4
Rook La. ME9 ...... 35 F6
Rookery Cl. Ashford TN24 . 139 D7
Rookery Cl. Bredgar ME9 .... 58 A6
Rookstone Cnr. CT5 ...... 48 D1
Roonagh Ct. ME10 ...... 36 E2
Roosevelt Ave. ME5 ...... 32 A8
Rope Walk Mews. CT13 ...... 93 F8
Rope Wlk. ME4 ...... 9 F5
Ropemakers Ct. ME4 ...... 10 A1
Roper Cl. Canterbury CT2 .... 66 E1
Roper Cl. Gillingham ME8 .... 33 C3
Roper Rd. Canterbury CT2 .... 66 E1
Roper Rd. Teynham ME9 ..... 38 B7
Rose Acre Rd. CT3 ...... 89 F7
Rose Ave. CT5 ...... 43 C5
Rose Cotts.
Lenham Heath ME17 ...... 119 B8
Rose Ct. ME17 ...... 96 D1
Rose Gdns.
Birchington CT7 ...... 26 F6
Rose Gdns. Eythorne CT15 . 131 D7
Rose Gdns. Herne Bay C6 .. 23 C4
Rose Gdns. Minster,
Thanet CT12 ...... 50 B6
Rose Hill. **9**
Ramsgate CT11 ...... 52 E6
Rose Hill.
Wittersham TN30 ...... 189 B5
Rose La.
Bishopsbourne CT4 ...... 111 C6
Rose La. Canterbury CT1 .... 87 F8
Rose La.
Lenham Heath ME17 ...... 119 B8
Rose St. Rochester ME1 ...... 9 D3
Rose St. Sheerness ME12 .... 1 C2
Rose Street
Cty Prim Sch. ME12 ...... 1 C2
Rose Terr. ME13 ...... 62 D5
Roseacre Cl. CT2 ...... 66 E1
Roseacre Ct. CT9 ...... 8 E2
Roseacre Gdns. ME14 ...... 76 A4
Roseacre Jun Sch. ME14 .... 76 A4
Roseacre La. ME14 ...... 76 A4
Rosebery Ave.
Herne Bay CT6 ...... 23 E5
Rosebery Ave.
Ramsgate CT11 ...... 52 B7
Rosebery Cl. ME10 ...... 37 D4

Rosebery Rd. Chatham ME4 .. 9 E2
Rosebery Rd.
Gillingham ME7 ...... 10 D7
Rosedale Rd. CT9 ...... 8 A1
Roseholme. ME16 ...... 74 D2
Roselands. CT14 ...... 117 C1
Roselands Gdns. CT2 ...... 66 D2
Roselawn Gdns. **3** CT9 ...... 28 B8
Roselea Ave. CT2 ...... 22 F3
Roseleigh Ave. ME14 ...... 74 C5
Roseleigh Rd. ME10 ...... 36 D2
Rosemary Cl.
Broadstairs CT10 ...... 30 A3
Rosemary Ave.
Halfway Houses ME12 ...... 3 D6
Rosemary Cl. **8** ME5 ...... 31 F4
Rosemary Cnr. TN29 ...... 197 D8
Rosemary Gdns.
Broadstairs CT10 ...... 29 F2
Rosemary Gdns.
Whitstable CT5 ...... 44 A8
Rosemary La. **16** CT1 ...... 87 F8
Rosemary Rd. ME15 ...... 76 A3
Rosemount Cl. ME15 ...... 96 F4
Rosetower Ct. CT10 ...... 29 F8
Rosiers Ct. **1** CT2 ...... 66 E1
Ross Gdns. CT2 ...... 66 B3
Ross St. ME1 ...... 9 D4
Ross Way. CT20 ...... 177 E5
Rossendale Cl. **9** CT20 ... 178 E6
Rossendale Gdns. **7**
CT20 ...... 178 E6
Rossendale Rd. CT20 ...... 178 E6
Rossetti Rd. CT7 ...... 26 F8
Rossland Rd. CT12 ...... 52 A8
Rosslyn Gn. ME16 ...... 74 B5
Rothbrook Dr. TN24 ...... 139 C7
Rother Ho. **6** ME15 ...... 97 D8
Rother Vale. ME5 ...... 32 C3
Rothley Cl. TN30 ...... 179 B8
Rothsay Ct. CT11 ...... 29 F1
Rough Common Rd. CT2 .... 66 B3
Roundel Cl. ME9 ...... 38 D2
Roundel The. ME10 ...... 36 F2
Roundwell. ME14 ...... 76 D3
Rover Rd. ME5 ...... 32 B2
Row The. Ash CT3 ...... 71 E5
Row The. Elham CT4 ...... 144 F5
Rowan Cl. Ashford TN23 ... 138 E2
Rowan Cl. Staple CT3 ...... 92 A6
Rowan Cl. Sturry CT2 ...... 67 F6
Rowan Cl. CT10 ...... 30 A4
Rowan Ho. **4** Chatham ME5 31 F5
Rowan Lea. ME5 ...... 10 B1
Rowan Wlk. ME4 ...... 9 E3
Rowans The. ME12 ...... 4 B7
Rowbrook Cl. ME8 ...... 33 D3
Rowe Cl. CT9 ...... 28 F7
Rowena Rd. CT8 ...... 7 C1
Rowetts Way. ME12 ...... 5 D3
Rowland Ave. ME7 ...... 10 E8
Rowland Cl. ME5 ...... 10 E1
Rowland Cres. CT6 ...... 23 E5
Rowland Dr. CT6 ...... 22 C2
Roxburgh Rd. CT8 ...... 7 D1
Royal Ave. CT5 ...... 43 C5
Royal Cinque Ports
Golf Links. CT13 ...... 95 B4
Royal Cres. Margate CT9 .... 7 H2
Royal Cres. Ramsgate CT11 . 52 D5
Royal Eagle Cl. ME2 ...... 9 E7
Royal Engineers' Rd. ME14 . 74 F7
Royal Espl. Margate CT9 ...... 7 F1
Royal Espl. Ramsgate CT11 . 52 C5
Royal Military Ave. CT20 ... 177 D5
Royal Military Rd.
Aldington TN25 ...... 173 D1
Royal Military Rd.
Hythe CT21 ...... 175 D1
Royal Par. CT11 ...... 52 E6
Royal Rd. Ramsgate CT11 .. 52 D6
Royal Rd. Sheerness ME12 .. 1 D2
Royal Sch
for Deaf Children. CT9 .. 7 J2
Royal Sea Bathing Hospl.
CT9 ...... 7 G2
Royal Sovereign Ave. CT10 . 10 B7
Royal St George's
Golf Links. CT13 ...... 73 E2
Royal Star Arc. **5** ME14 .... 74 F4
Royal Victoria Hospl.
CT19 ...... 178 C6
Royal Victoria Pl. **8**
CT16 ...... 166 D8
Royds Rd. TN24 ...... 156 D6
Royston Gdns. CT15 ...... 150 F6
Royston Rd. ME15 ...... 76 A3
Roystons Cl. ME8 ...... 11 F2
Royton Ave. ME17 ...... 101 D5

Rubery Dro. CT3 ...... 72 C7
Ruckinge Cnr. TN25 ...... 183 F8
Ruckinge Rd. TN26 ...... 183 A7
Ruckinge Way. ME8 ...... 11 C3
Rudge Cl. ME5 ...... 32 D2
Rugby Cl. Broadstairs CT10 . 29 F5
Rugby Cl. Chatham ME5 ..... 31 F4
Rugby Gdns. TN23 ...... 156 C8
Rugby Rd. CT17 ...... 166 A6
Ruins Barn Rd.
ME10 & ME9 ...... 58 D6
Rule Ct. ME12 ...... 3 B8
Rumfields Rd. CT10 ...... 29 C5
Rumstead La. ME17 & ME 9 . 56 D4
Rumstead Rd. ME9 ...... 56 E4
Rumwood Ct. ME17 ...... 98 B5
Runcie Ho. **6** CT1 ...... 87 F7
Runcie Pl. CT2 ...... 66 D1
Runham La. ME17 ...... 100 E3
Running Horse
Rndbt The. ME20 ...... 53 E1
Rush Cl. Chatham ME5 ...... 32 A3
Rush Cl. Dymchurch TN29 . 195 B6
Rusham Rd. CT3 ...... 70 C1
Rushenden Cl. ME11 ...... 2 F3
Rushenden Rd. ME11 ...... 3 A4
Rushmead Cl. CT2 ...... 66 D2
Rushmead Dr. ME15 ...... 97 A7
Russell Dr. CT5 ...... 21 D3
Russell Cl. ME10 ...... 36 C3
Russell Cl. ME4 ...... 10 B3
Russell Pl. ME13 ...... 40 B3
Russell Rd. **1**
Folkestone CT19 ...... 178 D6
Russell Rd. Kit's Coty ME20 . 53 D7
Russell St. Dover CT16 ...... 166 E7
Russell St. Sheerness ME12 .. 1 C2
Russells Ave. ME8 ...... 34 A8
Russet Ave. ME13 ...... 62 E5
Russet Ct. ME17 ...... 96 C5
Russet Rd. CT1 ...... 88 C8
Russets The.
Maidstone ME16 ...... 74 B5
Russets The.
Whitstable CT5 ...... 21 D1
Ruth Ho. ME16 ...... 74 E5
Rutherford Coll. CT2 ...... 66 E4
Rutherford Rd. TN24 ...... 139 B5
Rutland Ave. CT9 ...... 8 C2
Rutland Cl. CT1 ...... 88 D7
Rutland Gdns.
Birchington CT7 ...... 26 F7
Rutland Gdns. Margate CT9 .. 8 C2
Rutland Ho. **3** ME8 ...... 8 B2
Rutland Pl. ME8 ...... 33 C3
Rutland Rd. CT16 ...... 149 B3
Rutland Way. ME15 ...... 97 E8
Ryan Dr. ME15 ...... 76 A2
Rycaut Cl. ME8 ...... 33 D3
Rydal Ave. CT11 ...... 52 B7
Ryde Cl. ME5 ...... 32 B8
Ryde St. CT2 ...... 66 E1
Ryder's Ave. CT8 ...... 27 D8
Rye Ct. TN23 ...... 155 D7
Rye Wlk. CT6 ...... 23 C2
Ryecourt Cl. **4** ME16 ...... 74 E3
Ryeglass Cl. ME8 ...... 32 C6
Ryegrass Cl. ME8 ...... 32 C6
Ryland Ct. **4** CT20 ...... 178 E5
Ryland Pl. **5** CT20 ...... 178 E5
Rylands Rd. TN24 ...... 139 D5
Rype Cl. TN29 ...... 203 C5
Ryswick Mews. TN28 ...... 200 C8

Sabre Ct. ME7 ...... 11 A1
Sackett's Gap. CT9 ...... 8 C3
Sacketts Hill. CT10 ...... 29 C6
Sackville Cl. TN26 ...... 138 A7
Sackville Cres. TN23 ...... 139 A2
Saddler's Wall La. TN29 .. 191 B1
Saddlers Cl. ME14 ...... 75 E5
Saddlers Hill. CT3 ...... 91 D2
Saddlers Mews. CT5 ...... 21 D1
Saddlers Way. TN23 ...... 156 B5
Saddleton Gr. CT5 ...... 43 B8
Saddleton Rd. CT5 ...... 43 B8
Sadlers Cl. ME5 ...... 31 D2
Saffron Way. **1**
Chatham ME5 ...... 31 F5
Saffron Way.
Sittingbourne ME10 ...... 36 F7
Saffron's Pl. **12** CT20 ...... 178 E5
Sailfield Ct. ME14 ...... 9 F7
Sainsbury La. ME14 ...... 10 E2
St Agnes Gdns. ME12 ...... 1 D1
St Alban's Rd. CT3 ...... 46 E1
St Albans Cl. ME7 ...... 10 E7

St Alphege CE Inf Sch.
CT5 .... 20 D1
St Alphege Cl. CT5 .... 43 B7
St Alphege La. **6** CT1 .... 66 F1
St Alphege Rd. **4** CT16 ...... 149 C1
St Ambrose Gn. TN25 .... 123 E2
St Andrew Rd. ME7 .... 10 D7
St Andrew Terr. CT17 .... 149 A2
St Andrew's Cl.
  Maidstone ME16 .... 74 A2
St Andrew's Cl.
  Whitstable CT5 .... 43 E7
St Andrew's Gdns. CT15 ...... 130 E5
St Andrew's Lees. CT13 .... 94 A8
St Andrew's Rd.
  Deal CT14 .... 117 C6
St Andrew's Rd.
  Littlebourne-on-S TN28 ...... 200 E6
St Andrew's Rd.
  Maidstone ME16 .... 74 A3
St Andrew's Rd.
  Ramsgate CT11 .... 52 F8
St Andrews. CT19 .... 178 E5
St Andrews Cl.
  Canterbury CT1 .... 87 E7
St Andrews Cl.
  Herne Bay CT6 .... 23 A4
St Andrews Cl.
  Margate CT9 .... 28 F7
St Andrews Gdns. CT17 .... 149 B2
St Andrews Way. CT14 .... 115 A3
St Ann's Rd.
  Dymchurch TN29 .... 195 B7
St Ann's Rd.
  Faversham ME13 .... 62 B7
St Anne Cl. ME16 .... 74 A4
St Anne's Ct. **1**
  Dover CT16 .... 149 B2
St Anne's Ct.
  Herne Bay CT6 .... 22 E5
St Anne's Dr. CT6 .... 22 D4
St Anne's Gdns. CT9 .... 28 F8
St Anne's Rd.
  Ashford TN23 .... 155 F7
St Anne's Rd.
  Whitstable CT5 .... 20 F7
St Anselm's
  Cath Comp Sch. CT1 .... 88 C5
St Anthony's Sch. CT9 .... 8 C1
St Anthony's Way. CT9 .... 8 C1
St Augustine of Canterbury
  RC Prim Sch. ME8 .... 33 D3
St Augustine's Abbey.
  CT11 .... 52 D5
St Augustine's Ave. CT9 .... 28 F8
St Augustine's Coll. CT1 .... 88 A8
St Augustine's Cres. CT5 ...... 21 D3
St Augustine's Ct. CT1 .... 88 B8
St Augustine's
  Golf Course. CT12 .... 51 C4
St Augustine's Pk. CT11 .... 52 C6
St Augustine's
  RC Prim Sch. CT21 .... 176 E2
St Augustine's Rd.
  Canterbury CT1 .... 88 B7
St Augustine's Rd.
  Deal CT14 .... 116 F4
St Augustine's Rd.
  Ramsgate CT11 .... 52 D5
St Barnabas Cl.
  Ashford TN23 .... 155 F7
St Barnabas Cl.
  Gillingham ME7 .... 10 D3
St Barnabas Cl.
  Maidstone ME16 .... 74 C8
St Bart's Rd. CT13 .... 93 F8
St Bartholomew's Hospl.
  ME1 .... 9 E4
St Bartholomew's La. ME1 ..... 9 E4
St Bartholomew's Sch.
  ME10 .... 36 F7
St Bartholomew's Terr. ME1 .. 9 E4
St Benedict's Lawn. CT11 ..... 52 D5
St Benedicts
  RC Prim Sch. ME5 .... 32 C2
St Benet's Rd. CT8 .... 27 E7
St Benets Ct. TN30 .... 179 B8
St Benets Way. TN30 .... 179 B8
St Catherine's Dr. ME13 .... 62 D6
St Catherine's Gr. CT12 .... 28 D1
St Catherine's Hospl. ME1 .... 9 E4
St Catherines. CT9 .... 199 A7
St Catherines Ct. CT11 .... 29 F1
St Christopher Ct. CT9 .... 29 D8
St Christopher's Sch. CT1 ..... 88 B6
St Christophers Gn. CT10 ..... 29 F5
St Clare Rd. CT14 .... 117 C1
St Clement's Ct. CT6 .... 23 A3

St Clement's Ho. ME1 .... 9 D5
St Clement's Rd. CT8 .... 7 C1
St Clements. **8** CT13 .... 73 A1
St Clements Cl. ME1 .... 6 D2
St Clements Cl. CT10 .... 29 E6
St Clements Rd. ME12 .... 6 E2
St Cosmus Cl. TN25 .... 105 B1
St Crispin's
  Cty Inf Sch. CT8 .... 27 E7
St Crispin's Rd. CT8 .... 27 E7
St David's Cl.
  Birchington CT7 .... 27 B8
St David's Cl.
  Whitstable CT5 .... 43 E8
St David's Rd. Deal CT14 ..... 117 C6
St David's Rd.
  Ramsgate CT11 .... 29 F1
St Davids Ave. CT17 .... 166 A5
St Denys Rd. CT18 .... 163 B5
St Dunstan's Cl. CT2 .... 66 E1
St Dunstan's Rd. CT9 .... 8 A2
St Dunstan's St. CT2 .... 66 E1
St Dunstan's Terr. CT2 .... 66 E1
St Eanswythe Way. **15**
  CT20 .... 178 D5
St Eanswythe's
  CE Prim Sch. CT20 .... 178 D4
St Edmund's RC Sch.
  CT16 .... 149 D2
St Edmund's Rd. CT14 .... 116 E4
St Edmund's Sch. CT2 .... 66 C3
St Edmunds Rd. CT1 .... 87 F8
St Edmunds Way. ME8 .... 12 B1
St Edward's
  RC Prim Sch. ME12 .... 1 C2
St Ethelbert's
  RC Prim Sch. CT11 .... 52 F8
St Faith's La. ME14 .... 76 B4
St Faith's St. ME14 .... 74 F4
St Faiths Sch. CT3 .... 71 C1
St Francis Cl. Deal CT14 ..... 116 F4
St Francis Cl.
  Margate CT9 .... 29 D8
St Francis
  RC Prim Sch. ME14 .... 75 B7
St Francis Rd. CT19 .... 177 F6
St Francis Rd. ME14 .... 75 B7
St Gabriel's. **11** CT20 .... 178 E6
St George's Ave.
  Herne Bay CT6 .... 22 D4
St George's Ave.
  Sheerness ME12 .... 1 C1
St George's Bsns Ctr.
  TN23 .... 138 F2
St George's
  CE High Sch. CT10 .... 29 C5
St George's
  CE Mid Sch. ME12 .... 1 B1
St George's Cl. CT5 .... 43 E7
St George's Cl. ME12 .... 3 B8
St George's Lees. CT13 .... 94 A8
St George's Pass. CT14 ..... 117 D6
St George's Pl.
  Canterbury CT1 .... 88 A8
St George's Pl.
  Hythe CT21 .... 187 D8
St George's Rd.
  Broadstairs CT10 .... 30 A4
St George's Rd.
  Deal CT14 .... 117 D6
St George's Rd.
  Folkestone CT19 .... 177 F6
St George's Rd.
  Gillingham ME7 .... 10 C6
St George's Rd.
  Ramsgate CT11 .... 52 F8
St George's Rd.
  Sandwich CT3 .... 94 A8
St George's Sq. **3**
  Ashford TN23 .... 139 B2
St George's Sq.
  Maidstone ME16 .... 74 E3
St George's St. CT1 .... 88 A8
St George's Terr. CT6 .... 22 E5
St Georges Ave. ME12 .... 5 D2
St Georges Ct. CT17 .... 149 A2
St Georges La. CT1 .... 88 A8
St Georges Pl. CT15 .... 150 F6
St Georges St. CT1 .... 88 A8
St Giles Cl. CT17 .... 166 B5
St Giles Rd. CT17 .... 166 B5
St Giles Wlk. CT17 .... 166 B5
St Gregory's. **9** CT1 .... 67 A1
St Gregory's Cl. CT14 .... 116 F4
St Gregory's
  RC Prim Sch. CT9 .... 28 E8
St Gregory's Rd. CT1 .... 67 B1
St Helen's Rd. ME12 .... 1 E1
St Helier's Cl. ME16 .... 74 B2
St Hilda Rd. CT19 .... 177 E6

St Hilda's Rd. CT21 .... 176 B1
St Jacob's Pl. CT1 .... 87 D6
St James' Ave.
  Broadstairs CT10 .... 29 E5
St James' Ave.
  Ramsgate CT12 .... 29 A1
St James' Cl. ME12 .... 6 E4
St James' Gdns. CT5 .... 43 D8
St James La. **5** CT16 .... 166 E7
St James' Park Rd. CT9 .... 28 A8
St James Rd. CT14 .... 134 D5
St James St. CT16 .... 166 E7
St James's Terr. CT7 .... 27 B8
St Jean's Rd. CT8 .... 27 E7
St John Fisher
  Cath Comp Sch. ME4 .... 9 F2
St John Fisher Cath Sch
  (Lower Sch). ME4 .... 9 F2
St John's Ave.
  Ramsgate CT12 .... 29 A1
St John's Ave.
  Sittingbourne ME10 .... 37 B3
St John's CE Sch. ME4 .... 9 F2
St John's CE (VA)
  Prim Sch. ME14 .... 75 E4
St John's Church Rd.CT19 .. 178 C6
St John's Cl. CT18 .... 163 A7
St John's Commandery
  (rems of). CT15 .... 146 E4
St John's Ct. TN24 .... 157 A6
St John's Ct. TN24 .... 157 A6
St John's Hospl. **6** CT1 ..... 67 A1
St John's La.
  Ashford TN23 .... 139 C2
St John's La.
  Canterbury CT1 .... 87 F8
St John's Pl. CT1 .... 67 A1
St John's Rd. Dover CT17 ... 166 C7
St John's Rd.
  Faversham ME13 .... 62 D7
St John's Rd.
  Gillingham ME7 .... 10 C3
St John's Rd. Margate CT9 .... 7 J2
St John's Rd.
  New Romney TN28 .... 200 A6
St John's Rd.
  Whitstable CT5 .... 21 D3
St John's St.
  Folkestone CT20 .... 178 D5
St John's St. **7**
  Margate CT9 .... 7 J2
St John's Way. CT18 .... 163 A7
St Johns Cres. CT2 .... 66 D6
St Johns Rd.
  Elvington CT15 .... 114 B2
St Johns Rd. Hythe CT21 ... 176 A3
St Johns Way. ME1 .... 9 A2
St Joseph's
  RC Prim Sch. CT3 .... 113 A5
St Julien Ave. CT1 .... 67 D1
St Katherine Rd. ME12 .... 3 E7
St Laurence Ave. ME16 .... 74 C8
St Laurence
  CE Jun Sch. CT12 .... 52 B8
St Laurence Cl. ME9 .... 35 C7
St Laurence Cl. CT11 .... 52 C7
St Laurence Ct. CT11 .... 52 B5
St Laurence Cl. CT11 .... 88 B6
St Laurence Coll. CT11 .... 52 D8
St Laurence Coll
  (Jun Sch). CT11 .... 52 E8
St Laurence Ind Est. CT11 .. 52 B7
St Laurence Rd. CT11 .... 88 B6
St Leonard's
  CE Jun Sch. CT21 .... 176 B2
St Leonard's Rd. CT14 .... 117 B4
St Leonards Ave. ME4 .... 9 F2
St Leonards Cl. CT21 .... 176 B1
St Leonards Rd.
  Hythe CT21 .... 176 B1
St Leonards Rd.
  Maidstone ME16 .... 74 C8
St Louis Gr. CT6 .... 22 C4
St Luke's Ave.
  Maidstone ME14 .... 75 B5
St Luke's Ave.
  Ramsgate CT11 .... 52 B8
St Luke's Cl. CT8 .... 27 E8
St Luke's Rd.
  Maidstone ME14 .... 75 B5
St Luke's Rd.
  Ramsgate CT11 .... 52 E8
St Lukes Cl. CT5 .... 43 E7
St Lukes Ct. TN23 .... 155 F7
St Magnus Cl. CT7 .... 27 A8
St Margaret's at Cliffe
  Cty Prim Sch. CT15 .... 151 A6

St Margaret's at Troy Town
  CE Prim Sch. ME1 .... 9 C4
St Margaret's Banks. ME1 .... 9 D5
St Margaret's
  CE Inf Sch. ME8 .... 33 E8
St Margaret's CE Jun Sch.
  ME8 .... 33 E8
St Margaret's Cl. CT5 .... 43 A6
St Margaret's Mews. ME1 ..... 9 C5
St Margaret's Rd. St Margaret's
  at Cliffe CT15 .... 151 A5
St Margaret's Rd.
  Westgate-on-S CT8 .... 27 E7
St Margaret's St.
  Canterbury CT1 .... 87 F8
St Margaret's St.
  Rochester ME1 .... 9 C5
St Margarets Cl. ME16 .... 74 F3
St Margarets Cl. **1**
  CT20 .... 178 B5
St Margarets Dr.
  Deal CT14 .... 134 B8
St Margarets Dr.
  Gillingham ME8 .... 33 C5
St Margarets Rd. CT7 .... 27 F3
St Mark's Cl. CT20 .... 177 D5
St Marks Cl. CT5 .... 43 E8
St Marks Ho. ME7 .... 10 C5
St Martin's
  CE Prim Sch. CT18 .... 177 B5
St Martin's Cl.
  Detling ME14 .... 55 A1
St Martin's Cl.
  Dover CT17 .... 166 B5
St Martin's
  Cty Prim Sch. CT17 .... 166 A7
St Martin's Hill. CT1 .... 88 C8
St Martin's Hospl. CT1 .... 88 D8
St Martin's Pl. CT1 .... 88 B8
St Martin's Rd.
  Canterbury CT1 .... 67 B1
St Martin's Rd. Deal CT14 .. 116 F4
St Martin's Terr. CT1 .... 88 B8
St Martin's View. CT6 .... 46 A8
St Martins Ave. CT1 .... 88 B8
St Martins Cl.
  Canterbury CT1 .... 88 B8
St Martins Cl.
  Newington ME9 .... 35 C7
St Martins Rd.
  Folkestone CT20 .... 177 D6
St Martins Rd.
  New Romney TN28 .... 200 B6
St Mary Cl. **3** ME13 .... 62 D7
St Mary of Charity
  CE Inf Sch. ME13 .... 62 D7
St Mary of Charity
  CE Jun Sch. ME13 .... 62 D7
St Mary's Ave. CT9 .... 8 D1
St Mary's CE Prim Sch.
  Ashford TN23 .... 139 A3
St Mary's CE Prim Sch.
  Chilham CT4 .... 107 B8
St Mary's CE Prim Sch.
  Dover CT16 .... 166 E8
St Mary's CE Prim Sch.
  Folkestone CT19 .... 178 F6
St Mary's Church. CT6 .... 24 D7
St Mary's Cl. Eastry CT13 ... 93 C2
St Mary's Cl.
  Hamstreet TN26 .... 183 A8
St Mary's Cl.
  Nonington CT15 .... 113 C5
St Mary's Cl.
  Woodnesborough CT13 .... 93 B6
St Mary's Coll.
  Folkestone CT20 .... 178 A5
St Mary's Coll.
  Herne Bay CT6 .... 22 E4
St Mary's Cl. **17** CT1 .... 87 F8
St Mary's
  Cty Prim Sch. ME2 .... 9 B7
St Mary's Gdns.
  Gillingham ME7 .... 10 D6
St Mary's Gdns.
  St Mary's Bay TN29 .... 195 A5
St Mary's Gdns.
  Upstreet CT3 .... 47 E3
St Mary's Gr.
  Tilmanstone CT13 .... 115 A4
St Mary's Gr.
  Whitstable CT5 .... 42 F7
St Mary's Hospl. CT18 .... 161 D3
St Mary's Meadow. CT3 .... 91 A8
St Mary's Pl. ME9 .... 35 C7
St Mary's RC Prim Sch.
  Deal CT14 .... 116 F3
St Mary's RC Prim Sch.
  Gillingham ME7 .... 10 D6

St Mary's RC Prim Sch.
  Whitstable CT5 .... 20 F2
St Mary's Rd. **5**
  Broadstairs CT10 .... 30 B4
St Mary's Rd. Deal CT14 .... 117 C1
St Mary's Rd. Elham CT4 .... 144 F4
St Mary's Rd.
  Faversham ME13 .... 62 D7
St Mary's Rd.
  Gillingham ME7 .... 10 C6
St Mary's Rd. Minster,
  Thanet CT12 .... 50 B6
St Mary's Rd.
  Patrixbourne CT4 .... 89 B3
St Mary's Rd. Rochester ME2 .. 9 B7
St Mary's Rd.
  St Mary in the Marsh
  TN28 & TN29 .... 194 C5
St Mary's Rd.
  West Hythe CT21 .... 175 B1
St Mary's Row. ME12 .... 4 A6
St Mary's St. CT1 .... 87 F8
St Mary's Terr. **2** CT20 ... 178 E5
St Mary's View. ME9 .... 35 C7
St Marys Gn. TN24 .... 139 F7
St Marys Mews. TN24 .... 156 F8
St Matthew's
  CE (VC) Inf Sch. ME1 .... 9 A2
St Matthew's Cl. ME9 .... 35 C7
St Michael's Alley. **11** CT11 .. 52 E6
St Michael's CE Inf Sch.
  ME16 .... 74 E3
St Michael's CE Jun Sch.
  ME16 .... 74 E3
St Michael's CE Prim Sch.
  TN30 .... 167 A3
St Michael's Cl.
  Chatham ME4 .... 9 F3
St Michael's Cl. **5**
  Sittingbourne ME10 .... 36 F4
St Michael's Ct. **6**
  Folkestone CT20 .... 178 E5
St Michael's Ct.
  Rochester ME2 .... 9 B8
St Michael's Pl. CT2 .... 66 E2
St Michael's RC Prim Sch.
  ME4 .... 9 F3
St Michael's Rd.
  Canterbury CT2 .... 66 E2
St Michael's Rd.
  Maidstone ME16 .... 74 D3
St Michael's Rd.
  Sittingbourne ME10 .... 36 E4
St Michael's Rd.
  Sittingbourne ME10 .... 37 A4
St Michael's Terr. TN30 ...... 167 B3
St Michael's Wlk. CT18 ...... 162 F4
St Michaels Ave. CT9 .... 29 D8
St Michaels Cl.
  Canterbury CT2 .... 66 A1
St Michaels Cl. Pratling Street
  ME14 & ME20 .... 53 C3
St Mildred's Ave.
  Birchington CT7 .... 26 E8
St Mildred's Ave.
  Broadstairs CT10 .... 30 A4
St Mildred's Ave.
  Ramsgate CT11 .... 52 B5
St Mildred's Cl. **2** TN30 ... 179 A7
St Mildred's Cty Inf Sch.
  CT10 .... 30 A4
St Mildred's Gdns.
  CT8 & CT9 .... 7 D1
St Mildred's Rd.
  Margate CT9 .... 8 A2
St Mildred's Rd.
  Minster, Thanet CT12 .... 50 B5
St Mildred's Rd.
  Ramsgate CT11 .... 52 C6
St Mildred's Rd.
  Westgate-on-S CT8 .... 7 C1
St Mildreds Ct.
  Canterbury CT1 .... 87 E8
St Mildreds Ct. Deal CT14 .. 117 C1
St Mildreds Pl. CT1 .... 87 E8
St Monicas CT17 .... 166 C7
St Monicas Rd. CT14 .... 134 D6
St Nicholas at Wade
  CE Prim Sch. CT7 .... 25 E2
St Nicholas
  CE Inf Sch. ME2 .... 9 A7
St Nicholas Cl. Deal CT14 .. 116 F4
St Nicholas Cl. Sturry CT2 ... 67 F7
St Nicholas Cnr. CT7 .... 25 F1
St Nicholas Hospl. CT2 .... 66 C1
St Nicholas Rd.
  Canterbury CT1 .... 87 D6
St Nicholas Rd.
  Faversham ME13 .... 62 A7

St Nicholas Rd.
Hythe CT21 .... 176 A2
St Nicholas Rd.
Littlebourne-on-S TN28 .... 200 E6
St Nicholas Rdbt. CT7 .... 26 B2
St Nicholas Sch. CT1 .... 87 F6
St Nicholas & St John's
CE Prim Sch. CT14 .... 134 C5
St Nicholas Terr. **1** CT21 .. 176 B2
St Patrick's Cl.
Whitstable CT5 .... 43 E7
St Patrick's Rd. Deal CT14 ... 117 C6
St Patrick's Rd.
Ramsgate CT11 .... 52 F8
St Patricks Rd. CT17 .... 166 A4
St Paul's Ave. ME13 .... 62 A7
St Paul's Ct. CT20 .... 177 E4
St Paul's Rd. CT9 .... 8 A3
St Paul's Rd. **1** ME10 .... 36 E5
St Paul's Way. CT20 .... 177 F4
St Pauls Cres. ME13 .... 64 A3
St Pauls
Cty Inf Sch. ME14 .... 75 A7
St Pauls Rd. ME13 .... 64 A3
St Pauls Terr. CT1 .... 88 A8
St Peter St. ME1 .... 9 D4
St Peter's Bridge. ME16 ...... 74 F4
St Peter's CE Prim Sch.
Aylesford ME20 .... 53 A3
St Peter's CE Prim Sch.
Folkestone CT19 .... 178 E5
St Peter's Cl. ME12 .... 3 D6
St Peter's Ct.
Broadstairs CT10 .... 29 F5
St Peter's Ct.
Faversham ME13 .... 62 A7
St Peter's Cty Inf Sch. ME1 .. 9 C3
St Peter's Footpath.
Margate CT9 .... 7 J1
St Peter's Footpath.
Margate CT9 .... 29 A8
St Peter's Gr. CT1 .... 87 F8
St Peter's La. CT1 & CT2 ...... 66 F1
St Peter's Meth Prim Sch.
CT1 .... 87 F8
St Peter's Park Rd. CT10 ..... 29 F5
St Peter's Path. ME1 .... 9 D5
St Peter's Pl. CT1 & CT2 ..... 87 F8
St Peter's RC Prim Sch.
Sittingbourne ME10 .... 36 D2
St Peter's RC Prim Sch.
Sittingbourne ME10 .... 36 E4
St Peter's Rd.
Boughton Street ME13 .... 64 A3
St Peter's Rd.
Broadstairs CT10 .... 29 F5
St Peter's Rd. Margate CT9 .. 29 A7
St Peter's Rd.
Whitstable CT5 .... 20 D2
St Peter's St.
Canterbury CT1 & CT2 .... 87 F8
St Peter's St.
Sandwich CT13 .... 73 A1
St Peter's Way. TN26 .... 170 A8
St Peter's-in-Thanet
CE Jun Sch. CT10 .... 29 E5
St Peters Pl. ME9 .... 60 A6
St Peters St. ME16 .... 74 F4
St Philip Howard
RC Prim Sch. CT6 .... 22 F5
St Philip's Ave. ME15 .... 75 B2
St Philip's CE Prim Sch.
ME15 .... 75 A3
St Radigund's
Cty Prim Sch. CT17 .... 149 A1
St Radigund's Pl. CT1 .... 67 A1
St Radigund's Rd. CT17 ...... 149 A1
St Radigunds St. **2** CT1 .... 67 A1
St Richard's RC Prim Sch.
CT16 .... 149 D1
St Richard's Rd. CT14 .... 116 F3
St Richard's Wlk. CT17 ...... 166 A4
St Ronan's Cl. ME15 .... 97 C7
St Saviour's Cl. ME13 .... 62 E7
St Saviour's Hospl. CT21 .... 176 F2
St Saviours CE Jun Sch.
CT8 .... 27 E8
St Saviours Cl. CT19 .... 178 D7
St. Saviours Rd. ME15 .... 97 D6
St Simon of England
RC Prim Sch. TN23 .... 156 A8
St Simon Stock RC Sch.
ME16 .... 74 C4
St Stephen's CE Inf Sch.
ME15 .... 74 E2
St Stephen's Cl.
Canterbury CT2 .... 66 F2
St Stephen's Cl.
Newington ME9 .... 35 C7
St Stephen's Ct. CT2 .... 66 F2

St Stephen's Cty Inf Sch.
CT2 .... 66 F3
St Stephen's Cty Jun Sch.
CT1 .... 66 F3
St Stephen's Fields. CT2 ..... 66 F1
St Stephen's Gn. CT2 .... 66 F3
St Stephen's Hill. CT2 .... 66 E4
St Stephen's Lodge. CT2 ..... 66 F2
St Stephen's Rd. CT2 .... 66 F2
St Stephen's Sq. ME15 .... 74 E2
St Stephen's Way. CT20 .... 177 F4
St Stephen's Wlk. TN23 ..... 155 F7
St Swithin's Rd. CT5 .... 21 B3
St Teresa's RC Prim Sch.
TN24 .... 139 B4
St Theresa's Cl. TN24 .... 139 B3
St Thomas' Cross. TN26 ..... 170 E3
St Thomas Hill. CT2 .... 66 D3
St Thomas More
RC Prim Sch. ME5 .... 32 A5
St Thomas of Canterbury
Cath Prim Sch. ME1 .... 11 B2
St Thomas' RC Prim Sch.
CT1 .... 67 A1
St Thomas's Hospl. CT13 .... 93 D7
St Thomas's Sch. ME10 ...... 36 E7
St Vincent Rd. CT15 .... 150 F7
St Vincent's Cl.
Littlebourne CT3 .... 68 F1
St Vincent's Cl.
Whitstable CT5 .... 43 E7
St Welcume's Way.
ME17 .... 100 E6
St William of Perth
RC Prim Sch. ME1 .... 9 B2
St William's Way. ME1 .... 9 D2
St Williams Hospl. ME1 .... 9 D2
St Winifred Rd. CT19 .... 177 F6
Salem St. ME15 .... 75 A3
Salisbury Ave.
Broadstairs CT10 .... 29 F2
Salisbury Ave.
Gillingham ME8 .... 33 D8
Salisbury Ave.
Ramsgate CT11 .... 52 F8
Salisbury Cl. ME10 .... 37 C4
Salisbury Ho. **5** ME15 .... 97 D7
Salisbury Rd.
Chatham ME4 .... 10 A3
Salisbury Rd. Deal CT14 ..... 117 B2
Salisbury Rd. Dover CT16 . 149 D1
Salisbury Rd.
Folkestone CT19 .... 177 E7
Salisbury Rd.
Herne Bay CT6 .... 23 C5
Salisbury Rd.
Kit's Coty ME20 .... 53 D7
Salisbury Rd.
Maidstone ME14 .... 75 A6
Salisbury Rd. St Margaret's
at Cliffe CT15 .... 151 B6
Salisbury Rd.
Whitstable CT5 .... 43 D8
Sally Port. ME7 .... 10 A6
Sally Port Gdns. ME7 .... 10 B6
Salmestone
Cty Prim Sch. CT9 .... 28 E8
Salmestone Grange. CT9 .... 28 E8
Salmestone Rd. CT9 .... 28 F8
Salmestone Rise. CT9 .... 28 E8
Salmon Cres. ME12 .... 3 F6
Salt Marsh La. **15** CT15 ..... 20 D2
Salt's Ave. ME15 .... 96 F3
Salt's Dr. CT10 .... 29 F5
Salter's La. TN29 .... 199 C8
Salters La. ME13 .... 62 D4
Salthouse Cl. TN29 .... 197 D8
Saltings The.
Littlebourne-on-S TN28 ..... 200 E5
Saltings The. **10**
Whitstable CT5 .... 20 D2
Salts Cl. CT5 .... 20 D1
Salts La. ME15 .... 97 A4
Saltwood CE Prim Sch.
CT21 .... 176 B4
Saltwood Gdns. CT9 .... 8 E2
Saltwood Rd. ME15 .... 74 F1
Samara Cl. ME5 .... 32 A1
Samian Cres. CT19 .... 177 C6
Samphire Cl. ME14 .... 75 E4
Sancroft Ave. CT2 .... 66 C1
Sanctuary Cl. CT10 .... 29 F2
Sanctuary Rd. ME8 .... 11 A3
Sand Ct. ME12 .... 6 G2
Sandbanks Rd. ME13 .... 41 C2
Sandbourne Dr. ME14 .... 53 F1
Sanders Cl. ME12 .... 4 A5
Sandford Rd. ME10 .... 36 B5
Sandgate Cl. ME8 .... 33 F4

Sandgate Cty Prim Sch.
CT20 .... 177 F4
Sandgate Espl.
CT20 & CT21 .... 177 D2
Sandgate High St. CT20 .... 177 E3
Sandgate Hill. CT20 .... 178 A4
Sandgate Rd.
Folkestone CT20 .... 178 C4
Sandgate Rd.
Folkestone CT20 .... 178 D4
Sandhurst Cl.
Canterbury CT2 .... 67 A4
Sandhurst Cl.
Gillingham ME8 .... 11 C3
Sandhurst Rd. CT9 .... 8 F2
Sandilands. TN24 .... 139 E2
Sandle's Rd. CT7 .... 26 F7
Sandlewood Dr. CT7 .... 25 F1
Sandling Cl. TN23 .... 155 F6
Sandling Cty Prim Sch.
ME14 .... 75 B8
Sandling La. ME14 .... 75 A8
Sandling Rd.
Hythe CT21 .... 175 F6
Sandling Rd.
Maidstone ME14 .... 74 F6
Sandling Rd. Maidstone,
Ringlestone ME14 .... 74 F7
Sandling Sta. CT21 .... 175 F6
Sandown Cl. CT14 .... 95 D1
Sandown Cotts.
Margate CT9 .... 8 A3
Sandown Cotts.
Teynham ME9 .... 38 E1
Sandown Cty Prim Sch.
CT14 .... 117 C7
Sandown Dr.
Gillingham ME8 .... 33 D7
Sandown Dr.
Herne Bay CT6 .... 22 D4
Sandown Lees. CT13 .... 94 D8
Sandown Rd. Deal CT14 .... 117 D8
Sandown Rd.
Sandwich CT13 .... 94 B8
Sandpiper Ct. **3**
Birchington CT7 .... 26 E8
Sandpiper Rd.
Chatham ME5 .... 32 D2
Sandpiper Rd.
Whitstable CT5 .... 43 B7
Sandpit Hill. CT3 .... 47 C4
Sandringham Ho. ME1 .... 9 B4
Sandringham Rd. ME8 .... 33 E3
Sandstone Cl. CT20 .... 78 A3
Sandstone Rise. ME14 .... 54 C8
Sandway Rd. ME17 .... 100 F4
Sandwich Bay Bird Obsy.
CT13 .... 94 E7
Sandwich Cl. CT20 .... 177 F5
Sandwich Cty Inf Sch.
CT13 .... 72 F1
Sandwich Cty Jun Sch.
CT13 .... 93 F7
Sandwich Hill. CT3 .... 70 B1
Sandwich Ind Est. CT13 ..... 73 B1
Sandwich Rd. Ash CT3 .... 71 F1
Sandwich Rd. Ash CT3 .... 72 A2
Sandwich Rd.
Cliffs End CT12 .... 51 D4
Sandwich Rd. Eastry CT13 .. 93 C3
Sandwich Rd.
Eythorne CT15 .... 131 C8
Sandwich Rd.
Nonington CT15 & CT3 .... 113 F6
Sandwich Rd.
Sandwich CT13 .... 93 D7
Sandwich Rd.
Tilmanstone CT14 & CT15 115 B2
Sandwich Rd.
Whitfield CT15 .... 132 A2
Sandwich Rd.
Whitfield CT16 .... 149 A7
Sandwich Rd.
Woodnesborough CT13 ..... 93 D5
Sandwich Sta. CT13 .... 94 A8
Sandwich Tech Sch. CT13 .. 93 F6
Sandwood Rd.
Ramsgate CT10 .... 29 F1
Sandwood Rd.
Sandwich CT13 .... 93 F8
Sandy Cnr. TN26 .... 154 F5
Sandy Dell. ME7 .... 33 A3
Sandy La. Ashford TN24 ... 140 B1
Sandy La.
Daniel's Water TN26 .... 154 E6
Sandy La.
Hythe CT21 .... 177 B3
Sandy La. Maidstone,
Harbourland ME14 .... 75 C8

Sandy La. Maidstone,
Penenden Heath ME14 .... 75 C7
Sandy La. Maidstone,
Ware Street ME14 .... 76 B5
Sandy La. Tenterden TN30 . 179 B7
Sandy Mount. ME14 .... 76 B5
Sandy Pl. TN25 .... 158 D5
Sandyhurst La.
TN24 & TN25 & TN23 .... 139 B8
Sangro Pl. CT1 .... 67 D1
Sanspareil Ave. ME12 .... 4 A6
Santon La. CT3 .... 70 E8
Saracen Cl. ME7 .... 11 A1
Saracen Fields.
ME5 & ME14 .... 54 C8
Sarah Gdns. CT9 .... 29 D8
Sark Cl. TN29 .... 195 C8
Sarre Ct. CT3 .... 48 D6
Sarre Mill. CT7 .... 48 D7
Sarre Pl. CT13 .... 93 F8
Sarsen Hts. ME5 .... 31 F1
Satis Ave. ME10 .... 36 E7
Satmar La. CT15 & CT18 ... 164 E4
Saunders La. CT3 .... 71 F1
Saunders St. ME7 .... 10 C6
Saunders Way. TN31 .... 201 A2
Savage Rd. ME5 .... 32 B3
Savernake Dr. CT6 .... 23 B2
Saw Lodge Field. TN23 ..... 156 C4
Sawpit Rd. ME9 .... 59 B2
Sawyers Ct. ME4 .... 10 B2
Saxon Ave. ME2 .... 4 B6
Saxon Cl. CT21 .... 176 B2
Saxon Rd. Bridge CT4 .... 89 A1
Saxon Rd. Faversham ME13 . 62 C7
Saxon Rd. Ramsgate CT11 .. 52 B6
Saxon Rd. Westgate-on-S CT8 7 D1
Saxon St. **9** CT17 .... 166 D8
Saxons Cl. CT14 .... 117 C8
Saxons Dr. ME14 .... 75 B7
Saxton Rd. TN29 .... 204 E5
Saxton St. ME7 .... 10 C5
Sayer Rd. TN27 .... 120 C8
Sayers La. **4** TN30 .... 179 A7
Scanlons Bridge Rd. CT21 . 176 A2
Scarborough Dr. ME12 .... 4 C8
Scarlett Cl. ME5 .... 32 C5
Scene Cotts. CT20 .... 176 E4
Sceptre Way. CT5 .... 43 B7
School Ave. ME7 .... 10 C4
School Cl The. CT8 .... 7 C1
School Hall. CT14 .... 107 B8
School Hill. Bapchild ME9 ... 37 D2
School La. Bekesbourne CT4 89 C4
School La. Blean CT2 .... 66 A6
School La. Borden ME9 .... 35 F4
School La.
Boughton Street ME13 .... 63 F3
School La. Fordwich CT2 ..... 68 A4
School La. Goodnestone CT3 91 D2
School La. Herne Bay CT6 ... 23 B2
School La. Hoath CT3 .... 46 E6
School La. Ickham CT3 .... 90 C8
School La. Iwade ME9 .... 14 C4
School La.
Lower Halstow ME9 .... 13 B2
School La.
Lower Hardres CT4 .... 110 B6
School La. Maidstone ME15 . 75 E1
School La. Newington ME9 ... 35 B7
School La.
Platt's Heath ME17 .... 100 F2
School La. Ramsgate CT11 .. 52 C7
School La.
Stalisfield Green ME13 ..... 103 D6
School La. Staple CT3 .... 92 A6
School La. Stourmouth CT3 .. 48 E2
School La. Wingham CT3 ..... 91 B7
School Rd. Appledore TN26 181 C1
School Rd. Ash CT3 .... 71 C2
School Rd.
Bethersden TN26 .... 153 D4
School Rd. Charing TN27 ... 120 C8
School Rd. Densole CT18 .. 162 E7
School Rd. Faversham ME13 62 C6
School Rd. Hothfield TN26 . 138 A7
School Rd. Hythe CT21 ..... 176 B4
School Rd. Sandwich CT13 .. 72 F1
School Rd.
Sittingbourne ME10 .... 37 B3
School Rd.
Tilmanstone CT14 .... 114 F4
School View. ME9 .... 58 C8
Scimitar Cl. ME7 .... 11 A1
Scocles Cotts. ME12 .... 4 C5
Scocles Rd. ME12 .... 4 C5
Scoggers Hill. ME13 .... 85 A7
Scot's La. TN25 .... 159 F8
Scotby Ave. ME5 .... 32 B4
Scott Ave. ME8 .... 12 A1
Scott St. ME14 .... 74 F6

Scott's Terr. ME4 .... 9 F3
Scotteswood Ave. ME4 .... 9 F2
Scotton St. TN25 .... 123 F2
Scragged Oak Rd.
Detling ME14 .... 55 C5
Scragged Oak Rd.
Hucking ME14 .... 56 C1
Scraps Hill. ME9 .... 37 F4
Scrapsgate Rd. ME12 .... 4 A7
Scrubbs La. ME16 .... 74 D4
Sea App. ME12 .... 6 E4
Sea Rd. Hythe CT21 .... 177 A2
Sea Rd. Kingsdown CT14 ... 134 D6
Sea Rd.
Westgate-on-S CT7 & CT8 ... 7 C1
Sea St. Herne Bay CT6 .... 22 C3
Sea St. St Margaret's
at Cliffe CT15 .... 151 A6
Sea St. Whitstable CT5 .... 20 D2
Sea View Ave. CT7 .... 26 E8
Sea View Cl. CT18 .... 164 B1
Sea View Gdns. ME12 .... 6 E3
Sea View Hts. CT7 .... 26 D8
Sea View Rd.
Birchington CT7 .... 26 E8
Sea View Rd.
Broadstairs CT10 .... 30 A6
Sea View Rd.
Cliffs End CT12 .... 51 D6
Sea View Rd.
Herne Bay CT6 .... 23 C5
Sea View Rd. St Margaret's
at Cliffe CT15 .... 150 F4
Sea View Sq. CT6 .... 22 F5
Sea View Terr.
Folkestone CT20 .... 177 D3
Sea View Terr. Margate CT9 . 7 G2
Sea View Terr.
Minster ME12 .... 5 A5
Sea Wall.
Dymchurch TN29 .... 195 D8
Sea Wall. Whitstable CT5 ... 20 D2
Seabourne Way. TN29 ...... 195 B7
Seabrook Cl. CT21 .... 177 B3
Seabrook Gdns. CT21 .... 177 B2
Seabrook Gr. CT21 .... 177 A2
Seabrook Rd. CT21 .... 177 B2
Seabrook Vale. CT21 .... 177 B4
Seacroft Rd. CT10 .... 30 A1
Seadown Cl. CT21 .... 177 A4
Seafield Rd.
Broadstairs CT10 .... 30 A4
Seafield Rd.
Ramsgate CT11 .... 52 C6
Seafield Rd.
Whitstable CT5 .... 21 B3
Seaford Ct. ME1 .... 9 B5
Seagar Rd. ME13 .... 40 B1
Seager Rd. ME12 .... 1 F2
Seagrave Cres. CT19 .... 178 F6
Sealand Ct. ME1 .... 9 B5
Seamark Cl. CT12 .... 49 D7
Seamark Rd. CT12 & CT7 .. 26 E2
Seapoint Rd. CT10 .... 30 B3
Sealsalter Beach. CT5 .... 43 A7
Sealsalter Cl. ME12 .... 6 E4
Sealsalter La. CT5 .... 43 A5
Sealsalter Rd. CT5 & ME13 41 E3
Seaside Ave. ME12 .... 4 C8
Seathorpe Ave. ME12 .... 4 C8
Seaths Cr. CT3 .... 91 A7
Seaton Ave. CT21 .... 176 B3
Seaton Cotts. TN25 .... 122 E3
Seaton Rd. Gillingham ME7 . 10 E3
Seaton Rd.
Wickhambreaux CT3 .... 69 D2
Seaview Ave. ME12 .... 6 H1
Seaview Cotts. **6** CT10 ..... 30 B4
Seaview Cr. CT10 .... 30 B3
Seaview Rd.
Gillingham ME7 .... 10 C4
Seaview Rd.
Greatstone-on-S TN28 ..... 200 E1
Seaville Dr. CT6 .... 23 E5
Seaway Cres. TN29 .... 194 F4
Seaway Gdns. TN29 .... 194 F4
Seaway Rd. TN29 .... 195 A4
Second Ave.
Broadstairs CT10 .... 8 G2
Second Ave.
Chatham ME4 & ME5 .... 10 C1
Second Ave.
Eastchurch ME12 .... 5 F5
Second Ave.
Gillingham ME7 .... 10 E3
Second Ave. Margate CT9 .... 8 B3
Second Ave.
Rushenden ME11 .... 2 F3

Second Ave.
Sheerness ME12 .... 1 C1
Secretan Rd. ME1 .... 9 B1
Sedge Cres. ME5 .... 31 E4
Sedley Cl. ME8 .... 33 C3
Seesalter Cross. CT5 .... 43 A6
Seeshill Cl. CT5 .... 43 E8
Segrave Rd. CT19 .... 178 F5
Selby Cl. CT6 .... 23 C4
Selborne Rd. CT9 .... 29 B8
Selbourne Rd. ME7 .... 10 D7
Selbourne Wlk. ME15 ...... 97 F6
Selby Rd. ME15 .... 97 F4
Selkirk Rd. CT16 .... 149 B3
Sellens Cotts. ME12 .... 1 E2
Sellindge
Cty Prim Sch. TN25 ..... 159 C1
Selling CE Prim Sch. ME13 . 84 B5
Selling Cl. ME13 .... 84 C5
Selling Rd. Chilham CT4 .... 85 B3
Selling Rd.
Faversham ME13 .... 62 F3
Selling Rd. Selling ME13 .... 84 E6
Sellinge Gn. ME8 .... 11 C3
Selsea Ave. CT6 .... 22 D4
Selstead Cl. ME8 .... 11 C2
Selsted CE Prim Sch.
CT15 .... 146 C6
Selway Ct. CT14 .... 117 B3
Selwood Cl. ME12 .... 3 E6
Selwyn Cl. CT10 .... 29 F5
Selwyn Dr. CT10 .... 29 F5
Semaphore Rd. CT7 .... 26 F8
Semple Cl. CT12 .... 50 C7
Semple Gdns. ME4 .... 9 F3
Senacre La. ME15 .... 97 E6
Senacre Sq. ME15 .... 97 F7
Senacre Tech Coll. ME15 .... 97 D6
Senacre Wood
Cty Prim Sch. ME15 ...... 97 F7
Sene Pk. CT21 .... 176 D3
Sene Valley Golf Course.
CT21 .... 176 E4
Senlac Cl. CT11 .... 52 B6
Serene Ct. **12** CT10 .... 30 B4
Serene Pl. **9** CT10 .... 30 B4
Setford Rd. ME5 .... 32 C6
Setterfield Ho. CT21 .... 176 D2
Setterfield Rd. CT9 .... 7 J1
Settington Ave. ME5 .... 10 C1
Sevastopol Pl. CT1 .... 66 D1
Seven Stones Dr. CT10 .... 30 A1
Sevenacre Rd. ME13 .... 62 C8
Sevenscore Farm Cotts.
CT12 .... 51 A5
Severn Rd. ME5 .... 32 C5
Sevington La. TN24 .... 157 A7
Sevington Pk. ME15 .... 96 F6
Sewell Cl. CT7 .... 27 A6
Sexburga Dr. ME12 .... 4 B8
Sextant Pk. ME2 .... 9 E6
Seymour Ave.
Westgate-on-S CT9 .... 7 D1
Seymour Ave.
Whitstable CT5 .... 20 E1
Seymour Cl. CT6 .... 23 B7
Seymour Pl. CT1 .... 87 E7
Seymour Rd. **1**
Chatham ME4 .... 10 B3
Seymour Rd.
Gillingham ME8 .... 12 C1
Seymour Rd. St Margaret's
at Cliffe CT15 .... 150 F8
Shackleton Cl. ME5 .... 32 B6
Shadoxhurst Rd. TN26 .... 169 C7
Shaftesbury Ave. CT19 ... 177 E7
Shaftesbury Ct. CT14 ...... 117 D2
Shaftesbury Dr. ME16 ...... 74 C4
Shaftesbury Rd.
Canterbury CT2 .... 66 F3
Shaftesbury Rd.
Hersden CT3 .... 46 E1
Shaftesbury Rd.
Whitstable CT5 .... 20 D1
Shaftsbury St. CT11 .... 52 F7
Shah Pl. CT11 .... 52 D7
Shakespeare Ct. CT17 .... 166 B7
Shakespeare Pas. CT19 ...... 7 H2
Shakespeare Rd.
Birchington CT7 .... 27 A8
Shakespeare Rd.
Dover CT17 .... 166 B6
Shakespeare Rd.
Gillingham ME7 .... 10 C3
Shakespeare Rd.
Margate CT9 .... 7 J1
Shakespeare Rd.
Sittingbourne ME10 ...... 37 A4

Shakespeare Terr. **8**
CT20 .... 178 C4
Shalder Ho. ME7 .... 10 D7
Shalloak Rd. CT2 .... 67 D6
Shallows Rd. CT10 .... 29 C6
Shalmsford Ct. CT4 .... 86 B2
Shalmsford Rd. CT4 .... 85 E2
Shalmsford St. CT4 .... 86 B2
Shamel Bsns Ctr. ME2 ...... 9 C7
Shamley Rd. ME5 .... 32 D2
Shamrock Ave. CT5 .... 43 B7
Shanklin Cl. ME5 .... 32 C8
Shapland Cl. CT6 .... 23 C3
Share and Coulter Rd. CT5 . 21 D1
Sharon Cres. ME5 .... 31 F4
Sharsted Hill. ME9 .... 81 C8
Sharsted Way.
Gillingham ME7 .... 33 A3
Sharsted Way.
Maidstone ME14 .... 76 B5
Shatterlocks
Cty Inf Sch. CT17 .... 149 B2
Shaw Cross. TN24 .... 139 D5
Shawdon Ave. CT13 .... 95 A7
Shaws Way. ME1 .... 9 C3
Shawstead Rd. ME7 & ME7 . 32 D5
Sheal's Cres. ME15 .... 75 A2
Sheals Ct. ME15 .... 75 A2
Shear Way. TN29 .... 186 C5
Shearers Cl. ME14 .... 75 E4
Shearwater. ME16 .... 74 B5
Shearwater Ave. CT5 ...... 43 C7
Shearwater Ct. ME12 .... 3 B8
Shearwater Ho. TN29 ..... 195 A3
Shearway Rd. CT19 .... 177 F8
Sheepfold La. TN23 .... 156 C4
Sheerness Golf Course.
ME12 .... 3 F8
Sheerness Harbour Est.
ME12 .... 1 A3
Sheerness-on-Sea
(Terminus). ME12 .... 1 C2
Sheerstone. ME9 .... 14 D4
Sheerwater Rd. CT3 .... 70 F5
Sheerways. ME13 .... 62 A6
Sheet Glass Rd. ME11 .... 3 A3
Shelden Dr. ME8 .... 33 F8
Sheldon Bsns Ctr. ME2 ..... 9 D8
Sheldon Cl. CT3 .... 113 A6
Sheldwich Cl. TN23 .... 156 A6
Shellbeach. ME12 .... 19 D6
Shelley Ave. CT1 .... 67 C2
Shelley Rd. ME14 .... 74 C2
Shelley St. ME14 .... 74 C2
Shelliness Rd. ME12 .... 19 D7
Shellons St. CT20 .... 178 D5
Shelvin La. CT4 .... 129 C3
Shenley Gr. ME14 .... 53 F2
Shepherd Dr. TN24 .... 157 A8
Shepherd's Close Rd. CT4 .. 89 E1
Shepherd's Cross. CT15 . 132 B1
Shepherds Gate. ME7 ..... 32 F5
Shepherds Gate Dr. ME14 . 75 E6
Shepherds Way.
Langley Heath ME17 .... 98 E4
Shepherds Way.
Whitstable CT5 .... 44 C8
Shepherds Well Sta.
CT15 .... 130 D5
Shepherds Wlk.
Hythe CT21 .... 175 E1
Shepherds Wlk.
Whitstable CT5 .... 44 C8
Shepherdsgate. CT2 .... 66 F1
Shepherdsgate Dr. CT6 ... 46 A8
Shepherdswell Rd. CT15 . 131 A7
Shepperton Cl. ME5 .... 32 C4
Sheppey Cl. CT7 .... 27 A7
Sheppey Cotts. ME12 .... 1 C2
Sheppey Hospl. ME12 .... 4 C7
Sheppey Rd. ME15 .... 97 A7
Sheppey St. ME12 .... 1 B2
Sheppey Terr. ME12 .... 4 F5
Sheppey View. CT5 .... 43 C6
Sheppey Way.
Bobbing ME10 & ME9 ..... 36 B7
Sheppey Way. Iwade ME9 . 14 F6
Sheppey Way.
Queenborough ME12 & ME9 . 3 D2
Shepway. TN24 .... 139 E5
Shepway Cl. CT19 .... 178 D6
Shepway Cross. CT21 ..... 175 B3
Shepway Ct. ME15 .... 97 C8
Shepway
Cty Inf Sch. ME15 .... 97 E8
Shepway
Cty Jun Sch. ME15 .... 97 E8
Sheraton Cl. ME5 .... 31 F1
Sherborne Dr. ME16 .... 74 B2
Sheridan Cl. Chatham ME5 . 32 C7
Sheridan Cl.
Maidstone ME14 .... 74 E8

Sheridan Rd. CT16 .... 149 B3
Sheriff Dr. ME5 .... 32 A2
Sherman Cl. ME7 .... 11 B1
Shernold Sch. ME16 .... 74 D5
Shernolds. ME15 .... 97 B7
Sheron Cl. CT14 .... 117 A5
Sherriffs Court La. CT12 ... 49 E6
Sherwood Ave. ME5 .... 32 A2
Sherwood Cl.
Ashford TN24 .... 139 D7
Sherwood Cl.
Faversham ME13 .... 40 B1
Sherwood Cl.
Herne Bay CT6 .... 23 C2
Sherwood Cl.
Whitstable CT5 .... 43 C6
Sherwood Ct. CT8 .... 7 C1
Sherwood Dr. CT5 .... 43 C6
Sherwood Gdns. CT11 ..... 29 E1
Sherwood Ho. ME5 .... 32 A3
Sherwood Rd. CT7 .... 26 F5
Shillingheld Cl. ME14 .... 140 A1
Ship Cl. TN29 .... 195 C8
Ship La. ME1 .... 9 A4
Ship St. CT19 .... 178 D6
Shipland Hos. TN27 .... 136 D8
Shipley Ct. ME14 .... 75 A4
Shipman Ave. CT2 .... 87 C8
Shipmans Way. CT16 ..... 149 A3
Shipwrights Ave. ME4 ..... 10 B2
Shipwrights Lee. CT5 ...... 20 C2
Shire La. ME13 .... 103 C6
Shireway Cl. CT19 .... 178 A7
Shirley Ave. Chatham ME5 . 31 D5
Shirley Ave.
Ramsgate CT11 .... 29 E1
Shirley Way. ME15 .... 76 A3
Shoebury Terr. ME12 .... 5 A5
Sholden Bank. CT14 ...... 116 E4
Sholden
CE Prim Sch. CT14 .... 116 F5
Sholden New Rd. CT14 ... 116 F6
Shooter's Hill. **5**
CT16 & CT17 .... 149 C1
Shooters Hill. CT15 .... 131 C8
Shorefields. ME8 .... 12 B2
Shoregate La. ME9 .... 42 C1
Shoreham La. TN30 .... 167 A3
Shoreham Wlk. ME15 ...... 97 F7
Shoreland Ct. ME1 .... 9 C4
Shorncliffe Cres. CT20 ... 177 E5
Shorncliffe Ind Est. CT20 . 177 D4
Shorncliffe Rd.
Folkestone CT20 .... 177 F5
Shorncliffe Rd.
Folkestone CT20 .... 178 B5
Short La. Alkham CT15 ... 147 D1
Short La. Gillingham ME7 ... 11 A6
Short La. Snargate TN29 ... 191 D6
Short St. **3** Chatham ME4 . 10 B3
Short St. Chillenden CT3 ... 114 A8
Short St. **5** Sandwich CT13 . 73 A1
Short St. Sheerness ME12 .... 1 C2
Short's Prospect. ME2 .... 17 C8
Shortlands Gn. ME15 ...... 97 F5
Shortlands Rd. ME10 ...... 37 B4
Shorts Way. ME1 .... 9 A3
Shottendane Rd.
CT9 & CT7 & CT8 .... 28 C7
Shottenden Rd.
Leavenland CT4 & ME13 . 105 D8
Shottenden Rd.
Shottenden CT4 .... 84 B1
Shrimpton Cl. CT4 .... 85 B3
Shropshire Terr. **3** ME15 . 97 E7
Shrub Hill Rd. CT5 .... 44 D7
Shrubbery The.
Chatham 111 F1
Shrubbery The. Deal CT14 . 117 C1
Shrubcote. TN30 .... 179 C7
Shrubsole Ave. ME12 .... 1 C1
Shrubsole Dr. ME14 .... 53 F3
Shuart La. CT7 .... 25 F4
Shurland Ave.
Leysdown-on-S ME12 .... 6 H1
Shurland Ave. Minster ME12 . 4 B6
Shurland Ave.
Sittingbourne ME10 .... 36 F1
Shuttle Rd. CT10 .... 30 B5
Sibert's Cl. CT15 .... 130 F5
Sibertswold
CE Prim Sch. CT15 .... 130 E4
Sibton Park Prep Sch.
CT18 .... 161 B8
Sidings The. CT18 .... 161 C7
Sidney Rd. Gillingham ME7 . 10 C7
Sidney Rd. Rochester ME1 . 9 A2
Sidney St.
Folkestone CT19 .... 178 E7

Sidney St.
Maidstone ME16 .... 74 C2
Silchester Ct. ME14 .... 75 C7
Silecroft Ct. TN23 .... 138 E1
Silvanus Ho. CT11 .... 52 D7
Silver Ave. CT7 .... 27 B6
Silver Bank. ME5 .... 32 A6
Silver Birch Gr. TN23 .... 156 B4
Silver Birches.
Chatham ME5 .... 32 A3
Silver Birches.
Ruckinge TN26 .... 171 A5
Silver Birches.
Sheerness ME12 .... 1 H1
Silver Hill. Chatham ME4 .... 9 F3
Silver Hill.
Tenterden TN30 .... 167 B1
Silver Hill Gdns.
Ashford TN24 .... 140 A1
Silver Hill Gdns.
Chatham ME4 .... 9 F3
Silver Hill Rd. TN24 ...... 140 A1
Silver St. Deal CT14 ...... 117 D7
Silver St. Silver Street ME9 . 57 F5
Silver Tree. ME5 .... 32 B1
Silverdale. ME16 .... 74 A2
Silverdale Ave. ME12 .... 4 A6
Silverdale Dr.
Gillingham ME8 .... 33 F7
Silverdale Dr.
Herne Bay CT6 .... 23 D2
Silverdale Gr. ME10 .... 36 D3
Silverdale Rd. CT11 .... 52 A5
Silverlands Rd. CT18 ..... 161 C7
Silvers The. CT10 .... 29 C4
Silverspot Cl. ME8 .... 33 F7
Silverweed Rd. ME5 .... 31 F4
Simmonds La. ME15 .... 98 B6
Simmonds Rd. CT1 .... 87 E7
Simon Ave. CT9 .... 8 D2
Simon Langton
Sch for Boys. CT1 .... 88 A4
Simon Langton
Sch for Girls. CT1 .... 88 C5
Simon's Ave. TN23 .... 155 F7
Simone Weil Ave. TN24 .. 139 B4
Simpson Rd. ME10 .... 36 C5
Sinclair Cl. ME8 .... 33 E5
Singapore Dr. ME7 .... 10 B5
Singer Ave. CT6 .... 22 B4
Singledge Ave. CT16 ..... 148 F6
Singledge La. CT15 .... 131 C2
Singleton Cl. CT12 .... 50 B6
Singleton Ctr The. TN23 . 155 D8
Singleton Hill. TN23 ...... 155 D8
Singleton Rd. TN23 .... 138 C1
Sion Hill. CT11 .... 52 E6
Sir Evelyn Rd. ME1 .... 9 B1
Sir John Hawkins Way.
ME4 .... 9 F4
Sir John Moore Ave.
CT21 .... 176 B2
Sir John Moore Ct. **5**
CT20 .... 177 E3
Sir Joseph Williamson's
Mathematical Sch. ME1 .... 9 C1
Sir Roger Manwood's Sch.
CT13 .... 94 B8
Sir Thomas Longley Rd.
ME2 .... 9 E6
Sir William Nottidge
Tech Sch. CT5 .... 43 F8
Siskin Cl. CT18 .... 162 F4
Sissinghurst Dr. ME16 .... 74 B4
Sittingbourne
Comm Coll. ME10 .... 37 C2
Sittingbourne & Kemsley
Light Rly. ME10 .... 37 A7
Sittingbourne Rd.
Maidstone,Detling ME14 .. 75 E8
Sittingbourne Rd.
Maidstone, Penenden
Heath ME14 .... 75 B6
Six Fields Path. TN30 .... 179 A7
Sixth Ave. ME12 .... 6 A5
Skeete Rd. CT18 & TN25 . 160 E7
Skene Ct. ME8 .... 12 A1
Skinner Rd. TN29 .... 203 C6
Skinner St. Chatham ME4 ... 9 F3
Skinner St. Gillingham ME7 . 10 C5
Skinner St. Gillingham ME7 . 10 C6
Skinner Street
Cty Prim Sch. ME7 .... 10 C6
Skinner's Alley. **3** CT5 .. 20 D7
Skinner's Way. ME17 ...... 98 E4
Skinners Cl. ME20 .... 53 A6
Skye Cl. ME15 .... 97 A7
Slade Cl. ME5 .... 32 A2
Slade Rd.
ME8 & ME13 & ME13 ..... 102 D8
Slades Cl. CT5 .... 44 C8

Slatin Rd. ME2 .... 9 B8
Sleigh Rd. CT2 .... 67 F6
Slicketts Hill. CT4 .... 10 A4
Slip La. CT15 .... 147 C2
Slip Rd. ME4 .... 10 A8
Slipway Rd. ME12 .... 1 A3
Sloe La. CT10 & CT9 ...... 29 B6
Slough Rd. ME9 .... 59 A3
Smack Alley. ME13 .... 62 D8
Small Hythe Rd. TN30 .... 179 C3
Smallhythe Rd. TN30 ..... 179 A6
Smarden Cty Prim Sch.
TN27 .... 135 A1
Smarden Rd. TN27 .... 136 B6
Smarden Wlk. ME8 .... 12 B1
Smarts Cotts. ME14 .... 76 C4
Smeed Cl. ME10 .... 37 B4
Smeed-Dean Ctr The.
ME10 .... 37 A4
Smeeth Cty Prim Sch.
TN25 .... 158 D5
Smith Rd. ME5 .... 32 B3
Smith St. ME2 .... 9 A6
Smuggler's Way. CT7 ...... 27 A8
Snakes Hill. CT3 .... 91 A5
Snargate La. TN29 .... 191 C5
Snargate St. CT17 .... 166 D7
Snell Gdns. CT6 .... 22 B2
Snodhurst Ave. ME5 .... 31 E5
Snow Ho. ME7 .... 10 E7
Snowbell Rd. TN23 .... 156 B4
Snowdon Ave. ME14 ...... 75 B5
Snowdon Cl. ME5 .... 32 B7
Snowdon Caravan Site.
CT15 .... 113 A4
Snowdown Ct. CT3 .... 112 F5
Snowdown Sta. CT15 .... 113 B3
Snowdrop Cl. CT19 .... 178 C8
Sobraon Way. CT1 .... 67 D1
Sole Street Cotts. CT4 .. 125 B7
Solent Gdns. ME5 .... 32 B8
Soleshill Rd. CT4 .... 84 E1
Solihull Cotts. CT12 .... 49 E6
Solomon Ho. CT14 .... 117 B3
Solomon Rd. ME8 .... 12 A1
Solomons La. ME13 .... 62 D7
Solomons Rd. ME4 .... 9 F4
Somerfield Barn Ct. TN25 . 174 C8
Somerfield Cl. ME16 .... 74 D5
Somerfield Hospl The.
ME16 .... 74 E5
Somerfield La. ME16 ...... 74 D4
Somerfield Rd. ME16 ...... 74 D4
Somerset Cl. Chatham ME5 . 32 C8
Somerset Cl.
Sittingbourne ME10 ...... 36 C4
Somerset Cl.
Whitstable CT5 .... 43 B7
Somerset Ct. Deal CT14 . 117 B3
Somerset Ct.
Ramsgate CT12 .... 29 B2
Somerset Rd.
Ashford TN23 & TN24 ... 139 B3
Somerset Rd.
Canterbury CT1 .... 88 D8
Somerset Rd. Deal CT14 . 117 C3
Somerset Rd.
Folkestone CT19 .... 177 E6
Somerset Rd.
Maidstone ME15 .... 97 C8
Somme Ct. CT1 .... 67 D1
Sommerville Cl. ME13 ..... 62 E7
Somner Cl. CT2 .... 66 D1
Somner Wlk. ME15 .... 97 F4
Sondes Cl. CT6 .... 23 A2
Sondes Rd. Deal CT14 ... 117 D5
Sorrell Rd. ME5 .... 31 F4
Sotherton. TN24 .... 156 E7
Souberg Cl. CT14 .... 117 C8
South Ave. Aylesham CT15 . 113 A3
South Ave. Gillingham ME8 . 11 B2
South Ave.
Sittingbourne ME10 ...... 37 A3
South Avenue Cty Jun
& Inf Schs. ME10 .... 37 A3
South Barham Rd. CT4 .. 128 E6
South Borough
Cty Prim Sch. ME15 ..... 75 A8
South Brooks Rd. TN29 . 202 F2
South Bush La. ME8 .... 34 B6
South Camber Way. CT16 . 150 B1
South Canterbury Rd. CT1 . 88 A6
South Cl. CT1 .... 88 A8
South Cliff Par. CT10 ..... 30 B1
South Court Dr. CT3 .... 91 A7
South Cres. ME17 .... 96 C4
South Ct. Deal CT14 ..... 117 D6
South Ct. Ramsgate CT12 . 29 B2
South Cty Prim Sch. TN23 . 156 A8
South Deal Cty Prim Sch.
CT14 .... 117 B4

South Eastern Rd.
  Ramsgate CT11 .... 52 D7
South Eastern Rd.
  Rochester ME2 .... 9 C7
South Exit Rd. CT16 .... 166 G8
South Goodwin Ct. CT14 .. 117 D8
South Green La. ME9 .... 56 F6
South Kent Coll of Tech.
  Ashford TN23 .... 139 C1
South Kent Coll of Tech.
  Ashford TN23 .... 156 A8
South Kent Coll of Tech.
  Dover CT16 .... 166 D8
South Kent Coll of Tech.
  Folkestone CT20 .... 178 B5
South Lea. TN23 .... 156 A3
South Lodge Cl. CT5 .... 20 E3
South Military Rd. CT17 ... 166 C5
South Motto. TN23 .... 156 B5
South of England Rare
  Breeds Ctr The. TN26 .... 169 D1
South Park Bsns Village.
  ME15 .... 75 A1
South Park Rd. ME15 .... 75 C1
South Pondside Rd. ME4 ... 10 A8
South Rd. Dover CT17 ..... 166 B8
South Rd. Faversham ME13 . 62 C7
South Rd. Gillingham ME7 .. 10 A7
South Rd. Gillingham ME8 .. 10 B7
South Rd. Herne Bay CT6 .. 23 A5
South Rd. Hythe CT21 ..... 176 D1
South Rd.
  Kingsdown CT14 .... 134 D5
South Rd.
  Sandwich CT14 .... 73 A8
South Side Three Rd. ME4 .. 10 C8
South St.
  Boughton Street ME13 .... 84 F8
South St. Canterbury CT1 .. 67 C2
South St. Deal CT14 .... 117 D6
South St. Lydd TN29 ...... 203 C6
South St.
  Queenborough ME11 .... 2 F5
South St. Whitstable CT5 ... 44 A7
South Stour Ave. TN23 ... 156 C8
South Street Crossing.
  CT5 .... 44 A7
South Street Rd. ME9 ...... 56 C7
South View. CT14 .... 46 F1
South View Gdns. ME12 ...... 1 D1
South View Rd. CT5 .... 43 D6
South Wall. CT14 .... 117 B7
Southbourne. TN23 .... 155 E5
Southbourne Gr. ME5 .... 32 A4
Southbourne Rd. CT19 ... 178 E5
Southdown Rd. ME12 .... 3 E6
Southenay La. TN25 ...... 159 C4
Southernwood Rise. CT20 177 F4
Southfields. ME1 .... 9 C3
Southgate Rd. TN30 ...... 179 C7
Southill Rd. ME4 .... 9 F3
Southlands
  Comm Comp Sch. TN28 200 B7
Southlees La. ME9 .... 56 F3
Southmead Cl. CT19 ...... 178 A6
Southover CT. ME9 .... 2 D4
Southsea Ave. CT14 .... 4 C8
Southsea Dr. CT6 .... 22 D4
Southwall Rd. CT14 .... 117 B6
Southward Gdns. CT11 ..... 52 B7
Southwold Pl. CT8 .... 27 E7
Southwood Gdns. CT11 .... 52 B6
Southwood Rd.
  Ramsgate CT11 .... 52 C6
Southwood Rd.
  Whitstable CT5 .... 21 B2
Sovereign Bvd.
  Gillingham ME7 .... 10 F2
Sovereign Bvd.
  Gillingham,Twydall ME8 ... 11 A2
Sovereigns The. ME16 ..... 74 D4
Sowell St. CT10 .... 29 F5
Spade La. ME8 & ME9 ...... 34 C6
Spanton Cres. CT21 ...... 176 A3
Sparrow Castle. CT9 .... 7 J1
Spearhead Rd. ME14 .... 74 F7
Spearpoint Cnr. TN24 ..... 139 F5
Spectrum Bsns Ctr. ME2 ... 9 E8
Spectrum Bsns Est. ME15 . 97 F4
Speedwell Ave. ME5 ...... 31 F4
Speedwell Cl.
  Gillingham ME7 .... 10 E5
Speedwell Cl.
  Maidstone ME14 .... 75 E5
Speke Rd. CT10 .... 29 E6
Spekes Rd. ME7 .... 33 B6
Speldhurst Cl. TN23 ...... 155 E5
Speldhurst Ct. ME16 ...... 74 D4
Speldhurst Gdns. CT9 ...... 8 F3
Spencer Cl. ME5 .... 32 A5

Spencer Flats. ME5 .... 32 B8
Spencer Ho. 3 CT20 ...... 177 F5
Spencer Rd. CT7 .... 27 A8
Spencer Sq. CT11 .... 52 D6
Spencer St. 9 CT11 .... 52 D6
Spenlow Dr. ME5 .... 54 A8
Spenser Ct. CT6 .... 22 F4
Spicer Homes. ME10 .... 36 F2
Spicer's Pl. CT3 .... 69 C2
Spiers The. ME7 .... 11 C5
Spillett Cl. ME13 .... 62 B6
Spillway The. ME15 .... 74 D2
Spindle Glade. ME14 .... 75 C5
Spindlewood Cl. ME5 .... 32 B3
Spinnaker Cl. 3 ME1 .... 9 C1
Spinnens Acre
  Cty Jun Sch. ME5 .... 32 C1
Spinney La. Aylesham CT3 . 112 E4
Spinney La. Aylesham CT3 . 112 F5
Spinney The.
  Ashford TN23 .... 138 E3
Spinney The. Chatham ME5 . 32 B1
Spinney The.
  Maidstone ME15 .... 75 B2
Spinney The. Margate CT9 ... 8 E1
Spinney The. River CT17 .. 148 E2
Spire Ave. CT5 .... 44 A8
Spires The. ME16 .... 74 D4
Spitalfield La. TN28 ...... 199 F6
Spitfire Cl. ME5 .... 32 B6
Spitfire & Hurricane
  Memls Mus. CT12 .... 28 A2
Split La. CT4 .... 127 A5
Sportsfield. ME14 .... 75 B5
Spot La. ME15 .... 76 A2
Spratling La. CT12 .... 28 E1
Spratling St. CT12 .... 28 E1
Sprig The. ME14 .... 76 A4
Spring Farm Rd. TN29 .... 192 C5
Spring Grove Sch. TN25 .. 123 C2
Spring Ho. CT21 .... 176 C2
Spring Hollow. TN29 ...... 195 A4
Spring La. Canterbury CT1 .. 88 C7
Spring La. Fordwich CT2 ... 68 A4
Spring La. Hythe CT21 .... 177 A4
Spring Vale. ME14 .... 74 E4
Spring Wlk. CT5 .... 43 C7
Springett Way. ME17 ...... 96 D3
Springfield Ave.
  Maidstone ME14 .... 74 F7
Springfield Ave.
  St Michaels ME8 .... 167 C2
Springfield Cl. CT11 .... 29 E2
Springfield Pass. CT21 ... 176 B2
Springfield Rd.
  Dover CT16 .... 149 B2
Springfield Rd.
  Gillingham ME7 .... 10 E6
Springfield Rd. Margate CT9 . 8 E3
Springfield Rd.
  Sittingbourne ME10 .... 36 D5
Springfield Way. CT21 ... 177 B3
Springhead Rd. ME13 ...... 40 D1
Springside Terr. CT18 .... 161 C6
Springvale. Gillingham ME8 . 33 C6
Springvale. Iwade ME9 .... 14 D4
Springwood Cl.
  Ashford TN23 .... 138 E3
Springwood Cl.
  Maidstone ME16 .... 74 A3
Springwood Ct. TN28 .... 200 B6
Springwood Dr. TN23 .... 138 E3
Sprotlands Ave. ME16 ..... 74 A3
Sprotlands Ave. TN24 .... 139 F1
Sprotshill Cl. ME10 .... 36 E6
Spurgeons Cotts. ME17 ... 96 E2
Spurway. ME14 .... 76 A4
Square Hill. ME15 .... 75 B4
Square Hill Rd.
  ME14 & ME15 .... 75 B4
Square The.
  Birchington CT7 .... 27 A7
Square The. Chilham CT4 .. 107 B8
Square The. Elham CT4 ... 144 F4
Square The.
  Lenham ME17 .... 101 D5
Square The. Selling ME13 .. 84 A6
Square The.
  Sittingbourne ME10 .... 14 F1
Squeeze Gut Alley. 8 CT5 . 20 D2
Squire Ave. CT2 .... 87 C8
Squires Cl. ME12 .... 5 E3
Squires Way. CT16 .... 149 A3
Stable Cl. ME5 .... 32 D1
Stable Ct. ME13 .... 62 D6
Stable Mews. CT18 ...... 161 D4
Stablemead. CT19 .... 178 A7
Stace Cl. TN30 .... 179 C8
Staceys St. ME14 .... 74 F5
Stade St. CT21 .... 176 C1

Stade The. CT19 .... 178 E5
Staffa Rd. ME15 .... 97 A7
Stafford Cl. TN23 .... 138 F2
Stafford St. ME7 .... 10 C5
Staffordshire St. 8 CT11 .. 52 E7
Stag Rd. ME5 .... 32 B5
Staines Hill. CT2 .... 68 B7
Stains Pl. CT10 .... 30 B5
Stalham Ct. ME7 .... 33 B4
Stalin Ave. ME5 .... 32 B8
Stalisfield Rd.
  Charing ME13 & TN27 .... 103 E3
Stalisfield Rd. Stalisfield Green
  ME13 & ME17 & TN27 ... 103 C5
Stalisfield Rd.
  Throwley, Eastling ME13 .. 82 C6
Stampers The. ME15 ...... 74 D2
Stanbury Cres. CT19 ...... 178 F7
Stancomb Ave. CT11 ...... 52 C5
Standard Ave. 1 CT6 ...... 22 A4
Standen Cl. ME8 .... 33 E4
Standen La. CT18 .... 163 E5
Standen St. CT12 .... 52 A8
Staner Hill. CT12 .... 51 F8
Stanford Dr. ME16 .... 74 C3
Stanhope Ave. ME10 ...... 37 A3
Stanhope Cl. ME14 .... 74 E7
Stanhope Rd.
  Ashford TN23 .... 155 F7
Stanhope Rd.
  Ashford, Stanhope TN23 .. 155 E6
Stanhope Rd. Deal CT14 .. 117 D6
Stanhope Rd. Dover CT16 .. 149 C2
Stanhope Rd.
  Rochester ME2 .... 9 A7
Stanhope Sq. TN23 ...... 155 F6
Stanley Ave. Minster ME12 . 4 D7
Stanley Ave.
  Queenborough ME11 .... 3 A4
Stanley Cl. TN29 .... 187 B4
Stanley Gdns. CT6 .... 22 F3
Stanley Pl.
  Broadstairs CT10 .... 30 A4
Stanley Pl. Ramsgate CT11 . 52 E7
Stanley Rd.
  Broadstairs CT10 .... 30 A6
Stanley Rd. Chatham ME5 . 32 C6
Stanley Rd. Deal CT14 .... 117 D5
Stanley Rd.
  Folkestone CT19 .... 177 E6
Stanley Rd. Gillingham ME7 . 10 C6
Stanley Rd. Herne Bay CT6 . 22 F4
Stanley Rd. Margate CT9 ... 8 A3
Stanley Rd. Ramsgate CT11 . 52 D8
Stanley Rd. Whitstable CT5 . 43 D7
Stanley Sykes Cl. CT9 ...... 29 B8
Stanmore Ct. CT1 .... 88 B7
Stansted Cl. ME16 .... 74 D7
Staple Cl. ME10 .... 36 E5
Staple Rd. CT3 .... 91 C6
Staple St. ME13 .... 63 F5
Staple Vineyard. CT3 ...... 91 F5
Staplehurst Ave. CT10 .... 30 A2
Staplehurst Gdns. CT9 ..... 8 E2
Staplehurst Rd.
  Gillingham ME8 .... 11 B3
Staplehurst Rd.
  Sittingbourne ME10 .... 36 D5
Staplers Ln. ME14 .... 75 B8
Staplestreet Rd. ME13 .... 64 A4
Star Hill. ME1 .... 9 D5
Star La. Folkestone CT19 .. 177 D7
Star La. Gillingham ME7 ... 33 A7
Star La.
  Margate CT10 & CT9 ...... 29 A5
Star Mill Ct. ME5 .... 10 D2
Star Mill La. ME5 .... 10 D2
Star Rd. TN24 .... 139 D2
Starle Cl. CT1 .... 67 B1
Starnes Ct. 5 ME14 .... 75 A5
Starvation Cnr. 1 CT5 .... 20 D2
Station App. Adisham CT3 . 112 E8
Station App.
  Birchington CT7 .... 26 F7
Station App.
  Maidstone ME16 .... 74 F3
Station App.
  Martin Mill CT15 .... 133 C2
Station App. Minster.
  Thanet CT12 .... 50 C5
Station App.
  New Romney TN28 .... 200 C6
Station Approach Rd.
  CT11 .... 52 D8
Station Cotts. ME13 .... 84 E7
Station Dr. CT14 .... 117 A1
Station Rd. Adisham CT3 .. 94 A8
Station Rd. Ashford TN23 . 139 C2
Station Rd. Birchington CT7 . 27 A7
Station Rd. Bridge CT4 .... 88 F2
Station Rd. Charing TN27 . 120 C7

Station Rd. Deal CT14 .... 117 B1
Station Rd.
  Dymchurch TN29 .... 195 B7
Station Rd.
  East Farleigh ME15 .... 96 A7
Station Rd.
  Faversham ME13 .... 62 D6
Station Rd.
  Folkestone CT19 .... 177 F5
Station Rd. Gillingham ME8 . 12 A2
Station Rd.
  Harrietsham ME17 .... 100 D6
Station Rd. Herne Bay CT6 . 22 E4
Station Rd. Hythe CT21 ... 176 D3
Station Rd. Lydd TN29 .... 203 D7
Station Rd. Lyminge CT18 . 161 C6
Station Rd.
  Maidstone ME14 .... 74 F5
Station Rd. Margate CT9 ... 7 H2
Station Rd.
  Martin Mill CT15 .... 133 D1
Station Rd. Minster.
  Thanet CT12 .... 50 C5
Station Rd.
  New Romney TN28 .... 200 C6
Station Rd. Newington ME9 . 35 B6
Station Rd.
  Patrixbourne CT4 .... 89 C4
Station Rd. Pluckley TN27 . 136 C5
Station Rd. Rochester ME2 . 9 C7
Station Rd.
  Shepherdswell CT15 ...... 130 D5
Station Rd. Smeeth TN25 . 158 B3
Station Rd. St Margaret's
  at Cliffe CT15 .... 150 E8
Station Rd.
  Tenterden TN30 .... 179 A7
Station Rd. Teynham ME9 . 38 D2
Station Rd.
  Westgate-on-S CT8 .... 7 D1
Station Rd. Whitstable CT5 . 20 E2
Station Rd E. CT1 .... 87 F7
Station Rd W. CT1 .... 66 F1
Station Row. ME9 .... 38 D3
Station St. ME10 .... 36 F4
Stede Hill. ME17 .... 78 F3
Steed Cl. CT16 .... 49 A6
Steeds Cl. TN23 .... 156 A1
Steeds La. TN23 & TN26 .. 156 B1
Steele St. ME2 .... 9 A8
Steerforth Cl. ME1 .... 9 C2
Stella Maris
  RC Prim Sch. CT19 ...... 178 C6
Stelling Minnis
  CE Prim Sch. CT4 .... 126 F6
Stembrook Ct. CT16 ...... 166 D8
Stembrook Ct. 4 CT16 ... 166 D7
Step Style. ME10 .... 37 B2
Stephen Cl. CT10 .... 30 A4
Stephen Ct. 2 CT20 ...... 178 D5
Stephen's Cl. CT9 .... 28 B7
Stephens Cl.
  Faversham ME13 .... 62 B8
Stephens Cl.
  Ramsgate CT11 .... 52 C8
Stephenson Rd. CT2 .... 66 F3
Steps Hill Rd. ME9 .... 56 D6
Sterling Ave. ME16 .... 74 C5
Sterling Cl. CT19 .... 178 D8
Sterling Rd.
  Queenborough ME11 .... 3 A5
Sterling Rd.
  Sittingbourne ME10 .... 36 D1
Stevens Cl. ME13 .... 74 F3
Stickfast La. ME9 .... 14 A1
Stiles Cl. CT19 .... 178 A7
Stirling Cl. Gillingham ME8 . 33 E4
Stirling Cl. Rochester ME1 ... 9 A3
Stirling Way. CT12 .... 29 A2
Stirling Rd. TN24 .... 156 D7
Stisted Way. TN27 .... 118 F3
Stock La. TN25 .... 158 A4
Stockbury Dr. ME16 .... 74 D7
Stockbury Gdns. CT9 .... 8 E2
Stockdale Gdns. CT14 ... 117 C4
Stocker's Hill. ME13 .... 63 E4
Stockers Brow. ME9 .... 57 A4
Stockers Hill. ME10 & ME9 . 57 A7
Stockett La. ME15 .... 96 D6
Stockham Ct. CT19 .... 177 E7
Stocks Rd. TN30 .... 188 F3
Stocks The. ME13 .... 83 C6
Stockton Cl. ME14 .... 75 B8
Stockwood Chase. CT2 .... 66 A2
Stoddart Rd. CT19 .... 177 E6
Stodmarsh National
  Nature Reserve. CT3 ...... 69 D8
Stodmarsh Rd. CT3 .... 68 C3
Stombers La. CT18 .... 163 C6
Stonar Cl. Ramsgate CT11 . 29 E1
Stonar Cl. Sandwich CT13 . 73 A1

Stonar Gdns. CT13 .... 73 A2
Stone Abbage. TN27 ...... 136 D4
Stone Barn Ave. CT7 .... 27 A6
Stone Bay Sch. CT10 ...... 30 B6
Stone Cnr. TN30 .... 189 A6
Stone Cross Lees. CT13 .... 93 F7
Stone Gdns. CT10 .... 30 B5
Stone Gn. TN30 .... 189 F4
Stone Hill. TN23 .... 159 A2
Stone Hill Rd. TN27 ...... 118 F2
Stone Ho. CT10 .... 30 B7
Stone Ho. CT10 .... 30 B5
Stone St. Faversham ME13 . 62 C7
Stone St.
  Lympne CT21 & TN25 .... 175 A4
Stone St. Stanford TN25 . 160 C3
Stone St. Stelling Minnis
  CT4 & CT18 .... 126 D4
Stone St.
  Westenhanger TN25 ..... 175 B6
Stoneacre Cl. ME8 .... 33 D5
Stoneacre La. ME15 .... 98 B7
Stoneacre (NT). ME15 ..... 98 B7
Stonebridge Cotts. TN23 . 156 B8
Stonebridge Green Rd.
  TN27 .... 119 A4
Stonecross. Way. ME15 ... 63 B7
Stonecross Lea. ME5 .... 10 C1
Stonedane Ct. ME13 .... 62 C8
Stonehall Rd. CT15 ...... 147 F8
Stoneheap Rd.
  CT14 & CT15 .... 115 E1
Stonestile Farm Rd. TN27 103 A3
Stoney Bank. ME7 .... 10 F1
Stoney Rd. ME13 .... 64 B3
Stony La. ME5 .... 31 C5
Stonyway La. CT15 ...... 165 C5
Stopford Rd. ME7 .... 10 D4
Storehouse Wharf. ME12 ... 1 A3
Stour Cl. Ashford TN23 .. 138 E1
Stour Cl. Chartham CT4 ... 86 D2
Stour Cres. CT1 .... 67 D3
Stour Ct. 7 Canterbury CT1 . 87 F8
Stour Ct. Sandwich CT13 . 72 F1
Stour Ho. CT17 .... 97 D8
Stour Rd. CT14 .... 86 D2
Stour St. CT1 .... 87 F8
Stour Valley Cl. CT13 ..... 47 D3
Stourmouth Rd. CT3 ...... 70 C8
Stourside Studios. 2 CT2 .. 66 F1
Stowting
  CE Prim Sch. CT18 ...... 160 B8
Stowting Hill. TN25 ...... 143 A1
Straight La. TN29 .... 191 F1
Strakers Hill. CT15 .... 132 D8
Strand Approach Rd. ME7 . 10 E7
Strand St. CT13 .... 72 F1
Strand The. CT14 .... 117 D4
Stranger's Cl. CT1 .... 87 C6
Stranger's La. CT1 .... 87 C6
Strangford Pl. CT6 .... 23 B2
Strangford Rd. CT5 .... 20 F2
Strasbourg St. CT9 .... 9 A6
Stratford Ave. ME8 .... 33 C8
Stratford La. ME8 .... 33 F8
Straw Mill Hill. ME15 ..... 74 E1
Stream Wlk. CT5 .... 20 D2
Street End. CT3 .... 71 E1
Street End Rd. ME5 .... 10 B1
Street The. Acol CT7 .... 27 B3
Street The. Adisham CT3 . 112 C8
Street The.
  Appledore TN26 .... 190 D8
Street The. Ash CT3 .... 71 D1
Street The. Ashford TN24 . 157 B8
Street The.
  Barfrestone CT15 .... 113 D1
Street The. Barham CT4 . 111 F1
Street The.
  Bethersden TN26 .... 153 D5
Street The.
  Bishopsbourne CT4 .... 111 C6
Street The. Borden ME9 ... 36 B2
Street The.
  Bossingham CT4 .... 127 A7
Street The.
  Boughton Street ME13 .... 64 A3
Street The. Boxley ME14 . 54 C3
Street The.
  Brabourne TN25 .... 159 C8
Street The. Bredgar ME9 .. 58 A5
Street The. Bredhurst ME7 . 33 B1
Street The. Brook TN25 .. 141 B6
Street The. Chilham CT4 . 107 B8
Street The. Deal CT14 ... 116 F6

Street The. Denton CT4 .... 129 B3
Street The. Detling ME14 ..... 55 A1
Street The.
  Doddington ME9 .... 80 E7
Street The.
  East Langdon CT15 .... 133 A1
Street The. Eastling ME13 ... 81 E6
Street The. Egerton TN27 ... 118 F3
Street The.
  Eythorne CT15 .... 131 D7
Street The.
  Finglesham CT14 .... 116 B8
Street The.
  Godmersham CT4 .... 107 B2
Street The.
  Goodnestone CT3 .... 91 D2
Street The.
  Great Chart TN23 .... 138 C1
Street The. Guston CT15 ... 149 E6
Street The.
  Hamstreet TN26 .... 183 A7
Street The. Hartlip ME9 ... 34 D5
Street The.
  Hastingleigh TN25 .... 142 B6
Street The.
  Hawkinge CT18 .... 163 B5
Street The.
  Hothfield TN26 .... 138 A6
Street The. Ickham CT3 ... 69 C2
Street The. Iwade ME9 ... 14 E4
Street The. Kingston CT4 ... 111 D3
Street The.
  Lower Halstow ME9 .... 13 B3
Street The. Lympne CT21 ... 174 F2
Street The. Lynsted ME9 ... 60 A6
Street The.
  Maidstone ME14 .... 76 C4
Street The. Martin CT15 ... 133 B3
Street The. Mersham TN25 157 E4
Street The.
  Newington CT18 .... 177 A7
Street The. Newnham ME9 ... 81 C8
Street The.
  Northbourne CT14 .... 116 A5
Street The. Oare ME13 ... 40 B2
Street The.
  Patrixbourne CT4 .... 89 B3
Street The. Petham CT4 ... 109 B3
Street The. Postling CT21 ... 160 F2
Street The. Preston CT3 ... 70 C6
Street The.
  Shadoxhurst TN26 .... 170 A8
Street The.
  Silver Street ME9 .... 57 F5
Street The.
  St Nicholas at Wade CT7 ... 25 F2
Street The. Staple CT3 ... 91 F6
Street The.
  Stone in Oxney TN30 ... 190 A5
Street The. Stourmouth CT3 ... 48 E1
Street The. Upchurch ME9 ... 12 F4
Street The.
  West Hougham CT15 ... 164 F5
Street The.
  Wickhambreaux CT3 ... 69 C1
Street The.
  Wittersham TN30 .... 188 D3
Street The.
  Womenswold CT4 .... 112 D2
Street The.
  Woodnesborough CT13 ... 93 C7
Street The. Wormshill ME9 ... 79 A7
Street The. Worth CT14 ... 94 B5
Streete Court Rd. CT8 .... 27 F8
Streete Ct. CT8 .... 27 F8
Streetfield. CT6 .... 46 B8
Streetfield Rd. ME8 ...... 11 F1
Stringer Dr. CT7 .... 27 A6
Strode Cres. ME12 .... 1 D2
Strode Park Rd. CT6 ..... 23 A2
Strond St. CT17 .... 166 D6
Strood Sta. ME2 .... 9 C7
Strood Rd. TN23 .... 155 D7
Strover St. ME7 .... 10 C7
Stuart Cl. ME14 .... 75 C6
Stuart Ct. CT17 .... 166 C8
Stuart Ho. CT17 .... 117 A5
Stuart Rd.
  Folkestone CT19 .... 178 E6
Stuart Rd. Gillingham ME7 ... 10 D3
Studds Cotts. CT6 ..... 22 A3
Studfall Cl. CT21 ...... 187 D8
Studio Cl. TN24 .... 139 E6
Stumble La. TN23 & TN26 . 156 B1
Stuppington Court Farm.
  CT1 .... 87 E5
Stuppington La. CT1 ... 87 F4
Sturdee Ave. ME7 ...... 10 E4
Sturdy Cl. CT21 .... 176 D2
Sturges Rd. TN24 ..... 139 B3
Sturla Rd. ME4 .... 10 A3
Sturmer Cl. CT1 .... 88 C7
Sturry CE Prim Sch. CT2 ... 68 A7
Sturry Court Mews. CT2 ... 67 F5
Sturry Hill. CT2 .... 67 F6
Sturry Rd. CT1 & CT2 ... 67 C3
Sturry Sta. CT2 .... 67 F5
Sturry Way. ME8 ...... 11 C2
Stutfall Castle (rems of).
  CT21 .... 174 F1
Style Cl. ME8 .... 33 E4
Sudbury Pl. CT8 .... 27 E7
Suffolk Ave. Gillingham ME8 11 F1
Suffolk Ave.
  Westgate-on-S CT8 ... 27 D7
Suffolk Dr. TN23 ...... 139 A2
Suffolk Gdns. CT17 ... 165 F7
Suffolk Rd. Canterbury CT1 . 88 D8
Suffolk Rd.
  Maidstone ME15 ...... 97 D8
Suffolk St. CT5 .... 43 D8
Sugarloaf Wlk. CT19 ... 178 D8
Sultan Rd. ME5 .... 32 C2
Summer Cl. Hythe CT21 ... 175 F2
Summer Cl.
  Tenterden TN30 ...... 167 C1
Summer Ct. CT2 ...... 66 C1
Summer Hill. CT2 ..... 66 C1
Summer Hill Pk. TN24 . 157 C7
Summer La. CT2 ...... 66 C6
Summer Leeze. TN24 . 156 E8
Summer Leeze Gdns.TN24 156 E8
Summer Rd. CT7 ...... 25 E1
Summerfield Ave. CT5 ... 20 F1
Summerfield Rd. CT9 ... 8 E2
Summerhill. TN23 ..... 155 E6
Summerville Ave. ME12 ... 4 A5
Sumpter Way. ME13 ... 61 F7
Sun La. Hythe CT21 ... 176 C2
Sun La.
  St Nicholas at Wade CT7 ... 25 F2
Sun St. CT1 .... 87 F8
Sun Terr. ME5 .... 32 B4
Sunbeam Ave. CT6 ... 21 F4
Sunderland Cl. ME1 ... 9 A3
Sunderland Dr. ME8 ... 34 A8
Sunderland Ho. ME7 ... 10 C7
Sunder Gr. CT11 ...... 52 E8
Sundridge Cl. CT2 ... 67 A4
Sundridge Dr. ME5 ... 32 A4
Sunningdale Ave.
  CT19 .... 178 A7
Sunningdale Cl. ME8 ... 33 D6
Sunningdale Cl. ME15 ... 75 B4
Sunningdale Dr. ME8 ... 33 D6
Sunningdale Wlk. CT6 ... 22 D1
Sunny Bank. Hythe CT21 ... 175 F2
Sunny Bank.
  Sittingbourne ME10 ... 37 B5
Sunny Cnr. CT17 ..... 166 B5
Sunnyfields Cl. ME8 ... 33 E8
Sunnyfields Dr. ME12 ... 3 C6
Sunnyhill Rd. CT6 ... 22 C4
Sunnymead. CT2 ..... 66 D7
Sunnymead Ave. ME7 ... 10 E5
Sunnyside. Doddington ME9 80 E7
Sunnyside.
  Littlestone-on-S TN28 ... 200 D6
Sunnyside. Lydd TN29 ... 203 B6
Sunnyside Ave. ME12 ... 4 A6
Sunnyside Cl. CT14 ... 116 D1
Sunnyside Gdns. CT13 ... 93 E8
Sunnyside Rd. CT20 ... 177 D3
Sunray Ave. CT5 ..... 43 B7
Sunrise Ind
  Pre-Prep Sch. ME17 ... 98 D4
Sunset Cl. Eastchurch ME12 ... 5 F6
Sunset Cl. Whitstable CT5 ... 43 C6
Superabbey Est. ME20 ... 53 B2
Surf Cres. ME12 ...... 5 F6
Surrenden. TN27 ..... 136 F7
Surrenden Rd. CT19 ... 177 F6
Surrey Gdns. CT7 ... 26 F7
Surrey Rd. Canterbury CT1 88 D7
Surrey Rd. Maidstone ME15 . 97 D8
Surrey Rd. Margate CT9 ... 8 B3
Susan's Hill. TN26 ... 168 E3
Sussex Ave. Ashford TN24 139 B3
Sussex Ave.
  Canterbury CT1 .... 88 D7
Sussex Ave. Margate CT9 ... 7 J1
Sussex Cl. CT4 .... 22 D4
Sussex Dr. ME5 .... 32 A4
Sussex Gdns.
  Birchington CT7 ..... 26 F7
Sussex Gdns.
  Herne Bay CT6 .... 22 B4
Sussex Gdns.
  Westgate-on-S CT8 ... 7 D1
Sussex Mansions. CT8 ... 7 D1
Sussex Rd. **5**
  Folkestone CT19 ..... 178 D6
Sussex Rd.
  Maidstone ME15 ..... 97 D8
Sussex Rd.
  New Romney TN28 ... 200 A6
Sussex St. CT11 ...... 52 E7
Sussex Wlk. CT1 ...... 88 D7
Sutherland Cl. CT21 ... 176 A2
Sutherland Dr. CT7 ... 27 B6
Sutherland Gdns. ME8 ... 33 E6
Sutherland Rd. CT14 ... 117 C6
Sutton Cl.
  Folkestone CT19 ..... 178 A7
Sutton Cl. Gillingham ME8 ... 34 A8
Sutton Cotts. ME13 ... 84 C3
Sutton La. Ringwould CT14 133 F5
Sutton La. Ripple CT14 ... 133 C8
Sutton Rd. Hersden CT3 ... 46 E1
Sutton Rd. Langley ME17 ... 98 C5
Sutton Rd. Maidstone ME15 . 97 D6
Sutton St. ME14 ...... 76 D4
Suttons The. TN31 ... 201 A1
Swadelands Cl. ME17 ... 101 C5
Swadelands Sch. ME17 ... 101 C5
Swain Rd. Gillingham ME8 ... 33 B6
Swain Rd.
  St Michaels TN30 .... 167 D3
Swakeley Wlk. CT5 ... 21 D3
Swale Ave. Rushenden ME11 . 2 F3
Swale Ave. Sheerness ME12 ... 1 C1
Swale Cl. CT6 .... 23 A3
Swale Halt. ME9 ...... 15 A7
Swale Ho. **1** ME15 ... 97 E7
Swale View. ME13 ... 64 B6
Swalecliffe Ave. CT6 ... 22 B4
Swalecliffe Court Dr. CT5 ... 21 D3
Swalecliffe
  Cty Prim Sch. CT5 ... 21 B2
Swallow Ave. CT5 ... 43 B6
Swallow Cl. CT9 ...... 28 C8
Swallow Ho. **4** ME16 ... 74 E4
Swallow Rise. ME5 ... 32 A5
Swallowfield. TN24 ... 156 E7
Swamp Rd. TN29 ..... 199 B4
Swan Apartments. **10**
  ME15 .... 97 E5
Swan Cl. ME10 .... 37 B4
Swan Cotts. TN30 ... 188 D4
Swan Gn. TN25 ...... 159 D1
Swan La. TN25 ...... 159 E2
Swan St. TN30 ...... 188 C3
Swanfield Rd. CT5 ... 43 D8
Swanstree Ave. ME10 ... 37 B2
Swanton La.
  Canterbury CT3 ..... 68 D2
Swanton La. Lydden CT15 . 147 C6
Swanton Mill. TN25 ... 157 B2
Swarling Hill Rd. CT4 ... 109 C7
Swaynes Way. CT13 ... 93 B2
Sweechbridge Rd. CT6 ... 23 F3
Sweechgate. CT2 & CT3 ... 67 E7
Sweetbriar La. CT15 ... 114 B2
Sweetlove Pl. CT3 ... 91 A8
Sweyn Rd. CT9 .... 8 A3
Swift Cres. ME5 ..... 32 C6
Swift Ho. **6** ME16 ... 74 E4
Swinburne Ave. CT10 ... 30 A3
Swinford Gdns. CT9 ... 29 C8
Swingate Cl. ME5 ... 32 B2
Swingate
  Cty Inf Sch. ME5 ... 32 C1
Sycamore Ave. CT3 ... 112 E5
Sycamore Cl.
  Broadstairs CT10 ... 29 C4
Sycamore Cl.
  Dymchurch TN29 ... 195 C8
Sycamore Cl.
  Herne Bay CT6 ...... 23 C5
Sycamore Cl. Hythe CT21 . 175 E1
Sycamore Cl. Lydd TN29 ... 203 D7
Sycamore Cl. Margate CT9 . 28 E7
Sycamore Cres. ME16 ... 74 C5
Sycamore Gdns. TN29 ... 195 C8
Sycamore Ho. ME12 ... 1 C2
Sycamores The. CT3 ... 68 E8
Sydcot Dr. CT14 ..... 117 D8
Sydenham Rd. CT14 ... 117 D7
Sydenham St. CT5 ... 20 D2
Sydney Ave. ME10 ... 36 C4
Sydney Cooper Cl. CT2 ... 66 B2
Sydney Rd. Chatham ME4 ... 10 A3
Sydney Rd. Deal CT14 ... 117 A1
Sydney Rd. Ramsgate CT11 . 52 F8
Sydney Rd. Whitstable CT5 . 43 E8
Sydney St. TN23 ..... 156 C8
Sylewood Cl. ME1 ... 31 B8
Sylvan Glade. ME5 ... 54 A4
Sylvan Rd. ME8 ...... 33 C8
Symmonds Dr. ME10 ... 37 A6
Symons Ave. ME4 ... 10 A2
Syndale Pl. **1** CT11 ... 52 F7
Tabret Cl. TN24 ..... 139 D6
Tadburn Gn. ME5 ... 32 B4
Taddington Wood La. ME5 . 31 E2
Taddy Gdns. CT9 .... 29 C8
Tadley Cl. ME7 ...... 10 F6
Tadworth Rd. TN24 ... 139 D5
Tail Race The. ME15 ... 74 E2
Tailbur Cl. ME8 ...... 36 F7
Talavera Rd. CT1 .... 88 D8
Talbot Ave. CT6 ..... 22 B3
Talbot Rd. Maidstone ME16 . 74 C6
Talbot Rd. Margate CT9 ... 8 B2
Tall Trees Cl. ME17 ... 99 D2
Tally Ho Rd. TN26 ... 155 C2
Tamar Ho. **4** ME15 ... 97 E8
Tamarind Cl. ME4 ... 33 A4
Tamarisk. ME12 ...... 19 E5
Tame La. TN29 ...... 185 F6
Tamley La. TN25 ..... 142 B6
Tangier Cl. CT16 ..... 149 E3
Tanglewood Cl. ME8 ... 33 C6
Tangmere Cl. ME7 ... 10 F5
Tanker Hill. ME8 ..... 33 D6
Tankerton Cir. CT5 ... 20 F3
Tankerton Cl. CT5 ... 21 B3
Tankerton Mews. CT5 ... 20 E3
Tankerton Rd. CT5 ... 20 F3
Tanner's Hill CT16 ... 176 C3
Tanner's Hill Gdns. CT21 ... 176 C3
Tanners St. ME13 .... 62 C7
Tannery Cl. **3** ME10 ... 36 E5
Tannery La. TN23 & TN24 . 139 C2
Tapleys Hill. CT14 ... 110 B5
Target Bsns Ctr. ME15 ... 97 F4
Target Firs. CT16 .... 148 D5
Tariff Reform Cotts. ME13 . 62 D5
Tartane La. TN29 .... 195 C8
Tasker Cl. ME15 ..... 76 B3
Tassell's Wlk. CT5 ... 21 D3
Taswell Cl. CT16 .... 166 E8
Taswell Rd. ME8 ..... 12 A1
Taswell St. CT16 .... 166 E8
Tatler Cl. ME5 .... 32 D2
Tatsfield Cl. ME8 .... 11 A2
Taunton Cl. ME15 ... 97 F6
Taverners Rd. ME8 ... 33 E7
Tavistock Cl. Chatham ME5 . 31 F1
Tavistock Cl.
  Gillingham ME8 ..... 33 E7
Tavistock Cl.
  Sittingbourne ME10 ... 36 D4
Tavistock Rd. CT11 ... 29 E1
Tay Cl. ME5 .... 32 B5
Taylor Rd. Folkestone CT19 177 E6
Taylor Rd.
  Lydd-on-S TN29 ..... 204 E6
Taylor Rd. Minster,
  Thanet CT12 .... 50 B6
Taylor's La. ME2 ..... 9 B7
Taylors Cl. TN29 .... 194 F3
Taylors Hill. CT17 ... 107 B8
Taylors La. TN29 .... 194 F3
Taylors Yd. TN25 ... 123 E2
Taywood Cl. TN24 ... 139 F1
Teasaucer Hill. ME15 ... 96 F8
Teasel Cl. ME14 ..... 75 F4
Teasel Rd. ME5 ..... 31 F4
Teddars Leas Rd. CT18 161 E4
Tedder Ave. ME5 .... 32 A7
Teddington Cl. CT1 ... 67 B2
Teelin Cl. TN29 ..... 195 A4
Tees Ho. **9** ME15 ... 97 E7
Telegraph Rd. CT14 ... 117 B3
Telford Cl.
  Folkestone CT19 .... 178 E6
Telford Ct. Herne Bay CT6 . 22 C2
Telford Ho. **1** ME14 ... 75 A6
Telford St. CT6 ..... 22 E5
Telham Ave. CT12 ... 52 B8
Templar Rd. CT16 ... 148 D5
Templar St. CT17 ... 166 C8
Temple Cl. CT16 .... 148 D6
Temple Cl. CT2 ..... 66 D1
Temple Ewell
  CE Prim Sch. CT16 ... 148 D6
Temple Gdns.
  Rochester ME2 ..... 9 A6
Temple Gdns.
  Sittingbourne ME10 ... 37 B3
Temple Mews. **10** CT1 ... 87 F8
Temple Rd. CT11 .... 66 D1
Temple Side. CT16 ... 148 D6
Temple Way. CT14 ... 94 A4
Templeman Liby. CT2 ... 66 E4
Ten Acre Way. ME8 ... 12 B1
Ten Perch Rd. CT1 ... 87 D6
Tennyson Ave. CT1 ... 67 D3
Tennyson Gdns. CT3 ... 112 F6
Tennyson Pl. CT19 ... 178 E7
Tennyson Rd.
  Ashford TN23 .... 156 A6
Tennyson Rd.
  Gillingham ME7 ..... 10 C3
Tenterden CE Jun Sch.
  TN30 .... 179 B7
Tenterden Cty Inf Sch.
  TN30 .... 179 B7
Tenterden Dr. CT2 ... 67 A4
Tenterden Rd.
  Appledore TN26 & TN30 . 181 B1
Tenterden Rd.
  Chatham ME5 .... 32 B5
Tenterden Town Sta.
  TN30 .... 179 A8
Tenterden Way. CT9 ... 8 C1
Terence Cl. ME4 ..... 10 A2
Terminus Dr. CT6 ... 23 D5
Terminus Rd. ME16 ... 74 A2
Terrace Cotts. CT14 ... 127 A6
Terrace Rd.
  Elvington CT15 ..... 114 B1
Terrace Rd.
  Maidstone ME16 .... 74 E3
Terrace The.
  Sittingbourne ME10 ... 37 B3
Terrace The.
  Canterbury CT2 ..... 66 F3
Terrace The. Chatham ME4 . 9 F7
Terrace The.
  Faversham ME13 .... 62 A7
Terrace The.
  Little Chart TN26 ... 120 A1
Terrace The. Rochester ME1 . 9 C5
Terrace The.
  Shepherdswell CT15 . 130 D5
Terry's La. CT15 ..... 20 D2
Teynham Cl. CT9 .... 8 F2
Teynham Dr. CT5 .... 20 F2
Teynham Gn. ME8 ... 11 A4
Teynham Parochial
  CE Prim Sch. ME9 ... 38 C2
Teynham Rd. CT5 ... 20 F2
Teynham Sta. ME9 ... 38 D3
Thames Ave.
  Gillingham ME8 ..... 33 E8
Thames Ave.
  Sheerness ME12 ..... 1 C1
Thames Cl. ME12 .... 6 G2
Thames Ho. **3** ME15 ... 97 D8
Thames View
  Cty Inf Sch. ME8 ... 11 D2
Thames View
  Cty Prim Sch (Jun). ME8 . 11 D2
Thanet Cl. CT10 ..... 30 B5
Thanet Coll.
  Broadstairs CT10 ... 30 A3
Thanet Coll. Margate CT9 ... 7 I2
Thanet Pl. CT19 ..... 178 F6
Thanet Place Gdns. CT10 ... 30 B6
Thanet Rd.
  Broadstairs CT10 ... 30 B4
Thanet Rd. Margate CT9 ... 7 J2
Thanet Rd. Ramsgate CT11 . 52 F7
Thanet Rd.
  Westgate-on-S CT8 ... 27 D8
Thanet Terr. TN26 ... 138 A6
Thanet View.
  Eythorne CT15 ...... 131 B8
Thanet View.
  St Nicholas at Wade CT7 . 25 F2
Thanet Way.
  Boughton Street ME13 . 63 D6
Thanet Way. Hawthorn Cnr
  CT3 & CT6 & CT7 ... 24 C4
Thanet Way.
  Herne Bay CT6 & CT5 . 22 D3
Thanet Way.
  Whitstable CT5 ..... 21 C2
Thanet Way.
  Whitstable CT5 ..... 43 D6
Thanet Way.
  Yorklets CT5 & ME13 . 42 E2
Thanington Rd. CT1 ... 87 C6
Thatchers The. ME16 ... 74 B5
Theatre Sq. **5** TN30 ... 179 A7
Theatre St. CT21 .... 176 C2
Theodore Pl. ME7 ... 10 C5
Theresa Rd. CT21 ... 176 B1
Third Ave.
  Chatham ME4 & ME5 ... 10 C1
Third Ave. Eastchurch ME12 . 5 F6
Third Ave. Gillingham ME7 . 10 F4
Third Ave. Margate CT9 ... 8 B3
Thirlmere. TN24 ..... 139 D6
Thirlmere Ave. CT11 ... 52 A7
Thirlmere Cl. ME7 ... 10 F4
Thirlmere Gdns. CT3 ... 112 F6

Thistle Wlk. ME10 .... 37 B5
Thistlebank. ME5 .... 32 A3
Thistledown. ME14 .... 75 F4
Thistledown Cl. ME7 .... 33 A4
Thomas Aveling Sch The.
ME1 .... 31 C8
Thomas Ct. ME10 .... 37 B4
Thomas Rd.
Faversham ME13 .... 62 D7
Thomas Rd.
Sittingbourne ME10 .... 37 B4
Thomas St. ME1 .... 9 C3
Thompson Cl. Deal CT14 .. 134 B8
Thompson Cl.
Folkestone CT19 .... 178 B7
Thompson Cl.
Gillingham ME8 .... 34 A8
Thorn Cl. ME5 .... 31 D1
Thorn Est The. TN27 .. 136 B6
Thorn Gdns. CT11 .... 29 E1
Thorn Hill Rd. ME12 .... 6 D4
Thorn La. CT4 .... 126 C2
Thorn Wlk. ME10 .... 37 C5
Thornbridge Rd. CT14 .. 117 B2
Thorndale Cl. ME5 .... 31 D4
Thornden Cl. CT6 .... 22 B2
Thornden Ct. CT2 .... 66 C4
Thornden Wood Rd.
Herne Bay CT6 .... 22 B1
Thornden Wood Rd.
Whitstable CT2 & CT6 .. 44 E4
Thorndike Cl. ME4 .... 31 F8
Thorndike Rd. TN29 .. 186 C4
Thorne Hill. CT12 .... 51 A6
Thorne Rd. CT12 .... 50 B6
Thorney Croft Cl. ME17 .. 99 D2
Thorneycroft Rd. ME13 .. 103 D5
Thornham Rd. ME8 .... 11 C3
Thornhill Pl. ME14 .... 75 A6
Thornhurst. CT6 .... 23 D4
Thornlea. TN23 .... 138 E2
Thornton La. CT13 & CT14 . 114 E7
Thornton's La. [7] CT16 .. 166 E7
Thorold Rd. ME4 .... 10 B3
Thorpe Wlk. ME8 .... 33 D3
Thrale Way. ME8 .... 33 E4
Thread La. ME13 .... 64 B4
Three Acres Site. CT19 .... 178 B8
Three King's Yd. CT13 .. 73 A1
Threshers Dr. ME14 .... 75 E5
Throwley Dr. CT6 .... 22 C4
Throwley Rd. ME13 .... 82 D5
Thrupp Paddock. CT10 .. 8 G1
Thrush Cl. ME5 .... 32 B7
Thruxted La. CT4 .... 86 B1
Thunderland Rd. CT6 .... 23 B4
Thurlow Ave. CT6 .... 23 C5
Thurnham CE Inf Sch.
ME14 .... 76 A4
Thurnham La. ME14 .... 76 C6
Thurston Pk. CT5 .... 20 E1
Thurstone Ct. ME14 .... 74 F6
Tiber Cl. CT19 .... 177 C6
Tichborne Cl. ME16 .... 74 C6
Tickham La. ME9 .... 60 C5
Tickner's La. TN29 .... 192 B1
Tideway The. ME1 .... 31 C8
Tilbury Rd. ME8 .... 12 A2
Tilden Cl. TN26 .... 167 D7
Tilden Gill Rd. TN30 .. 179 C7
Tile Fields. ME17 .... 77 D2
Tile Ho The. CT21 .... 176 C2
Tile Kiln Hill. CT2 .... 66 B5
Tile Kiln La. CT19 .... 177 F7
Tile Kiln Rd. TN24 .... 139 C7
Tile Lodge Cotts. TN27 .... 119 E8
Tile Lodge Rd. TN27 .... 119 E8
Tillard Cl. CT14 .... 109 B3
Tillery La. TN29 .... 198 A8
Timber Tops. ME14 .... 54 D8
Timberbank. ME5 .... 32 A6
Timperley Cl. CT14 .... 117 B6
Tina Gdns. CT10 .... 30 A6
Tinbridge Pk. ME13 .... 63 A5
Tintagel Manor. ME7 .... 10 C6
Tintern Rd. ME16 .... 74 C4
Titchfield Cl. [5] ME15 .. 97 F6
Titchfield Rd. ME15 .... 97 F6
Tithe Barn La. TN23 .. 155 D8
Tithe The. ME17 .... 101 D5
Tivoli Brooks. CT9 .... 7 I1
Tivoli Park Ave. CT9 .... 7 H1
Tivoli Rd. CT9 .... 28 E8
Tobruk Way. ME5 .... 31 F6
Toby Rd. TN29 .... 200 F4
Todd Cres. ME10 .... 37 A8
Toddington Cres. ME5 .... 31 D1
Toke Cl. TN23 .... 138 C1
Tolgate La. ME7 .... 53 B8
Tolgate Way. ME14 .... 53 E4
Toll Gate. CT14 .... 117 A4

Toll La. TN27 .... 120 E7
Tollemache Cl. CT12 .... 27 F2
Tollgate Ct. CT15 .... 43 C8
Tolsford Cl.
Etchinghill CT18 .... 161 D3
Tolsford Cl.
Folkestone CT19 .... 177 D6
Tomay Cotts. CT6 .... 24 A3
Tomlin Dr. CT9 .... 29 C8
Tonbridge Ct. ME16 .... 74 D3
Tonford La. Canterbury CT1 . 87 B6
Tonford La.
Harbledown CT2 .... 87 A7
Tong Rd. ME10 .... 37 B4
Tonge Rd. ME10 .... 37 C4
Tontine St. CT20 .... 178 E5
Tookey Rd. TN28 .... 200 B6
Top Rd. TN30 .... 189 E3
Tormore Mews. CT14 .. 117 A4
Tormore Pk. CT14 .... 117 A4
Toronto Cl. [6] CT16 .. 149 B3
Toronto Rd. ME7 .... 10 E4
Torrington Cotts. CT12 .. 50 D7
Torrington Rd. TN23 .. 156 C8
Tothill St. CT12 .... 50 C7
Tournay Cl. TN23 .... 155 F8
Tourney Cl. CT21 .... 174 F3
Tourney Rd. TN29 .. 203 C5
Tourtel Rd. CT1 .... 67 A1
Tovil Gn. ME15 .... 74 E1
Tovil Green Bsns Pk. ME15 . 74 E1
Tovil Hill. ME15 .... 74 E2
Tovil Rd. ME15 .... 74 F2
Tower Bglws. CT7 .... 27 A8
Tower Ct. [4] CT20 .... 177 E3
Tower East. TN29 .... 186 E2
Tower Gdns. Hythe CT21 . 176 C1
Tower Gdns.
Maidstone ME14 .... 76 B4
Tower Hamlets Rd. CT17 .. 166 C8
Tower Hamlets St. [1]
CT17 .... 166 C8
Tower Hill. Dover CT17 .. 166 C8
Tower Hill. Whitstable CT5 .. 20 E3
Tower La. ME14 .... 76 B4
Tower Par. CT5 .... 20 E3
Tower Rd. CT5 .... 20 E2
Tower St. CT17 .... 166 C8
Tower Way. [1] CT1 .... 87 F8
Towers Sch The. TN24 .. 139 D8
Towers The. TN27 .... 103 E1
Towers View. TN24 .... 139 C7
Town La. CT4 .... 86 C6
Town Rd. CT10 .... 109 C5
Town Wlk. CT20 .... 178 D4
Townley St. CT11 .... 52 D6
Townsend Farm Rd. CT15 . 150 F6
Townsend Terr. CT17 .. 166 B5
Townwall St. CT16 .... 166 E7
Tracies The. ME9 .... 35 C6
Trafalgar Pl. ME12 .... 4 B6
Trafalgar Rd. CT7 .... 27 F3
Trafalgar St. ME7 .... 10 C5
Tram Rd The. CT20 .... 178 E5
Transom Ho. [2] ME1 .... 9 C1
Trapfield Cl. ME14 .... 76 C4
Trapfield La. ME14 .... 76 C4
Trapham Rd. ME16 .... 74 D5
Travers Gdns. ME9 .... 57 F5
Travers Rd. CT14 .... 117 A5
Travertine Rd. ME5 .... 32 B1
Treasury View. CT3 .... 90 C8
Trefoil The. ME9 & ME13 .. 60 E6
Trefor Jones Ct. CT16 .. 149 C4
Trelawn Cres. ME5 .... 32 B2
Trent Ho. [2] ME15 .... 97 E7
Trent Rd. ME5 .... 32 B5
Trenton Cl. ME16 .... 74 B7
Trevale Rd. ME1 .... 9 B1
Trevino Dr. ME5 .... 31 F2
Trevor Dr. ME16 .... 74 C5
Tribune Cl. ME12 .... 3 B8
Tribune Dr. ME10 .... 36 F6
Trident Cl. ME2 .... 9 D7
Trigg's Row. ME9 .... 38 D2
Trimworth Rd. CT9 .... 177 F6
Trinity Cres. CT20 .... 178 B4
Trinity Ct. Aylesford ME20 .. 53 A3
Trinity Ct. Margate CT9 .... 7 J3
Trinity Gdns. CT20 .... 178 C4
Trinity Hill. CT11 .... 52 E7
Trinity Homes. CT14 .... 117 A4
Trinity Pl. Deal CT14 .... 117 A4
Trinity Pl. Ramsgate CT11 .. 52 F7
Trinity Rd. Ashford TN24 .. 139 B6
Trinity Rd.
Folkestone CT20 .... 178 B4
Trinity Rd. Gillingham ME7 .. 10 E8
Trinity Rd. Sheerness ME12 .. 1 D2
Trinity Rd.
Sittingbourne ME10 .... 36 F7
Trinity Sq. CT10 .... 29 F7

Trinity Trad Est. ME10 .. 36 F6
Trinity Hill. CT9 .... 7 J3
Trinity Sq. CT9 .... 7 J3
Tritton Cl. TN24 .... 139 F7
Tritton Fields. TN24 .... 139 F7
Tritton Gdns. TN29 .. 186 D1
Tritton La. TN28 .... 200 B6
Troodos Hill. ME14 .... 74 F8
Trotts Hall Gdns. ME10 .. 36 F3
Trotwood Cl. ME5 .... 31 F1
Troughton La. TN24 .. 157 B7
Troughton Mews. CT9 .... 7 H1
Trove Ct. [5] CT1 .... 52 F7
Troy Town La. TN25 .. 141 B5
Troys Mead. ME17 .... 77 D2
Trueman Cl. CT2 .... 66 A7
Trumpet Ho. TN23 .. 156 B8
Truro Cl. ME8 .... 11 D3
Truro Rd. CT11 .... 52 F7
Tudor Ave.
Dymchurch TN29 .. 186 D1
Tudor Ave.
Maidstone ME14 .... 75 B6
Tudor Byway. TN24 .. 139 D6
Tudor Cl. CT7 .... 27 B8
Tudor End. TN24 .... 139 D5
Tudor Gr. ME8 .... 33 F8
Tudor Ho. CT14 .... 117 A5
Tudor Rd. Ashford TN24 .. 139 D5
Tudor Rd. Canterbury CT1 .. 87 E7
Tudor Rd.
Folkestone CT19 .... 177 D6
Tufa Cl. ME5 .... 32 B1
Tufton Rd. Ashford TN24 .. 139 B6
Tufton Rd. Gillingham ME8 .. 11 F1
Tufton St. Hothfield TN26 .. 138 A7
Tufton St. Maidstone ME14 .. 75 A4
Tufton Wlk. [9] TN23 .. 139 B2
Tunbury Ave.
Chatham ME5 .... 31 F1
Tunbury Ave.
Chatham ME5 .... 31 F2
Tunbury Cty Prim Sch.
ME5 .... 31 F1
Tunis Ct. CT1 .... 67 D1
Tunis Row. CT10 .... 30 B5
Tunstall CE Prim Sch. ME9 . 58 C8
Tunstall Rd.
Canterbury CT2 .... 67 A4
Tunstall Rd.
Sittingbourne ME10 & ME9 . 58 D8
Tupman Cl. ME1 .... 9 B4
Turgis Cl. ME17 .... 98 E4
Turketel Rd. CT20 .... 178 A4
Turmine Ct. ME12 .... 4 A5
Turnagain La. [3] CT1 .. 87 F8
Turnden Gdns. CT9 .... 8 E2
Turner Cl. ME10 .... 37 A7
Turner Ct. [5]
Folkestone CT20 .... 177 F5
Turner Ct. Margate CT9 .... 8 A2
Turner St. CT11 .... 52 E7
Turners Ave. TN30 .... 179 B8
Turners Cl. ME17 .... 1 D1
Turnpike Cl. CT11 .... 176 A2
Turnpike Hill. CT21 .... 176 A3
Turnstone Cl. TN29 .. 195 A3
Turnstone Rd. ME5 .... 32 C1
Tuscan Dr. ME5 .... 32 C1
Twelve Acres. TN24 .. 156 F8
Twiss Ave. CT21 .... 176 D2
Twiss Gr. CT21 .... 176 D2
Twiss Rd. CT21 .... 176 D2
Two Chimneys Holiday Pk.
CT7 .... 25 E5
Twydall Cl. ME8 & ME8 .. 11 B2
Twydall Cty Prim Jun Sch.
ME8 .... 11 B2
Twydall Gn. ME8 .... 11 B3
Twydall La. ME8 .... 11 B2
Twyford Cl. ME8 .... 12 A2
Twyford Ct. ME14 .... 75 D6
Twyne Cl. CT2 .... 68 A6
Tydeman Rd. ME5 .... 75 F2
Tydeman's Ave. CT5 .... 21 C1
Tyland La. ME14 .... 53 F3
Tyler Cl. CT2 .... 66 F3
Tyler Dr. ME8 .... 12 A3
Tyler Hill Rd. CT2 .... 66 D6
Tyler Way. CT5 .... 21 E3
Tyndale Pk. CT6 .... 23 B5
Tyne Cl. ME5 .... 32 C5
Tyne Ho. [10] ME15 .. 97 E7
Tysoe Ct. ME12 .... 4 A5
Tyson Ave. CT9 .... 7 J3
Tyson Rd. CT19 .... 178 E7
Uden Rd. TN29 .... 187 B4
Uffington Ct. CT3 .... 91 A2

Ufton Cl. ME15 .... 75 E1
Ufton La. ME10 .... 36 E3
Ulcombe Gdns. CT2 .... 67 A3
Ulcombe Hill. ME17 .... 99 F1
Ulcombe Rd. ME17 .... 98 E3
Ulley Rd. TN24 .... 139 D7
Ullswater Gdns. CT3 .. 112 F6
Ulster Rd. CT9 .... 8 B3
Undercliff. CT20 .... 177 E3
Undercliffe Rd. CT14 .. 134 D5
Underdown Ave. ME4 .... 9 F1
Underdown La. CT6 .... 22 F2
Underdown Rd.
Dover CT17 .... 166 B7
Underdown Rd.
Herne Bay CT6 .... 22 F5
Underhill Cotts. CT18 .. 177 B8
Underhill Rd. CT20 .... 177 B5
Underwood. CT18 .... 163 C6
Underwood Cl.
Ashford TN24 .... 139 D6
Underwood Cl.
Canterbury CT1 .... 88 B5
Underwood Cl.
Maidstone ME15 .... 74 F2
Underwood Ct. CT1 .... 88 B6
Unicorn Cotts. CT4 .... 89 B5
Unicumes La. ME16 .... 74 C2
Union Cres. CT9 .... 7 J2
Union Pk. ME15 .... 97 F4
Union Pl. [4] CT1 .... 67 A1
Union Rd. Bridge CT4 .... 88 F1
Union Rd. Deal CT14 .... 117 D6
Union Rd. Minster ME12 .... 4 C7
Union Rd. Ramsgate CT11 .. 52 F8
Union Row. CT9 .... 7 J2
Union Sq. [3] CT10 .... 30 B4
Union St. Canterbury CT1 .. 67 A1
Union St. Chatham ME4 .... 10 A3
Union St. Dover CT17 .... 166 D6
Union St. Faversham ME13 . 62 C7
Union St. Maidstone ME14 .. 75 A5
Union St.
Ramsgate CT11 .... 52 E7
Union St. Rochester ME1 .... 9 C5
Union St. Sheerness ME12 .. 1 B2
Unity Pl. [2] CT1 .... 52 F7
Unity St. Sheerness ME12 .. 1 E2
Unity St.
Sittingbourne ME10 .... 36 E3
Univ of Kent at Canterbury.
CT2 .... 66 D4
University Rd. CT2 .... 66 D3
Unwin Cl. ME20 .... 53 A3
Upbury Manor High Sch.
ME7 .... 10 B4
Upbury Way. ME4 .... 10 A4
Upchurch Wlk. CT9 .... 8 E2
Uphill. CT18 .... 163 B4
Uplands. CT2 .... 66 F4
Uplands Way. ME12 .... 3 C5
Uplees Cotts. ME13 .... 39 F5
Uplees Rd. ME13 .... 40 A3
Upnor Rd. ME2 .... 9 D8
Upper Approach Rd. CT10 .. 30 A3
Upper Brents. ME13 .... 62 D8
Upper Bridge St.
Canterbury CT1 .... 88 A8
Upper Bridge St.
Wye TN25 .... 123 F2
Upper Britton Pl. ME7 .. 10 B5
Upper Chantry La. CT1 .. 88 A7
Upper Corniche. CT20 .. 177 C3
Upper Dane Rd. CT9 .... 8 B1
Upper Denmark Rd. TN23 . 156 B8
Upper Dumpton Park Rd.
CT11 .... 52 E8
Upper East Rd. ME4 .... 10 B8
Upper Fant Rd. ME16 .... 74 D2
Upper Field Rd. ME10 .... 37 B5
Upper Free Down. CT6 .. 23 B2
Upper Gore La. CT13 .. 93 A2
Upper Gr. CT9 .... 7 J2
Upper Grange Rd. ME15 .. 96 B3
Upper Luton Rd.
ME4 & ME5 .... 10 C2
Upper Malthouse Hill.
CT21 .... 176 B2
Upper Rd.
Dover CT15 & CT16 .. 150 C2
Upper Rd. Dover CT16 .. 166 H8
Upper Rd. Maidstone ME15 . 75 B2
Upper St.
Hollingbourne ME17 .... 77 E3
Upper St.
Kingsdown CT14 .... 134 D5
Upper St. Leeds ME17 .. 99 E8
Upper St.
Tilmanstone CT13 .... 115 A3
Upper St Ann's Rd. ME13 .. 62 B6
Upper Stone St. ME15 .. 75 A3

Upper Strand St. CT13 .. 73 A1
Upper Tickham Cotts.
ME9 .... 60 D6
Upper Vicarage Rd. TN24 . 139 D7
Upstreet. CT18 .... 161 D3
Upton Cl. CT19 .... 178 A7
Upton Cty Jun Sch. CT10 .. 29 F4
Upton Rd. CT10 .... 29 F5
Urquhart Cl. ME5 .... 32 A5
Ursuline Dr. CT8 .... 27 D7

Vale Cotts. ME9 .... 57 A8
Vale Dr. ME5 .... 31 E6
Vale Pl. CT11 .... 52 D6
Vale Rd. Broadstairs CT10 .. 29 F4
Vale Rd. Loose ME15 .... 96 E4
Vale Rd. Ramsgate CT11 .. 52 D6
Vale Rd.
Ripple CT14 & CT15 .. 133 B8
Vale Rd. Whitstable CT5 .. 43 D8
Vale Sq. CT11 .... 52 D6
Vale The. CT10 .... 30 A3
Vale View Cty Prim Sch.
CT17 .... 166 B7
Vale View Rd.
Aylesham CT3 .... 112 E5
Vale View Rd.
Dover CT17 .... 166 B7
Valebrook Cl. CT20 .... 177 C5
Valence Ho. ME15 .... 97 C7
Valenciennes Rd. ME10 .. 36 E3
Valentine Cl. ME7 .... 11 A1
Valentine Rd. ME15 .... 97 E7
Valerian Cl. ME5 .... 31 E4
Valestone Cl.
CT20 & CT21 .... 177 B4
Valiant Rd. ME5 .... 32 C2
Valkyrie Ave. CT5 .... 43 C7
Vallance The. ME9 .... 60 A6
Valley Cotts. Alkham CT15 . 147 C1
Valley Cotts.
Stalisfield Green ME13 .. 103 D8
Valley Dr. ME15 .... 96 F6
Valley Rd. Barham CT4 .. 111 E2
Valley Rd. Canterbury CT1 .. 87 E6
Valley Rd.
Folkestone CT20 .... 177 E4
Valley Rd. Gillingham ME7 .. 10 E4
Valley Rd. Lydden CT9 .... 28 E4
Valley Rd. River CT17 .. 148 E3
Valley Rise. ME5 .... 31 F1
Valley The. ME17 .... 96 D3
Valley View. CT15 .... 131 C8
Valley View Rd. ME1 .... 9 B1
Valley Wlk. CT21 .... 177 B3
Vancouver Dr. ME8 .... 11 C1
Vancouver Rd. CT16 .. 149 C3
Vange Cottage Mews. ME1 .. 9 B4
Vanity La. ME17 .... 96 D1
Vanity Rd. ME12 .... 6 F2
Varne Cl. [6] CT20 .... 177 F3
Varne Lodge. [3] CT20 .. 177 F3
Varne Pl. CT19 .... 178 F5
Varne Rd. CT19 .... 178 F5
Vaughan Dr. ME10 .... 36 F8
Vauxhall Ave.
Canterbury CT1 .... 67 C3
Vauxhall Ave.
Herne Bay CT6 .... 22 A3
Vauxhall Cres. CT1 .... 67 C3
Vauxhall Industrial Rd.
CT1 .... 67 C4
Vauxhall Lakes
(Nature Reserve). CT1 .. 67 B3
Vauxhall Rd. CT1 & CT2 .. 67 C4
Vectis Dr. ME10 .... 36 F8
Ventnor Cl. ME5 .... 32 C8
Ventnor La. [12] CT9 .... 7 J2
Venture Cl. TN29 .... 186 D1
Vere Rd. CT10 .... 30 A4
Vereth Rd. [2] CT11 .... 52 D6
Vernon Holme (Kent Coll
Inf & Jun Sch). CT2 .. 66 A1
Vernon Pl. Canterbury CT1 .. 88 A7
Vernon Pl. Deal CT14 .. 117 D8
Verwood Cl. CT2 .... 66 E2
Vesper Ct. TN27 .... 135 A1
Vestey Ct. CT8 .... 7 C1
Viaduct Cl. CT12 .... 52 C8
Viaduct Terr. TN26 .. 182 F7
Viaduct The. CT17 .... 166 D5
Viburnum Cl. TN23 .... 138 E2
Vicarage Cl. ME20 .... 53 A3
Vicarage Cres. [8] CT9 .... 7 J2
Vicarage Ct. ME8 .... 35 B7
Vicarage Gdn. CT12 .... 49 C7
Vicarage Gdns. CT3 .... 91 A7
Vicarage Hill. CT4 .... 109 B4

Vicarage La.
Ashford TN23 .... 139 C2
Vicarage La. Blean CT2 ...... 66 A6
Vicarage La. Deal CT14 ..... 116 F5
Vicarage La.
East Farleigh ME15 .... 96 B6
Vicarage La. Elham CT4 ... 144 F4
Vicarage La.
Faversham ME13 .... 62 A4
Vicarage La.
Lower Halstow ME9 .... 13 C3
Vicarage La.
Nonington CT15 .... 113 C5
Vicarage La.
Sandwich CT13 .... 72 F1
Vicarage La. Selling ME13 ... 84 C6
Vicarage La.
Tilmanstone CT14 .... 115 A3
Vicarage Pl. CT9 .... 7 J1
Vicarage Rd.
Folkestone CT20 .... 177 F3
Vicarage Rd.
Gillingham ME7 .... 10 C5
Vicarage Rd. Minster ME12 ... 4 D7
Vicarage Rd.
Rochester ME2 .... 9 B8
Vicarage Rd.
Sittingbourne ME10 .... 36 E6
Vicarage St.
Broadstairs CT10 .... 29 E5
Vicarage St.
Faversham ME13 .... 62 D8
Vicary Way. ME16 .... 74 D5
Vickers Cl. CT18 .... 163 A4
Victor Ave. CT9 .... 8 D2
Victoria Ave.
Broadstairs CT10 .... 29 E8
Victoria Ave. Hythe CT21 ... 176 B2
Victoria Ave. Margate CT9 ... 8 B1
Victoria Ave. St Margaret's
at Cliffe CT15 .... 151 B6
Victoria Cl. ME5 .... 31 D2
Victoria Cres.
Ashford TN23 .... 139 B1
Victoria Cres. Dover CT16 . 166 D8
Victoria Ct. Hythe CT21 ... 176 C1
Victoria Ct. 6
Maidstone ME16 .... 74 E3
Victoria Dr. CT6 .... 22 C5
Victoria Gr. 9
Folkestone CT20 .... 178 D5
Victoria Gr. Hythe CT21 ... 177 B2
Victoria Ho. 7 CT5 .... 20 D2
Victoria Hospl. CT14 .... 117 B5
Victoria Par.
Broadstairs CT10 .... 30 B4
Victoria Par.
Ramsgate CT11 .... 52 F7
Victoria Pk. Dover CT16 ... 166 E8
Victoria Pk. Herne Bay CT6 .. 23 A5
Victoria Pl.
Faversham ME13 .... 62 C7
Victoria Pl. Hythe CT21 ... 176 B4
Victoria Rd. Ashford TN23 . 139 B1
Victoria Rd.
Broadstairs CT10 .... 29 E6
Victoria Rd.
Canterbury CT1 .... 87 E7
Victoria Rd.
Capel-le-F CT18 .... 164 B1
Victoria Rd.
Chatham,Luton ME4 .... 10 B2
Victoria Rd. Chatham,
Walderslade ME5 .... 31 E3
Victoria Rd. Deal CT14 ..... 117 D5
Victoria Rd.
Folkestone CT20 .... 178 C5
Victoria Rd. Hythe CT21 ... 176 C1
Victoria Rd.
Kingsdown CT14 .... 134 C4
Victoria Rd.
Littlestone-on-S TN28 ..... 200 E5
Victoria Rd. Lydden CT9 .... 28 D4
Victoria Rd. Margate CT9 .... 7 J2
Victoria Rd.
Ramsgate CT11 .... 52 F7
Victoria Rd.
Sittingbourne ME10 .... 36 D4
Victoria Rd W. TN28 .... 200 E5
Victoria Road
Cty Prim Sch. TN23 .... 139 B1
Victoria Row. CT1 .... 67 A1
Victoria St. Dover CT17 ... 149 B1
Victoria St. Gillingham ME7 .. 10 D6
Victoria St.
Maidstone ME16 .... 74 E3

Victoria St.
New Romney TN28 .... 200 A6
Victoria St. Rochester ME2 .... 9 B7
Victoria St.
Rochester,Troy Town ME1 ... 9 D5
Victoria St. Sheerness ME12 .. 1 D1
Victoria St. Whitstable CT5 .. 20 D2
Victoria Terr. Minster ME12 ... 5 A5
Victoria Terr.
Rochester ME1 .... 9 A2
Victoria Terr.
Sittingbourne ME10 .... 36 D4
Victory Pk. ME2 .... 9 E7
Victory Rd. CT15 .... 133 F1
Victory St. ME12 .... 1 C2
Vidal Manor. ME7 .... 10 C5
Vigo Terr. ME9 .... 38 B1
Viking Cl. CT7 .... 26 D8
Viking Cl. Broadstairs CT10 . 30 B3
Viking Ct. Canterbury CT2 ... 66 F2
Viking Ct. Margate CT9 .... 8 A2
Village Way. TN26 .... 183 A7
Villas The. CT3 .... 47 A1
Villiers Cl. CT17 .... 166 C7
Villiers Ho. CT10 .... 30 B7
Villiers Rd. CT1 .... 67 D1
Vincent Cl.
Broadstairs CT10 .... 29 C3
Vincent Cl.
Folkestone CT20 .... 177 E5
Vincent Ct. ME12 .... 1 D1
Vincent Gdns. ME12 .... 1 D1
Vincent Rd.
Kit's Coty ME20 .... 53 C7
Vincent Rd. Lydden CT9 ... 28 C4
Vincent Rd.
Sittingbourne ME10 .... 37 C3
Vine Cl. CT11 .... 29 E2
Vine End. CT11 .... 29 E2
Vine Lands. TN29 .... 203 B6
Vineries The. ME7 .... 10 E5
Viners Cl. ME10 .... 36 F1
Vines La. ME1 .... 9 C5
Viney's Gdns. TN30 .... 167 C1
Vineyard Cres. ME8 .... 12 B1
Vinson Cl. ME13 .... 41 D1
Vinten Cl. CT6 .... 46 M8
Vinters Rd. ME14 .... 75 B4
Vinters Sch for Boys.
  ME14 .... 75 C4
Vintners Way. ME14 .... 75 E4
Violet Ave. CT12 .... 29 C2
Violet Cl. ME5 .... 54 A8
Virginia Rd.
  Gillingham ME7 .... 10 C7
Virginia Rd.
  Whitstable CT5 .... 44 A8
Vixen Cl. ME5 .... 32 C6
Vlissingen Dr. CT14 .... 117 C8
Volante Dr. ME10 .... 36 E7
Vulcan Cl. Chatham ME5 .... 32 B7
Vulcan Cl. Whitstable CT5 .. 43 C7

Wacher Cl. CT2 .... 66 F2
Waddenhall Farm. CT4 ..... 126 B6
Waddle Cnr. TN30 .... 189 D3
Wades Cl. TN29 .... 194 B4
Wadham Pl. ME10 .... 37 B2
Waghorn St. ME4 .... 10 B3
Wagoners Cl. ME14 .... 75 E4
Wain Ct. ME12 .... 4 A5
Wainwright Pl. TN24 .... 156 D8
Wake Rd. ME1 .... 31 C8
Wakefield Way. CT21 .... 176 B1
Wakefield Wlk. CT21 .... 176 D1
Wakehurst Cl. ME17 .... 96 B3
Wakeley
  Cty Jun Sch. ME8 .... 12 A1
Wakeley Rd. ME8 .... 12 A2
Wakeleys Cotts. ME8 .... 34 B8
Walcheren Cl. CT14 .... 117 C8
Waldens The. ME17 .... 99 E2
Waldershare Ave. CT13 ..... 95 A7
Waldershare Rd. CT15 ..... 132 A5
Walderslade
  Cty Prim Sch. ME5 .... 32 A3
Walderslade Girls Sch.
  ME5 .... 31 F5
Walderslade Rd. ME5 .... 31 F6
Walderslade Woods.
  Chatham ME5 .... 31 E2
Walderslade Woods.
  Chatham ME5 & ME14 ..... 54 B8
Waldron Dr. ME15 .... 96 F6
Waldron Rd. CT10 .... 30 B2
Walk The. ME17 .... 99 E2
Walker La. CT7 .... 26 D8
Walkers Outland
  (RSPB Reserve). TN28 .... 204 B1
Wall Rd. TN24 .... 139 B3
Wall The. ME10 .... 36 E5

Wallace Mews. CT19 .... 178 D7
Wallace Rd. ME1 .... 31 E8
Wallace Way. CT10 .... 29 E4
Wallbridge La. ME8 & ME9 .. 12 D3
Waller Rd. TN29 .... 204 E7
Wallers Rd. ME13 .... 62 A7
Wallis Ave. ME15 .... 97 E5
Wallis Rd. TN24 .... 139 D2
Wallwood Rd. CT11 .... 52 F8
Walmer Castle. CT14 .... 117 D1
Walmer Castle Rd. CT14 .. 117 C1
Walmer Ct. 3 ME14 .... 75 A5
Walmer Gdns.
  Cliffs End CT12 .... 51 D5
Walmer Gdns. Deal CT14 .. 117 A2
Walmer Gdns.
  Sittingbourne ME10 .... 36 D5
Walmer & Kingsdown
  Golf Links. CT14 .... 134 D2
Walmer Rd. CT5 .... 43 E8
Walmer Sch. CT14 .... 117 B2
Walmer Sta. CT14 .... 117 A1
Walmer Way. CT14 .... 117 A2
Walmsley Ho. 3 CT19 ..... 178 E6
Walmsley Rd. CT10 .... 29 F5
Walner Gdns. TN28 .... 200 B7
Walner La. TN28 .... 200 B7
Walnut Cl. Ashford TN24 ... 139 D6
Walnut Cl. Chatham ME5 .... 32 B8
Walnut Ridge. TN25 .... 173 A6
Walnut Tree Ave. ME15 ..... 97 A5
Walnut Tree Cotts. ME13 ... 84 E8
Walnut Tree Dr. ME10 .... 36 D4
Walnut Tree La.
  Loose ME15 .... 97 A5
Walnut Tree La.
  Westbere CT2 .... 68 D7
Walpole Rd. CT10 .... 7 J3
Walsby Dr. ME10 .... 37 A8
Walseley Terr. TN29 .... 203 C5
Walsham Rd. ME5 .... 31 F1
Walshaw Ho. 2 ME14 .... 75 A6
Walsingham Cl. ME8 .... 33 D3
Walsingham Ho. 3 ME14 .. 75 A6
Waltham Cl. CT19 .... 8 E2
Waltham Rd.
  Gillingham ME8 .... 11 C3
Waltham Rd.
  Waltham CT4 .... 108 F1
Walton Gdns. CT19 .... 178 D7
Walton Manor Cl. CT19 .... 178 D7
Walton Rd. CT10 .... 178 D6
Waltons The. CT19 .... 178 C8
Wanden La. TN27 .... 135 C8
Wanstall Ct. CT7 .... 27 A7
Wansted House Sch. CT9 ..... 8 A3
Wantsum Mews. CT13 .... 72 F1
Wantsum Way. CT7 .... 25 E3
Wantsume Lees. CT13 .... 72 E2
Warblers Cl. ME2 .... 9 A7
Warden Bay Rd. ME12 .... 6 A3
Warden Cl. ME16 .... 74 C4
Warden Ct. 10 CT17 .... 149 C1
Warden House
  Cty Prim Sch. CT14 .... 117 A5
Warden Rd. Rochester ME1 .. 9 C2
Warden Rd. Warden ME12 ..... 6 B5
Warden Terr. ME12 .... 5 A6
Warden View Gdns. ME12 .... 6 D1
Warden Way. ME12 .... 6 B5
Wardour Cl. CT10 .... 30 B4
Wards Hill Rd. ME12 .... 4 A9
Wardwell La. ME9 .... 13 C1
Ware St. ME14 .... 76 A5
Warehorne Rd. TN26 .... 183 A7
Warlingham Ct. ME8 .... 12 A1
Warmlake. ME17 .... 98 F1
Warmlake Est. ME17 .... 98 F1
Warmlake Rd. ME17 .... 98 C1
Warner St. ME4 .... 9 F3
Warnford Gdns. ME15 .... 97 A8
Warre Ave. CT11 .... 52 C5
Warren Cl.
  Folkestone CT19 .... 178 F6
Warren Cl.
  Sittingbourne ME10 .... 37 B2
Warren Dr. CT10 .... 29 E5
Warren Dr The. CT8 .... 27 D7
Warren Ho. TN27 .... 119 E8
Warren Hts. TN25 .... 158 E5
Warren La.
  Ashford TN23 & TN24 .... 139 A4
Warren La. Hartlip ME9 ...... 34 C3
Warren La. Lydden CT15 ... 147 D6
Warren Rd.
  Folkestone CT19 .... 178 F6
Warren Rd.
  Kit's Coty ME5 & ME20 .... 53 D7
Warren Rd.
  Littlestone-on-S TN28 .... 200 D6
Warren Rd.
  Warren Rd Pk. TN24 .... 139 B4

Warren St.
  Stalisfield Green TN27 ... 103 A3
Warren St.
  Warren Street ME17 .... 102 D7
Warren The.
  Brabourne Lees TN25 .... 158 E5
Warren The.
  Whitstable CT5 .... 43 C6
Warren View. TN23 .... 138 F4
Warren Way. CT19 .... 178 F6
Warren Wood
  Cty Prim Sch. ME1 .... 31 C8
Warren Wood Rd. ME1 .... 31 C7
Warten Rd. CT10 & CT11 .... 29 F1
Warwick Cres. ME14 .... 75 E5
Warwick Dr. CT11 .... 52 B5
Warwick Pl. ME16 .... 74 E3
Warwick Rd.
  Ashford TN24 .... 139 E5
Warwick Rd.
  Canterbury CT1 .... 88 C8
Warwick Rd. Deal CT14 .... 117 D2
Warwick Rd. Margate CT9 .... 8 B2
Warwick Rd.
  Whitstable CT5 .... 20 D2
Washford Farm Rd. TN23 . 155 E5
Washington Cl. 4 CT16 ... 149 B3
Washington La. TN29 .... 198 C6
Wass Dro. CT3 .... 71 B7
Wat Tyler Way. ME15 .... 75 A4
Watchester Ave. CT11 .... 52 C5
Watchester La. CT12 .... 50 B5
Water Farm. CT4 .... 144 F4
Water La. Bayfield ME13 ..... 61 B3
Water La. Canterbury CT1 .... 87 F2
Water La. 6
  Faversham ME13 .... 62 C7
Water La.
  Harrietsham ME17 .... 100 B5
Water La. Kingswood ME17 .. 99 F3
Water La. 4
  Maidstone ME15 .... 75 A4
Water La. Maidstone,
  Bearsted ME14 .... 76 E6
Water La. Smarden TN2 ... 135 A2
Water St. CT14 .... 117 D7
Watercress La. TN23 .... 155 F8
Waterditch La.
  ME17 & TN27 .... 102 E5
Waterfall Rd. TN26 .... 138 B6
Waterham Rd. ME13 .... 42 C1
Waterlock Cotts. CT3 .... 91 A7
Waterloo Cres.
  CT16 & CT17 .... 166 E7
Waterloo Hill. ME12 .... 4 D6
Waterloo Mansions. 12
  CT16 & CT17 .... 166 E7
Waterloo Pl. 8 CT11 .... 52 F7
Waterloo Rd.
  Folkestone CT20 .... 177 D5
Waterloo Rd.
  Gillingham ME7 .... 10 C4
Waterloo Rd.
  Sittingbourne ME10 .... 36 D5
Waterloo St. ME15 .... 75 A3
Waterloo Terr. ME12 .... 5 A5
Waterloo Rd. ME14 .... 75 A6
Waterman Ho. TN23 .... 156 B8
Watermead Cl. TN23 .... 155 E7
Watermeadow Cl. ME7 .... 32 F6
Watermill Cl.
  Maidstone ME16 .... 74 B5
Watermill Cl.
  Rochester ME2 .... 9 C8
Waters Edge. ME15 .... 74 F2
Waters Pl. ME7 .... 33 A6
Watersend. CT16 .... 148 D5
Waterside. TN24 .... 139 F1
Waterside Ct. 5 CT21 ...... 176 B2
Waterside Dr. CT8 .... 7 D1
Waterside La. ME7 .... 10 F7
Waterside View. ME12 .... 6 A4
Waterstone Pl. ME13 .... 62 A6
Waterworks Hill. CT15 ...... 133 B3
Waterworks La. CT15 .... 133 B3
Watery La. CT4 .... 109 C5
Watkin Rd. CT19 .... 178 C6
Watling Ave. ME5 .... 10 D2
Watling Pl. ME10 .... 37 A3
Watling St. Canterbury CT1 . 87 F8
Watling St.
  Chatham ME5 & ME7 .... 10 D2
Watling St.
  Gillingham ME5 & ME7 ..... 10 D2
Watson Ave. ME5 .... 31 D5
Watsons Cl. TN25 .... 139 C8
Watsons Hill. ME10 .... 36 C5
Wattle Cnr. TN30 .... 189 D3
Watts' Ave. ME1 .... 9 C4

Watts Cotts. TN24 .... 139 D7
Watts' St. ME4 .... 9 E3
Watts Yd. CT13 .... 72 F1
Wauchope Rd. CT5 .... 42 F6
Wave Crest. CT5 .... 20 C1
Waveney Ho. 7 ME15 .... 97 E8
Waverley Ave. ME12 .... 4 B7
Waverley Cl. Chatham ME5 .. 32 D2
Waverley Cl.
  Coxheath ME17 .... 96 C3
Waverley Rd. CT9 .... 28 C8
Way Farm Cotts. CT12 .... 50 E7
Way Hill. CT12 .... 50 E7
Wayborough Hill. CT12 ...... 50 D7
Wayfield
  Cty Prim Sch. ME5 .... 32 A7
Wayfield Rd. ME5 .... 32 A7
Wayne Cl. CT10 .... 29 E5
Wayside. TN30 .... 167 B2
Wayside Ave. TN30 .... 167 B3
Wayside Flats. TN30 .... 167 B2
Weald Cl. ME15 .... 97 C6
Weald Ct. ME10 .... 36 C3
Weald The. TN24 .... 139 C3
Wealden Ave. TN30 .... 167 B1
Wealden Ct. 5 ME4 .... 10 B3
Wealden Forest Pk.
  CT2 &CT6 .... 45 D4
Wealdhurst Pk. CT10 .... 29 D5
Wear Bay Cres. CT19 .... 178 F6
Wear Bay Rd. CT19 .... 178 F5
Weatherly Cl. ME1 .... 9 C4
Weatherly Dr. CT10 .... 29 F2
Weaving Cotts. ME14 .... 75 E3
Weavering St. ME14 .... 75 F4
Weavers The. ME16 .... 74 B5
Weavers Way.
  Ashford TN23 .... 155 E7
Weavers Way. Dover CT16 .. 149 A3
Webb Cl. CT19 .... 178 A7
Webster Rd. ME8 .... 11 F1
Weddington La. CT3 .... 71 E2
Wedgewood Cl. ME16 .... 74 B5
Wedgewood Dr. ME5 .... 32 A7
Weeds Wood Rd. ME5 .... 31 F4
Week St. ME14 .... 75 A4
Weeks Ct. ME11 .... 3 A6
Weighall Pl. CT11 .... 52 C7
Weighbridge Way. CT16 ... 166 M8
Welcombe Ct. ME8 .... 33 D8
Well Cl. CT2 .... 68 A6
Well La. Bayfield ME13 ...... 61 B3
Well La.
  Fordwich CT2 & CT3 .... 68 A3
Well La. St Margaret's
  at Cliffe CT15 .... 150 F6
Well Rd. Lyminge CT18 ... 161 C6
Well Rd. Maidstone ME14 ... 75 A5
Well Rd.
  Queenborough ME11 .... 3 A5
Well Rd. Rushenden ME11 .... 2 F3
Well St. ME15 & ME17 .... 96 E4
Well Winch Rd. ME10 .... 36 D5
Welland Ho. 8 ME15 .... 97 E8
Weller Ave. ME1 .... 9 C4
Wellesley Ave. CT14 .... 117 C3
Wellesley Cl.
  Broadstairs CT10 .... 29 E3
Wellesley Cl.
  Westgate-on-S CT8 .... 27 E7
Wellesley Rd.
  Ashford TN23 .... 139 C2
Wellesley Rd. Dover CT16 . 166 E7
Wellesley Rd. Margate CT9 .. 8 B1
Wellesley Rd.
  Sheerness ME12 .... 1 E2
Wellesley Rd.
  Westgate-on-S CT8 .... 27 E7
Wellfield Rd. CT20 .... 178 A5
Wellington Cl. CT8 .... 7 C1
Wellington Cres. CT11 .... 52 F6
Wellington Ct. CT14 .... 117 D7
Wellington Gdns. 2
  Dover CT16 .... 149 B3
Wellington Gdns.
  Margate CT9 .... 7 J3
Wellington Ho. 6 ME15 ..... 97 E5
Wellington Par.
  Kingsdown CT14 .... 134 D7
Wellington Par.
  Kingsdown CT14 .... 134 C6
Wellington Pl.
  Folkestone CT20 .... 177 D3
Wellington Pl.
  Maidstone ME14 .... 74 F6
Wellington Rd. Deal CT14 . 117 D5
Wellington Rd.
  Folkestone CT20 .... 177 D5
Wellington Rd.
  Gillingham ME7 .... 10 C4

Wellington Rd. Lydden CT9 . 28 D4
Wellington Rd.
  Sittingbourne ME10 .... 36 B5
Wellington Rd.
  Temple Ewell CT16 .... 148 D5
Wellington Rd.
  Westgate-on-S CT8 .... 27 E7
Wellington St. CT5 .... 43 D5
Wellington St. CT5 .... 43 D5
Wellington Terr. CT20 ...... 177 D3
Wellis Gdns. CT9 .... 7 G1
Wells Ave. CT1 .... 88 B7
Wells Cl.
  New Romney TN28 .... 200 C6
Wells Cl. Tenterden TN30 .. 179 B8
Wells Ho. ME10 .... 37 B4
Wells Rd. CT19 .... 177 F6
Wells Way. ME13 .... 40 B1
Welsdene Rd. CT9 .... 28 B8
Welson Rd. CT20 .... 178 A5
Wemmick Cl. ME1 .... 31 D7
Wemyss Cl. **13** CT1 .... 67 B2
Wemyss Ho. **14** CT1 .... 67 B2
Wemyss Way. CT1 .... 67 C1
Wenham's La. TN29 .... 192 E2
Wents Wood. ME14 .... 75 F5
Wentworth Ave. CT9 .... 7 E1
Wentworth Cl. CT18 .... 161 C6
Wentworth Dr.
  Gillingham ME8 .... 33 E7
Wentworth Dr.
  Ramsgate CT12 .... 29 A1
Wentworth Dr.
  Sittingbourne ME10 .... 36 C5
Wentworth Gdns. CT6 .... 22 C2
Wentworth Ho. ME10 .... 36 C5
Wesley Terr. CT18 .... 161 C7
West Beach. CT5 .... 20 C1
West Borough
  Cty Prim Sch. ME16 .... 74 B3
West Cliff. CT5 .... 20 D1
West Cliff Arc. **8** CT11 ...... 52 E6
West Cliff Ave. CT10 .... 30 B3
West Cliff Dr. CT6 .... 22 B4
West Cliff Gdns.
  Folkestone CT20 .... 178 D4
West Cliff Gdns.
  Herne Bay CT6 .... 22 B4
West Cliff Prom. CT11 .... 52 D5
West Cliff Rd.
  Broadstairs CT10 .... 30 B3
West Cliff Rd.
  Ramsgate CT11 .... 52 D6
West Cliff Terr. CT11 .... 52 B5
West Dr. ME5 .... 31 D5
West Dumpton La.
  CT10 & CT11 .... 29 E1
West End. TN26 .... 168 F3
West End Cotts. ME9 .... 80 D7
West Gn. ME10 .... 14 F1
West Hill Rd. CT6 .... 22 C5
West Hythe Rd. CT21 .... 187 A8
West La. Sheerness ME12 ..... 1 B2
West La.
  Sittingbourne ME10 .... 37 A4
West Lane Trad Est. ME10 .. 37 A4
West Lawn Gdns. CT20 ..... 177 D3
West Lea. CT14 .... 117 C7
West Minster
  Cty Prim Sch. ME12 .... 3 B8
West Norman Rd. CT16 ..... 166 E8
West Par. CT21 .... 176 B1
West Park Ave. CT9 .... 8 D1
West Park Farm North
  Ret Pk. CT19 .... 178 B8
West Park Rd. ME15 .... 75 B2
West Pas. ME12 .... 1 B2
West Pl. TN29 .... 197 D8
West Ramp. CT16 .... 166 G8
West Rd. Folkestone CT20 .. 177 C4
West Rd. Gillingham ME4 ... 10 A7
West Rd. Sandwich CT12 ...... 51 A1
West Ridge. ME10 .... 36 D3
West Rise. CT12 .... 29 B1
West Side. CT15 .... 133 A1
West St. Ashford TN23 ...... 139 B2
West St. Deal CT14 .... 117 D6
West St. Dover CT17 .... 166 C8
West St. Faversham ME13 .. 62 C7
West St. Gillingham ME7 .... 10 B6
West St.
  Harrietsham ME17 .... 100 C6
West St. Hothfield TN26 .... 137 F7
West St. Lenham ME17 .... 99 F2
West St.
  New Romney TN28 .... 200 A6
West St.
  Queenborough ME11 .... 2 F5
West St. Sheerness ME12 ..... 1 B2
West St.
  Sittingbourne ME10 .... 36 E4

West Street Cotts. CT13 ...... 94 A1
West Terr. CT20 .... 178 D4
West View. CT19 .... 178 D8
West View Cl. CT6 .... 22 C2
West Wlk. ME16 .... 74 B3
West Wood Rd. ME9 .... 56 B8
Westbere La. CT2 .... 68 B7
Westbourne. TN23 .... 155 D6
Westbourne Gdns. CT20 .. 178 B4
Westbourne St. ME10 .... 36 E4
Westbrook Ave. CT9 .... 7 F1
Westbrook Cotts. CT9 .... 7 G1
Westbrook Gdns. CT9 .... 7 G1
Westbrook House Sch.
  CT20 .... 178 B5
Westbrook La. CT6 .... 22 B3
Westbrook Prom. CT9 .... 7 G2
Westbrook Rd. CT9 .... 7 G2
Westbrook Wlk. **8** ME13 ... 62 C7
Westbrooke Cl. ME10 .... 10 A2
Westbury Cres. CT17 .... 166 B6
Westbury Hts. CT17 .... 166 B6
Westbury Rd. Dover CT17 .. 166 B6
Westbury Rd.
  Westgate-on-S CT8 .... 27 E8
Westcliff Dr. ME12 .... 4 D8
Westcliff Gdns. CT9 .... 7 F1
Westcliff Ho. **4** CT20 ..... 178 D4
Westcliff Rd. CT9 .... 7 G1
Westcourt La. CT15 .... 130 C5
Westcourt Rd. ME4 .... 10 A6
Westdean Cl. CT17 .... 148 E2
Westenhanger Sta. TN25 .. 175 B7
Western Cl.
  Broadstairs CT10 .... 8 F1
Western Cl.
  Canterbury CT2 .... 67 A4
Western Cl.
  Gillingham ME8 .... 11 B3
Western Rd. Margate CT9 .... 8 C2
Western Ave. CT14 .... 117 C4
Westerhout Rd. CT14 .... 117 C4
Western Ave.
  Ashford TN23 .... 139 A3
Western Ave. Bridge CT4 ... 89 A1
Western Ave.
  Halfway Houses ME12 .... 3 D6
Western Ave.
  Herne Bay CT6 .... 22 E4
Western Cl. CT17 .... 166 C6
Western Espl.
  Broadstairs CT10 .... 8 F1
Western Espl.
  Herne Bay CT6 .... 22 C5
Western Gdns. TN24 .... 156 E8
Western Heights Rdbt.
  CT17 .... 166 C5
Western Ho. CT14 .... 117 C7
Western Link. ME13 .... 62 A8
Western Rd. Deal CT14 .... 117 C7
Western Rd.
  Maidstone ME16 .... 74 C2
Western Rd. Margate CT9 .... 29 C8
Western Service Rd.
  CT16 .... 166 G8
Western Undercliff. CT11 ... 52 C5
Westfield. CT2 .... 66 A6
Westfield Bsns Ctr. ME2 .... 9 C7
Westfield Cotts. ME9 .... 13 A2
Westfield La. CT18 .... 161 C3
Westfield Rd.
  Birchington CT7 .... 27 A7
Westfield Rd. Margate CT9 .. 28 A8
Westfield Sole Rd. ME14 .... 54 D8
Westfields. TN27 .... 136 D8
Westgate Ave. CT7 .... 28 A4
Westgate Bay Ave.
  CT8 & CT9 .... 7 C1
Westgate & Birchington
  Golf Course. CT8 .... 27 C8
Westgate Cl. CT2 .... 66 C1
Westgate Court Ave. CT2 .. 66 D1
Westgate Garden Flats.
  CT2 .... 87 E8
Westgate Gr. CT2 .... 66 F1
Westgate Hall Rd. **3**
  CT1 & CT2 .... 66 F1
Westgate Rd. ME13 .... 62 A8
Westgate Terr. CT5 .... 20 E2
Westgate-on-Sea Sta. CT8 . 27 E8
Westlands Ave. ME10 .... 36 B4
Westlands High Sch The.
  ME10 .... 36 B4
Westlands Rd. CT6 .... 22 C5
Westleigh Rd. CT18 .... 27 D8
Westmarsh Cl. ME15 .... 97 F7
Westmarsh Dr. TN23 .... 8 E2
Westmeads Cty Inf Sch.
  CT5 .... 20 E2
Westmeads Rd. CT5 .... 20 E2
Westminster Rd. CT1 .... 67 C4

Westminster Wlk. CT12 .... 29 C1
Westmoors. TN23 .... 155 E6
Westmoreland Dr. ME9 .... 13 C3
Westmorland Cl. ME15 .... 97 E7
Westmorland Gn. ME15 ..... 97 E7
Westmorland Rd. ME15 ..... 97 E7
Westmount Ave. ME4 .... 9 F5
Westmount Ho. **4** CT9 ..... 8 B2
Weston Rd. ME2 .... 9 A8
Westonville Ave. CT9 .... 7 F1
Westover Gdns. CT10 .... 29 E7
Westover Rd. CT10 .... 29 E6
Westree Rd. ME16 .... 74 E3
Westway. ME17 .... 96 C3
Westwell La.
  Charing TN25 & TN27 ..... 120 F5
Westwell La. Potters Corner
  TN24 & TN25 .... 138 E7
Westwell La.
  Westwell TN25 .... 121 B4
Westwood Ind Est. CT19 ..... 29 A6
Westwood Pl. ME13 .... 62 D5
Westwood Rd.
  Broadstairs CT10 .... 29 C4
Westwood Rd.
  Maidstone ME15 .... 97 A7
Wetheral Dr. ME5 .... 32 B4
Wey Cl. ME5 .... 32 C5
Wey St. TN26 .... 183 D3
Weybridge Cl. ME5 .... 32 C4
Weyburn Dr. CT12 .... 29 A1
Weyhill Cl. ME14 .... 75 C6
Weymouth Cl. CT19 .... 177 D7
Weymouth Rd. CT19 .... 177 D6
Weymouth Terr. CT19 .... 177 D7
Wharf Rd. Gillingham ME7 .. 10 C7
Wharf Rd.
  Maidstone ME15 .... 74 F2
Wharfedale Rd. CT9 .... 8 A1
Wharton Gdns. TN24 .... 156 E8
Whatman Cl. ME14 .... 75 C6
Whatmer Cl. CT2 .... 68 A6
Wheatcroft Cl. ME10 .... 37 B4
Wheatcroft Gr. ME8 .... 33 F7
Wheatear Way. ME5 .... 32 B7
Wheatfields.
  Chatham ME5 .... 32 D2
Wheatfields.
  Maidstone ME14 .... 75 D4
Wheatley Rd.
  Ramsgate CT12 .... 29 C1
Wheatley Rd.
  Whitstable CT5 .... 20 E2
Wheatsheaf Cl.
  Boughton Street ME13 .... 64 A3
Wheatsheaf Cl.
  Maidstone ME15 .... 97 B8
Wheatsheaf Gdns. ME12 ...... 1 C2
Wheeler St. ME14 .... 75 A5
Wheelers The. ME8 .... 33 B6
Wheelwrights Way. CT13 .. 93 B2
Wheler Rd. TN27 .... 120 C8
Whewell Terr. **1** CT20 .... 178 E5
Whiffen's Ave. ME4 .... 9 F5
Whiffen's Ave W. ME4 .... 9 F5
Whigham Cl. TN23 .... 155 D7
Whimbrel Ho. ME10 .... 36 F8
Whimbrel Wlk. ME5 .... 32 C1
Whinfell Ave. CT11 .... 51 F7
Whiteless Rd. CT17 .... 166 A8
Whiston Ave. TN26 .... 153 C4
Whitby Rd. CT10 .... 177 D6
Whitchurch Cl. ME16 .... 74 F4
Whitcombe Cl. ME5 .... 110 A8
White Acre Dr. CT14 .... 134 B8
White Cliffs. **11** CT20 ..... 178 E4
White Cliffs Bsns Pk.
  CT16 .... 149 A6
White Cl. **8** CT20 .... 177 E3
White Hart Mansions. CT9 .. 7 J3
White Hill. Boughton Aluph
  TN25 & CT4 .... 122 B6
White Hill. Chailock TN25 .. 105 E1
White Hill Rd. ME14 .... 33 D1
White Horse La. **6**
  Canterbury CT1 .... 87 F8
White Horse La.
  Otham Hole ME15 .... 98 A6
White Horse La.
  Rhodes Minnis CT4 .... 144 A3
White House Farm Ct.
  CT15 .... 113 E5
White Marsh Ct. CT5 .... 20 F2
White Mill Folk Mus. CT13 .. 72 E2
White Post. ME17 .... 78 B3
White Post Gdns. CT3 .... 71 F1
White Rd. ME4 .... 10 A2
White Rock Ct. ME16 .... 74 E3
White Rock Pl. **5** ME16 .. 74 E3
White Wood Rd. CT13 .... 93 B1

Whiteacre La. CT4 .... 125 E4
Whitebeam Dr. ME17 .... 96 B3
Whitecliff Way. CT19 .... 178 F6
Whitefriars Meadow. CT13 . 94 A8
Whitefriars Way. CT13 ...... 72 F1
Whitehall. TN29 .... 199 F8
Whitehall Bridge Rd. CT2 .. 87 E8
Whitehall Cl. CT2 .... 87 E8
Whitehall Dr. ME17 .... 99 D3
Whitehall Gdns. CT2 .... 66 E1
Whitehall Rd.
  Broad Street ME14 .... 77 A6
Whitehall Rd.
  Canterbury CT2 .... 87 D7
Whitehall Rd.
  Canterbury CT2 .... 87 E8
Whitehall Rd.
  Ramsgate CT12 .... 29 C1
Whitehall Rd.
  Sittingbourne ME10 .... 36 E2
Whitehall Way. TN25 .... 159 D1
Whiteheads La. ME14 .... 76 B4
Whitehorse Hill. ME41 .... 103 B3
Whitehouse Cres. ME1 ...... 53 A8
Whitehouse Dro.
  CT13 & CT3 .... 72 D7
Whitelocks Cl. CT14 .... 111 D3
Whitenbrook. CT21 .... 177 B2
Whiterow Gn. CT10 .... 8 F1
Whiteness Rd. CT10 .... 8 G2
Whites Hill. CT14 .... 115 B2
Whitewall Ctr. ME2 .... 9 D8
Whitewall Rd. ME2 .... 9 D8
Whitewall Way. ME2 .... 9 D7
Whiteway Rd. ME11 .... 2 F6
Whitfeld Rd. TN23 .... 156 B8
Whitfield Ave.
  Broadstairs CT10 .... 29 E7
Whitfield Ave. Dover CT16 . 149 B2
Whitfield Cotts. TN23 ...... 156 B8
Whitfield
  Cty Prim Sch. CT16 .... 149 A7
Whitfield Hill.
  Temple Ewell CT16 .... 148 F4
Whitfield Hill.
  Whitfield CT16 .... 148 F5
Whitfield Rdbt. CT16 .... 149 A6
Whitgift Cl. CT2 .... 66 D1
Whiting Cres. ME13 .... 62 A8
Whiting Ho. TN29 .... 203 C5
Whitmore St. ME16 .... 74 D2
Whitstable
  Cty Jun Sch. CT5 .... 20 D1
Whitstable Rd.
  Canterbury CT2 .... 66 D2
Whitstable Rd.
  Faversham ME13 .... 62 E7
Whitstable Rd. Faversham,
  Goodnestone ME13 .... 63 B6
Whitstable Rd.
  Herne Bay CT6 & CT6 ...... 21 F3
Whitstable Rd.
  Herne Bay, Studd Hill CT6 .. 22 B3
Whitstable Rd.
  Rough Common CT2 .... 66 B4
Whitstable & Seasalter
  Endowed CE Jun Sch.
  CT5 .... 20 D1
Whitstable & Tankerton
  Hospl. CT5 .... 21 A2
Whitstable & Tankerton
  Sta. CT5 .... 20 E1
Whittaker St. ME4 .... 10 A4
Whittington Terr. CT15 ..... 130 D4
Whybornes Chase. ME12 ...... 4 C7
Whyman Ave. ME4 .... 10 A3
Whytecliffs. CT10 .... 30 A2
Wichling Cl. CT2 .... 67 A3
Wick La. CT4 .... 129 E7
Wicken Ho. ME16 .... 74 E4
Wicken La. TN25 & TN27 .. 120 E6
Wickenden Cres. TN24 .... 157 A8
Wickets The. TN24 .... 156 F7
Wickham Ave. CT11 .... 52 G8
Wickham Cl. ME9 .... 35 B6
Wickham Court La. CT3 .... 69 B3
Wickham La. CT3 .... 69 B1
Wickham Mill. CT3 .... 69 C2
Wickham Pl. ME17 .... 101 D5
Wickham Rd. CT3 .... 69 B2
Wickham St. ME1 .... 9 D3
Wickhambreaux
  CE Prim Sch. CT3 .... 69 C2
Widred Rd. CT17 .... 166 C8
Wierton La. ME17 .... 97 E1
Wife Of Bath Hill. CT2 .... 87 C8
Wigmore La. CT15 .... 131 C8
Wigmore Rd.
  Gillingham ME8 .... 33 B4
Wigmore Rd.
  Gillingham ME8 .... 33 B5

Wigwam Paddocks. CT7 ..... 27 A8
Wihtred Rd. ME9 .... 37 D2
Wilberforce Rd.
  Coxheath ME17 .... 96 D3
Wilberforce Rd.
  Folkestone CT20 .... 177 E3
Wilbrough Rd. CT7 .... 27 A7
Wilcox Cl. CT3 .... 112 D5
Wilderness Hill. CT9 .... 8 A2
Wildfell Cl. ME14 .... 54 C8
Wildish Rd. ME13 .... 62 B8
Wildman Cl. ME8 .... 33 D3
Wildwood Cl. ME17 .... 99 E2
Wildwood Glade. ME7 .... 33 B4
Wildwood Rd. CT2 .... 67 F6
Wiles Ave. TN28 .... 200 B6
Wiles Ho. TN28 .... 200 B6
Wilfred Rd. CT11 .... 52 C8
Wilgate Green Rd. ME13 .... 82 F6
Wilkes Rd. CT10 .... 29 E4
Wilkie Rd. CT7 .... 27 A8
Will Adams Ct. ME7 .... 10 C6
Will Adams Way. ME7 .... 10 F1
Willement Rd. ME13 .... 62 B7
Willesborough Ct. TN24 ... 140 A2
Willesborough
  Cty Inf Sch. TN24 .... 157 A8
Willesborough Ind Pk.
  TN24 .... 140 A1
Willesborough Rd. TN24 .. 139 F4
Willetts Hill. CT12 .... 49 D7
William Ave.
  Folkestone CT19 .... 178 B7
William Ave. Margate CT9 .. 29 C8
William Gibbs Ct. **14**
  ME13 .... 62 D7
William Harvey
  Hospl The. TN24 .... 140 C1
William Judge Cl. TN30 ... 179 D7
William Pitt Ave. CT14 ..... 117 B6
William Pitt Cl. CT21 .... 176 D2
William Rd. TN23 .... 156 B8
William St.
  Faversham ME13 .... 62 D7
William St. Gillingham ME8 . 12 A1
William St. Herne Bay CT6 . 22 F5
William St.
  Sittingbourne ME10 .... 36 E4
William St. Whitstable CT5 . 20 D2
Williamson Rd. TN29 .... 204 E5
Willington Dr. TN23 .... 155 E5
Willington Pl. CT14 .... 117 C1
Willington Gn. ME15 .... 97 E7
Willington St. ME15 .... 75 F2
Willis Cl. ME12 .... 3 F5
Willis Ho. ME1 .... 9 C4
Willop Cl. TN29 .... 186 F3
Willop Way. TN29 .... 186 F3
Willoughby Ct. **11** CT1 .. 87 F8
Willow Ave.
  Broadstairs CT10 .... 29 D4
Willow Ave.
  Faversham ME13 .... 62 A7
Willow Cl. Canterbury CT2 . 67 A2
Willow Cl. Hythe CT21 ...... 175 E1
Willow Cl. Margate CT9 .... 8 C2
Willow Ct.
  Broadstairs CT10 .... 30 A5
Willow Ct. Folkestone CT20 177 E4
Willow Dr.
  Hamstreet TN26 .... 183 A7
Willow Dr.
  St Mary's Bay TN29 .... 194 F3
Willow Ho. **2**
  Chatham ME5 .... 31 F5
Willow Ho.
  Sheerness ME12 .... 1 C2
Willow Ho.
  Sittingbourne ME10 .... 37 B3
Willow Rd.
  Great Mongeham CT14 ... 116 C3
Willow Rd. Whitstable CT5 . 43 C5
Willow Rise. ME15 .... 75 F1
Willow Tree Cl.
  Ashford TN24 .... 139 F1
Willow Tree Cl.
  Herne Bay CT6 .... 23 D5
Willow Way.
  Maidstone ME15 .... 75 B3
Willow Way. Margate CT9 .. 28 C8
Willow Way.
  Whitstable CT5 .... 44 C8
Willowbank Cl. TN29 .... 195 A4
Willowby Gdns. ME8 .... 33 E4
Willows Cl. CT2 .... 66 C4
Willows The.
  Gillingham ME8 .... 11 E2

Willows The.
Newington ME9 .... 35 B6
Willows The.
Sheerness ME12 .... 1 I1
Willows The.
Sittingbourne ME10 .... 14 F1
Willson's Rd. CT11 .... 52 D6
Wilmecote Ct. ME8 .... 33 D8
Wilmington Way. ME8 .... 11 B2
Wilmott Pl. CT13 .... 93 B2
Wilson Ave. Chatham ME1 ... 31 E7
Wilson Ave. Deal CT14 ...... 116 F4
Wilson Cl. Ashford TN24 ... 140 A1
Wilson Cl.
Maidstone ME15 .... 97 E7
Wilsons La. ME15 .... 96 A5
Wiltie Gdns. CT19 .... 178 C5
Wilton Cl. CT14 .... 117 C5
Wilton Rd.
Folkestone CT19 .... 178 B6
Wilton Rd. Margate CT12 ... 28 F1
Wilton Terr. ME10 .... 36 B5
Wiltshire Cl. ME5 .... 32 C8
Wiltshire Way. ME15 .... 97 E8
Wimborne Pl. CT12 .... 52 B8
Wimbourne Dr. ME8 .... 33 D6
Win Pine Ho. CT21 .... 176 A1
Winant Way. CT16 .... 149 B3
Wincheap. CT1 .... 87 E7
Wincheap Gn. ◪ CT1 .... 87 F7
Wincheap Ind Est. CT1 ...... 87 D7
Wincheap Prim Sch. CT1 ... 87 E6
Winchelsea Ct. CT17 .... 166 C7
Winchelsea Rd.
Chatham ME5 .... 32 B5
Winchelsea Rd.
Dover CT11 .... 166 B7
Winchelsea St. CT17 .... 166 B7
Winchelsea Terr. CT17 ..... 166 B7
Winchester Ave. ME5 .... 31 F4
Winchester Gdns. CT1 ...... 88 A6
Winchester Ho. ◪ ME15 .... 97 D7
Winchester Pl. ◪ ME14 ..... 75 A5
Winchester Way. ME8 .... 34 A8
Wind Hill. TN27 .... 119 E7
Wind Hill La. TN27 .... 119 E7
Windermere. ME13 .... 62 E6
Windermere Ave. CT11 ..... 52 A7
Windermere Ct. TN24 ...... 139 C4
Windermere Dr. ME8 .... 33 D7
Windermere Gdns. CT3 .... 112 F6
Windermere Gr. ME10 .... 36 D3
Winding Hill. ME13 .... 83 F6
Windmill Ave. CT12 .... 29 B3
Windmill Cl.
Ashford TN24 .... 140 A1
Windmill Cl. Bridge CT4 .... 89 A1
Windmill Cl.
Canterbury CT1 .... 88 C8
Windmill Cl.
Herne Bay CT6 .... 23 A2
Windmill Cl. Boughton
Monchelsea ME17 .... 97 B3
Windmill Cl.
Whitstable CT5 .... 43 C7
Windmill Hill. ME17 .... 100 B1
Windmill Hts. ME14 .... 76 B4
Windmill Quay Rd. ME12 ... 4 E2
Windmill Rd.
Canterbury CT1 .... 88 C8
Windmill Rd.
Gillingham ME7 .... 10 C4
Windmill Rd.
Herne Bay CT6 .... 23 A2
Windmill Rd.
Sittingbourne ME10 .... 36 D6
Windmill Rd.
Whitstable CT5 .... 43 D7
Windmill Rise. ME12 .... 4 E6
Windmill Row. ME17 .... 98 D2
Windmill St. CT21 .... 176 B1
Windmill View. CT9 .... 29 A8
Windmill Wlk. CT12 .... 29 B1
Windsor Ave.
Chatham ME4 .... 9 F2
Windsor Ave. Margate CT9 ... 8 B1

Windsor Cl.
Broadstairs CT10 .... 29 E5
Windsor Cl.
Maidstone ME14 .... 75 B6
Windsor Cl. Deal CT14 ..... 117 C2
Windsor Ct. Margate CT9 .... 8 B1
Windsor Dr. ME10 .... 36 D2
Windsor Gdns.
Herne Bay CT6 .... 22 B3
Windsor Gdns.
Warden ME12 .... 6 D4
Windsor Ho. Deal CT14 .... 117 A5
Windsor Ho. ◪
Dover CT17 .... 166 D7
Windsor Ho.
Whitstable CT5 .... 20 D1
Windsor Mews. ◪
Margate CT9 .... 7 J2
Windsor Mews.
New Romney TN28 .... 200 C8
Windsor Rd.
Canterbury CT1 .... 87 C6
Windsor Rd. Cliffs End CT12 51 D7
Windsor Rd.
Gillingham ME7 .... 10 D5
Windward Rd. ME1 .... 9 C1
Windyridge. ME7 .... 10 E1
Winehouse La. CT18 .... 164 D3
Wineycock. ME9 .... 81 C8
Wing Ho. ME12 .... 6 H1
Wing Rd. ME12 .... 6 H1
Wingate Rd. CT19 .... 178 D7
Wingham Bird Pk. CT3 ...... 70 C1
Wingham Cl.
Gillingham ME8 .... 11 C3
Wingham Cl.
Maidstone ME15 .... 97 F7
Wingham Cty Prim Sch.
CT3 .... 91 A7
Wingham Rd. CT3 .... 90 D8
Wingrove Dr.
Rochester ME2 .... 9 C8
Wingrove Hill. CT17 .... 148 E2
Wings Ct. CT10 .... 30 B5
Winifred Ave. CT12 .... 29 C2
Winifred Rd. ME15 .... 75 F3
Winnipeg Cl. CT16 .... 149 C3
Winstanley Cres. CT11 ...... 52 D8
Winstanley Rd. ME12 .... 1 D2
Winston Cl. CT1 .... 88 C7
Winston Ct. CT7 .... 27 A8
Winston Gdns. CT6 .... 23 D4
Winston Ho. ◪ CT20 .... 177 F5
Winterage La. CT18 .... 162 C7
Winterstoke Cres. CT11 .... 52 G8
Winterstoke Way. CT11 .... 52 F8
Winton Way. TN29 .... 195 A5
Wirrals The. ME5 .... 32 A4
Wises La. ME10 & ME9 ...... 36 A4
Wish The. TN26 .... 181 F6
Wissenden La. TN26 .... 153 B6
Withersdane Cotts. TN25 . 124 A2
Witley Wlk. CT16 .... 149 B7
Wittersham CE
(VA) Prim Sch. TN30 ..... 188 D2
Wittersham Cl. ME5 .... 32 B5
Wittersham Rd.
Stone in Oxney TN30 ...... 189 C3
Wittersham Rd.
Wittersham TN30 .... 188 C5
Wivenhoe. TN23 .... 155 E5
Wivenhoe Cl. ME8 .... 12 A2
Wolfe Rd. ME16 .... 74 B2
Wollaston Cl. ME8 .... 33 D3
Wollaston Rd. CT14 .... 117 D4
Wolmer Way. ◪ CT20 ...... 177 F5
Wolseley Ave. CT6 .... 22 A4
Wolseley Pl. ◪ TN24 .... 139 B3
Wood Ave. CT19 .... 178 E7
Wood Cottage La. CT19 ... 177 D7
Wood Hill. CT2 .... 66 E6
Wood Rd. CT21 .... 176 B1
Wood St. Dover CT16 ...... 166 D8
Wood St. Gillingham ME7 ... 10 A6
Wood St. Lynsted ME9 ...... 59 F8
Wood St. Sheerness ME12 ... 1 D2
Wood View. CT3 .... 46 E5

Wood Yd. CT14 .... 117 D6
Wood's Pl. CT17 .... 149 B2
Woodberry Dr. ME10 .... 37 C3
Woodbridge Dr. ME15 .... 74 F1
Woodbrook. TN27 .... 120 D7
Woodbury La. TN30 .... 179 A7
Woodbury Rd. ME5 .... 31 F1
Woodchurch
CE Prim Sch. TN26 .... 169 A2
Woodchurch Cl. ME5 .... 32 B5
Woodchurch Cres. ME8 ..... 11 C2
Woodchurch Rd.
Appledore TN26 & TN30 ... 181 C4
Woodchurch Rd.
Margate CT7 & CT9 .... 28 A5
Woodchurch Rd.
Shadoxhurst TN26 .... 155 A1
Woodchurch Rd.
Tenterden TN30 .... 179 D8
Woodchurch Rd.
Westgate-on-S CT12 & CT7 27 F3
Woodcock Gdns. CT18 ..... 163 A4
Woodcote. CT5 .... 21 D1
Woodcourt Cl. ME10 .... 36 E2
Woodcut. ME14 .... 75 A8
Woodfield Ave. CT19 .... 177 E7
Woodfield Cl. CT19 .... 177 E7
Woodford Ave.
CT11 & CT12 .... 29 D1
Woodford Ct. CT7 .... 27 A7
Woodford Rd. ME16 .... 74 B2
Woodgate. CT4 .... 110 E3
Woodgate Cl. ME13 .... 62 C8
Woodgate Cl. ME13 .... 84 E7
Woodgate La. ME9 .... 35 C2
Woodhall Terr. ME11 .... 3 A5
Woodhurst. ME5 .... 31 D4

Woodland Ave.
Aylesham CT3 .... 112 E5
Woodland Ave.
Birchington CT7 .... 27 B6
Woodland Cl. CT17 .... 148 E2
Woodland Cotts. CT18 ..... 161 B7
Woodland Dr. ME12 .... 4 A7
Woodland Rd.
Herne Bay CT6 .... 22 B2
Woodland Rd.
Lyminge CT18 & TN25 .... 160 E8
Woodland View. TN30 ..... 188 E4
Woodland Way.
Broadstairs CT10 .... 8 G1
Woodland Way.
Canterbury CT2 .... 66 D4
Woodland Way.
Dymchurch TN29 .... 187 A5
Woodland Way.
Maidstone ME14 .... 75 B7
Woodland Way.
Woodnesborough CT13 ...... 93 C6
Woodlands. Blean CT2 ...... 64 B5
Woodlands. Chatham ME5 ... 32 A2
Woodlands.
Coxheath ME17 .... 96 B3
Woodlands. Hernhill ME13 ... 64 E7
Woodlands Cl. ME14 .... 75 B7
Woodlands
Cty Prim Sch. ME7 .... 10 F4
Woodlands Dr. CT21 .... 177 A4
Woodlands High Sch. ME7 . 10 F4
Woodlands Rd.
Adisham CT3 .... 112 C8
Woodlands Rd.
Ashford TN24 .... 139 F2
Woodlands Rd.
Gillingham ME7 .... 10 F4
Woodlands Rd.
Sittingbourne ME10 .... 37 B3
Woodlawn St. CT5 .... 20 D2
Woodlea. TN24 .... 139 C3
Woodman Ave. CT5 .... 21 E3
Woodnesborough La. CT13 93 B3
Woodnesborough Rd.
CT13 .... 93 E7
Woodpecker Glade. ME8 .... 33 D6
Woodrow Chase. CT6 .... 23 A1
Woodruff Cl. ME8 .... 12 D4
Woods Hill. CT4 .... 125 C5
Woods Ley. CT3 .... 71 D2

Woodshale Cotts. ME9 ...... 14 D1
Woodside. Ashford TN23 ... 155 E6
Woodside. Boughton
Street ME13 .... 64 B2
Woodside. Gillingham ME8 ... 33 C6
Woodside Ave. CT14 .... 86 D2
Woodside Cl. CT16 .... 148 E4
Woodside Gdns. ME10 ...... 36 D2
Woodside Rd.
Maidstone ME15 .... 97 C7
Woodside Rd. Sturry CT2 ... 67 F7
Woodstock Rd. Deal CT14 . 117 C4
Woodstock Rd.
Rochester ME2 .... 9 A7
Woodstock Rd.
Sittingbourne ME10 .... 36 E1
Woodstock Way. TN24 .... 139 C6
Woodvale Ave. CT5 .... 44 C8
Woodville Cl. CT1 .... 87 D6
Woodville Rd.
Maidstone ME15 .... 75 A2
Woodville Rd.
Ramsgate CT12 .... 29 C1
Woolaston Cl. ME15 .... 74 F1
Woolcomber St. CT16 ..... 166 E7
Wooldeys Rd. ME8 .... 11 F2
Woolett Rd. ME10 .... 36 C5
Woollets Cl. CT6 .... 22 C3
Woollett St. ME14 .... 75 A5
Woolley Rd. ME15 .... 97 F7
Woolmer Dr. TN24 .... 157 A7
Woolpack Hill. TN25 .... 158 D5
Woolreeds Rd. TN23 .... 156 A7
Woolwich Cl. ME5 .... 32 A7
Wootton Gn. ME8 .... 11 D3
Wootton La. CT15 & CT4 . 146 D7
Wopsle Cl. ME14 .... 31 D7

Worcester Cl.
Faversham ME13 .... 62 E6
Worcester Cl. Minster ME12 . 4 C6
Worcester Dr. ME10 .... 36 D6
Worcester La. CT33 & CT4 ... 88 E7
Worcester Rd. ME15 .... 97 D7
Wordsworth Cl. ME5 .... 32 C7
Wordsworth Gdns. CT3 .... 112 F6
Wordsworth Rd. ME14 ..... 75 B7
Workhouse La. ME15 .... 96 C4
Workhouse Rd.
Sutton Valence ME17 .... 99 A1
Workhouse Rd.
Throwley ME13 .... 82 F1
World's End. ME9 .... 60 E7
Wormdale Hill. ME9 .... 35 B3
Wormdale Rd. ME9 .... 35 B4
Worth Cty Prim Sch. CT14 . 94 B5
Worth La. CT20 .... 177 E3
Worthgate Pl. ◪ CT1 .... 87 F7
Worthington St. ◪
CT16 .... 166 D8
Wotton Cl. ME15 .... 97 E5
Wotton Rd. TN23 .... 156 B6
Wraightsfield Ave. TN29 .. 195 D8
Wraik Hill. CT5 .... 43 C5
Wrangleden Cl. ME15 .... 97 E5
Wrangleden Rd. ME15 ...... 97 E5
Wreight Ct. ME13 .... 40 B1
Wren Ind Est. ME15 .... 97 F4
Wren Way. ME5 .... 32 B6
Wrens Ct. ME9 .... 58 A8
Wrens Rd. ME9 .... 58 A7
Wrentham Ave. CT6 .... 22 B2
Wright Cl. ME8 .... 11 C2
Wright's Way. ME12 .... 17 C8
Wrights Cl. TN30 .... 179 A8
Wrotham Ave. ◪ CT10 ...... 30 B4
Wrotham Rd. CT10 .... 30 B4
Wyatt Ho. ◪ ME2 .... 9 A7
Wyatt Pl. ME2 .... 9 A7
Wyatt St. ME14 .... 75 A4
Wych Elm Way. CT21 ...... 187 E8
Wycherley Cres. CT16 ..... 149 B4
Wye Coll (Univ of London).
TN25 .... 123 F2
Wye Gdns. CT9 .... 8 F2
Wye High Sch (Prep).
TN25 .... 123 E2
Wye Rd. TN25 .... 122 F3
Wye Sta. TN25 .... 123 D2
Wyke Manor Rd. ME14 ..... 75 A4

Wykeham Cl. ME11 .... 2 F3
Wykeham Cotts. ME17 ..... 96 F2
Wykeham Gr. ME17 .... 99 A7
Wykeham Rd. ME10 .... 37 B4
Wykeham St. ME2 .... 9 B8
Wyles Rd. ME4 .... 9 E2
Wyles St. ME7 .... 10 C7
Wyllie Ct. ME10 .... 36 E7
Wynd The. TN27 .... 103 D1
Wyndam Rd. ME4 .... 9 E2
Wyndham Ave. CT9 .... 8 B2
Wyndham Rd. CT17 .... 166 B8
Wynn Ellis Ho. CT5 .... 20 E3
Wynn Rd. CT5 .... 21 A2
Wytchlings The. ME17 ...... 99 D2
Wytherling Cl. ME14 .... 75 F5
Wyvern Way. TN24 .... 139 E3
Wyvill Cl. ME8 .... 33 E5

Yard The. CT4 .... 111 F1
Yardhurst Gdns. CT9 .... 8 F3
Yardley Ho. CT10 .... 30 B7
Yarrow Cl. CT10 .... 30 A3
Yarrow Ct. ME14 .... 75 F5
Yarrow Rd. ME5 .... 31 F4
Yates Cl. TN31 .... 201 A3
Yaugher La. ME9 .... 34 C3
Yeates Dr. ME10 .... 37 A8
Yellow Sands. ME12 .... 19 F6
Yelsted La. Chatham ME14 . 54 D7
Yelsted La. Yelsted ME9 .... 34 A1
Yelsted Rd. ME9 .... 56 A7
Yeoman Ct. ME14 .... 76 B3
Yeoman Dr. ME7 .... 10 F1
Yeoman Gdns. TN24 .... 157 B8
Yeoman La. ME14 .... 76 B4
Yeoman Way. ME15 .... 76 A2
Yeomans Sq. TN23 .... 155 D8
Yeoman's Sq. TN23 .... 155 D8
Yevele Cl. ME11 .... 3 A5
Yew Cl. TN23 .... 138 E2
Yew Tree Cl.
Broadstairs CT10 .... 29 D4
Yew Tree Cl. Chatham ME5 . 32 D1
Yew Tree Cl. Deal CT14 ... 117 A4
Yew Tree Cl.
Stanford TN25 .... 160 B1
Yew Tree Cotts. ME14 .... 53 F1
Yew Tree Farm. CT3 .... 114 A8
Yew Tree Gdns.
Birchington CT7 .... 27 A7
Yew Tree Gdns.
Fordwich CT2 .... 68 A4
Yew Tree Pl. ME7 .... 33 B1
Yew Tree Rd. TN29 .... 194 F3
Yewhedges. ME13 .... 81 E4
Yewtree Cross. CT18 .... 161 C8
Yoakes La. TN29 .... 192 F1
Yoakley Sq. CT9 .... 28 F8
York and Albany Cl. CT14 117 B1
York Ave. ◪
Broadstairs CT10 .... 30 B4
York Ave. Chatham ME5 .... 31 F3
York Ave. Gillingham ME7 . 10 C4
York Cl. CT6 .... 22 D4
York Hill. ME4 .... 10 C2
York Ho. ◪ CT17 .... 166 D7
York Mews. CT19 .... 177 E7
York Rd. Ashford TN24 .... 139 D5
York Rd. Canterbury CT1 ... 87 E7
York Rd. Deal CT14 .... 117 D4
York Rd. Herne Bay CT6 .... 22 D5
York Rd. Maidstone ME15 ... 75 C2
York Rd. Rochester ME1 ..... 9 C3
York St. Broadstairs CT10 ... 30 B4
York St.
Dover CT16 & CT17 .... 166 D7
York St. Ramsgate CT11 .... 52 E6
York Street Rdbt. CT16 ... 166 D7
York Terr. CT7 .... 27 B7
Young Cl. CT14 .... 117 B6
Young's Pl. CT15 .... 164 F5
Ypres Ct. CT1 .... 67 D1
Ypres Dr. ME10 .... 14 F1

Zarena Ct. ◪ CT20 .... 177 F3
Zealand Rd. CT1 .... 87 F6
Zetland Ave. ME7 .... 10 E2
Zion Pl. CT9 .... 7 J3

Acol 27 B3
Adisham 112 D8
Aldington 173 A6
Alkham 147 C1
Appledore 190 C7
Appledore Heath 181 D1
Ash 71 D2
Ashbank 99 B7
Ashford 139 A2
Aylesford 53 A3
Aylesham 112 F5
Badlesmere 83 C1
Bagham 107 D8
Bapchild 37 E3
Barfrestone 113 E1
Barham 111 F1
Bekesbourne 89 D4
Bethersden 153 E5
Biddenden Green 135 B2
Bilsington 172 C1
Birchington 26 E7
Bishopsbourne 111 B5
Blean 66 A6
Bobbing 36 A7
Bonnington 172 F3
Borden 36 B3
Bossingham 127 A6
Boughton Aluph 123 A5
Boughton Lees 122 F3
Boughton Malherbe 118 A8
Boughton Moncholsea ... 97 B3
Boughton Street 63 E4
Boxley 54 D2
Boyden Gate 47 C8
Brabourne 159 C4
Brabourne Lees 158 D5
Bredgar 58 A6
Bredhurst 33 B1
Brenzett 192 A3
Bridge 89 A1
Broad Oak 67 D7
Broad Street 77 B6
Broadstairs 30 C5
Brook 141 B5
Brookland 197 D8
Broomfield (Maidstone) .. 99 D5
Burmarsh 186 C5
Calcott 42 E2
Camber 201 A2
Canterbury 87 D7
Capel-le-Ferne 164 B2
Challock 105 B1
Chamber's Green 136 C3
Charing 120 D8
Charing Heath 119 C7
Chart Sutton 98 B1
Chartham 86 E2

Chatham 31 E6
Chestnut Street 35 E4
Chilham 107 C7
Chillenden 113 F8
Chislet 47 D5
Church Hougham 165 B5
Cliffs End 51 D6
Cock Street 97 D2
Conyer 38 F5
Coxheath 96 C2
Danaway 35 C3
Deal 117 E6
Deans Hill 57 D6
Densole 163 A8
Denton 129 B3
Detling 55 B1
Doddington 80 E7
Dover 166 F7
Dungeness 205 H6
Dunkirk 64 E3
Dymchurch 195 D7
East Farleigh 96 B7
East Guldeford 196 A1
East Langdon 133 A1
East Stourmouth 48 E1
East Studdal 132 D7
Eastchurch 5 E3
Eastling 81 F6
Eastry 93 A2
Eccles 53 A6
Egerton 118 F4
Elham 144 E5
Elvington 114 C1
Etchinghill 161 C3
Ewell Minnis 147 E3
Eyhorne Street 77 C2
Eythorne 131 C8
Fairbourne Heath 100 B1
Faversham 62 B5
Folkestone 178 F4
Fordwich 68 A4
Further Quarter 152 C3
Gillingham 10 D3
Godmersham 107 A2
Goodnestone (Dover) 91 D2
Graveney 41 E2
Great Chart 138 C1
Great Mongeham 116 C3
Greatstone-on-Sea 200 E1
Guston 149 E6
Haffenden Quarter 152 A7
Halfway Houses 3 A5
Hamstreet 183 B7
Harrietsham 100 D5
Hartlip 34 E5
Hartlip Hill 34 E7
Hastingleigh 142 B6

Hawkinge 163 B5
Hawthorn Corner 24 A3
Hazel Street 57 A3
Herne 46 B8
Herne Bay 22 E6
Hernhill 64 B6
Hersden 46 F1
High Halden 167 D7
Hinxhill 140 D1
Hoath 46 F5
Hollingbourne 77 F2
Hothfield 138 A7
Hythe 176 D1
Ickham 69 C1
Ivychurch 192 E3
Iwade 14 D4
Kearsney 148 D3
Kemsley 14 F1
Kenardington 182 A6
Key Street 36 A5
Kingsdown 134 D5
Kingsnorth (Ashford) ... 156 A3
Kingston 111 D3
Kingswood 99 E3
Langley Heath 98 F4
Leadingcross Green 101 C3
Leeds 99 A7
Lenham 101 D5
Leysdown-on-Sea 6 H2
Little Chart 120 B1
Littlebourne 89 E8
Littleton-on-Sea 200 F5
Loose 96 F4
Lower Halstow 13 C3
Lower Hardres 110 A6
Lydd 203 D6
Lydd-on-Sea 204 F3
Lydden (Broadstairs) 28 E4
Lydden (Dover) 147 E8
Lyminge 161 B6
Lympne 175 A3
Lynsted 60 A6
Maidstone 75 C3
Manston 28 E1
Margate 7 H2
Martin 133 B3
Martin Mill 133 C2
Mersham 157 F4
Middle Quarter 152 D1
Milstead 58 F2
Minster (Isle of Sheppey) .. 4 B7
Minster (Isle of Thanet) . 50 A6
Molash 105 F4
Monkton 49 D7
Munday Bois 135 F8
New Romney 200 B5
Newchurch 184 E3

Newington (Folkestone) 177 A8
Newington (Gillingham) .. 35 A6
Newnham 81 C7
Nonington 113 D5
Northbourne 116 A4
Oad Street 35 E1
Oare 40 A3
Old Romney 199 B7
Old Wives Lees 85 C3
Otham 98 B7
Painter's Forstal 61 E3
Park Wood 97 E3
Patrixbourne 89 C3
Pedlinge 175 D4
Petham 109 B3
Platt's Heath 100 E1
Pluckley 136 D7
Postling 160 F2
Potter's Forstal 118 B2
Potters Corner 138 E6
Preston 70 B6
Queenborough 3 A5
Rainham 33 E8
Ram Lane 120 F2
Ramsgate 52 C4
Rhodes Minnis 144 A3
Ringwould 133 F5
Ripple 116 E1
River 148 E3
Rochester 9 E5
Rodmersham 59 C8
Rough Common 66 B3
Rushenden 2 F3
St Margaret's at Cliffe ... 151 A6
St Mary in the Marsh 194 B4
St Michaels 167 B4
St Nicholas at Wade 25 E1
Sandling 53 F1
Sandway 101 E3
Sandwich 73 B1
Sarre 48 D7
Sellindge 159 D1
Selling 84 C6
Sevington 157 B6
Shadoxhurst 170 A8
Sheerness 1 D3
Sheldwich 83 C6
Shepherdswell or
    Sibertswold 130 E5
Shottenden 84 D1
Silver Street 57 F5
Sittingbourne 36 C6
Smarden 135 B1
Smeeth 158 C4
Snargate 191 E6
South Green 57 A5

South Street 56 C7
Stalisield Green 103 D6
Stanford 160 B1
Staple 92 A5
Stelling Minnis 126 F2
Stiff Street 57 E7
Stockbury 56 E8
Stone in Oxney 189 F4
Stowting 160 A8
Stubb's Cross 155 C2
Sturry 67 F6
Sutton 133 A7
Swanton Street 57 F3
Temple Ewell 148 D6
Tenterden 179 C8
Teynham 38 C3
The Quarter 135 B5
Throwley Forstal 82 D1
Thurnham 76 D8
Tilmanstone 115 A3
Tunstall 58 D8
Tyler Hill 66 E6
Upchurch 12 F4
Upper Harbledown 65 F1
Upstreet 47 C3
Walderslade 31 F1
Waltham 125 E6
Warden 6 D4
Warren Street 102 D7
Wateringham 42 C2
West Hougham 164 F5
West Hythe 175 B1
Westbere 68 C7
Westbrook 7 F1
Westenhanger 175 B6
Westfield Sole 54 C7
Westgate-on-Sea 7 B1
Westwell 121 E4
Whitfield 149 A7
Whitstable 20 C3
Wichling 80 C5
Wickhambreaux 69 B2
Wingham 91 B7
Wittersham 188 D3
Womenswold 112 D2
Woodchurch 169 A2
Woodnesborough 93 C6
Woolage Green 129 F8
Wootton 129 D1
Wormshill 79 A7
Worth 94 B4
Wye 123 F1
Yelsted 34 A1
Yorkletts 42 F2

The Street Atlases are available from all good bookshops or by mail order direct from the publisher. Orders can be made in the following ways.

By phone Ring our special Credit Card Hotline on **01933 443863** during office hours (9am to 5pm) or leave a message on the answering machine, quoting your full credit card number plus expiry date and your full name and address.

By post or fax Fill out the order form below (you may photocopy it) and post it to: **Philip's Direct, 27 Sanders Road, Wellingborough, Northants NN8 4NL** or fax it to: **01933 443849.**

Before placing an order by post, by fax or on the answering machine, please telephone to check availability and prices.

STREET ATLASES ORDER FORM

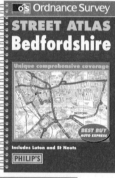

PHILIP'S

COLOUR REGIONAL ATLASES				
	SPIRAL	PAPERBACK	POCKET spiral	POCKET paperback	
	Quantity @ £7.99 each	Quantity @ £6.99 each	Quantity @ £5.99 each	Quantity @ £4.99 each	£ Total
LONDON	☐ 0 540 07812 3	☐ 0 540 07811 5	☐ 0 540 07810 7	☐ 0 540 07809 3 ➤	

COLOUR REGIONAL ATLASES				
	HARDBACK	SPIRAL	POCKET	
	Quantity @ £12.99 each	Quantity @ £9.99 each	Quantity @ £5.99 each	£ Total
BEDFORDSHIRE	☐ 0 540 07801 8	☐ 0 540 07802 6	☐ 0 540 07803 4 ➤	
BIRMINGHAM & WEST MIDLANDS	☐ 0 540 07603 1	☐ 0 540 07604 X	☐ 0 540 07605 8 ➤	
BUCKINGHAMSHIRE	☐ 0 540 07466 7	☐ 0 540 07467 5	☐ 0 540 07468 3 ➤	
CHESHIRE	☐ 0 540 07507 8	☐ 0 540 07508 6	☐ 0 540 07509 4 ➤	
DERBYSHIRE	☐ 0 540 07531 0	☐ 0 540 07532 9	☐ 0 540 07533 7 ➤	
EDINBURGH & East Central Scotland	☐ 0 540 07653 8	☐ 0 540 07654 6	☐ 0 540 07656 2 ➤	
NORTH ESSEX	☐ 0 540 07289 3	☐ 0 540 07290 7	☐ 0 540 07292 3 ➤	
SOUTH ESSEX	☐ 0 540 07294 X	☐ 0 540 07295 8	☐ 0 540 07297 4 ➤	
GLASGOW & West Central Scotland	☐ 0 540 07648 1	☐ 0 540 07649 X	☐ 0 540 07651 1 ➤	
NORTH HAMPSHIRE	☐ 0 540 07471 3	☐ 0 540 07472 1	☐ 0 540 07473 X ➤	
SOUTH HAMPSHIRE	☐ 0 540 07476 4	☐ 0 540 07477 2	☐ 0 540 07478 0 ➤	
HERTFORDSHIRE	☐ 0 540 06174 3	☐ 0 540 06175 1	☐ 0 540 06176 X ➤	
EAST KENT	☐ 0 540 07483 7	☐ 0 540 07276 1	☐ 0 540 07287 7 ➤	
WEST KENT	☐ 0 540 07366 0	☐ 0 540 07367 9	☐ 0 540 07369 5 ➤	
LEICESTERSHIRE	☐ 0 540 07854 9	☐ 0 540 07855 7	☐ 0 540 07856 5 ➤	
NORTHAMPTONSHIRE	☐ 0 540 07745 3	☐ 0 540 07746 1	☐ 0 540 07748 8 ➤	
OXFORDSHIRE	☐ 0 540 07512 4	☐ 0 540 07513 2	☐ 0 540 07514 0 ➤	
SURREY	☐ 0 540 07794 1	☐ 0 540 07795 X	☐ 0 540 07796 8 ➤	
EAST SUSSEX	☐ 0 540 07306 7	☐ 0 540 07307 5	☐ 0 540 07312 1 ➤	
WEST SUSSEX	☐ 0 540 07319 9	☐ 0 540 07323 7	☐ 0 540 07327 X ➤	
WARWICKSHIRE	☐ 0 540 07560 4	☐ 0 540 07561 2	☐ 0 540 07562 0 ➤	
SOUTH YORKSHIRE	☐ 0 540 06330 4	☐ 0 540 07667 8	☐ 0 540 07669 4 ➤	
WEST YORKSHIRE	☐ 0 540 07671 6	☐ 0 540 07672 4	☐ 0 540 07674 0 ➤	

COLOUR REGIONAL ATLASES

	HARDBACK	SPIRAL	POCKET	
	Quantity @ £10.99 each	Quantity @ £8.99 each	Quantity @ £4.99 each	£ Total
MERSEYSIDE	☐ 0 540 06480 7	☐ 0 540 06481 5	☐ 0 540 06482 3	➤
	Quantity @ £12.99 each	Quantity @ £8.99 each	Quantity @ £5.99 each	£ Total
BERKSHIRE	☐ 0 540 06170 0	☐ 0 540 06172 7	☐ 0 540 06173 5	➤
	Quantity @ £12.99 each	Quantity @ £9.99 each	Quantity @ £4.99 each	£ Total
DURHAM	☐ 0 540 06365 7	☐ 0 540 06366 5	☐ 0 540 06367 3	➤
	Quantity @ £12.99 each	Quantity @ £9.99 each	Quantity @ £5.50 each	£ Total
GREATER MANCHESTER	☐ 0 540 06485 8	☐ 0 540 06486 6	☐ 0 540 06487 4	➤
TYNE AND WEAR	☐ 0 540 06370 3	☐ 0 540 06371 1	☐ 0 540 06372 X	➤

COLOUR REGIONAL ATLASES

	HARDBACK	SPIRAL	POCKET	
	Quantity @ £14.99 each	Quantity @ £9.99 each	Quantity @ £5.99 each	£ Total
LANCASHIRE	☐ 0 540 06440 8	☐ 0 540 06441 6	☐ 0 540 06443 2	➤
NOTTINGHAMSHIRE	☐ 0 540 07541 8	☐ 0 540 07542 6	☐ 0 540 07543 4	➤
	Quantity @ £14.99 each	Quantity @ £10.99 each	Quantity @ £5.99 each	£ Total
STAFFORDSHIRE	☐ 0 540 07549 3	☐ 0 540 07550 7	☐ 0 540 07551 5	➤

BLACK AND WHITE REGIONAL ATLASES

	HARDBACK	SOFTBACK	POCKET	
	Quantity @ £11.99 each	Quantity @ £8.99 each	Quantity @ £3.99 each	£ Total
BRISTOL & AVON	☐ 0 540 06140 9	☐ 0 540 06141 7	☐ 0 540 06142 5	➤
	Quantity @ £12.99 each	Quantity @ £9.99 each	Quantity @ £4.99 each	£ Total
CARDIFF, SWANSEA & GLAMORGAN	☐ 0 540 06186 7	☐ 0 540 06187 5	☐ 0 540 06207 3	➤

COLOUR LOCAL ATLASES

	PAPERBACK	Quantity @ £3.50 each	£ Total
CANNOCK, LICHFIELD, RUGELEY		☐ 0 540 07625 2	➤
DERBY AND BELPER		☐ 0 540 07608 2	➤
NORTHWICH, WINSFORD, MIDDLEWICH		☐ 0 540 07589 2	➤
PEAK DISTRICT TOWNS		☐ 0 540 07609 0	➤
STAFFORD, STONE, UTTOXETER		☐ 0 540 07626 0	➤
WARRINGTON, WIDNES, RUNCORN		☐ 0 540 07588 4	➤

Name.....................................

Address.....................................

....

....

.....................................Postcode.....................

◆ Add £2 postage and packing per order

◆ All available titles will normally be dispatched within 5 working days of receipt of order but please allow up to 28 days for delivery

☐ Please tick this box if you do not wish your name to be used by other carefully selected organisations that may wish to send you information about other products and services

Registered Office: 2-4 Heron Quays, London E14 4JP
Registered in England number: 3597451

Total price of order £☐

(including postage and packing at £2 per order)

I enclose a cheque/postal order, for £☐

made payable to *Octopus Publishing Group Ltd,*

or please debit my ☐ Mastercard ☐ American Express

☐ Visa account by £☐

Account no

☐☐☐☐ ☐☐☐☐ ☐☐☐☐ ☐☐☐☐

Expiry date ☐☐ ☐☐

Signature.....................................

Post to: Philip's Direct, 27 Sanders Road, Wellingborough, Northants NN8 4NL

O|S Ordnance Survey

STREET ATLASES ORDER FORM

O|S Ordnance Survey

STREET ATLAS Leicestershire and Rutland
LEICESTER CITY CENTRE AT EXTRA-LARGE SCALE
Plus town maps of Corby, Grantham, Nuneaton and Rugby
Unique comprehensive coverage
Includes Stamford and Swadlincote
BEST BUY AUTO EXPRESS
PHILIP'S

O|S Ordnance Survey
STREET ATLAS Tyne and W
COMPLETE COUNT

O|S Ordnance Survey
STREET ATLAS Glasgow and West Central Scotland
Comprehensive coverage from Stirling to Ayr and Greenock to Lanark

O|S Ordnance Survey
STREET ATLAS North Essex
BEST BUY AUTO EXPRESS
Unique comprehensive coverage
Plus Bishop's Stortford, Felixstowe, Ipswich
PHILIP'S

PHILIP'S

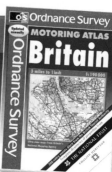

The best-selling *OS Motoring Atlas Britain* uses unrivalled and up-to-date mapping from the Ordnance Survey digital database. The exceptionally clear mapping is at a large scale of 3 miles to 1 inch (Orkney/Shetland Islands at 5 miles to 1 inch).

A special feature of the atlas is its wealth of tourist and leisure information. It contains comprehensive directories, including descriptions and location details, of the properties of the National Trust in England and Wales, the National Trust for Scotland, English Heritage and Historic Scotland. There is also a useful diary of British Tourist Authority Events listing more than 300 days out around Britain during the year.

Available from all good bookshops or direct from the publisher:
Tel: 01933 443863

The atlas includes:

- ◆ 112 pages of fully updated mapping
- ◆ 45 city and town plans
- ◆ 8 extra-detailed city approach maps
- ◆ route-planning maps
- ◆ restricted motorway junctions
- ◆ local radio information
- ◆ distances chart
- ◆ county boundaries map
- ◆ multi-language legend